FAVOURITE FAMILY
COOKBOOK

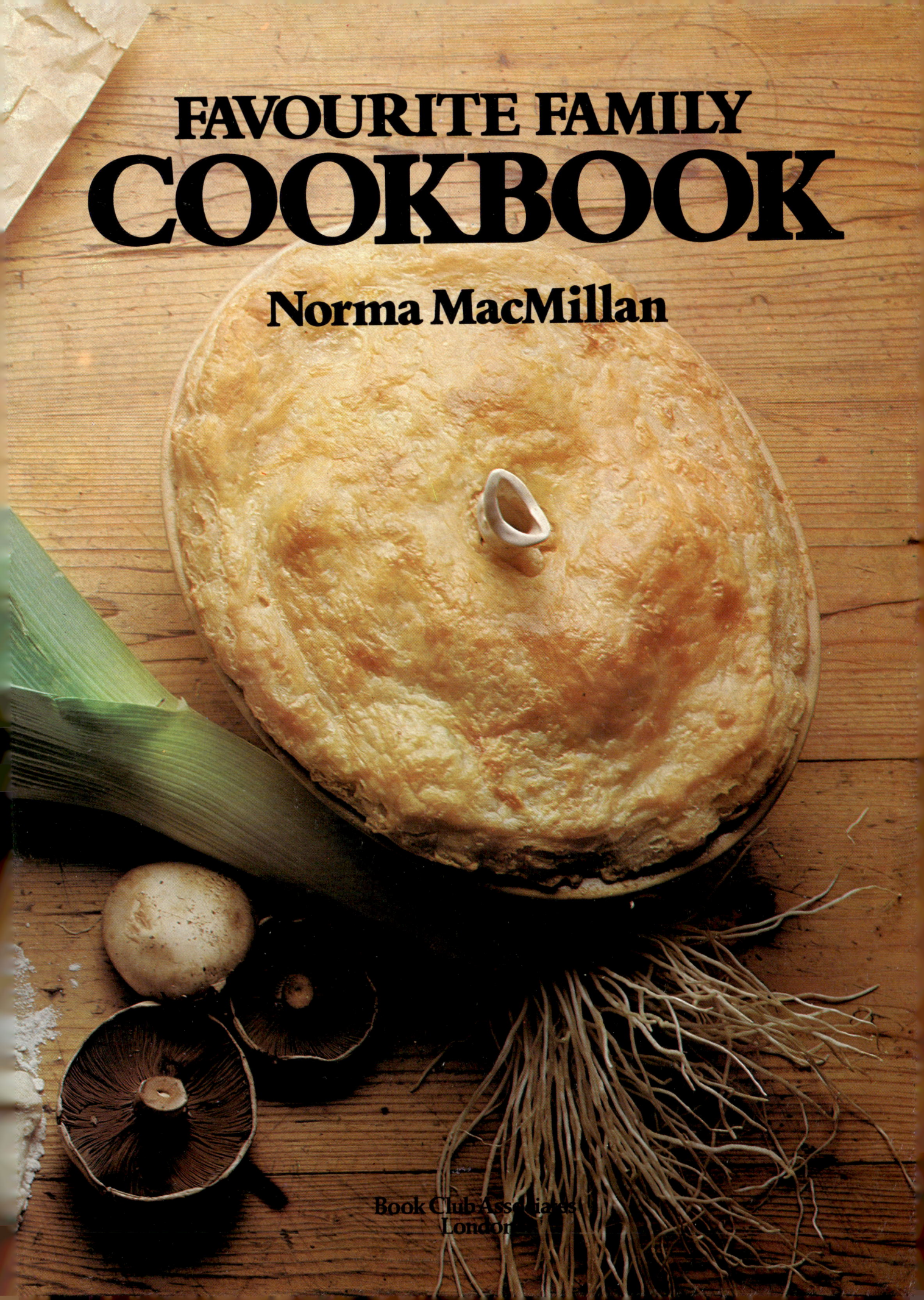
FAVOURITE FAMILY COOKBOOK

Norma MacMillan

Book Club Associates
London

CONTENTS

BASICS 6
APPETIZERS 20
SOUPS 34
FISH 48
MEAT 72
POULTRY & GAME 146
OFFAL 178
MEATLESS DISHES 188
BARBECUES & PICNICS 202
BUDGET DISHES 212
PASTA & RICE 228

238 EGGS & CHEESE
248 VEGETABLES & SALADS
276 DESSERTS
302 CAKES & COOKIES
336 BREADS & TEABREADS
356 SPECIAL OCCASIONS
376 FEAST DAYS
386 PARTY SNACKS
392 DRINKS
396 INDEX

This edition published 1978 by Book Club Associates
By arrangement with Octopus Books Limited, 59 Grosvenor Street, London W.1

© 1978 Octopus Books Limited ISBN 0 7064 0896 9

Printed in Czechoslovakia

50372

BASICS

Beef stock

METRIC/IMPERIAL
about 1kg/2lb beef marrow
  or shin bones
1 onion, peeled and halved
1 large carrot, peeled and
  thickly sliced
1 bouquet garni
6 black peppercorns
salt

AMERICAN
about 2lb beef marrow or
  shin bones
1 onion, peeled and halved
1 large carrot, peeled and
  thickly sliced
1 bouquet garni
6 black peppercorns
salt

Put the bones in a large saucepan or stockpot and pour over water to cover. Bring to the boil, then half cover and simmer for 2 hours, skimming off the scum.
   Add the remaining ingredients with salt to taste and continue simmering for 2 hours. Add more boiling water, when necessary, to keep the bones covered.
   Strain the stock and allow to cool. Skim off the layer of fat which will set on the surface. If not for immediate use, store the stock in the refrigerator.
Note: Ham or veal bones may be used to make stock in the same way.

Chicken stock

METRIC/IMPERIAL
1 chicken carcass
1 onion, peeled and halved
1 large carrot, peeled and
  thickly sliced
1 celery stick, thickly
  sliced, or celery leaves
6 black peppercorns
1 bay leaf
1 × 5ml spoon/1 teaspoon
  dried thyme or 2 sprigs of
  fresh thyme
salt

AMERICAN
1 chicken carcass
1 onion, peeled and halved
1 large carrot, peeled and
  thickly sliced
1 celery stalk, thickly
  sliced, or celery leaves
6 black peppercorns
1 bay leaf
1 teaspoon dried thyme or
  2 sprigs of fresh thyme
salt

Put the carcass in a large saucepan or stockpot and add the remaining ingredients with salt to taste. Pour in enough water to cover the carcass and bring to the boil. Cover and simmer for at least 2 hours. Add more boiling water, when necessary, to keep the carcass covered.
   Strain the stock and allow to cool. Skim off the layer of fat which will set on the surface. If not for immediate use, store the stock in the refrigerator.

Vegetable stock

METRIC/IMPERIAL
3 × 15ml spoons/
  3 tablespoons vegetable oil
1 onion, peeled and chopped
3 large carrots, peeled and
  chopped
2 celery sticks, with leaves,
  thickly sliced
1 swede or parsnip,
  peeled and chopped
mushroom stalks
1 bouquet garni
6 black peppercorns
salt

AMERICAN
3 tablespoons vegetable oil
1 onion, peeled and chopped
3 large carrots, peeled and
  chopped
2 celery stalks, with leaves,
  thickly sliced
1 swede or parsnip,
  peeled and chopped
mushroom stalks
1 bouquet garni
6 black peppercorns
salt

Heat the oil in a large saucepan or stockpot. Add the vegetables and cook gently for 10 minutes, being careful not to let the vegetables brown.
   Stir in the remaining ingredients with salt to taste and pour in water almost to fill the pan. Bring to the boil, then half cover and simmer for 45 minutes.
   Strain the stock and allow to cool. If not for immediate use, store in the refrigerator.

Fish stock

METRIC/IMPERIAL
about 0.5kg/1lb white fish
  heads and trimmings
  (bones, tails, etc.)
1 onion, peeled and halved
1 celery stick, thickly sliced
1 bouquet garni
6 black peppercorns
salt

AMERICAN
about 1lb white fish heads
  and trimmings (bones,
  tails, etc.)
1 onion, peeled and halved
1 celery stalk, thickly sliced
1 bouquet garni
6 black peppercorns
salt

Put all the ingredients, with salt to taste, in a large saucepan or stockpot. Pour in enough water to cover and bring to the boil. Half cover and simmer for 45 minutes, skimming off the scum that rises to the surface.
   Strain the stock. Use the same day.

Court bouillon

METRIC/IMPERIAL
600ml/1 pint dry white
  wine
600ml/1 pint water
1 × 15ml spoon/
  1 tablespoon lemon juice
1 onion, peeled and sliced
fresh herbs, such as fennel
  or dill, parsley or chervil,
  or 1 × 5ml spoon/
  1 teaspoon dried mixed
  herbs
6 black peppercorns
salt

AMERICAN
2½ cups dry white wine
2½ cups water
1 tablespoon lemon juice
1 onion, peeled and sliced
fresh herbs, such as fennel
  or dill, parsley or chervil,
  or 1 teaspoon mixed dried
  herbs
6 black peppercorns
salt

Put all the ingredients, with salt to taste, in a large saucepan and bring to the boil. Cover and simmer for 30 minutes.
  Strain and allow to cool. Use the same day for poaching fish.
Makes 900ml/1½ pints/3¾ cups

Horseradish sauce

METRIC/IMPERIAL
2 × 15ml spoons/
  2 tablespoons grated
  horseradish
150ml/¼ pint sour cream
pinch of caster sugar
salt
freshly ground pepper

AMERICAN
2 tablespoons grated
  horseradish root
⅔ cup sour cream
pinch of sugar
salt
freshly ground pepper

Mix together all the ingredients with salt and pepper to taste. Serve slightly chilled.
Makes about 150ml/¼ pint/⅔ cup

White sauce

METRIC/IMPERIAL
25g/1oz butter
25g/1oz plain flour
300ml/½ pint milk
salt
freshly ground pepper
pinch of grated nutmeg

AMERICAN
2 tablespoons butter
¼ cup all-purpose flour
1¼ cups milk
salt
freshly ground pepper
pinch of grated nutmeg

Melt the butter in a saucepan. Add the flour and cook, stirring, for 1 minute. Remove from the heat and gradually stir in the milk. Return to the heat and bring to the boil, stirring. Simmer for 1 to 2 minutes or until thickened and smooth. Season to taste with salt and pepper and the nutmeg.
Note: This sauce may also be made using half milk and half stock or cooking liquid from the vegetables, meat or fish, with which the sauce is to be served.
Makes 300ml/½ pint/1¼ cups
Variations
Add 1 × 15ml spoon/1 tablespoon made French mustard to the finished sauce.
Add 2 × 15ml spoons/2 tablespoons chopped fresh parsley to the finished sauce.
Add 50g/2oz/⅓ cup chopped peeled (shelled) shrimps to the finished sauce.

Bread sauce

METRIC/IMPERIAL
450ml/¾ pint milk
slice of onion
4 black peppercorns
1 bay leaf
2 whole cloves
100g/4oz fresh white
  breadcrumbs
25g/1oz butter
salt

AMERICAN
2 cups milk
slice of onion
4 black peppercorns
1 bay leaf
2 whole cloves
2 cups fresh white
  breadcrumbs
2 tablespoons butter
salt

Put the milk, onion, peppercorns, bay leaf and cloves in a saucepan and bring to just under boiling point. Remove from the heat, cover and leave to infuse for 10 minutes. Strain the milk.
  Return the milk to the saucepan and stir in the breadcrumbs, butter and salt to taste. Heat through gently, stirring to melt the butter. Serve hot.
Makes about 450ml/¾ pint/2 cups

Béchamel sauce

METRIC/IMPERIAL	AMERICAN
300ml/½ pint milk	1¼ cups milk
1 bay leaf	1 bay leaf
6 black peppercorns	6 black peppercorns
slice of onion	slice of onion
1 mace blade	1 mace blade
25g/1oz butter	2 tablespoons butter
25g/1oz plain flour	¼ cup all-purpose flour
salt	salt
freshly ground pepper	freshly ground pepper

Put the milk, bay leaf, peppercorns, onion and mace blade in a saucepan and bring to just under boiling point. Remove from the heat, cover and allow to infuse for 10 minutes. Strain the milk.

Melt the butter in a saucepan. Add the flour and cook, stirring, for 1 minute. Remove from the heat and gradually stir in the hot strained milk. Return to the heat and bring to the boil, stirring. Simmer for 1 to 2 minutes or until thickened and smooth. Season to taste with salt and pepper and serve hot.
Makes about 300ml/½ pint/1¼ cups

Hollandaise sauce

METRIC/IMPERIAL	AMERICAN
3 egg yolks	3 egg yolks
1 × 15ml spoon/ 1 tablespoon cold water	1 tablespoon cold water
1 × 15ml spoon/ 1 tablespoon lemon juice	1 tablespoon lemon juice
salt	salt
freshly ground pepper	freshly ground pepper
175g/6oz butter, melted and cooled	¾ cup butter, melted and cooled

Put the egg yolks, water, lemon juice and a pinch each of salt and pepper in the top of a double boiler or in a heatproof bowl placed over a pan of hot water. Beat well together until the mixture is thick. Add the butter, drop by drop, beating constantly. As the sauce begins to thicken to a heavy creamy consistency, the butter may be added more quickly. Do not let the pan or bowl become too hot or the sauce will curdle.

Taste and adjust the seasoning, adding more lemon juice if the sauce is too bland. Serve warm.
Makes about 300ml/½ pint/1¼ cups

Mint sauce

METRIC/IMPERIAL	AMERICAN
1 × 15ml spoon/ 1 tablespoon sugar	1 tablespoon sugar
1 × 15ml spoon/ 1 tablespoon boiling water	1 tablespoon boiling water
2 × 15ml spoons/ 2 tablespoons vinegar	2 tablespoons vinegar
4 × 15ml spoons/ 4 tablespoons finely chopped fresh mint leaves	4 tablespoons finely chopped fresh mint leaves

Dissolve the sugar in the water and stir in the vinegar. Add the mint leaves and mash well. Leave to infuse for 15 minutes before serving.

Mustard butter

METRIC/IMPERIAL	AMERICAN
100g/4oz unsalted butter	½ cup unsalted butter
2 × 5ml spoons/2 teaspoons dry English mustard	2 teaspoons dry English mustard
1 × 5ml spoon/1 teaspoon lemon juice	1 teaspoon lemon juice
salt	salt
freshly ground pepper	freshly ground pepper

Cream the butter with a wooden spoon until it is softened. Beat in the remaining ingredients with salt and pepper to taste. Form the butter into a roll and wrap in foil. Alternatively, spread the butter on a sheet of foil and cover with another sheet of foil. Chill until firm.

To use, slice the roll or cut the sheet of butter into squares or decorative shapes.

Chinese plum sauce

METRIC/IMPERIAL
75g/3oz butter
1 onion, peeled and finely chopped
225g/8oz plum jam, sieved
2 × 15ml spoons/
  2 tablespoons soy sauce
1 × 15ml spoon/
  1 tablespoon wine vinegar
1 × 2.5ml spoon/
  ½ teaspoon ground ginger
pinch of dry mustard

AMERICAN
⅓ cup butter
1 onion, peeled and finely chopped
¾ cup plum jam, strained
2 tablespoons soy sauce
1 tablespoon wine vinegar
½ teaspoon ground ginger
pinch of dry mustard

Melt the butter in a saucepan. Add the onion and fry until it is soft but not brown. Stir in the remaining ingredients and heat through gently, stirring occasionally. Serve hot.
Makes about 350ml/12fl oz/1½ cups

Mornay sauce

METRIC/IMPERIAL
2 × 5ml spoons/2 teaspoons made French mustard
150g/5oz cheese, grated (preferably half Cheddar and half Gruyère)
300ml/½ pint hot white or béchamel sauce★

AMERICAN
2 teaspoons prepared French mustard
1¼ cups grated cheese (preferably half Cheddar and half Gruyère)
1¼ cups hot white or béchamel sauce★

Add the mustard and cheese to the hot sauce and stir until the cheese has melted and the sauce is smooth.
Makes about 300ml/½ pint/1¼ cups

Cranberry sauce

METRIC/IMPERIAL
175g/6oz sugar
150ml/¼ pint water
225g/8oz cranberries
medium sherry (optional)

AMERICAN
¾ cup sugar
⅔ cup water
½ lb cranberries
medium sherry (optional)

Put the sugar and water in a saucepan and heat gently, stirring to dissolve the sugar. Add the cranberries and simmer for about 10 minutes or until the fruit is just soft. Remove from the heat and allow to cool.
If you like, add a little sherry to taste before serving.
Makes about 600ml/1 pint/2½ cups

Tartare sauce

METRIC/IMPERIAL
2 eggs, hard-boiled, separated and whites discarded
150ml/¼ pint mayonnaise★
1 × 5ml spoon/1 teaspoon chopped capers
1 × 5ml spoon/1 teaspoon chopped gherkins
1 × 5ml spoon/1 teaspoon chopped fresh parsley
1 × 5ml spoon/1 teaspoon chopped fresh chives
1 × 5ml spoon/1 teaspoon lemon juice

AMERICAN
2 eggs, hard-cooked, separated and whites discarded
⅔ cup mayonnaise★
1 teaspoon chopped capers
1 teaspoon chopped dill pickles
1 teaspoon chopped fresh parsley
1 teaspoon chopped fresh chives
1 teaspoon lemon juice

Rub the egg yolks through a sieve (strainer) into a mixing bowl. Add the remaining ingredients and mix well. Serve chilled.
Makes about 150ml/¼ pint/⅔ cup

Apple sauce

METRIC/IMPERIAL
0.5kg/1lb cooking apples, peeled, cored and roughly chopped
25g/1oz unsalted butter
2 × 15ml spoons/ 2 tablespoons water
1 × 15ml spoon/ 1 tablespoon lemon juice
sugar
1 × 2.5ml spoon/ ½ teaspoon ground cinnamon or grated nutmeg

AMERICAN
1lb baking apples, peeled, cored and roughly chopped
2 tablespoons unsalted butter
2 tablespoons water
1 tablespoon lemon juice
sugar
½ teaspoon ground cinnamon or grated nutmeg

Put the apples, butter, water and lemon juice in a saucepan and cook gently for 10 to 15 minutes or until the apples are soft and pulpy. Remove from the heat and beat well until smooth. If necessary, rub the apple mixture through a sieve (strainer) or purée in an electric blender.

Return the apple sauce to the saucepan and reheat. Stir in sugar to taste and the spice. Serve warm.

Béarnaise sauce

METRIC/IMPERIAL
4 × 15ml spoons/ 4 tablespoons tarragon vinegar
1 shallot, peeled and chopped
1 sprig of fresh tarragon
salt
freshly ground pepper
3 egg yolks
100g/4oz butter, cut into small pieces
1 × 15ml spoon/ 1 tablespoon chopped fresh tarragon
1 × 15ml spoon/ 1 tablespoon chopped fresh parsley

AMERICAN
4 tablespoons tarragon vinegar
1 shallot, peeled and chopped
1 sprig of fresh tarragon
salt
freshly ground pepper
3 egg yolks
½ cup butter, cut into small pieces
1 tablespoon chopped fresh tarragon
1 tablespoon chopped fresh parsley

Put the vinegar, shallot, tarragon sprig and a pinch each of salt and pepper in a saucepan. Bring to the boil and simmer until the liquid has reduced by half. Strain the vinegar and allow to cool.

Put the egg yolks in the top of a double boiler or in a heatproof bowl over a pan of hot water. Beat the yolks together, then beat in the strained vinegar. Add the butter, piece by piece, beating constantly and waiting for one piece to be incorporated before adding the next. Do not let the pan or bowl become too hot or the sauce will curdle.

When all the butter has been added and the sauce is thick and smooth, adjust the seasoning and add the herbs. Serve hot.
Makes about 150ml/¼ pint/⅔ cup

Cumberland sauce

METRIC/IMPERIAL
thinly pared rind and juice
 of 2 oranges
150ml/¼ pint water
2 × 5ml spoons/2 teaspoons
 cornflour
150ml/¼ pint chicken stock
juice of 1 lemon
2 × 5ml spoons/2 teaspoons
 made mustard
2 × 15ml spoons/
 2 tablespoons port wine
75g/3oz redcurrant jelly
salt
freshly ground pepper

AMERICAN
thinly pared rind and juice
 of 2 oranges
⅔ cup water
2 teaspoons cornstarch
⅔ cup chicken stock
juice of 1 lemon
2 teaspoons prepared
 mustard
2 tablespoons port wine
¼ cup redcurrant jelly
salt
freshly ground pepper

Cut the orange rind into thin strips and put in a saucepan with the water. Bring to the boil and simmer for 15 to 20 minutes or until the rind is tender and the liquid has reduced to about 3 × 15ml spoons/ 3 tablespoons.
 Dissolve the cornflour (cornstarch) in the stock and add to the saucepan with the orange and lemon juices. Bring to the boil, stirring. Simmer until thickened. Stir in the mustard, port, jelly and salt and pepper to taste. Heat through gently. Serve hot.
Makes about 450ml/¾ pint/2 cups

Tomato sauce

METRIC/IMPERIAL
2 × 15ml spoons/
 2 tablespoons vegetable oil
1 onion, peeled and chopped
2 × 400g/14oz cans
 tomatoes
3 × 15ml spoons/
 3 tablespoons tomato purée
1 × 5ml spoon/1 teaspoon
 sugar
salt
freshly ground black pepper
1 × 15ml spoon/
 1 tablespoon chopped
 fresh herbs (basil, oregano,
 marjoram) or 1.5 × 5ml
 spoons/1½ teaspoons dried
 herbs

AMERICAN
2 tablespoons vegetable oil
1 onion, peeled and chopped
2 × 14oz cans tomatoes
3 tablespoons tomato paste
1 teaspoon sugar
salt
freshly ground black pepper
1 tablespoon chopped fresh
 herbs (basil, oregano,
 marjoram) or 1½ teaspoons
 dried herbs

Heat the oil in a saucepan. Add the onion and fry until it is soft but not brown. Add the tomatoes with the can juice, the tomato purée (paste), sugar, salt and pepper to taste and the herbs. Bring to simmering point, stirring to break up the tomatoes. Half cover and simmer for 45 minutes.
 If you prefer a smooth sauce, press through a sieve (strainer) and return to the saucepan to reheat. Serve hot.
Makes about 300ml/½ pint/1¼ cups

Custard sauce

METRIC/IMPERIAL
3 egg yolks
1 × 15ml spoon/
 1 tablespoon sugar
300ml/½ pint milk
thinly pared rind of ½ lemon

AMERICAN
3 egg yolks
1 tablespoon sugar
1¼ cups milk
thinly pared rind of ½ lemon

Mix the egg yolks and sugar together in a mixing bowl. Put the milk and lemon rind in a heavy saucepan and heat gently until just below boiling point. Remove from the heat, cover and leave to infuse for 10 minutes.
 Remove the lemon rind and add the milk to the egg yolk mixture, stirring well. Strain back into the saucepan. Stir over very gentle heat until the sauce thickens enough to coat the back of the spoon. Serve hot or cold.
Makes about 300ml/½ pint/1¼ cups

Chocolate sauce

METRIC/IMPERIAL
175g/6oz plain eating
 chocolate, broken into
 small pieces
1 × 15ml spoon/
 1 tablespoon brandy or
 light rum
15g/½oz butter

AMERICAN
6 squares semisweet
 chocolate, broken into
 small pieces
1 tablespoon brandy or
 light rum
1 tablespoon butter

Put the chocolate, brandy or rum and butter in a heavy-based saucepan or in the top of a double boiler. Melt the chocolate gently, stirring frequently. Heat through until the mixture is smooth and hot.
Makes about 120ml/4fl oz/½ cup

Melba sauce

METRIC/IMPERIAL
225g/8oz raspberries
4 × 15ml spoons/
 4 tablespoons redcurrant
 jelly
75g/3oz sugar
2 × 5ml spoons/2 teaspoons
 arrowroot
1 × 15ml spoon/
 1 tablespoon water

AMERICAN
½lb raspberries
4 tablespoons redcurrant
 jelly
⅓ cup sugar
2 teaspoons arrowroot flour
1 tablespoon water

Push the raspberries through a sieve (strainer) to make a smooth purée. There should be 150ml/¼ pint/⅔ cup of purée.
 Put the raspberry purée, jelly and sugar in a saucepan and heat gently, stirring to dissolve the sugar. Bring to the boil. Dissolve the arrowroot in the water and add to the saucepan. Simmer, stirring, until the mixture thickens and becomes clear.
 Strain and allow to cool.
Makes about 250ml/8fl oz/1 cup

Coating batter for deep frying

METRIC/IMPERIAL
100g/4oz plain flour
pinch of salt
1 × 15ml spoon/
 1 tablespoon vegetable oil
150ml/¼ pint lukewarm
 water
2 egg whites

AMERICAN
1 cup all-purpose flour
pinch of salt
1 tablespoon vegetable oil
⅔ cup lukewarm water
2 egg whites

Sift the flour and salt into a mixing bowl. Stir in the oil and enough water to form a smooth batter that will coat the back of the spoon.
 Beat the egg whites until stiff and fold into the batter. Use immediately.
Makes 100g/4oz/1 cup quantity

Chestnut and sausage meat stuffing

METRIC/IMPERIAL
15g/½oz butter
1 onion, peeled and finely chopped
2 large cooking apples, peeled, cored and chopped
225g/8oz pork sausage meat
100g/4oz fresh white breadcrumbs
1 × 425g/15oz can unsweetened chestnut purée
salt
freshly ground black pepper

AMERICAN
1 tablespoon butter
1 onion, peeled and finely chopped
2 large baking apples, peeled, cored and chopped
1 cup pork sausage meat
2 cups fresh white breadcrumbs
1 × 15oz can unsweetened chestnut purée
salt
freshly ground black pepper

Melt the butter in a frying pan (skillet). Add the onion and fry until it is soft but not brown. Remove from the heat and stir in the remaining ingredients with salt and pepper to taste. Allow to cool before using.
Makes enough to stuff a 1.5–1.75kg/3½–4lb chicken

Parsley and thyme stuffing

METRIC/IMPERIAL
100g/4oz fresh white breadcrumbs
25g/1oz shredded suet
2 × 15ml spoons/ 2 tablespoons chopped fresh parsley
1 × 15ml spoon/1 tablespoon chopped fresh thyme, or 1 × 5ml spoon/1 teaspoon dried thyme
1 small egg, lightly beaten
salt
freshly ground black pepper

AMERICAN
2 cups fresh white breadcrumbs
3 tablespoons shredded suet
2 tablespoons chopped fresh parsley
1 tablespoon chopped fresh thyme or 1 teaspoon dried thyme
1 egg, lightly beaten
salt
freshly ground black pepper

Mix together all the ingredients with salt and pepper to taste.
Makes enough to stuff a 1.5–1.75kg/3½–4lb chicken

Sage and onion stuffing

METRIC/IMPERIAL
25g/1oz butter
2 onions, peeled and finely chopped
100g/4oz fresh white breadcrumbs
1 × 15ml spoon/ 1 tablespoon chopped fresh sage leaves
1 small egg, lightly beaten
salt
freshly ground black pepper

AMERICAN
2 tablespoons butter
2 onions, peeled and finely chopped
2 cups fresh white breadcrumbs
1 tablespoon chopped fresh sage leaves
1 egg, lightly beaten
salt
freshly ground black pepper

Melt the butter in a frying pan (skillet). Add the onions and fry until they are soft but not brown. Remove from the heat and stir in the remaining ingredients with salt and pepper to taste. Allow to cool and use the same day.
Makes enough to stuff a 1.5–1.75kg/3½–4lb chicken

Rice and apricot stuffing

METRIC/IMPERIAL
100g/4oz long-grain rice, cooked and drained
100g/4oz dried apricots, soaked overnight, drained and chopped
50g/2oz hazelnuts, chopped
1 egg, lightly beaten
salt
freshly ground black pepper

AMERICAN
⅔ cup long-grain rice, cooked and drained
⅔ cup dried apricots, soaked overnight, drained and chopped
½ cup chopped hazelnuts
1 egg, lightly beaten
salt
freshly ground black pepper

Mix together all the ingredients with salt and pepper to taste.
Makes enough to stuff a 1.5–1.75kg/3½–4lb chicken

Crêpes

METRIC/IMPERIAL
100g/4oz plain flour
pinch of salt or sugar
1 egg, lightly beaten
300ml/½ pint milk
1 × 5ml spoon/1 teaspoon
vegetable oil

AMERICAN
1 cup all-purpose flour
pinch of salt or sugar
1 egg, lightly beaten
1¼ cups milk
1 teaspoon vegetable oil

Sift the flour and salt or sugar (depending on whether you are using a savoury or sweet filling) into a mixing bowl. Beat in the egg and half the milk until the mixture is smooth, then stir in the remaining milk and the oil. Transfer the batter to a jug (pitcher) for easy pouring.

Lightly grease a 25cm/10 inch diameter crêpe pan or frying pan (skillet). Heat the pan and pour a little of the batter into the centre. Quickly tilt and rotate the pan so the batter covers the bottom in a thin layer. Cook for about 1 minute or until the underside of the crêpe is golden brown. Turn or flip the crêpe and cook the other side for about 30 seconds. Slide the crêpe out of the pan and keep hot while you cook the remaining crêpes in the same way. As you cook the crêpes, stack them, interleaving with greaseproof (waxed) paper or foil. Fill the crêpes with the chosen filling and serve hot.
Makes about 12

Mayonnaise

METRIC/IMPERIAL
2 egg yolks
1 × 2.5ml spoon/
½ teaspoon dry mustard
salt
freshly ground pepper
300ml/½ pint olive or corn
oil
1 × 15ml spoon/
1 tablespoon lemon juice
or vinegar

AMERICAN
2 egg yolks
½ teaspoon dry mustard
salt
freshly ground pepper
1¼ cups olive or corn oil
1 tablespoon lemon juice or
vinegar

Put the egg yolks, mustard and salt and pepper to taste in a mixing bowl. Stir together to mix well, then begin adding the oil, drop by drop, beating constantly. When half the oil has been incorporated, the remainder may be added in a thin stream.

If the mayonnaise becomes too thick to beat, add a little of the lemon juice or vinegar. When all the oil has been incorporated, beat in the remaining lemon juice or vinegar.

If you prefer a thinner mayonnaise, dilute it with more lemon juice or vinegar, or with single (light) cream.
Makes about 300ml/½ pint/1¼ cups

Aïoli (garlic mayonnaise)

METRIC/IMPERIAL
2 garlic cloves, crushed
2 egg yolks
300ml/½ pint olive or corn oil
1 × 15ml spoon/
 1 tablespoon lemon juice
salt
freshly ground pepper

AMERICAN
2 garlic cloves, crushed
2 egg yolks
1¼ cups olive or corn oil
1 tablespoon lemon juice
salt
freshly ground pepper

Put the garlic and egg yolks in a mixing bowl and mix well together. Begin adding the oil, drop by drop, beating constantly. When half the oil has been incorporated the remainder may be added in a thin stream. Beat in the lemon juice with salt and pepper to taste.
Makes about 300ml/½ pint/1¼ cups

French dressing

METRIC/IMPERIAL
150ml/¼ pint olive, corn or nut oil
4–5 × 15ml spoons/
 4–5 tablespoons wine vinegar or lemon juice
1 garlic clove, peeled (optional)
pinch of sugar
2 × 5ml spoons/2 teaspoons made French mustard (optional)
salt
freshly ground pepper

AMERICAN
⅔ cup olive, corn or nut oil
4–5 tablespoons wine vinegar or lemon juice
1 garlic clove, peeled (optional)
pinch of sugar
2 teaspoons prepared French mustard (optional)
salt
freshly ground pepper

Put all the ingredients, with salt and pepper to taste, in a screwtop jar. Cover tightly and shake well to mix all the ingredients. Allow to infuse for at least 1 hour.
   Remove the garlic clove and shake well again before using.
Makes about 250ml/8fl oz/1 cup
Vinaigrette dressing: Add 1 × 15ml spoon/
1 tablespoon chopped fresh herbs to the basic French dressing.

Thousand island dressing

METRIC/IMPERIAL
300ml/½ pint mayonnaise*
5 × 15ml spoons/
 5 tablespoons mild chilli sauce
2 × 15ml spoons/
 2 tablespoons tomato ketchup
2 spring onions, finely chopped
1 egg, hard-boiled and chopped
2 gherkins, finely chopped
1 × 5ml spoon/1 teaspoon made French mustard

AMERICAN
1¼ cups mayonnaise*
⅓ cup mild chili sauce
2 tablespoons tomato ketchup
2 scallions, finely chopped
1 egg, hard-cooked and chopped
1 large dill pickle, finely chopped
1 teaspoon prepared French mustard

Mix together all the ingredients and serve chilled.
Makes about 400ml/14fl oz/1¾ cups

Yogurt dressing

METRIC/IMPERIAL
150ml/¼ pint natural yogurt
2 × 15ml spoons/
 2 tablespoons vegetable oil
2 × 5ml spoons/2 teaspoons vinegar or lemon juice
salt
freshly ground pepper

AMERICAN
⅔ cup unflavored yogurt
2 tablespoons vegetable oil
2 teaspoons vinegar or lemon juice
salt
freshly ground pepper

Mix together all the ingredients with salt and pepper to taste. Serve chilled.
Makes about 175ml/6fl oz/¾ cup

Flaky pastry

METRIC/IMPERIAL
225g/8oz plain flour
pinch of salt
75g/3oz butter, cut into small pieces
4–5 × 15ml spoons/
 4–5 tablespoons ice-cold water
75g/3oz lard, cut into small pieces

AMERICAN
2 cups all-purpose flour
pinch of salt
⅓ cup butter, cut into small pieces
4–5 tablespoons ice-cold water
⅓ cup shortening, cut into small pieces

Sift the flour and salt into a mixing bowl. Add half the butter and rub into the flour until the mixture resembles breadcrumbs. Stir in enough water to bind the mixture and knead the dough lightly until smooth.

Roll out the dough to an oblong and dot half the lard (shortening) over the top two-thirds. Fold up the bottom third, then fold down the top third. Give the dough a quarter turn and roll out again into an oblong. Dot the remaining butter over the top two-thirds of the oblong and fold and turn as before. Repeat with the rest of the lard (shortening).

Chill the dough for 30 minutes before using.
Makes 225g/8oz/2 cup quantity dough

Pepper sauce

METRIC/IMPERIAL
2 green and red peppers, deseeded, pith removed and finely chopped
2 × 15ml spoons/
 2 tablespoons olive oil
2–3 × 15ml spoons/
 2–3 tablespoons white wine vinegar
1 × 5ml spoon/1 teaspoon made French mustard
salt
freshly ground black pepper

AMERICAN
2 green and red peppers, deseeded, pith removed and finely chopped
2 tablespoons olive oil
2–3 tablespoons white wine vinegar
1 teaspoon prepared French mustard
salt
freshly ground black pepper

Mix the green and red peppers together. Blend the olive oil, vinegar, mustard and salt and pepper to taste. Pour into a screw-top jar and shake well. Pour over the peppers and allow to stand for 1 hour.

Choux pastry

METRIC/IMPERIAL
150ml/¼ pint water
50g/2oz butter
pinch of salt
65g/2½oz plain flour
2 eggs, lightly beaten

AMERICAN
⅔ cup water
¼ cup butter
pinch of salt
10 tablespoons all-purpose flour
2 eggs, lightly beaten

Put the water, butter and salt in a saucepan and heat gently, stirring to melt the butter. Bring to the boil, then remove from the heat. Sift the flour into the pan and beat until the mixture draws away from the sides then gradually beat in the eggs until the dough is smooth and glossy. The dough is then ready for use.
Makes 65g/2½oz/10 tablespoon quantity dough, enough for 8 éclairs or profiteroles

Puff pastry

METRIC/IMPERIAL
225g/8oz plain flour
pinch of salt
225g/8oz butter
6–7 × 15ml spoons/
 6–7 tablespoons ice-cold water

AMERICAN
2 cups all-purpose flour
pinch of salt
1 cup butter
6–7 tablespoons ice-cold water

Sift the flour and salt into a mixing bowl. Add one-third of the butter and cut into small pieces, then rub the butter into the flour until the mixture resembles breadcrumbs. Add enough water to bind the mixture. Turn the dough onto a lightly floured surface and knead for 2 to 3 minutes.
 Form the remaining butter into a slab about 5mm/¼ inch thick.
 Roll out the dough to an oblong about 1cm/½ inch thick. Place the slab of butter in the centre and fold the dough over it to form a parcel. Turn the parcel over so the folds are on the bottom and roll out again into an oblong. Fold in three and give the dough a quarter turn. Roll out again into an oblong. Repeat the folding, turning and rolling three times, then chill for 30 minutes before using.
Makes 225g/8oz/2 cup quantity dough

French flan pastry (pâte sucrée)

METRIC/IMPERIAL
100g/4oz plain flour
pinch of salt
50g/2oz butter, cut into small pieces
2 egg yolks
1 × 15ml spoon/
 1 tablespoon caster sugar

AMERICAN
1 cup all-purpose flour
pinch of salt
¼ cup butter, cut into small pieces
2 egg yolks
1 tablespoon sugar

Sift the flour and salt onto a work surface. Make a well in the centre and add the pieces of butter, the egg yolks and sugar. Work these last three ingredients together with the fingertips of one hand, then draw in the flour until a soft dough is formed. Chill for 30 minutes before using.
Makes 100g/4oz/1 cup quantity dough, enough to line a 20cm/8 inch diameter flan ring (pie pan).

Rough puff pastry

METRIC/IMPERIAL
225g/8oz plain flour
pinch of salt
150g/5oz butter
25g/1oz lard
150ml/¼ pint ice-cold water

AMERICAN
2 cups all-purpose flour
pinch of salt
⅔ cup butter
2 tablespoons shortening
⅔ cup ice-cold water

Sift the flour and salt into a mixing bowl. Add the butter and lard (shortening) and cut into small pieces. Stir in enough water to bind the mixture and press together gently to form a lumpy dough.
 Roll out the dough on a floured surface to an oblong. Fold in three and give the dough a quarter turn. Roll out again into an oblong. Repeat the folding, turning and rolling three times, then chill the dough for 30 minutes before using.
Makes 225g/8oz/2 cup quantity dough

Rich shortcrust (pie) pastry

METRIC/IMPERIAL
175g/6oz plain flour
pinch of salt
75g/3oz butter
1 egg yolk
1–2 × 15ml spoons/
  1–2 tablespoons cold water

AMERICAN
1½ cups all-purpose flour
pinch of salt
⅓ cup butter
1 egg yolk
1–2 tablespoons cold water

Sift the flour and salt into a mixing bowl. Add the butter and cut into small pieces, then rub the butter into the flour until the mixture resembles breadcrumbs. Stir in the egg yolk and enough water to bind the mixture. Knead the dough lightly until smooth. Chill for 30 minutes before using.
Makes 175g/6oz/1½ cup quantity dough, enough to line a 20cm/8 inch diameter flan ring (pie pan).
Variation: Add 2 × 5ml spoons/2 teaspoons sugar if making a sweet pie.

Suet crust pastry

METRIC/IMPERIAL
225g/8oz self-raising flour
1 × 5ml spoon/1 teaspoon
  salt
100g/4oz shredded suet
150ml/¼ pint water

AMERICAN
2 cups self-rising flour
1 teaspoon salt
¾ cup shredded suet
⅔ cup water

Sift the flour and salt into a mixing bowl. Stir in the suet, then add enough water to bind the mixture. Knead the dough lightly until smooth and elastic. The dough is then ready for use.
Makes 225g/8oz/2 cup quantity dough

Shortcrust (pie) pastry

METRIC/IMPERIAL
100g/4oz plain flour
pinch of salt
50g/2oz butter
1–2 × 15ml spoons/
  1–2 tablespoons cold water

AMERICAN
1 cup all-purpose flour
pinch of salt
¼ cup butter
1–2 tablespoons cold water

Sift the flour and salt into a mixing bowl. Add the butter and cut into small pieces, then rub the butter into the flour until the mixture resembles breadcrumbs. Stir in enough water to bind the mixture. Knead the dough lightly until smooth. Chill for 30 minutes before using.
Makes 100g/4oz/1 cup quantity dough, enough to line an 18cm/7 inch diameter flan ring (pie pan).
Variation: Add 1 × 5ml spoon/1 teaspoon sugar if making a sweet pie.

Almond paste (marzipan)

METRIC/IMPERIAL
225g/8oz ground almonds
225g/8oz icing sugar, sifted
225g/8oz caster sugar
1 egg, lightly beaten
2 × 5ml spoons/2 teaspoons
  lemon juice
1 × 2.5ml spoon/½ teaspoon
  almond essence
1 × 2.5ml spoon/½ teaspoon
  vanilla essence

AMERICAN
2 cups ground almonds
2 cups confectioners' sugar,
  sifted
1 cup sugar
1 egg, lightly beaten
2 teaspoons lemon juice
½ teaspoon almond extract
½ teaspoon vanilla extract

Mix together all the ingredients to form a soft, but not sticky, paste. Turn onto a board sprinkled lightly with icing (confectioners') sugar and knead until smooth. Use immediately or wrap in polythene (plastic wrap).
Makes enough to cover the top and sides of a 23cm/9 inch diameter cake

Chocolate frosting

METRIC/IMPERIAL
100g/4oz plain chocolate, broken into small pieces
1 × 15ml spoon/ 1 tablespoon milk
100g/4oz butter
225g/8oz icing sugar, sifted

AMERICAN
4 squares semisweet chocolate, broken into small pieces
1 tablespoon milk
½ cup butter
2 cups confectioners' sugar, sifted

Melt the chocolate with the milk over a very gentle heat. Remove from the heat and allow to cool slightly.
Meanwhile, cream the butter with a wooden spoon until it is soft. Gradually beat in the icing (confectioners') sugar, then stir in the chocolate mixture. Use immediately, or cover the bowl with a damp cloth.
Makes enough to fill and ice an 18cm/7 inch diameter sandwich (layer) cake

Royal icing

METRIC/IMPERIAL
2 egg whites
0.5kg/1lb icing sugar, sifted
2 × 5ml spoons/2 teaspoons lemon juice

AMERICAN
2 egg whites
3½ cups confectioners' sugar, sifted
2 teaspoons lemon juice

Beat the egg whites until they are frothy. Gradually beat in the icing (confectioners') sugar and continue beating until the icing is stiff. Beat in the lemon juice.
Use the icing immediately or cover the bowl with a damp cloth.
Makes enough to ice a 23cm/9 inch diameter cake

Maître d'hôtel butter

METRIC/IMPERIAL
100g/4oz unsalted butter
1 × 15ml spoon/ 1 tablespoon chopped fresh parsley
1 × 5ml spoon/1 teaspoon lemon juice
salt
freshly ground pepper

AMERICAN
½ cup unsalted butter
1 tablespoon chopped fresh parsley
1 teaspoon lemon juice
salt
freshly ground pepper

Cream the butter with a wooden spoon until it is softened. Beat in the remaining ingredients with salt and pepper to taste. Form the butter into a roll and wrap in foil. Alternatively, spread the butter on a sheet of foil and cover with another sheet of foil. Chill until firm.
To use, slice the roll or cut the sheet of butter into squares or decorative shapes.
Variation: Cream unsalted butter with other chopped fresh herbs, such as chives or fennel, or a mixture of fresh herbs.

Brandy butter

METRIC/IMPERIAL
75g/3oz unsalted butter
75g/3oz icing sugar, sifted
2–3 × 15ml spoons/ 2–3 tablespoons brandy

AMERICAN
⅓ cup unsalted butter
¾ cup confectioners' sugar, sifted
2–3 tablespoons brandy

Cream the butter with a wooden spoon until it is soft. Gradually beat in the icing (confectioners') sugar, then the brandy. Pile into a serving dish and chill until firm.

APPETIZERS

Country-style pâté

METRIC/IMPERIAL
225g/8oz chicken livers, minced
100g/4oz lean veal, minced
225g/8oz fat belly pork, minced
3 juniper berries, crushed
1 garlic clove, crushed
pinch of ground mace
salt
freshly ground black pepper
2 × 15ml spoons/
 2 tablespoons dry white wine
2 × 15ml spoons/
 2 tablespoons brandy
9 streaky bacon rashers, rinds removed

AMERICAN
1 cup ground chicken livers
½ cup ground lean veal
1 cup ground pork fat
3 juniper berries, crushed
1 garlic clove, crushed
pinch of ground mace
salt
freshly ground black pepper
2 tablespoons dry white wine
2 tablespoons brandy
9 bacon slices

Mix together the chicken livers, veal, pork belly (fat), juniper berries, garlic, mace, salt and pepper to taste, wine and brandy. Line a pâté dish or mould with 6 of the bacon rashers (slices). Spoon the meat mixture into the dish and smooth the top. Cover with the remaining bacon rashers (slices).

Place the dish or mould in a roasting tin and add enough boiling water to come halfway up the sides of the dish. Bake in a preheated cool oven (150°C/300°F, Gas Mark 2) for 1½ hours or until the pâté has shrunk away from the sides of the dish.

Remove the dish from the roasting tin and allow to cool. Cover with greaseproof (waxed) paper or foil and place a heavy weight on top. Keep in the refrigerator overnight.
Serves 6 to 8

Kipper pâté

METRIC/IMPERIAL
25g/1oz unsalted butter
225g/8oz kipper fillets
225g/8oz cream cheese
½ garlic clove, crushed
juice of ½ lemon
freshly ground black pepper

AMERICAN
2 tablespoons unsalted butter
½lb kipper fillets
1 cup cream cheese
½ garlic clove, crushed
juice of ½ lemon
freshly ground black pepper

Melt the butter in a frying pan (skillet). Add the kipper fillets, in batches, and cook gently until the fish is soft. Remove from the pan and allow to cool slightly. Remove the skins and flake the fish.

Put the fish, cream cheese, garlic, lemon juice and pepper to taste in the goblet of an electric blender. Blend until smooth.

Spoon into a serving dish and smooth the top. Chill for about 20 minutes. Serve sprinkled with more pepper.
Serves 4 to 6

Beef and vegetable stock (page 6)

Melon vinaigrette (page 33); Avocado stuffed with crab (page 356)

Speedy spiced pâté

METRIC/IMPERIAL
225g/8oz liverwurst
100g/4oz cream cheese
2 × 15ml spoons/
  2 tablespoons mayonnaise*
3 × 15ml spoons/
  3 tablespoons single cream
1 × 5ml spoon/1 teaspoon
  Worcestershire sauce
1 × 2.5ml spoon/
  ½ teaspoon mild curry
  powder
salt
freshly ground black pepper

AMERICAN
1 cup liver sausage
½ cup cream cheese
2 tablespoons mayonnaise*
3 tablespoons light cream
1 teaspoon Worcestershire
  sauce
½ teaspoon mild curry
  powder
salt
freshly ground black pepper

Cream the liverwurst (liver sausage) and cream cheese together until well mixed. Beat in the mayonnaise, cream, Worcestershire sauce, curry powder and salt and pepper to taste. Spoon into a serving dish and chill for at least 1 hour.
Serves 6 to 8

Chopped chicken livers

METRIC/IMPERIAL
25g/1oz chicken fat
1 onion, peeled and finely
  chopped
0.5kg/1lb chicken livers
3 eggs, hard-boiled and
  halved
salt
freshly ground black pepper

AMERICAN
2 tablespoons chicken fat
1 onion, peeled and finely
  chopped
1lb chicken livers
3 eggs, hard-cooked and
  halved
salt
freshly ground black pepper

Melt the chicken fat in a frying pan (skillet). Add the onion and fry until it is soft but not brown. Add the chicken livers and fry until they are lightly browned. Remove from the heat.
  Mince (grind) the onion and chicken livers. Set aside one of the egg yolks and finely chop the remainder. Stir into the liver mixture with salt and pepper to taste. Spoon the chicken livers into a serving dish. Push the reserved egg yolk through a sieve (strainer) and sprinkle over the livers.
Serves 6 to 8

Egg mayonnaise

METRIC/IMPERIAL
4 large lettuce leaves
8 sprigs of watercress
4 eggs, hard-boiled and
  halved
300ml/½ pint mayonnaise*
pinch of paprika

AMERICAN
4 large lettuce leaves
8 sprigs of watercress
4 eggs, hard-cooked and
  halved
1¼ cups mayonnaise*
pinch of paprika

Put a lettuce leaf on 4 individual serving plates. Add 2 watercress sprigs to each plate, then place the eggs in the centre, cut sides down. Pour over the mayonnaise and sprinkle each serving with a little paprika.
Serves 4

Watercress eggs

METRIC/IMPERIAL
4 eggs, hard-boiled and
  halved
salt
freshly ground pepper
squeeze of lemon juice
2 × 15ml spoons/
  2 tablespoons skimmed
  milk powder
4 × 15ml spoons/
  4 tablespoons chopped
  watercress
watercress to serve

AMERICAN
4 eggs, hard-cooked and
  halved
salt
freshly ground pepper
squeeze of lemon juice
2 tablespoons skimmed
  milk powder
4 tablespoons chopped
  watercress
watercress to serve

Remove the yolks from the eggs and mash until smooth with salt and pepper to taste and the lemon juice. Beat in the skimmed milk powder, then stir in the chopped watercress. Fill the egg white halves with this mixture. Arrange the stuffed eggs on a bed of watercress and serve slightly chilled.
Serves 4

Pears with blue cheese dressing (page 32)

Tuna and bean salad

METRIC/IMPERIAL
1 garlic clove, halved
1 × 200g/7oz can tuna fish
3 × 15ml spoons/
  3 tablespoons lemon juice
salt
freshly ground black pepper
100g/4oz dried haricot
  beans, soaked overnight,
  drained and cooked
chopped parsley to garnish

AMERICAN
1 garlic clove, halved
1 × 7oz can tuna fish
3 tablespoons lemon juice
salt
freshly ground black pepper
½ cup dried navy beans,
  soaked overnight, drained
  and cooked
chopped parsley to garnish

Rub the inside of a salad bowl with the cut sides of the garlic. Discard the garlic. Drain the tuna and put the oil from the can in the salad bowl. Add the lemon juice and salt and pepper to taste and mix well together. Fold in the beans.
  Flake the tuna and pile on top of the beans. Sprinkle with chopped parsley and serve.
Serves 4

Pickled herring salad

METRIC/IMPERIAL
4 rollmop herrings, cut into
  strips
2 dessert apples, peeled,
  cored and diced
3 gherkins, diced
2 × 5ml spoons/2 teaspoons
  capers
2 × 15ml spoons/
  2 tablespoons French
  dressing★
2 × 15ml spoons/
  2 tablespoons mayonnaise★
4–6 lettuce leaves
4 × 15ml spoons/
  4 tablespoons diced pickled
  beetroot
watercress to garnish

AMERICAN
4 rollmop herrings, cut into
  strips
2 dessert apples, peeled,
  cored and diced
3 small dill pickles, diced
2 teaspoons capers
2 tablespoons French
  dressing★
2 tablespoons mayonnaise★
4–6 lettuce leaves
4 tablespoons diced pickled
  beets
watercress to garnish

Mix together the herrings, apples, gherkins (pickles), capers, dressing and mayonnaise. Line a salad bowl with the lettuce leaves and pile the herring mixture in the centre. Top with the beetroot (beets) and garnish with watercress.
Serves 4 to 6

Prawn and grapefruit cocktails

METRIC/IMPERIAL
2 grapefruit
100g/4oz peeled prawns
4 × 15ml spoons/
 4 tablespoons mayonnaise★
4 × 15ml spoons/
 4 tablespoons natural
 yogurt
shredded lettuce
4 unpeeled prawns to
 garnish

AMERICAN
2 grapefruit
⅔ cup shelled shrimp
4 tablespoons mayonnaise★
4 tablespoons unflavored
 yogurt
shredded lettuce
4 unshelled shrimp to
 garnish

Halve the grapefruit and loosen the segments with a grapefruit knife. Tip the segments into a mixing bowl and remove the seeds. Add the prawns (shrimp), mayonnaise and yogurt and fold together gently.
　Put some shredded lettuce in the bottom of 4 glasses. Spoon in the grapefruit mixture. Garnish each serving with an unpeeled prawn (shrimp).
Serves 4
Note: The grapefruit and prawn (shrimp) mixture may be served in the grapefruit shells.

Baked anchovy tomatoes

METRIC/IMPERIAL
4 large tomatoes
8 anchovy fillets, finely
 chopped
25g/1oz fresh white
 breadcrumbs
1 garlic clove, crushed
1 × 15ml spoon/
 1 tablespoon olive oil
salt
freshly ground black pepper
1 egg, beaten
parsley sprigs to garnish

AMERICAN
4 large tomatoes
8 anchovy fillets, finely
 chopped
½ cup fresh white
 breadcrumbs
1 garlic clove, crushed
1 tablespoon olive oil
salt
freshly ground black pepper
1 egg, beaten
parsley sprigs to garnish

Cut the tops off the tomatoes, then scoop out the insides. Turn the tomatoes upside down on absorbent paper to drain.
　Mix together the anchovies, breadcrumbs, garlic, oil, salt and pepper to taste and enough of the beaten egg to bind the mixture. Spoon the anchovy mixture into the tomato cases and replace the tops. Place in a baking dish and bake in a preheated moderately hot oven (190°C/375°F, Gas Mark 5) for 20 minutes.
　Serve hot, garnished with parsley.
Serves 4

Shellfish cocktail

METRIC/IMPERIAL
225g/8oz peeled and cooked shellfish (prawns, crab, lobster, etc.)
150ml/¼ pint mayonnaise★
2 × 5ml spoons/2 teaspoons lemon juice
1 × 15ml spoon/ 1 tablespoon tomato purée
2 × 5ml spoons/2 teaspoons Worcestershire sauce
1 tomato, peeled, deseeded and very finely chopped
shredded lettuce
pinch of cayenne pepper

AMERICAN
½lb shelled and cooked shellfish (shrimp, crab, lobster, etc.)
⅔ cup mayonnaise★
2 teaspoons lemon juice
1 tablespoon tomato paste
2 teaspoons Worcestershire sauce
1 tomato, peeled, deseeded and very finely chopped
shredded lettuce
pinch of cayenne pepper

Flake the fish or cut into bite-sized pieces.
   Mix together the mayonnaise, lemon juice, tomato purée (paste), Worcestershire sauce and tomato. Half fill 4 glasses with shredded lettuce and pile the shellfish on top. Spoon over the mayonnaise mixture and sprinkle each serving with cayenne.
Serves 4

Taramasalata

METRIC/IMPERIAL
2 slices of white bread, crusts removed
milk
225g/8oz smoked cod's roe, skinned
1 garlic clove, crushed
150ml/¼ pint olive or corn oil
4 × 15ml spoons/ 4 tablespoons lemon juice
freshly ground black pepper

AMERICAN
2 slices of white bread, crusts removed
milk
1 × 8oz jar tarama
1 garlic clove, crushed
⅔ cup olive or corn oil
4 tablespoons lemon juice
freshly ground black pepper

Soak the bread in milk to cover for 10 minutes. Squeeze out the excess milk and tear the bread into small pieces.
   Beat the cod's roe (tarama) until it is smooth. Beat in the bread and garlic, then add the oil drop by drop, beating constantly. When all the oil has been incorporated, add the lemon juice and pepper to taste.
   Spoon into a serving dish and chill for at least 30 minutes. Serve sprinkled with more pepper.
Serves 4

Smoked salmon eggs

METRIC/IMPERIAL
4 eggs, hard-boiled and halved
15g/½oz butter, softened
1 × 2.5ml spoon/½ teaspoon lemon juice
salt
freshly ground black pepper
50g/2oz smoked salmon, finely chopped
8 lettuce leaves
4 lemon wedges

AMERICAN
4 eggs, hard-cooked and halved
1 tablespoon butter, softened
½ teaspoon lemon juice
salt
freshly ground black pepper
¼ cup finely chopped smoked salmon
8 lettuce leaves
4 lemon wedges

Remove the yolks from the whites and mash until smooth with the butter, lemon juice and salt and pepper to taste. Fold in the salmon. Fill the hollows in the egg whites with the salmon mixture.
   Arrange the lettuce leaves on 4 serving plates. Place 2 egg halves, cut sides up, on each plate and garnish with a lemon wedge.
Serves 4

Smoked trout with hot sauce

METRIC/IMPERIAL
2 smoked trout, halved lengthways
watercress
Sauce:
2 × 15ml spoons/ 2 tablespoons single cream
1 × 15ml spoon/ 1 tablespoon grated horseradish
1 × 5ml spoon/1 teaspoon lemon juice
Tabasco sauce

AMERICAN
2 smoked trout, halved lengthwise
watercress
Sauce:
2 tablespoons light cream
1 tablespoon grated horseradish root
1 teaspoon lemon juice
Tabasco sauce

Place the trout halves on 4 serving plates and garnish with watercress. Mix together the sauce ingredients with Tabasco sauce to taste. (Add the sauce drop by drop as it is very hot.) Spoon the sauce over the trout.
Serves 4

Mushroom fritters

METRIC/IMPERIAL
350g/12oz button mushrooms
100g/4oz quantity coating batter★
vegetable oil for deep frying
salt
freshly ground black pepper

AMERICAN
3 cups button mushrooms
1 cup quantity coating batter★
vegetable oil for deep frying
salt
freshly ground black pepper

Coat the mushrooms with the batter.
    Heat the oil in a deep frying pan (deep fat fryer) until it is 190°C/375°F. Fry the mushrooms, in batches, until they are crisp and golden. Drain on absorbent paper. Pile the fritters on a warmed serving plate. Serve sprinkled with salt and pepper.
Serves 4

Mushrooms à la grecque

METRIC/IMPERIAL
300ml/½ pint water
1 small onion, chopped
2 × 15ml spoons/ 2 tablespoons olive oil
1 × 5ml spoon/ 1 teaspoon tomato purée
salt
freshly ground black pepper
1 bouquet garni
juice of ½ lemon
350g/12oz small button mushrooms
chopped fresh parsley to garnish

AMERICAN
1¼ cups water
1 small onion, chopped
2 tablespoons olive oil
1 teaspoon tomato paste
salt
freshly ground black pepper
1 bouquet garni
juice of ½ lemon
3 cups small button mushrooms
chopped fresh parsley to garnish

Put the water, onion, oil, tomato purée (paste), salt and pepper to taste, the bouquet garni and lemon juice into a saucepan and simmer for 5 minutes. Add the mushrooms to the pan and simmer for a further 10 minutes. Remove the mushrooms from the pan.
    Boil the liquid rapidly until it is reduced to 3–4 × 15ml spoons/3–4 tablespoons. Discard the bouquet garni and pour over the mushrooms. Chill and serve garnished with parsley.
Serves 4 to 5

Blue cheese mousse

METRIC/IMPERIAL
175g/6oz blue cheese
100g/4oz cream cheese
1 × 2.5ml spoon/½ teaspoon anchovy essence
pinch of cayenne pepper
2 × 15ml spoons/ 2 tablespoons chopped spring onions
15g/½oz gelatine
4 × 15ml spoons/ 4 tablespoons water
175ml/6fl oz mayonnaise★
175ml/6fl oz double cream

AMERICAN
6oz blue cheese
½ cup cream cheese
½ teaspoon anchovy paste
pinch of cayenne pepper
2 tablespoons chopped scallions
2 envelopes unflavored gelatin
4 tablespoons water
¾ cup mayonnaise★
¾ cup heavy cream

Push the blue cheese through a sieve (strainer) into a mixing bowl and beat in the cream cheese. Add the anchovy essence (paste), cayenne and spring onions (scallions).
    Dissolve the gelatine in the water and strain into the cheese mixture. Stir well, then stir in the mayonnaise and cream. Spoon into a 900ml/1½ pint/4 cup mould and chill until set.
Serves 8

Salami hors d'oeuvre

METRIC/IMPERIAL
350g/12oz salami, sliced
1 lettuce
4 tomatoes, sliced
¼ cucumber, sliced

AMERICAN
¾lb salami, sliced
1 lettuce
4 tomatoes, sliced
¼ cucumber, sliced

Arrange slices of salami on a bed of lettuce. Garnish with tomato and cucumber slices and serve with pickles.
Serves 6 to 8

Ham mousse

METRIC/IMPERIAL
225g/8oz cooked ham, finely minced
1 × 5ml spoon/1 teaspoon tomato purée
2 × 15ml spoons/ 2 tablespoons gelatine
150ml/¼ pint chicken or ham stock
150ml/¼ pint béchamel sauce★
salt
freshly ground black pepper
150ml/¼ pint double cream
2 egg whites
watercress to garnish

AMERICAN
1 cup finely ground cooked ham
1 teaspoon tomato paste
2 tablespoons unflavored gelatin
⅔ cup chicken or ham stock
⅔ cup béchamel sauce★
salt
freshly ground black pepper
⅔ cup whipping cream
2 egg whites
watercress to garnish

Put the ham and tomato purée (paste) in the goblet of an electric blender and blend until very smooth. Turn into a mixing bowl. Dissolve the gelatine in the stock and strain into the ham purée. Mix well. Beat in the béchamel sauce with salt and pepper to taste. Chill until beginning to set.

Whip the cream until it is thick and fold into the ham mixture. Beat the egg whites until they are stiff and fold into the ham mixture. Spoon into a soufflé dish or individual serving dishes and chill until set.

Serve garnished with watercress.
Serves 6

Ham, tuna and fennel appetizer

METRIC/IMPERIAL
8 slices of cooked ham
1 × 200g/7oz can tuna fish, drained
150ml/¼ pint mayonnaise★
3 × 15ml spoons/ 3 tablespoons grated fennel
1 small red pepper, pith and seeds removed and cut into strips
8 black olives
parsley sprigs to garnish

AMERICAN
8 slices of cooked ham
1 × 7oz can tuna fish, drained
⅔ cup mayonnaise★
3 tablespoons grated Florence fennel
1 small pimiento, pith and seeds removed and cut into strips
8 black olives
parsley sprigs to garnish

Roll up the ham slices and arrange on a serving plate. Flake the tuna into large chunks and spoon a few onto each ham roll. Mix together the mayonnaise and fennel and spoon over the tuna. Decorate with strips of pepper (pimiento) and olives and garnish the dish with parsley sprigs.
Serves 4

Hare terrine

METRIC/IMPERIAL
1 hare
1 medium carrot, peeled and grated
1 medium onion, peeled and grated
0.75kg/1½lb pork sausage meat
4 egg yolks
300g/11oz raisins
4 × 15ml spoons/
 4 tablespoons chicken stock
salt
freshly ground black pepper
12 streaky bacon rashers, rinds removed

AMERICAN
1 hare
1 medium carrot, peeled and grated
1 medium onion, peeled and grated
1½lb pork sausage meat
4 egg yolks
2 cups raisins
4 tablespoons chicken stock
salt
freshly ground black pepper
12 bacon slices

Remove the skin from the hare and take the meat from the bones. Try to keep the breasts in neat pieces. Set the breast pieces aside and mince (grind) the remaining hare meat. Mix the minced (ground) hare with the carrot, onion, sausage meat, egg yolks, raisins, stock and salt and pepper to taste.

Line a terrine or baking dish with 8 or 9 of the bacon rashers (slices). Spoon in one-third of the minced (ground) mixture. Cover with half the hare breast pieces, then add another third of the minced (ground) mixture. Arrange the remaining hare breast pieces on top and cover with the rest of the minced (ground) mixture. Smooth the top and place the remaining bacon rashers (slices) on top.

Bake in a preheated moderate oven (180°C/350°F, Gas Mark 4) for 2½ hours. Pour off most of the fat and allow to cool.

Serve cold, cut into thick slices.
Serves 8 to 10

Stuffed courgettes (zucchini)

METRIC/IMPERIAL
8 small courgettes
225g/8oz peeled shrimps
2 × 15ml spoons/
 2 tablespoons lemon juice
salt
freshly ground black pepper
100g/4oz cottage cheese

AMERICAN
8 small zucchini
1 cup shelled shrimp
2 tablespoons lemon juice
salt
freshly ground black pepper
½ cup cottage cheese

Cut a thin slice, lengthways, from each courgette (zucchini) and scoop out the seeds. Blanch in boiling water for 4 minutes. Refresh under cold running water and allow to cool.

Mix together the shrimps, 1 × 15ml spoon/ 1 tablespoon of the lemon juice and salt and pepper to taste. Fill the courgettes (zucchini) with the shrimps.

Push the cottage cheese through a sieve (strainer) until it is smooth. Beat in the remaining lemon juice and salt and pepper to taste.

Arrange the courgettes (zucchini) on 4 serving plates and spoon over the cheese dressing. Chill lightly before serving.
Serves 4

Celeriac rémoulade

METRIC/IMPERIAL
1 celeriac (about 225g/8oz), peeled and grated
½ small onion, peeled and grated
250ml/8fl oz mayonnaise★
2 × 5ml spoons/2 teaspoons lemon juice
1 × 15ml spoon/
1 tablespoon made French mustard
4–6 lettuce leaves
chopped chives to garnish

AMERICAN
1 celery root (about ½lb), peeled and grated
½ small onion, peeled and grated
1 cup mayonnaise★
2 teaspoons lemon juice
1 tablespoon prepared French mustard
4–6 lettuce leaves
chopped chives to garnish

Mix together the celeriac (celery root), onion, mayonnaise, lemon juice and mustard. Line a salad bowl with the lettuce leaves and pile the celeriac mixture in the centre. Sprinkle with chives and serve.
Serves 4

Stuffed peaches

METRIC/IMPERIAL
25g/1oz sultanas, chopped
175g/6oz cream cheese
25g/1oz walnuts, chopped
2 large peaches, peeled, halved and stoned

AMERICAN
3 tablespoons chopped seedless white raisins
¾ cup cream cheese
¼ cup chopped walnuts
2 large peaches, peeled, halved and pitted

Soak the sultanas (raisins) in boiling water for 5 minutes. Drain and fold into the cream cheese with the walnuts. Form the cream cheese mixture into 4 balls.
Arrange the peach halves in 4 small dishes and place a cheese ball in the hollow of each.
Serves 4

Pears with blue cheese dressing

METRIC/IMPERIAL
lettuce leaves
4 pears, halved and cored
4 black grapes, halved and deseeded
Dressing:
175g/6oz blue cheese, crumbled
150ml/¼ pint mayonnaise★

AMERICAN
lettuce leaves
4 pears, halved and cored
4 black grapes, halved and deseeded
Dressing:
6oz blue cheese, crumbled
⅔ cup mayonnaise★

Arrange lettuce leaves on a serving plate, piling them up in the centre. Place the pear halves, cut sides down, around the lettuce.
To make the dressing, cream the cheese with enough of the mayonnaise to make a smooth thick dressing. Pour over the pears and garnish with the grapes and extra crumbled blue cheese. Serve lightly chilled.
Serves 4

Avocado with cheese dressing

METRIC/IMPERIAL
3 avocado pears
lemon juice
50g/2oz cottage cheese
50g/2oz blue cheese, diced

AMERICAN
3 avocado pears
lemon juice
¼ cup cottage cheese
¼ cup diced blue cheese

Halve the avocado pears and remove the stones (seeds). Sprinkle the cut surfaces with lemon juice to prevent discoloration and place the avocado halves on 6 serving plates.
Push the cottage cheese through a sieve (strainer) until it is smooth. Fold in the diced blue cheese. Fill the hollows in the avocado halves with the cheese mixture and serve.
Serves 6

Grilled (broiled) grapefruit

METRIC/IMPERIAL
2 large grapefruit, halved
4 × 5ml spoons/
  4 teaspoons medium sherry
4 × 15ml spoons/
  4 tablespoons brown sugar
15g/½oz butter, cut into 4 pieces

AMERICAN
2 large grapefruit, halved
4 teaspoons medium sherry
4 tablespoons brown sugar
1 tablespoon butter, cut into 4 pieces

Loosen the grapefruit segments and remove any seeds. Turn the halves, cut sides down, on absorbent paper to drain for 5 minutes.
  Arrange the grapefruit halves, cut sides up, in a grill (broiler) pan. Sprinkle each with 1 × 5ml spoon/ 1 teaspoon sherry, then with 1 × 15ml spoon/ 1 tablespoon sugar. Top each with a piece of butter. Grill (broil) for about 5 minutes or until bubbling.
Serves 4

Gingered grapefruit

METRIC/IMPERIAL
2 large grapefruit, peeled and segmented
4 × 15ml spoons/
  4 tablespoons sweet sherry
pinch of ground ginger
pinch of grated nutmeg
2 × 15ml spoons/
  2 tablespoons finely chopped preserved ginger

AMERICAN
2 large grapefruit, peeled and segmented
4 tablespoons sweet sherry
pinch of ground ginger
pinch of grated nutmeg
2 tablespoons finely chopped preserved ginger

Remove all the skin from the grapefruit segments and arrange the segments in 4 individual serving dishes. Sprinkle each serving with 1 × 15ml spoon/ 1 tablespoon sherry. Mix together the ginger and nutmeg and sprinkle over the grapefruit with the preserved ginger. Serve lightly chilled.
Serves 4

Minted melon cocktail

METRIC/IMPERIAL
100g/4oz sugar
120ml/4fl oz water
3 × 15ml spoons/
  3 tablespoons chopped fresh mint
juice of 1 lemon
juice of 1 orange
1 large honeydew or cantaloup melon, peeled, deseeded and cut into cubes or balls and chilled
mint sprigs to garnish

AMERICAN
½ cup sugar
½ cup water
3 tablespoons chopped fresh mint
juice of 1 lemon
juice of 1 orange
1 large honeydew or cantaloup melon, peeled, deseeded and cut into cubes or balls and chilled
mint sprigs to garnish

Put the sugar and water in a saucepan and heat gently, stirring to dissolve the sugar. Bring to the boil and boil for 5 minutes. Put the mint in a mixing bowl and pour over the hot syrup. Leave to infuse until cold.
  Strain the mint syrup and stir in the lemon and orange juices. Chill. Divide the melon cubes or balls between 6 glasses and pour over the mint syrup. Garnish with sprigs of mint and serve.
Serves 4 to 6

Melon vinaigrette

METRIC/IMPERIAL
2 small melons, peeled, deseeded and cut into cubes or balls and chilled
Vinaigrette:
1 × 5ml spoon/
  1 teaspoon caster sugar
salt
freshly ground black pepper
good pinch dry mustard
1 × 15ml spoon/
  1 tablespoon wine vinegar
3–4 × 15ml spoons/
  3–4 tablespoons olive oil
1 × 15ml spoon/
  1 tablespoon chopped fresh herbs (mint, parsley, chives, etc.)

AMERICAN
2 small melons, peeled, deseeded and cut into cubes or balls and chilled
Vinaigrette:
1 teaspoon sugar
salt
freshly ground black pepper
good pinch dry mustard
1 tablespoon wine vinegar
3–4 tablespoons olive oil
1 tablespoon chopped fresh herbs (mint, parsley, chives, etc.)

First prepare the vinaigrette dressing. Put the sugar, salt and pepper to taste, the mustard and vinegar into a bowl and mix well until the sugar dissolves. Add the oil, a little at a time, until well blended. Stir in the herbs. Add the melon cubes or balls to the dressing and mix well. Serve in individual glass dishes.
Serves 4

SOUPS

Thick carrot, leek and potato soup

METRIC/IMPERIAL
25g/1oz butter
3 medium carrots, peeled and chopped
3 medium leeks, thoroughly cleaned and chopped
3 medium potatoes, peeled and diced
1.2 litres/2 pints beef stock
salt
freshly ground black pepper
pinch of sugar
1 × 2.5ml spoon/½ teaspoon grated nutmeg
4 × 15ml spoons/ 4 tablespoons single cream

AMERICAN
2 tablespoons butter
3 medium carrots, peeled and chopped
3 medium leeks, thoroughly cleaned and chopped
3 medium potatoes, peeled and diced
5 cups beef stock
salt
freshly ground black pepper
pinch of sugar
½ teaspoon grated nutmeg
4 tablespoons light cream

Melt the butter in a saucepan. Add the carrots, leeks and potatoes and cook gently for 10 minutes. Stir in the stock and bring to the boil. Half cover and simmer for 30 minutes or until all the vegetables are very tender. Remove from the heat and allow to cool slightly.

Pour the vegetable mixture into the goblet of an electric blender and blend until smooth. Return to the saucepan and stir in salt and pepper to taste, the sugar and nutmeg. Reheat gently.

Stir in the cream and serve hot.
Serves 4

Bortsch

METRIC/IMPERIAL
25g/1oz butter
1 large onion, peeled and sliced
1 large carrot, peeled and grated
2 large cooked beetroots, peeled and sliced
½ small red cabbage, cored and shredded
1.2 litres/2 pints beef stock
1 × 15ml spoon/ 1 tablespoon tomato purée
1 × 15ml spoon/ 1 tablespoon vinegar
1 × 15ml spoon/ 1 tablespoon sugar
salt
freshly ground black pepper
300ml/½ pint sour cream to serve

AMERICAN
2 tablespoons butter
1 large onion, peeled and sliced
1 large carrot, peeled and grated
2 large cooked beets, peeled and sliced
½ small head red cabbage, cored and shredded
5 cups beef stock
1 tablespoon tomato paste
1 tablespoon vinegar
1 tablespoon sugar
salt
freshly ground black pepper
1¼ cups sour cream to serve

Melt the butter in a saucepan. Add the onion, carrot, beetroot (beets) and cabbage and cook gently for 5 minutes. Stir in the stock, tomato purée (paste), vinegar, sugar and salt and pepper to taste and bring to the boil. Cover and simmer for 20 to 30 minutes or until all the vegetables are tender.

Serve hot, with sour cream handed separately.
Serves 4

Watercress soup

METRIC/IMPERIAL
100g/4oz butter
50g/2oz plain flour
750ml/1¼ pints chicken stock
300ml/½ pint milk
salt
freshly ground black pepper
1 small onion, peeled and chopped
2 bunches of watercress, chopped
toasted bread croûtons to garnish

AMERICAN
½ cup butter
½ cup all-purpose flour
3 cups chicken stock
1¼ cups milk
salt
freshly ground black pepper
1 small onion, peeled and chopped
2 bunches of watercress, chopped
toasted bread croûtons to garnish

Melt 75g/3oz/⅓ cup of the butter in a saucepan. Stir in the flour and cook, stirring, for 1 minute. Remove from the heat and gradually stir in the stock and milk. Return to the heat and bring to the boil, stirring. Simmer until thickened and smooth. Remove from the heat and add salt and pepper to taste. Keep hot.

Melt the remaining butter in a frying pan (skillet). Add the onion and fry until it is soft but not brown. Stir in the watercress, cover and cook for 4 minutes.

Stir the watercress mixture into the stock mixture in the saucepan. Pour into the goblet of an electric blender and blend until smooth. Alternatively, push the mixture through a sieve (strainer).

Return to the saucepan and reheat gently. Serve hot, garnished with croûtons.
Serves 6

Cream of celery and tomato soup

METRIC/IMPERIAL
75g/3oz butter
1 medium onion, peeled and chopped
1 large head celery, sliced
0.75kg/1½lb tomatoes, peeled and chopped
1.2 litres/2 pints chicken stock
1 × 2.5ml spoon/½ teaspoon dried basil
50g/2oz plain flour
300ml/½ pint milk
salt
freshly ground black pepper
300ml/½ pint single cream

AMERICAN
⅓ cup butter
1 medium onion, peeled and chopped
1 large head celery, sliced
3 cups peeled and chopped tomatoes
5 cups chicken stock
½ teaspoon dried basil
½ cup all-purpose flour
1¼ cups milk
salt
freshly ground black pepper
1¼ cups light cream

Melt 25g/1oz/2 tablespoons of the butter in a saucepan. Add the onion and fry until it is soft but not brown. Stir in the celery and continue frying for 3 minutes.

Add the tomatoes, stock and basil and bring to the boil. Cover and simmer for 45 minutes. Pour into the goblet of an electric blender and blend until smooth. Alternatively, push through a sieve (strainer).

Melt the remaining butter in a saucepan. Stir in the flour and cook, stirring, for 1 minute. Gradually stir in the milk and bring to the boil, stirring. Simmer until thickened. Add the puréed vegetable mixture with salt and pepper to taste and simmer for a further 15 minutes. Just before serving, stir in the cream and reheat, but do not allow to boil.
Serves 6

Thick tomato soup

METRIC/IMPERIAL
25g/1oz butter
25g/1oz lean bacon, rind removed and chopped
1 onion, peeled and chopped
1 carrot, peeled and chopped
1 celery stick, chopped
1kg/2lb tomatoes, chopped
1.2 litres/2 pints chicken stock
1 bay leaf
3 × 15ml spoons/ 3 tablespoons cornflour
3 × 15ml spoons/ 3 tablespoons milk
2 × 15ml spoons/ 2 tablespoons tomato purée
salt
freshly ground black pepper
sugar
chopped parsley to garnish

AMERICAN
2 tablespoons butter
2 Canadian bacon slices, chopped
1 onion, peeled and chopped
1 carrot, peeled and chopped
1 celery stalk, chopped
4 cups chopped tomatoes
5 cups chicken stock
1 bay leaf
3 tablespoons cornstarch
3 tablespoons milk
2 tablespoons tomato paste
salt
freshly ground black pepper
sugar
chopped parsley to garnish

Melt the butter in a saucepan. Add the bacon and fry until it is softened. Add the onion, carrot and celery and fry gently until the vegetables are soft but not brown. Stir in the tomatoes, stock and bay leaf and bring to the boil. Simmer for 1½ hours.

Remove the bay leaf. Purée the soup in an electric blender or by pushing it through a sieve (strainer). Return the puréed soup to the saucepan. Dissolve the cornflour (cornstarch) in the milk and stir into the soup. Simmer, stirring, until thickened. Stir in the tomato purée (paste). Season to taste with salt, pepper and sugar.

Serve hot, garnished with parsley.
Serves 4 to 6

Pea soup

METRIC/IMPERIAL
25g/1oz butter
1 × 15ml spoon/ 1 tablespoon olive oil
1 small onion, peeled and chopped
2 celery sticks, chopped
275g/10oz shelled peas
1 small ham bone
450ml/¾ pint chicken stock or water
1 × 15ml spoon/ 1 tablespoon cornflour
300ml/½ pint milk
salt
freshly ground black pepper

AMERICAN
2 tablespoons butter
1 tablespoon olive oil
1 small onion, peeled and chopped
2 celery stalks, chopped
2 cups shelled peas
1 small ham bone
2 cups chicken stock or water
1 tablespoon cornstarch
1¼ cups milk
salt
freshly ground black pepper

Melt the butter with the oil in a saucepan. Add the onion and celery and fry until the onion is soft but not brown. Add the peas and cook for 5 minutes.

Add the ham bone and stock or water. Bring to the boil, cover and simmer gently for 30 to 40 minutes or until the peas are very tender.

Remove the ham bone, then purée the soup in an electric blender or by pushing it through a sieve (strainer). Return the puréed soup to the saucepan.

Dissolve the cornflour (cornstarch) in the milk and add to the soup. Simmer, stirring, until thickened. Season to taste with salt and pepper and serve hot.
Serves 4

Creamy potato soup

METRIC/IMPERIAL
2 × 15ml spoons/
  2 tablespoons olive oil
1 large onion, peeled and
  chopped
4 large potatoes, peeled and
  grated
1 small ham bone
1.2 litres/2 pints chicken
  stock
salt
freshly ground black pepper
3 × 15ml spoons/
  3 tablespoons single cream
grated nutmeg

AMERICAN
2 tablespoons olive oil
1 large onion, peeled and
  chopped
4 large potatoes, peeled and
  grated
1 small ham bone
5 cups chicken stock
salt
freshly ground black pepper
3 tablespoons light cream
grated nutmeg

Heat the oil in a saucepan. Add the onion and fry until it is soft but not brown. Add the potatoes with the ham bone, stock and salt and pepper to taste and bring to the boil. Cover and simmer for 20 minutes.

Remove the ham bone, then stir in the cream. If the soup is too thick, dilute with a little more cream or stock. Reheat gently.

Serve sprinkled with nutmeg.
Serves 4

Courgette (zucchini) and carrot soup

METRIC/IMPERIAL
50g/2oz butter
225g/8oz carrots, peeled
  and thinly sliced
225g/8oz courgettes, thinly
  sliced
pinch of dried thyme
1 bay leaf
1.2 litres/2 pints chicken
  stock
2 × 5ml spoons/2 teaspoons
  tomato purée
3 × 15ml spoons/
  3 tablespoons instant
  mashed potato powder
salt
freshly ground black pepper
chopped parsley to garnish

AMERICAN
¼ cup butter
½lb carrots, peeled and
  thinly sliced
½lb zucchini, thinly sliced
pinch of dried thyme
1 bay leaf
5 cups chicken stock
2 teaspoons tomato paste
3 tablespoons instant
  mashed potato powder
salt
freshly ground black pepper
chopped parsley to garnish

Melt the butter in a saucepan. Add the carrots, courgettes (zucchini), thyme and bay leaf. Cover and cook gently, shaking the pan occasionally, for 10 minutes.

Stir in the stock and tomato purée (paste) and bring to the boil. Re-cover and simmer for 30 minutes.

Add the potato powder with salt and pepper to taste. Bring back to the boil, stirring. Remove the bay leaf and serve hot, garnished with parsley.
Serves 6

French onion soup

METRIC/IMPERIAL
25g/1oz butter
2 × 15ml spoons/
  2 tablespoons olive oil
1 garlic clove, crushed
3 large onions, peeled and
  thinly sliced
1.2 litres/2 pints beef stock
salt
freshly ground black pepper
8–12 slices of French bread
75g/3oz Gruyère or
  Cheddar cheese, grated

AMERICAN
2 tablespoons butter
2 tablespoons olive oil
1 garlic clove, crushed
3 large onions, peeled and
  thinly sliced
5 cups beef stock
salt
freshly ground black pepper
8–12 slices of French bread
¾ cup grated Gruyère or
  Cheddar cheese

Melt the butter with the oil in a saucepan. Add the garlic and onions and fry gently for about 20 minutes or until the onions are very soft and pale golden brown. Do not allow them to brown too much.

Stir in the stock with salt and pepper to taste and bring to the boil. Simmer, covered, for 30 minutes.

Meanwhile, toast the bread. Ladle the soup into individual flameproof soup bowls and float 1 or 2 slices of bread on each. Sprinkle with the cheese. Grill (broil) for 1 to 2 minutes or until the cheese melts and is lightly golden brown. Serve hot.
Serves 4 to 6

Minestrone

METRIC/IMPERIAL
2 × 15ml spoons/
  2 tablespoons olive oil
1 large onion, peeled and
  finely chopped
1 garlic clove, crushed
4 streaky bacon rashers,
  rinds removed and chopped
1 small white cabbage,
  cored and shredded
4 celery sticks, chopped
1.75 litres/3 pints beef
  stock
50g/2oz dried white haricot
  beans, soaked overnight
  and drained
salt
freshly ground black pepper
4 large tomatoes, peeled,
  deseeded and chopped
2 × 15ml spoons/
  2 tablespoons tomato purée
2 carrots, peeled and diced
50g/2oz French beans,
  sliced
50g/2oz shelled peas
50g/2oz broken macaroni
1 × 5ml spoon/1 teaspoon
  dried basil or thyme
grated Parmesan cheese to
  serve

AMERICAN
2 tablespoons olive oil
1 large onion, peeled and
  finely chopped
1 garlic clove, crushed
4 bacon slices, chopped
1 small head white cabbage,
  cored and shredded
4 celery stalks, chopped
7½ cups beef stock
⅓ cup dried navy beans,
  soaked overnight and
  drained
salt
freshly ground black pepper
4 large tomatoes, peeled,
  deseeded and chopped
2 tablespoons tomato paste
2 carrots, peeled and diced
¼ cup sliced green beans
⅓ cup shelled peas
½ cup broken macaroni
1 teaspoon dried basil or
  thyme
grated Parmesan cheese to
  serve

Heat the oil in a large saucepan. Add the onion, garlic and bacon and fry until the onion is soft but not brown and the bacon is crisp. Stir in the cabbage, celery, stock, beans and salt and pepper to taste and bring to the boil. Cover and simmer for 2½ hours or until the beans are tender.

Add the tomatoes, tomato purée (paste), carrots, French (green) beans, peas, macaroni and herbs and continue simmering for 20 minutes or until the vegetables and macaroni are tender. Serve hot, with Parmesan cheese passed separately.
Serves 6

Oxtail soup

METRIC/IMPERIAL
4 × 15ml spoons/
  4 tablespoons oil
1 medium oxtail, cut into
  pieces
2 onions, peeled and
  chopped
2 carrots, peeled and
  chopped
2 celery sticks, chopped
1 medium turnip, peeled
  and chopped
2 litres/3½ pints water
salt
freshly ground black pepper
1 × 400g/14oz can tomatoes
2 × 15ml spoons/
  2 tablespoons plain flour
4 × 15ml spoons/
  4 tablespoons medium
  sherry

AMERICAN
4 tablespoons oil
1 medium oxtail, cut into
  pieces
2 onions, peeled and
  chopped
2 carrots, peeled and
  chopped
2 celery stalks, chopped
1 medium turnip, peeled
  and chopped
4½ pints water
salt
freshly ground black pepper
1 × 14oz can tomatoes
2 tablespoons all-purpose
  flour
4 tablespoons medium
  sherry

Heat the oil in a saucepan. Add the oxtail pieces and brown on all sides. Remove the oxtail from the pan.

Add the onions, carrots, celery and turnip to the pan and fry until the vegetables are just soft but not brown. Stir in the water with salt and pepper to taste. Return the oxtail pieces to the pan and bring to the boil. Cover and simmer for 4 hours or until the meat is almost falling off the bones.

Remove the oxtail pieces from the pan and remove the meat from the bones. Cut into small pieces. Allow the soup liquid to cool, then skim off the fat from the surface.

Pour the soup liquid and tomatoes, with the can juice, into the goblet of an electric blender and blend until smooth. Return to the saucepan and add the pieces of oxtail meat. Dissolve the flour in the sherry and stir into the soup. Bring to the boil gently, stirring, and simmer until thickened. Serve hot.
Serves 6

Cock-a-leekie

METRIC/IMPERIAL
1 × 1.5kg/3lb boiling
  chicken
1 bouquet garni
salt
freshly ground black pepper
6 leeks, halved crossways,
  thoroughly cleaned and cut
  into strips
6 prunes, soaked overnight,
  drained, halved and stoned

AMERICAN
1 × 3lb stewing chicken
1 bouquet garni
salt
freshly ground black pepper
6 leeks, halved crosswise,
  thoroughly cleaned and cut
  into strips
6 prunes, soaked overnight,
  drained, halved and pitted

Put the chicken in a large saucepan with the bouquet garni. Add enough water to cover and salt and pepper to taste. Bring to the boil, then half cover and simmer gently for 2 hours. Skim off any scum that rises to the surface.

Add the leeks and more water, if necessary, so that the bird is covered. Simmer, uncovered, for a further 30 minutes. Add the prunes and simmer for a further 30 minutes or until the bird is tender.

Transfer the bird to a carving board. Discard the skin and carve some of the meat into bite-sized pieces. Discard the bouquet garni from the soup. Return the chicken pieces to the pan and reheat gently. Serve hot. (The remaining chicken may be eaten separately as a main course.)
Serves 4 to 6

Chicken and corn chowder

METRIC/IMPERIAL
25g/1oz butter
1 large onion, peeled and finely chopped
2 × 15ml spoons/ 2 tablespoons plain flour
600ml/1 pint chicken stock
225g/8oz cooked chicken meat, diced
3 large potatoes, peeled, parboiled and diced
1 × 300g/11oz can sweetcorn, drained
300ml/½ pint single cream or milk
salt
freshly ground black pepper

AMERICAN
2 tablespoons butter
1 large onion, peeled and finely chopped
2 tablespoons all-purpose flour
2½ cups chicken stock
1 cup diced cooked chicken meat
3 large potatoes, peeled, parboiled and diced
1 × 11oz can corn kernels, drained
1¼ cups light cream or milk
salt
freshly ground black pepper

Melt the butter in a saucepan. Add the onion and fry until it is soft but not brown. Sprinkle over the flour and cook, stirring, for 1 minute. Gradually stir in the stock. Bring to the boil, stirring, and simmer until thickened.

Add the chicken, potatoes and corn and simmer for 20 minutes.

Stir in the cream or milk with salt and pepper to taste and heat through gently for a further 10 minutes. Serve hot.

Serves 4 to 6

Ertwensoep

METRIC/IMPERIAL
225g/8oz dried split peas
1.75 litres/3 pints water
0.75kg/1½lb stewing meat (for soup)
1 marrow bone, sawn into pieces
225g/8oz potatoes, peeled and sliced
300ml/½ pint milk
salt
freshly ground black pepper
1 leek, thoroughly cleaned and chopped
1 celery stick, chopped
2 × 15ml spoons/ 2 tablespoons chopped fresh parsley

AMERICAN
1 cup dried split peas
7½ cups water
1½lb stewing meat (for soup)
1 marrow bone, sawn into pieces
½lb potatoes, peeled and sliced
1¼ cups milk
salt
freshly ground black pepper
1 leek, thoroughly cleaned and chopped
1 celery stalk, chopped
2 tablespoons chopped fresh parsley

Soak the peas in half the water overnight.

Put the meat and marrow bone in a saucepan and pour over the remaining water. Bring to the boil and simmer for 1 hour. Add the split peas and soaking water and simmer for a further 40 minutes. Stir in the potatoes and continue simmering for 20 minutes or until the peas and potatoes are tender.

Remove the marrow bone and meat. Keep the meat hot. Scrape the marrow out of the bone and add to the saucepan. Purée the split pea mixture in an electric blender or by pushing it through a sieve (strainer). Return to the saucepan and stir in enough of the milk to thin the mixture to a soup consistency. Add salt and pepper to taste, the leek and celery. Simmer for 20 minutes, stirring occasionally. Stir in the parsley.

Chop the meat and serve with the soup.
Serves 6

Spiced fish soup

METRIC/IMPERIAL
50g/2oz butter
1 onion, peeled and chopped
275g/10oz white fish fillets, skinned and cut into small pieces
1 × 15ml spoon/ 1 tablespoon plain flour
pinch of ground cinnamon
pinch of mild curry powder
750ml/1¼ pints water
1 × 5ml spoon/1 teaspoon Worcestershire sauce
2 tomatoes, peeled and chopped
salt
freshly ground black pepper
toasted bread croûtons to garnish

AMERICAN
¼ cup butter
1 onion, peeled and chopped
10oz white fish fillets, skinned and cut into small pieces
1 tablespoon all-purpose flour
pinch of ground cinnamon
pinch of mild curry powder
3 cups water
1 teaspoon Worcestershire sauce
2 tomatoes, peeled and chopped
salt
freshly ground black pepper
toasted bread croûtons to garnish

Melt the butter in a saucepan. Add the onion and fry until it is soft but not brown. Add the fish and cook for a further 5 minutes. Sprinkle over the flour, cinnamon and curry powder and stir well. Gradually stir in the water and bring to the boil, stirring. Simmer until thickened.

Add the Worcestershire sauce, tomatoes and salt and pepper to taste. Simmer for 10 minutes.

Serve hot, garnished with croûtons.
Serves 4 to 6

Clam chowder

METRIC/IMPERIAL
75g/3oz salt pork, diced
2 onions, peeled and finely chopped
175ml/6fl oz water or fish stock★
250ml/8fl oz milk
4 medium potatoes, peeled and diced
1 × 0.5kg/1lb can clams, drained and chopped
pinch of cayenne pepper
salt
freshly ground black pepper
150ml/¼ pint double cream

AMERICAN
⅓ cup diced salt or pickled pork
2 onions, peeled and finely chopped
¾ cup water or fish stock★
1 cup milk
4 medium potatoes, peeled and diced
1 × 1lb can clams, drained and chopped
pinch of cayenne pepper
salt
freshly ground black pepper
⅔ cup heavy cream

Fry the pork in a saucepan until it has rendered most of its fat. Add the onions and fry until they are soft but not brown. Stir in the water or stock, milk and potatoes and bring to the boil. Simmer for 15 to 20 minutes or until the potatoes are tender.

Add the clams, cayenne and salt and pepper to taste and heat through gently. Stir in the cream and continue cooking gently for 3 minutes. Serve hot.
Serves 4

Quick crab bisque

METRIC/IMPERIAL
50g/2oz butter
1 onion, peeled and finely chopped
50g/2oz mushrooms, thinly sliced
450ml/¾ pint fish stock★
1 × 425g/15oz can crabmeat, drained and flaked
300ml/½ pint single cream
2 egg yolks
2 × 15ml spoons/ 2 tablespoons sherry
salt
freshly ground black pepper

AMERICAN
¼ cup butter
1 onion, peeled and finely chopped
½ cup thinly sliced mushrooms
2 cups fish stock★
1 × 15oz can crabmeat, drained and flaked
1¼ cups light cream
2 egg yolks
2 tablespoons sherry
salt
freshly ground black pepper

Melt the butter in a saucepan. Add the onion and fry until it is soft but not brown. Add the mushrooms and fry for 3 minutes. Stir in the stock and crabmeat and simmer gently for 5 minutes.

Mix together the cream and egg yolks. Stir a little of the hot crab liquid into the egg mixture, then stir into the crab mixture in the saucepan. Heat through gently, stirring, until thickened. Stir in the sherry and salt and pepper to taste and serve hot.
Serves 4 to 6

Cheddar soup

METRIC/IMPERIAL
50g/2oz butter
50g/2oz plain flour
300ml/½ pint milk
450ml/¾ pint chicken stock
2 carrots, peeled and grated
175g/6oz Cheddar cheese, grated
salt
freshly ground black pepper
toasted bread croûtons to garnish

AMERICAN
¼ cup butter
½ cup all-purpose flour
1¼ cups milk
2 cups chicken stock
2 carrots, peeled and grated
1½ cups grated Cheddar cheese
salt
freshly ground black pepper
toasted bread croûtons to garnish

Melt the butter in a saucepan. Add the flour and cook, stirring, for 1 minute. Remove from the heat and gradually stir in the milk and stock. Return to the heat and bring to the boil, stirring. Simmer until thickened and smooth.

Add the carrots and simmer for 3 minutes, then stir in the cheese with salt and pepper to taste. When the cheese has melted, pour into soup bowls and serve hot, topped with croûtons.
Serves 4

Chilled tomato and parsley soup

METRIC/IMPERIAL
0.5kg/1lb tomatoes, peeled, deseeded and chopped
juice of ½ lemon
1 × 5ml spoon/1 teaspoon salt
1 slice of onion
3 parsley sprigs
1 × 425g/15oz can condensed consommé
chopped parsley to garnish

AMERICAN
2 cups peeled, deseeded and chopped tomatoes
juice of ½ lemon
1 teaspoon salt
1 slice of onion
3 parsley sprigs
1 × 15oz can condensed consommé
chopped parsley to garnish

Put the tomatoes, lemon juice, salt, onion and parsley sprigs in the goblet of an electric blender. Blend until smooth. Pour into a serving bowl and stir in the consommé. Chill well.

Just before serving, sprinkle with chopped parsley.
Serves 4 to 6

Chilled prawn soup

METRIC/IMPERIAL
1 large can evaporated milk, chilled
4 × 15ml spoons/ 4 tablespoons lemon juice
2 × 5ml spoons/2 teaspoons finely grated onion
1 × 5ml spoon/1 teaspoon made mustard
2 × 15ml spoons/ 2 tablespoons double cream
salt
175g/6oz peeled prawns, finely chopped
3 × 15ml spoons/ 3 tablespoons chopped fresh parsley
unpeeled prawns to garnish

AMERICAN
1 large can evaporated milk, chilled
4 tablespoons lemon juice
2 teaspoons finely grated onion
1 teaspoon prepared mustard
2 tablespoons heavy cream
salt
1 cup finely chopped shelled shrimp
3 tablespoons chopped fresh parsley
unshelled shrimp to garnish

Mix together the evaporated milk, lemon juice, onion, mustard, cream and salt to taste. Fold in the prawns (shrimp) and parsley. Pour into a serving tureen and chill for at least 1 hour.

Stir gently before serving, garnished with unpeeled prawns (shrimp).
Serves 4

Vichyssoise

METRIC/IMPERIAL
50g/2oz butter
4 leeks (white part only), thoroughly cleaned and thinly sliced
1 onion, peeled and thinly sliced
1.5 litres/2½ pints chicken stock
0.5kg/1lb potatoes, peeled and thinly sliced
150ml/¼ pint double cream
salt
freshly ground pepper
pinch of grated nutmeg
chopped chives to garnish

AMERICAN
¼ cup butter
4 leeks (white part only), thoroughly cleaned and thinly sliced
1 onion, peeled and thinly sliced
6¼ cups chicken stock
1lb potatoes, peeled and thinly sliced
⅔ cup heavy cream
salt
freshly ground pepper
pinch of grated nutmeg
chopped chives to garnish

Melt the butter in a saucepan. Add the leeks and onion and cook gently until they are soft but not brown. Stir in the stock and add the potatoes. Bring to the boil, cover and simmer for 30 minutes or until all the vegetables are very tender.

Purée the soup in an electric blender or by pushing it through a sieve (strainer). Allow to cool.

Stir in the cream with salt and pepper to taste and the nutmeg. Chill well. Serve cold, garnished with chives.
Serves 4 to 6

Chilled cream of spinach soup

METRIC/IMPERIAL
50g/2oz butter
1 onion, peeled and chopped
0.5kg/1lb spinach, stalks removed
900ml/1½ pints chicken stock
salt
freshly ground black pepper
2 × 5ml spoons/2 teaspoons lemon juice
1 bay leaf
2 × 15ml spoons/ 2 tablespoons plain flour
6 × 15ml spoons/ 6 tablespoons single cream

AMERICAN
¼ cup butter
1 onion, peeled and chopped
1lb spinach, stalks removed
3¾ cups chicken stock
salt
freshly ground black pepper
2 teaspoons lemon juice
1 bay leaf
2 tablespoons all-purpose flour
6 tablespoons light cream

Melt 25g/1oz/2 tablespoons of the butter in a saucepan. Add the onion and fry until it is soft but not brown. Add the spinach and cook for 5 minutes. Stir in the stock, salt and pepper to taste, the lemon juice and bay leaf and bring to the boil. Cover and simmer for 20 minutes.

Remove the bay leaf and purée the soup in an electric blender.

Melt the remaining butter in another saucepan. Add the flour and cook, stirring, for 1 minute. Gradually stir in the puréed spinach mixture and bring to the boil, stirring. Simmer for 5 minutes. Remove from the heat and allow to cool, then chill.

Just before serving stir in the cream.
Serves 4

Chilled cucumber soup

METRIC/IMPERIAL
900ml/1½ pints chicken stock
1 small onion, peeled and sliced
1 large cucumber, peeled and chopped
1 mint sprig
1 × 15ml spoon/ 1 tablespoon cornflour
2 × 15ml spoons/ 2 tablespoons water
3 × 15ml spoons/ 3 tablespoons double cream
salt
freshly ground black pepper
green food colouring
To garnish:
diced cucumber
sprig of mint

AMERICAN
3¾ cups chicken stock
1 small onion, peeled and sliced
1 large cucumber, peeled and chopped
1 mint sprig
1 tablespoon cornstarch
2 tablespoons water
3 tablespoons heavy cream
salt
freshly ground black pepper
green food coloring
To garnish:
diced cucumber
sprig of mint

Put the stock and onion in a saucepan and bring to the boil. Simmer for 15 minutes.

Add the cucumber and mint and simmer for a further 20 minutes. Pour into the goblet of an electric blender and blend until smooth. Alternatively, push through a sieve (strainer).

Return to the saucepan and reheat gently. Dissolve the cornflour (cornstarch) in the water and add to the saucepan. Bring to the boil, stirring, and simmer until thickened. Stir in the cream with salt and pepper to taste. Remove from the heat. Stir in enough food colouring to tint the soup a pale green. Allow to cool.

Pour the soup into a serving bowl or tureen and chill. Serve garnished with diced cucumber and a sprig of mint.
Serves 4

Gazpacho

METRIC/IMPERIAL
0.5kg/1lb tomatoes, peeled and chopped
1 small onion, peeled and chopped
1 small green pepper, pith and seeds removed and chopped
1 garlic clove, crushed
1 × 15ml spoon/ 1 tablespoon red wine vinegar
1 × 15ml spoon/ 1 tablespoon olive oil
1–2 × 15ml spoons/ 1–2 tablespoons lemon juice
salt
freshly ground black pepper
To garnish:
1 egg, hard-boiled and finely chopped
toasted bread croûtons

AMERICAN
2 cups peeled and chopped tomatoes
1 small onion, peeled and chopped
1 small green pepper, pith and seeds removed and chopped
1 garlic clove, crushed
1 tablespoon red wine vinegar
1 tablespoon olive oil
1–2 tablespoons lemon juice
salt
freshly ground black pepper
To garnish:
1 egg, hard-cooked and finely chopped
toasted bread croûtons

Put the tomatoes, onion, green pepper, garlic, vinegar and oil in the goblet of an electric blender. Blend until smooth, then pour into a mixing bowl. Stir in lemon juice and salt and pepper to taste. Chill for at least 1 hour.

Serve cold, sprinkled with the egg and croûtons.
Serves 4

Chilled cream of chicken soup

METRIC/IMPERIAL
600ml/1 pint chicken stock
1 onion, peeled and chopped
1 large potato, peeled and chopped
1 bouquet garni
100g/4oz cooked chicken meat, chopped
150ml/¼ pint single cream
salt
freshly ground black pepper
chopped chives to garnish

AMERICAN
2½ cups chicken stock
1 onion, peeled and chopped
1 large potato, peeled and chopped
1 bouquet garni
½ cup chopped cooked chicken meat
⅔ cup light cream
salt
freshly ground black pepper
chopped chives to garnish

Put the stock, onion, potato and bouquet garni in a saucepan and bring to the boil. Simmer for 20 minutes. Add the chicken and cook for a further 10 minutes.

Remove the bouquet garni and pour the chicken mixture into the goblet of an electric blender. Blend until smooth. Stir in the cream with salt and pepper to taste and allow to cool. Chill and serve sprinkled with chives.
Serves 4

Chilled apple and orange soup

METRIC/IMPERIAL
1 medium onion, peeled and chopped
150ml/¼ pint chicken stock
300ml/½ pint dry cider
300ml/½ pint orange juice
pinch of sugar
salt
freshly ground black pepper
1 cinnamon stick
1 dessert apple, cored and finely diced to garnish

AMERICAN
1 medium onion, peeled and chopped
⅔ cup chicken stock
1¼ cups hard cider
1¼ cups orange juice
pinch of sugar
salt
freshly ground black pepper
1 cinnamon stick
1 dessert apple, cored and finely diced to garnish

Put the onion and stock in a saucepan and bring to the boil. Simmer for 5 minutes, then cover and remove from the heat. Allow to cool.

Strain the stock into a mixing bowl and stir in the cider and orange juice. Add the sugar, salt and pepper to taste and the cinnamon stick. Chill for at least 30 minutes.

To serve, remove the cinnamon stick and pour into individual soup cups. Garnish with diced apple.
Serves 4

Chilled pumpkin soup

METRIC/IMPERIAL
1 onion, peeled and chopped
1 × 200g/7oz can tomatoes, drained
900ml/1½ pints beef stock
1 bay leaf
225g/8oz cooked pumpkin, puréed
salt
freshly ground black pepper
300ml/½ pint milk

AMERICAN
1 onion, peeled and chopped
1 × 7oz can tomatoes, drained
3¾ cups beef stock
1 bay leaf
1½ cups cooked puréed pumpkin
salt
freshly ground black pepper
1¼ cups milk

Put the onion, tomatoes, stock and bay leaf in a saucepan and bring to the boil. Cover and simmer for 15 minutes. Discard the bay leaf and pour the mixture into the goblet of an electric blender. Blend until smooth.
　Return to the pan and add the pumpkin with salt and pepper to taste. Cook for 5 minutes.
　Remove from the heat and stir in the milk. Allow to cool, then chill well before serving.
Serves 6

Tomato and mint soup

METRIC/IMPERIAL
25g/1oz butter
1 carrot, peeled and diced
1 onion, peeled and chopped
3 celery sticks, chopped
50g/2oz bacon rashers, chopped
0.75kg/1½lb tomatoes, peeled and chopped
750ml/1¼ pints stock
salt
freshly ground black pepper
1–2 × 5ml spoons/
　1–2 teaspoons sugar, or to taste
2 × 15ml spoons/
　2 tablespoons chopped fresh mint
15g/½oz cornflour
150ml/¼ pint milk
fresh mint leaves to garnish

AMERICAN
2 tablespoons butter
1 carrot, peeled and diced
1 onion, peeled and chopped
3 celery stalks, chopped
3 bacon slices, chopped
3 cups peeled and chopped tomatoes
3 cups stock
salt
freshly ground black pepper
1–2 teaspoons sugar, or to taste
2 tablespoons chopped fresh mint
2 tablespoons cornstarch
⅔ cup milk
fresh mint leaves to garnish

Melt the butter in a saucepan and gently fry the carrot, onion, celery and bacon until the butter is absorbed. Add the tomatoes and cook for 2 minutes. Add the stock, salt and pepper to taste, sugar and chopped mint. Cover and simmer for 45 minutes.
　Purée the soup in a blender, then rub through a sieve (strainer). Return to the rinsed pan. Blend the cornflour (cornstarch) with the milk and add to the purée. Boil for 3 minutes, stirring constantly. Adjust the seasoning. Serve hot, garnished with mint leaves, or serve cold with a swirl of sour cream added to each bowl.
Serves 4 to 5

FISH

Grilled (broiled) marinated fish

METRIC/IMPERIAL
4 large plaice fillets
4 large tomatoes, halved
8 flat mushrooms
Marinade:
5 × 15ml spoons/
  5 tablespoons olive oil
1 garlic clove, finely
  chopped
juice of 1 lemon
sprigs of fresh basil, thyme
  or sage
salt
freshly ground black pepper

AMERICAN
4 large flounder fillets
4 large tomatoes, halved
8 flat mushrooms
Marinade:
⅓ cup olive oil
1 garlic clove, finely
  chopped
juice of 1 lemon
sprigs of fresh basil, thyme
  or sage
salt
freshly ground black pepper

Mix together the ingredients for the marinade, with salt and pepper to taste. Add the fish fillets, tomato halves and mushrooms and turn to coat them with the marinade. Leave to marinate at room temperature for 1 hour.

Remove the fish from the marinade and arrange on a grill (broiler) rack. Arrange the tomato halves and mushrooms around the fish. Grill (broil) for 4 to 5 minutes on each side, brushing frequently with the marinade. Serve hot.
Serves 4

Plaice (flounder) rolls with tomato sauce

METRIC/IMPERIAL
4 large plaice fillets, skinned
salt
freshly ground black pepper
juice of ½ lemon
4 × 15ml spoons/
  4 tablespoons béchamel
  sauce★
pinch of cayenne pepper
300ml/½ pint court
  bouillon★
600ml/1 pint hot tomato
  sauce★
To garnish:
4 black olives, halved and
  stoned
1 gherkin, chopped

AMERICAN
4 large flounder fillets,
  skinned
salt
freshly ground black pepper
juice of ½ lemon
4 tablespoons béchamel
  sauce★
pinch of cayenne pepper
1¼ cups court bouillon★
2½ cups hot tomato sauce★
To garnish:
4 black olives, halved and
  pitted
1 small dill pickle, chopped

Cut the fillets in half lengthways. Trim the sides so they are straight. Chop the trimmings. Rub the fillets with salt, pepper and lemon juice.

Stir the trimmings into the béchamel sauce with the cayenne. Spread each fillet with a little of the béchamel sauce mixture and roll up. Place the fish rolls in a baking dish, cut sides down. Choose a dish that is just large enough to hold the fish rolls so they are packed quite closely together. Pour over the court bouillon. Cover and bake in a preheated moderate oven (180°C/350°F, Gas Mark 4) for 20 minutes.

Drain the fish rolls and arrange them in a warmed serving dish. Pour over the tomato sauce and garnish with the olives and gherkin (dill pickle). Serve hot.
Serves 4

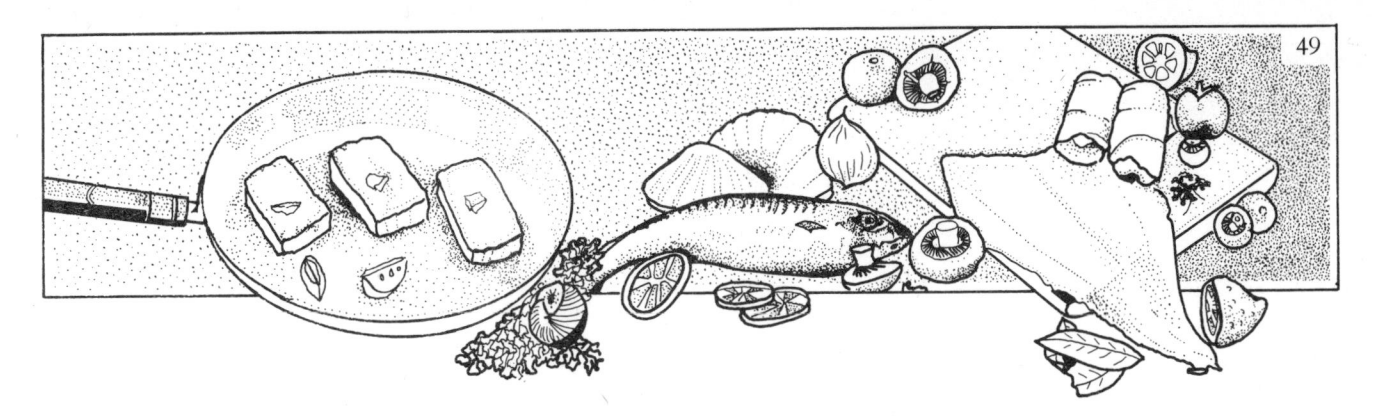

Whiting braised with vermouth

METRIC/IMPERIAL
8 whiting fillets, skinned
salt
freshly ground black pepper
75g/3oz butter, melted
50g/2oz fresh breadcrumbs
2 shallots, peeled and chopped
1 × 15ml spoon/
  1 tablespoon chopped fresh parsley
6 × 15ml spoons/
  6 tablespoons dry vermouth

AMERICAN
8 whiting fillets, skinned
salt
freshly ground black pepper
$\frac{1}{3}$ cup butter, melted
1 cup fresh breadcrumbs
2 shallots, peeled and chopped
1 tablespoon chopped fresh parsley
6 tablespoons dry vermouth

Rub the fillets with salt and pepper. Brush with about one-third of the melted butter, then coat with the breadcrumbs.

Put the shallots and parsley in the bottom of a greased baking dish. Place the fillets on top and sprinkle with the remaining melted butter. Spoon the vermouth around the fish.

Cook in a preheated hot oven (230°C/450°F, Gas Mark 8) for 10 to 15 minutes or until the fillets are tender.

Transfer the fillets to a warmed serving dish and keep hot. Strain the cooking liquid into a saucepan and bring to the boil. Boil until reduced to about half, then pour over the fish. Serve hot.
Serves 4

Cod with curry topping

METRIC/IMPERIAL
50g/2oz butter, melted
2 × 5ml spoons/2 teaspoons mild curry powder
1 × 5ml spoon/1 teaspoon Worcestershire sauce
2 × 15ml spoons/
  2 tablespoons sultanas
1 × 15ml spoon/
  1 tablespoon sweet chutney
salt
freshly ground black pepper
3 × 15ml spoons/
  3 tablespoons fresh breadcrumbs
4 cod steaks
halved lemon slices to garnish

AMERICAN
$\frac{1}{4}$ cup butter, melted
2 teaspoons mild curry powder
1 teaspoon Worcestershire sauce
2 tablespoons seedless white raisins
1 tablespoon sweet chutney
salt
freshly ground black pepper
3 tablespoons fresh breadcrumbs
4 cod steaks
halved lemon slices to garnish

Mix together the melted butter, curry powder, Worcestershire sauce, sultanas (raisins), chutney, salt and pepper to taste and the breadcrumbs. Arrange the fish in a greased baking dish and spread each with the curry topping. Bake in a preheated moderately hot oven (200°C/400°F, Gas Mark 6) for 25 minutes. Serve hot, garnished with halved lemon slices.
Serves 4

Cod or haddock with green sauce

METRIC/IMPERIAL
1 medium onion, peeled and grated
2 × 15ml spoons/
 2 tablespoons chopped fresh parsley
2 × 5ml spoons/2 teaspoons capers
2 gherkins, finely chopped
½ × 50g/2oz can anchovy fillets, drained
1 × 15ml spoon/
 1 tablespoon fresh breadcrumbs
1 × 15ml spoon/
 1 tablespoon olive oil
juice of 1 lemon
salt
freshly ground black pepper
4 cod or haddock steaks

AMERICAN
1 medium onion, peeled and grated
2 tablespoons chopped fresh parsley
2 teaspoons capers
2 small dill pickles, finely chopped
½ × 2oz can anchovy fillets, drained
1 tablespoon fresh breadcrumbs
1 tablespoon olive oil
juice of 1 lemon
salt
freshly ground black pepper
4 cod or haddock steaks

Put the onion, parsley, capers, gherkins (pickles), anchovies, breadcrumbs, oil and lemon juice in the goblet of an electric blender. Blend until the mixture is smooth. Season to taste with salt and pepper.
 Arrange the fish in a baking dish and pour over the green sauce. Cover the dish and bake in a preheated moderately hot oven (200°C/400°F, Gas Mark 6) for 15 minutes or until the fish is tender.
 Serve hot.
Serves 4

Italian-style cod steaks

METRIC/IMPERIAL
4 large cod steaks
salt
freshly ground black pepper
25g/1oz butter, melted
2 × 15ml spoons/
 2 tablespoons olive oil
1 onion, peeled and finely chopped
1 garlic clove, crushed
2 large tomatoes, peeled and chopped
5 × 15ml spoons/
 5 tablespoons dry white wine
175g/6oz mushrooms, sliced
2 × 15ml spoons/
 2 tablespoons toasted breadcrumbs
1 × 15ml spoon/
 1 tablespoon chopped fresh marjoram or oregano

AMERICAN
4 large cod steaks
salt
freshly ground black pepper
2 tablespoons butter, melted
2 tablespoons olive oil
1 onion, peeled and finely chopped
1 garlic clove, crushed
2 large tomatoes, peeled and chopped
⅓ cup dry white wine
1½ cups sliced mushrooms
2 tablespoons toasted breadcrumbs
1 tablespoon chopped fresh marjoram or oregano

Rub the cod steaks with salt and pepper and arrange on the rack in a grill (broiler) pan. Brush with half the melted butter and grill (broil) for 5 to 7 minutes on each side or until cooked through, basting with the remaining melted butter when necessary.
 Meanwhile, heat the oil in a saucepan. Add the onion and garlic and fry until the onion is soft but not brown. Stir in the tomatoes and wine and bring to the boil. Simmer for 5 minutes.
 Add the mushrooms with salt and pepper to taste and simmer for a further 5 minutes. Remove from the heat.
 Arrange the cod steaks on a warmed serving plate and pour over the tomato sauce. Sprinkle with the breadcrumbs and herbs and serve hot.
Serves 4

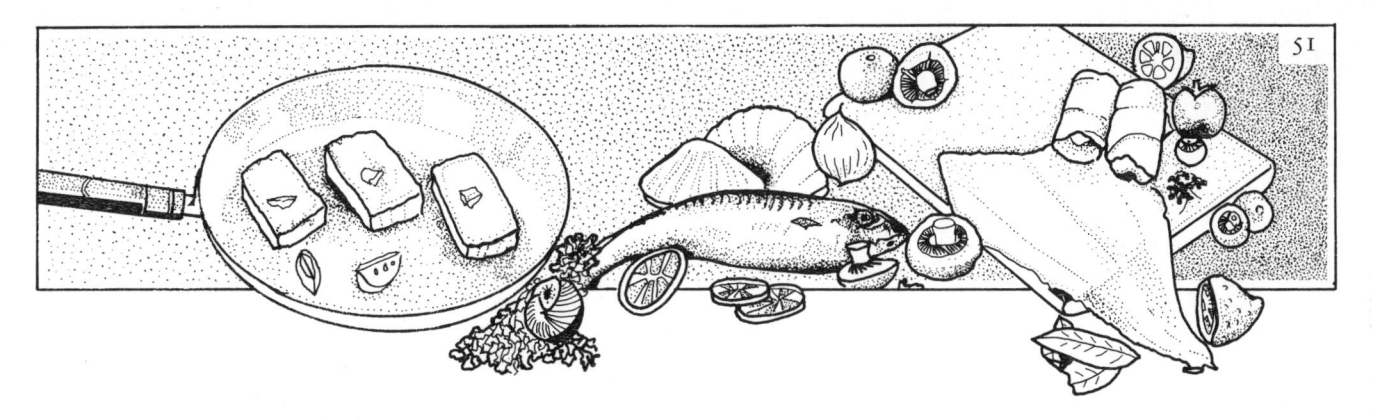

Cod and green pepper sauté

METRIC/IMPERIAL
0.75kg/1½lb cod fillet, skinned
50g/2oz flour
salt
freshly ground black pepper
2 streaky bacon rashers, rinds removed and chopped
1 green pepper, deseeded, pith removed and sliced
4 × 15ml spoons/ 4 tablespoons oil
4 tomatoes, skinned and chopped
75g/3oz Gruyère cheese, grated

AMERICAN
1½lb cod fillet, skinned
½ cup flour
salt
freshly ground black pepper
2 bacon slices, chopped
1 green pepper, deseeded, pith removed and sliced
4 tablespoons oil
4 tomatoes, skinned and chopped
¾ cup grated Gruyère cheese

Cut the fish into fairly large pieces and coat in the flour, seasoned with salt and pepper. Put the bacon and pepper in a frying pan (skillet) and fry gently. Add half the oil and half the fish. Turn the fish to brown on both sides, taking care not to break up. Remove from the pan and drain on absorbent paper. Heat the rest of the oil and fry the remaining fish. Add the chopped tomatoes and return all cooked ingredients to the pan. Reheat and season to taste with salt and pepper.

Transfer the fish mixture to a flameproof serving dish, sprinkle over the grated cheese and place under a hot grill (broiler) until browned and bubbling. Serve immediately with creamed potatoes and courgettes (zucchini).
Serves 4

Haddock with fennel and celery sauce

METRIC/IMPERIAL
1kg/2lb haddock fillet
65g/2½oz butter
salt
freshly ground black pepper
3 celery sticks, chopped
1 small head fennel, chopped
600ml/1 pint milk
50g/2oz flour
1 × 15ml spoon/ 1 tablespoon grated Parmesan cheese
To garnish:
1 lemon, sliced
fennel leaves

AMERICAN
2lb haddock fillet
5 tablespoons butter
salt
freshly ground black pepper
3 celery stalks, chopped
1 small head fennel, chopped
2½ cups milk
½ cup flour
1 tablespoon grated Parmesan cheese
To garnish:
1 lemon, sliced
fennel leaves

Place the fish in a greased ovenproof dish, dot with 15g/½oz/1 tablespoon butter and season to taste with salt and pepper. Put the celery and fennel in a pan of boiling salted water and simmer for 15 minutes. Drain well. Spoon the vegetables over the fish and pour over the milk. Cover the dish, place in a preheated moderate oven (180°C/350°F, Gas Mark 4) and cook for 12 to 15 minutes until the fish is just cooked. Drain the liquor from the fish and reserve.

Melt the remaining butter in a pan, stir in the flour and cook for 2 minutes. Gradually stir in the reserved fish liquor, bring to the boil and cook, stirring, for 3 minutes. Pour the sauce over the fish, sprinkle over the Parmesan cheese and return to the oven for about 20 minutes until heated through and bubbling. If the top is not browned, put under a hot grill (broiler) for a few minutes. Serve hot, garnished with lemon slices and fennel leaves.
Serves 4

Red mullet (snapper) provençale

METRIC/IMPERIAL
25g/1oz butter, cut into small pieces
2 tomatoes, peeled and sliced
1 small green pepper, pith and seeds removed and sliced
100g/4oz mushrooms, sliced
salt
freshly ground black pepper
4 medium red mullet
6 × 15ml spoons/
6 tablespoons dry red wine
2 × 15ml spoons/
2 tablespoons chopped fresh chives

AMERICAN
2 tablespoons butter, cut into small pieces
2 tomatoes, peeled and sliced
1 small green pepper, pith and seeds removed and sliced
1 cup sliced mushrooms
salt
freshly ground black pepper
4 small red snapper
6 tablespoons dry red wine
2 tablespoons chopped fresh chives

Dot half the butter pieces over the bottom of a shallow baking dish or casserole large enough to take the fish in one layer. Mix together the tomatoes, green pepper, mushrooms and salt and pepper to taste and spoon into the dish. Arrange the fish on top, laying them head to tail. Sprinkle over the wine and chives and dot with the remaining butter.

Cover the dish or casserole tightly with a lid or foil and bake in a preheated moderate oven (180°C/350°F, Gas Mark 4) for 30 to 35 minutes or until the fish are tender. Serve hot.
Serves 4

Salmon steaks with herbs

METRIC/IMPERIAL
4 salmon steaks
50g/2oz butter, cut into 4 pieces
2 bay leaves, halved
4 thin onion slices
4 slivers of thinly pared lemon rind
4 fresh parsley sprigs
4 fresh thyme sprigs
salt
freshly ground black pepper

AMERICAN
4 salmon steaks
¼ cup butter, cut into 4 pieces
2 bay leaves, halved
4 thin onion slices
4 slivers of thinly pared lemon rind
4 fresh parsley sprigs
4 fresh thyme sprigs
salt
freshly ground black pepper

Put the salmon steaks on 4 squares of foil large enough to enclose the steaks. Place a piece of butter, half a bay leaf, a slice of onion, a sliver of lemon rind, a parsley sprig and a thyme sprig on each steak. Sprinkle with salt and pepper.

Fold up the foil to enclose the steaks completely. Place in a baking dish. Add a little water to the dish to cover the bottom.

Bake in a preheated moderate oven (180°C/350°F, Gas Mark 4) for 15 to 20 minutes or until the salmon is cooked. Unwrap the steaks and discard the herbs and seasonings. Serve hot.
Serves 4

Stuffed trout braised in white wine

METRIC/IMPERIAL
50g/2oz butter
1 small onion, peeled and finely chopped
225g/8oz button mushrooms, sliced
1 × 15ml spoon/ 1 tablespoon lemon juice
1 × 15ml spoon/ 1 tablespoon chopped fresh chervil
salt
freshly ground black pepper
4 trout, cleaned
150ml/¼ pint dry white wine

AMERICAN
¼ cup butter
1 small onion, peeled and finely chopped
2 cups sliced button mushrooms
1 tablespoon lemon juice
1 tablespoon chopped fresh chervil
salt
freshly ground black pepper
4 trout, cleaned
⅔ cup dry white wine

Melt the butter in a frying pan (skillet). Add the onion and fry until it is soft but not brown. Stir in the mushrooms and fry for 3 minutes. Add the lemon juice, chervil and salt and pepper to taste. Remove from the heat.

Divide the mushroom mixture between the trout and stuff into the cavity in the bodies. Arrange the fish in a baking dish, in one layer. Pour over the wine. Cover the dish.

Braise in a preheated moderately hot oven (190°C/ 375°F, Gas Mark 5) for 30 minutes, or until the fish are cooked. Serve hot.
Serves 4

Trout with almonds

METRIC/IMPERIAL
25g/1oz plain flour
salt
freshly ground black pepper
4 large trout, cleaned
75g/3oz butter
50g/2oz blanched almonds, flaked
2 × 5ml spoons/2 teaspoons lemon juice
To garnish:
lemon wedges
parsley sprigs

AMERICAN
¼ cup all-purpose flour
salt
freshly ground black pepper
4 large trout, cleaned
⅓ cup butter
½ cup blanched slivered almonds
2 teaspoons lemon juice
To garnish:
lemon wedges
parsley sprigs

Mix the flour with salt and pepper. Use to coat the trout.

Melt the butter in a frying pan (skillet). Add the trout and brown quickly on both sides. Reduce the heat and continue cooking until the trout are tender. Transfer the fish to a warmed serving dish. Keep hot.

Add the almonds to the pan and cook until they are golden. Stir in the lemon juice and heat through. Pour the almonds and liquid over the fish and garnish with lemon wedges and parsley sprigs. Serve hot.
Serves 4

Sole Colbert

METRIC/IMPERIAL
4 × 225g/8oz soles, skinned
2 × 15ml spoons/
  2 tablespoons lemon juice
25g/1oz plain flour
salt
freshly ground black pepper
2 eggs, lightly beaten
75g/3oz dry breadcrumbs
vegetable oil for deep frying
8 parsley sprigs
50g/2oz maître d'hôtel
  butter★, cut into 4 pats
lemon slices to garnish

AMERICAN
4 × ½lb soles, skinned
2 tablespoons lemon juice
¼ cup all-purpose flour
salt
freshly ground black pepper
2 eggs, lightly beaten
¾ cup dry breadcrumbs
vegetable oil for deep frying
8 parsley sprigs
¼ cup maître d'hôtel
  butter★, cut into 4 pats
lemon slices to garnish

On the white side of each sole make a cut down the centre to the bone, 2.5cm/1 inch in from the top and bottom. Carefully slice the fish away from the bones on each side and roll the flesh of the fillet back. Carefully snip through the rib bones in the opening using scissors. Sprinkle the fish with the lemon juice.

Mix the flour with salt and pepper and use to coat the fish. Dip the fish in the beaten egg, then coat with the breadcrumbs.

Heat the oil in a deep frying pan (deep fat fryer) until it is 190°C/375°F. Fry the fish, one at a time, until golden. Drain on absorbent paper and keep hot. Remove the bones from the openings.

Fry the parsley sprigs for about 30 seconds or until they are crisp. Drain on absorbent paper.

Arrange the fish on a warmed serving dish. Put 2 parsley sprigs and a pat of maître d'hôtel butter in the opening of each fish. Garnish with lemon slices and serve.
Serves 4

Sole with Marsala cream sauce

METRIC/IMPERIAL
25g/1oz plain flour
salt
freshly ground black pepper
8 small sole fillets
50g/2oz butter
1.5 × 15ml spoons/
  1½ tablespoons olive oil
4 × 15ml spoons/
  4 tablespoons Marsala
4 × 15ml spoons/
  4 tablespoons double cream

AMERICAN
¼ cup all-purpose flour
salt
freshly ground black pepper
8 small sole fillets
¼ cup butter
1½ tablespoons olive oil
4 tablespoons Marsala
4 tablespoons heavy cream

Mix the flour with salt and pepper and use to coat the sole fillets. Melt the butter with the oil in a frying pan (skillet). Add the fillets and fry for about 6 minutes, turning once. Transfer the fillets to a warmed serving dish and keep hot.

Add the Marsala and cream to the pan and heat gently, stirring. Pour the sauce over the fish and serve.
Serves 4

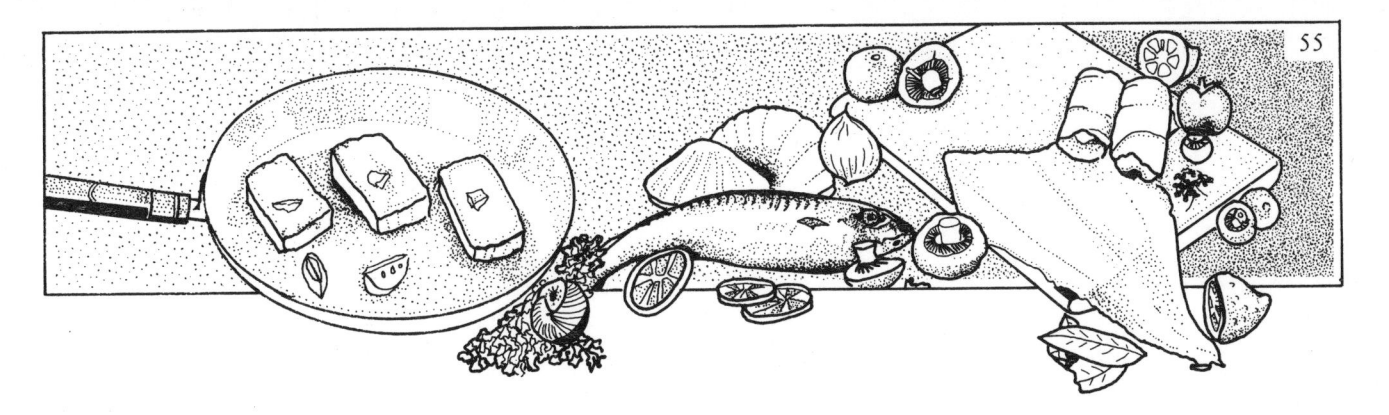

Sole duglére

METRIC/IMPERIAL
25g/1oz butter
1 medium onion, peeled and finely chopped
25g/1oz plain flour
salt
freshly ground black pepper
4 sole fillets, skinned
300ml/½ pint dry white wine
300ml/½ pint fish stock★
4 tomatoes, peeled, deseeded and chopped
4 × 15ml spoons/ 4 tablespoons single cream
chopped parsley to garnish

AMERICAN
2 tablespoons butter
1 medium onion, peeled and finely chopped
¼ cup all-purpose flour
salt
freshly ground black pepper
4 sole fillets, skinned
1¼ cups dry white wine
1¼ cups fish stock★
4 tomatoes, peeled, deseeded and chopped
4 tablespoons light cream
chopped parsley to garnish

Melt the butter in a frying pan (skillet). Add the onion and fry until it is soft but not brown. Meanwhile, mix the flour with salt and pepper and use to coat the fish fillets.

Add the fillets to the pan, in batches, and brown lightly on both sides. Return all the fillets to the pan and add the wine, stock and tomatoes. Bring to the boil, then simmer gently for 15 to 20 minutes or until the sole is cooked.

Stir in the cream with salt and pepper to taste and reheat gently. Serve hot, garnished with chopped parsley.
Serves 4

Sole with sherry sauce

METRIC/IMPERIAL
8 small sole fillets
250ml/8fl oz dry white wine
salt
freshly ground black pepper
1 bay leaf
chopped chervil to garnish
Sauce:
25g/1oz butter
25g/1oz plain flour
150ml/¼ pint milk
2 egg yolks
2 × 15ml spoons/ 2 tablespoons medium sherry

AMERICAN
8 small sole fillets
1 cup dry white wine
salt
freshly ground black pepper
1 bay leaf
chopped chervil to garnish
Sauce:
2 tablespoons butter
¼ cup all-purpose flour
⅔ cup milk
2 egg yolks
2 tablespoons medium sherry

Fold the fillets in half and arrange in a shallow saucepan. Pour over the wine and add salt and pepper to taste and the bay leaf. Bring to the boil, then simmer gently for 6 to 7 minutes or until cooked.

Meanwhile, make the sauce. Melt the butter in another saucepan. Add the flour and cook, stirring, for 1 minute. Remove from the heat and gradually stir in the milk. Return to the heat and bring to the boil, stirring. Simmer until thickened and smooth.

Transfer the sole fillets to a warmed serving dish and keep hot. Strain the cooking liquid into the saucepan with the sauce and stir well. Beat together the egg yolks and sherry. Stir in a little of the hot sauce, then add to the remaining sauce in the saucepan. Heat through gently, stirring. Taste and add more salt and pepper if necessary.

Pour the sherry sauce over the fish and sprinkle with chervil. Serve hot.
Serves 4

Fish cakes

METRIC/IMPERIAL
0.5kg/1lb smoked haddock
0.75kg/1½lb potatoes, peeled and quartered
50g/2oz butter
salt
freshly ground black pepper
1 × 2.5ml spoon/½ teaspoon dried thyme
1 large egg, lightly beaten
100g/4oz dry breadcrumbs
vegetable oil

AMERICAN
1lb smoked haddock
1½lb potatoes, peeled and quartered
¼ cup butter
salt
freshly ground black pepper
½ teaspoon dried thyme
1 egg, lightly beaten
1 cup dry breadcrumbs
vegetable oil

Poach the fish in simmering water until tender, then drain well. Remove the skin and flake the flesh. Allow to cool.

Meanwhile, cook the potatoes in boiling water until tender. Drain well, then mash until smooth. Beat in the butter and salt and pepper to taste. Mix the fish and thyme with the mashed potatoes. If necessary, bind the mixture with a little of the beaten egg.

Divide the mixture into 8 portions and shape into flat patties. Coat with the beaten egg, then with the breadcrumbs.

Heat about 1cm/½ inch of oil in a frying pan (skillet). Add the fish cakes, in batches, and fry until crisp and golden on both sides. Drain on absorbent paper and serve hot.
Serves 4

Finnan haddie

METRIC/IMPERIAL
0.75kg/1½lb smoked haddock, cut into small pieces
300ml/½ pint milk
150ml/¼ pint single cream
25g/1oz butter
freshly ground black pepper
6 eggs

AMERICAN
1½lb smoked haddock, cut into small pieces
1¼ cups milk
⅔ cup light cream
2 tablespoons butter
freshly ground black pepper
6 eggs

Put the haddock pieces in a baking dish. Put the milk, cream, butter and pepper to taste in a saucepan and heat gently until the butter has melted and the mixture is hot. Pour over the fish.

Bake in a preheated moderate oven (180°C/350°F, Gas Mark 4) for 20 minutes or until the fish is cooked.

Five minutes before the fish is ready, poach the eggs in boiling water, or using an egg poacher. Top the fish mixture with the poached eggs and serve.
Serves 6

Mushrooms à la grecque (page 29) and Tomato and mint soup (page 47)

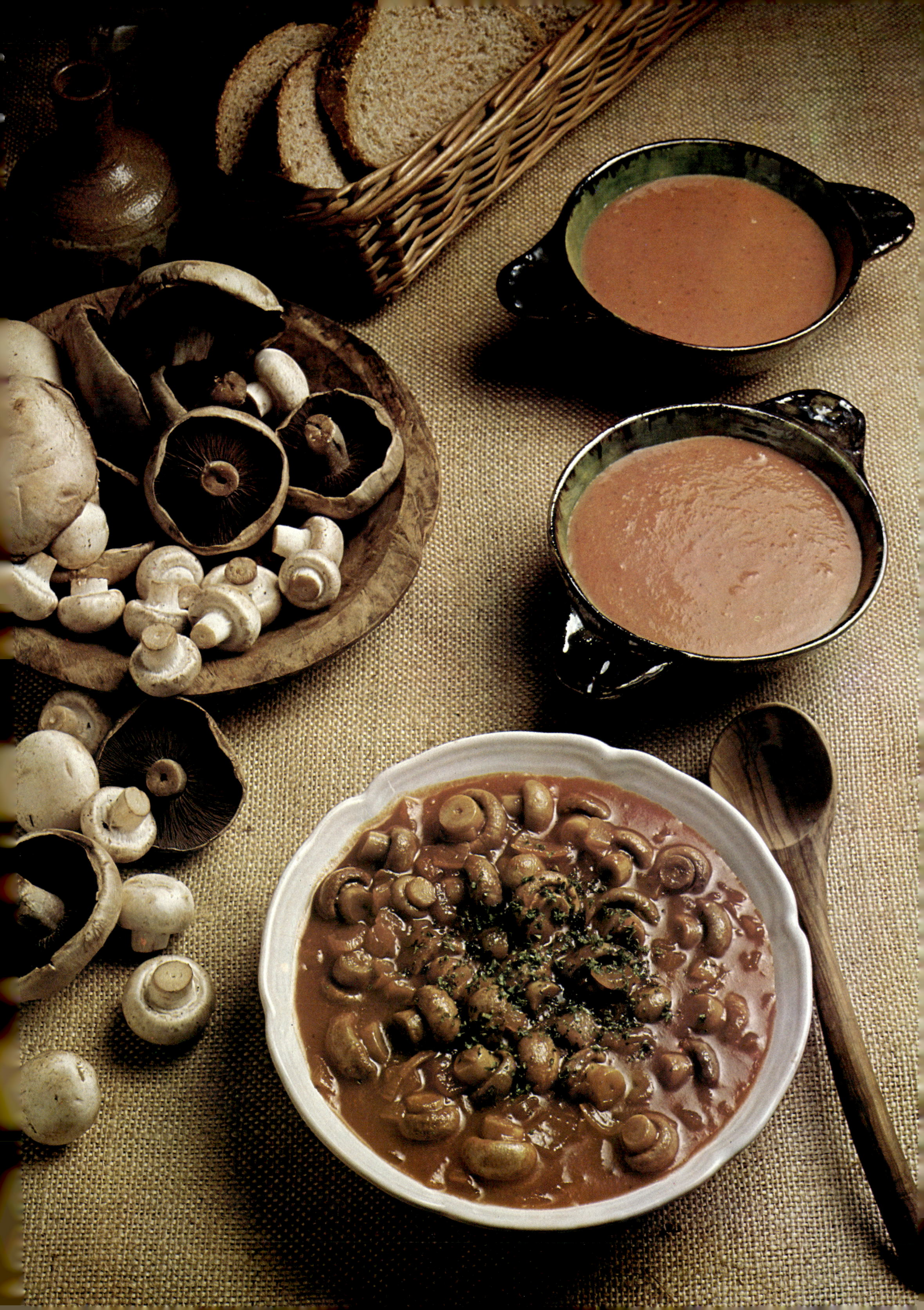

Chilled cucumber soup (page 45); French onion soup (page 38)

GRAND VIN DE
BORDEAU
APPELLATIO
PREMIÈRES COTES DE B
CONTROLÉE
PRODUCE OF FRANCE

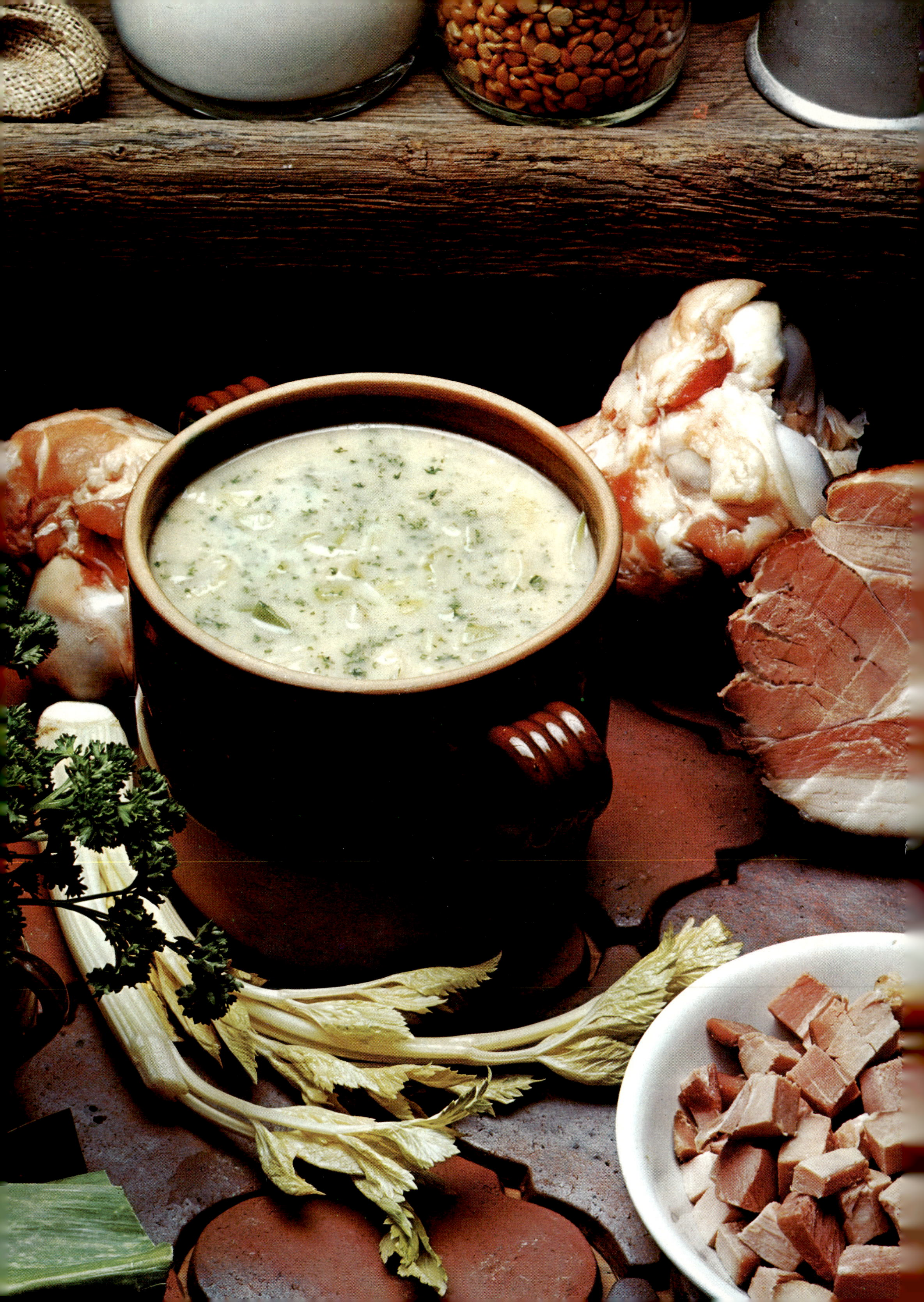

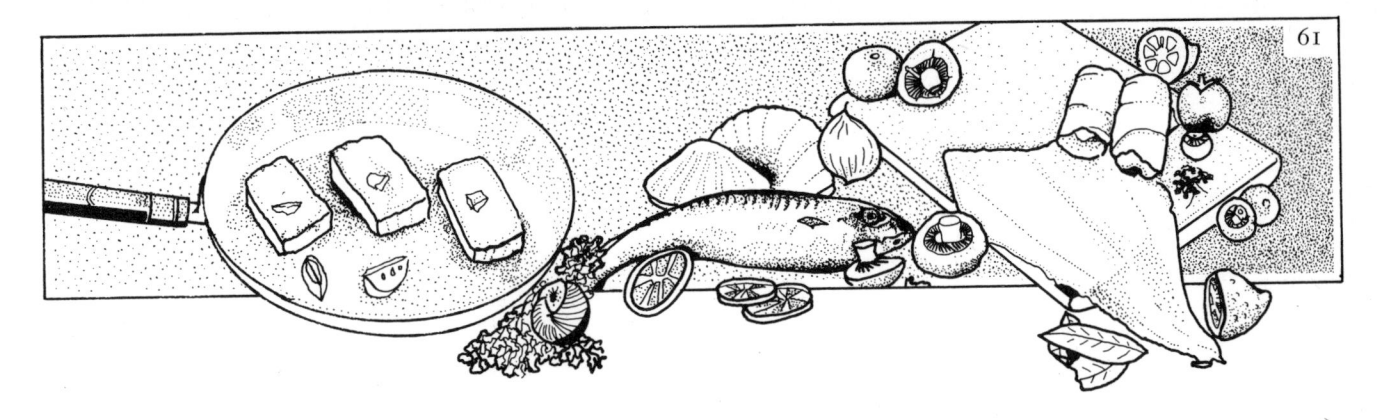

Tuna provençale

METRIC/IMPERIAL
2 × 200g/7oz cans tuna fish
juice of ½ lemon
salt
freshly ground black pepper
4 anchovy fillets
1 × 15ml spoon/
 1 tablespoon olive oil
1 onion, peeled and
 chopped
1 garlic clove, crushed
4 tomatoes, peeled,
 deseeded and chopped
1 × 15ml spoon/
 1 tablespoon tomato purée
150ml/¼ pint dry white
 wine
1 × 5ml spoon/1 teaspoon
 dried basil

AMERICAN
2 × 7oz cans tuna fish
juice of ½ lemon
salt
freshly ground black pepper
4 anchovy fillets
1 tablespoon olive oil
1 onion, peeled and chopped
1 garlic clove, crushed
4 tomatoes, peeled,
 deseeded and chopped
1 tablespoon tomato paste
⅔ cup dry white wine
1 teaspoon dried basil

Remove the tuna carefully from the cans so the round shapes are intact. Place side by side in a baking dish. Sprinkle with the lemon juice and salt and pepper. Place the anchovy fillets on top.

Heat the oil in a saucepan. Add the onion and garlic and fry until the onion is soft but not brown. Stir in the tomatoes, tomato purée (paste), wine and basil and bring to the boil. Simmer until thickened.

Pour the tomato sauce over the tuna. Cover and bake in a preheated moderate oven (180°C/350°F, Gas Mark 4) for 15 minutes.

Serve hot.
Serves 2 to 4

Tuna mould

METRIC/IMPERIAL
450ml/¾ pint sour cream
4 × 15ml spoons/
 4 tablespoons mayonnaise*
salt
freshly ground black pepper
1 × 5ml spoon/1 teaspoon
 Worcestershire sauce
1 × 15ml spoon/
 1 tablespoon chopped
 fresh chives
15g/½oz gelatine
4 × 15ml spoons/
 4 tablespoons water
2 × 200g/7oz cans tuna
 fish, drained and flaked
4 eggs, hard-boiled and
 chopped
To garnish:
tomato wedges
watercress
chopped spring onions

AMERICAN
2 cups sour cream
4 tablespoons mayonnaise*
salt
freshly ground black pepper
1 teaspoon Worcestershire
 sauce
1 tablespoon chopped fresh
 chives
2 envelopes unflavored
 gelatin
4 tablespoons water
2 × 7oz cans tuna fish,
 drained and flaked
4 eggs, hard-cooked and
 chopped
To garnish:
tomato wedges
watercress
chopped scallions

Mix together the sour cream, mayonnaise, salt and pepper to taste, the Worcestershire sauce and chives. Dissolve the gelatine in the water and strain into the sour cream mixture. Stir well. Fold in the tuna and eggs and spoon into a plain or decorative mould. Chill until set.

To serve, turn out of the mould onto a serving plate. Garnish with tomato wedges, watercress and spring onions (scallions).
Serves 6 to 8

Ertwensoep (page 40)

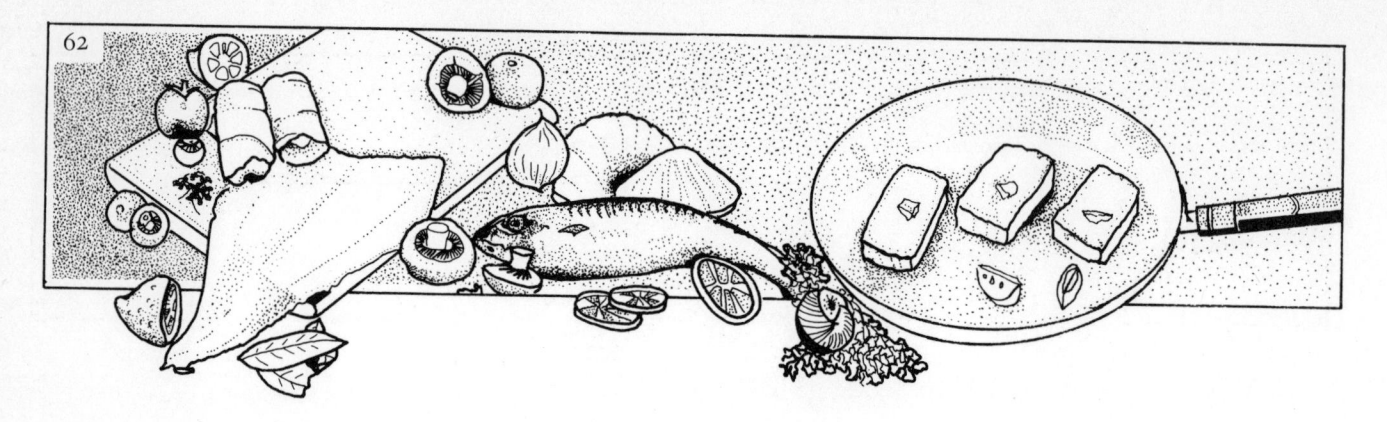

Mackerel baked with tomatoes

METRIC/IMPERIAL
2 × 15ml spoons/
　2 tablespoons olive oil
0.75kg/1½lb tomatoes,
　peeled, deseeded and
　chopped
salt
freshly ground black pepper
25g/1oz butter
4 medium mackerel (or
　other oily fish), cleaned
3 × 15ml spoons/
　3 tablespoons fresh
　breadcrumbs
1 × 15ml spoon/
　1 tablespoon chopped
　fresh parsley
1 garlic clove, finely
　chopped

AMERICAN
2 tablespoons olive oil
1½lb tomatoes, peeled,
　deseeded and chopped
salt
freshly ground black pepper
2 tablespoons butter
4 medium mackerel (or
　other oily fish), cleaned
3 tablespoons fresh
　breadcrumbs
1 tablespoon chopped
　fresh parsley
1 garlic clove, finely
　chopped

Heat the oil in a frying pan (skillet). Add the tomatoes and fry for 3 minutes. Season with salt and pepper to taste. Spoon the tomatoes into a baking dish.

Add the butter to the pan and melt it. Add the mackerel and fry for about 5 minutes on each side. Remove from the heat. Arrange the mackerel on top of the tomatoes in the dish.

Mix together the breadcrumbs, parsley, garlic and salt and pepper to taste and sprinkle over the mackerel. Pour over the fat from the frying pan (skillet).

Bake in a preheated moderately hot oven (200°C/400°F, Gas Mark 6) for 25 minutes or until the fish are cooked. Serve hot, from the dish.
Serves 4

Herrings in cider

METRIC/IMPERIAL
100g/4oz mushrooms, sliced
50g/2oz fresh breadcrumbs
1 dessert apple, cored and
　chopped
1 small onion, peeled and
　chopped
40g/1½oz butter, melted
6 herrings (or other oily
　fish), filleted
1 × 5ml spoon/1 teaspoon
　dried thyme
150ml/¼ pint dry cider

AMERICAN
1 cup sliced mushrooms
1 cup fresh breadcrumbs
1 dessert apple, cored and
　chopped
1 small onion, peeled and
　chopped
3 tablespoons butter, melted
6 herrings (or other oily
　fish), filleted
1 teaspoon dried thyme
⅔ cup hard cider

Mix together half the mushrooms, the breadcrumbs, apple, onion and melted butter. Divide this stuffing between the herrings, placing it at the head end. Fold over the herrings to enclose the stuffing.

Put the remaining mushrooms in a baking dish or casserole and sprinkle with the thyme. Arrange the folded herrings on top and pour over the cider. Cover tightly with a lid or foil and bake in a preheated cool oven (150°C/300°F, Gas Mark 2) for 20 to 25 minutes or until the fish are tender. Serve hot, from the casserole.
Serves 6

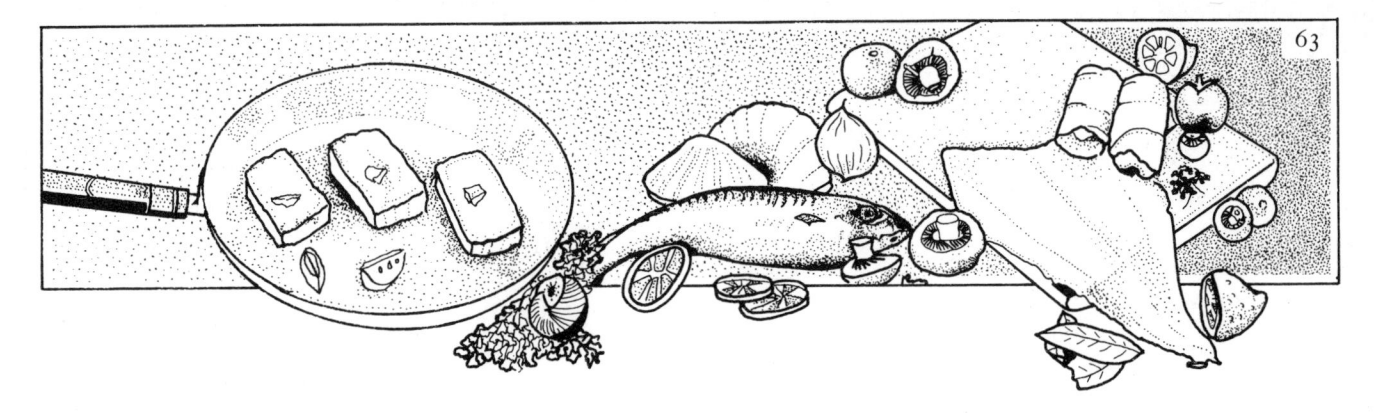

Fish meunière

METRIC/IMPERIAL
50g/2oz plain flour
salt
freshly ground black pepper
4 medium white fish (sole, whiting, etc.), filleted
1 egg, lightly beaten
100g/4oz clarified butter
1 × 15ml spoon/
  1 tablespoon chopped
  fresh parsley
1 × 15ml spoon/
  1 tablespoon lemon juice

AMERICAN
½ cup all-purpose flour
salt
freshly ground black pepper
4 medium white fish (sole, whiting, etc.), filleted
1 egg, lightly beaten
½ cup clarified butter
1 tablespoon chopped fresh parsley
1 tablespoon lemon juice

Mix the flour with salt and pepper and use to coat the fillets. Dip the fillets into the beaten egg to coat well.

Heat the butter in a frying pan (skillet). Add the fillets and fry until they are golden brown on both sides and cooked through. Transfer the fish to a warmed serving dish and keep hot.

Pour off all but 4 × 15ml spoons/4 tablespoons of the butter from the pan. Stir in the parsley and lemon juice and heat through gently. Pour the flavoured butter over the fish and serve.
Serves 4

Creamy fish mould

METRIC/IMPERIAL
0.5kg/1lb white fish fillets (sole, whiting, etc.), skinned
300ml/½ pint water
1 bay leaf
salt
freshly ground black pepper
15g/½oz gelatine
2 × 15ml spoons/
  2 tablespoons medium sherry
3 × 15ml spoons/
  3 tablespoons mayonnaise*
150ml/¼ pint double cream
1 × 15ml spoon/
  1 tablespoon chopped fresh parsley
shredded lettuce to serve

AMERICAN
1lb white fish fillets (sole, whiting, etc.), skinned
1¼ cups water
1 bay leaf
salt
freshly ground black pepper
2 envelopes unflavored gelatin
2 tablespoons medium sherry
3 tablespoons mayonnaise*
⅔ cup heavy cream
1 tablespoon chopped fresh parsley
shredded lettuce to serve

Put the fish in a saucepan and pour over the water. Add the bay leaf and salt and pepper and bring to the boil. Simmer gently until the fish is just cooked.

Drain the fish, reserving the cooking liquid. Discard the bay leaf and make the liquid up to 300ml/½ pint/1¼ cups again with water, if necessary. Flake the fish.

Soften the gelatine in the sherry and stir into the hot cooking liquid. Stir until dissolved, then strain into a mixing bowl. Leave until just beginning to set, then stir in the fish and mayonnaise.

Whip the cream until it is thick and fold into the fish mixture with the parsley. Add salt and pepper to taste. Pour into an oiled 1.2 litre/2 pint/5 cup decorative mould and chill until set.

To serve, turn out onto a bed of shredded lettuce.
Serves 4

Halibut with egg and lemon sauce

METRIC/IMPERIAL
1 onion, peeled and sliced
1 large carrot, peeled and sliced
4 × 225g/8oz halibut steaks
300ml/½ pint water
salt
freshly ground black pepper
1.5 × 15ml spoons/
 1½ tablespoons cornflour
juice of 2 large lemons
2 eggs, lightly beaten
lemon slices to garnish

AMERICAN
1 onion, peeled and sliced
1 large carrot, peeled and sliced
4 × ½lb halibut steaks
1¼ cups water
salt
freshly ground black pepper
1½ tablespoons cornstarch
juice of 2 large lemons
2 eggs, lightly beaten
lemon slices to garnish

Put the onion and carrot in a frying pan (skillet). Arrange the fish steaks on top and pour over the water. Add salt and pepper to taste and bring to the boil. Cover and cook gently for 15 minutes or until the fish is cooked.

Transfer the fish to a warmed serving dish. Keep hot. Strain the cooking liquid into a saucepan and bring to the boil.

Dissolve the cornflour (cornstarch) in the lemon juice and stir in a little of the boiling cooking liquid. Add to the remaining liquid in the pan and simmer for 1 minute or until thickened and smooth. Remove from the heat and allow to cool slightly, then gradually stir into the beaten eggs. Add salt and pepper to taste and pour over the fish. Serve hot, garnished with lemon slices.
Serves 4

Turbot steaks with mussel and shrimp sauce

METRIC/IMPERIAL
6 turbot steaks
450ml/¾ pint fish stock★
100g/4oz butter
½ small onion, peeled and chopped
4 × 15ml spoons/
 4 tablespoons dry white wine
2 dozen mussels or clams, scrubbed and beards scraped off
50g/2oz plain flour
225g/8oz peeled shrimps
2 egg yolks, lightly beaten
salt
freshly ground black pepper
1 × 15ml spoon/
 1 tablespoon lemon juice

AMERICAN
6 turbot steaks
2 cups fish stock★
½ cup butter
½ small onion, peeled and chopped
4 tablespoons dry white wine
2 dozen mussels or clams, scrubbed and beards scraped off
½ cup all-purpose flour
1 cup shelled shrimp
2 egg yolks, lightly beaten
salt
freshly ground black pepper
1 tablespoon lemon juice

Arrange the turbot steaks in one layer in a baking dish. Pour over the fish stock and cover with buttered foil. Bake in a preheated moderate oven (160°C/325°F, Gas Mark 3) for 20 minutes or until the fish is cooked.

Melt 25g/1oz/2 tablespoons of the butter in a saucepan. Add the onion and fry until it is soft but not brown. Stir in the wine. Add the mussels or clams, cover and steam for 5 minutes or until the shells open. (Discard any that do not open.) Remove the fish from the shells and return the fish to their cooking liquid. Remove from the heat and keep hot.

Transfer the turbot steaks to a warmed serving dish and keep hot. Strain the cooking liquid and reserve.

Melt the remaining butter in a saucepan. Add the flour and cook, stirring, for 1 minute. Gradually stir in the turbot cooking liquid and bring to the boil, stirring. Simmer until thickened and smooth. Stir in the shrimps and mussels or clams with their cooking liquid. Add a little of the hot liquid to the egg yolks and beat well, then stir into the sauce mixture. Heat through gently without boiling. Add salt and pepper to taste and the lemon juice. Pour the sauce over the turbot steaks.
Serves 6

Prawns (shrimp) with tarragon dressing

METRIC/IMPERIAL
4 dozen peeled prawns
lemon or lime wedges to garnish
Dressing:
150ml/¼ pint olive oil
1 × 15ml spoon/
 1 tablespoon tarragon vinegar
2 eggs, hard-boiled
2 sprigs of fresh tarragon
salt
freshly ground black pepper
sugar
lemon juice

AMERICAN
4 dozen shelled shrimp
lemon or lime wedges to garnish
Dressing:
⅔ cup olive oil
1 tablespoon tarragon vinegar
2 eggs, hard-cooked
2 sprigs of fresh tarragon
salt
freshly ground black pepper
sugar
lemon juice

To make the dressing, put the oil, vinegar, eggs, tarragon and salt and pepper to taste in the goblet of an electric blender. Blend until smooth, then add sugar and lemon juice to taste. Pour this dressing into a small serving bowl.

Arrange the prawns (shrimp) on a serving dish and garnish with lemon or lime wedges. Serve chilled, with the tarragon dressing.
Serves 4 to 6

Crab soufflé

METRIC/IMPERIAL
100g/4oz butter
50g/2oz flour
450ml/¾ pint milk
4 egg yolks
275g/10oz frozen crabmeat, thawed
150ml/¼ pint double cream
2 × 15ml spoons/
 2 tablespoons sherry
50g/2oz Cheddar cheese, grated
salt
freshly ground black pepper

AMERICAN
½ cup butter
½ cup flour
2 cups milk
4 egg yolks
10oz frozen crabmeat, thawed
⅔ cup heavy cream
2 tablespoons sherry
½ cup grated Cheddar cheese
salt
freshly ground black pepper

Melt the butter in a saucepan, add the flour and cook, stirring, for 5 minutes. Gradually add the milk and continue to cook until thickened and smooth, stirring constantly. Bring to the boil, then remove from the heat. Beat in the egg yolks, one at a time, then stir in the crabmeat, cream, sherry and half the grated cheese. Add salt and pepper to taste. Whisk the egg whites until stiff, then fold into the crab mixture.

Pour the mixture into a buttered 1.75 litre/3 pint/7½ cup soufflé dish. Sprinkle with the remaining grated cheese. Place in a preheated moderately hot oven (190°C/375°F, Gas Mark 5) and bake for 35 to 40 minutes until well risen and golden brown on top. The mixture should be creamy in the centre. Serve at once.
Serves 4

Shrimp curry

METRIC/IMPERIAL
2 × 15ml spoons/
　2 tablespoons oil
1 large onion, peeled and
　finely chopped
1 garlic clove, crushed
1 × 2.5ml spoon/
　½ teaspoon turmeric
1 × 2.5ml spoon/
　½ teaspoon mustard seeds
1 × 5ml spoon/1 teaspoon
　ground ginger
1 × 5ml spoon/1 teaspoon
　mild chilli powder
1 × 400g/14oz can
　tomatoes, sieved
0.5kg/1lb peeled shrimps
juice of ½ lemon
150ml/¼ pint natural
　yogurt

AMERICAN
2 tablespoons oil
1 large onion, peeled and
　finely chopped
1 garlic clove, crushed
½ teaspoon turmeric
½ teaspoon mustard seeds
1 teaspoon ground ginger
1 teaspoon mild chili
　powder
1 × 14oz can tomatoes,
　strained
1lb shelled shrimp
juice of ½ lemon
⅔ cup unflavored yogurt

Heat the oil in a frying pan (skillet). Add the onion and garlic and fry until the onion is soft but not brown. Stir in the spices and fry for 2 minutes. Add the tomatoes and cook for a further 10 minutes, stirring frequently.
　Stir in the shrimps and lemon juice and simmer for 15 minutes. Add the yogurt and heat through gently. Serve hot with rice.
Serves 4

Fried scampi

METRIC/IMPERIAL
0.75kg/1½lb shelled scampi
　or Dublin Bay prawns
vegetable oil for deep frying
lemon wedges to garnish
tartare sauce★ to serve
Batter:
100g/4oz plain flour
1 egg
1 × 15ml spoon/
　1 tablespoon olive oil
150ml/¼ pint milk
salt
freshly ground black pepper

AMERICAN
1½lb shelled scampi or
　jumbo shrimp
vegetable oil for deep frying
lemon wedges to garnish
tartare sauce★ to serve
Batter:
1 cup all-purpose flour
1 egg
1 tablespoon olive oil
⅔ cup milk
salt
freshly ground black pepper

First make the batter. Sift the flour into a mixing bowl. Add the egg, oil and half the milk and mix well together with a wooden spoon. Stir in the remaining milk and beat until the batter is smooth. Season to taste with salt and pepper. Coat the scampi or prawns (shrimp) with the batter.
　Heat the oil in a deep frying pan (deep fat fryer) until it is 190°C/375°F. Fry the scampi until crisp and golden, then drain on absorbent paper.
　Pile on a warmed serving dish and garnish with lemon wedges. Serve hot, with tartare sauce.
Serves 4

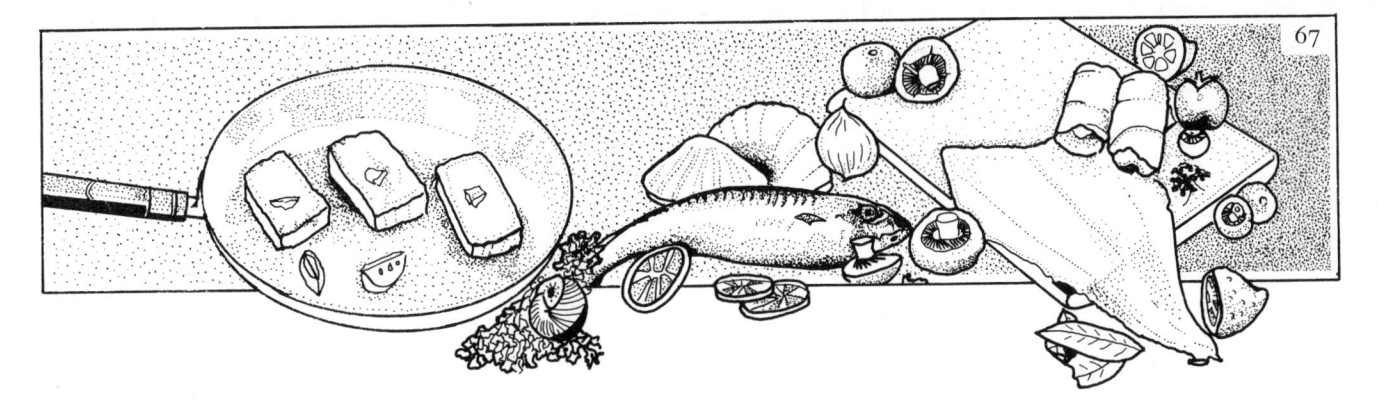

Butterfly prawns (shrimp)

METRIC/IMPERIAL	AMERICAN
20 Mediterranean prawns	12 Pacific shrimp
3 × 15ml spoons/ 3 tablespoons dry sherry	3 tablespoons dry sherry
vegetable oil for deep frying	vegetable oil for deep frying
2 eggs, lightly beaten	2 eggs, lightly beaten
6 × 15ml spoons/ 6 tablespoons cornflour	6 tablespoons cornstarch

Holding the prawns (shrimp) by the tails, remove the rest of the shell, keeping the tail intact, attached to the fish. Split the prawns (shrimp) in half lengthways to the tail and remove the intestinal vein. Flatten the prawns (shrimp) to look like butterflies. Sprinkle them with the sherry and leave to marinate for 10 minutes.

Meanwhile, heat the oil in a deep frying pan (deep fat fryer) until it is hot enough to turn a stale bread cube brown in 50 seconds.

Coat the prawns (shrimp) in the eggs, then dip in the cornflour (cornstarch). Fry for 2 to 3 minutes or until golden brown and crisp. Drain on absorbent paper and serve hot.

Serves 4

Mussels or clams au gratin

METRIC/IMPERIAL	AMERICAN
4 dozen mussels or clams, scrubbed and beards removed	4 dozen mussels or clams, scrubbed and beards removed
300ml/½ pint dry white wine	1¼ cups dry white wine
150ml/¼ pint water	⅔ cup water
salt	salt
freshly ground black pepper	freshly ground black pepper
1 small bunch of parsley	1 small bunch of parsley
65g/2½oz butter	5 tablespoons butter
40g/1½oz plain flour	6 tablespoons all-purpose flour
4 × 15ml spoons/ 4 tablespoons single cream	4 tablespoons light cream
4 × 15ml spoons/ 4 tablespoons grated Parmesan cheese	4 tablespoons grated Parmesan cheese
4 × 15ml spoons/ 4 tablespoons dry breadcrumbs	4 tablespoons dry breadcrumbs

Put the mussels or clams in a saucepan with the wine, water, salt and pepper to taste and the parsley. Bring to the boil, then cover tightly and cook for 10 minutes.

Drain the mussels or clams, reserving the cooking liquid. Discard any mussels or clams that have not opened. Remove the fish from the shells and keep hot. Strain the cooking liquid.

Melt 40g/1½oz/3 tablespoons of the butter in a saucepan. Add the flour and cook, stirring, for 1 minute. Gradually stir in 450ml/¾ pint/2 cups of the reserved cooking liquid. Bring to the boil, stirring, and simmer until thickened and smooth.

Add the mussels or clams and heat through gently for 2 to 3 minutes. Remove from the heat and stir in the cream. Spoon into a warmed flameproof serving dish. Mix together the cheese and breadcrumbs and sprinkle over the top. Dot with the remaining butter, cut into small pieces. Grill (broil) until the top is lightly browned and bubbling. Serve hot, from the dish.

Serves 4

Seafood quiche

METRIC/IMPERIAL
100g/4oz quantity
  shortcrust pastry★
100g/4oz peeled shrimps,
  chopped
50g/2oz crabmeat, flaked
3 eggs, lightly beaten
150ml/¼ pint single cream
salt
freshly ground black pepper
2 × 15ml spoons/
  2 tablespoons chopped
  fresh parsley

AMERICAN
1 cup quantity pie pastry★
½ cup shelled shrimp,
  chopped
⅓ cup crabmeat, flaked
3 eggs, lightly beaten
⅔ cup light cream
salt
freshly ground black pepper
2 tablespoons chopped
  fresh parsley

Roll out the pastry dough and use to line an 18cm/7 inch diameter flan ring (pie pan). Arrange the shrimps and crabmeat in the pastry case (pie shell).

Mix together the eggs, cream, salt and pepper to taste and the parsley. Pour into the pastry case (pie shell). Place on a baking sheet.

Bake in a preheated moderately hot oven (190°C/375°F, Gas Mark 5) for 20 to 25 minutes or until the pastry is golden and the filling is set. Serve warm or cold.

Serves 4

Bouillabaisse

METRIC/IMPERIAL
1kg/2lb assorted fish, to
  include white fish, oily
  fish and shellfish
2 × 15ml spoons/
  2 tablespoons olive oil
1 medium onion, peeled
  and chopped
1 large leek, thoroughly
  cleaned and sliced
1 garlic clove, crushed
600ml/1 pint fish stock★
1 × 425g/15oz can
  tomatoes, chopped
3 parsley sprigs
1 bay leaf
pinch of powdered saffron
salt
freshly ground black pepper

AMERICAN
2lb assorted fish, to include
  white fish, oily fish and
  shellfish
2 tablespoons olive oil
1 medium onion, peeled
  and chopped
1 large leek, thoroughly
  cleaned and sliced
1 garlic clove, crushed
2½ cups fish stock★
1 × 15oz can tomatoes,
  chopped
3 parsley sprigs
1 bay leaf
pinch of powdered saffron
salt
freshly ground black pepper

Cut all the boned fish into bite-sized pieces. Prepare the shellfish. Shell prawns (shrimp), but keep mussels in their shells.

Heat the oil in a large saucepan and fry the onion, leek and garlic until transparent and softened. Add the oily fish, and cook gently for 10 minutes, then add the remaining fish, fish stock and all remaining ingredients with salt and pepper to taste. Simmer for about 10 minutes, until the fish is tender. Adjust the seasoning, discard the parsley and bay leaf. Serve with French bread.

Serves 6 to 8

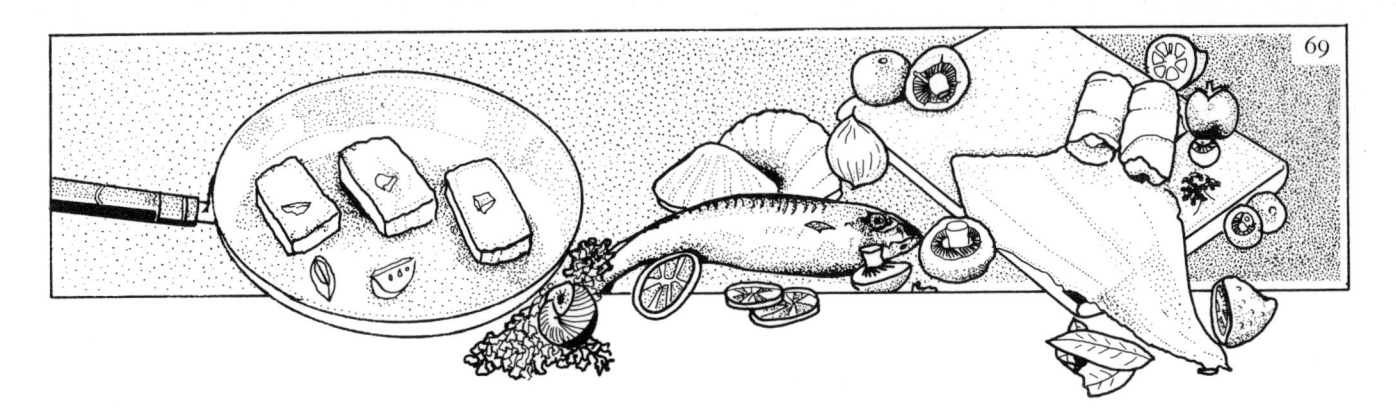

Scallops in mushroom sauce

METRIC/IMPERIAL
0.5kg/1lb shelled scallops
150ml/¼ pint dry white wine
1 slice of onion
1 parsley sprig
1 bay leaf
50g/2oz butter
100g/4oz button mushrooms, sliced
50g/2oz plain flour
450ml/¾ pint milk
salt
freshly ground black pepper
75g/3oz cheese, grated (preferably a mixture of Gruyère and Parmesan)

AMERICAN
1lb shelled bay or sea scallops
⅔ cup dry white wine
1 slice of onion
1 parsley sprig
1 bay leaf
¼ cup butter
1 cup sliced button mushrooms
½ cup all-purpose flour
2 cups milk
salt
freshly ground black pepper
¾ cup grated cheese (preferably a mixture of Gruyère and Parmesan)

Quarter the scallops (sea scallops) and put in a saucepan with the wine, onion, parsley and bay leaf. Bring to the boil and simmer for 5 minutes. Drain the scallops, reserving the cooking liquid. Keep the scallops hot. Strain the cooking liquid.

Melt the butter in another saucepan. Add the mushrooms and fry for 3 minutes. Remove the mushrooms from the pan with a slotted spoon.

Stir the flour into the fat in the saucepan and cook, stirring, for 1 minute. Remove from the heat and gradually stir in the milk and reserved cooking liquid. Return to the heat and bring to the boil, stirring. Simmer until thickened and smooth. Stir in the mushrooms, salt and pepper to taste and 50g/2oz/ ½ cup of the cheese.

Fold in the scallops and heat through gently. Spoon into a warmed flameproof serving dish and sprinkle over the remaining cheese. Grill (broil) until the top is lightly browned. Serve hot.
Serves 4 to 6

Scallops and bacon

METRIC/IMPERIAL
16–20 shelled scallops
salt
freshly ground black pepper
lemon juice
16–20 streaky bacon rashers, rinds removed
tartare sauce★ to serve

AMERICAN
16–20 shelled bay scallops
salt
freshly ground black pepper
lemon juice
16–20 bacon slices
tartare sauce★ to serve

Sprinkle the scallops with salt, pepper and lemon juice. Stretch the bacon rashers (slices) with a flat-bladed knife. Wrap a rasher (slice) around each scallop and secure with wooden cocktail sticks (toothpicks).

Grill (broil) slowly – about 5 minutes on each side – or until cooked through. Serve hot with tartare sauce.
Serves 4

Fish in a jacket

METRIC/IMPERIAL
225g/8oz quantity puff
 pastry★ (made with
 225g/8oz plain flour, etc.)
4 large white fish fillets
salt
freshly ground black pepper
1 egg, beaten
1 × 15ml spoon/
 1 tablespoon water
Sauce:
25g/1oz butter
25g/1oz flour
150ml/¼ pint milk
100g/4oz mushrooms,
 chopped
To garnish:
lemon wedges
parsley sprigs

AMERICAN
2 cup quantity puff pastry★
 (made with 2 cups
 all-purpose flour, etc.)
4 large white fish fillets
salt
freshly ground black pepper
1 egg, beaten
1 tablespoon water
Sauce:
2 tablespoons butter
¼ cup flour
⅔ cup milk
1 cup chopped mushrooms
To garnish:
lemon wedges
parsley sprigs

Roll out the pastry on a floured surface and cut into 4 squares large enough to cover the fish. Lay the fish fillets on a board and season to taste with salt and pepper.

To make the sauce, melt the butter in a saucepan, add the flour and cook, stirring, for 1 minute. Stir in the milk and bring to the boil, stirring constantly. Simmer for 1 minute until very thick and smooth. Stir in the chopped mushrooms. Season to taste with salt and pepper.

Spread the mushroom sauce over half of each fillet, then fold the other half of the fish over the sauce. Lay on the squares of pastry, moisten the edges and fold over to make triangles, sealing the edges securely.

Place on a baking sheet and brush with the beaten egg mixed with the water. Put in a preheated very hot oven (240°C/475°F, Gas Mark 9) and bake for 10 minutes, then lower the temperature to moderate (180°C/350°F, Gas Mark 4) and bake for a further 20 to 25 minutes until golden brown and puffed up. Serve garnished with lemon wedges and parsley sprigs.
Serves 4 to 6

Crispy skin fish

METRIC/IMPERIAL
3–4 slices root ginger,
 peeled and chopped
1 × 15ml spoon/
 1 tablespoon salt
0.75kg/1½lb medium fish
 (whiting, small trout,
 etc.), cleaned
1.5 × 15ml spoons/
 1½ tablespoons flour
oil for deep frying
parsley sprigs to garnish

AMERICAN
3–4 slices green ginger
 peeled and chopped
1 tablespoon salt
1½lb medium fish (whiting,
 small trout, etc.), cleaned
1½ tablespoons flour
oil for deep frying
parsley sprigs to garnish

Mix the ginger with the salt. Rub this mixture over the fish, inside and outside, and leave for 3 hours. Then rub the fish with the flour and leave for a further 30 minutes.

Heat the oil in a deep frying pan (deep fat fryer) until very hot. Place half the fish in a deep frying basket and carefully lower into the hot oil. Fry for 3 to 4 minutes, or until the fish are crisp and golden brown. Remove from the oil and drain on absorbent paper. Keep hot while you fry the remaining fish in the same way. When the fish have been drained thoroughly, return them to the oil for a second frying for 2½ to 3 minutes, or until very crisp – even the bones and heads should be crisp enough to eat. Drain well on absorbent paper and transfer to a warmed serving dish. Garnish with parsley sprigs and serve with plain boiled rice.
Serves 4 to 6

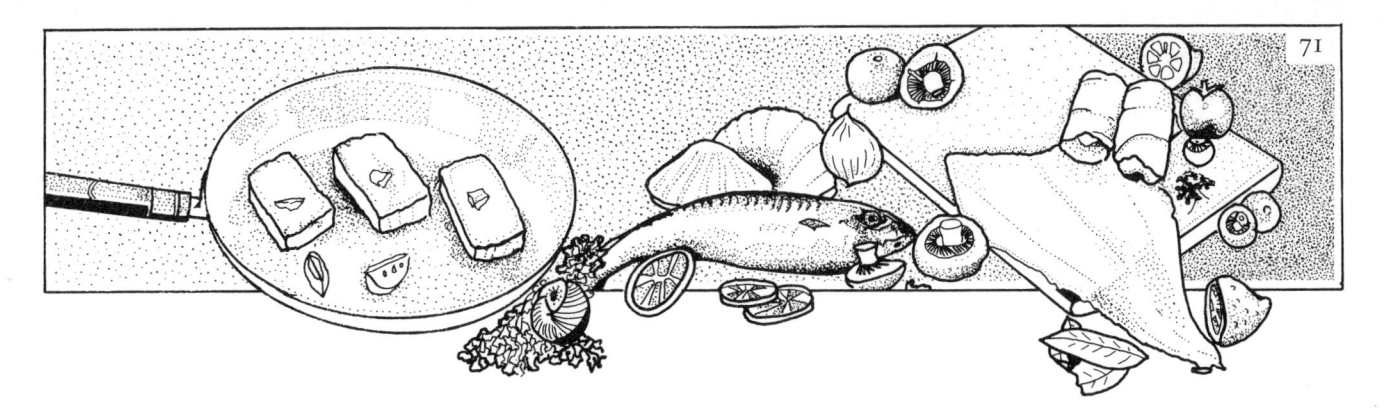

Fish pie

METRIC/IMPERIAL
0.75kg/1½lb cod or haddock, skinned
salt
freshly ground black pepper
75g/3oz butter
1 onion, peeled and finely chopped
0.75kg/1½lb potatoes, peeled
25g/1oz flour
150ml/¼ pint milk
2 × 15ml spoons/
   2 tablespoons chopped fresh parsley
2 hard-boiled eggs, chopped
1 × 15ml spoon/
   1 tablespoon lemon juice
pinch of cayenne pepper
25g/1oz Cheddar cheese, grated

AMERICAN
1½lb cod or haddock, skinned
salt
freshly ground black pepper
⅓ cup butter
1 onion, peeled and finely chopped
1½lb potatoes, peeled
¼ cup flour
⅔ cup milk
2 tablespoons chopped fresh parsley
2 hard-cooked eggs, chopped
1 tablespoon lemon juice
pinch of cayenne pepper
¼ cup grated Cheddar cheese

Poach the fish in water seasoned with salt and pepper for 10 to 15 minutes. Drain and retain 150ml/¼ pint/⅔ cup of the cooking liquid.

Melt a third of the butter in a frying pan (skillet), add the onion and fry until soft but not brown. Set aside.

Cook the potatoes and mash with half the remaining butter, adding a little milk if liked, and salt and pepper to taste. Allow to cool. Melt the remaining butter in a saucepan add the flour and cook, stirring, for 1 minute. Gradually add the milk and reserved cooking liquid. Bring to the boil, then simmer until thickened and smooth, stirring constantly.

Flake the fish and add to the sauce with the onion, parsley, egg, lemon juice and cayenne pepper. Season to taste, then spoon into a pie dish. Sprinkle the grated cheese over the top. Pipe the creamed potato over the fish. Place in a preheated moderately hot oven (190°C/375°F, Gas Mark 5) and bake for 20 to 30 minutes.
Serves 4

Pissaladière niçoise

METRIC/IMPERIAL
lightly cooked 20cm/8 inch flan case of rich shortcrust pastry★, made with 200g/7oz flour and 90g/3½oz fat
0.75kg/1½lb onions, peeled and chopped
4 × 15ml spoons/
   4 tablespoons oil
1 bouquet garni
salt
freshly ground black pepper
2 cloves garlic, crushed
few drops of anchovy essence
1 small can anchovy fillets
black olives

AMERICAN
lightly cooked 8 inch pie shell of rich pie pastry★, made with 1¾ cups flour and 7 tablespoons fat
1½lb onions, peeled and chopped
4 tablespoons oil
1 bouquet garni
salt
freshly ground black pepper
2 cloves garlic, crushed
few drops of anchovy extract
1 small can anchovy fillets
black olives

Put the flan case (pie shell) onto a baking tray. Cook the onions slowly in 3 × 15ml spoons/3 tablespoons oil with the bouquet garni and salt and pepper to taste, for about 45 minutes. The onions should almost melt and acquire a rich golden colour. Stir in the garlic and anchovy essence (extract) after about 20 minutes.

Discard the bouquet garni. Transfer the onion mixture to the pastry case (pie shell) and spread evenly. Arrange the drained anchovy fillets in a lattice pattern on top and dot with black olives.

Sprinkle over the remaining oil and place in a preheated moderately hot oven (200°C/400°F, Gas Mark 6) and bake for 15 minutes or until really hot.
Serves 4

BEEF

Steak and kidney pudding

METRIC/IMPERIAL
225g/8oz quantity suet
 crust pastry★
25g/1oz plain flour
salt
freshly ground black pepper
350g/12oz stewing steak,
 cut into small cubes
100g/4oz kidney, skinned,
 cored and sliced
1 onion, peeled and
 chopped
3 × 15ml spoons/
 3 tablespoons water

AMERICAN
2 cup quantity suet crust
 pastry★
¼ cup all-purpose flour
salt
freshly ground black pepper
¾lb stewing steak, cut into
 small cubes
¼lb kidney, skinned, cored
 and sliced
1 onion, peeled and chopped
3 tablespoons water

Roll out three-quarters of the pastry dough and use to line a greased 900ml/1½ pint/3¾ cup pudding basin (steaming mold).

Mix the flour with salt and pepper and use to coat the steak and kidney. Spoon into the pastry-lined basin (mold) and add the onion and water.

Roll out the remaining quarter of dough and use to cover the basin (mold). Dampen the edges and press together to seal. Cover the basin (mold) with foil, making a pleat to allow for expansion. Tie on securely with string and steam for 4 hours. Add more boiling water when necessary.

Serve hot.
Serves 4

Beef upside-down pie

METRIC/IMPERIAL
50g/2oz dripping
2 onions, peeled and finely
 chopped
3 tomatoes, peeled and
 chopped
25g/1oz mushrooms,
 chopped
300ml/½ pint beef stock
350g/12oz beef, minced
salt
freshly ground black pepper
Topping:
175g/6oz self-raising flour
50g/2oz butter
50g/2oz Cheddar cheese,
 grated
1 egg yolk
milk

AMERICAN
¼ cup drippings
2 onions, peeled and finely
 chopped
3 tomatoes, peeled and
 chopped
¼ cup chopped mushrooms
1¼ cups beef stock
1½ cups ground beef
salt
freshly ground black pepper
Topping:
1½ cups self-rising flour
¼ cup butter
½ cup grated Cheddar
 cheese
1 egg yolk
milk

Melt the dripping in a saucepan. Add the onions, tomatoes and mushrooms and fry until the onions are soft but not brown. Stir in the stock and beef with salt and pepper to taste and bring to the boil. Simmer for 15 minutes.

Meanwhile, sift the flour with salt and pepper into a mixing bowl. Rub in the butter until the mixture resembles breadcrumbs. Stir in the cheese. Add the egg yolk and enough milk to bind the mixture to a soft dough. Shape the dough into a 20cm/8 inch round.

Spoon the meat mixture into a 20cm/8 inch diameter deep cake tin or baking dish. Place the dough round on top. Bake in a preheated moderate oven (180°C/350°F, Gas Mark 4) for 50 minutes or until the dough topping is cooked through.

To serve, invert onto a warmed serving dish.
Serves 4

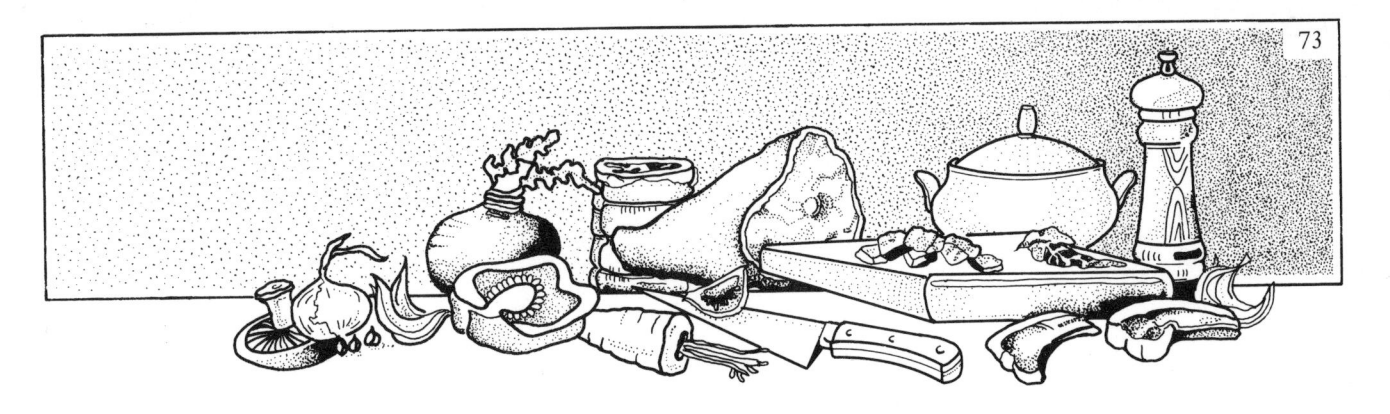

Beef and spinach curry

METRIC/IMPERIAL
25g/1oz butter
1 × 15ml spoon/
  1 tablespoon oil
2 medium onions, peeled
  and finely chopped
1 garlic clove, crushed
1 × 5ml spoon/1 teaspoon
  ground ginger
1 × 5ml spoon/1 teaspoon
  turmeric
1 × 2.5ml spoon/
  ½ teaspoon mild chilli
  powder
1 × 15ml spoon/
  1 tablespoon ground
  coriander
1 × 5ml spoon/1 teaspoon
  dry English mustard
1kg/2lb chuck steak, cut
  into cubes
0.5kg/1lb spinach
300ml/½ pint natural yogurt

AMERICAN
2 tablespoons butter
1 tablespoon oil
2 medium onions, peeled
  and finely chopped
1 garlic clove, crushed
1 teaspoon ground ginger
1 teaspoon turmeric
½ teaspoon mild chili
  powder
1 tablespoon ground
  coriander
1 teaspoon dry English
  mustard
2lb chuck steak, cut into
  cubes
1lb spinach
1¼ cups unflavored yogurt

Melt the butter with the oil in a flameproof casserole. Add the onions and garlic and fry until the onions are soft but not brown. Stir in the spices and mustard and cook for 2 minutes. Add the beef and brown well on all sides.

Meanwhile, put the spinach in a saucepan. Cook for about 6 minutes or until it is tender (do not add any water: there should be enough left on the leaves after washing). Drain the spinach, pressing out all excess moisture, and chop roughly.

Add the spinach to the casserole with half the yogurt. Stir well. Cover and transfer to a preheated moderate oven (160°C/325°F, Gas Mark 3). Cook for 2 to 2½ hours or until the meat is tender.

Stir in the remaining yogurt just before serving.
Serves 4 to 6

Chilli con carne

METRIC/IMPERIAL
2 × 15ml spoons/
  2 tablespoons oil
1 large onion, peeled and
  chopped
0.75kg/1½lb beef, minced
150ml/¼ pint beef stock
1 × 400g/14oz can
  tomatoes, drained
2 × 15ml spoons/
  2 tablespoons tomato purée
1 × 5ml spoon/1 teaspoon
  sugar
1 × 5ml spoon/1 teaspoon
  mild chilli powder (or to
  taste), or 2 × 5ml spoons/
  2 teaspoons chilli
  seasoning
salt
freshly ground black pepper
1 × 400g/14oz can red
  kidney beans, drained

AMERICAN
2 tablespoons oil
1 large onion, peeled and
  chopped
3 cups ground beef
⅔ cup beef stock
1 × 14oz can tomatoes,
  drained
2 tablespoons tomato paste
1 teaspoon sugar
1 teaspoon mild chili
  powder (or to taste), or
  2 teaspoons chili seasoning
salt
freshly ground black pepper
1 × 14oz can red kidney
  beans, drained

Heat the oil in a saucepan. Add the onion and fry until it is soft but not brown. Add the beef and brown well. Stir in the stock, tomatoes, tomato purée (paste), sugar, chilli powder or seasoning and salt and pepper to taste. Bring to the boil, then cover and simmer for 25 minutes.

Add the kidney beans and simmer for a further 5 minutes. Serve hot.
Serves 4

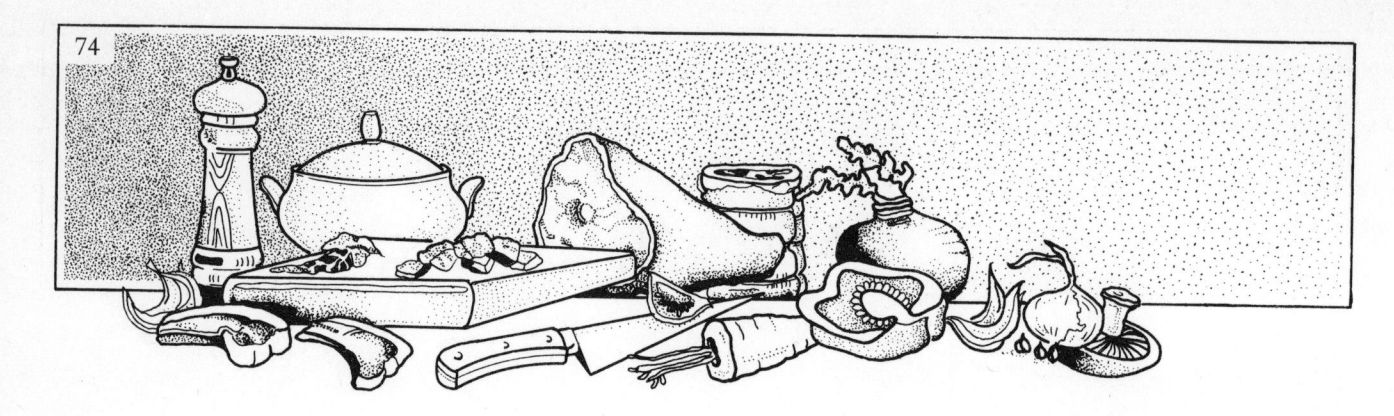

Beef and apricot stew

METRIC/IMPERIAL
100g/4oz dried apricots
600ml/1 pint boiling beef stock
25g/1oz plain flour
salt
freshly ground black pepper
0.75kg/1½lb chuck steak, cut into cubes
4 × 15ml spoons/ 4 tablespoons oil
grated rind and juice of 1 lemon
2 × 5ml spoons/2 teaspoons sugar
1 × 100g/4oz can tomatoes, drained

AMERICAN
⅔ cup dried apricots
2½ cups boiling beef stock
¼ cup all-purpose flour
salt
freshly ground black pepper
1½lb chuck steak, cut into cubes
4 tablespoons oil
grated rind and juice of 1 lemon
2 teaspoons sugar
1 × ¼lb can tomatoes, drained

Put the apricots in a mixing bowl and pour over the stock. Leave to soak for at least 8 hours.

Mix the flour with salt and pepper in a polythene (plastic) bag. Add the beef cubes and shake to coat with the seasoned flour. Heat the oil in a saucepan. Add the beef cubes, in batches, and brown on all sides. Remove from the casserole as they are browned.

Return the beef to the saucepan. Strain the stock from the apricots and add to the pan with the lemon rind and juice and sugar. Finely chop about one-third of the apricots and add to the pan. Bring to the boil, stirring. Cover and simmer for 1¾ hours.

Add the remaining apricots and simmer for 15 minutes. Stir in the tomatoes and simmer for a further 15 minutes. Taste and adjust the seasoning. Serve hot.
Serves 4

Argentinian beef stew

METRIC/IMPERIAL
2 × 15ml spoons/ 2 tablespoons oil
2 onions, peeled and chopped
3 streaky bacon rashers, rinds removed and chopped
1 red pepper, pith and seeds removed and diced
0.75kg/1½lb stewing steak, cut into small cubes
2 × 5ml spoons/2 teaspoons paprika
1.2 litres/2 pints beef stock
225g/8oz garlic sausage, peeled and chopped
100g/4oz dried white haricot beans, soaked overnight and drained
1 × 200g/7oz can sweetcorn, drained
salt
freshly ground black pepper

AMERICAN
2 tablespoons oil
2 onions, peeled and chopped
3 bacon slices, chopped
1 pimiento, pith and seeds removed and diced
1½lb stewing steak, cut into small cubes
2 teaspoons paprika
5 cups beef stock
1 cup chopped peeled garlic sausage
½ cup dried navy beans, soaked overnight and drained
1 × 7oz can corn kernels, drained
salt
freshly ground black pepper

Heat the oil in a flameproof casserole. Add the onions, bacon and red pepper (pimiento) and fry until the onions are soft but not brown. Add the meat and brown on all sides.

Sprinkle over the paprika and stir well, then stir in the stock. Bring to the boil. Add the sausage and beans, cover and transfer to a cool oven (150°C/300°F, Gas Mark 2). Cook for 2½ hours.

Stir in the corn with salt and pepper to taste and cook for a further 30 minutes. Serve hot, from the casserole.
Serves 6

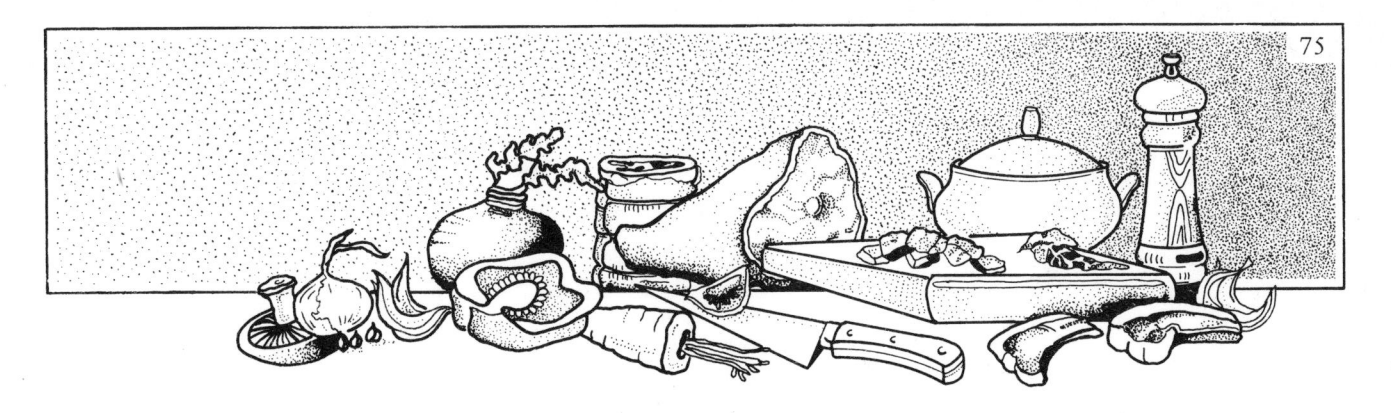

Beef, mushroom and olive casserole

METRIC/IMPERIAL
25g/1oz plain flour
salt
freshly ground black pepper
0.5kg/1lb stewing steak, cut into cubes
25g/1oz butter
1 × 15ml spoon/1 tablespoon olive oil
225g/8oz button onions, peeled
1 garlic clove, crushed
2 carrots, peeled and sliced
600ml/1 pint beef stock
50g/2oz mushrooms, sliced
10 black olives, stoned

AMERICAN
¼ cup all-purpose flour
salt
freshly ground black pepper
1lb stewing steak, cut into cubes
2 tablespoons butter
1 tablespoon olive oil
½lb baby onions, peeled
1 garlic clove, crushed
2 carrots, peeled and sliced
2½ cups beef stock
½ cup sliced mushrooms
10 black olives, pitted

Mix the flour with salt and pepper in a polythene (plastic) bag. Add the beef cubes and shake to coat with the seasoned flour.

Melt the butter with the oil in a flameproof casserole. Add the beef cubes, in batches, and brown on all sides. Remove from the casserole as they are browned.

Add the onions, garlic and carrots to the casserole and fry until the onions are golden brown. Stir in the stock. Return the beef cubes to the casserole and stir well. Bring to the boil.

Cover and transfer to a preheated moderate oven (160°C/325°F, Gas Mark 3). Cook for 2 hours.

Stir in the mushrooms and olives and cook for a further 30 minutes or until the meat is tender. Serve hot, from the casserole.
Serves 4

Beef carbonnade

METRIC/IMPERIAL
25g/1oz plain flour
salt
freshly ground black pepper
1kg/2lb chuck steak, cut into cubes
25g/1oz butter
1 × 15ml spoon/1 tablespoon olive oil
1 large onion, peeled and thinly sliced
1 garlic clove, crushed
300ml/½ pint stout
1 × 5ml spoon/1 teaspoon made French mustard
1 × 5ml spoon/1 teaspoon vinegar
pinch of sugar
1 bouquet garni

AMERICAN
¼ cup all-purpose flour
salt
freshly ground black pepper
2lb chuck steak, cut into cubes
2 tablespoons butter
1 tablespoon olive oil
1 large onion, peeled and thinly sliced
1 garlic clove, crushed
1¼ cups stout or dark beer
1 teaspoon prepared French mustard
1 teaspoon vinegar
pinch of sugar
1 bouquet garni

Mix the flour with salt and pepper in a polythene (plastic) bag. Add the beef cubes and shake to coat them with the seasoned flour.

Melt the butter with the oil in a flameproof casserole. Add the beef cubes, in batches, and brown on all sides. Remove from the casserole as they are browned.

Add the onion and garlic to the casserole. Fry until the onion is soft but not brown. Stir in the stout (beer), mustard, vinegar, sugar and salt and pepper to taste. Return the beef to the casserole and add the bouquet garni. Bring to the boil, then cover and transfer to a preheated moderate oven (160°C/325°F, Gas Mark 3). Cook for 2 to 2½ hours or until the meat is tender.

Discard the bouquet garni and serve hot, from the casserole.
Serves 4 to 5

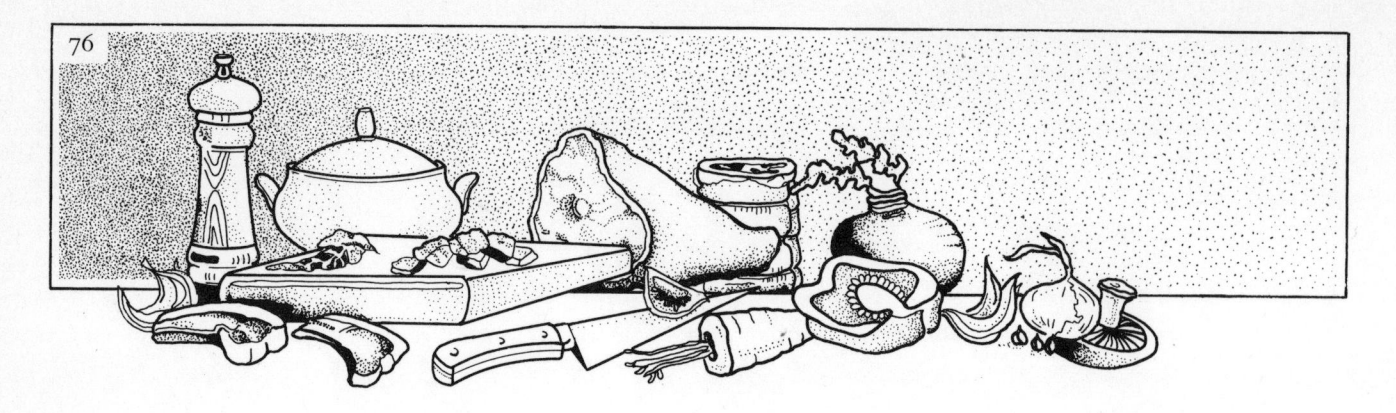

French beef stew

METRIC/IMPERIAL
0.75kg/1½lb chuck steak, cut into cubes
1 carrot, peeled and sliced
1 onion, peeled and sliced
2 celery sticks, chopped
150ml/¼ pint dry red wine
1 garlic clove, crushed
salt
freshly ground black pepper
225g/8oz streaky bacon, rinds removed and diced
300ml/½ pint beef stock
100g/4oz stoned black olives
1 bouquet garni

AMERICAN
1½lb chuck steak, cut into cubes
1 carrot, peeled and sliced
1 onion, peeled and sliced
2 celery stalks, chopped
⅔ cup dry red wine
1 garlic clove, crushed
salt
freshly ground black pepper
½lb bacon, diced
1¼ cups beef stock
¾ cup pitted black olives
1 bouquet garni

Put the steak, carrot, onion and celery in a mixing bowl. Pour over the wine and add the garlic with salt and pepper to taste. Stir well, then leave to marinate for at least 4 hours, stirring occasionally.

Remove the meat from the marinade and pat dry with absorbent paper. Reserve the marinade and vegetables.

Fry the bacon in a flameproof casserole until it is crisp and has rendered its fat. Add the steak cubes and brown on all sides. Pour in the stock, reserved marinade, vegetables and olives and bring to the boil. Add the bouquet garni, cover tightly and transfer to a preheated moderate oven (160°C/325°F/Gas Mark 3). Cook for 2 to 2½ hours or until the meat is tender.

Remove the bouquet garni and serve hot, from the casserole.
Serves 4

Boiled beef with dumplings

METRIC/IMPERIAL
1kg/2lb salt brisket of beef, soaked overnight and drained
2 onions, peeled and quartered
4 carrots, peeled and cut into 2.5cm/1 inch pieces
1 medium turnip, peeled and roughly chopped
freshly ground black pepper
Dumplings:
100g/4oz self-raising flour
pinch of salt
50g/2oz shredded suet
water

AMERICAN
2lb corned beef
2 onions, peeled and quartered
4 carrots, peeled and cut into 1 inch pieces
1 medium turnip, peeled and roughly chopped
freshly ground black pepper
Dumplings:
1 cup self-rising flour
pinch of salt
½ cup shredded suet
water

Put the beef in a saucepan and add the vegetables and pepper to taste. Add water to cover and bring to the boil. Simmer for 1½ hours.

To make the dumplings, sift the flour and salt into a mixing bowl. Stir in the suet and enough water to make a slightly sticky dough. Form into 8 small balls.

Add the dumplings to the boiling liquid and simmer for a further 15 to 20 minutes or until the dumplings are well risen and light and the beef is tender. Serve hot.
Serves 4

Crispy skin fish (page 70)

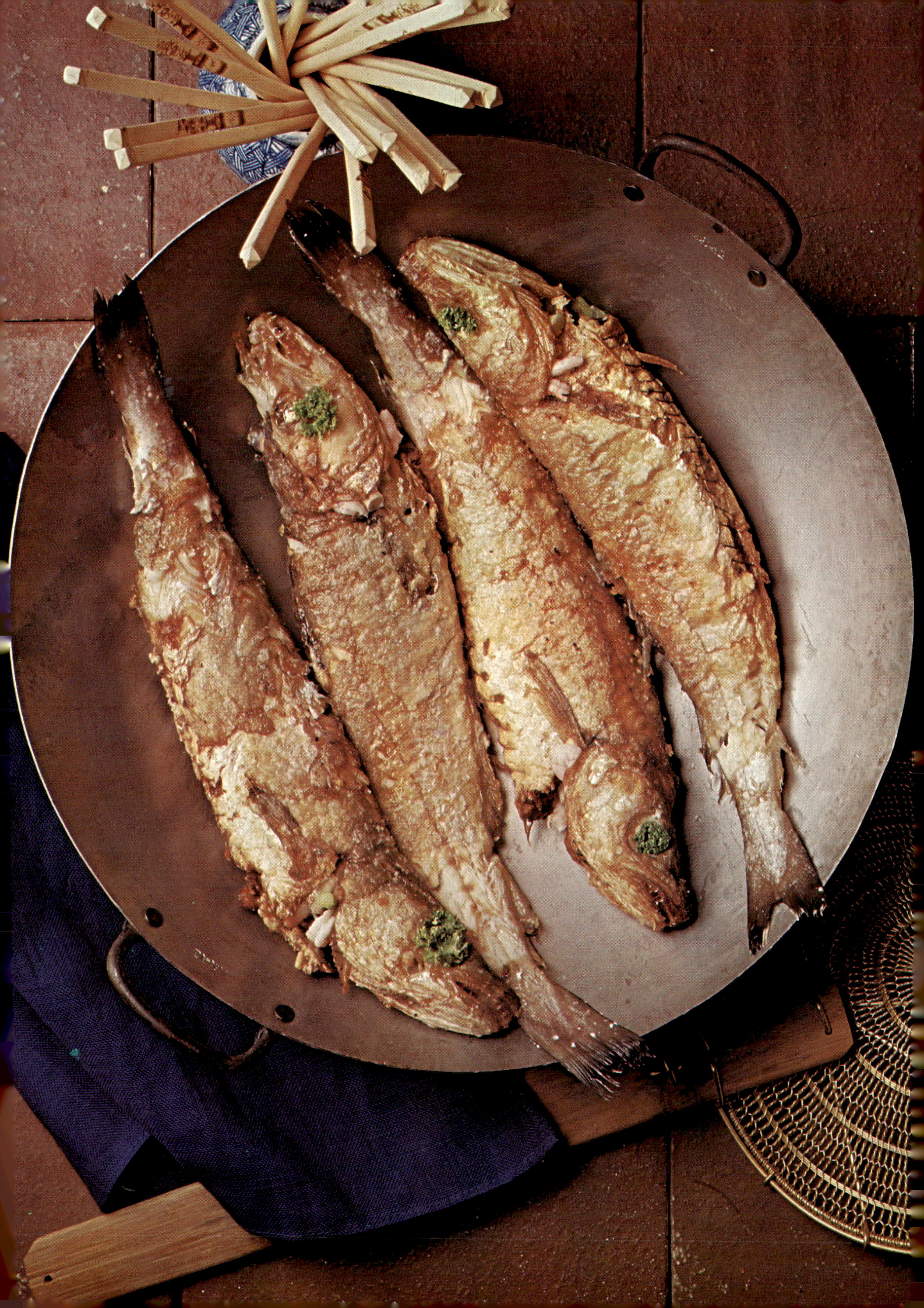

Trout with almonds (page 53); Pissaladière niçoise (page 71)

Bottled at the Domaine de Chasseloir
of Production - Saint-Fiacre-sur-Maine

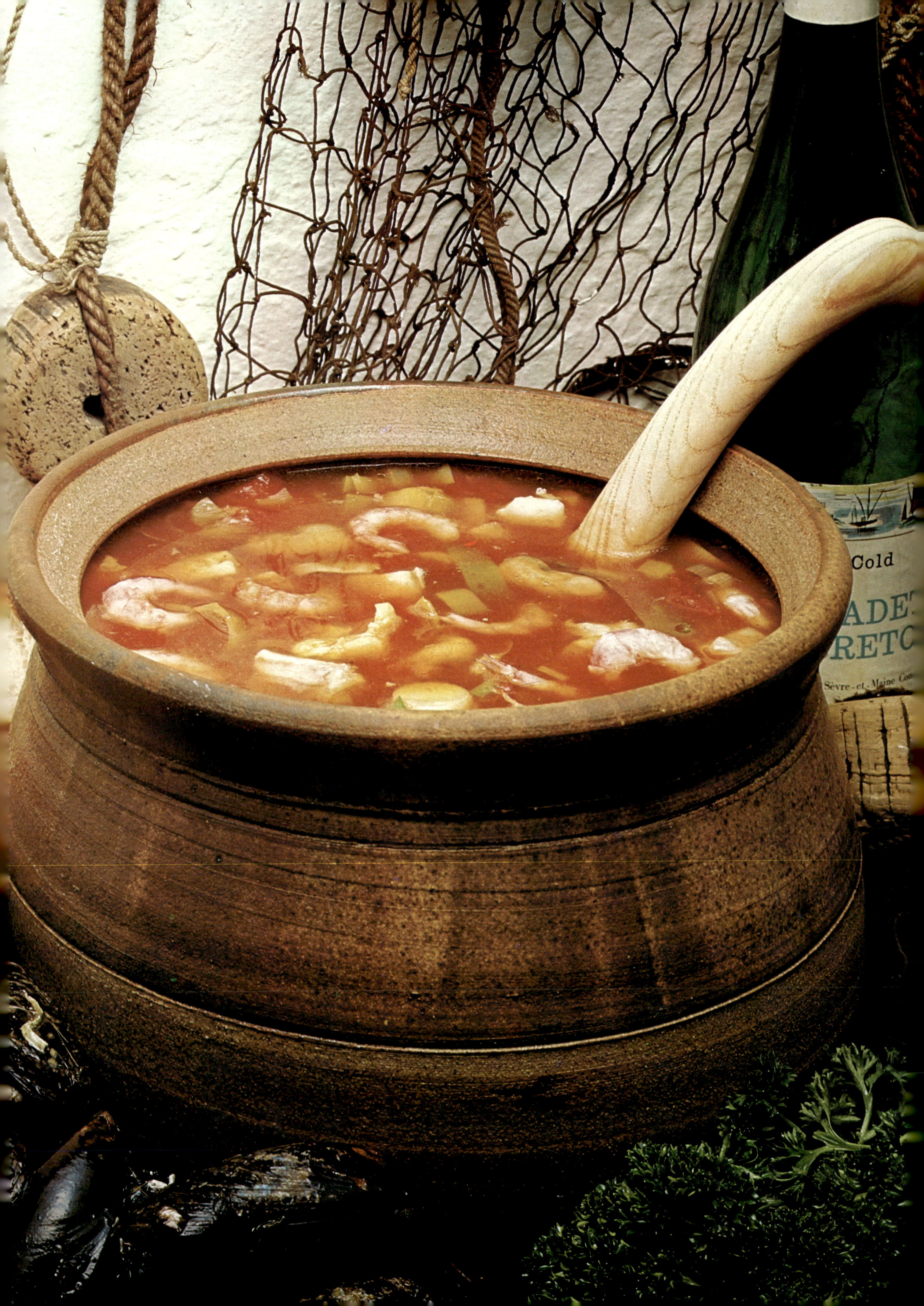
Cold

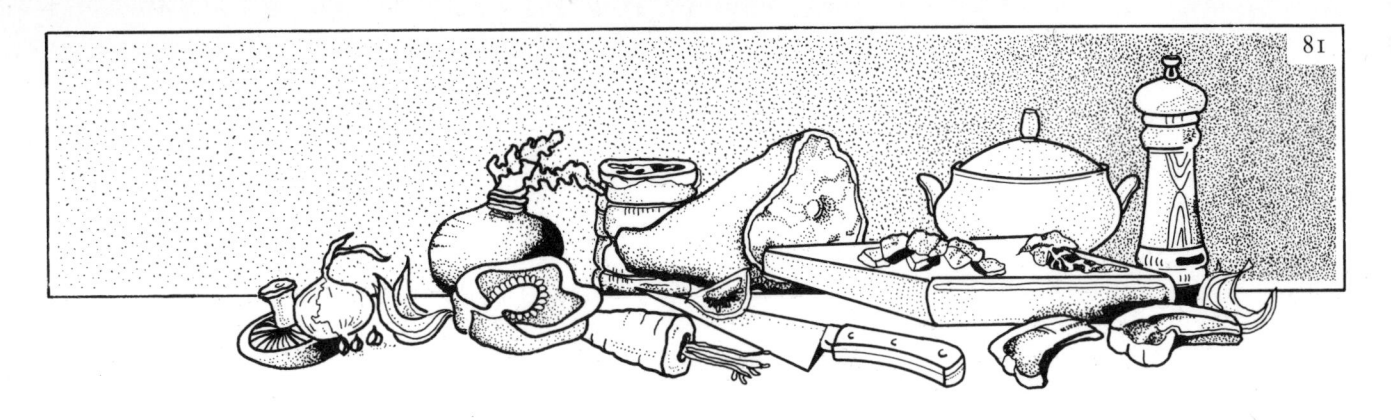

Boeuf bourguignonne

METRIC/IMPERIAL
100g/4oz streaky bacon, rinds removed and cut into strips
50g/2oz butter
2 × 15ml spoons/ 2 tablespoons olive oil
12 very small onions, peeled
1kg/2lb chuck steak, cut into 5cm/2 inch cubes
25g/1oz plain flour
150ml/¼ pint brown stock
1 garlic clove, crushed
1 bouquet garni
salt
freshly ground black pepper
½ bottle dry red wine (Burgundy)
100g/4oz button mushrooms
chopped parsley to garnish

AMERICAN
¼lb bacon, cut into strips
¼ cup butter
2 tablespoons olive oil
12 very small onions, peeled
2lb chuck steak, cut into 2 inch cubes
¼ cup all-purpose flour
⅔ cup beef stock
1 garlic clove, crushed
1 bouquet garni
salt
freshly ground black pepper
½ bottle dry red wine (Burgundy)
1 cup button mushrooms
chopped parsley to garnish

Blanch the bacon strips in boiling water for 5 minutes. Drain well.

Melt 25g/1oz/2 tablespoons of the butter with the oil in a flameproof casserole. Add the onions and brown on all sides. Remove the onions and set aside. Add the beef cubes and bacon strips to the casserole and fry until the beef cubes are well browned. Sprinkle over the flour and cook, stirring, for 2 minutes. Stir in the stock, then add the garlic, bouquet garni and salt and pepper to taste.

Add the wine and bring to the boil, stirring well. Cover and transfer to a preheated cool oven (150°C/300°F, Gas Mark 2). Cook for 1½ hours.

Melt the remaining butter in a frying pan (skillet) and add the mushrooms. Fry until they are just tender. Add the mushrooms and onions to the casserole and cook for a further 30 minutes or until the meat is tender. Remove the bouquet garni.

Serve hot, from the casserole, garnished with parsley.
Serves 4 to 6

Beef stroganoff

METRIC/IMPERIAL
25g/1oz plain flour
salt
freshly ground black pepper
0.75kg/1½lb rump steak, cut into 5mm × 5cm/ ¼ × 2 inch strips
50g/2oz butter
1 onion, peeled and thinly sliced
225g/8oz button mushrooms, sliced
300ml/½ pint sour cream
1 × 15ml spoon/ 1 tablespoon tomato purée
1 × 5ml spoon/1 teaspoon made mustard

AMERICAN
¼ cup all-purpose flour
salt
freshly ground black pepper
1½lb boneless sirloin steak, cut into ¼ × 2 inch strips
¼ cup butter
1 onion, peeled and thinly sliced
2 cups sliced button mushrooms
1¼ cups sour cream
1 tablespoon tomato paste
1 teaspoon prepared mustard

Mix the flour with salt and pepper and use to coat the steak strips. Melt the butter in a frying pan (skillet). Add the onion and fry until it is soft but not brown. Push the onion to the side of the pan and add the steak strips. Fry for about 5 minutes or until well browned and tender.

Stir in the mushrooms and cook for 3 minutes. Mix together the sour cream, tomato purée (paste) and mustard and stir into the pan. Heat through gently without boiling and serve hot.
Serves 4

Bouillabaisse (page 68)

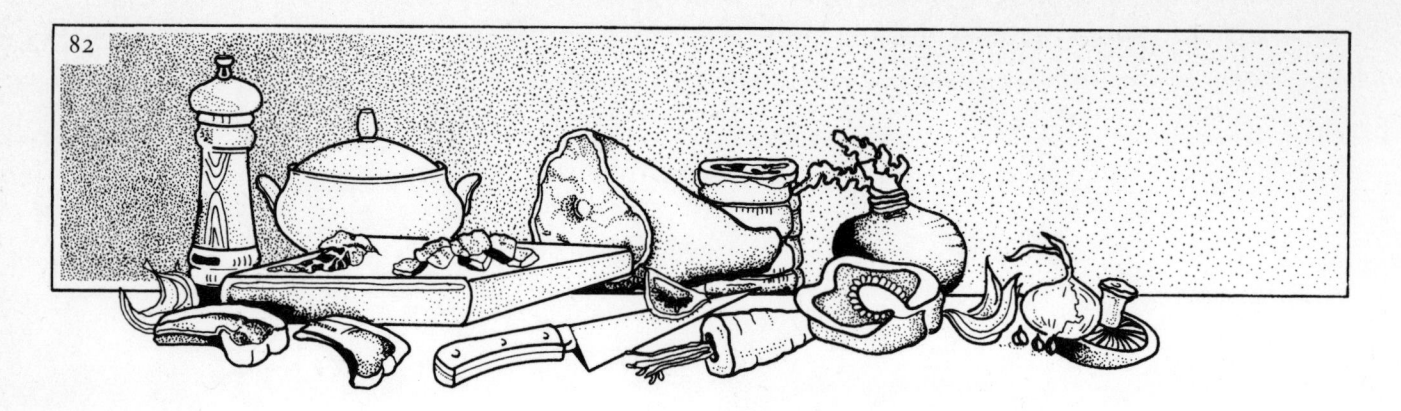

Fondue bourguignonne

METRIC/IMPERIAL
1kg/2lb fillet steak, cut into 2.5cm/1 inch cubes
vegetable oil
To serve:
At least 3 of the following sauces: horseradish★, mayonnaise★, béarnaise★, tomato★, tartare★, mustard★, thousand island dressing★

AMERICAN
2lb boneless sirloin steak, cut into 1 inch cubes
vegetable oil
To serve:
At least 3 of the following sauces: horseradish★, mayonnaise★, béarnaise★, tomato★, tartare★, mustard★, thousand island dressing★

Arrange the steak cubes on a serving plate and put on the table with the sauces and accompaniments. (Baked potatoes and a green salad are convenient to serve with a meat fondue.)

Heat the oil in a saucepan on top of the stove until a cube of stale bread dropped into the oil turns golden in 1 minute. Pour the oil carefully into a meat fondue pot and place over a spirit burner. Each person spears a cube of meat on a fondue fork and cooks it in the hot oil. When the meat is cooked, it is transferred to the individual plates and dipped with a dinner fork into a sauce.
Serves 4

Quick-fried steak with celery and cabbage

METRIC/IMPERIAL
1 × 5ml spoon/1 teaspoon cornflour
2 × 15ml spoons/ 2 tablespoons water
0.5kg/1lb rump steak, cut into paper-thin slices
2 × 15ml spoons/ 2 tablespoons oil
2 celery sticks, shredded
4 spring onions, finely chopped
100g/4oz white cabbage, shredded
1 × 15ml spoon/ 1 tablespoon soy sauce
salt
freshly ground black pepper

AMERICAN
1 teaspoon cornstarch
2 tablespoons water
1lb boneless sirloin steak, cut into paper-thin slices
2 tablespoons oil
2 celery stalks, shredded
4 scallions, finely chopped
$\frac{1}{4}$lb white cabbage, shredded
1 tablespoon soy sauce
salt
freshly ground black pepper

Dissolve the cornflour (cornstarch) in the water. Coat the steak slices in this mixture. Heat the oil in a frying pan (skillet). Add the steak slices and fry quickly, stirring, for 3 minutes. Remove the steak from the pan.

Add the celery, spring onions (scallions) and cabbage to the pan and fry gently for 5 minutes. Stir in the soy sauce with salt and pepper to taste, then stir in the meat. Cook for a further 2 to 3 minutes. Serve hot.
Serves 4

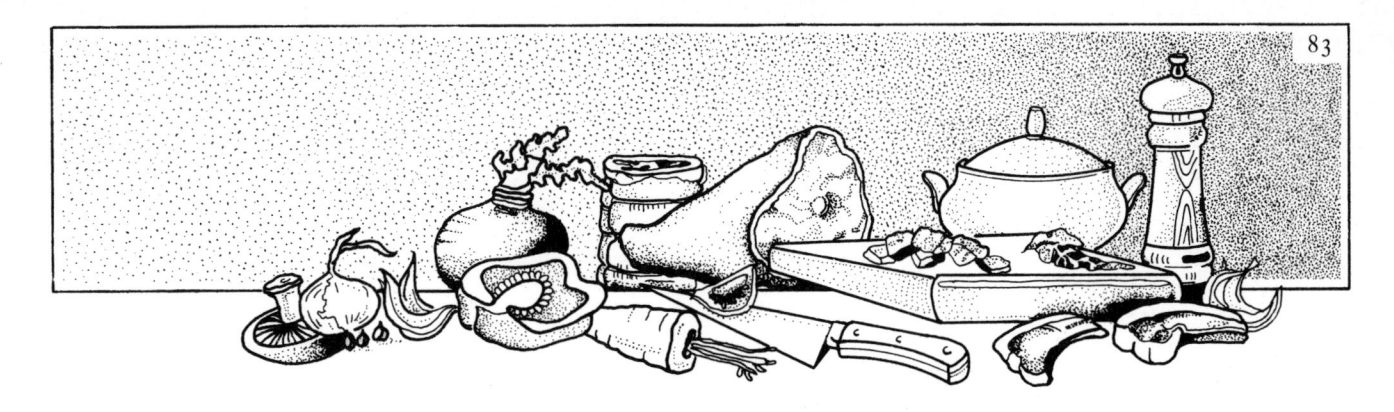

Neapolitan steak

METRIC/IMPERIAL
0.75kg/1½lb tomatoes, peeled and chopped
2 × 15ml spoons/ 2 tablespoons olive oil
2 garlic cloves, finely chopped
1 × 15ml spoon/ 1 tablespoon chopped fresh parsley
1 × 2.5ml spoon/ ½ teaspoon dried oregano
1 × 5ml spoon/1 teaspoon sugar
salt
freshly ground black pepper
4 rump steaks

AMERICAN
3 cups peeled and chopped tomatoes
2 tablespoons olive oil
2 garlic cloves, finely chopped
1 tablespoon chopped fresh parsley
½ teaspoon dried oregano
1 teaspoon sugar
salt
freshly ground black pepper
4 boneless sirloin steaks

Put the tomatoes, oil, garlic, parsley, oregano, sugar and salt and pepper to taste in a saucepan. Bring to the boil, then simmer for 15 minutes.

Just before the sauce is ready, grill (broil) the steaks for 3 to 7 minutes on each side or until cooked to your preference.

Transfer the steaks to a warmed serving dish and pour over the sauce. Serve hot.
Serves 4

Apple-stuffed steaks

METRIC/IMPERIAL
4 rump steaks (2.5cm/ 1 inch thick)
4 × 15ml spoons/ 4 tablespoons fresh breadcrumbs
grated rind and juice of 1 orange
1 cooking apple, cored and grated
25g/1oz butter, melted
1 egg yolk
salt
freshly ground black pepper
pinch of dried thyme
1 × 15ml spoon/ 1 tablespoon oil

AMERICAN
4 boneless sirloin steaks (1 inch thick)
4 tablespoons fresh breadcrumbs
grated rind and juice of 1 orange
1 baking apple, cored and grated
2 tablespoons butter, melted
1 egg yolk
salt
freshly ground black pepper
pinch of dried thyme
1 tablespoon oil

Make a slit in the steaks to form a pocket. Mix together the breadcrumbs, orange rind, apple, butter, egg yolk, salt and pepper to taste and the thyme. Fill the steaks with this mixture.

Place the steaks on the grill (broiler) rack and brush with a little oil. Grill (broil) for 3 to 7 minutes on each side, or until cooked to your preference.

Transfer the steaks to a warmed serving dish and pour over the orange juice. Serve hot.
Serves 4

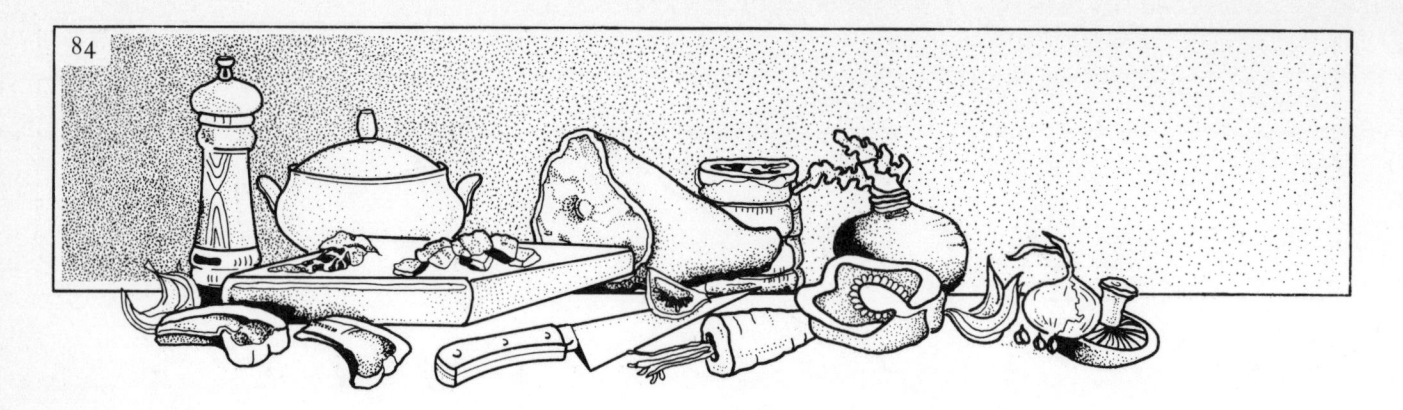

Steaks with mustard sauce

METRIC/IMPERIAL
4 fillet steaks
salt
freshly ground black pepper
50g/2oz butter
1 × 15ml spoon/
  1 tablespoon olive oil
150ml/¼ pint double cream
1 × 15ml spoon/
  1 tablespoon made French mustard

AMERICAN
4 boneless sirloin steaks
salt
freshly ground black pepper
¼ cup butter
1 tablespoon olive oil
⅔ cup heavy cream
1 tablespoon prepared French mustard

Rub the steaks with salt and pepper. Melt the butter with the oil in a frying pan (skillet). Add the steaks and fry for 3 to 5 minutes on each side or until cooked to your preference. Transfer the steaks to a warmed serving plate and keep hot.

Pour the cream into the pan and stir well. Heat through gently without boiling, then stir in the mustard. Pour over the steaks and serve.
Serves 4

Tournedos provençale

METRIC/IMPERIAL
50g/2oz butter
1 onion, peeled and thinly sliced
0.5kg/1lb tomatoes, peeled, deseeded and chopped
2 × 15ml spoons/
  2 tablespoons tomato purée
150ml/¼ pint water
1 bay leaf
pinch of dried basil
1 garlic clove, halved
2 × 15ml spoons/
  2 tablespoons olive oil
4 × 175g/6oz tournedos
  (3.5cm/1½ inches thick)
100g/4oz button mushrooms
watercress to garnish
salt
freshly ground black pepper

AMERICAN
¼ cup butter
1 onion, peeled and thinly sliced
2 cups peeled, deseeded and chopped tomatoes
2 tablespoons tomato paste
⅔ cup water
1 bay leaf
pinch of dried basil
1 garlic clove, halved
2 tablespoons olive oil
4 × 6oz tournedos
  (1½ inches thick)
1 cup button mushrooms
watercress to garnish
salt
freshly ground black pepper

Melt 25g/1oz/2 tablespoons of the butter in a saucepan. Add the onion and fry until it is soft but not brown. Stir in the tomatoes, tomato purée (paste), water, bay leaf and basil and bring to the boil. Cover and simmer for 15 minutes or until reduced to a thick sauce.

Meanwhile, rub a frying pan (skillet) with the cut sides of the garlic. Discard the garlic. Melt the remaining butter with the oil in the pan. Add the tournedos and fry for about 5 minutes on each side for rare steaks (increase the time if you prefer them well done). When you turn the steaks over, add the mushrooms to the pan and cook with the steaks.

Transfer the steaks and mushrooms to a warmed serving dish. Garnish with watercress and keep hot. Season the tomato sauce with salt and pepper to taste and pour into a sauceboat. Serve with the steaks.
Serves 4

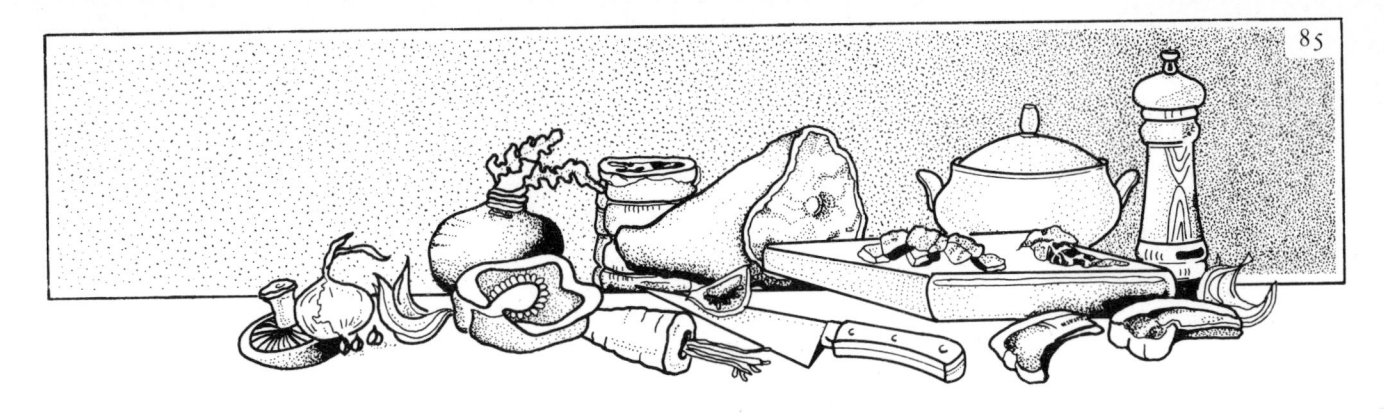

Sukiyaki

METRIC/IMPERIAL
0.75kg/1½lb rump steak, cut into very thin strips
150ml/¼ pint beef stock
2 × 15ml spoons/ 2 tablespoons sake or dry sherry
1 × 15ml spoon/ 1 tablespoon soy sauce
1 × 5ml spoon/1 teaspoon sugar
salt
freshly ground black pepper
4 × 15ml spoons/ 4 tablespoons oil
1 onion, peeled and thinly sliced
50g/2oz French beans, thinly sliced
100g/4oz mushrooms, sliced
1 green pepper, pith and seeds removed and thinly sliced
1 × 5ml spoon/1 teaspoon cornflour

AMERICAN
1½lb boneless sirloin steak, cut into very thin strips
⅔ cup beef stock
2 tablespoons sake or dry sherry
1 tablespoon soy sauce
1 teaspoon sugar
salt
freshly ground black pepper
4 tablespoons oil
1 onion, peeled and thinly sliced
¼ cup thinly sliced green beans
1 cup sliced mushrooms
1 green pepper, pith and seeds removed and thinly sliced
1 teaspoon cornstarch

Put the steak strips in a shallow dish. Mix together the stock, sake or sherry, soy sauce, sugar and salt and pepper to taste and pour over the meat. Leave to marinate for 2 hours.

Drain the meat, reserving the marinade.

Heat the oil in a frying pan (skillet). Add the onion and fry until it is soft but not brown. Add the meat strips and fry, stirring, until they are browned. Add the green beans, mushrooms and green pepper and continue to stir-fry for 3 minutes.

Dissolve the cornflour (cornstarch) in a little of the reserved marinade and add with the remaining marinade to the pan. Bring to the boil, stirring, and simmer until thickened. Serve hot.

Serves 4

Baked marinated steak

METRIC/IMPERIAL
4 rump steaks
25g/1oz butter
2 × 5ml spoons/2 teaspoons made French mustard
4 small shallots, peeled and finely chopped
4 bay leaves
4 fresh marjoram sprigs
Marinade:
300ml/½ pint dry red wine
2 × 15ml spoons/ 2 tablespoons olive oil
salt
freshly ground black pepper

AMERICAN
4 boneless sirloin steaks
2 tablespoons butter
2 teaspoons prepared French mustard
4 small shallots, peeled and finely chopped
4 bay leaves
4 fresh marjoram sprigs
Marinade:
1¼ cups dry red wine
2 tablespoons olive oil
salt
freshly ground black pepper

Mix together the ingredients for the marinade with salt and pepper to taste in a shallow dish. Lay the steaks in the marinade, in one layer. Leave to marinate for at least 6 hours, turning occasionally.

Cut out 4 pieces of foil large enough to enclose the steaks. Coat the centre of each foil piece with the butter and mustard.

Remove the steaks from the marinade and place on the foil. Top each with shallots, a bay leaf and a marjoram sprig. Fold up the foil to make neat parcels. Arrange the parcels on a baking sheet.

Bake in a preheated moderately hot oven (200°C/400°F, Gas Mark 6) for 15 minutes. Serve hot, in the foil parcels.

Serves 4

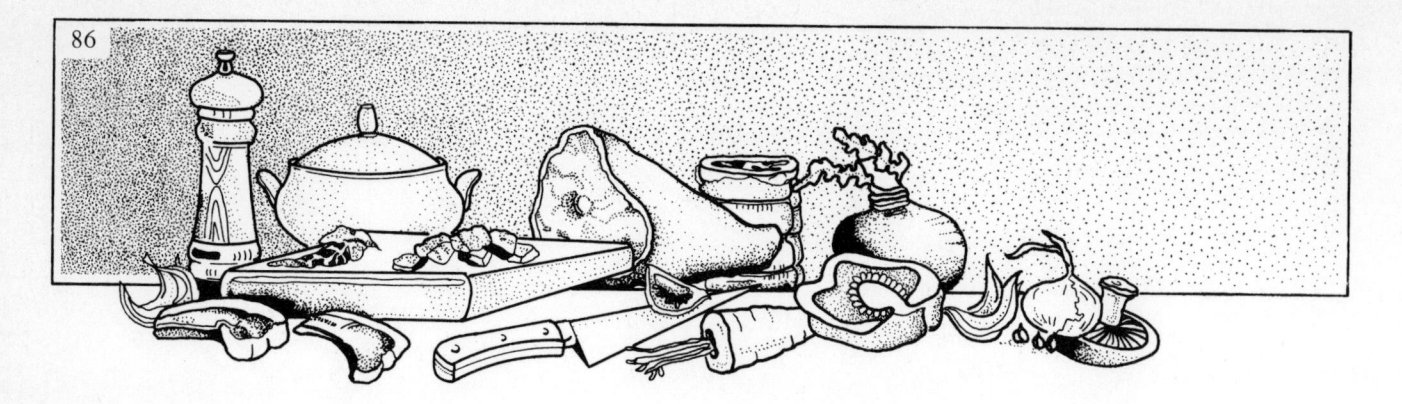

Peppered steak

METRIC/IMPERIAL
2 × 15ml spoons/
 2 tablespoons black or
 green peppercorns,
 crushed
1kg/2lb rump steak, cut
 into 4 pieces
100g/4oz butter
2 × 15ml spoons/
 2 tablespoons brandy

AMERICAN
2 tablespoons black or green
 peppercorns, crushed
2lb boneless sirloin steak,
 cut into 4 pieces
½ cup butter
2 tablespoons brandy

Press the peppercorns into both sides of the steaks and leave at room temperature for 1 hour.

Melt the butter in a frying pan (skillet). Add 2 of the steaks and fry for 2 minutes on each side until well browned. Remove from the pan and brown the remaining 2 steaks in the same way. Return the first 2 steaks to the pan and cook gently for a further 2 to 3 minutes on each side or until cooked to your taste.

Transfer the steaks to a warmed serving dish and keep hot.

Add the brandy to the pan and stir well. Pour this mixture over the steaks and serve hot.
Serves 4

Stuffed beef fillet

METRIC/IMPERIAL
50g/2oz dripping
2 onions, peeled and finely
 chopped
2 anchovy fillets, chopped
1 × 15ml spoon/
 1 tablespoon chopped
 bacon
freshly ground black pepper
pinch of dried thyme
1 × 5ml spoon/1 teaspoon
 chopped fresh parsley
1 egg yolk
1 × 0.75kg/1½lb beef fillet
watercress to garnish

AMERICAN
¼ cup drippings
2 onions, peeled and finely
 chopped
2 anchovy fillets, chopped
1 tablespoon chopped bacon
freshly ground black pepper
pinch of dried thyme
1 teaspoon chopped fresh
 parsley
1 egg yolk
1 × 1½lb beef fillet
 (tenderloin)
watercress to garnish

Melt 25g/1oz/2 tablespoons of the dripping in a frying pan (skillet). Add the onions and fry until they are soft but not brown. Remove from the heat and stir in the anchovies, bacon, pepper to taste, thyme, parsley and egg yolk.

Make 4 cuts lengthways in the beef, not cutting all the way through. Fill the cuts with the stuffing. Tie the beef into shape with string or secure with wooden cocktail sticks (toothpicks).

Place the beef on a sheet of foil and dot with the remaining dripping. Fold up the foil to enclose the beef and place in a roasting tin. Roast in a preheated cool oven (150°C/300°F, Gas Mark 2) for 1 to 1¼ hours or until tender. Serve hot, garnished with watercress.
Serves 4

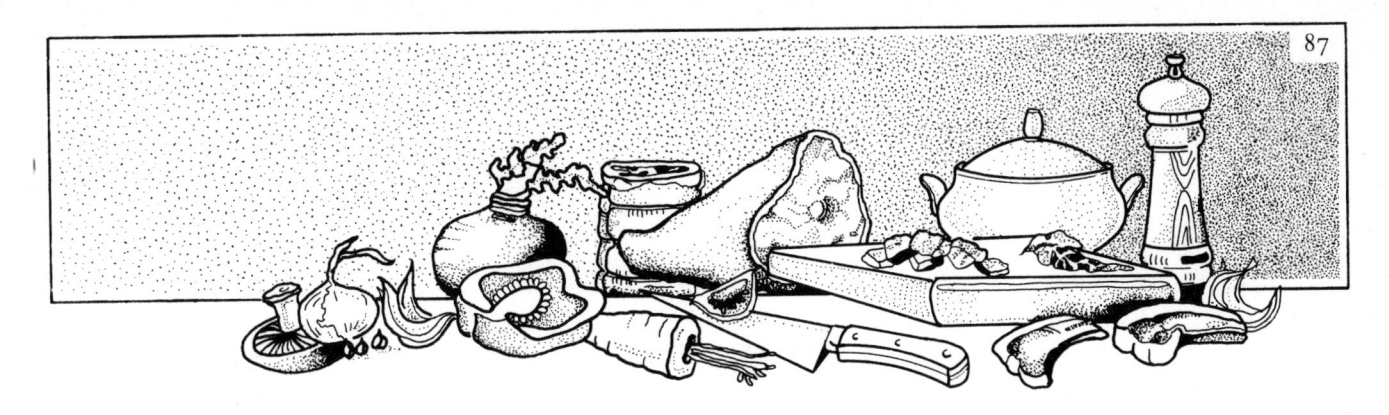

Braised beef topside (top round)

METRIC/IMPERIAL
1 × 1kg/2lb beef topside
salt
freshly ground black pepper
25g/1oz butter
225g/8oz carrots, peeled and sliced
2 large onions, peeled and sliced
300ml/½ pint brown ale
1 × 2.5ml spoon/
 ½ teaspoon dried thyme
2 × 5ml spoons/2 teaspoons brown sugar
1 × 15ml spoon/
 1 tablespoon cornflour
1 × 15ml spoon/
 1 tablespoon water

AMERICAN
1 × 2lb beef top round
salt
freshly ground black pepper
2 tablespoons butter
½lb carrots, peeled and sliced
2 large onions, peeled and sliced
1¼ cups dark beer
½ teaspoon dried thyme
2 teaspoons brown sugar
1 tablespoon cornstarch
1 tablespoon water

Rub the beef all over with salt and pepper. Melt the butter in a flameproof casserole. Add the beef and brown on all sides. Remove the beef from the pan. Add the carrots and onions to the pan and fry until the onions are soft but not brown. Return the beef to the pan and pour over the ale (beer). Add the thyme and sugar and bring to the boil. Braise on top of the stove or in a preheated moderate oven (160°C/325°F, Gas Mark 3) for 2 to 2½ hours or until tender.

Transfer the beef to a carving board. Drain the vegetables, reserving the cooking liquid, and arrange the vegetables on a warmed serving dish. Carve the meat and arrange the slices, overlapping, down the centre of the dish. Keep hot.

Dissolve the cornflour (cornstarch) in the water and add to the cooking liquid. Return to the casserole and simmer, stirring, until thickened and smooth. Pour over the meat and serve.
Serves 4 to 6

Roast beef

METRIC/IMPERIAL
1 × 2.75kg/6lb rib roast of beef
salt
freshly ground black pepper
25g/1oz beef dripping
2 × 15ml spoons/
 2 tablespoons plain flour
300ml/½ pint beef stock

AMERICAN
1 × 6lb rib roast of beef
salt
freshly ground black pepper
2 tablespoons beef drippings
2 tablespoons all-purpose flour
1¼ cups beef stock

Rub the beef with salt and pepper. Melt the dripping in a roasting tin and place the roast in the tin, fat side up. Roast in a preheated moderate oven (180°C/350°F, Gas Mark 4) for 20 minutes to the 0.5kg/1lb plus 20 minutes over. This will produce medium rare meat. If you prefer it well done, roast for 25 minutes to the 0.5kg/1lb plus 25 minutes over.

Transfer the meat to a carving board and keep hot.

Pour off most of the fat from the roasting tin. Sprinkle over the flour and stir in well, scraping up any sediment. Place over the heat on top of the stove and cook until brown. Gradually stir in the stock and simmer, stirring, until thickened. Season to taste with salt and pepper. Pour into a gravy boat and serve with the meat.
Serves 8

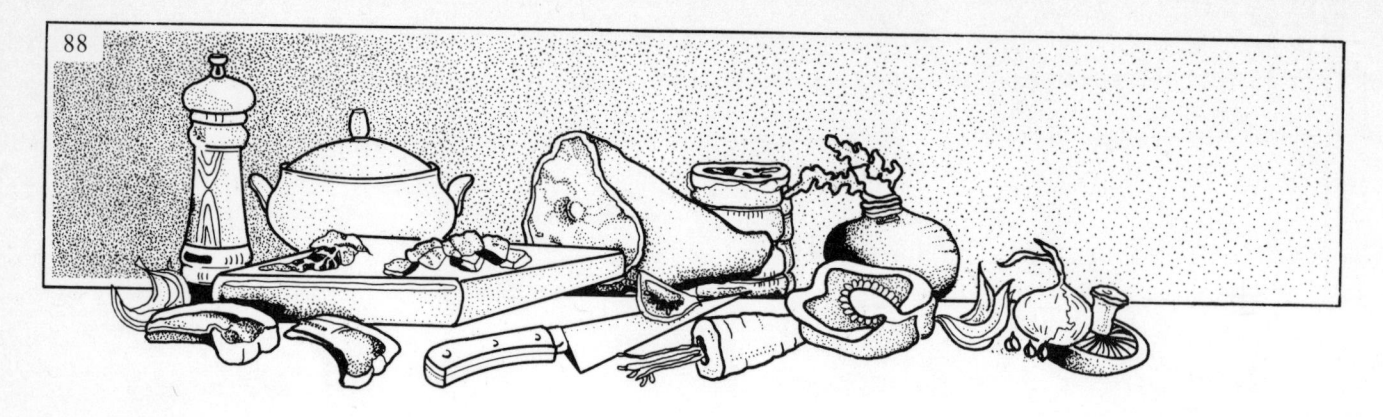

Stuffed beef rolls

METRIC/IMPERIAL
6 thin steaks
6 lean bacon rashers, rinds removed
50g/2oz butter
2 × 15ml spoons/ 2 tablespoons olive oil
2 large onions, peeled and finely chopped
175g/6oz fresh white breadcrumbs
50g/2oz Parmesan cheese, grated
1 × 5ml spoon/1 teaspoon dried marjoram
25g/1oz sultanas
25g/1oz blanched almonds, chopped
salt
freshly ground black pepper
3 × 15ml spoons/ 3 tablespoons tomato purée
300ml/½ pint beef stock

AMERICAN
6 thin steaks
6 Canadian bacon slices
¼ cup butter
2 tablespoons olive oil
2 large onions, peeled and finely chopped
3 cups fresh white breadcrumbs
½ cup grated Parmesan cheese
1 teaspoon dried marjoram
3 tablespoons seedless white raisins
¼ cup chopped blanched almonds
salt
freshly ground black pepper
3 tablespoons tomato paste
1¼ cups beef stock

Roll out the steaks with a rolling pin until they are very thin. Grill (broil) the bacon, then place a rasher (slice) on each steak.

Melt the butter with 1 × 15ml spoon/1 tablespoon of the oil in a frying pan (skillet). Add the onions and fry until they are soft but not brown. Remove from the heat. Remove half the onions from the pan and set aside.

Add the breadcrumbs, cheese, marjoram, sultanas (raisins), almonds and salt and pepper to taste to the pan and mix well. Divide this stuffing between the steaks and press down firmly. Roll up the steaks and secure with wooden cocktail sticks (toothpicks).

Heat the remaining oil in a flameproof casserole. Add the beef rolls and brown on all sides. Mix the tomato purée (paste) with the stock and add to the casserole with the reserved onion. Bring to the boil, then cover and transfer to a preheated moderate oven (160°C/325°F, Gas Mark 3). Braise for 1 hour or until the meat is tender.

Remove the cocktail sticks (toothpicks). Serve hot, from the casserole.
Serves 6

Beef and bacon rolls

METRIC/IMPERIAL
1kg/2lb topside of beef, thinly sliced and pounded
salt
freshly ground black pepper
0.5kg/1lb lean bacon rashers, rinds removed
25g/1oz butter
1 × 15ml spoon/ 1 tablespoon oil
1 large onion, peeled and finely chopped
2 × 15ml spoons/ 2 tablespoons plain flour
350ml/12fl oz dry red wine

AMERICAN
2lb top round of beef, thinly sliced and pounded
salt
freshly ground black pepper
1lb Canadian bacon slices
2 tablespoons butter
1 tablespoon oil
1 large onion, peeled and finely chopped
2 tablespoons all-purpose flour
1½ cups dry red wine

Rub the beef slices with salt and pepper. Place a bacon rasher (slice) on each beef slice and roll up. Secure with string or a wooden cocktail stick (toothpick).

Melt the butter with the oil in a saucepan. Add the beef rolls, in batches, and brown on all sides. As they are browned, remove from the pan.

Add the onion to the pan and fry until it is soft but not brown. Sprinkle over the flour and stir well. Cook, stirring, for 2 minutes. Gradually stir in the wine and bring to the boil. Simmer until thickened.

Return the beef rolls to the pan and spoon the sauce over. Cover and simmer for 1½ hours or until the beef is tender. Serve hot.
Serves 6

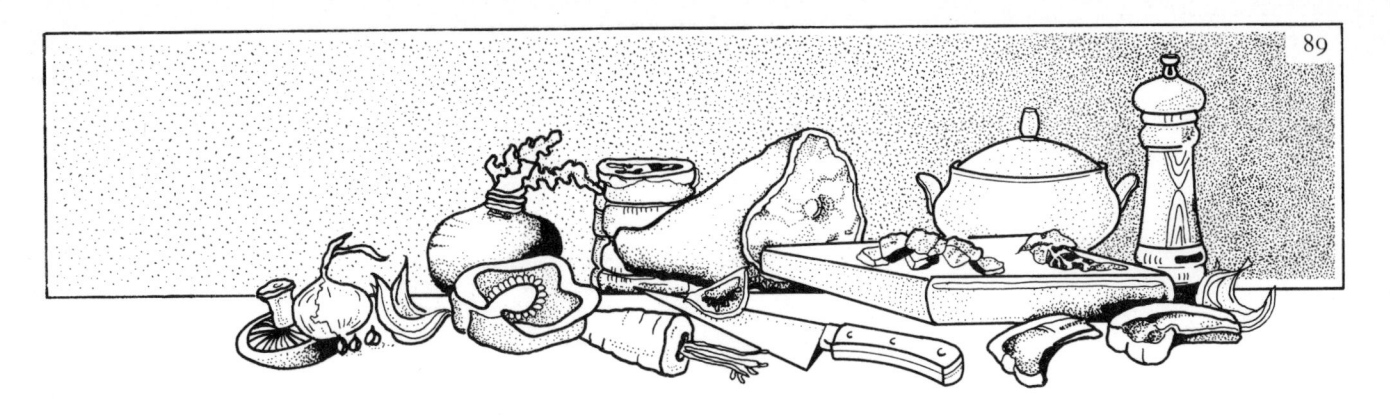

Steak and kidney pie

METRIC/IMPERIAL
50g/2oz dripping
1 large onion, peeled and finely chopped
1kg/2lb stewing steak, cut into small cubes
225g/8oz kidney, skinned, cored and chopped
50g/2oz plain flour
225g/8oz mushrooms, sliced
1 carrot, peeled and sliced
300ml/½ pint beef stock
1 bay leaf
salt
freshly ground black pepper
225g/8oz quantity puff pastry*

AMERICAN
¼ cup drippings
1 large onion, peeled and finely chopped
2lb stewing steak, cut into small cubes
½lb kidney, skinned, cored and chopped
½ cup all-purpose flour
2 cups sliced mushrooms
1 carrot, peeled and sliced
1¼ cups beef stock
1 bay leaf
salt
freshly ground black pepper
2 cup quantity puff pastry*

Melt the dripping in a saucepan. Add the onion and fry until soft but not brown. Coat the steak and kidney in the flour, then add to the pan and brown on all sides. Add the mushrooms and carrot and sprinkle over any remaining flour. Cook for 1 minute then gradually stir in the stock, bay leaf and salt and pepper to taste. Bring to the boil, stirring, then cover and simmer for 1 to 2 hours or until the meat is tender.

Remove the bay leaf and turn the meat into an ovenproof pie dish. Roll out the pastry on a floured surface. Dampen the edge of the pie dish with a little water and cover with the pastry. Cut an air vent in the centre and use the pastry trimmings to decorate. Put in a preheated hot oven (220°C/425°F, Gas Mark 7) for 25 to 30 minutes. Cover with foil if the pastry browns too quickly.
Serves 6

Sweet and sour meatballs

METRIC/IMPERIAL
0.75kg/1½lb beef, minced
1 garlic clove, finely chopped
50g/2oz plain flour
25g/1oz fresh breadcrumbs
1 large egg yolk
salt
freshly ground black pepper
40g/1½oz butter
Sauce:
115g/4½oz sugar
6 × 15ml spoons/ 6 tablespoons cider vinegar
6 × 15ml spoons/ 6 tablespoons soy sauce
2 × 15ml spoons/ 2 tablespoons cornflour
450ml/¾ pint water
1 large green pepper, pith and seeds removed and thinly sliced
350g/12oz tomatoes, peeled and quartered
1 × 300g/11oz can crushed pineapple, drained

AMERICAN
3 cups ground beef
1 garlic clove, finely chopped
½ cup all-purpose flour
½ cup fresh breadcrumbs
1 egg yolk
salt
freshly ground black pepper
3 tablespoons butter
Sauce:
½ cup plus 1 tablespoon sugar
6 tablespoons cider vinegar
6 tablespoons soy sauce
2 tablespoons cornstarch
2 cups water
1 large green pepper, pith and seeds removed and thinly sliced
¾lb tomatoes, peeled and quartered
1 × 11oz can crushed pineapple, drained

Mix together the beef, garlic, 25g/1oz/¼ cup of the flour, the breadcrumbs, egg yolk and salt and pepper to taste. Form into walnut-sized balls and coat with the remaining flour. Melt the butter in a frying pan (skillet) and add the meatballs. Fry for 20 minutes, turning occasionally to brown evenly.

Meanwhile, put the sugar, vinegar and soy sauce in a saucepan. Heat gently, stirring, to dissolve the sugar. Dissolve the cornflour (cornstarch) in the water and add to the pan. Bring to the boil, stirring, and simmer for 5 minutes. Add the pepper, tomatoes and pineapple and simmer for a further 10 minutes.

Drain the meatballs on absorbent paper and add to the saucepan. Spoon the sauce over them and simmer gently for a further 3 minutes. Serve hot.
Serves 4

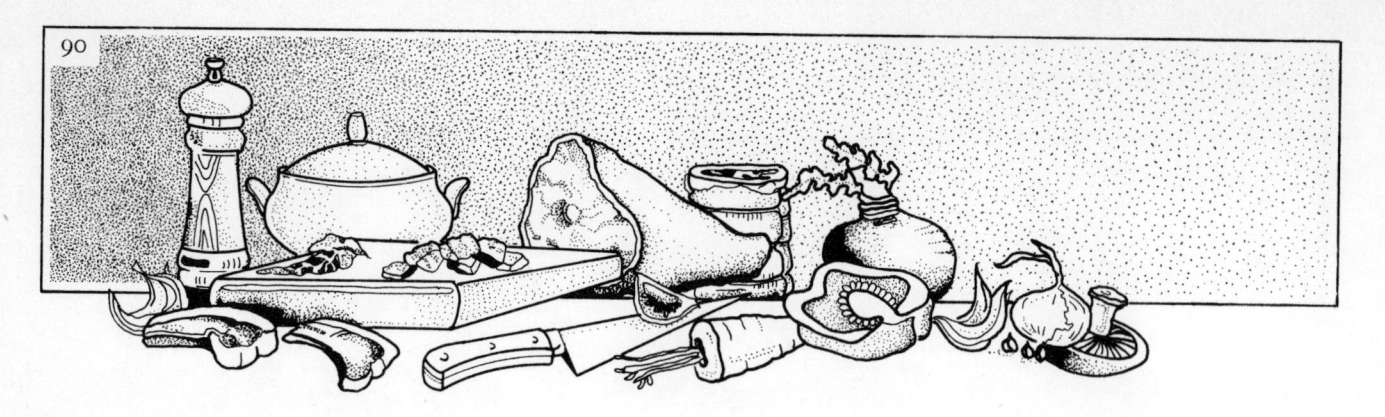

Boeuf catalan

METRIC/IMPERIAL
1 × 2lb beef topside
oil for frying
4 bacon rashers, rinds removed and chopped
1 medium onion, peeled and sliced
2 carrots, peeled and sliced
50g/2oz mushrooms, sliced
1 garlic clove, crushed
1 bouquet garni
pinch of grated nutmeg
1 × 225g/8oz can tomatoes
1 × 5ml spoon/
  1 teaspoon black treacle
250ml/8fl oz cider
salt
freshly ground black pepper
watercress to garnish

AMERICAN
1 × 2lb beef top round
oil for frying
4 bacon slices, chopped
1 medium onion, peeled and sliced
2 carrots, peeled and sliced
½ cup sliced mushrooms
1 garlic clove, crushed
1 bouquet garni
pinch of grated nutmeg
1 × ½lb can tomatoes
1 teaspoon molasses
1 cup hard cider
salt
freshly ground black pepper
watercress to garnish

Brown the beef in the oil in a flameproof casserole. When the beef is browned on all sides, remove from the pot and drain on absorbent paper. Add the bacon, onion and carrots to the pot and fry until the onions are soft but not brown. Add the mushrooms, garlic, bouquet garni and nutmeg. Place the meat on top. Mix together the tomatoes, treacle (molasses), cider and salt and pepper to taste and pour over the beef. Bring to the boil on top of the stove, then place in a preheated moderate oven (160°C/325°F, Gas Mark 3) for 2½ hours or until tender. Lift the meat onto a warmed serving dish; leave whole or cut into thick slices. Keep hot.

Remove the bouquet garni and quickly sieve (strain) the sauce or purée in a blender. Reheat in a separate pan and adjust the seasoning. Pour the sauce over the meat and serve, garnished with watercress.
Serves 4 to 6

Greek meatballs

METRIC/IMPERIAL
0.75kg/1½lb beef, minced
1 onion, peeled and grated
1 garlic clove, finely chopped
2 × 15ml spoons/
  2 tablespoons chopped fresh parsley
2 × 15ml spoons/
  2 tablespoons long-grain rice
salt
freshly ground black pepper
750ml/1¼ pints beef stock
Sauce:
4 eggs
3 × 15ml spoons/
  3 tablespoons water
120ml/4fl oz lemon juice

AMERICAN
3 cups ground beef
1 onion, peeled and grated
1 garlic clove, finely chopped
2 tablespoons chopped fresh parsley
2 tablespoons long-grain rice
salt
freshly ground black pepper
3 cups beef stock
Sauce:
4 eggs
3 tablespoons water
½ cup lemon juice

Mix together the beef, onion, garlic, parsley, rice and salt and pepper to taste. Form into walnut-sized balls. Put the stock in a saucepan and bring to the boil. Add the meatballs, cover and simmer for 45 minutes.

To make the sauce, beat the eggs and water together in a heatproof bowl over a pan of hot water. Beat until the mixture is light and fluffy. Gradually beat in 4 × 15ml spoons/4 tablespoons of the meatball stock.

Add the lemon juice and continue beating until the sauce is thick and smooth. Add salt to taste and remove from the heat. Keep warm.

Drain the meatballs and arrange in a warmed serving dish. Pour over the sauce and serve hot.
Serves 4 to 6

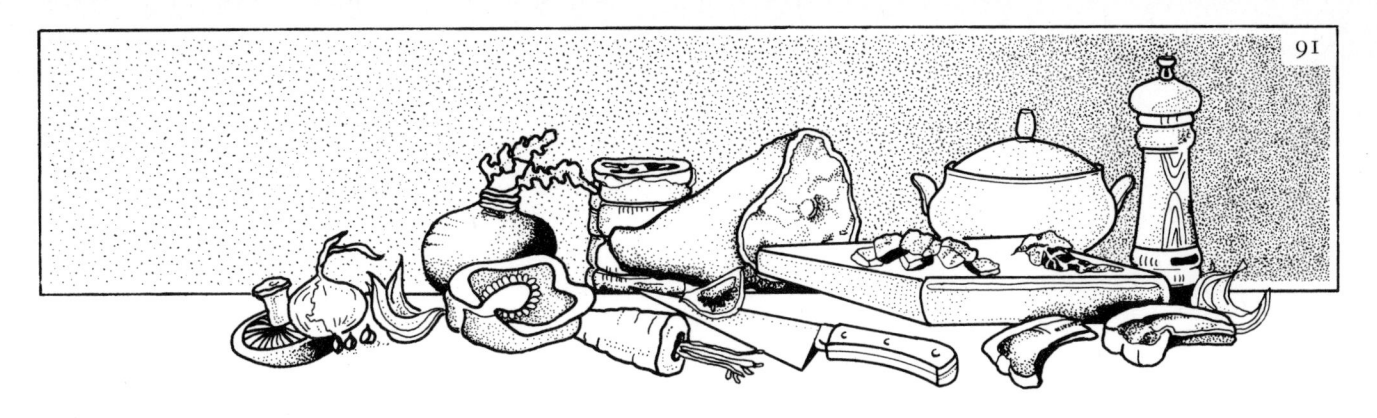

Goulash

METRIC/IMPERIAL
2 × 15ml spoons/
  2 tablespoons oil
0.5kg/1lb braising steak,
  cut into cubes
2 × 5ml spoons/
  2 teaspoons paprika
2 × 5ml spoons/
  2 teaspoons flour
300ml/½ pint stock
25g/1oz butter
4 onions, peeled and
  chopped
225g/8oz carrots, peeled
  and diced
1 bay leaf
1 × 2.5ml spoon/
  ½ teaspoon dried thyme
1 × 400g/14oz can
  tomatoes
1 × 15ml spoon/
  1 tablespoon tomato purée
salt
freshly ground black pepper
1 large potato, peeled and
  diced
1 × 15ml spoon/
  1 tablespoon sour cream to
finish

AMERICAN
2 tablespoons oil
1lb braising steak, cut into
  cubes
2 teaspoons paprika
2 teaspoons flour
1¼ cups stock
2 tablespoons butter
4 onions, peeled and
  chopped
½lb carrots, peeled and
  diced
1 bay leaf
½ teaspoon dried thyme
1 × 14oz can tomatoes
1 tablespoon tomato paste
salt
freshly ground black pepper
1 large potato, peeled and
  diced
1 tablespoon sour cream to
  finish

Heat the oil in frying pan (skillet) and fry the beef cubes until brown on all sides. Reduce the heat and sprinkle over the paprika and flour. Turn the meat over to absorb the flour and cook for 2 to 3 minutes. Add the stock and stir gently. Pour into a casserole.

Rinse the pan, melt the butter and gently fry the onions and carrots over a low heat. Add the herbs, tomatoes, tomato purée (paste) and salt and pepper to taste. Add the potato to the tomato mixture. Pour the mixture over the meat in the casserole. Place in a preheated moderate oven (160°C/325°F, Gas Mark 3) and cook for 1¾ hours.

Before serving, remove the bay leaf, taste and adjust the seasoning and stir in the sour cream.
Serves 4

African beef curry

METRIC/IMPERIAL
1kg/2lb chuck steak, cut
  into cubes
25g/1oz flour
1 × 2.5ml spoon/
  ½ teaspoon paprika
good pinch chilli powder
corn oil for frying
2 large onions, peeled and
  chopped
1 × 15ml spoon/
  1 tablespoon desiccated
  coconut
2 × 15ml spoons/
  2 tablespoons curry powder
1 × 15ml spoon/
  1 tablespoon curry paste
1 garlic clove, crushed
600ml/1 pint beef stock

AMERICAN
2lb chuck steak, cut into
  cubes
¼ cup flour
½ teaspoon paprika
good pinch chili powder
corn oil for frying
2 large onions, peeled and
  chopped
1 tablespoon shredded
  coconut
2 tablespoons curry powder
1 tablespoon curry paste
1 garlic clove, crushed
2½ cups beef stock

Coat the beef cubes in the flour, seasoned with paprika and chilli powder. Heat 1.5 × 15ml spoons/ 1½ tablespoons oil in a large saucepan and fry the onions gently until soft and evenly browned. Add the coconut, curry powder, curry paste, garlic and stock. Bring to the boil.

Using a large frying pan (skillet), heat enough oil just to cover the base. Add the beef cubes to the pan, in batches, and fry until browned all over. When all the meat has been browned, drain and add to the curry sauce. Cover the pan and simmer for 2 hours, or until the meat is tender.

Serve with sliced fresh fruit and raw vegetables, desiccated (shredded) coconut and poppadums.
Serves 4

VEAL

Saltimbocca

METRIC/IMPERIAL
8 thin slices of cooked ham, trimmed to 15 × 10cm/ 6 × 4 inches
8 veal escalopes, pounded thin and trimmed to 15 × 10cm/6 × 4 inches
8 fresh sage leaves
freshly ground black pepper
50g/2oz butter
120ml/4fl oz dry white wine

AMERICAN
8 thin slices of cooked ham, trimmed to 6 × 4 inches
8 veal scallops, pounded thin and trimmed to 6 × 4 inches
8 fresh sage leaves
freshly ground black pepper
¼ cup butter
½ cup dry white wine

Put a slice of ham on each veal escalope (scallop), then a sage leaf and finally a sprinkling of pepper. Roll up and secure with wooden cocktail sticks (toothpicks).

Melt the butter in a frying pan (skillet). Add the veal rolls and fry until golden brown. Pour in the wine and bring to the boil. Cover and simmer for 15 minutes, or until tender.

Transfer the veal rolls to a warmed serving dish and remove the cocktail sticks (toothpicks). Pour over the cooking juices and serve hot.
Serves 4

Veal parcels with yogurt sauce

METRIC/IMPERIAL
4 streaky bacon rashers, rinds removed and cut into strips
100g/4oz mushrooms, sliced
1 × 15ml spoon/ 1 tablespoon chopped fresh parsley
1 small onion, peeled and grated
50g/2oz butter
75g/3oz fresh breadcrumbs
1 egg
salt
freshly ground black pepper
4 large veal chops
Sauce:
300ml/½ pint natural yogurt
2 × 15ml spoons/ 2 tablespoons medium sherry
1 × 5ml spoon/1 teaspoon made mustard

AMERICAN
4 bacon slices, cut into strips
1 cup sliced mushrooms
1 tablespoon chopped fresh parsley
1 small onion, peeled and grated
¼ cup butter
1½ cups fresh breadcrumbs
1 egg
salt
freshly ground black pepper
4 large veal chops
Sauce:
1¼ cups unflavored yogurt
2 tablespoons medium sherry
1 teaspoon prepared mustard

Mix together the bacon, mushrooms, parsley, onion, butter, breadcrumbs, egg and salt and pepper to taste. Cut out 4 squares of foil each large enough to enclose a chop. Grease the foil.

Place a chop in the centre of each piece of foil. Spoon the bacon mixture on top of the chops and fold up the foil to make neat parcels. Arrange the parcels in a roasting tin and cook in a preheated hot oven (220°C/425°F, Gas Mark 7) for 40 to 45 minutes.

Meanwhile, put the yogurt, sherry and mustard in a heatproof bowl over a pan of hot water. Heat gently, stirring occasionally. Season to taste with salt and pepper.

Unwrap the parcels and serve hot with the yogurt sauce.
Serves 4

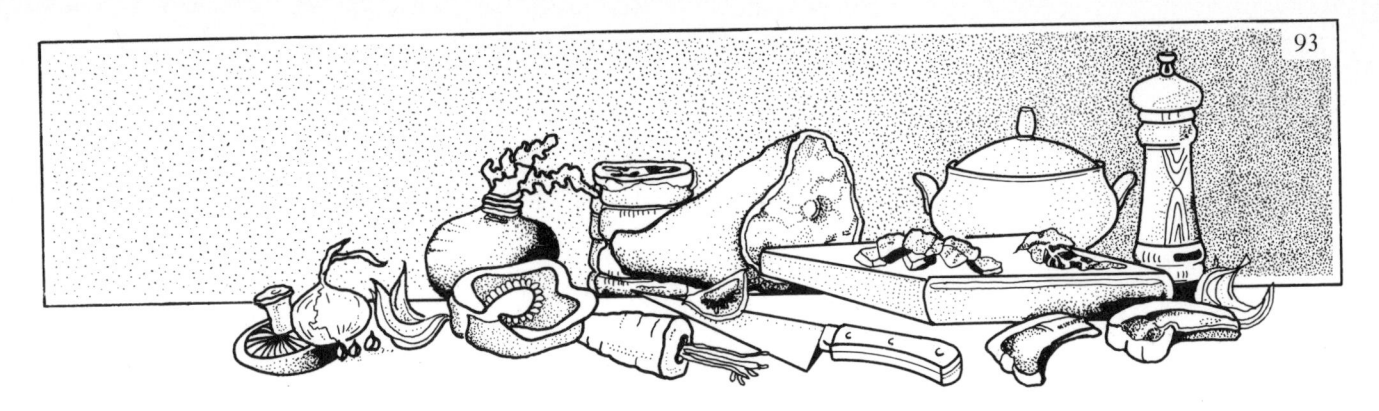

Veal escalopes (scallops) with vermouth

METRIC/IMPERIAL
25g/1oz plain flour
salt
freshly ground black pepper
4 veal escalopes, halved and pounded thin
50g/2oz butter
6 spring onions, chopped
1 lemon, thinly sliced
2 × 5ml spoons/2 teaspoons chopped fresh rosemary
dash of Tabasco sauce
150ml/¼ pint dry vermouth

AMERICAN
¼ cup all-purpose flour
salt
freshly ground black pepper
4 veal scallops, halved and pounded thin
¼ cup butter
6 scallions, chopped
1 lemon, thinly sliced
2 teaspoons chopped fresh rosemary
dash of Tabasco sauce
⅔ cup dry vermouth

Mix the flour with salt and pepper and use to coat the veal. Melt the butter in a frying pan (skillet). Add the veal and fry until it is golden on both sides. Remove from the pan and keep hot.

Add the chopped white part of the spring onions (scallions) and fry for 3 minutes. Replace the veal in the pan and cover with the lemon slices. Sprinkle with the rosemary and Tabasco and pour the vermouth into the pan. Bring to the boil and simmer for 3 minutes.

Serve hot, garnished with the chopped green part of the spring onions (scallions).
Serves 4

Veal Cordon Bleu

METRIC/IMPERIAL
4 slices of lean cooked ham
4 slices of Gruyère cheese
4 veal escalopes, pounded thin
50g/2oz butter
3 × 15ml spoons/ 3 tablespoons olive oil
300ml/½ pint beef stock
150ml/¼ pint Madeira
salt
freshly ground black pepper

AMERICAN
4 slices of lean cooked ham
4 slices of Gruyère cheese
4 veal scallops, pounded thin
¼ cup butter
3 tablespoons olive oil
1¼ cups beef stock
⅔ cup Madeira
salt
freshly ground black pepper

Place a slice of ham and a slice of cheese on one half of each escalope (scallop). Fold over the veal to cover and secure with wooden cocktail sticks (toothpicks).

Melt the butter with the oil in a frying pan (skillet). Add the veal and brown quickly on both sides. Reduce the heat and cook for a further 6 minutes on each side or until tender.

Add the stock and Madeira with salt and pepper to taste and bring to the boil. Simmer for 5 minutes.

Transfer the veal to a warmed serving dish. Keep hot. Boil the cooking liquid until it has reduced to half the original quantity.

Remove the cocktail sticks (toothpicks) from the veal. Pour over the cooking liquid and serve.
Serves 4

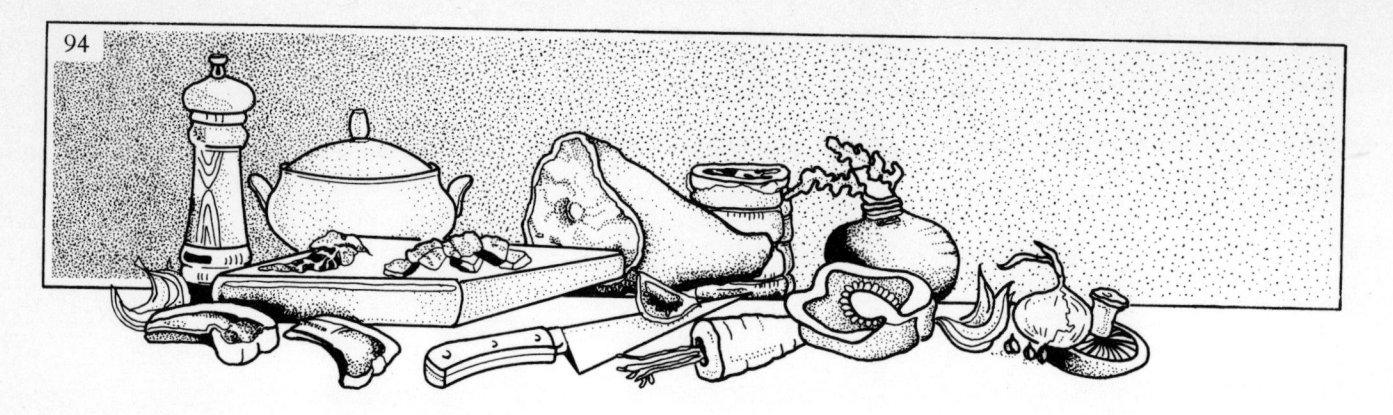

Escalopes (scallops) bolognese

METRIC/IMPERIAL
4 veal escalopes, pounded thin
1 egg, lightly beaten
50g/2oz dry breadcrumbs
100g/4oz butter
4 slices cooked ham
50g/2oz Parmesan cheese, grated

AMERICAN
4 veal scallops, pounded thin
1 egg, lightly beaten
½ cup dry breadcrumbs
½ cup butter
4 slices cooked ham
½ cup grated Parmesan cheese

Coat the veal in the egg, then in the breadcrumbs. Melt 75g/3oz/⅓ cup of the butter in a frying pan (skillet). Add the veal and fry for 4 to 5 minutes on each side or until golden brown and cooked through.

Place a slice of ham on each escalope (scallop), then sprinkle with the cheese. Cut the remaining butter into small pieces and dot over the top. Cover the pan and cook for a further 3 to 4 minutes or until the cheese has melted. Serve hot.
Serves 4

Veal paupiettes

METRIC/IMPERIAL
4 veal escalopes, pounded thin
25g/1oz plain flour
25g/1oz butter
1 × 15ml spoon/
 1 tablespoon olive oil
150ml/¼ pint dry white wine
150ml/¼ pint chicken stock
Stuffing:
25g/1oz butter
1 small onion, peeled and finely chopped
100g/4oz mushrooms, finely chopped
75g/3oz fresh breadcrumbs
2 × 15ml spoons/
 2 tablespoons chopped fresh parsley
finely grated rind and juice of 1 lemon
salt
freshly ground black pepper

AMERICAN
4 veal scallops, pounded thin
¼ cup all-purpose flour
2 tablespoons butter
1 tablespoon olive oil
⅔ cup dry white wine
⅔ cup chicken stock
Stuffing:
2 tablespoons butter
1 small onion, peeled and finely chopped
1 cup finely chopped mushrooms
1½ cups fresh breadcrumbs
2 tablespoons chopped fresh parsley
finely grated rind and juice of 1 lemon
salt
freshly ground black pepper

First make the stuffing. Melt the butter in a saucepan. Add the onion and fry until it is soft but not brown. Stir in the mushrooms and fry for 2 to 3 minutes. Remove from the heat and stir in the remaining stuffing ingredients with salt and pepper to taste.

Lay the veal flat and spread each escalope (scallop) with the stuffing. Roll up and tie with string. Coat with the flour.

Melt the butter with the oil in a flameproof casserole. Add the veal rolls and brown on all sides. Pour in the wine and stock and bring to the boil. Add salt and pepper to taste, then cover and simmer for 45 minutes to 1 hour or until the veal is tender.
Serves 4

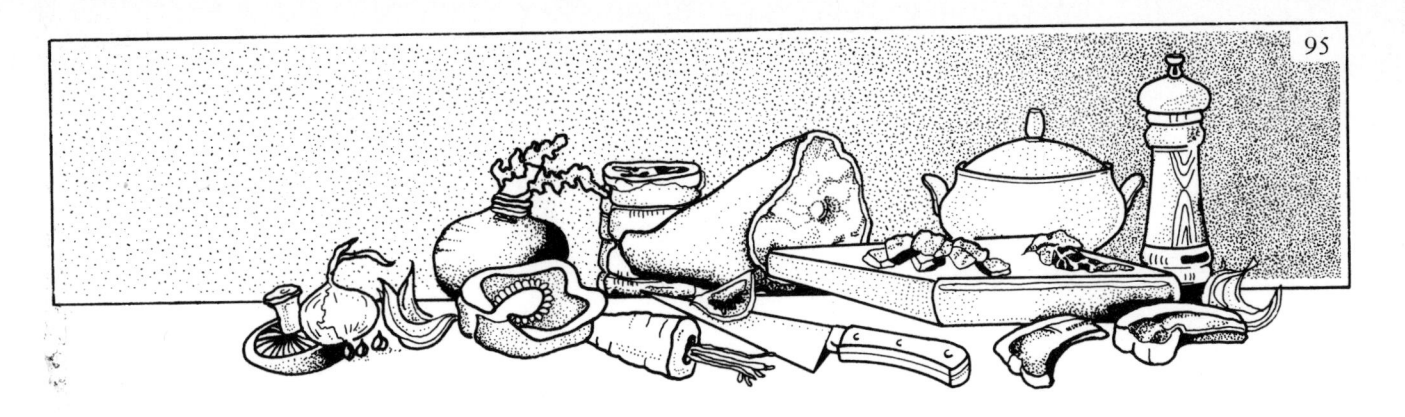

Escalopes (scallops) Parmesan

METRIC/IMPERIAL
25g/1oz plain flour
salt
freshly ground black pepper
4 veal escalopes, pounded thin
50g/2oz dry breadcrumbs
50g/2oz Parmesan cheese, grated
1 × 5ml spoon/1 teaspoon grated lemon rind
1 egg, lightly beaten
50g/2oz butter
1 × 15ml spoon/ 1 tablespoon olive oil

AMERICAN
¼ cup all-purpose flour
salt
freshly ground black pepper
4 veal scallops, pounded thin
½ cup dry breadcrumbs
½ cup grated Parmesan cheese
1 teaspoon grated lemon rind
1 egg, lightly beaten
¼ cup butter
1 tablespoon olive oil

Mix the flour with salt and pepper and use to coat the veal. Mix together the breadcrumbs, cheese and lemon rind. Dip the veal in the egg, then coat with the cheese mixture. Chill for 1 hour.

Melt the butter with the oil in a frying pan (skillet). Add the escalopes (scallops), two at a time, and fry for 2 minutes on each side or until browned. When all the escalopes (scallops) have been browned, put them all in the pan and cook for a further 3 to 4 minutes or until cooked through.

Serve hot, with tomato sauce★.

Serves 4

Wiener schnitzel

METRIC/IMPERIAL
4 veal escalopes, pounded thin
juice of 2 lemons
salt
freshly ground black pepper
1 large egg, lightly beaten
100g/4oz dry breadcrumbs
40g/1½oz butter
lemon wedges to garnish

AMERICAN
4 veal scallops, pounded thin
juice of 2 lemons
salt
freshly ground black pepper
1 egg, lightly beaten
1 cup dry breadcrumbs
3 tablespoons butter
lemon wedges to garnish

Put the veal in a shallow dish and sprinkle with the lemon juice and salt and pepper. Leave to marinate for 1 hour.

Dip the veal in the egg, then coat in the breadcrumbs.

Melt the butter in a frying pan (skillet). Add the veal, in batches, and fry for about 3 to 4 minutes on each side or until golden brown and cooked through.

Serve hot, garnished with lemon wedges.

Serves 4

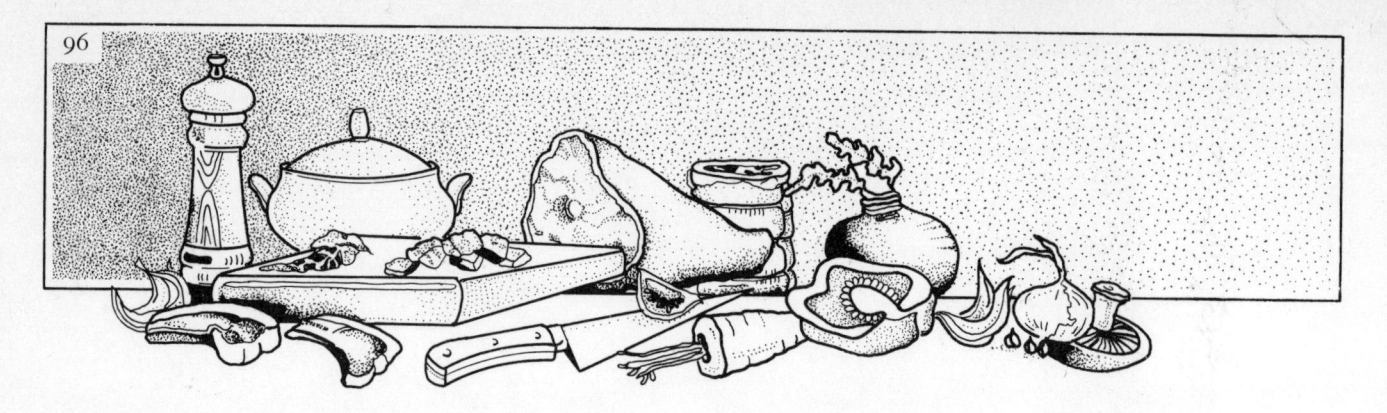

Hungarian veal chops

METRIC/IMPERIAL
25g/1oz plain flour
salt
freshly ground black pepper
4 large veal chops
25g/1oz butter
1 onion, peeled and sliced
1 × 15ml spoon/
 1 tablespoon paprika
150ml/¼ pint chicken or
 veal stock
3 × 15ml spoons/
 3 tablespoons tomato purée
2 × 15ml spoons/
 2 tablespoons lemon juice
175g/6oz button
 mushrooms, sliced
150ml/¼ pint sour cream

AMERICAN
¼ cup all-purpose flour
salt
freshly ground black pepper
4 large veal chops
2 tablespoons butter
1 onion, peeled and sliced
1 tablespoon paprika
⅔ cup chicken or veal stock
3 tablespoons tomato paste
2 tablespoons lemon juice
1½ cups sliced button
 mushrooms
⅔ cup sour cream

Mix the flour with salt and pepper and use to coat the veal chops. Melt the butter in a frying pan (skillet). Add the onion and fry until it is soft but not brown. Push the onion to one side and add the veal chops to the pan. Brown well on both sides. Remove the chops from the pan.

Stir the paprika into the onion and cook for 1 minute. Gradually stir in the stock, tomato purée (paste) and lemon juice and bring to the boil. Return the chops to the pan, cover tightly and simmer for 10 to 15 minutes or until the chops are cooked through.

Stir in the mushrooms and cook for a further 3 minutes or until tender. Add all but 2 × 15ml spoons/2 tablespoons of the sour cream and heat through gently.

Place the chops on a bed of freshly boiled rice and pour over the sauce. Spoon over the remaining sour cream and serve.
Serves 4

Veal chops with creamy mushroom sauce

METRIC/IMPERIAL
50g/2oz butter
4 veal chops
1 small onion, peeled and
 grated
150ml/¼ pint dry white
 wine
salt
freshly ground black pepper
175g/6oz small button
 mushrooms
5 × 15ml spoons/
 5 tablespoons double cream

AMERICAN
¼ cup butter
4 veal chops
1 small onion, peeled and
 grated
⅔ cup dry white wine
salt
freshly ground black pepper
1½ cups small button
 mushrooms
⅓ cup heavy cream

Melt the butter in a frying pan (skillet). Add the chops and brown on both sides. Remove the chops from the pan.

Add the onion to the pan and fry until it is soft but not brown. Stir in the wine with salt and pepper to taste. Return the chops to the pan and turn over in the liquid. Bring to the boil, then cover and simmer gently for 30 minutes.

Add the mushrooms, re-cover and simmer for a further 5 to 10 minutes or until the chops are tender.

Stir in the cream and heat very gently. Serve hot.
Serves 4

Beef Wellington (page 362)

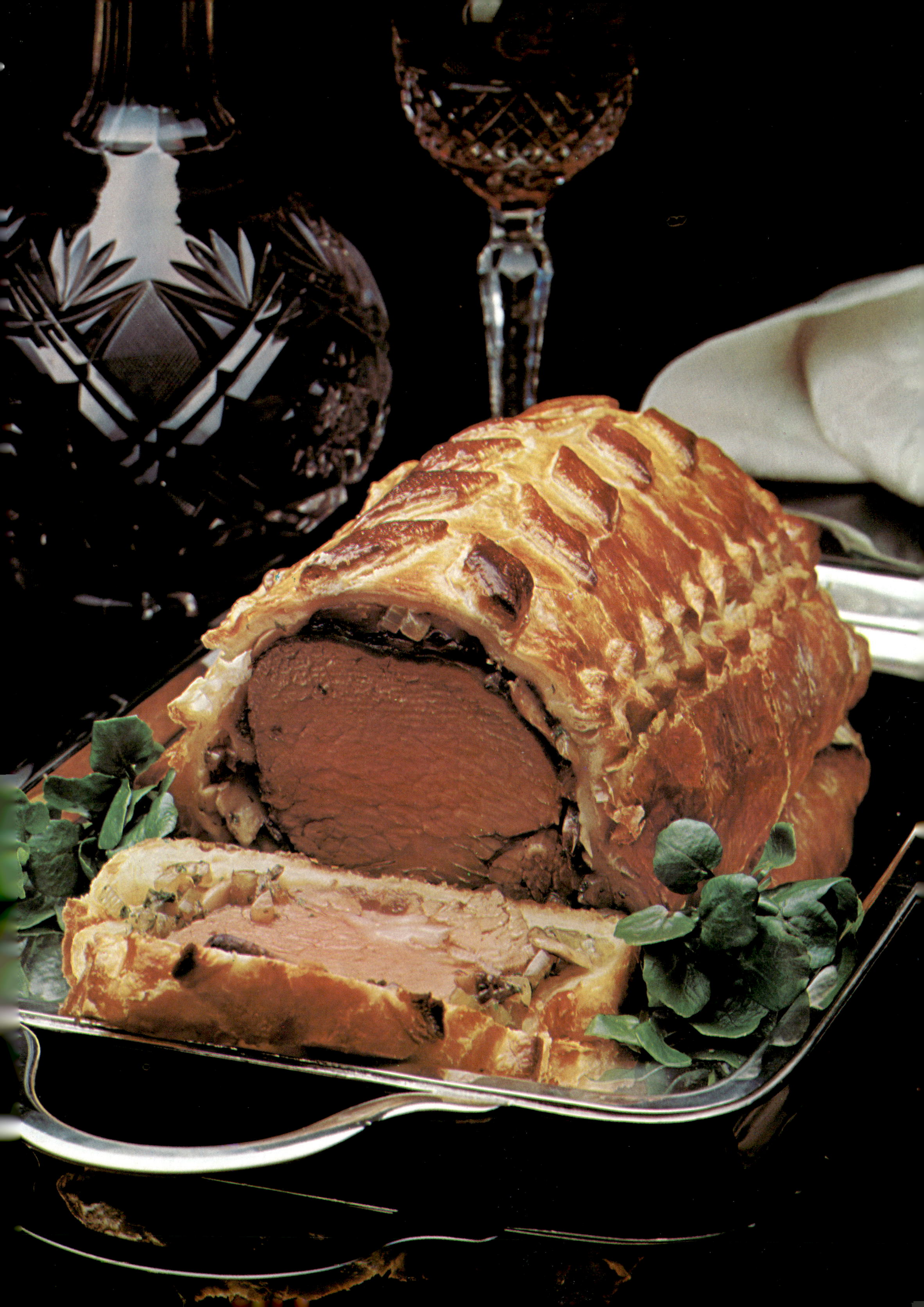

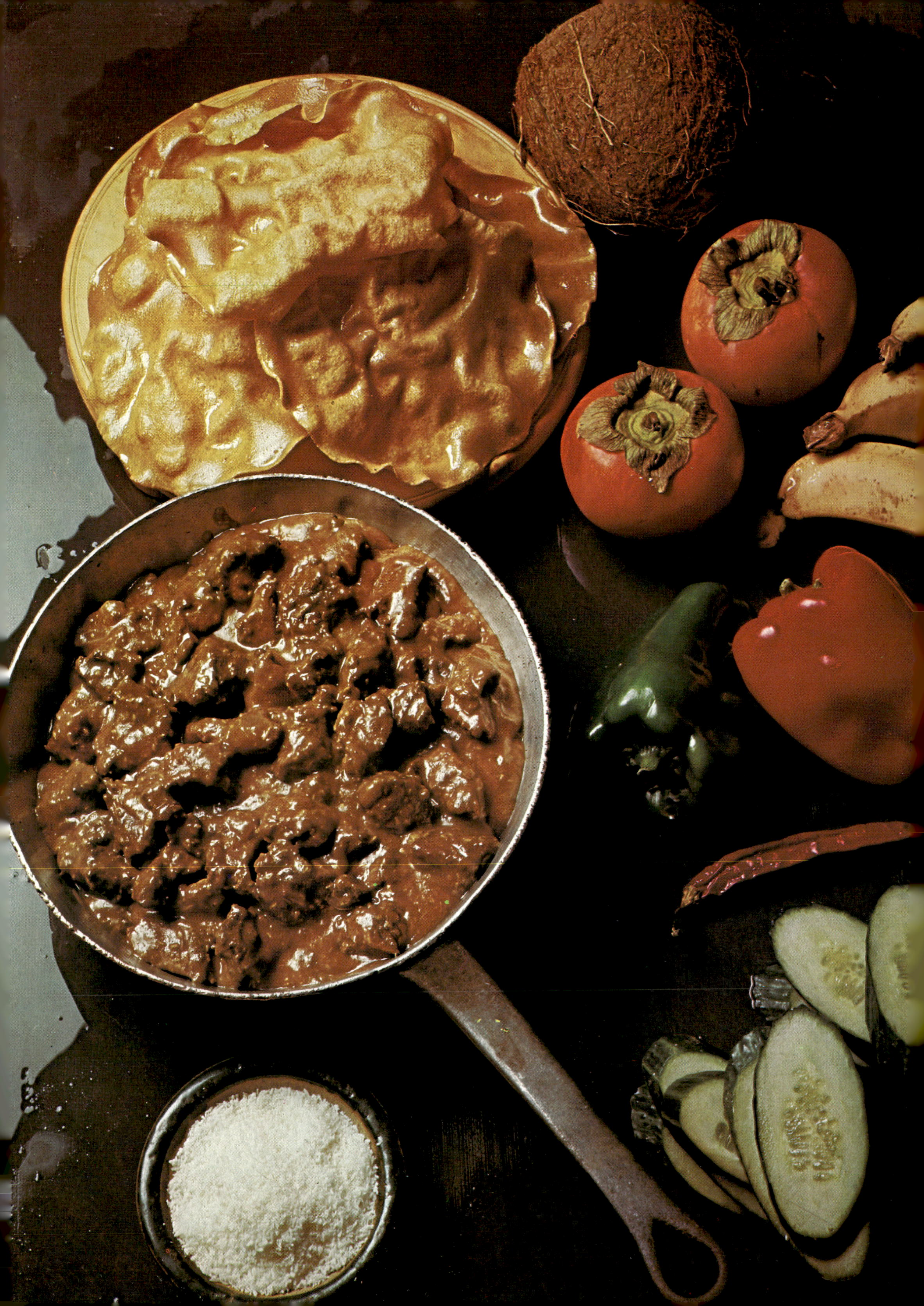

African beef curry (page 91); Quick-fried steak with celery and cabbage (page 82)

1870
EMBOTELLADO
ESTATE BOTTLED
EN LA PROPIEDAD
TORRES
Tres
Miguel Torres

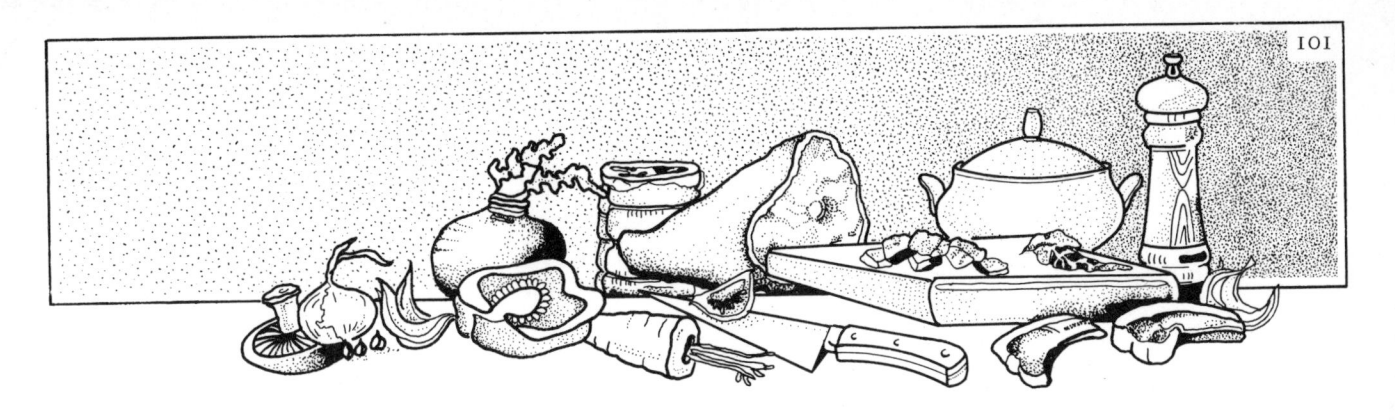

Veal stew niçoise

METRIC/IMPERIAL
25g/1oz butter
1 × 15ml spoon/
　1 tablespoon vegetable oil
0.75kg/1½lb stewing veal,
　cut into 2.5cm/1 inch
　cubes
4 shallots, peeled and
　chopped
1 garlic clove, crushed
4 tomatoes, peeled,
　deseeded and quartered
25g/1oz plain flour
150ml/¼ pint dry white
　wine
300ml/½ pint veal or
　chicken stock
salt
freshly ground black pepper
175g/6oz button
　mushrooms
10 black olives, stoned

AMERICAN
2 tablespoons butter
1 tablespoon vegetable oil
1½lb stewing veal, cut into
　1 inch cubes
4 shallots, peeled and
　chopped
1 garlic clove, crushed
4 tomatoes, peeled,
　deseeded and quartered
¼ cup all-purpose flour
⅔ cup dry white wine
1¼ cups veal or chicken
　stock
salt
freshly ground black pepper
1½ cups button mushrooms
10 black olives, pitted

Melt the butter with the oil in a flameproof casserole. Add the veal cubes, in batches, and brown on all sides. Add the shallots and garlic and fry for a further 3 minutes. Stir in the tomatoes.
　Sprinkle over the flour and stir in well, then gradually stir in the wine and stock with salt and pepper to taste. Bring to the boil, stirring. Cover and transfer to a preheated moderate oven (180°C/350°F, Gas Mark 4). Cook for 45 minutes.
　Stir in the mushrooms and olives and cook for a further 15 minutes or until the veal is tender. Serve hot, from the casserole.
Serves 4

Osso bucco

METRIC/IMPERIAL
50g/2oz plain flour
salt
freshly ground black pepper
1.5–1.75kg/3–4lb shin of
　veal, cut into 8cm/3 inch
　pieces
6 × 15ml spoons/
　6 tablespoons olive oil
1 onion, peeled and thinly
　sliced
1 carrot, peeled and grated
1 celery stick, finely
　chopped
150ml/¼ pint dry white
　wine
150ml/¼ pint veal or
　chicken stock
225g/8oz tomatoes, peeled
　and chopped
2 × 15ml spoons/
　2 tablespoons tomato purée
2 garlic cloves, finely
　chopped
4 × 15ml spoons/
　4 tablespoons chopped
　fresh parsley
finely grated rind of 1 small
　lemon

AMERICAN
½ cup all-purpose flour
salt
freshly ground black pepper
3–4lb foreshank of veal, cut
　into 3 inch pieces
6 tablespoons olive oil
1 onion, peeled and thinly
　sliced
1 carrot, peeled and grated
1 celery stalk, finely
　chopped
⅔ cup dry white wine
⅔ cup veal or chicken stock
1 cup peeled and chopped
　tomatoes
2 tablespoons tomato paste
2 garlic cloves, finely
　chopped
4 tablespoons chopped fresh
　parsley
finely grated rind of 1 small
　lemon

Mix the flour with salt and pepper and use to coat the veal pieces. Heat the oil in a flameproof casserole. Add the veal pieces, in batches, and brown well on all sides. Remove the veal from the pot.
　Add the onion, carrot and celery to the casserole and fry until the onion is soft but not brown. Stir in the wine and stock and bring to the boil. Add the tomatoes and tomato purée (paste) and stir well, then return the veal pieces to the casserole. Spoon the sauce over the veal. Cover the casserole and transfer to a preheated moderate oven (160°C/325°F, Gas Mark 3). Cook for 2 hours. Taste and add salt and pepper if necessary.
　Mix together the garlic, parsley and lemon rind. Sprinkle over the osso bucco and serve from the casserole.
Serves 6

Boeuf catalan (page 90)

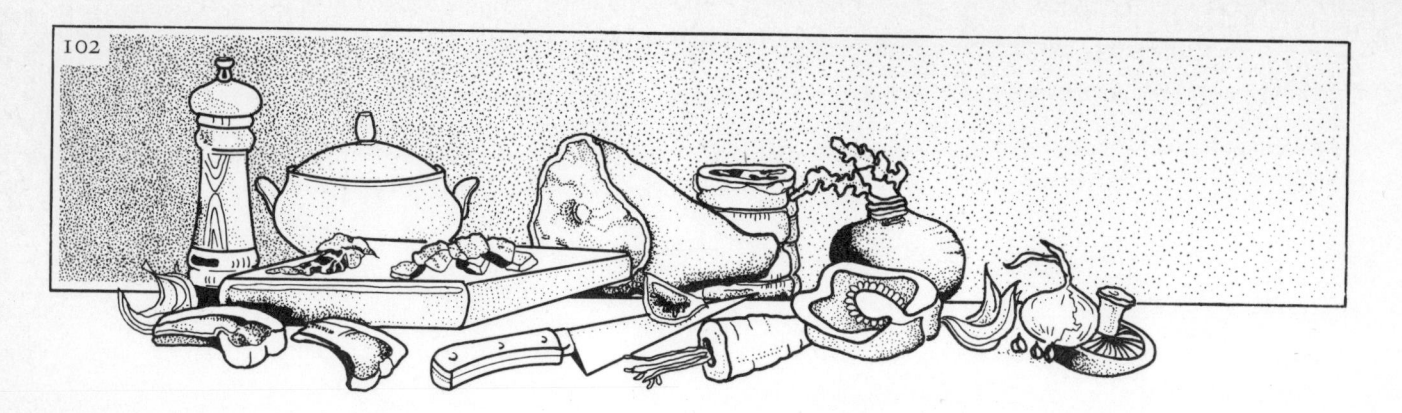

Blanquette de veau

METRIC/IMPERIAL
50g/2oz butter
0.75kg/1½lb stewing veal, cut into 5cm/2 inch cubes
10 small onions, peeled
50g/2oz plain flour
900ml/1½ pints veal or chicken stock
1 bouquet garni
6 black peppercorns
100g/4oz button mushrooms
2 × 5ml spoons/2 teaspoons lemon juice
150ml/¼ pint single cream
salt
freshly ground black pepper
chopped parsley to garnish

AMERICAN
¼ cup butter
1½lb stewing veal, cut into 2 inch cubes
10 small onions, peeled
½ cup all-purpose flour
3¾ cups veal or chicken stock
1 bouquet garni
6 black peppercorns
1 cup button mushrooms
2 teaspoons lemon juice
⅔ cup light cream
salt
freshly ground black pepper
chopped parsley to garnish

Melt the butter in a saucepan. Add the veal and fry until it turns pale cream but not brown. Remove the meat from the pan.

Add the onions to the pan and fry for 5 minutes without browning. Remove the onions from the pan.

Stir the flour into the fat in the pan and cook, stirring, for 1 minute. Gradually stir in the stock and bring to the boil, stirring. Add the bouquet garni, peppercorns and the stalks from the mushrooms. Simmer for 20 minutes.

Strain the stock mixture and return to the pan. Add the veal and onions and stir well. Cover and simmer for 1 to 1½ hours or until the veal is tender. Stir in the mushrooms and cook for a further 10 minutes.

Add the lemon juice, cream and salt and pepper to taste and heat through gently. Serve hot, garnished with parsley.
Serves 4

Italian veal stew

METRIC/IMPERIAL
25g/1oz butter
1 × 15ml spoon/ 1 tablespoon olive oil
1 medium onion, peeled and finely chopped
1 garlic clove, finely chopped
0.75kg/1½lb pie veal, cut into cubes
4 tomatoes, peeled and chopped
150ml/¼ pint dry white wine
1 × 15ml spoon/ 1 tablespoon tomato purée
5 × 15ml spoons/ 5 tablespoons chopped fresh parsley
2 × 5ml spoons/2 teaspoons chopped fresh basil
1 red pepper, pith and seeds removed and chopped
2 celery sticks, chopped
salt
freshly ground black pepper

AMERICAN
2 tablespoons butter
1 tablespoon olive oil
1 medium onion, peeled and finely chopped
1 garlic clove, finely chopped
1½lb stewing veal, cut into cubes
4 tomatoes, peeled and chopped
⅔ cup dry white wine
1 tablespoon tomato paste
⅓ cup chopped fresh parsley
2 teaspoons chopped fresh basil
1 pimiento, pith and seeds removed and chopped
2 celery stalks, chopped
salt
freshly ground black pepper

Melt the butter with the oil in a saucepan. Add the onion and garlic and fry until the onion is soft but not brown. Add the veal cubes and brown lightly on all sides.

Stir in the tomatoes, wine, tomato purée (paste), parsley, basil, red pepper (pimiento), celery and salt and pepper to taste. Bring to the boil, cover and simmer for 1½ to 2 hours or until the veal is tender. Serve hot.
Serves 4

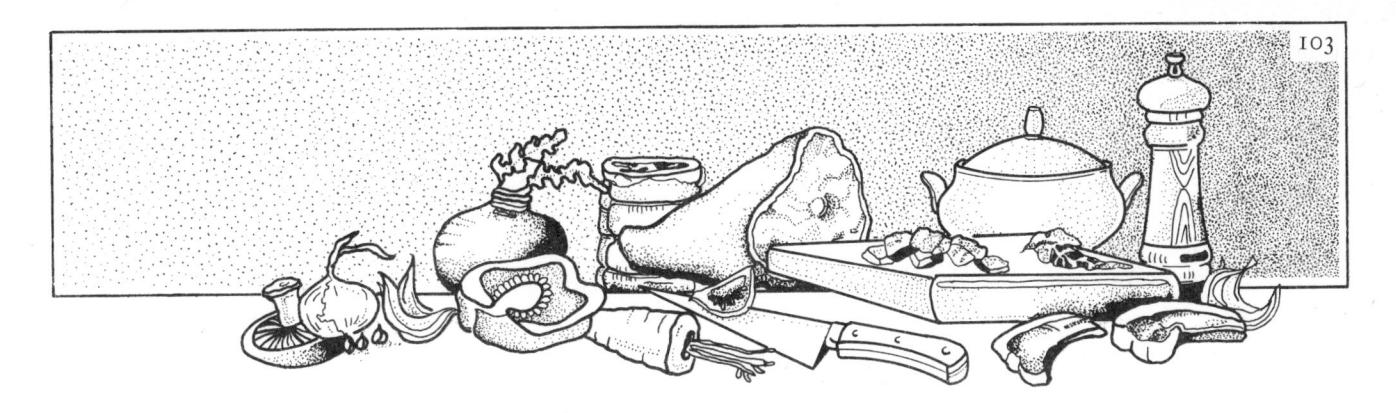

Hungarian goulash

METRIC/IMPERIAL
50g/2oz dripping
0.75kg/1½lb pie veal, cut into cubes
3 medium onions, peeled and sliced
1 garlic clove, finely chopped
0.5kg/1lb tomatoes, peeled and chopped
salt
freshly ground black pepper
1 × 15ml spoon/
  1 tablespoon paprika
600ml/1 pint beef stock
0.5kg/1lb potatoes, peeled and sliced
150ml/¼ pint sour cream to serve

AMERICAN
¼ cup drippings
1½lb stewing veal, cut into cubes
3 medium onions, peeled and sliced
1 garlic clove, finely chopped
2 cups peeled and chopped tomatoes
salt
freshly ground black pepper
1 tablespoon paprika
2½ cups beef stock
1lb potatoes, peeled and sliced
⅔ cup sour cream to serve

Melt the dripping in a saucepan. Add the veal and brown on all sides. Remove the veal from the pan.
  Add the onions and garlic to the pan and fry until they are soft but not brown. Stir in the tomatoes with salt and pepper to taste. Mix the paprika with the stock and add to the pan. Return the veal to the pan and stir well.
  Bring to the boil, then cover and simmer for 1¾ hours.
  Add the potatoes, re-cover and simmer for a further 45 minutes or until the veal is tender.
  Serve hot, with the sour cream handed separately.
Serves 4 to 6

Veal casserole with dumplings

METRIC/IMPERIAL
25g/1oz butter
1 × 15ml spoon/
  1 tablespoon oil
1 onion, peeled and chopped
1kg/2lb breast of veal (boned weight), cut into cubes
2 × 15ml spoons/
  2 tablespoons plain flour
150ml/¼ pint beef stock
150ml/¼ pint dry red wine
pinch of ground cloves
pinch of dried thyme
salt
freshly ground black pepper
100g/4oz button mushrooms
chopped parsley to garnish
Dumplings:
100g/4oz self-raising flour
1 × 2.5ml spoon/½ teaspoon dried thyme
25g/1oz butter
water

AMERICAN
2 tablespoons butter
1 tablespoon oil
1 onion, peeled and chopped
2lb breast of veal (boned weight), cut into cubes
2 tablespoons all-purpose flour
⅔ cup beef stock
⅔ cup dry red wine
pinch of ground cloves
pinch of dried thyme
salt
freshly ground black pepper
1 cup button mushrooms
chopped parsley to garnish
Dumplings:
1 cup self-rising flour
½ teaspoon dried thyme
2 tablespoons butter
water

Melt the butter with the oil in a flameproof casserole. Add the onion and fry until it is soft but not brown. Add the veal cubes, in batches, and brown on all sides. Remove from the casserole as they are browned.
  Sprinkle over the flour and stir in well. Cook, stirring, for 1 minute. Gradually stir in the stock and wine and bring to the boil, stirring. Add the cloves, thyme and salt and pepper to taste.
  Return the veal cubes to the casserole with the mushrooms and mix well. Cover and transfer to a preheated moderate oven (160°C/325°F, Gas Mark 3). Cook for 1½ hours.
  To make the dumplings, sift the flour, thyme and salt and pepper into a mixing bowl. Rub in the butter until the mixture resembles breadcrumbs, then bind with a little water to a fairly stiff dough. Form into small balls and add to the casserole. Re-cover and cook for a further 30 minutes or until the veal is tender.
  Serve hot, sprinkled with chopped parsley.
Serves 4 to 6

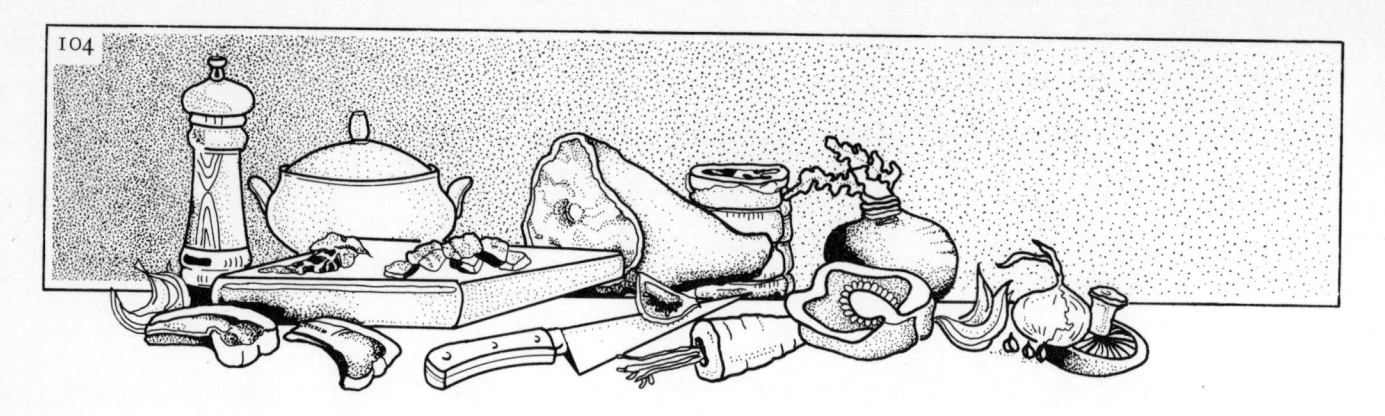

Veal and orange casserole

METRIC/IMPERIAL
50g/2oz plain flour
salt
freshly ground black pepper
1kg/2lb lean pie veal, cut into cubes
4 × 15ml spoons/
 4 tablespoons oil
2 onions, peeled and sliced
2 celery sticks, chopped
1 × 15ml spoon/
 1 tablespoon grated orange rind
1 × 5ml spoon/1 teaspoon dried rosemary
250ml/8fl oz orange juice
250ml/8fl oz chicken stock
1.5 × 15ml spoons/
 1½ tablespoons cornflour
3 × 15ml spoons/
 3 tablespoons water

AMERICAN
½ cup all-purpose flour
salt
freshly ground black pepper
2lb lean stewing veal, cut into cubes
4 tablespoons oil
2 onions, peeled and sliced
2 celery stalks, chopped
1 tablespoon grated orange rind
1 teaspoon dried rosemary
1 cup orange juice
1 cup chicken stock
1½ tablespoons cornstarch
3 tablespoons water

Mix the flour with salt and pepper in a polythene (plastic) bag. Add the veal cubes and shake to coat with the seasoned flour. Heat the oil in a saucepan. Add the veal cubes, in batches, and brown on all sides. As they are browned remove them from the pan.

Add the onions and celery to the pan and fry until the onions are soft but not brown. Stir in the orange rind, rosemary, orange juice, stock and salt and pepper to taste. Return the veal cubes to the pan and bring to the boil. Cover and simmer for 1¼ to 1½ hours or until the veal is tender.

Dissolve the cornflour (cornstarch) in the water and add to the pan. Simmer, stirring, until thickened. Serve hot.

Serves 4 to 6

Emincé de veau

METRIC/IMPERIAL
4 × 15ml spoons/
 4 tablespoons oil
1 large onion, peeled and sliced
1 garlic clove, crushed
1 red pepper, pith and seeds removed and thinly sliced
1 × 400g/14oz can tomatoes
salt
freshly ground black pepper
pinch of cayenne pepper
0.75kg/1½lb lean cooked veal, cut into strips

AMERICAN
4 tablespoons oil
1 large onion, peeled and sliced
1 garlic clove, crushed
1 pimiento, pith and seeds removed and thinly sliced
1 × 14oz can tomatoes
salt
freshly ground black pepper
pinch of cayenne pepper
1½lb lean cooked veal, cut into strips (about 3 cups)

Heat the oil in a frying pan (skillet). Add the onion, garlic and red pepper (pimiento) and fry until the onion is soft but not brown. Stir in the tomatoes, with the can juice, salt and pepper to taste and the cayenne. Bring to the boil and simmer for 10 minutes.

Stir in the veal strips and continue simmering for 5 to 10 minutes or until the veal is heated through. Serve hot.

Serves 4

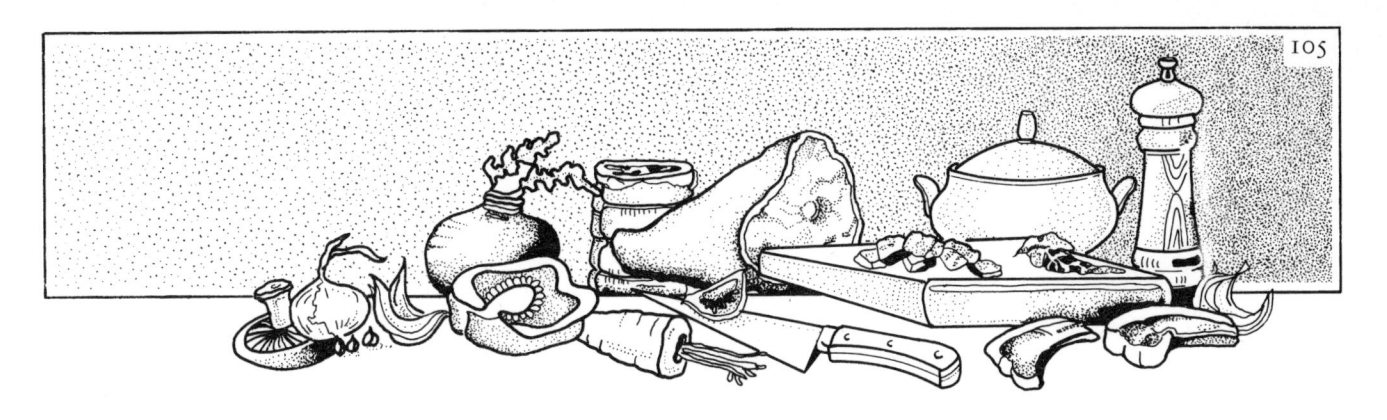

Fricadelles de veau smetana

METRIC/IMPERIAL
0.75kg/1½lb lean veal, minced
75g/3oz fresh breadcrumbs
1 × 2.5ml spoon/½ teaspoon dried sage
salt
freshly ground black pepper
25g/1oz butter, melted
1 egg, lightly beaten
50g/2oz plain flour
4 × 15ml spoons/ 4 tablespoons oil
150ml/¼ pint chicken stock
150ml/¼ pint sour cream

AMERICAN
3 cups ground lean veal
1½ cups fresh breadcrumbs
½ teaspoon dried sage
salt
freshly ground black pepper
2 tablespoons butter, melted
1 egg, lightly beaten
½ cup all-purpose flour
4 tablespoons oil
⅔ cup chicken stock
⅔ cup sour cream

Mix together the veal, breadcrumbs, sage, salt and pepper to taste, butter and egg. Divide into 8 portions and shape each into a patty. Coat with the flour.

Heat the oil in a frying pan (skillet). Add the veal patties and brown on both sides. Pour in the stock and bring to the boil. Simmer for 10 to 15 minutes or until the veal patties are cooked.

Stir in the sour cream with salt and pepper to taste and heat through gently. Serve hot.
Serves 4

Roast stuffed shoulder of veal

METRIC/IMPERIAL
1 × 1.5kg/3½lb shoulder of veal (boned weight)
salt
freshly ground black pepper
225g/8oz streaky bacon rashers, rinds removed
Stuffing:
1 small onion, peeled and finely chopped
100g/4oz mushrooms, chopped
1 garlic clove, crushed
1 × 5ml spoon/1 teaspoon grated lemon rind
3 × 15ml spoons/ 3 tablespoons chopped fresh parsley
100g/4oz fresh breadcrumbs
1 egg, lightly beaten
25g/1oz butter, melted

AMERICAN
1 × 3½lb shoulder of veal (boned weight)
salt
freshly ground black pepper
½lb bacon slices
Stuffing:
1 small onion, peeled and finely chopped
1 cup chopped mushrooms
1 garlic clove, crushed
1 teaspoon grated lemon rind
3 tablespoons chopped fresh parsley
2 cups fresh breadcrumbs
1 egg, lightly beaten
2 tablespoons butter, melted

Lay the shoulder of veal out flat and pound until it is a fairly even thickness. Sprinkle with salt and pepper.

Mix together the ingredients for the stuffing with salt and pepper to taste. Spread over the veal and roll up loosely. Tie at intervals with string.

Stretch the bacon rashers (slices) with a flat-bladed knife and use to cover the meat completely. Place in a roasting tin and cover with foil. Roast in a preheated hot oven (220°C/425°F, Gas Mark 7) for 2½ hours or until the veal is cooked. Remove the foil for the last 30 minutes.
Serves 8

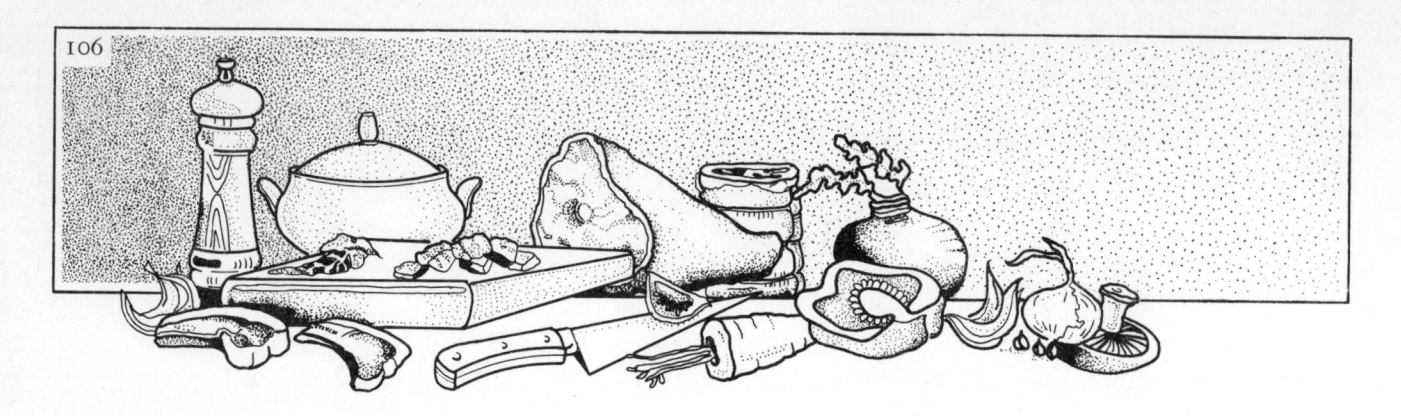

Stuffed loin of veal

METRIC/IMPERIAL
1 × 1.75kg/4lb loin of veal (boned weight)
salt
freshly ground black pepper
1 quantity sage and onion stuffing★
2 × 15ml spoons/ 2 tablespoons oil
450ml/¾ pint chicken stock
1 × 15ml spoon/ 1 tablespoon finely grated orange rind
pinch of dried sage
2 × 15ml spoons/ 2 tablespoons cornflour
3 × 15ml spoons/ 3 tablespoons water

AMERICAN
1 × 4lb loin of veal (boned weight)
salt
freshly ground black pepper
1 quantity sage and onion stuffing★
2 tablespoons oil
2 cups chicken stock
1 tablespoon finely grated orange rind
pinch of dried sage
2 tablespoons cornstarch
3 tablespoons water

Lay the veal flat and rub with salt and pepper. Spread over the stuffing and roll up. Tie at intervals with string.

Heat the oil in a flameproof casserole. Add the veal and brown on all sides. Pour over the stock and bring to the boil. Stir in the orange rind and sage and cover. Transfer to a preheated moderately hot oven (190°C/375°F, Gas Mark 5). Cook for 2 to 2½ hours or until the veal is cooked.

Transfer the veal to a warmed serving plate and remove the string. Keep hot.

Put the casserole on top of the stove and boil the cooking liquid until it has reduced to about two-thirds the original quantity. Dissolve the cornflour (cornstarch) in the water and stir into the cooking liquid. Simmer, stirring, until thickened. Serve this sauce with the veal.
Serves 8

Veal Orloff

METRIC/IMPERIAL
3 × 15ml spoons/ 3 tablespoons olive oil
1 × 1.5kg/3lb leg or loin of veal (boned weight), tied into shape
1 onion, peeled and quartered
2 carrots, peeled and thickly sliced
1 bouquet garni
salt
freshly ground black pepper
150ml/¼ pint hot mornay sauce★
3 × 15ml spoons/ 3 tablespoons grated Parmesan cheese
Garnish:
25g/1oz butter
1 large onion, peeled and finely chopped
175g/6oz mushrooms, chopped

AMERICAN
3 tablespoons olive oil
1 × 3lb leg or loin of veal (boned weight), tied into shape
1 onion, peeled and quartered
2 carrots, peeled and thickly sliced
1 bouquet garni
salt
freshly ground black pepper
⅔ cup hot mornay sauce★
3 tablespoons grated Parmesan cheese
Garnish:
2 tablespoons butter
1 large onion, peeled and finely chopped
1½ cups chopped mushrooms

Heat the oil in a flameproof casserole. Add the veal and brown on all sides. Add the onion, carrots, bouquet garni and salt and pepper to taste, then pour in just enough water to cover the bottom of the pot. Cover and transfer to a moderately hot oven (200°C/400°F, Gas Mark 6). Braise for 30 minutes, then lower the temperature to moderate (180°C/350°F, Gas Mark 4). Continue braising for 1½ hours or until the veal is cooked.

To make the garnish, melt the butter in a saucepan. Add the onion and fry until it is soft but not brown. Stir in the mushrooms with salt and pepper to taste and cook for 3 to 4 minutes. Remove from the heat and keep hot.

Remove the veal from the casserole and carve into thick slices. Arrange the slices in a warmed flameproof serving dish. Spoon the onion and mushroom garnish around the veal and between the slices. Pour the mornay sauce over the veal and sprinkle with the Parmesan. Grill (broil) for 3 to 4 minutes or until the top is lightly browned and bubbling. Serve hot.
Serves 6

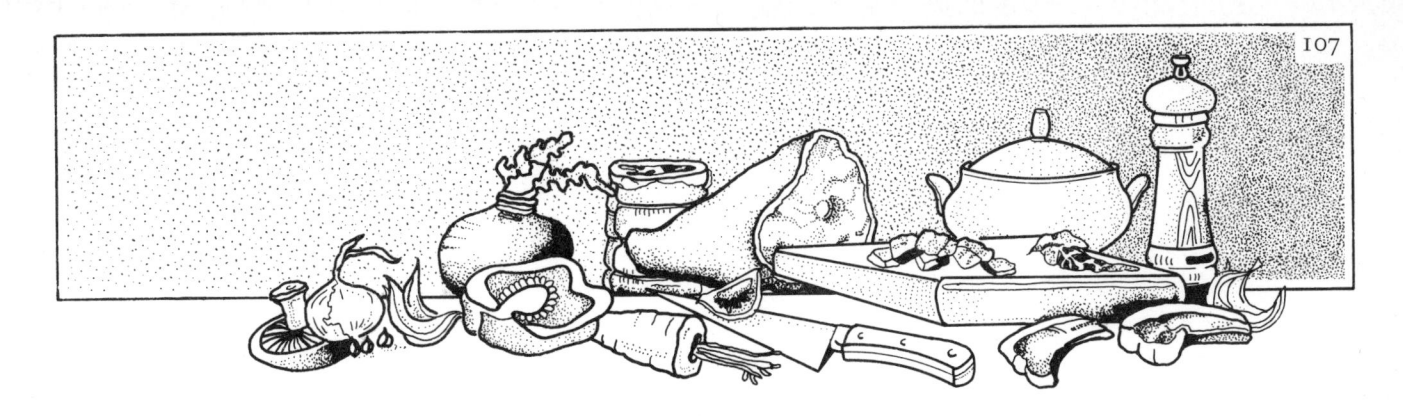

Veal and ham pie

METRIC/IMPERIAL
0.75kg/1½lb pie veal, cut into cubes
100g/4oz cooked ham, diced
1 small onion, peeled and chopped
1 × 15ml spoon/ 1 tablespoon chopped fresh parsley
1 × 5ml spoon/1 teaspoon grated lemon rind
salt
freshly ground black pepper
600ml/1 pint chicken stock
225g/8oz quantity puff pastry*
beaten egg to glaze

AMERICAN
1½lb stewing veal, cut into cubes
½ cup diced cooked ham
1 small onion, peeled and chopped
1 tablespoon chopped fresh parsley
1 teaspoon grated lemon rind
salt
freshly ground black pepper
2½ cups chicken stock
2 cup quantity puff pastry*
beaten egg to glaze

Mix together the veal, ham, onion, parsley, lemon rind and salt and pepper to taste. Put into a deep pie dish and pour over enough stock to three-quarters fill the dish.

Roll out the pastry dough to about 2.5cm/1 inch thick and use to cover the dish. Make a slit in the centre. Brush with beaten egg.

Bake in a preheated hot oven (220°C/425°F, Gas Mark 7) for 30 minutes. Cover the pastry with foil and reduce the temperature to moderate (160°C/325°F, Gas Mark 3). Continue baking for 1 hour or until the veal is tender.

Bring any remaining stock to the boil and pour through the slit in the centre of the pie. Serve hot or cold.
Serves 6

Vitello tonnato

METRIC/IMPERIAL
0.75kg/1½lb cold roast veal, thinly sliced
1 × 200g/7oz can tuna fish
300ml/½ pint mayonnaise*
1 × 15ml spoon/ 1 tablespoon lemon juice
veal or chicken stock
freshly ground black pepper
8 anchovy fillets
1 × 15ml spoon/ 1 tablespoon capers
To garnish:
parsley sprigs
1 lemon, cut into quarters

AMERICAN
1½lb cold roast veal, thinly sliced
1 × 7oz can tuna fish
1¼ cups mayonnaise*
1 tablespoon lemon juice
veal or chicken stock
freshly ground black pepper
8 anchovy fillets
1 tablespoon capers
To garnish:
parsley sprigs
1 lemon, cut into quarters

Arrange the veal slices, overlapping, on a serving plate. Add the tuna, with the oil from the can, to the mayonnaise and mash together with a fork until the mixture is quite smooth. Stir in the lemon juice and enough stock to thin the mixture to the consistency of cream. Add pepper to taste.

Spoon the sauce over the veal. Cover and chill for at least 8 hours.

Just before serving, decorate with the anchovy fillets and capers and garnish the dish with parsley sprigs and lemon quarters. Serve cold.
Serves 6

LAMB

Grilled (broiled) marinated lamb chops

METRIC/IMPERIAL
6–8 lamb chops
watercress sprigs to garnish
Marinade:
25g/1oz butter, melted
2 × 15ml spoons/
  2 tablespoons
  Worcestershire sauce
2 × 15ml spoons/
  2 tablespoons lemon juice
2 × 15ml spoons/
  2 tablespoons gin
pinch of garlic powder
salt
freshly ground black pepper

AMERICAN
6–8 lamb chops
watercress sprigs to garnish
Marinade:
2 tablespoons butter, melted
2 tablespoons
  Worcestershire sauce
2 tablespoons lemon juice
2 tablespoons gin
pinch of garlic powder
salt
freshly ground black pepper

Mix together the ingredients for the marinade with salt and pepper to taste in a shallow dish. Add the lamb chops and turn to coat them with the marinade. Leave to marinate at room temperature for 15 minutes.

Remove the chops from the marinade and arrange on a grill (broiler) rack. Grill (broil) the chops for about 5 minutes on each side, brushing frequently with any remaining marinade.

Serve hot, garnished with watercress.
Serves 4

Mixed grill maître d'hôtel

METRIC/IMPERIAL
4 lamb chops
2 lamb's kidneys, halved
  and cored
salt
freshly ground black pepper
4 tomatoes, halved
dried basil
8 button mushrooms
melted butter or oil
225g/8oz chipolata sausages
4 lean bacon rashers, rinds
  removed
watercress to garnish
4 pats maître d'hôtel butter★

AMERICAN
4 lamb chops
2 lamb kidneys, halved and
  cored
salt
freshly ground black pepper
4 tomatoes, halved
dried basil
8 button mushrooms
melted butter or oil
½lb link sausages
4 Canadian bacon slices
watercress to garnish
4 pats maître d'hôtel butter★

Rub the chops and kidneys with salt and pepper. Place the tomatoes, cut sides up, on a grill (broiler) pan and sprinkle with basil. Put the mushrooms on the pan, undersides up, and brush with melted butter or oil. Put the grill (broiler) rack in position over the tomatoes and mushrooms.

Arrange the sausages, chops and kidneys on the grill (broiler) rack. Brush with melted butter or oil and grill (broil) for 10 minutes, turning frequently.

Transfer the sausages and kidneys to a warmed serving dish and keep hot. Add the bacon to the rack and grill (broil) with the chops for a further 3 to 5 minutes. Add the chops and bacon to the serving dish, with the tomatoes and mushrooms. Garnish with watercress and top each chop with a pat of maître d'hôtel butter. Serve hot.
Serves 4

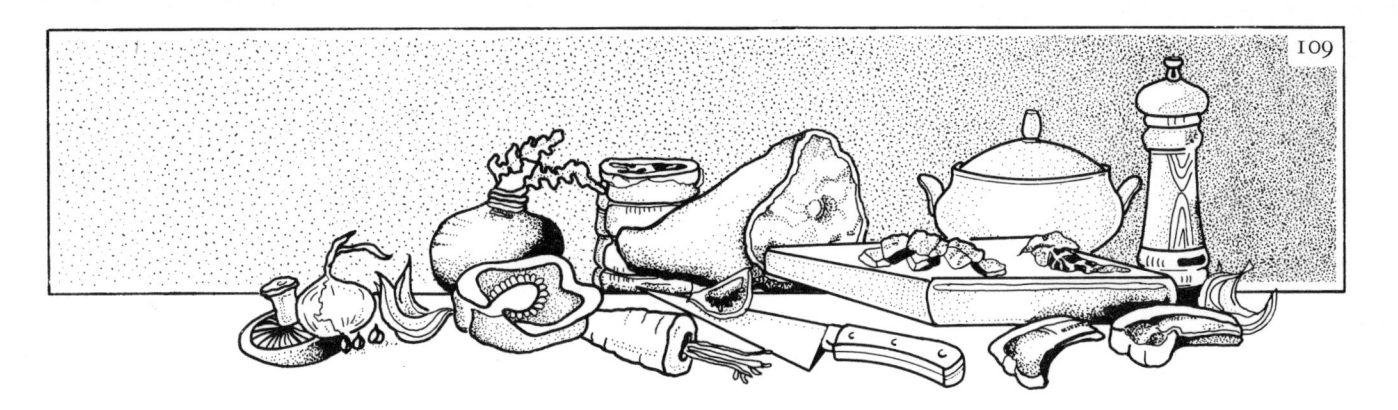

Turkish lamb

METRIC/IMPERIAL
50g/2oz plain flour
2 × 5ml spoons/2 teaspoons ground cumin
salt
freshly ground black pepper
8 thick lamb chops
4 × 15ml spoons/ 4 tablespoons olive oil
2 onions, peeled and chopped
1 garlic clove, crushed
2 green peppers, pith and seeds removed and chopped
900ml/1½ pints tomato juice
juice of 1 lemon
chopped mint to garnish

AMERICAN
½ cup all-purpose flour
2 teaspoons ground cumin
salt
freshly ground black pepper
8 thick lamb chops
4 tablespoons olive oil
2 onions, peeled and chopped
1 garlic clove, crushed
2 green peppers, pith and seeds removed and chopped
3¾ cups tomato juice
juice of 1 lemon
chopped mint to garnish

Mix the flour with the cumin and salt and pepper. Use to coat the lamb chops. Heat the oil in a flameproof casserole. Add the chops, in batches, and brown on both sides. Remove the chops from the pan as they are browned.

Add the onions, garlic and green peppers to the pan and fry until the onions are soft but not brown. Sprinkle over any remaining seasoned flour and stir well. Stir in the tomato juice and lemon juice.

Return the chops to the casserole and bring to the boil. Cover and transfer to a cool oven (150°C/300°F, Gas Mark 2). Cook for 3 hours or until the lamb is very tender and the sauce thickened.

Taste and add salt and pepper if necessary. Serve hot, sprinkled with chopped mint.
Serves 4

Lyonnaise lamb chops

METRIC/IMPERIAL
0.5kg/1lb potatoes, peeled and sliced
2 large onions, peeled and sliced
salt
freshly ground black pepper
1 × 5ml spoon/1 teaspoon dried rosemary
8 thick lean lamb chops
4 × 15ml spoons/ 4 tablespoons beef stock
25g/1oz butter, cut into small pieces

AMERICAN
1lb potatoes, peeled and sliced
2 large onions, peeled and sliced
salt
freshly ground black pepper
1 teaspoon dried rosemary
8 thick lean lamb chops
4 tablespoons beef stock
2 tablespoons butter, cut into small pieces

Put half the potato slices in the bottom of a long shallow baking dish. Cover with half the onion slices and sprinkle with salt, pepper and rosemary. Arrange the chops on top, in one layer. Cover with the remaining onion and then the remaining potatoes, to cover completely. Sprinkle over the stock.

Cover the dish with foil and bake in a preheated moderate oven (180°C/350°F, Gas Mark 4) for 45 minutes. Remove the foil and dot the pieces of butter over the top. Continue baking for 30 minutes or until the chops are tender and the top is lightly browned.

Serve hot, from the dish.
Serves 4

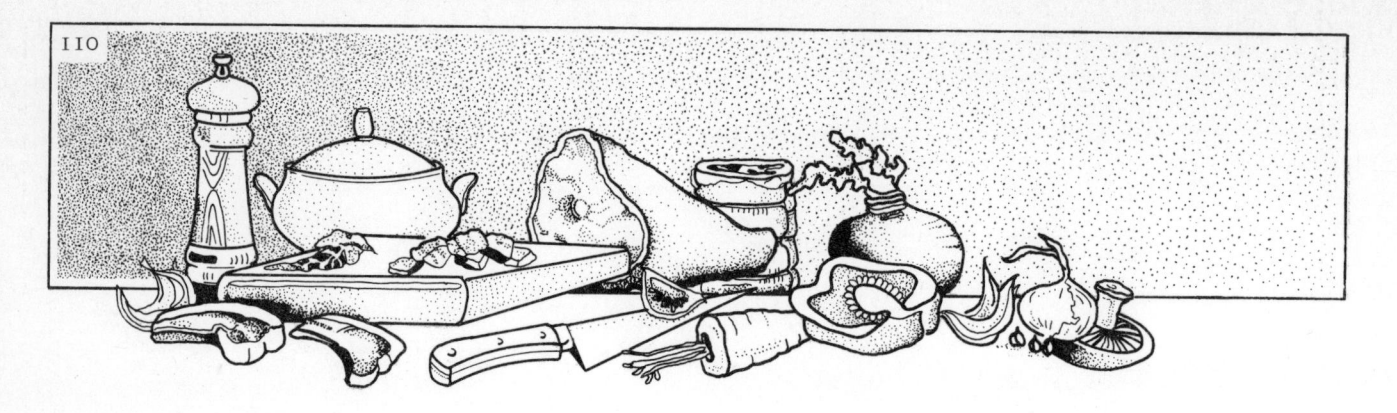

Milanaise lamb noisettes

METRIC/IMPERIAL
8 lamb noisettes
salt
freshly ground black pepper
100g/4oz butter
0.5kg/1lb spaghetti
25g/1oz Parmesan cheese, grated
300ml/½ pint hot tomato sauce★

AMERICAN
8 lamb noisettes (boned lamb chops)
salt
freshly ground black pepper
½ cup butter
1lb spaghetti
¼ cup grated Parmesan cheese
1¼ cups hot tomato sauce★

Rub the noisettes with salt and pepper. Melt 75g/3oz/⅓ cup of the butter in a frying pan (skillet). Add the noisettes and brown on both sides. Reduce the heat and fry for a further 5 minutes on each side or until cooked through.

Meanwhile, cook the spaghetti in boiling salted water until *al dente* (just tender to the bite). Drain well and return to the saucepan. Add the remaining butter and half the cheese and toss well together.

Arrange the spaghetti on a warmed serving dish. Top with the noisettes and pour over the hot tomato sauce. Sprinkle with the remaining cheese and serve hot.
Serves 4

Lemon and ginger chops

METRIC/IMPERIAL
8 lamb chops
120ml/4fl oz oil
grated rind of 2 lemons
4 × 15ml spoons/ 4 tablespoons lemon juice
2 × 15ml spoons/ 2 tablespoons brown sugar
1 × 5ml spoon/1 teaspoon ground ginger
salt
freshly ground black pepper

AMERICAN
8 lamb chops
½ cup oil
grated rind of 2 lemons
4 tablespoons lemon juice
2 tablespoons brown sugar
1 teaspoon ground ginger
salt
freshly ground black pepper

Put the lamb chops in a shallow dish. Mix together the remaining ingredients with salt and pepper to taste and pour over the chops. Leave to marinate for 4 hours.

Remove the chops from the marinade and arrange on the rack in a grill (broiler) pan. Grill (broil) for 5 to 8 minutes on each side, basting with the marinade from time to time. Serve hot.
Serves 4

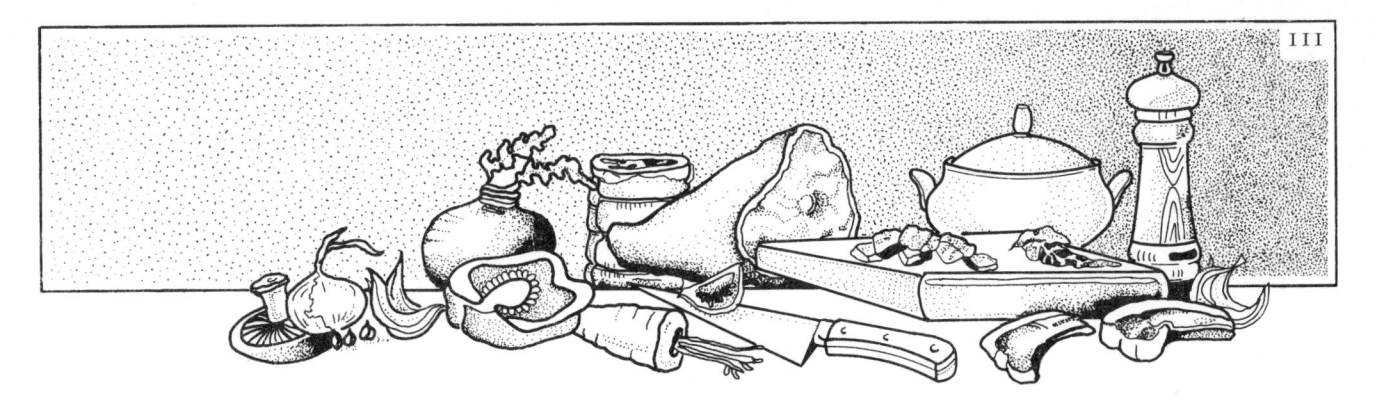

Crumbed lamb chops

METRIC/IMPERIAL
50g/2oz plain flour
salt
freshly ground black pepper
8 lamb chops
1 large egg, lightly beaten
1 × 5ml spoon/1 teaspoon
  Worcestershire sauce
100g/4oz dry breadcrumbs
25g/1oz butter
2 × 15ml spoons/
  2 tablespoons oil

AMERICAN
½ cup all-purpose flour
salt
freshly ground black pepper
8 lamb chops
1 egg, lightly beaten
1 teaspoon Worcestershire
  sauce
1 cup dry breadcrumbs
2 tablespoons butter
2 tablespoons oil

Mix the flour with salt and pepper and use to coat the chops. Mix the egg with the Worcestershire sauce. Dip the chops in the egg mixture, then coat with the breadcrumbs.

Melt the butter with the oil in a frying pan (skillet). Add the chops and brown on both sides. Reduce the heat and cook gently for a further 5 minutes on each side or until cooked through. Serve hot.
Serves 4

Lamb rissoles

METRIC/IMPERIAL
25g/1oz butter
50g/2oz plain flour
150ml/¼ pint milk
50g/2oz fresh breadcrumbs
350g/12oz cooked lamb,
  minced
salt
freshly ground black pepper
pinch of cayenne pepper
1 large egg, lightly beaten
50g/2oz dry breadcrumbs
vegetable oil for deep frying

AMERICAN
2 tablespoons butter
½ cup all-purpose flour
⅔ cup milk
1 cup fresh breadcrumbs
1½ cups ground cooked lamb
salt
freshly ground black pepper
pinch of cayenne pepper
1 egg, lightly beaten
½ cup dry breadcrumbs
vegetable oil for deep frying

Melt the butter in a saucepan. Add 25g/1oz/¼ cup of the flour and cook, stirring, for 1 minute. Remove from the heat and gradually stir in the milk. Return to the heat and bring to the boil, stirring. Simmer until thickened and smooth.

Remove from the heat and stir in the fresh breadcrumbs, lamb, salt and pepper to taste and the cayenne. Allow to cool, then divide into 8 portions. Form each into a patty.

Mix the remaining flour with salt and pepper and use to coat the patties. Dip in the egg, then coat in the dry breadcrumbs.

Heat the oil in a deep frying pan (deep fat fryer) until it is 190°C/375°F. Fry the rissoles until they are golden brown. Drain on absorbent paper and serve hot.
Serves 4

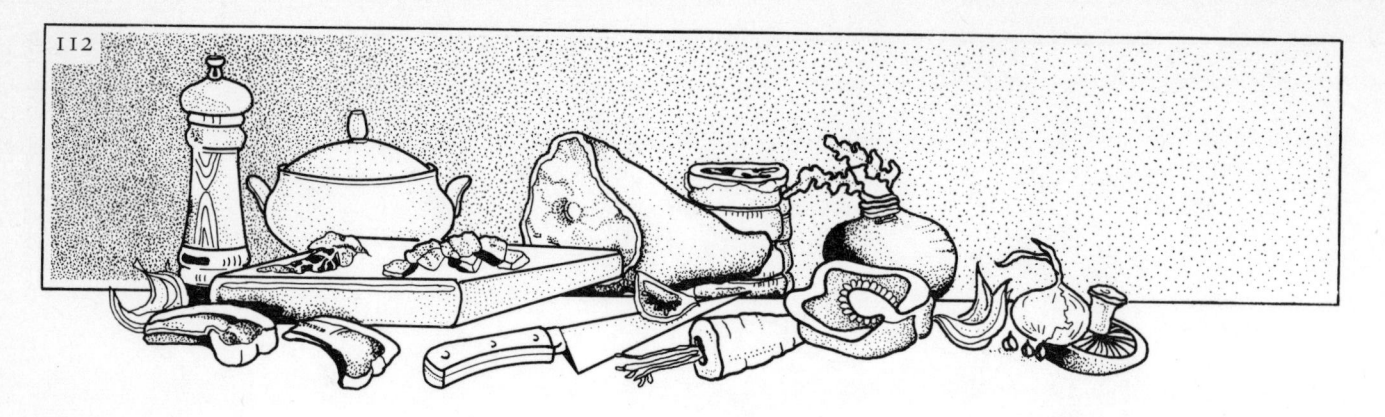

Bobotee

METRIC/IMPERIAL
25g/1oz butter
2 onions, peeled and chopped
0.5kg/1¼lb lean lamb, minced
3 tomatoes, peeled and chopped
150ml/¼ pint beef stock
1 × 15ml spoon/ 1 tablespoon mild curry powder
3 × 15ml spoons/ 3 tablespoons blanched flaked almonds
salt
freshly ground black pepper
2 eggs, lightly beaten
300ml/½ pint milk

AMERICAN
2 tablespoons butter
2 onions, peeled and chopped
2½ cups ground lean lamb
3 tomatoes, peeled and chopped
⅔ cup beef stock
1 tablespoon mild curry powder
3 tablespoons blanched slivered almonds
salt
freshly ground black pepper
2 eggs, lightly beaten
1¼ cups milk

Melt the butter in a frying pan (skillet). Add the onions and fry until they are soft but not brown. Stir in the lamb and cook until it is browned. Add the tomatoes, stock and curry powder and stir well. Bring to the boil and simmer for 30 minutes.

Stir in the almonds with salt and pepper to taste and spoon into a baking dish. Mix together the eggs and milk and pour over the top. Bake in a preheated moderate oven (160°C/325°F, Gas Mark 3) for 45 minutes or until the topping is firm and set. Serve hot, from the dish.
Serves 4

Lamb and aubergine (eggplant) casserole

METRIC/IMPERIAL
1 large aubergine, peeled and diced
salt
2 × 15ml spoons/ 2 tablespoons olive oil
1 small onion, peeled and finely chopped
1 garlic clove, crushed
0.5kg/1lb cooked lamb, diced
0.5kg/1lb tomatoes, peeled and chopped
2 × 15ml spoons/ 2 tablespoons chopped fresh parsley
1 × 5ml spoon/1 teaspoon chopped fresh rosemary
1 × 5ml spoon/1 teaspoon chopped fresh thyme
1 bay leaf
freshly ground black pepper
4 black olives, stoned and sliced
2 × 15ml spoons/ 2 tablespoons grated Parmesan cheese
50g/2oz dry breadcrumbs

AMERICAN
1 large eggplant, peeled and diced
salt
2 tablespoons olive oil
1 small onion, peeled and finely chopped
1 garlic clove, crushed
2 cups diced cooked lamb
2 cups peeled and chopped tomatoes
2 tablespoons chopped fresh parsley
1 teaspoon chopped fresh rosemary
1 teaspoon chopped fresh thyme
1 bay leaf
freshly ground black pepper
4 black olives, pitted and sliced
2 tablespoons grated Parmesan cheese
½ cup dry breadcrumbs

Put the aubergine (eggplant) in a colander and sprinkle with salt. Leave for 20 minutes, then rinse and pat dry with absorbent paper.

Heat the oil in a frying pan (skillet). Add the onion and garlic and fry until the onion is soft but not brown. Stir in the lamb and brown lightly. Add the aubergine (eggplant), tomatoes, herbs, salt and pepper to taste and the olives.

Transfer the mixture to a baking dish. Mix together the cheese and breadcrumbs and sprinkle over the top. Bake in a preheated moderately hot oven (200°C/400°F, Gas Mark 6) for 15 minutes. Serve hot, from the casserole.
Serves 4 to 6

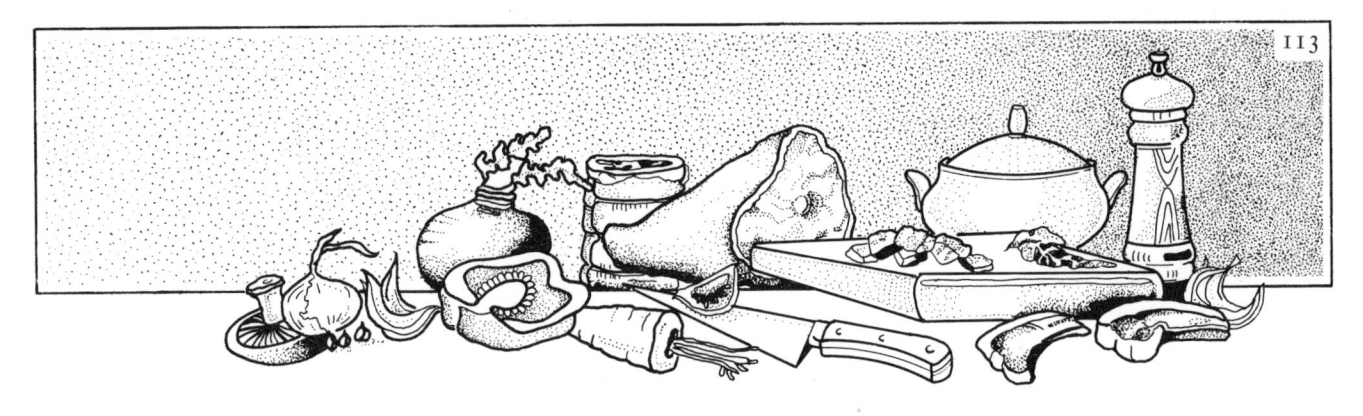

Roast leg of lamb with apricot stuffing

METRIC/IMPERIAL
1 × 2kg/4½lb leg of lamb (boned weight)
225g/8oz carrots, peeled and sliced
1 large onion, peeled and sliced
1 bay leaf
3 parsley sprigs
150ml/¼ pint dry red wine
2 × 15ml spoons/ 2 tablespoons plain flour

Stuffing:
½ medium onion, peeled and finely chopped
100g/4oz dried apricots, chopped
100g/4oz fresh white breadcrumbs
25g/1oz butter, melted
1 × 15ml spoon/ 1 tablespoon clear honey
pinch of dried thyme
1 egg, lightly beaten
salt
freshly ground black pepper

AMERICAN
1 × 4½lb leg of lamb (boned weight)
½lb carrots, peeled and sliced
1 large onion, peeled and sliced
1 bay leaf
3 parsley sprigs
⅔ cup dry red wine
2 tablespoons all-purpose flour

Stuffing:
½ medium onion, peeled and finely chopped
⅔ cup chopped dried apricots
2 cups fresh white breadcrumbs
2 tablespoons butter, melted
1 tablespoon clear honey
pinch of dried thyme
1 egg, lightly beaten
salt
freshly ground black pepper

To make the stuffing, mix all the ingredients together with salt and pepper to taste. Spoon the stuffing into the cavity in the lamb, packing it in firmly. Sew up with a trussing needle and string. (Do not sew too tightly or the skin may split while roasting.)

Put the stuffed leg of lamb into a polythene (plastic) bag and add the carrots, onion, bay leaf, parsley and wine. Leave to marinate for 6 hours. Remove the lamb from the bag and reserve the marinade.

Place the lamb in a roasting tin. Roast in a preheated moderate oven (180°C/350°F, Gas Mark 4) for about 1¾ hours or until the lamb is cooked. Place the lamb on a warmed serving dish and remove the trussing string. Keep hot.

Pour off the fat from the roasting tin. Sprinkle over the flour and stir well. Cook on top of the stove for 2 to 3 minutes, stirring. Add 3 × 15ml spoons/ 3 tablespoons of the strained marinade and simmer, stirring, for 5 minutes. Taste and adjust the seasoning.
Serves 8

Roast leg of lamb with Marsala

METRIC/IMPERIAL
1 × 1.75kg/4lb leg of lamb
2 garlic cloves, slivered
1 × 5ml spoon/1 teaspoon dried rosemary
75g/3oz butter, melted
salt
freshly ground black pepper
150ml/¼ pint Marsala

AMERICAN
1 × 4lb leg of lamb
2 garlic cloves, slivered
1 teaspoon dried rosemary
⅓ cup butter, melted
salt
freshly ground black pepper
⅔ cup Marsala

Make incisions in the lamb and insert the garlic slivers and rosemary. Put the lamb in a roasting tin and pour over the melted butter. Roast in a preheated hot oven (220°C/425°F, Gas Mark 7) for 15 minutes.

Sprinkle the lamb with salt and pepper and reduce the temperature to moderate (180°C/350°F, Gas Mark 4). Continue roasting for 1½ hours.

Pour the wine over the lamb and roast for a further 15 minutes, basting frequently. Transfer the lamb to a carving board or warmed serving plate. Keep hot.

Skim the fat from the juices in the roasting tin and bring to the boil on top of the stove. Boil until thick and syrupy. Serve this sauce with the lamb.
Serves 6 to 8

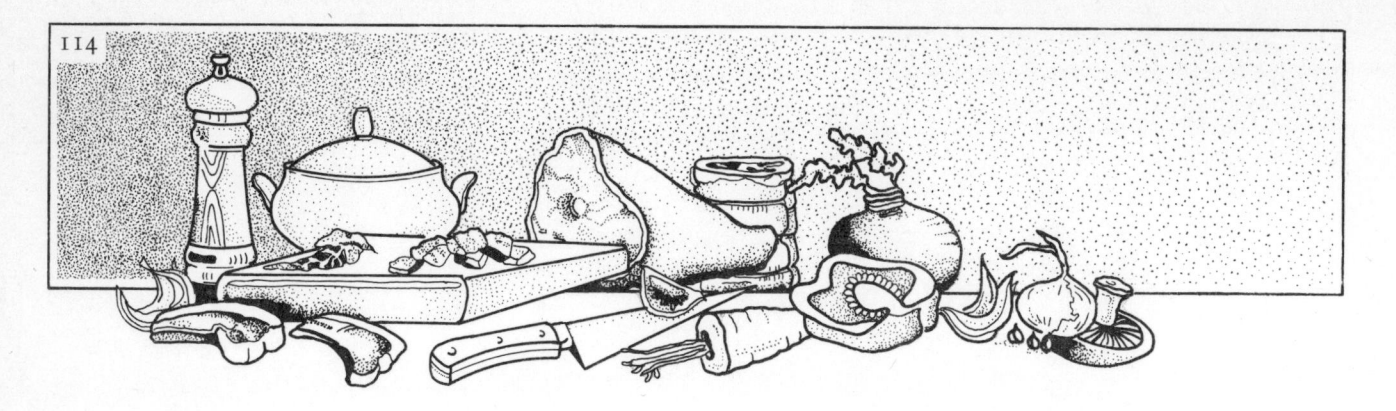

Stuffed shoulder of lamb

METRIC/IMPERIAL
1 × 1.5kg/3lb shoulder of
  lamb (boned weight)
25g/1oz dripping, melted
1 × 15ml spoon/
  1 tablespoon plain flour
300ml/½ pint beef or lamb
  stock
Stuffing:
25g/1oz butter
1 small onion, peeled and
  chopped
75g/3oz lamb's liver,
  chopped
50g/2oz raisins
75g/3oz long-grain rice,
  cooked
1 × 2.5ml spoon/½ teaspoon
  dried rosemary
½ egg, lightly beaten
salt
freshly ground black pepper

AMERICAN
1 × 3lb shoulder of lamb
  (boned weight)
2 tablespoons drippings,
  melted
1 tablespoon all-purpose
  flour
1¼ cups beef or lamb stock
Stuffing:
2 tablespoons butter
1 small onion, peeled and
  chopped
⅓ cup chopped lamb liver
⅓ cup raisins
½ cup long-grain rice,
  cooked
½ teaspoon dried rosemary
½ egg, lightly beaten
salt
freshly ground black pepper

First make the stuffing. Melt the butter in a saucepan. Add the onion and fry until it is soft but not brown. Add the liver and fry until well browned. Remove from the heat and stir in the remaining stuffing ingredients with salt and pepper to taste.

Fill the hollow in the lamb with the stuffing and tie securely with string. Place on a rack in a roasting tin and brush the lamb with the dripping. Sprinkle with salt and pepper.

Roast in a preheated hot oven (230°C/450°F, Gas Mark 8) for 20 minutes, then reduce the temperature to moderate (180°C/350°F, Gas Mark 4). Roast for a further 1 to 1½ hours or until the lamb is cooked.

Transfer the lamb to a serving dish and keep hot. Skim off most of the fat from the roasting tin. Sprinkle over the flour and cook on top of the stove, stirring, for 2 to 3 minutes or until well browned. Gradually stir in the stock and bring to the boil. Simmer, stirring, until the gravy is thickened and smooth. Add salt and pepper to taste and serve with the lamb.
Serves 6

Spring lamb

METRIC/IMPERIAL
1 × 1.5kg/3lb shoulder of
  lamb, chined
1 quantity parsley and
  thyme stuffing★
2 × 15ml spoons/
  2 tablespoons oil
450ml/¾ pint chicken stock
4 small carrots, peeled
8 new potatoes, peeled
salt
freshly ground black pepper
2 × 15ml spoons/
  2 tablespoons plain flour
2 × 15ml spoons/
  2 tablespoons water
mint sprigs to garnish

AMERICAN
1 × 3lb shoulder of lamb,
  chined
1 quantity parsley and
  thyme stuffing★
2 tablespoons oil
2 cups chicken stock
4 small carrots, peeled
8 new potatoes, peeled
salt
freshly ground black pepper
2 tablespoons all-purpose
  flour
2 tablespoons water
mint sprigs to garnish

Lay the meat flat with the cut side towards you and fill with the stuffing. Secure with string.

Heat the oil in a roasting tin. Add the meat and brown on all sides. Pour over the stock and add the carrots and potatoes with salt and pepper to taste. Transfer to a preheated hot oven (220°C/425°F, Gas Mark 7). Roast for 20 minutes, then reduce the temperature to moderately hot (190°C/375°F, Gas Mark 5). Continue roasting for 1¼ hours or until the lamb is cooked.

Transfer the lamb and vegetables to a warmed serving dish. Keep hot.

Dissolve the flour in the water and add to the liquid in the roasting tin. Place over heat on top of the stove and bring to the boil, stirring. Simmer until thickened and serve with the meat. Garnish with mint sprigs.
Serves 4 to 6

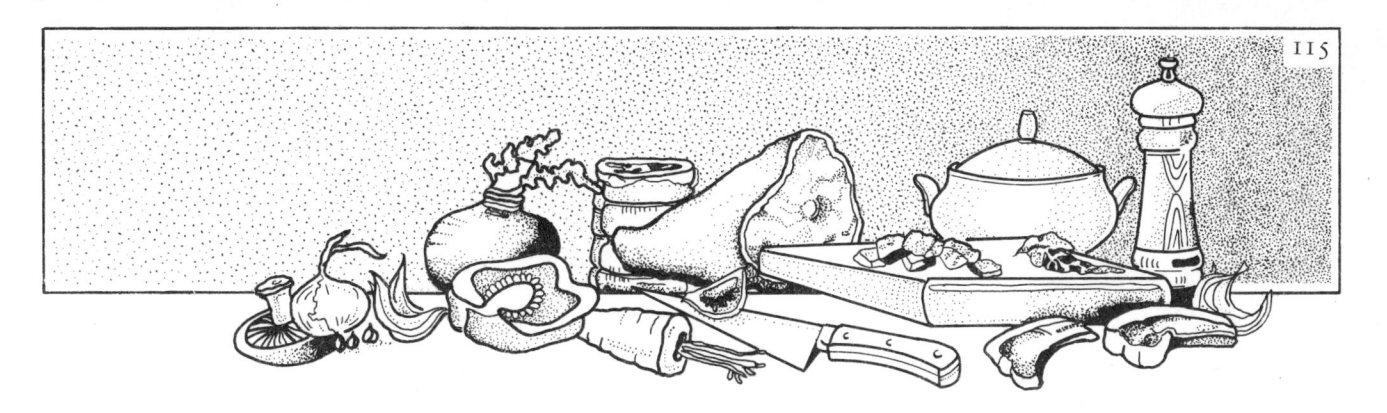

Lamb and bean stew

METRIC/IMPERIAL
3 × 15ml spoons/
  3 tablespoons oil
1kg/2lb lean lamb, cut into cubes
1 large onion, peeled and chopped
1 garlic clove, crushed
600ml/1 pint chicken stock
6 × 15ml spoons/
  6 tablespoons tomato purée
350g/12oz dried white haricot beans, soaked overnight and drained
2 carrots, peeled and sliced
2 celery sticks, chopped
2 parsnips, peeled and chopped
1 bouquet garni
salt
freshly ground black pepper

AMERICAN
3 tablespoons oil
2lb lean lamb, cut into cubes
1 large onion, peeled and chopped
1 garlic clove, crushed
2½ cups chicken stock
6 tablespoons tomato paste
1¾ cups dried navy beans, soaked overnight and drained
2 carrots, peeled and sliced
2 celery stalks, chopped
2 parsnips, peeled and chopped
1 bouquet garni
salt
freshly ground black pepper

Heat the oil in a saucepan. Add the lamb cubes, in batches, and brown on all sides. Remove the lamb from the pan as it is browned.

Add the onion and garlic to the pan and fry until the onion is soft but not brown. Stir in the stock and tomato purée (paste) and mix well. Return the lamb cubes to the pan and stir in the beans, carrots, celery, parsnips, bouquet garni and salt and pepper to taste. Bring to the boil, then cover and simmer for 2½ hours or until the lamb is tender. Serve hot.
Serves 6

Cranberry lamb stew

METRIC/IMPERIAL
4 × 15ml spoons/
  4 tablespoons oil
1kg/2lb lean lamb, cut into cubes
1 onion, peeled and chopped
300ml/½ pint dry red wine
150ml/¼ pint chicken stock
3 tomatoes, peeled and chopped
150ml/¼ pint cranberry sauce*
1 × 2.5ml spoon/
  ½ teaspoon ground ginger
sugar
salt
freshly ground black pepper

AMERICAN
4 tablespoons oil
2lb lean lamb, cut into cubes
1 onion, peeled and chopped
1¼ cups dry red wine
⅔ cup chicken stock
3 tomatoes, peeled and chopped
⅔ cup cranberry sauce*
½ teaspoon ground ginger
sugar
salt
freshly ground black pepper

Heat the oil in a saucepan. Add the lamb cubes, in batches, and brown on all sides. Remove the lamb from the pan as it is browned.

Add the onion to the pan and fry until it is soft but not brown. Stir in the wine, stock and tomatoes and bring to the boil. Return the lamb to the pan and mix well. Simmer for 45 minutes.

Stir in the cranberry sauce and ginger and simmer for a further 30 minutes or until the lamb is tender.

Taste and add sugar and salt and pepper, if necessary. Serve hot.
Serves 4 to 6

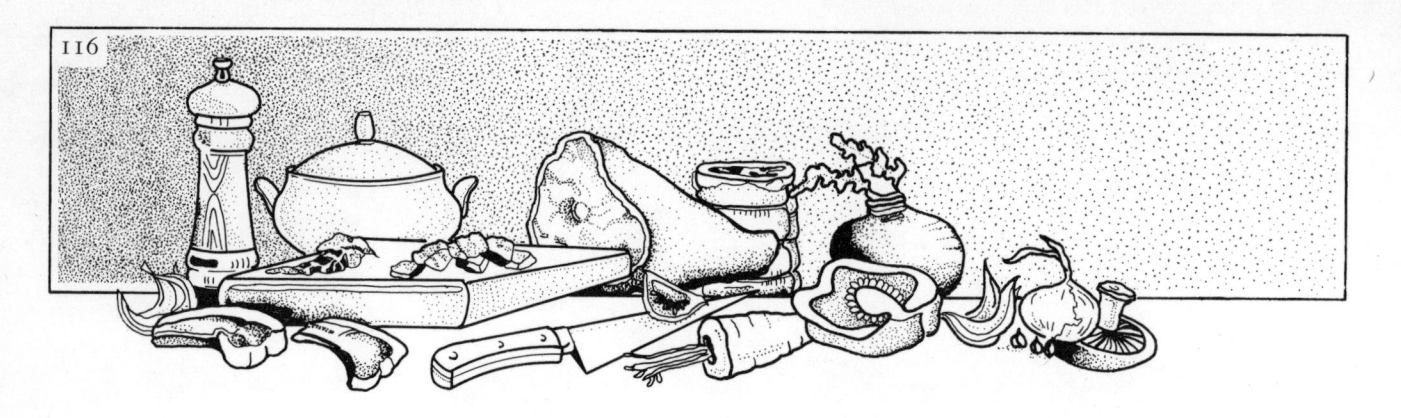

Lamb curry

METRIC/IMPERIAL
150ml/¼ pint natural yogurt
2 × 5ml spoons/2 teaspoons garam masala
1 × 15ml spoon/ 1 tablespoon mild curry powder
1kg/2lb lean lamb, cut into cubes
25g/1oz butter
2 × 15ml spoons/ 2 tablespoons oil
2 onions, peeled and chopped
1 garlic clove, crushed
2 × 5ml spoons/2 teaspoons chopped root ginger
salt
freshly ground black pepper
1 × 15ml spoon/ 1 tablespoon lemon juice
50g/2oz dried apricots, chopped
50g/2oz sultanas
2 × 15ml spoons/ 2 tablespoons blanched flaked almonds, toasted

AMERICAN
⅔ cup unflavored yogurt
2 teaspoons garam masala
1 tablespoon mild curry powder
2lb lean lamb, cut into cubes
2 tablespoons butter
2 tablespoons oil
2 onions, peeled and chopped
1 garlic clove, crushed
2 teaspoons chopped green ginger
salt
freshly ground black pepper
1 tablespoon lemon juice
⅓ cup chopped dried apricots
⅓ cup seedless white raisins
2 tablespoons blanched slivered almonds, toasted

Mix together the yogurt, garam masala and curry powder in a shallow dish. Add the lamb cubes and turn to coat with the yogurt mixture. Leave to marinate for 4 hours.

Melt the butter with the oil in a saucepan. Add the onions, garlic and ginger and fry until the onions are soft but not brown. Stir in the lamb with the yogurt mixture, salt and pepper to taste and the lemon juice. Cook for 5 minutes.

Add the apricots and sultanas (raisins), cover and simmer for 1¼ hours or until the lamb is tender. Serve hot, sprinkled with the almonds.
Serves 4 to 6

Spanish lamb stew

METRIC/IMPERIAL
4 × 15ml spoons/ 4 tablespoons oil
1kg/2lb lean lamb, cut into cubes
2 onions, peeled and chopped
2 red peppers, pith and seeds removed and chopped
1 × 2.5ml spoon/½ teaspoon powdered saffron
350ml/12fl oz chicken stock
salt
freshly ground black pepper
3 × 15ml spoons/ 3 tablespoons dry sherry

AMERICAN
4 tablespoons oil
2lb lean lamb, cut into cubes
2 onions, peeled and chopped
2 pimientos, pith and seeds removed and chopped
½ teaspoon powdered saffron
1½ cups chicken stock
salt
freshly ground black pepper
3 tablespoons dry sherry

Heat the oil in a saucepan. Add the lamb cubes, in batches, and brown on all sides. Remove the lamb from the pan as it is browned.

Add the onions and red peppers (pimientos) to the pan and fry until the onions are soft but not brown. Dissolve the saffron in the stock and add to the pan with salt and pepper to taste. Stir well.

Return the lamb cubes to the pan and bring to the boil. Simmer for 1 hour.

Stir in the sherry. Simmer for a further 15 minutes or until the lamb is tender. Serve hot.
Serves 4 to 6

Osso bucco (page 101)

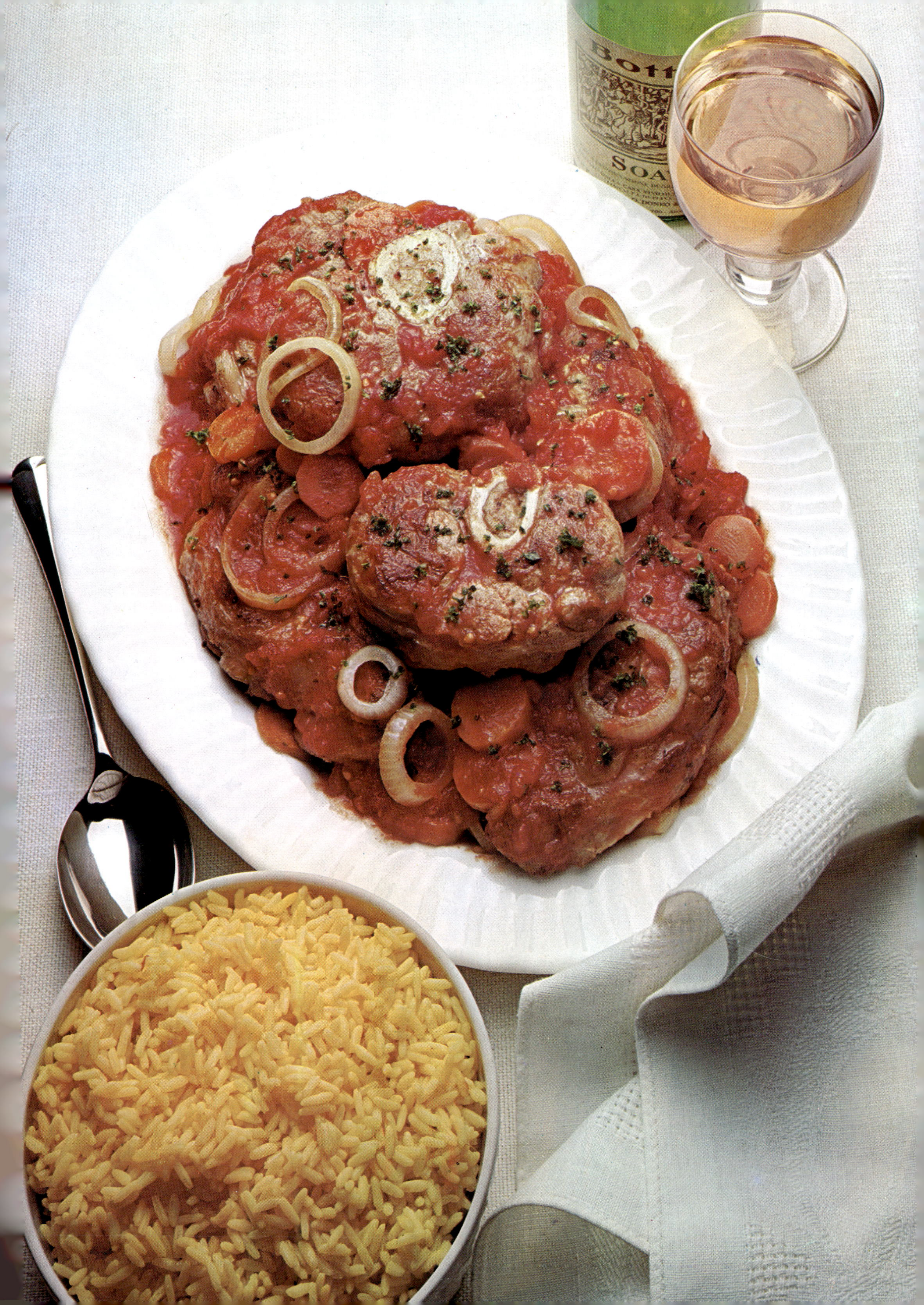

Lamb and yogurt casserole (page 123); Braised orange lamb (page 124)

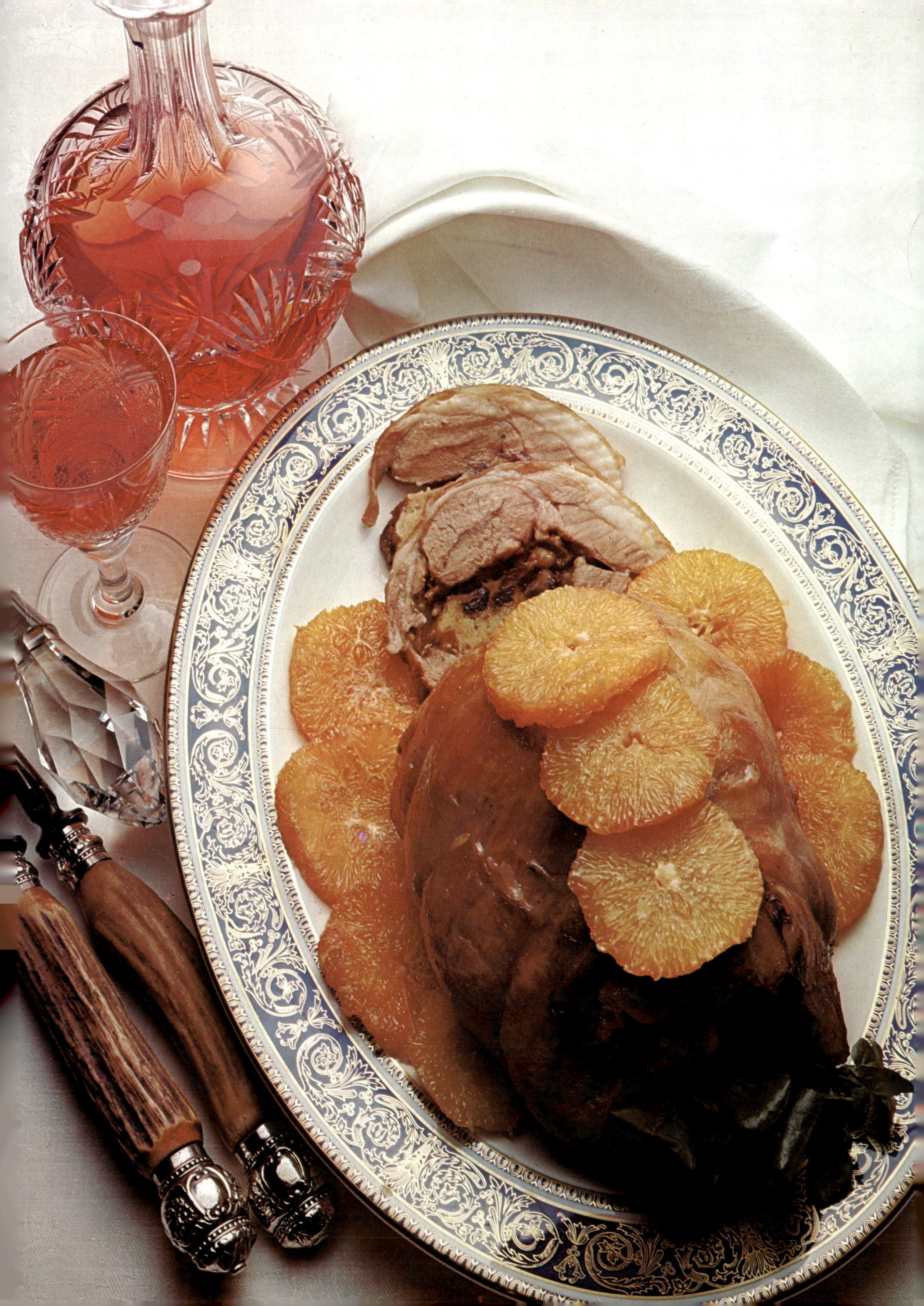

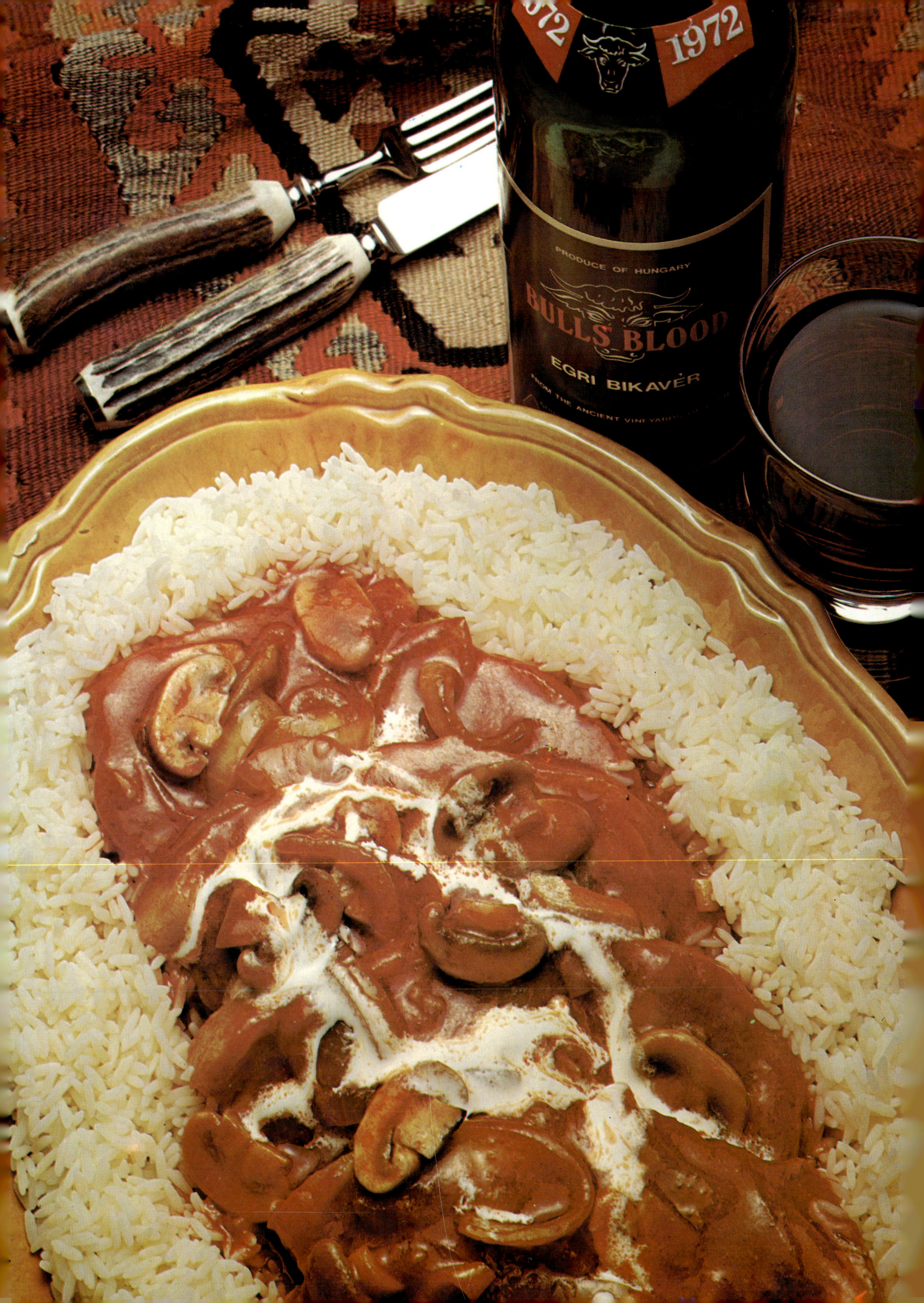
1972
PRODUCE OF HUNGARY
BULLS BLOOD
EGRI BIKAVÉR

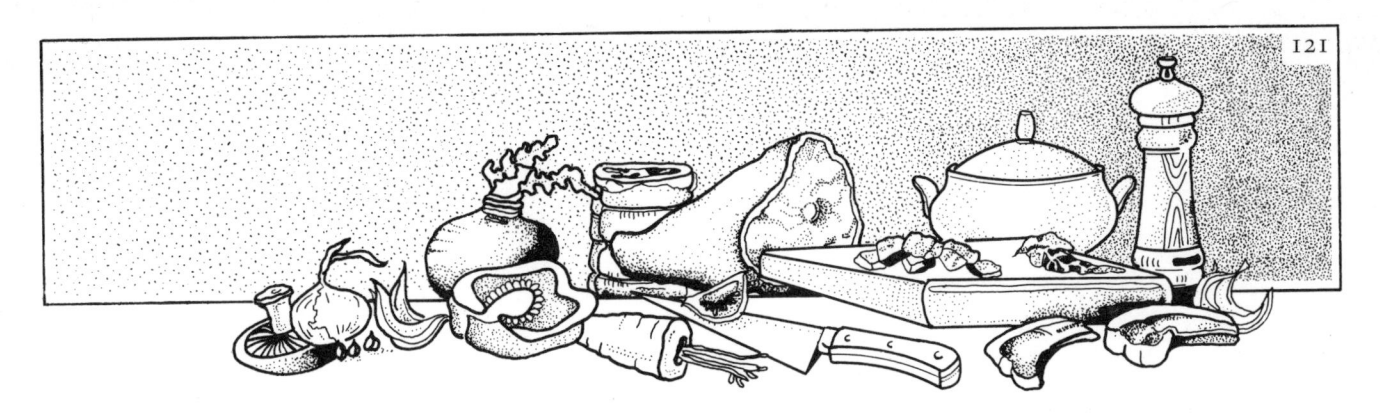

Lancashire hotpot

METRIC/IMPERIAL
1kg/2lb potatoes, peeled and sliced
25g/1oz dripping
1kg/2lb middle neck lamb chops
2 lamb's kidneys, cored and chopped
1 large onion, peeled and chopped
1 × 2.5ml spoon/½ teaspoon dried thyme
salt
freshly ground black pepper
600ml/1 pint hot beef stock

AMERICAN
2lb potatoes, peeled and sliced
2 tablespoons drippings
2lb middle neck lamb slices
2 lamb kidneys, cored and chopped
1 large onion, peeled and chopped
½ teaspoon dried thyme
salt
freshly ground black pepper
2½ cups hot beef stock

Cover the bottom of a deep casserole with half the potato slices.

Melt the dripping in a frying pan (skillet). Add the chops (neck slices) and kidneys and brown on both sides. Remove from the heat. Arrange the chops (neck slices) and kidneys in the casserole. Sprinkle with the onion, thyme and salt and pepper to taste and pour over the stock. Cover with the remaining potato slices.

Cover and bake in a preheated moderate oven (180°C/350°F, Gas Mark 4) for 2 hours. Remove the lid and bake for a further 15 to 20 minutes to brown the potatoes on top.

Serve hot, from the casserole.
Serves 4

Irish stew with parsley dumplings

METRIC/IMPERIAL
25g/1oz plain flour
salt
freshly ground black pepper
1.5kg/3lb middle neck or scrag end of lamb, cut into pieces
3 large onions, peeled and chopped
0.5kg/1lb potatoes, peeled and quartered
1 × 2.5ml spoon/½ teaspoon dried thyme
900ml/1½ pints boiling beef stock
Dumplings:
100g/4oz self-raising flour
50g/2oz shredded suet
2 × 15ml spoons/ 2 tablespoons chopped fresh parsley
about 4 × 15ml spoons/ 4 tablespoons cold water

AMERICAN
¼ cup all-purpose flour
salt
freshly ground black pepper
3lb lamb middle neck slices
3 large onions, peeled and chopped
1lb potatoes, peeled and quartered
½ teaspoon dried thyme
3¾ cups boiling beef stock
Dumplings:
1 cup self-rising flour
½ cup shredded suet
2 tablespoons chopped fresh parsley
about 4 tablespoons cold water

Mix the flour with salt and pepper and use to coat the lamb pieces. Put into a casserole and add the onions, potatoes, thyme and stock. Cover and cook in a preheated moderate oven (160°C/325°F, Gas Mark 3) for 2½ hours.

To make the dumplings, sift the flour with salt and pepper into a mixing bowl. Stir in the suet, then add the parsley and enough water to bind to a soft dough. Divide into 8 portions and shape into balls. Add to the casserole and cook for a further 30 minutes. Serve hot, from the casserole.
Serves 4 to 6

Hungarian veal chops (page 96)

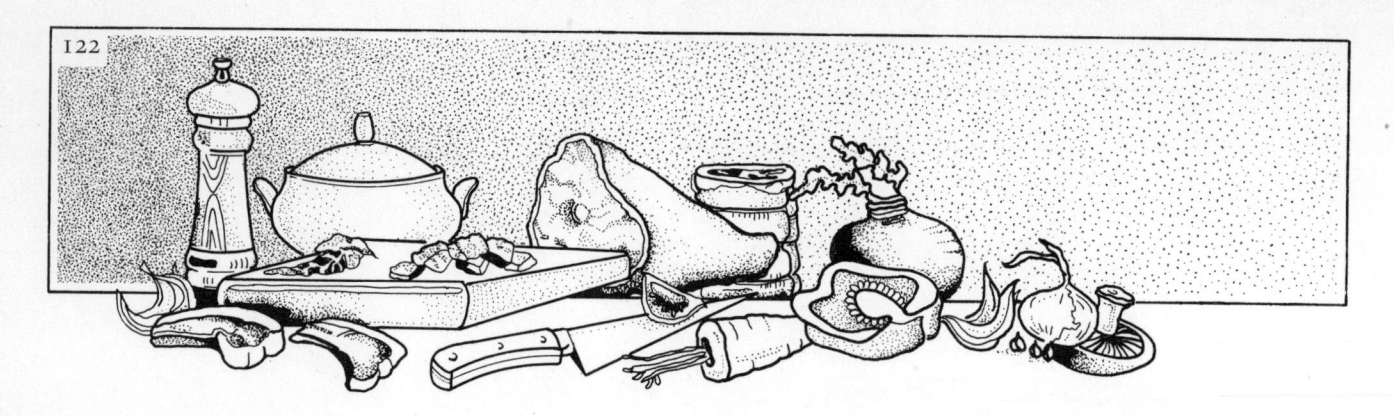

Lamb stew

METRIC/IMPERIAL
25g/1oz plain flour
salt
freshly ground black pepper
1kg/2lb lean lamb, cut into cubes
40g/1½oz dripping
1 large onion, peeled and chopped
1 × 400g/14oz can tomatoes
1 × 15ml spoon/ 1 tablespoon tomato purée
2 large carrots, peeled and sliced
2 medium turnips, peeled and chopped
1 bouquet garni
1 × 5ml spoon/1 teaspoon sugar
300ml/½ pint beef stock

AMERICAN
¼ cup all-purpose flour
salt
freshly ground black pepper
2lb lean lamb, cut into cubes
3 tablespoons drippings
1 large onion, peeled and chopped
1 × 14oz can tomatoes
1 tablespoon tomato paste
2 large carrots, peeled and sliced
2 medium turnips, peeled and chopped
1 bouquet garni
1 teaspoon sugar
1¼ cups beef stock

Mix the flour with salt and pepper in a polythene (plastic) bag. Add the lamb cubes and shake to coat with the seasoned flour.

Melt the dripping in a flameproof casserole. Add the onion and fry until it is soft but not brown. Add the lamb cubes, in batches, and brown on all sides. Remove the lamb cubes as they are browned.

Return all the lamb to the casserole and stir in the tomatoes, tomato purée (paste), carrots, turnips, bouquet garni, sugar and salt and pepper to taste. Pour over the stock. Bring to the boil, then cover and transfer to a moderate oven (160°C/325°F, Gas Mark 3). Cook for 2 hours or until the meat is tender.

Discard the bouquet garni and serve hot, from the casserole.
Serves 4 to 6

Lamb stew with dumplings

METRIC/IMPERIAL
25g/1oz plain flour
salt
freshly ground black pepper
1 × 5ml spoon/1 teaspoon mild curry powder
1kg/2lb shoulder of lamb, cut into cubes
3 × 15ml spoons/ 3 tablespoons vegetable oil
900ml/1½ pints chicken stock
8 very small onions, peeled
8 small carrots, peeled
Dumplings:
40g/1½oz butter
50g/2oz fresh white breadcrumbs
225g/8oz self-raising flour
salt
pinch of garlic powder
3 × 15ml spoons/ 3 tablespoons vegetable oil
milk

AMERICAN
¼ cup all-purpose flour
salt
freshly ground black pepper
1 teaspoon mild curry powder
2lb shoulder of lamb, cut into cubes
3 tablespoons vegetable oil
3¾ cups chicken stock
8 very small onions, peeled
8 small carrots, peeled
Dumplings:
3 tablespoons butter
1 cup fresh white breadcrumbs
2 cups self-rising flour
salt
pinch of garlic powder
3 tablespoons vegetable oil
milk

Sift the flour with salt and pepper and the curry powder into a polythene (plastic) bag. Add the lamb cubes and shake to coat with the seasoned flour.

Heat the oil in a flameproof casserole. Add the lamb cubes and brown on all sides. Stir in any remaining seasoned flour, then the stock. Bring to the boil and add the onions. Cover and transfer to a preheated moderate oven (160°C/325°F, Gas Mark 3). Cook for 1 hour.

To make the dumplings, melt the butter in a frying pan (skillet). Add the breadcrumbs and fry until they are golden. Remove from the heat.

Sift together the flour, salt and garlic powder. Add the oil and enough milk to give a soft dough. Form into walnut-sized balls and roll in the breadcrumbs to coat on all sides.

Add the dumplings to the casserole with the carrots. Re-cover and cook for a further 1 hour or until the meat is tender. Serve hot, from the casserole.
Serves 4 to 6

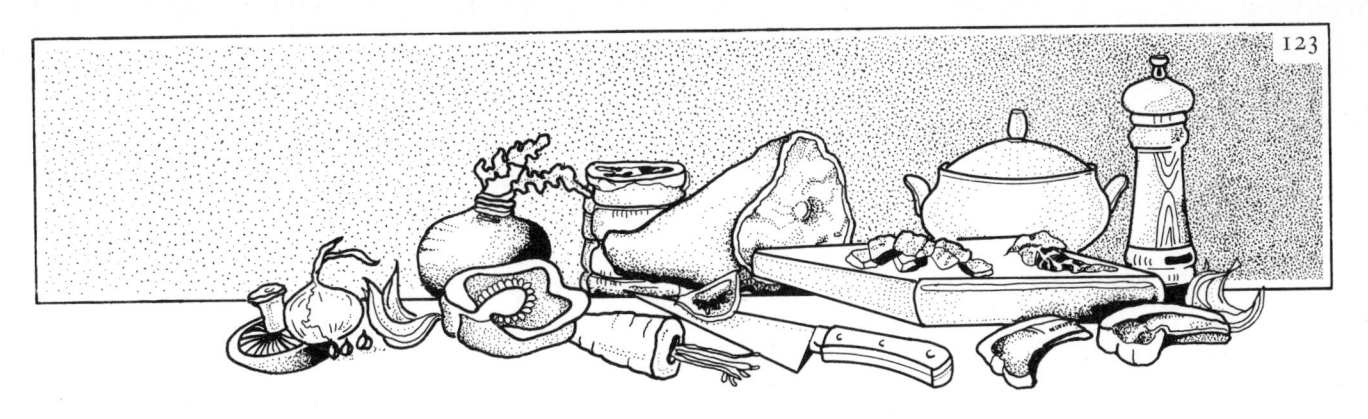

Lamb and yogurt casserole

METRIC/IMPERIAL
25g/1oz butter
1 × 15ml spoon/
 1 tablespoon olive oil
0.75kg/1½lb lean lamb, cut into 2.5cm/1 inch cubes
1 large onion, peeled and chopped
25g/1oz plain flour
300ml/½ pint chicken stock
1 × 15ml spoon/
 1 tablespoon capers
2 dill pickled cucumbers, sliced
finely grated rind of 1 lemon
1 × 15ml spoon/
 1 tablespoon chopped fresh parsley
salt
freshly ground black pepper
300ml/½ pint natural yogurt

AMERICAN
2 tablespoons butter
1 tablespoon olive oil
1½lb lean lamb, cut into 1 inch cubes
1 large onion, peeled and chopped
¼ cup all-purpose flour
1¼ cups chicken stock
1 tablespoon capers
2 dill pickles, sliced
finely grated rind of 1 lemon
1 tablespoon chopped fresh parsley
salt
freshly ground black pepper
1¼ cups unflavored yogurt

Melt the butter with the oil in a flameproof casserole. Add the lamb cubes, in batches, and brown on all sides. Remove the lamb from the casserole.

Add the onion to the casserole and fry until it is soft but not brown. Stir in the flour and cook, stirring, for 1 minute. Gradually add the stock and bring to the boil, stirring. Add the capers, pickled cucumbers (pickles), lemon rind, parsley and salt and pepper to taste and stir well. Return the lamb cubes to the casserole and stir into the liquid. Cover and transfer to a preheated moderate oven (160°C/325°F, Gas Mark 3). Cook for 1½ hours or until the lamb is tender.

Remove the casserole from the oven and allow to cool slightly before stirring in the yogurt. Serve hot, from the casserole.
Serves 4

Lamb and orange stew

METRIC/IMPERIAL
1kg/2lb lean lamb, cut into 1cm/½ inch cubes
1 × 15ml spoon/
 1 tablespoon soy sauce
1 × 15ml spoon/
 1 tablespoon dry sherry
1 × 5ml spoon/1 teaspoon ground ginger
2 × 15ml spoons/
 2 tablespoons finely grated orange rind
1 × 5ml spoon/1 teaspoon salt
1.2 litres/2 pints plus 2 × 15ml spoons/
 2 tablespoons water or stock
1 × 15ml spoon/
 1 tablespoon cornflour

AMERICAN
2lb lean lamb, cut into ½ inch cubes
1 tablespoon soy sauce
1 tablespoon dry sherry
1 teaspoon ground ginger
2 tablespoons finely grated orange rind
1 teaspoon salt
5 cups plus 2 tablespoons water or stock
1 tablespoon cornstarch

Put the lamb in a saucepan and add the soy sauce, sherry, ginger, orange rind, salt and all but 2 × 15ml spoons/2 tablespoons of the water or stock. Stir well and bring to the boil. Cover and simmer for 2 hours or until the lamb is tender.

Dissolve the cornflour (cornstarch) in the remaining water or stock and stir into the lamb mixture. Simmer, stirring, until lightly thickened. Serve hot.
Serves 4 to 6

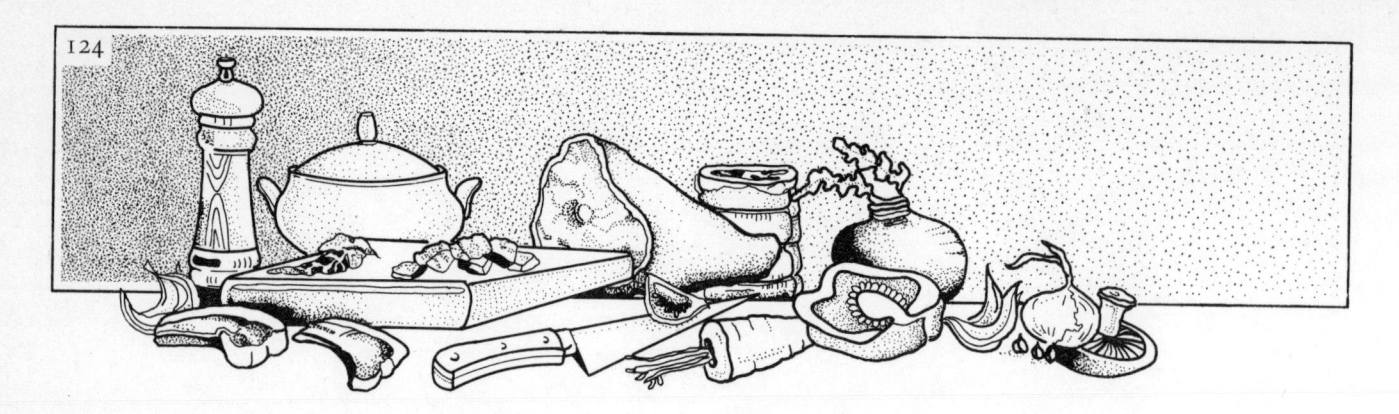

Leg of lamb with cherry sauce

METRIC/IMPERIAL
1 × 1.75kg/4lb leg of lamb
4 fresh rosemary sprigs
4 strips of lemon rind
2 × 15ml spoons/
 2 tablespoons oil
Sauce:
25g/1oz plain flour
450ml/¾ pint chicken stock
1 × 400g/14oz can black cherries, drained
150ml/¼ pint port wine
salt
freshly ground black pepper

AMERICAN
1 × 4lb leg of lamb
4 fresh rosemary sprigs
4 strips of lemon rind
2 tablespoons oil
Sauce:
¼ cup all-purpose flour
2 cups chicken stock
1 × 14oz can black cherries, drained
⅔ cup port wine
salt
freshly ground black pepper

Make 8 incisions in the lamb and insert the rosemary sprigs and lemon rind strips. Rub the lamb with the oil and place in a roasting tin. Roast in a preheated moderately hot oven (200°C/400°F, Gas Mark 6) for 20 minutes, then reduce the temperature to moderate (160°C/325°F, Gas Mark 3). Roast for a further 1½ hours or until the lamb is cooked.

Transfer the lamb to a warmed serving dish and keep hot. Pour off most of the fat from the roasting tin. Sprinkle over the flour and stir well to scrape up the sediment. Place over heat on top of the stove and cook, stirring, for 1 minute. Gradually stir in the stock and bring to the boil, stirring. Simmer until thickened and smooth.

Stir in the cherries, port and salt and pepper to taste and simmer for a further 5 minutes or until hot. Serve with the lamb.
Serves 8

Braised orange lamb

METRIC/IMPERIAL
100g/4oz fresh white breadcrumbs
50g/2oz raisins
50g/2oz shredded suet
pinch of dried marjoram
salt
freshly ground black pepper
2 large oranges, rinds grated
1 egg, beaten
1 × 1.5kg/3lb shoulder of lamb (boned weight)
25g/1oz lard
150ml/¼ pint brown stock
2 × 15ml spoons/
 2 tablespoons red wine
2 × 15ml spoons/
 2 tablespoons redcurrant jelly
watercress to garnish

AMERICAN
2 cups fresh white breadcrumbs
⅓ cup raisins
½ cup shredded suet
pinch of dried marjoram
salt
freshly ground black pepper
2 large oranges, rinds grated
1 egg, beaten
1 × 3lb shoulder of lamb (boned weight)
2 tablespoons lard
⅔ cup brown stock
2 tablespoons red wine
2 tablespoons redcurrant jelly
watercress to garnish

Mix together the breadcrumbs, raisins, suet, marjoram, salt and pepper and grated orange rinds. Bind together with the beaten egg. Spread the mixture evenly over the lamb, roll up and tie at intervals with string. Season well.

Heat the lard in a frying pan (skillet) and brown the lamb all over. Remove all pith from the oranges, slice thickly and place in a casserole. Place the drained lamb on top and pour over the stock and wine. Cover and place in a preheated moderate oven (180°C/350°F, Gas Mark 4) and cook for 2 hours or until the meat is tender. Just before serving, stir the redcurrant jelly into the cooking liquid and baste the lamb. Place the lamb on a warmed serving dish. Arrange the orange slices round the meat and garnish with watercress.
Serves 6

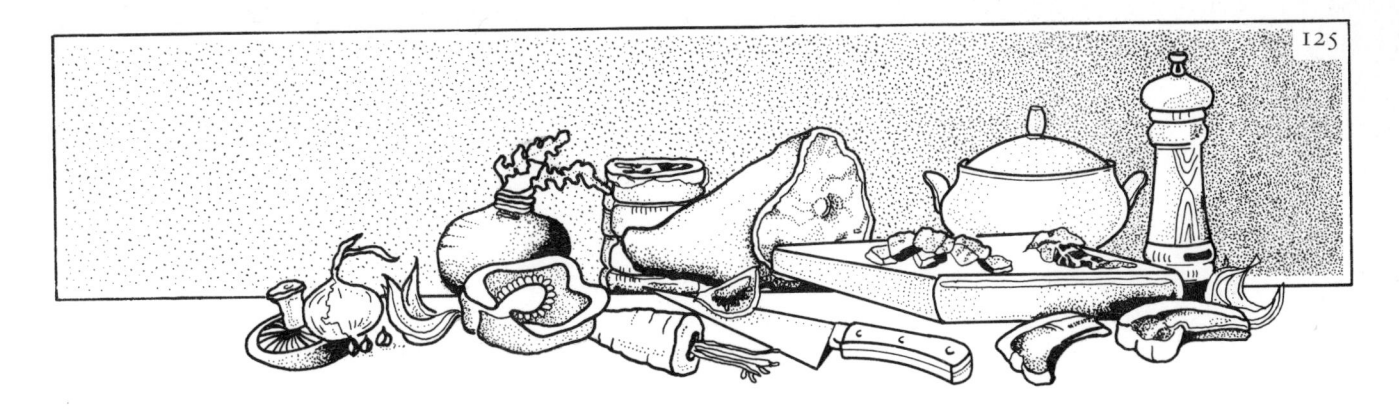

Stuffed leg of lamb en croûte

METRIC/IMPERIAL
1 × 2kg/4½lb leg of lamb
  (boned weight)
150ml/¼ pint dry red wine
0.5kg/1lb pork sausage
  meat
100g/4oz streaky bacon
  rashers, rinds removed and
  diced
salt
freshly ground black pepper
1 × 2.5ml spoon/½ teaspoon
  dried thyme
25g/1oz butter
1 large onion, peeled and
  sliced
1 bay leaf
3 parsley sprigs
1 × 425g/15oz can
  consommé
225g/8oz quantity puff or
  flaky pastry★
2 eggs, lightly beaten
2 × 15ml spoons/
  2 tablespoons cornflour
3 × 15ml spoons/
  3 tablespoons water

AMERICAN
1 × 4½lb leg of lamb
  (boned weight)
⅔ cup dry red wine
2 cups pork sausage meat
¼lb bacon slices, diced
salt
freshly ground black pepper
½ teaspoon dried thyme
2 tablespoons butter
1 large onion, peeled and
  sliced
1 bay leaf
3 parsley sprigs
1 × 15oz can consommé
2 cup quantity puff or flaky
  pastry★
2 eggs, lightly beaten
2 tablespoons cornstarch
3 tablespoons water

Put the lamb in a polythene (plastic) bag and pour in the wine. Allow to marinate for 3 hours.

Remove the lamb from the bag and pat dry. Reserve the wine. Mix together the sausage meat, bacon, salt and pepper to taste and the thyme. Stuff the cavity in the lamb with this mixture and sew up securely.

Melt the butter in a frying pan (skillet). Add the lamb and turn to brown on all sides. Transfer the lamb to a casserole.

Add the onion to the frying pan (skillet) and fry until it is soft but not brown. Add the onion to the casserole with the bay leaf, parsley, consommé and marinating wine. Cover and cook in a preheated moderate oven (160°C/325°F, Gas Mark 3) for 2 hours.

Remove the lamb from the casserole and allow to cool. Skim the fat from the cooking juices and strain into a saucepan.

Roll out the dough to an oblong large enough to enclose the lamb. Brush the meat with beaten egg and place in the centre of the dough oblong. Wrap the lamb in the dough, pressing the edges together and sealing with beaten egg. Use the dough trimmings to decorate.

Place the wrapped lamb, join side down, on a baking sheet and brush again with beaten egg. Bake in a preheated hot oven (230°C/450°F, Gas Mark 8) for 45 minutes.

Ten minutes before the lamb is ready, make the gravy. Dissolve the cornflour (cornstarch) in the water and add to the cooking juices. Bring to the boil and simmer, stirring, until thickened and smooth. Adjust the seasoning if necessary.

Serve the lamb hot, with the gravy.
Serves 8 to 10

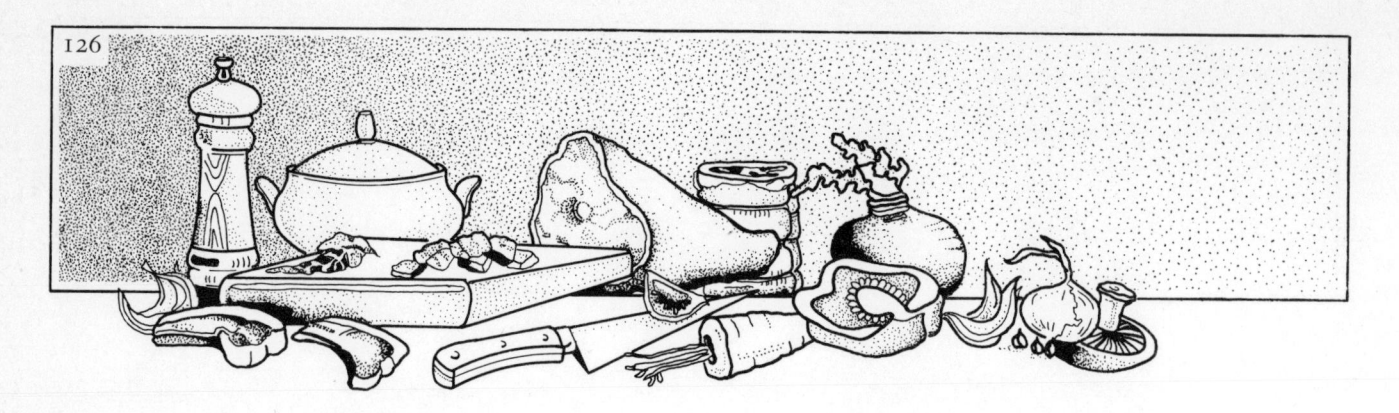

Boiled breast of lamb with caper sauce

METRIC/IMPERIAL
1 × 1.75kg/4lb breast of lamb, excess fat removed and tied into shape
12 peppercorns
1 bouquet garni
1 × 15ml spoon/
 1 tablespoon chopped fresh rosemary
1 carrot, peeled and sliced
40g/1½oz butter
40g/1½oz plain flour
300ml/½ pint milk
salt
freshly ground black pepper
1 × 2.5ml spoon/½ teaspoon vinegar
1.5 × 15ml spoons/
 1½ tablespoons capers

AMERICAN
1 × 4lb breast of lamb, excess fat removed and tied into shape
12 peppercorns
1 bouquet garni
1 tablespoon chopped fresh rosemary
1 carrot, peeled and sliced
3 tablespoons butter
6 tablespoons all-purpose flour
1¼ cups milk
salt
freshly ground black pepper
½ teaspoon vinegar
1½ tablespoons capers

Put the lamb in a saucepan with the peppercorns, bouquet garni, rosemary and carrot. Add enough water to cover and bring to the boil, skimming off the scum that rises to the surface. Cover and simmer for 2½ hours or until the lamb is cooked.
 Transfer the lamb to a warmed serving dish. Keep hot. Strain the cooking liquid and reserve 300ml/ ½ pint/1¼ cups.
 Melt the butter in another saucepan. Add the flour and cook, stirring, for 1 minute. Remove from the heat and gradually stir in the reserved cooking liquid and milk. Return to the heat and bring to the boil, stirring. Simmer until thickened and smooth.
 Stir in salt and pepper to taste, the vinegar and capers and heat through gently. Serve hot with the lamb.
Serves 6

Stuffed breast of lamb

METRIC/IMPERIAL
1 × 1.5kg/3lb breast of lamb (boned weight)
salt
freshly ground black pepper
25g/1oz butter
1 onion, peeled and finely chopped
100g/4oz lean veal, minced
75g/3oz lean bacon, minced
75g/3oz fresh breadcrumbs
cayenne pepper
1 egg, lightly beaten

AMERICAN
1 × 3lb breast of lamb (boned weight)
salt
freshly ground black pepper
2 tablespoons butter
1 onion, peeled and finely chopped
½ cup ground lean veal
⅓ cup ground Canadian bacon
1½ cups fresh breadcrumbs
cayenne pepper
1 egg, lightly beaten

Lay the lamb flat and rub with salt and pepper. Melt the butter in a frying pan (skillet). Add the onion and fry until it is soft but not brown. Remove from the heat and stir in the veal, bacon, breadcrumbs, cayenne to taste and the egg. Spread this stuffing over the lamb and roll up loosely. Tie in several places with string.
 Place the lamb on a rack in a roasting tin. Roast in a preheated moderate oven (180°C/350°F, Gas Mark 4) for 2 to 2½ hours or until the meat is cooked.
 Serve hot, cut in thick slices.
Serves 4 to 6

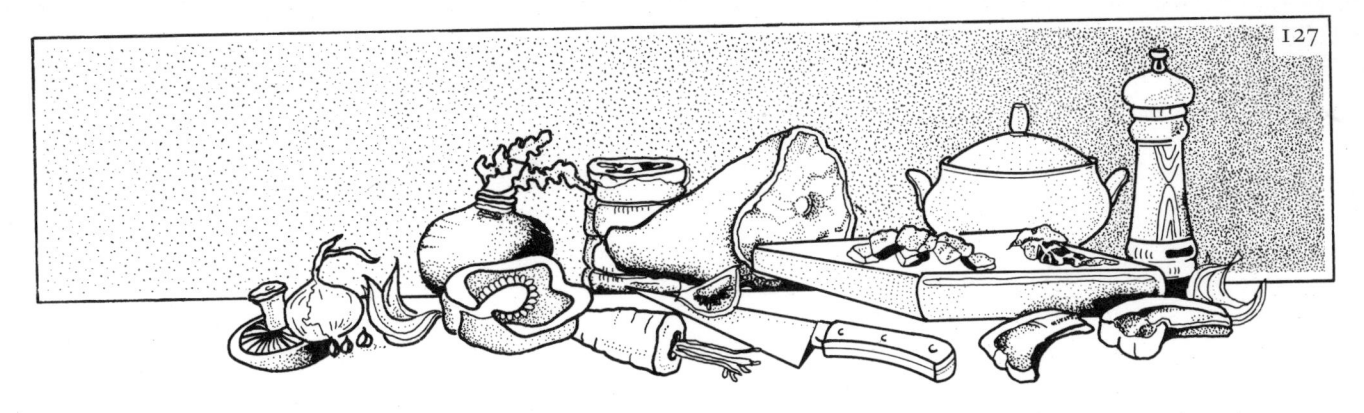

Lamb noisettes with tomato sauce

METRIC/IMPERIAL
50g/2oz butter
4 lamb noisettes
salt
freshly ground black pepper
1 garlic clove, crushed
25g/1oz flour
150ml/¼ pint red wine (Burgundy)
2 × 15ml spoons/ 2 tablespoons tomato purée
300ml/½ pint beef stock
100g/4oz button mushrooms, sliced
parsley sprigs to garnish

AMERICAN
¼ cup butter
4 lamb noisettes (boned lamb chops)
salt
freshly ground black pepper
1 garlic clove, crushed
¼ cup flour
⅔ cup red wine (Burgundy)
2 tablespoons tomato paste
1¼ cups beef stock
1 cup sliced button mushrooms
parsley sprigs to garnish

Melt half the butter in a frying pan (skillet). Season the lamb with salt and pepper and put into the pan. Cover and cook gently for 8 to 10 minutes until cooked through.

Meanwhile, fry the garlic in the remaining butter for 1 minute. Sprinkle over the flour and cook, stirring, for 1 minute. Gradually add the wine, tomato purée (paste) and stock. Bring to the boil and simmer, stirring, until thickened and smooth. Stir in the mushrooms and continue cooking for 10 minutes. Add salt and pepper to taste.

Drain the noisettes on absorbent paper. Transfer to a warmed serving dish and spoon over the sauce. Serve garnished with parsley sprigs.
Serves 4

Lamb cutlets with bean sprouts

METRIC/IMPERIAL
4 lamb cutlets, trimmed
salt
freshly ground black pepper
300ml/½ pint chicken stock
2 × 15ml spoons/ 2 tablespoons tomato purée
2 × 5ml spoons/2 teaspoons cornflour
1 × 15ml spoon/ 1 tablespoon oil
1 onion, peeled and sliced
1 green pepper, deseeded, pith removed and sliced
200g/6oz button mushrooms, sliced
1 × 500g/1lb can bean sprouts, drained
2 × 15ml spoons/ 2 tablespoons sherry
3 eggs
25g/1oz butter

AMERICAN
4 lamb cutlets, trimmed
salt
freshly ground black pepper
1¼ cups chicken stock
2 tablespoons tomato paste
2 teaspoons cornstarch
1 tablespoon oil
1 onion, peeled and sliced
1 green pepper, deseeded, pith removed and sliced
1½ cups sliced button mushrooms
1 × 1lb can bean sprouts, drained
2 tablespoons sherry
3 eggs
2 tablespoons butter

Season the cutlets with salt and pepper. Place on the rack in a grill (broiler) pan and cook under a moderate heat for 8 to 10 minutes on each side.

Meanwhile, make the sauce. Pour the stock, tomato purée (paste) and soy sauce into a saucepan. Add salt and pepper to taste. Mix the cornflour (cornstarch) with a little cold water and stir into the sauce. Bring to the boil and boil for 3 minutes, stirring continuously.

Heat the oil in a frying pan (skillet) and fry the onion and pepper until soft. Add the mushrooms to the pan and continue frying for 3 minutes. Stir in the bean sprouts, sherry and one-third of the sauce. Simmer for 5 minutes.

Beat the eggs with a little water and add salt and pepper to taste. Melt the butter in an omelette pan and use the egg mixture to cook two large flat omelettes. When cooked, turn out of the pan and cut each in half.

Put the bean sprout mixture on a warmed serving dish and arrange the cutlets on top. Fold the omelette halves and place on the cutlets. Serve with the remaining sauce passed separately.
Serves 4

PORK & HAM

Baked pork chops with fruit cocktail sauce

METRIC/IMPERIAL
25g/1oz plain flour
salt
freshly ground black pepper
4 large pork chops
1 egg, lightly beaten
½ quantity sage and onion stuffing★
Sauce:
25g/1oz butter
1 onion, peeled and chopped
1 green pepper, pith and seeds removed and diced
4 × 15ml spoons/ 4 tablespoons tomato ketchup
1 × 5ml spoon/1 teaspoon lemon juice
1 × 15ml spoon/ 1 tablespoon brown sugar
1 × 400g/14oz can fruit cocktail
1 × 15ml spoon/ 1 tablespoon cornflour

AMERICAN
¼ cup all-purpose flour
salt
freshly ground black pepper
4 large pork chops
1 egg, lightly beaten
½ quantity sage and onion stuffing★
Sauce:
2 tablespoons butter
1 onion, peeled and chopped
1 green pepper, pith and seeds removed and diced
4 tablespoons tomato ketchup
1 teaspoon lemon juice
1 tablespoon brown sugar
1 × 14oz can fruit cocktail
1 tablespoon cornstarch

Mix the flour with salt and pepper and use to coat the chops. Dip in the egg, then coat in the stuffing, pressing it on well. Arrange on a rack in a roasting tin and roast in a preheated moderate oven (180°C/ 350°F, Gas Mark 4) for 1 hour.

Meanwhile, make the sauce. Melt the butter in a saucepan, add the onion and green pepper and fry until the onion is soft but not brown. Stir in the ketchup, lemon juice and sugar.

Drain the fruit cocktail, reserving the juice. Dissolve the cornflour (cornstarch) in the juice and add to the saucepan. Bring to the boil, stirring, and simmer for 10 minutes.

Stir in the fruit cocktail with salt and pepper to taste and heat through gently.

Transfer the chops to a warmed serving dish. Pour over the sauce and serve hot.
Serves 4

Spicy pork chops

METRIC/IMPERIAL
1 × 15ml spoon/ 1 tablespoon coriander seeds, crushed
6 black peppercorns, crushed
4 × 15ml spoons/ 4 tablespoons soy sauce
1 garlic clove, crushed
1 × 5ml spoon/1 teaspoon sugar
4 large pork chops

AMERICAN
1 tablespoon coriander seeds, crushed
6 black peppercorns, crushed
4 tablespoons soy sauce
1 garlic clove, crushed
1 teaspoon sugar
4 large pork chops

Mix together the coriander seeds, peppercorns, soy sauce, garlic and sugar in a shallow dish. Add the chops and turn to coat with the spicy mixture. Leave to marinate for 1 hour, turning occasionally.

Arrange the chops on the rack in a grill (broiler) pan. Grill (broil) for about 10 minutes on each side or until cooked. Baste occasionally with the marinade. Serve hot.
Serves 4

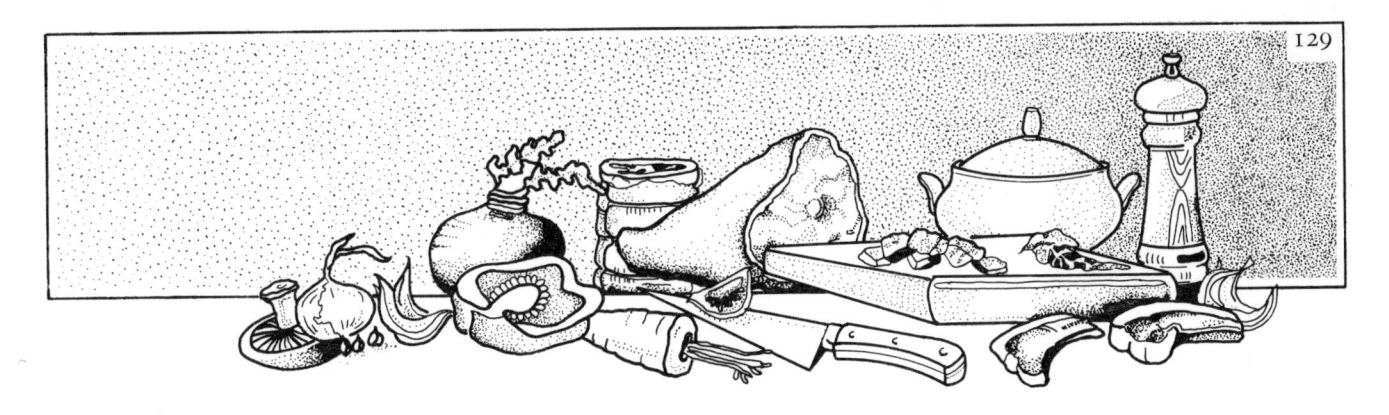

Pork chops with spicy plum sauce

METRIC/IMPERIAL
4 pork loin chops
350g/12oz plums, stoned
2 × 15ml spoons/
  2 tablespoons sugar
2 × 15ml spoons/
  2 tablespoons water
pinch of ground cinnamon
pinch of ground cloves
150ml/¼ pint dry red wine
salt
freshly ground black pepper

AMERICAN
4 pork loin chops
¾lb plums, pitted
2 tablespoons sugar
2 tablespoons water
pinch of ground cinnamon
pinch of ground cloves
⅔ cup dry red wine
salt
freshly ground black pepper

Grill (broil) the chops until they are lightly browned on both sides.

Meanwhile, put the plums, sugar, water and spices in a saucepan. Poach gently for 15 minutes or until the plums are very soft. Pour into the goblet of an electric blender and purée until smooth. Stir in the wine with salt and pepper to taste.

Arrange the chops in a baking dish. Pour over the plum sauce and cover. Cook in a preheated moderate oven (180°C/350°F, Gas Mark 4) for 1 hour or until the chops are tender. Serve hot.
Serves 4

Pork 'n' beans

METRIC/IMPERIAL
4 pork chops
1 × 400g/14oz can tomatoes
1 × 425g/15oz can baked beans
1 onion, peeled and chopped
0.75kg/1½lb potatoes, peeled and thinly sliced
salt
freshly ground black pepper
15g/½oz butter, cut into small pieces

AMERICAN
4 pork chops
1 × 14oz can tomatoes
1 × 15oz can baked beans
1 onion, peeled and chopped
1½lb potatoes, peeled and thinly sliced
salt
freshly ground black pepper
1 tablespoon butter, cut into small pieces

Grill (broil) the pork chops until they are lightly browned on both sides.

Meanwhile, mix together the tomatoes with the can juice, the baked beans and onion. Make a layer of half the potatoes in a greased casserole. Cover with half the bean mixture.

Lay the chops on top and season with salt and pepper. Add the remaining bean mixture. Top with the remaining potatoes, to cover.

Cover the casserole and cook in a preheated cool oven (150°C/300°F, Gas Mark 2) for 2½ hours.

Remove the lid and dot the top with the butter pieces. Cook for a further 30 minutes or until the potato topping is golden brown. Serve hot, from the casserole.
Serves 4

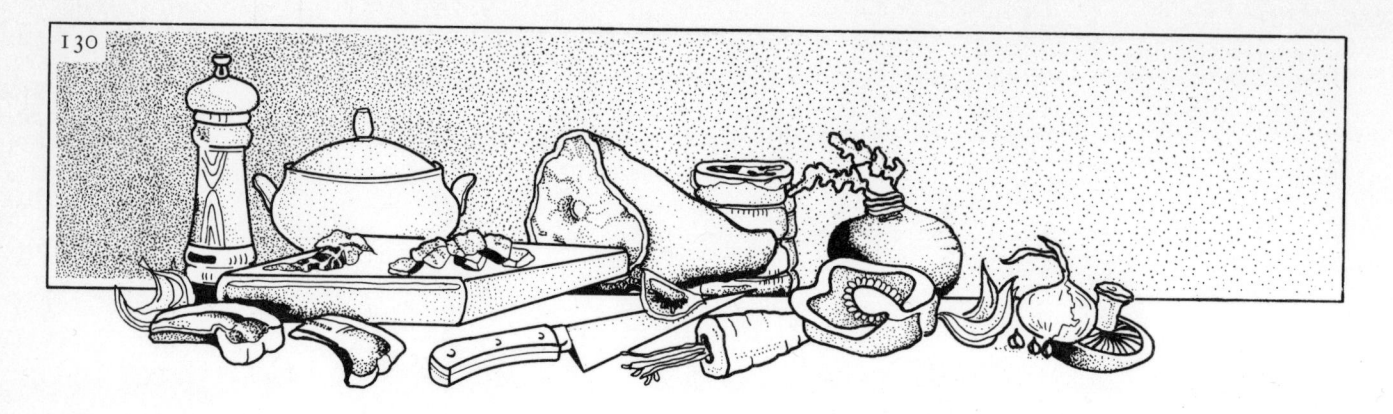

Orange-braised pork chops

METRIC/IMPERIAL
75g/3oz butter
1 large onion, peeled and thinly sliced
1 × 5ml spoon/1 teaspoon dry mustard
2 × 5ml spoons/2 teaspoons brown sugar
salt
freshly ground black pepper
4 pork chops
1 × 15ml spoon/1 tablespoon plain flour
grated rind and juice of 2 oranges
150ml/¼ pint dry white wine
1 orange, peeled and segmented

AMERICAN
⅓ cup butter
1 large onion, peeled and thinly sliced
1 teaspoon dry mustard
2 teaspoons brown sugar
salt
freshly ground black pepper
4 pork chops
1 tablespoon all-purpose flour
grated rind and juice of 2 oranges
⅔ cup dry white wine
1 orange, peeled and segmented

Melt 25g/1oz/2 tablespoons of the butter in a flameproof casserole. Add the onion and fry until it is soft but not brown. Remove from the casserole.

Mix together the mustard, sugar, salt and pepper to taste and blend into the remaining butter. Spread this mixture onto one side of each chop. Fry the chops until golden on both sides. Remove the chops from the pot.

Stir the flour into the fat in the casserole. Add the orange rind and onion. Make up the orange juice to 150ml/¼ pint/⅔ cup with water and stir into the onion mixture with the wine. Bring to the boil, stirring. Return the chops to the casserole and spoon the onion mixture over them. Add the orange segments.

Cover and simmer for 40 minutes or until the chops are cooked. Serve hot.
Serves 4

Pork chop casserole

METRIC/IMPERIAL
25g/1oz butter
1 × 15ml spoon/1 tablespoon olive oil
100g/4oz button onions, peeled
4 large pork chops
3 × 15ml spoons/3 tablespoons plain flour
300ml/½ pint chicken stock
150ml/¼ pint dry cider
225g/8oz tomatoes, peeled and quartered
2 celery sticks, cut into 2.5cm/1 inch pieces
2 dessert apples, cored and sliced
100g/4oz button mushrooms
1 × 5ml spoon/1 teaspoon dried thyme
salt
freshly ground black pepper

AMERICAN
2 tablespoons butter
1 tablespoon olive oil
½ cup peeled baby onions
4 large pork chops
3 tablespoons all-purpose flour
1¼ cups chicken stock
⅔ cup hard cider
½lb tomatoes, peeled and quartered
2 celery stalks, cut into 1 inch pieces
2 dessert apples, cored and sliced
1 cup button mushrooms
1 teaspoon dried thyme
salt
freshly ground black pepper

Melt the butter with the oil in a flameproof casserole. Add the onions and fry until they are lightly browned. Add the chops and brown on both sides. Remove the chops and onions from the pot.

Stir the flour into the fat in the casserole and cook, stirring, for 1 minute. Gradually stir in the stock and cider and bring to the boil, stirring. Return the chops and onions to the casserole and add the tomatoes, celery, apples, mushrooms, thyme and salt and pepper to taste.

Cover the casserole and transfer to a preheated moderate oven (180°C/350°F, Gas Mark 4). Cook for 45 minutes. Serve hot, from the casserole.
Serves 4

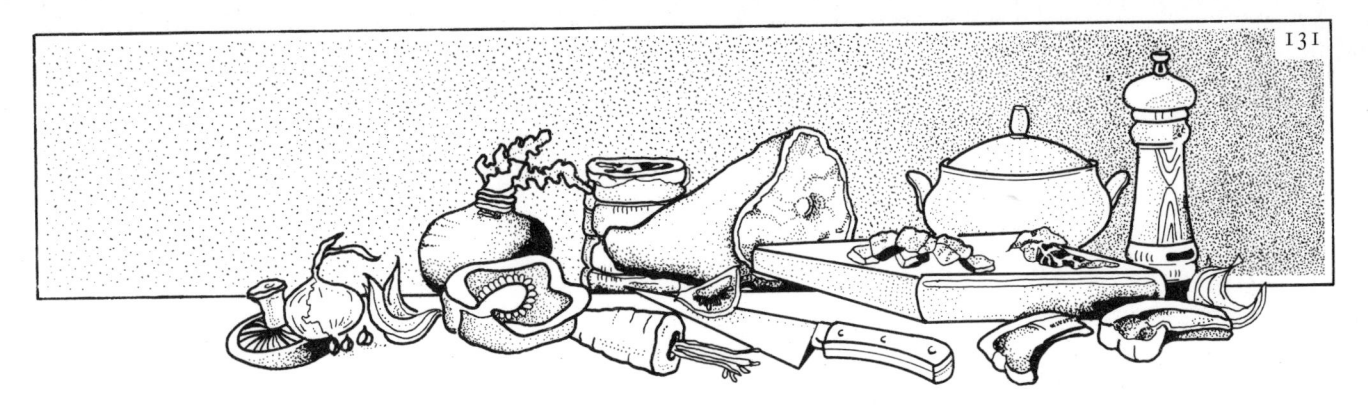

Deep-fried Chinese pork

METRIC/IMPERIAL
0.5kg/1lb lean pork, cut into cubes
450ml/¾ pint water
2 × 15ml spoons/
  2 tablespoons soy sauce
1 × 5ml spoon/1 teaspoon sugar
1 × 15ml spoon/
  1 tablespoon dry sherry
salt
vegetable oil for deep frying
Batter:
100g/4oz self-raising flour
1 egg
150ml/¼ pint water

AMERICAN
1lb lean pork, cut into cubes
2 cups water
2 tablespoons soy sauce
1 teaspoon sugar
1 tablespoon dry sherry
salt
vegetable oil for deep frying
Batter:
1 cup self-rising flour
1 egg
⅔ cup water

Put the pork in a saucepan and add the water, soy sauce, sugar, sherry and salt to taste. Bring to the boil and simmer for 15 minutes or until the pork is tender. Drain well and pat dry with absorbent paper.

To make the batter, sift the flour and a pinch of salt into a mixing bowl. Add the egg and water and beat to a smooth batter. Coat the pork cubes in the batter.

Heat the oil in a deep frying pan (deep fat fryer) until it is 190°C/375°F. Add the pork cubes, in batches, and fry until they are crisp and golden. Drain on absorbent paper and serve hot.
Serves 3 to 4

Pork and vegetable casserole

METRIC/IMPERIAL
25g/1oz butter
2 × 15ml spoons/
  2 tablespoons oil
2 onions, peeled and chopped
2 carrots, peeled and sliced
2 celery sticks, chopped
1 small green pepper, pith and seeds removed and chopped
25g/1oz plain flour
salt
freshly ground black pepper
0.75kg/1½lb lean pork, cut into cubes
600ml/1 pint milk
1 bay leaf

AMERICAN
2 tablespoons butter
2 tablespoons oil
2 onions, peeled and chopped
2 carrots, peeled and sliced
2 celery stalks, chopped
1 small green pepper, pith and seeds removed and chopped
¼ cup all-purpose flour
salt
freshly ground black pepper
1½lb lean pork, cut into cubes
2½ cups milk
1 bay leaf

Melt the butter with the oil in a saucepan. Add the vegetables and cook gently until they are soft but not brown.

Mix the flour with salt and pepper in a polythene (plastic) bag. Add the pork cubes and shake to coat with the seasoned flour. Add the pork to the saucepan, in batches, and fry until browned on all sides. Stir in any remaining seasoned flour and cook, stirring, for 1 minute.

Add the milk and bay leaf and bring to the boil. Cover and simmer for 1¼ to 1½ hours or until the pork is tender. Remove the bay leaf and serve hot.
Serves 4

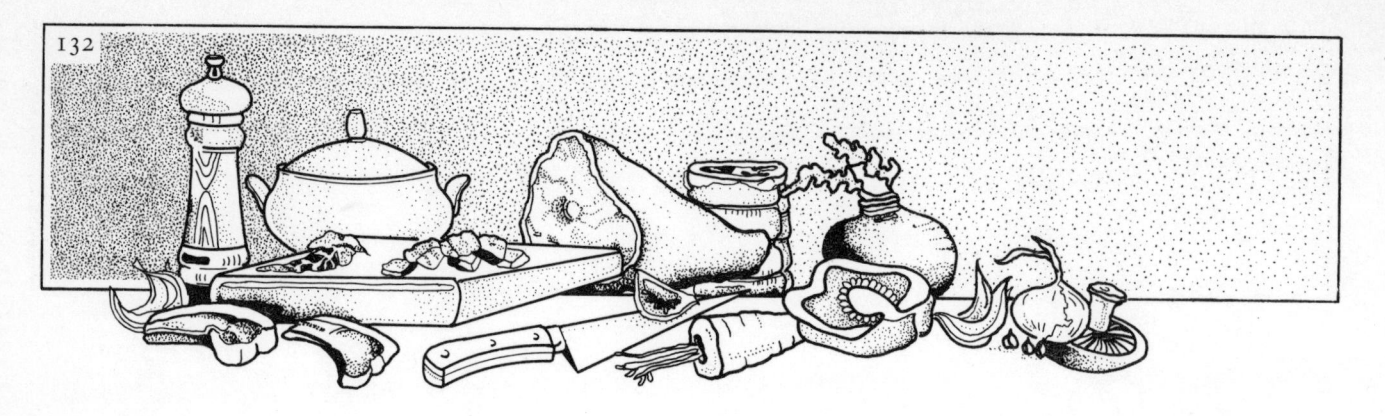

Pork and mushroom stew

METRIC/IMPERIAL
50g/2oz plain flour
salt
freshly ground black pepper
0.75kg/1½lb lean stewing pork, cut into cubes
25g/1oz butter
2 × 15ml spoons/ 2 tablespoons oil
1 onion, peeled and sliced
1 garlic clove, crushed
600ml/1 pint chicken stock
225g/8oz button mushrooms
1 × 5ml spoon/1 teaspoon dried thyme

AMERICAN
½ cup all-purpose flour
salt
freshly ground black pepper
1½lb lean stewing pork, cut into cubes
2 tablespoons butter
2 tablespoons oil
1 onion, peeled and sliced
1 garlic clove, crushed
2½ cups chicken stock
2 cups button mushrooms
1 teaspoon dried thyme

Mix the flour with salt and pepper in a polythene (plastic) bag. Add the pork cubes and shake to coat with the seasoned flour.

Melt the butter with the oil in a saucepan. Add the onion and garlic and fry until the onion is soft but not brown. Add the pork cubes, in batches, and brown on all sides. Stir in the stock and bring to the boil.

Add the mushrooms and thyme, stir well and cover. Simmer for 1½ to 2 hours or until the meat is tender. Serve hot.
Serves 4

Chinese-style quick fried pork

METRIC/IMPERIAL
2 × 15ml spoons/ 2 tablespoons oil
0.5kg/1lb lean pork, cut into thin strips
4 spring onions, chopped
1 × 15ml spoon/ 1 tablespoon soy sauce
2 × 15ml spoons/ 2 tablespoons chicken stock
1 × 5ml spoon/1 teaspoon sugar
0.5kg/1lb bean sprouts
2 canned pineapple rings, finely chopped
freshly ground black pepper

AMERICAN
2 tablespoons oil
1lb lean pork, cut into thin strips
4 scallions, chopped
1 tablespoon soy sauce
2 tablespoons chicken stock
1 teaspoon sugar
1lb bean sprouts
2 canned pineapple rings, finely chopped
freshly ground black pepper

Heat the oil in a frying pan (skillet). Add the pork and stir-fry until browned on all sides. Add the spring onions (scallions) and fry for 2 minutes.

Mix together the soy sauce, stock and sugar and stir into the pan. Add the beans sprouts, pineapple and pepper to taste and bring to the boil. Simmer for 5 minutes or until the pork is cooked. Serve hot.
Serves 4

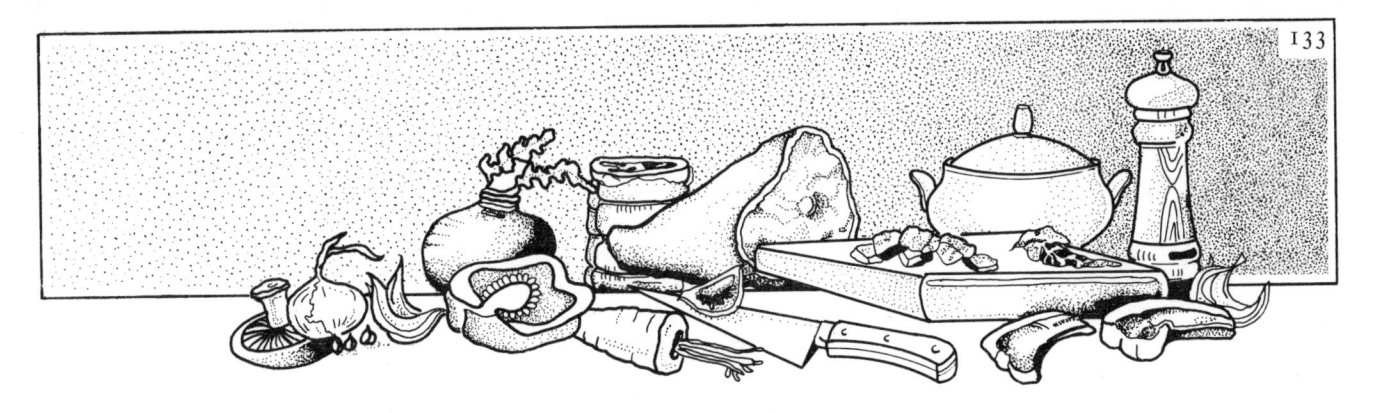

Pork with chestnuts and spinach

METRIC/IMPERIAL
1kg/2lb lean pork, cut into small cubes
600ml/1 pint water
0.5kg/1lb dried skinned chestnuts
4 × 15ml spoons/ 4 tablespoons soy sauce
3 × 15ml spoons/ 3 tablespoons dry sherry
1 × 5ml spoon/1 teaspoon brown sugar
0.5kg/1lb spinach, finely shredded

AMERICAN
2lb lean pork, cut into small cubes
2½ cups water
1lb dried skinned chestnuts
4 tablespoons soy sauce
3 tablespoons dry sherry
1 teaspoon brown sugar
1lb spinach, finely shredded

Put the pork in a saucepan with the water and bring to the boil. Skim off any scum from the surface, then cover the pan and simmer for 1 hour.

Meanwhile, put the chestnuts in another saucepan and cover with cold water. Bring to the boil, cover and simmer for 1 hour. Drain the chestnuts and add to the pork with the soy sauce, sherry and sugar. Continue simmering for 20 minutes.

Put the spinach in a frying pan (skillet) with 2 × 15ml spoons/2 tablespoons of the pork cooking liquid. Stir-fry for about 5 minutes or until the spinach is just tender.

Drain the spinach, put in a warmed serving bowl and pour over the pork and chestnut mixture. Serve hot, with freshly cooked rice.

Serves 4 to 6

Marinated roast loin of pork

METRIC/IMPERIAL
1 × 1.5kg/3lb loin of pork, chined and trimmed of excess fat
1 garlic clove, slivered
salt
freshly ground black pepper
1 × 2.5ml spoon/½ teaspoon dried thyme
150ml/¼ pint dry red wine
3 × 15ml spoons/ 3 tablespoons fresh breadcrumbs
3 × 15ml spoons/ 3 tablespoons chopped fresh parsley

AMERICAN
1 × 3lb loin of pork, chined and trimmed of excess fat
1 garlic clove, slivered
salt
freshly ground black pepper
½ teaspoon dried thyme
⅔ cup dry red wine
3 tablespoons fresh breadcrumbs
3 tablespoons chopped fresh parsley

Make small cuts in the pork and insert the garlic slivers in them. Rub the pork with salt, pepper and the thyme and place it in a polythene (plastic) bag. Pour in the wine and leave to marinate for 3 hours.

Transfer the pork to a roasting tin, fat side up, and pour over the marinade. Cover with foil and roast in a preheated moderate oven (180°C/350°F, Gas Mark 4) for 1¼ hours.

Remove the foil. Mix together the breadcrumbs and parsley and spread over the fat on the pork. Press on well. Baste with the marinade in the tin and continue roasting in a cool oven (150°C/300°F, Gas Mark 2) for 45 minutes, basting occasionally.

Transfer to a warmed serving plate and carve into chops to serve.

Serves 4 to 6

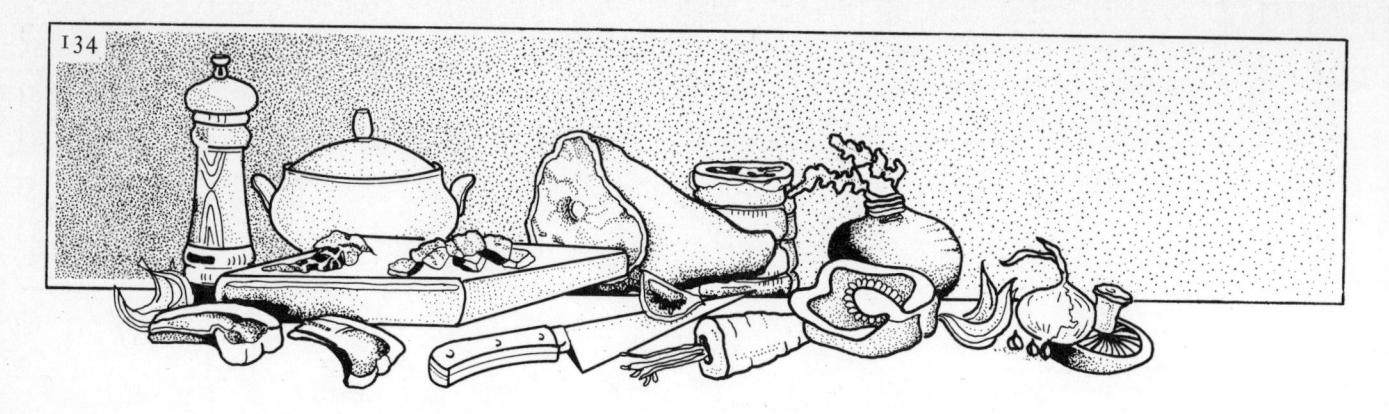

Alsace-style pork

METRIC/IMPERIAL
1 × 1.25kg/2½lb loin or leg
  or pork (boned weight)
25g/1oz dripping, melted
salt
1 small white cabbage,
  cored and shredded
25g/1oz butter
1 small onion, peeled and
  finely chopped
2 cooking apples, peeled,
  cored and sliced
300ml/½ pint dry white
  wine
1 × 5ml spoon/1 teaspoon
  caraway seeds
freshly ground black pepper

AMERICAN
1 × 2½lb loin or leg of pork
  (boned weight)
2 tablespoons drippings,
  melted
salt
1 small head white cabbage,
  cored and shredded
2 tablespoons butter
1 small onion, peeled and
  finely chopped
2 baking apples, peeled,
  cored and sliced
1¼ cups dry white wine
1 teaspoon caraway seeds
freshly ground black pepper

Put the pork in a roasting tin and brush with the dripping. Sprinkle with salt. Roast in a preheated moderately hot oven (200°C/400°F, Gas Mark 6) for 1 hour.

Meanwhile, partially cook the cabbage in boiling water for 5 minutes. Drain and refresh under cold running water.

Melt the butter in a saucepan. Add the onion and fry until it is soft but not brown. Stir in the cabbage, apples, wine, caraway seeds and salt and pepper to taste. Bring to the boil.

Pour off the fat from the roasting tin. Add the cabbage mixture and roast for a further 1 hour or until the pork is cooked. Serve hot.
Serves 4

Loin of pork with apricot stuffing

METRIC/IMPERIAL
1 × 2kg/4½lb loin of pork
  (boned weight)
vegetable oil
Stuffing:
1 × 225g/8oz can apricots
100g/4oz fresh breadcrumbs
50g/2oz butter, melted
75g/3oz raisins
salt
freshly ground black pepper

AMERICAN
1 × 4½lb loin of pork
  (boned weight)
vegetable oil
Stuffing:
1 × ½lb can apricots
2 cups fresh breadcrumbs
¼ cup butter, melted
½ cup raisins
salt
freshly ground black pepper

To make the stuffing, drain the apricots, reserving the syrup. Chop the apricots and mix with the breadcrumbs, butter, raisins and salt and pepper to taste. Add enough of the apricot syrup to bind the mixture.

Lay the pork loin flat and spread with the stuffing. Roll up and tie at intervals with string. Place in a roasting tin and brush with a little oil. Roast in a preheated hot oven (220°C/425°F, Gas Mark 7) for 45 minutes, then reduce the temperature to moderately hot (200°C/400°F, Gas Mark 6). Continue roasting for 1¼ hours or until the pork is cooked. Serve hot.
Serves 6 to 8

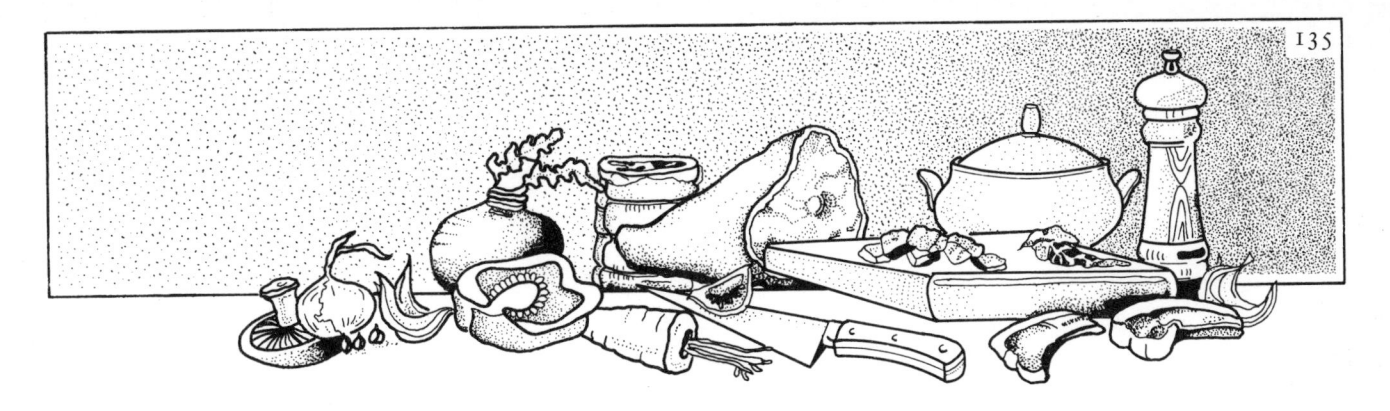

Cold loin of pork oriental

METRIC/IMPERIAL
1 × 2.25kg/5lb loin of pork (boned weight), rolled and tied into shape
2 × 15ml spoons/ 2 tablespoons dry mustard
150ml/¼ pint dry sherry
150ml/¼ pint soy sauce
1 × 5ml spoon/1 teaspoon ground ginger
1 garlic clove, crushed
225g/8oz redcurrant jelly
watercress to garnish

AMERICAN
1 × 5lb loin of pork (boned weight), rolled and tied into shape
2 tablespoons dry mustard
⅔ cup dry sherry
⅔ cup soy sauce
1 teaspoon ground ginger
1 garlic clove, crushed
¾ cup redcurrant jelly
watercress to garnish

Rub the pork with the mustard and put in a polythene (plastic) bag. Mix together 120ml/4fl oz/½ cup each of the sherry and soy sauce, the ginger and garlic and pour into the bag. Leave to marinate for 2 hours.

Remove the pork from the bag and place on a rack in a roasting tin. Pour over the marinade. Roast in a preheated moderate oven (180°C/350°F, Gas Mark 4) for 2½ to 3 hours or until the pork is cooked. Baste occasionally with the marinade.

Put the redcurrant jelly in a saucepan and melt gently. Stir in the remaining sherry and soy sauce and remove from the heat.

Remove the pork from the oven and pour off the marinade from the tin. Allow to cool, then spoon the jelly mixture over the pork to glaze. Allow to set, then serve cold, garnished with watercress.
Serves 8 to 10

Braised loin of pork Normandy

METRIC/IMPERIAL
1 × 1kg/2lb loin of pork (boned weight), rolled and tied into shape
2 cooking apples, peeled, cored and sliced
salt
freshly ground black pepper
25g/1oz butter
1 × 15ml spoon/ 1 tablespoon oil
1 onion, peeled and finely chopped
150ml/¼ pint dry cider
150ml/¼ pint water
1 × 15ml spoon/ 1 tablespoon plain flour
1 × 5ml spoon/1 teaspoon made mustard
150ml/¼ pint sour cream

AMERICAN
1 × 2lb loin of pork (boned weight), rolled and tied into shape
2 baking apples, peeled, cored and sliced
salt
freshly ground black pepper
2 tablespoons butter
1 tablespoon oil
1 onion, peeled and finely chopped
⅔ cup hard cider
⅔ cup water
1 tablespoon all-purpose flour
1 teaspoon prepared mustard
⅔ cup sour cream

Make about 10 slits on both sides of the rolled pork and insert about half the apple slices. Rub the pork with salt and pepper. Melt the butter with the oil in a flameproof casserole. Add the pork and brown on all sides. Remove the pork from the pot.

Add the onion and remaining apple slices to the casserole and fry until the onion is soft but not brown. Return the pork to the casserole and pour over the cider and water. Cover and transfer to a preheated moderate oven (160°C/325°F, Gas Mark 3). Braise for 1½ to 2 hours or until the pork is cooked.

Transfer the pork to a warmed serving dish and keep hot.

Mix together the flour, mustard and sour cream, stirring well to dissolve the flour. Put the casserole on top of the stove and stir in the sour cream mixture. Heat gently, stirring, until the liquid thickens. Serve hot with the pork.
Serves 4

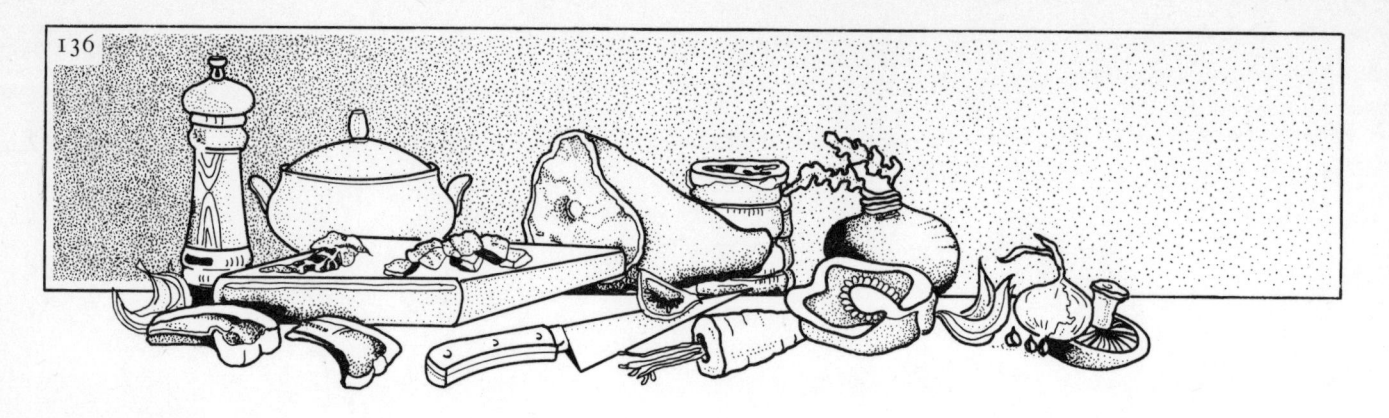

Stuffed pork rolls

METRIC/IMPERIAL
4 × 175g/6oz slices pork fillet, pounded thin
3 × 15ml spoons/
  3 tablespoons plain flour
25g/1oz butter
1 × 15ml spoon/
  1 tablespoon oil
1 small onion, peeled and finely chopped
6 × 15ml spoons/
  6 tablespoons dry white wine
1 × 2.5ml spoon/½ teaspoon paprika
600ml/1 pint chicken stock
Stuffing:
25g/1oz butter
100g/4oz lean bacon, rind removed and diced
1 small onion, peeled and chopped
100g/4oz fresh breadcrumbs
225g/8oz pork sausage meat
1 × 2.5ml spoon/½ teaspoon dried thyme
salt
freshly ground black pepper

AMERICAN
4 × 6oz slices pork tenderloin, pounded thin
3 tablespoons all-purpose flour
2 tablespoons butter
1 tablespoon oil
1 small onion, peeled and finely chopped
6 tablespoons dry white wine
½ teaspoon paprika
2½ cups chicken stock
Stuffing:
2 tablespoons butter
¼lb Canadian bacon, diced
1 small onion, peeled and chopped
2 cups fresh breadcrumbs
1 cup pork sausage meat
½ teaspoon dried thyme
salt
freshly ground black pepper

First make the stuffing. Melt the butter in a frying pan (skillet). Add the bacon and onion and fry until the onion is soft but not brown. Remove from the heat and stir in the remaining stuffing ingredients with salt and pepper to taste. Divide the stuffing between the pork slices and roll up. Tie with string. Coat the pork rolls with the flour.

Melt the butter with the oil in a flameproof casserole. Add the pork rolls and brown on all sides. Remove the pork rolls from the pot.

Add the onion to the casserole and fry until it is soft but not brown. Stir in the wine, paprika and stock and bring to the boil. Return the pork rolls to the casserole and spoon the liquid over them. Transfer the casserole to a preheated moderate oven (180°C/350°F, Gas Mark 4) and cook for 1½ hours.

Transfer the pork rolls to a warmed serving dish. Remove the string. Skim any fat from the surface of the cooking liquid and pour over the pork rolls.
Serves 4

Roast leg of pork

METRIC/IMPERIAL
1 × 1.75kg/4lb leg of pork
1 × 15ml spoon/
  1 tablespoon oil
salt

AMERICAN
1 × 4lb leg of pork
1 tablespoon oil
salt

Score the fat of the pork so that it will come off in strips. Rub with the oil, then liberally with salt. Place in a roasting tin.

Roast in a preheated hot oven (220°C/425°F, Gas Mark 7) for 20 minutes, then reduce the temperature to moderate (180°C/350°F, Gas Mark 4). Continue roasting for 1¾ hours or until the pork is cooked.

Transfer the pork to a carving board. Remove the fat (now crackling) and break into the strips. Carve the pork and serve hot with the crackling.
Serves 6

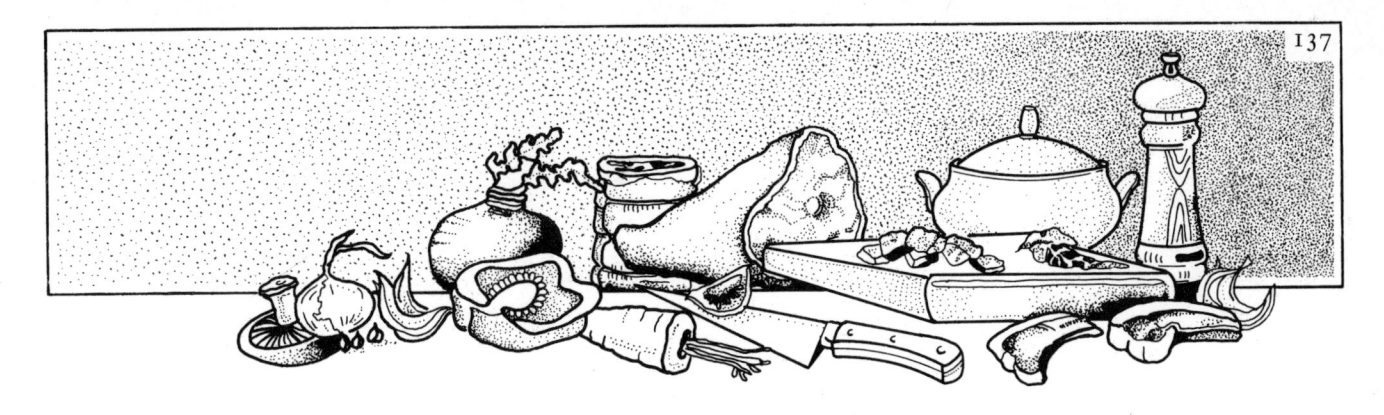

Pork and orange stew

METRIC/IMPERIAL
25g/1oz plain flour
salt
freshly ground black pepper
0.75kg/1½lb pork fillet, cut into cubes
25g/1oz butter
1 small onion, peeled and chopped
1 green pepper, pith and seeds removed and chopped
finely grated rind and juice of 2 oranges
1 × 15ml spoon/ 1 tablespoon Worcestershire sauce
150ml/¼ pint beef stock
1 orange, peeled and segmented

AMERICAN
¼ cup all-purpose flour
salt
freshly ground black pepper
1½lb pork tenderloin, cut into cubes
2 tablespoons butter
1 small onion, peeled and chopped
1 green pepper, pith and seeds removed and chopped
finely grated rind and juice of 2 oranges
1 tablespoon Worcestershire sauce
⅔ cup beef stock
1 orange, peeled and segmented

Mix the flour with salt and pepper in a polythene (plastic) bag. Add the pork cubes and shake to coat with the seasoned flour. Melt the butter in a saucepan. Add the onion and green pepper and fry until the onion is soft but not brown.

Push the vegetables to one side and add the pork cubes, in batches. Brown on all sides. Stir in the orange rind and juice, Worcestershire sauce, stock and salt and pepper to taste. Bring to the boil and simmer for 10 minutes.

Stir in the orange segments and cook for a further 2 to 3 minutes. Serve hot.

Serves 4

Sweet and sour pork

METRIC/IMPERIAL
25g/1oz cornflour
salt
freshly ground black pepper
0.75kg/1½lb pork fillet, cut into cubes
2 × 15ml spoons/ 2 tablespoons oil
3 canned pineapple rings, chopped
4 × 15ml spoons/ 4 tablespoons pineapple syrup (from the can)
3 × 15ml spoons/ 3 tablespoons cocktail onions
2 × 15ml spoons/ 2 tablespoons vinegar
300ml/½ pint chicken stock
1 × 15ml spoon/ 1 tablespoon clear honey
2 × 15ml spoons/ 2 tablespoons medium sherry
2 × 5ml spoons/2 teaspoons soy sauce
1 × 15ml spoon/ 1 tablespoon tomato ketchup

AMERICAN
¼ cup cornstarch
salt
freshly ground black pepper
1½lb pork tenderloin, cut into cubes
2 tablespoons oil
3 canned pineapple rings, chopped
4 tablespoons pineapple syrup (from the can)
3 tablespoons cocktail onions
2 tablespoons vinegar
1¼ cups chicken stock
1 tablespoon clear honey
2 tablespoons medium sherry
2 teaspoons soy sauce
1 tablespoon tomato ketchup

Mix all but 1 × 15ml spoon/1 tablespoon of the cornflour (cornstarch) with salt and pepper in a polythene (plastic) bag. Add the pork and shake to coat with the seasoned cornflour (cornstarch). Heat the oil in a frying pan (skillet). Add the pork cubes, in batches, and brown on all sides. When all the pork cubes have been browned, return to the pan and continue to cook until tender.

Meanwhile, put the pineapple, pineapple syrup, onions, vinegar, stock, honey, the remaining cornflour (cornstarch) dissolved in the sherry, the soy sauce and ketchup in a saucepan. Bring to the boil, stirring, and simmer until thickened and smooth.

Transfer the pork to a warmed serving dish. Pour over the sauce and serve hot.

Serves 4

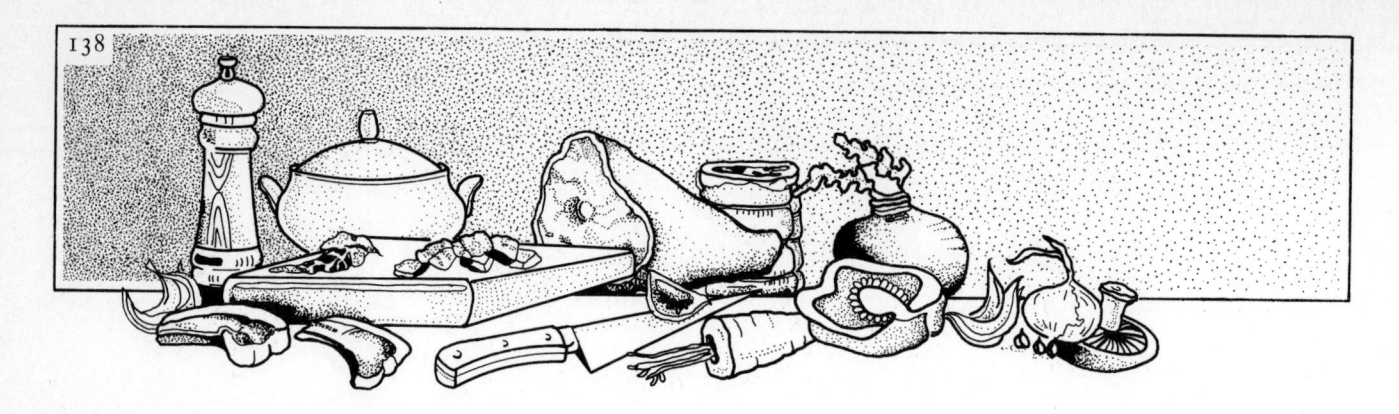

Pork in creamy prune sauce

METRIC/IMPERIAL	AMERICAN
25g/1oz butter	2 tablespoons butter
1 × 15ml spoon/ 1 tablespoon olive oil	1 tablespoon olive oil
1 onion, peeled and finely chopped	1 onion, peeled and finely chopped
1kg/2lb pork fillet, cut into cubes	2lb pork tenderloin, cut into cubes
1 × 15ml spoon/ 1 tablespoon plain flour	1 tablespoon all-purpose flour
salt	salt
freshly ground black pepper	freshly ground black pepper
12 prunes, stoned and soaked overnight in 300ml/½ pint dry white wine	12 prunes, pitted and soaked overnight in 1¼ cups dry white wine
1 × 15ml spoon/ 1 tablespoon redcurrant jelly	1 tablespoon redcurrant jelly
150ml/¼ pint double cream	⅔ cup heavy cream

Melt the butter with the oil in a flameproof casserole. Add the onion and fry until it is soft but not brown. Add the pork, in batches, and brown on all sides. Remove the pork from the casserole.

Sprinkle the flour over the onion with salt and pepper to taste. Cook, stirring, for 1 minute. Gradually stir in the wine used for soaking the prunes and bring to the boil. Add the prunes and return the pork cubes to the casserole. Stir well.

Cover and transfer to a preheated moderate oven (180°C/350°F, Gas Mark 4). Cook for 45 minutes to 1 hour or until the pork is tender.

Stir in the jelly, then gradually stir in the cream. Reheat gently on top of the stove but do not allow to boil. Serve hot.
Serves 4

Pork fillet (tenderloin) with vermouth

METRIC/IMPERIAL	AMERICAN
1kg/2lb pork fillet, cut into 4 pieces	2lb pork tenderloin, cut into 4 pieces
salt	salt
freshly ground black pepper	freshly ground black pepper
50g/2oz butter	¼ cup butter
300ml/½ pint dry vermouth	1¼ cups dry vermouth
2 × 5ml spoons/2 teaspoons cornflour	2 teaspoons cornstarch
2 × 15ml spoons/ 2 tablespoons water	2 tablespoons water
4 × 15ml spoons/ 4 tablespoons double cream	4 tablespoons heavy cream

Rub the pork with salt and pepper. Melt the butter in a flameproof casserole. Add the pork and brown on all sides. Pour in the vermouth and bring to the boil. Cover and transfer to a preheated moderate oven (180°C/350°F, Gas Mark 4). Cook for 45 minutes or until the pork is tender.

Transfer the pork to a warmed serving plate and keep hot.

Dissolve the cornflour (cornstarch) in the water. Put the casserole on top of the stove and stir in the cornflour (cornstarch) mixture. Bring to the boil, stirring, and simmer until reduced and thickened. Remove from the heat and stir in the cream. Pour the sauce over the pork and serve hot.
Serves 4

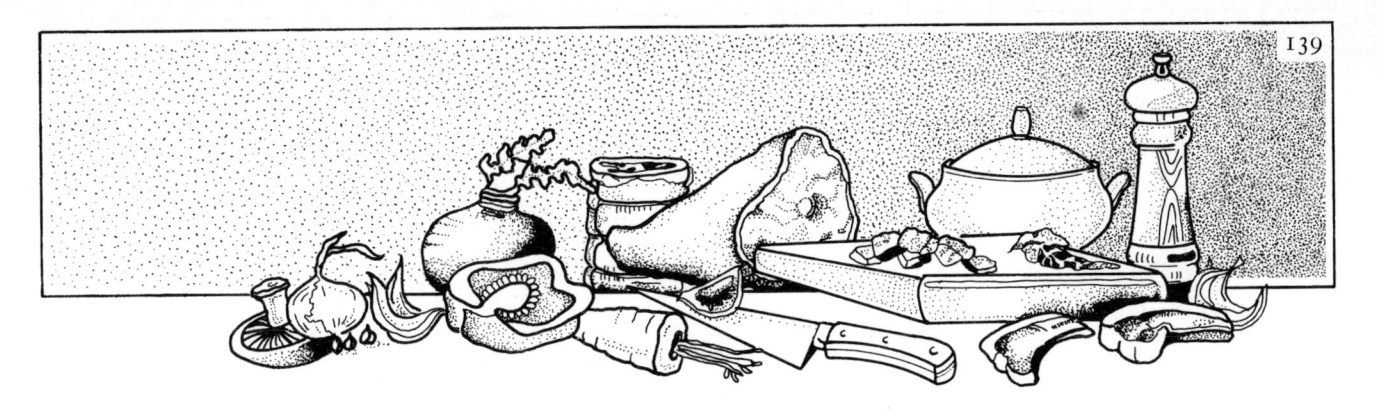

Chinese quick-roast pork

METRIC/IMPERIAL
2.5 × 15ml spoons/
  2½ tablespoons soy sauce
1 × 2.5ml spoon/½ teaspoon salt
1.5 × 15ml spoons/
  1½ tablespoons vegetable oil
1.5 × 5ml spoons/
  1½ teaspoons sugar
1 × 0.75kg/1½lb pork fillet

AMERICAN
2½ tablespoons soy sauce
½ teaspoon salt
1½ tablespoons vegetable oil
1½ teaspoons sugar
1 × 1½lb pork tenderloin

Mix together the soy sauce, salt, oil and sugar in a long shallow dish. Add the pork and turn to coat with the marinade. Leave to marinate for 2 hours, turning every 30 minutes.

Transfer the pork to a rack in a roasting tin. Roast in a preheated hot oven (230°C/450°F, Gas Mark 8) for 15 minutes, turning once and basting with any remaining marinade.

Cut the pork across the grain into slices and transfer to a warmed serving dish. Serve hot.
Serves 4

Pork fillet (tenderloin) with cheese

METRIC/IMPERIAL
1 × 1kg/2lb pork fillet
salt
freshly ground black pepper
50g/2oz butter
1 × 5ml spoon/1 teaspoon dried sage
225g/8oz Gruyère cheese, cut into 12 slices
1 × 15ml spoon/
  1 tablespoon made French mustard
150ml/¼ pint single cream

AMERICAN
1 × 2lb pork tenderloin
salt
freshly ground black pepper
¼ cup butter
1 teaspoon dried sage
½lb Gruyère cheese, cut into 12 slices
1 tablespoon prepared French mustard
⅔ cup light cream

Rub the pork with salt and pepper. Melt the butter in a frying pan (skillet). Add the pork and brown on all sides. Sprinkle over the sage, cover and cook gently for 40 minutes.

Remove the pork from the pan and make 12 cuts in it. Insert a cheese slice in each cut. Return to the pan and cook, uncovered, for a further 5 to 10 minutes or until the cheese has melted.

Transfer the pork to a warmed serving plate and keep hot.

Stir the mustard and cream into the cooking juices in the pan. Heat through gently, then pour over the pork. Serve hot.
Serves 4

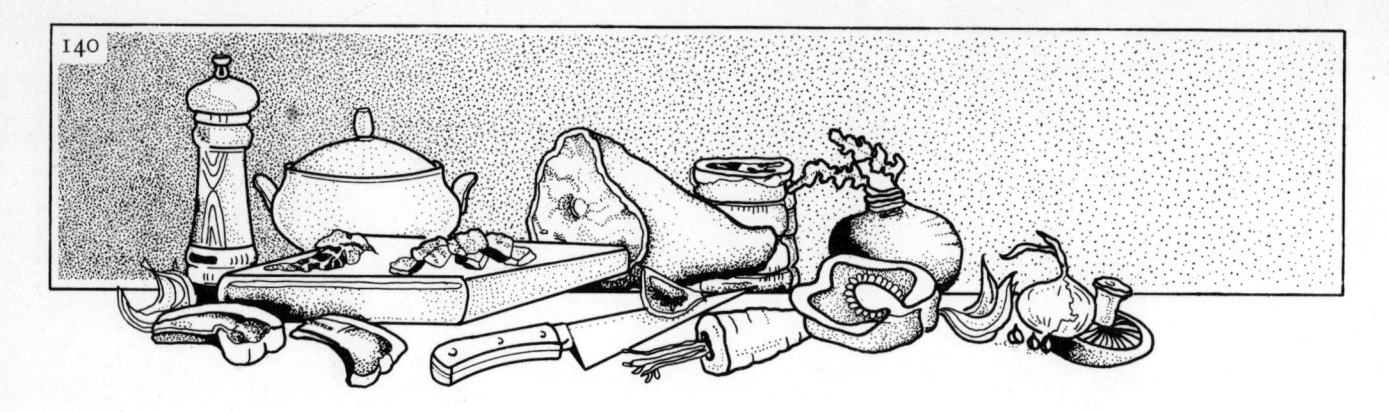

Sweet and sour spareribs

METRIC/IMPERIAL
1.75kg/4lb pork spareribs, or sparerib chops
salt
2 × 15ml spoons/ 2 tablespoons oil
1 large onion, peeled and finely chopped
1 garlic clove, crushed
1 × 15ml spoon/ 1 tablespoon tomato purée
2 × 15ml spoons/ 2 tablespoons soy sauce
1 × 15ml spoon/ 1 tablespoon brown sugar
1 × 15ml spoon/ 1 tablespoon clear honey
freshly ground black pepper
300ml/½ pint chicken stock
juice of ½ lemon

AMERICAN
4lb pork spareribs
salt
2 tablespoons oil
1 large onion, peeled and finely chopped
1 garlic clove, crushed
1 tablespoon tomato paste
2 tablespoons soy sauce
1 tablespoon brown sugar
1 tablespoon clear honey
freshly ground black pepper
1¼ cups chicken stock
juice of ½ lemon

Put the spareribs or chops in a roasting tin and sprinkle with salt. Roast in a preheated moderately hot oven (190°C/375°F, Gas Mark 5) for 30 minutes.

Meanwhile, heat the oil in a saucepan. Add the onion and garlic and fry until soft but not brown. Remove from the heat. Stir in the tomato purée (paste), soy sauce, sugar, honey, pepper to taste, the stock and lemon juice.

Remove the pork from the roasting tin and pour off the fat. Cut the spareribs into two-rib pieces. (Cut the chops into bite-sized pieces.) Return to the tin and pour over the sauce. Roast for a further 1 to 1½ hours or until the meat is tender. Serve hot.
Serves 4 to 6

Pork sausages in white wine sauce

METRIC/IMPERIAL
0.5kg/1lb pork sausages
50g/2oz butter
1 medium onion, peeled and thinly sliced
225g/8oz lean bacon rashers, rinds removed and diced
2 × 15ml spoons/ 2 tablespoons plain flour
300ml/½ pint chicken stock
4 × 15ml spoons/ 4 tablespoons dry white wine
salt
freshly ground black pepper
chopped parsley to garnish

AMERICAN
1lb pork sausages
¼ cup butter
1 medium onion, peeled and thinly sliced
½lb Canadian bacon, diced
2 tablespoons all-purpose flour
1¼ cups chicken stock
4 tablespoons dry white wine
salt
freshly ground black pepper
chopped parsley to garnish

Twist the sausages in the centre and cut into 2 smaller sausages. Melt the butter in a frying pan (skillet). Add the sausages and brown quickly on all sides. Remove the sausages from the pan.

Add the onion and bacon to the pan and fry until the onion is soft but not brown. Stir in the flour, then gradually stir in the stock and wine. Bring to the boil, stirring.

Return the sausages to the pan with salt and pepper to taste. Cover and simmer for 6 to 8 minutes or until the sausages are cooked through.

Serve hot, garnished with parsley.
Serves 4

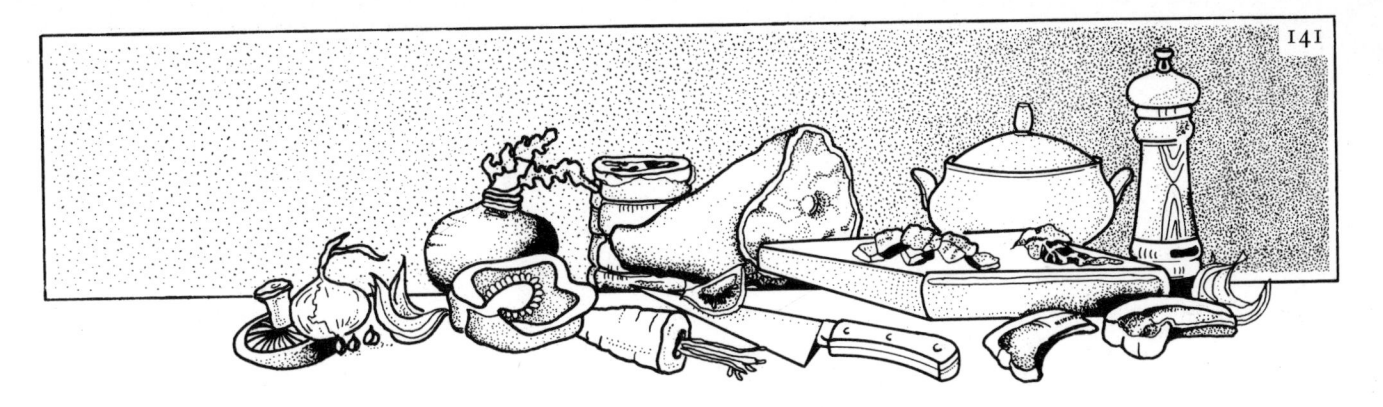

Glazed baked gammon (ham)

METRIC/IMPERIAL
1 × 2.25kg/5lb gammon joint, soaked in cold water and drained
6 black peppercorns
12 juniper berries, lightly crushed
2 onions, skinned and quartered
1 bay leaf
350g/12oz brown sugar
about 30 whole cloves

AMERICAN
1 × 5lb unprocessed smoked ham
6 black peppercorns
12 juniper berries, lightly crushed
2 onions, skinned and quartered
1 bay leaf
2 cups brown sugar
about 30 whole cloves

Put the gammon (ham) in a large saucepan and add the peppercorns, juniper berries, onions and bay leaf. Add enough cold water to cover and bring to the boil. Simmer, allowing 20 minutes per 0.5kg/1lb plus 20 minutes over. Drain the gammon (ham) well. Allow to cool slightly, then remove the skin.

Place the gammon (ham) in a roasting tin and score the fat in a diamond pattern. Sprinkle the sugar over the fat to cover well. Press a clove into the centre of each diamond shape.

Bake in a preheated moderately hot oven (200°C/400°F, Gas Mark 6) for 20 minutes or until the fat is crisp and golden. Serve hot or cold.

Serves 8 to 10

Spareribs with maple syrup sauce

METRIC/IMPERIAL
1.75kg/4lb pork spareribs, cut into 2 rib pieces
175ml/6fl oz maple syrup
1 garlic clove, crushed
2 × 15ml spoons/ 2 tablespoons tomato purée
1 × 5ml spoon/1 teaspoon lemon juice
1 × 15ml spoon/ 1 tablespoon made French mustard

AMERICAN
4lb pork spareribs, cut into 2 rib pieces
¾ cup maple syrup
1 garlic clove, crushed
2 tablespoons tomato paste
1 teaspoon lemon juice
1 tablespoon prepared French mustard

Put the spareribs in a roasting tin. Roast in a preheated moderately hot oven (200°C/400°F, Gas Mark 6) for 30 minutes.

Meanwhile, mix together the remaining ingredients.

Pour off the fat from the roasting tin. Pour the maple syrup mixture over the spareribs and return to a moderate oven (180°C/350°F, Gas Mark 4). Roast for a further 45 minutes or until the ribs are tender and glazed. Serve hot.

Serves 4 to 6

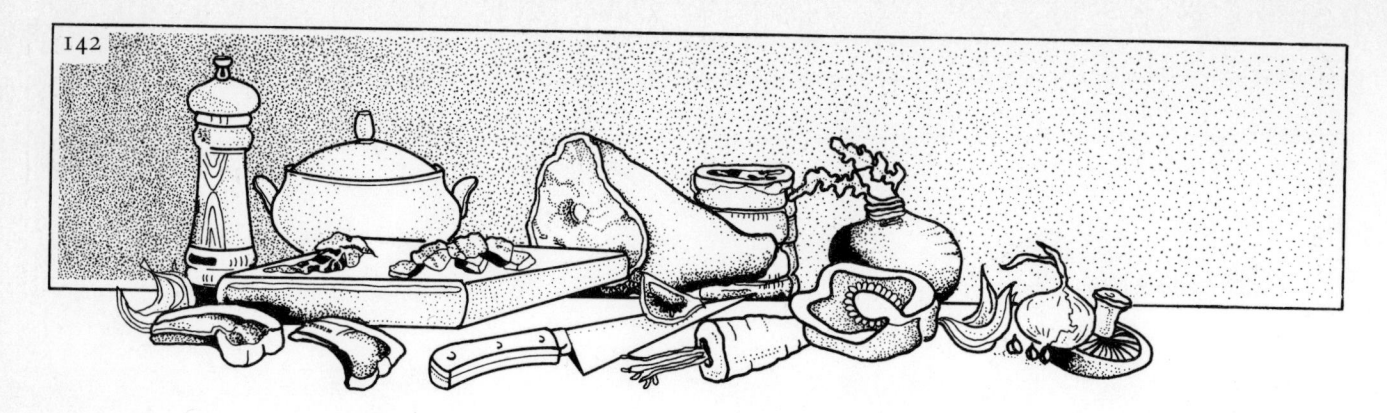

Spiced orange gammon (ham)

METRIC/IMPERIAL
1 × 2.25kg/5lb gammon joint, soaked in cold water and drained
6 black peppercorns
12 juniper berries, lightly crushed
1 bay leaf
175g/6oz butter
150g/5oz soft brown sugar
grated rind and juice of 3 oranges
5 × 15ml spoons/ 5 tablespoons cider vinegar
1 × 2.5ml spoon/ ½ teaspoon ground ginger
salt
freshly ground black pepper
2 oranges, sliced

AMERICAN
1 × 5lb unprocessed smoked ham
6 black peppercorns
12 juniper berries, lightly crushed
1 bay leaf
¾ cup butter
¾ cup brown sugar
grated rind and juice of 3 oranges
⅓ cup cider vinegar
½ teaspoon ground ginger
salt
freshly ground black pepper
2 oranges, sliced

Put the gammon (ham) in a large saucepan and add the peppercorns, juniper berries and bay leaf. Add enough cold water to cover and bring to the boil. Simmer, allowing 20 minutes per 0.5kg/1lb plus 20 minutes over. Drain the gammon (ham) well. Allow to cool slightly, then remove the skin. Wrap in foil and place in a roasting tin. Keep warm.

Put the butter and sugar in a saucepan and heat gently, stirring to dissolve the sugar. Bring to the boil and boil until golden. Remove from the heat and stir in the orange rind and juice, vinegar, ginger and salt and pepper to taste. Return to the heat and simmer gently for 10 minutes.

Meanwhile, poach the orange slices in water to cover until the rinds are soft. Drain and add to the orange caramel. Simmer for a further 5 minutes.

Unwrap the gammon (ham) and coat with a little of the orange caramel. Bake in a preheated hot oven (220°C/425°F, Gas Mark 7) for 20 minutes.

Serve hot with the remaining orange caramel sauce.
Serves 8 to 10

Gammon (ham) braised in beer

METRIC/IMPERIAL
1 × 1.5kg/3lb gammon joint, soaked in cold water and drained
1 onion, peeled and chopped
50g/2oz brown sugar
1 × 2.5ml spoon/½ teaspoon dried thyme
300ml/½ pint beer

AMERICAN
1 × 3lb unprocessed smoked ham
1 onion, peeled and chopped
⅓ cup brown sugar
½ teaspoon dried thyme
1¼ cups dark beer

Put the gammon (ham) in a saucepan and add the onion, 1 × 15ml spoon/1 tablespoon of the sugar and the thyme. Pour over water to cover and bring to the boil. Cover and simmer for 1½ hours or until the ham is cooked.

Drain the ham and place it in a baking dish. Pour over the beer and sprinkle with the remaining sugar. Braise in a preheated moderately hot oven (200°C/400°F, Gas Mark 6) for 45 minutes, basting occasionally with the beer. Serve hot, with the cooking juices as a sauce.
Serves 6 to 8

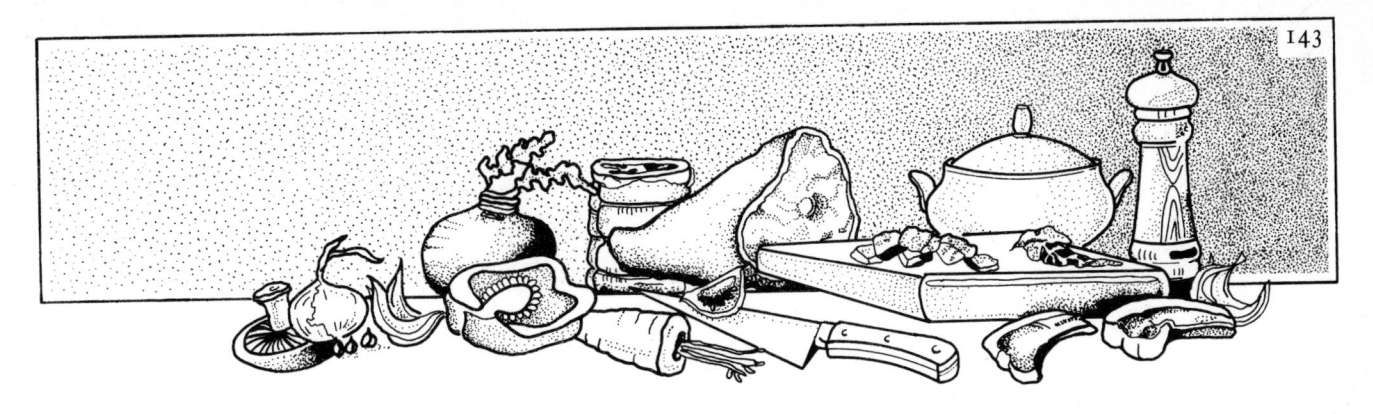

Ham with corn sauce

METRIC/IMPERIAL
75g/3oz butter
8 thick slices cooked ham
1 small onion, peeled and finely chopped
25g/1oz plain flour
300ml/½ pint milk
salt
freshly ground black pepper
6 × 15ml spoons/ 6 tablespoons canned sweetcorn
pinch of cayenne pepper

AMERICAN
⅓ cup butter
8 thick slices cooked ham
1 small onion, peeled and finely chopped
¼ cup all-purpose flour
1¼ cups milk
salt
freshly ground black pepper
6 tablespoons canned corn kernels
pinch of cayenne pepper

Melt 50g/2oz/¼ cup of the butter in a frying pan (skillet). Add the ham slices and cook gently, turning occasionally, for 10 minutes or until heated through.

Meanwhile, melt the remaining butter in a saucepan. Add the onion and fry until it is soft but not brown. Stir in the flour and cook, stirring, for 1 minute. Remove from the heat and gradually stir in the milk. Return to the heat and bring to the boil, stirring. Simmer until thickened.

Add salt and pepper to taste, the corn and cayenne. Remove from the heat and keep hot.

Transfer the ham slices to a warmed serving dish. Pour over the corn sauce and serve hot.
Serves 4

Gammon (ham) French style

METRIC/IMPERIAL
1 × 1.5kg/3lb gammon joint, soaked in cold water and drained
1 onion, peeled
4 whole cloves
4 peppercorns
1 bouquet garni
1 carrot, peeled and sliced
½ bottle dry red wine
2 × 5ml spoons/2 teaspoons arrowroot
1 × 15ml spoon/ 1 tablespoon water

AMERICAN
1 × 3lb unprocessed smoked ham
1 onion, peeled
4 whole cloves
4 peppercorns
1 bouquet garni
1 carrot, peeled and sliced
½ bottle dry red wine
2 teaspoons arrowroot flour
1 tablespoon water

Put the gammon (ham) in a saucepan and add the onion, cloves, peppercorns, bouquet garni and carrot. Pour over enough water to cover and bring to the boil. Simmer for 1 hour.

Drain the gammon (ham), reserving 600ml/1 pint/ 2½ cups of the cooking liquid. Remove the skin and place the gammon (ham) in a baking dish or casserole. Pour over the wine and reserved cooking liquid. Braise in a preheated moderate oven (160°C/325°F, Gas Mark 3) for 1 hour, basting occasionally.

Transfer to a carving board or warmed serving plate and keep hot. Strain the cooking liquid into a saucepan. Dissolve the arrowroot in the water and add to the liquid. Bring to the boil, stirring, and simmer for 3 minutes or until thickened. Serve with the gammon (ham).
Serves 6 to 8

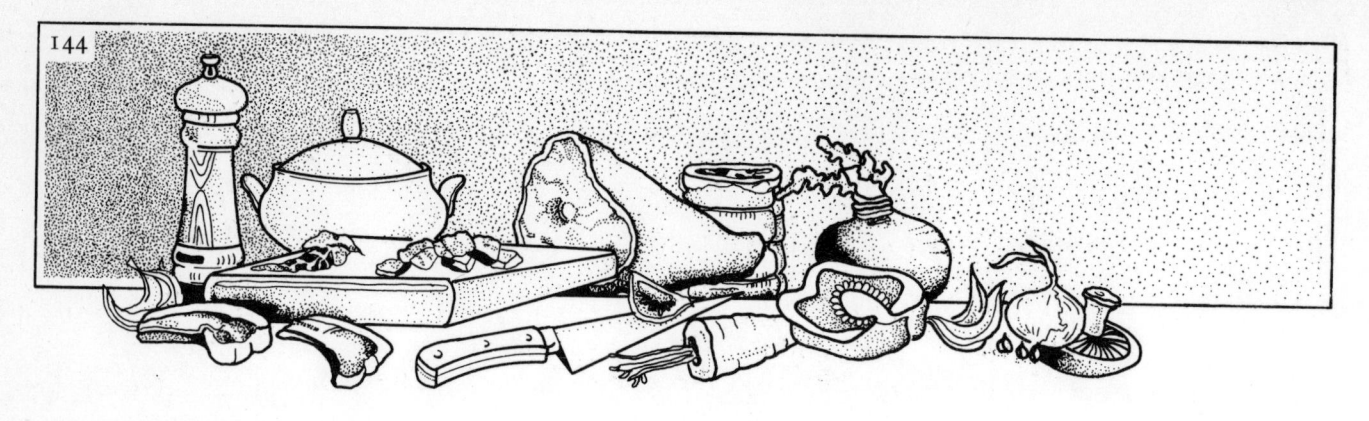

Ham rolls with curried rice

METRIC/IMPERIAL
175g/6oz long-grain rice
salt
1 × 2.5ml spoon/½ teaspoon powdered saffron
1 bay leaf
75g/3oz butter, melted
1 small cooking apple, peeled, cored and finely chopped
1 small onion, peeled and finely chopped
2 × 5ml spoons/2 teaspoons mild curry powder
6 × 15ml spoons/ 6 tablespoons single cream
grated rind and juice of 1 small lemon
freshly ground black pepper
1 small red pepper, pith and seeds removed and diced
12 slices of lean cooked ham
parsley sprigs to garnish

AMERICAN
1 cup long-grain rice
salt
½ teaspoon powdered saffron
1 bay leaf
⅓ cup butter, melted
1 small baking apple, peeled, cored and finely chopped
1 small onion, peeled and finely chopped
2 teaspoons mild curry power
6 tablespoons light cream
grated rind and juice of 1 small lemon
freshly ground black pepper
1 small pimiento, pith and seeds removed and diced
12 slices of lean cooked ham
parsley sprigs to garnish

Cook the rice in boiling salted water, to which the saffron and bay leaf have been added, according to the directions on the package. Remove from the heat and discard the bay leaf. Add 40g/1½oz/3 tablespoons of the butter and stir into the rice. Allow to cool.

Put the remaining melted butter in a frying pan (skillet) and heat. Add the apple and onion and fry until the onion is soft but not brown. Stir in the curry powder and cook for 1 minute, stirring.

Remove from the heat and stir in the cream. Stir the apple mixture into the rice with the lemon rind and juice, salt and pepper to taste and the red pepper (pimiento). Mix well and allow to cool.

Divide the rice mixture between the ham slices and roll up. Arrange on a serving dish and garnish with parsley sprigs. Serve cold.
Serves 6

Ham Italiana

METRIC/IMPERIAL
4 thick gammon steaks
1 × 5ml spoon/1 teaspoon dried sage
225g/8oz fettucine verde
salt
25g/1oz butter
300ml/½ pint hot tomato sauce★
8 black olives, halved and stoned

AMERICAN
4 thick ham steaks
1 teaspoon dried sage
½lb fettucine verde
salt
2 tablespoons butter
1¼ cups hot tomato sauce★
8 black olives, halved and pitted

Rub the gammon (ham) steaks with the sage and arrange on a rack in a grill (broiler) pan. Grill (broil) for 6 to 7 minutes on each side or until cooked through.

Meanwhile, cook the fettucine in boiling salted water until *al dente* (just tender to the bite). Drain well and stir in the butter. Arrange on a warmed serving plate.

Place the gammon (ham) steaks on top of the fettucine and pour over the tomato sauce. Sprinkle with the olive halves and serve hot.
Serves 4

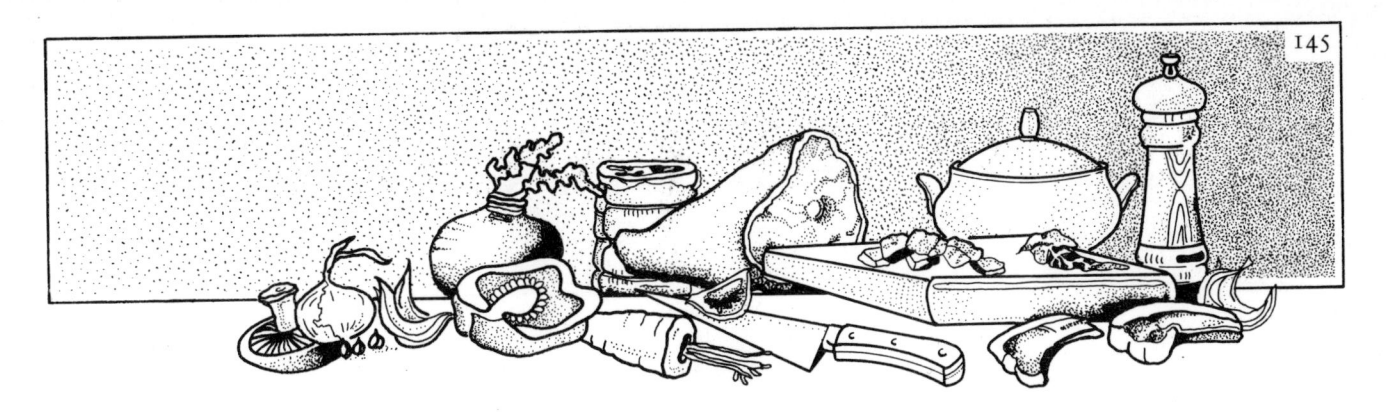

Ham and asparagus rolls

METRIC/IMPERIAL
1 × 425g/15oz can asparagus spears, drained
6 large slices cooked ham
300ml/½ pint hot mornay sauce★

AMERICAN
1 × 15oz can asparagus spears, drained
6 large slices cooked ham
1¼ cups hot mornay sauce★

Divide the asparagus between the ham slices and roll up. Arrange the ham rolls in a baking dish. Pour over the sauce.
  Bake in a preheated moderate oven (180°C/350°F, Gas Mark 4) for 20 minutes or until heated through. Serve hot.
Serves 4 to 6

Ham in Madeira sauce

METRIC/IMPERIAL
25g/1oz butter
1 small onion, peeled and finely chopped
2 × 15ml spoons/ 2 tablespoons plain flour
300ml/½ pint chicken stock
4 × 15ml spoons/ 4 tablespoons Madeira
4 × 15ml spoons/ 4 tablespoons double cream
salt
freshly ground black pepper
8 thick slices cooked ham

AMERICAN
2 tablespoons butter
1 small onion, peeled and finely chopped
2 tablespoons all-purpose flour
1¼ cups chicken stock
4 tablespoons Madeira
4 tablespoons heavy cream
salt
freshly ground black pepper
8 thick slices cooked ham

Melt the butter in a frying pan (skillet). Add the onion and fry until it is soft but not brown. Sprinkle over the flour and cook, stirring, for 1 minute. Gradually stir in the stock and bring to the boil, stirring. Simmer until thickened.
  Stir in the Madeira and cream with salt and pepper to taste. Place the ham slices in the pan and spoon the sauce over them. Heat through gently for 5 minutes. Serve hot.
Serves 4

POULTRY & GAME

Chicken pie

METRIC/IMPERIAL
1 × 1.75kg/4lb chicken
1 small onion, peeled and halved
1 carrot, peeled
1 leek, thoroughly cleaned and halved
6 peppercorns
salt
175g/6oz quantity puff pastry★ (made with 175g/6oz plain flour, etc.)
1 egg, lightly beaten
Sauce:
50g/2oz butter
1 onion, peeled and chopped
2 red peppers, pith and seeds removed and chopped
25g/1oz plain flour
100g/4oz Cheddar cheese, grated
freshly ground black pepper

AMERICAN
1 × 4lb chicken
1 small onion, peeled and halved
1 carrot, peeled
1 leek, thoroughly cleaned and halved
6 peppercorns
salt
1½ cup quantity puff pastry★ (made with 1½ cups all-purpose flour, etc.)
1 egg, lightly beaten
Sauce:
¼ cup butter
1 onion, peeled and chopped
2 pimientos, pith and seeds removed and chopped
¼ cup all-purpose flour
1 cup grated Cheddar cheese
freshly ground black pepper

Put the chicken, onion, carrot, leek, peppercorns and salt to taste in a saucepan. Add enough cold water to cover and bring to the boil. Simmer for 2 hours or until the chicken is tender.

Remove the chicken from the pan. Bring the cooking liquid back to the boil and boil until it has reduced to 600ml/1 pint/2½ cups. Strain and reserve.

When the chicken is cool enough to handle, remove the meat from the carcass and cut it into bite-sized pieces.

Melt the butter in a saucepan. Add the onion and peppers (pimientos) and fry until the onion is soft but not brown. Stir in the flour and cook, stirring, for 1 minute. Gradually stir in the reserved chicken stock and bring to the boil, stirring. Simmer until thickened. Stir in the cheese with salt and pepper to taste. When the cheese has melted, remove from the heat and fold in the chicken. Spoon into a 1.75 litre/3 pint/7½ cup pie dish with a funnel. Allow to cool.

Roll out the dough and use to cover the pie dish. Use the trimmings to decorate the top. Brush with the beaten egg. Bake in a preheated hot oven (230°C/450°F, Gas Mark 8) for 30 minutes. Reduce the temperature to moderate (160°C/325°F, Gas Mark 3) and continue baking for 30 minutes. Serve hot.
Serves 6

Roast chicken with sweetsour stuffing

METRIC/IMPERIAL
0.5kg/1lb sausage meat
3 × 15ml spoons/ 3 tablespoons raisins
3 × 15ml spoons/ 3 tablespoons chopped walnuts
3 × 15ml spoons/ 3 tablespoons chopped gherkins
2 × 5ml spoons/2 teaspoons chopped fresh parsley
1 egg, lightly beaten
chicken stock
1 × 1.75kg/4lb chicken
watercress to garnish

AMERICAN
2 cups sausage meat
3 tablespoons raisins
3 tablespoons chopped walnuts
3 tablespoons chopped dill pickles
2 teaspoons chopped fresh parsley
1 egg, lightly beaten
chicken stock
1 × 4lb chicken
watercress to garnish

Mix together the sausage meat, raisins, walnuts, gherkins (pickles), parsley and egg. If the mixture is too stiff and dry, add a little chicken stock. Stuff the chicken with this mixture and truss or secure the opening with a skewer.

Wrap the chicken in foil and place in a roasting tin. Roast in a preheated moderately hot oven (200°C/400°F, Gas Mark 6) for 1½ to 1¾ hours or until the chicken is cooked. Open the foil for the last 30 minutes so the breast can brown.

Transfer the chicken to a warmed serving dish and untruss or remove the skewer. Garnish with watercress and serve with roast potatoes and corn.
Serves 4

Hindle wakes

METRIC/IMPERIAL
1 × 2.75kg/6lb boiling
  chicken
120ml/4fl oz vinegar
1 × 15ml spoon/
  1 tablespoon sugar
Stuffing:
275g/10oz prunes, stoned
  and chopped
50g/2oz shredded suet
50g/2oz fresh breadcrumbs
1 × 5ml spoon/1 teaspoon
  grated lemon rind
2 × 5ml spoons/2 teaspoons
  chopped fresh parsley
salt
freshly ground black pepper

AMERICAN
1 × 6lb stewing chicken
½ cup vinegar
1 tablespoon sugar
Stuffing:
2 cups chopped pitted prunes
½ cup shredded suet
1 cup fresh breadcrumbs
1 teaspoon grated lemon
  rind
2 teaspoons chopped fresh
  parsley
salt
freshly ground black pepper

Mix together the ingredients for the stuffing with salt and pepper to taste. Fill the chicken with the stuffing and secure the cavity with a skewer or trussing needle and string. Put the chicken in a saucepan and cover with water. Add the vinegar and sugar and bring to the boil.

Cover and simmer for 2½ hours or until the chicken is cooked. Remove from the heat and allow to cool in the liquid. When cold, drain and carve. Serve cold.
Serves 8

Curried chicken

METRIC/IMPERIAL
25g/1oz butter
2 × 15ml spoons/
  2 tablespoons vegetable oil
4 chicken quarters
1 onion, peeled and chopped
2 × 15ml spoons/
  2 tablespoons mild curry
  powder
1 × 15ml spoon/
  1 tablespoon plain flour
salt
freshly ground black pepper
150ml/¼ pint chicken stock
50g/2oz sultanas

AMERICAN
2 tablespoons butter
2 tablespoons vegetable oil
4 chicken quarters
1 onion, peeled and chopped
2 tablespoons mild curry
  powder
1 tablespoon all-purpose
  flour
salt
freshly ground black pepper
⅔ cup chicken stock
⅓ cup seedless white raisins

Melt the butter with the oil in a flameproof casserole or saucepan. Add the chicken quarters, in batches, and brown well on all sides. Remove the chicken from the pan. Add the onion and fry until it is soft but not brown. Sprinkle over the curry powder, flour and salt and pepper to taste and cook, stirring, for 2 minutes. Remove from the heat and gradually stir in the stock.

Return to the heat and bring to the boil, stirring. Simmer until thickened and smooth. Stir in the sultanas (raisins). Return the chicken quarters to the pan and spoon the sauce over them. Cover and simmer gently for 20 to 25 minutes or until the chicken is cooked through.

Serve hot, on a bed of freshly boiled rice, with curry accompaniments.
Serves 4

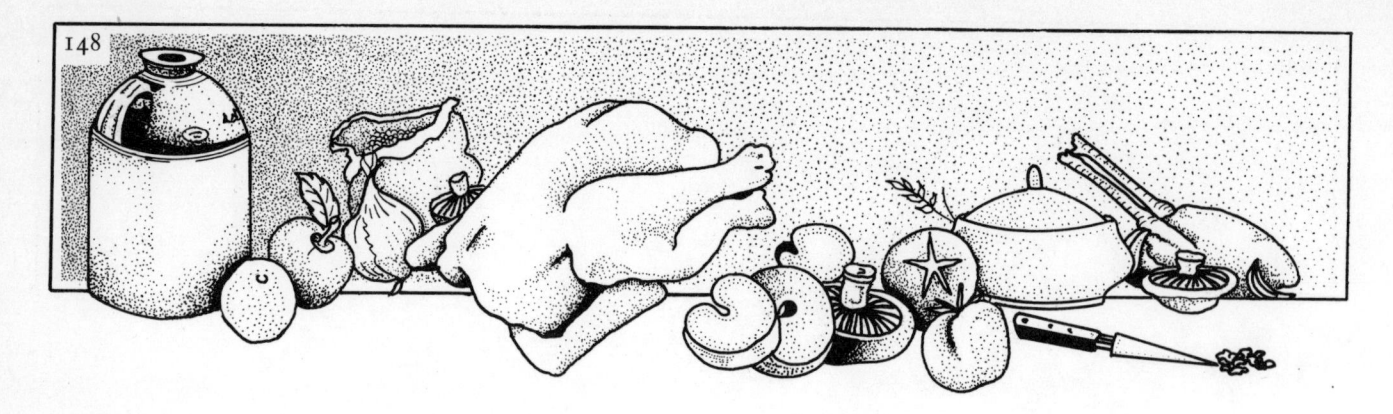

Devilled chicken

METRIC/IMPERIAL
4 chicken quarters
Devil sauce:
3 × 15ml spoons/
  3 tablespoons olive oil
1 × 15ml spoon/
  1 tablespoon
  Worcestershire sauce
1 × 15ml spoon/
  1 tablespoon tarragon
  vinegar
1 × 15ml spoon/
  1 tablespoon minced onion
1 × 5ml spoon/1 teaspoon
  made French mustard
salt
freshly ground black pepper
To garnish:
1 red pepper, pith and seeds
  removed and cut into thin
  strips
watercress

AMERICAN
4 chicken quarters
Devil sauce:
3 tablespoons olive oil
1 tablespoon Worcestershire
  sauce
1 tablespoon tarragon
  vinegar
1 tablespoon ground onion
1 teaspoon prepared French
  mustard
salt
freshly ground black pepper
To garnish:
1 pimiento, pith and seeds
  removed and cut into thin
  strips
watercress

Mix together the ingredients for the devil sauce in a shallow dish. Score the skin of the chicken quarters and place in the dish. Turn over to coat with the sauce. Leave to marinate for 15 minutes.

Arrange the chicken quarters on the rack in a grill (broiler) pan. Grill (broil) for about 20 minutes, turning and basting with the devil sauce, or until the chicken is cooked.

Serve hot, garnished with red pepper (pimiento) strips and watercress.
Serves 4

Marsala chicken

METRIC/IMPERIAL
50g/2oz butter
6 chicken quarters
150ml/¼ pint Marsala
150ml/¼ pint double cream
pinch of paprika
100g/4oz Cheddar cheese,
  grated
salt
freshly ground black pepper
rosemary sprigs to garnish

AMERICAN
¼ cup butter
6 chicken quarters
⅔ cup Marsala
⅔ cup heavy cream
pinch of paprika
1 cup grated Cheddar cheese
salt
freshly ground black pepper
rosemary sprigs to garnish

Melt the butter in a flameproof casserole. Add the chicken quarters, two at a time, and brown well on all sides. Remove from the pan and pour off the fat. Return the chicken quarters to the casserole and pour over the Marsala. Cover tightly and simmer for about 40 minutes or until the chicken is cooked.

Meanwhile, whip the cream until it is thick. Stir in the paprika, cheese and salt and pepper to taste.

Transfer the chicken quarters to a flameproof serving dish and pour over the juices from the casserole. Top with the cheese mixture and grill (broil) until the topping melts and browns lightly. Serve hot, garnished with rosemary sprigs.
Serves 6

Poulet bonne femme

METRIC/IMPERIAL
50g/2oz butter
4 chicken quarters
12 small onions, peeled
100g/4oz streaky bacon, rinds removed and diced
15g/½oz plain flour
150ml/¼ pint dry white wine
150ml/¼ pint chicken stock
1 bouquet garni
salt
freshly ground black pepper
100g/4oz button mushrooms

AMERICAN
¼ cup butter
4 chicken quarters
12 small onions, peeled
¼lb bacon, diced
2 tablespoons all-purpose flour
⅔ cup dry white wine
⅔ cup chicken stock
1 bouquet garni
salt
freshly ground black pepper
1 cup button mushrooms

Melt the butter in a saucepan. Add the chicken quarters and fry until golden on all sides. Remove the chicken from the pan.

Add the onions and bacon to the pan and fry until the bacon is crisp and the onions are golden brown. Stir in the flour and cook, stirring, for 2 minutes. Gradually stir in the wine and stock and bring to the boil, stirring. Add the bouquet garni with salt and pepper to taste.

Return the chicken quarters to the pan with the mushrooms. Cover and simmer for 40 to 45 minutes or until the chicken is tender. Remove the bouquet garni and serve hot.
Serves 4

Coq au vin

METRIC/IMPERIAL
75g/3oz butter
4 chicken quarters
4 streaky bacon rashers, rinds removed and diced
8 small onions, peeled
3 × 15ml spoons/ 3 tablespoons brandy, warmed
300ml/½ pint dry red wine
300ml/½ pint chicken stock
salt
freshly ground black pepper
1 garlic clove, crushed
1 bouquet garni
100g/4oz button mushrooms
25g/1oz plain flour

AMERICAN
6 tablespoons butter
4 chicken quarters
4 bacon slices, diced
8 small onions, peeled
3 tablespoons brandy, warmed
1¼ cups dry red wine
1¼ cups chicken stock
salt
freshly ground black pepper
1 garlic clove, crushed
1 bouquet garni
1 cup button mushrooms
¼ cup all-purpose flour

Melt 50g/2oz/¼ cup of the butter in a saucepan. Add the chicken quarters and brown on all sides. Remove the chicken from the pan.

Add the bacon and onions to the pan and fry until the bacon is crisp and the onions are golden brown. Return the chicken to the pan, pour over the brandy and set alight. When the flames have died down, add the wine, stock, salt and pepper to taste, the garlic and bouquet garni. Bring to the boil, cover and simmer for 30 minutes.

Add the mushrooms and simmer, covered, for a further 10 to 15 minutes or until the chicken is tender. Remove the bouquet garni. Transfer the chicken, onions and mushrooms to a warmed serving dish. Keep hot.

Mix together the flour and remaining butter to make a paste. Add in small pieces to the pan, stirring, and simmer until the liquid has thickened. Pour over the chicken and serve.
Serves 4

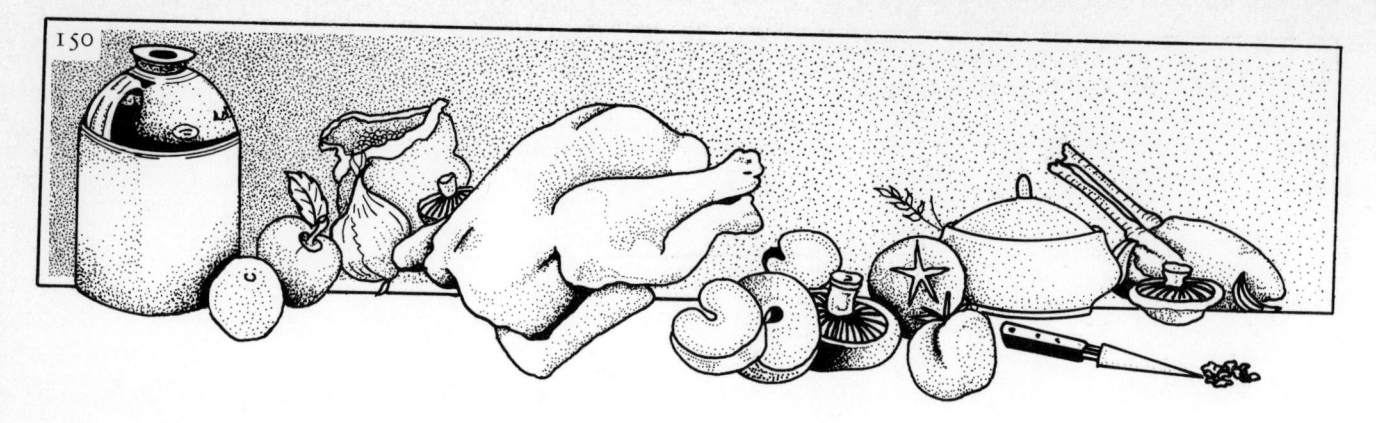

Chicken cacciatora

METRIC/IMPERIAL
25g/1oz plain flour
salt
freshly ground black pepper
4 chicken quarters
50g/2oz butter
1 × 15ml spoon/
 1 tablespoon olive oil
1 large onion, peeled and chopped
2 garlic cloves, finely chopped
8 tomatoes, peeled and chopped
3 × 15ml spoons/
 3 tablespoons tomato purée
1 × 5ml spoon/1 teaspoon sugar
150ml/¼ pint chicken stock
225g/8oz mushrooms, sliced
4 × 15ml spoons/
 4 tablespoons Marsala
225g/8oz spaghetti
grated Parmesan cheese

AMERICAN
¼ cup all-purpose flour
salt
freshly ground black pepper
4 chicken quarters
¼ cup butter
1 tablespoon olive oil
1 large onion, peeled and chopped
2 garlic cloves, finely chopped
8 tomatoes, peeled and chopped
3 tablespoons tomato paste
1 teaspoon sugar
⅔ cup chicken stock
2 cups sliced mushrooms
4 tablespoons Marsala
½lb spaghetti
grated Parmesan cheese

Mix the flour with salt and pepper and use to coat the chicken pieces. Melt the butter with the oil in a saucepan. Add the chicken pieces and fry until golden brown on all sides. Remove the chicken from the pan.

Add the onion and garlic to the pan and fry until the onion is soft but not brown. Stir in the tomatoes, tomato purée (paste), sugar, stock and salt and pepper to taste and bring to the boil. Return the chicken pieces to the pan and spoon the sauce over them. Cover and simmer for 30 to 45 minutes or until the chicken is cooked and tender.

Add the mushrooms and Marsala and continue simmering for 10 minutes.

Meanwhile, cook the spaghetti in boiling salted water until it is *al dente* (just tender to the bite). Drain well and arrange on a warmed serving dish. Keep hot.

Place the chicken pieces on top of the spaghetti and pour over the tomato sauce. Sprinkle with Parmesan and serve hot.

Serves 4

Chicken with ham sauce

METRIC/IMPERIAL
6 chicken quarters
salt
freshly ground black pepper
2 × 15ml spoons/
 2 tablespoons oil
1 onion, peeled and thinly sliced
1 garlic clove, crushed
300ml/½ pint chicken stock
300ml/½ pint dry white wine
1 bouquet garni
1 small cucumber, peeled and thinly sliced
4 egg yolks
2 × 15ml spoons/
 2 tablespoons milk
100g/4oz lean cooked ham, chopped

AMERICAN
6 chicken quarters
salt
freshly ground black pepper
2 tablespoons oil
1 onion, peeled and thinly sliced
1 garlic clove, crushed
1¼ cups chicken stock
1¼ cups dry white wine
1 bouquet garni
1 small cucumber, peeled and thinly sliced
4 egg yolks
2 tablespoons milk
½ cup chopped lean cooked ham

Rub the chicken pieces with salt and pepper. Heat the oil in a flameproof casserole. Add the chicken pieces, two at a time, and brown on all sides. Remove the chicken from the pot and pour off the fat.

Put the onion, garlic, chicken stock, wine and bouquet garni in the casserole and stir well. Return the chicken pieces to the casserole and spoon the liquid over them. Bring to the boil, cover and simmer for 45 minutes or until tender.

Remove the bouquet garni. Add the cucumber to the casserole and simmer for a further 5 minutes.

Transfer the chicken pieces, onion and cucumber to a warmed serving dish. Keep hot.

Beat together the egg yolks and milk. Add a little of the hot cooking liquid, then beat this mixture into the remaining cooking liquid in the casserole. Heat gently, without boiling, until the sauce thickens. Stir in the ham and heat through.

Pour the ham sauce over the chicken and serve hot.
Serves 6

Normandy chicken

METRIC/IMPERIAL
25g/1oz butter
1 × 15ml spoon/
 1 tablespoon olive oil
4 chicken quarters
1 onion, peeled and chopped
1 garlic clove, crushed
3 streaky bacon rashers,
 rinds removed and chopped
25g/1oz plain flour
450ml/¾ pint dry cider
2 dessert apples, cored and
 diced
150ml/¼ pint single cream
salt
freshly ground black pepper

AMERICAN
2 tablespoons butter
1 tablespoon olive oil
4 chicken quarters
1 onion, peeled and chopped
1 garlic clove, crushed
3 bacon slices, chopped
¼ cup all-purpose flour
2 cups hard cider
2 dessert apples, cored and
 diced
⅔ cup light cream
salt
freshly ground black pepper

Melt the butter with the oil in a saucepan. Add the chicken quarters and brown on all sides. Remove the chicken from the pan.

Add the onion, garlic and bacon to the pan and fry until the onion is soft but not brown. Stir in the flour and cook, stirring, for 1 minute. Gradually stir in the cider and bring to the boil, stirring. Simmer until thickened.

Return the chicken pieces to the pan and spoon the sauce over them. Cover and simmer gently for 30 minutes.

Stir the apples and cream into the chicken mixture. Heat through gently without boiling. Season to taste with salt and pepper. Serve hot.
Serves 4

Chicken and walnuts

METRIC/IMPERIAL
6 chicken quarters, skinned
2 × 15ml spoons/
 2 tablespoons medium
 sherry
2 × 5ml spoons/2 teaspoons
 sugar
3 × 15ml spoons/
 3 tablespoons oil
225g/8oz button
 mushrooms, sliced
600ml/1 pint chicken stock
2 × 15ml spoons/
 2 tablespoons cornflour
3 × 15ml spoons/
 3 tablespoons water
salt
freshly ground black pepper
25g/1oz butter
100g/4oz walnut halves

AMERICAN
6 chicken quarters, skinned
2 tablespoons medium sherry
2 teaspoons sugar
3 tablespoons oil
2 cups sliced button
 mushrooms
2½ cups chicken stock
2 tablespoons cornstarch
3 tablespoons water
salt
freshly ground black pepper
2 tablespoons butter
1 cup walnut halves

Put the chicken quarters in a shallow dish and sprinkle with the sherry and sugar. Leave to marinate for 2 hours.

Remove the chicken pieces from the marinade and pat dry with absorbent paper. Heat the oil in a frying pan (skillet). Add the chicken pieces and brown on all sides. Remove from the heat.

Put the mushrooms in a casserole. Arrange the chicken pieces on top and pour over any marinade, the juices from the frying pan (skillet) and the stock. Cover and cook in a preheated moderate oven (180°C/350°F, Gas Mark 4) for 2 hours.

Transfer the chicken pieces and mushrooms to a warmed serving dish. Keep hot.

Strain the cooking liquid into a saucepan. Dissolve the cornflour (cornstarch) in the water and add to the cooking liquid. Bring to the boil, stirring, and simmer until thickened. Remove from the heat and season to taste with salt and pepper. Keep this sauce hot.

Melt the butter in a frying pan (skillet). Add the walnut halves and fry for 4 to 5 minutes or until browned. Remove from the pan and drain on absorbent paper.

Pour some of the sauce over the chicken and garnish with the walnut halves. Serve the remaining sauce in a sauceboat.
Serves 6

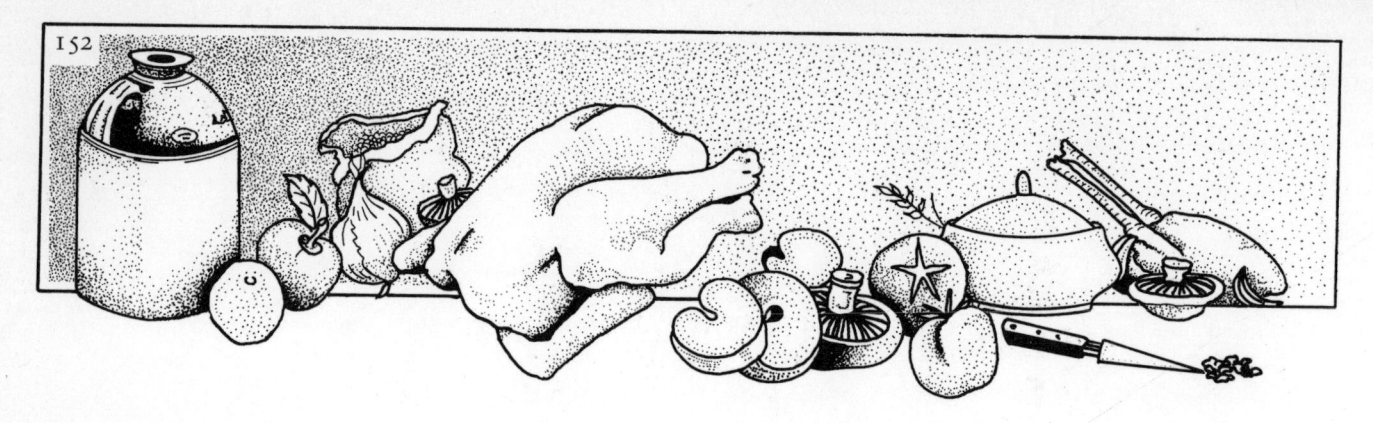

Chicken and avocado casserole

METRIC/IMPERIAL
75g/3oz plain flour
salt
freshly ground black pepper
pinch of dried thyme
finely grated rind and juice of 1 lemon
6 chicken quarters
75g/3oz butter
2 onions, peeled and sliced
300ml/½ pint dry white wine
150ml/¼ pint chicken stock
2 avocado pears
150ml/¼ pint double cream
1 × 15ml spoon/
1 tablespoon oil

AMERICAN
¾ cup all-purpose flour
salt
freshly ground black pepper
pinch of dried thyme
finely grated rind and juice of 1 lemon
6 chicken quarters
⅓ cup butter
2 onions, peeled and sliced
1¼ cups dry white wine
⅔ cup chicken stock
2 avocado pears
⅔ cup heavy cream
1 tablespoon oil

Mix all but 1 × 15ml spoon/1 tablespoon of the flour with salt and pepper, the thyme and lemon rind. Use to coat the chicken pieces.

Melt 50g/2oz/¼ cup of the butter in a large saucepan. Add the chicken pieces, in batches, and brown on all sides. Transfer the chicken pieces to a casserole.

Add the remaining butter to the saucepan. When it has melted, add the onions and fry until they are soft but not brown. Sprinkle over the reserved flour and stir well. Gradually stir in the wine and stock and bring to the boil, stirring. Simmer until thickened. Pour over the chicken in the casserole. Cover and cook in a preheated moderately hot oven (190°C/375°F, Gas Mark 5) for 1 hour.

Just before the chicken is ready, peel the avocado pears, halve and remove the stones (seeds). Slice the avocados and sprinkle with the lemon juice to prevent discoloration.

Remove the casserole from the oven and allow to cool just until the liquid stops bubbling. Stir in the cream. Arrange the avocado slices on top of the chicken and brush with the oil.

Return to the oven and bake for a further 10 minutes. Serve hot, from the casserole.
Serves 6

Chicken with orange and almond sauce

METRIC/IMPERIAL
1 × 5ml spoon/1 teaspoon paprika
salt
freshly ground black pepper
4 chicken quarters
50g/2oz butter
juice of 2 oranges
2 × 5ml spoons/2 teaspoons sugar
1 orange, peeled and segmented
50g/2oz blanched almonds, flaked and toasted

AMERICAN
1 teaspoon paprika
salt
freshly ground black pepper
4 chicken quarters
¼ cup butter
juice of 2 oranges
2 teaspoons sugar
1 orange, peeled and segmented
½ cup blanched slivered almonds, toasted

Mix the paprika with salt and pepper and rub all over the chicken. Melt the butter in a frying pan (skillet). Add the chicken pieces and brown on all sides. Reduce the heat, cover and cook for 30 minutes or until tender.

Transfer the chicken to a warmed serving dish and keep hot.

Pour off the fat from the pan. Add the orange juice and sugar to the pan and stir over a gentle heat to dissolve the sugar. Stir in the orange segments and bring to the boil. Boil for 3 minutes. Add salt and pepper to taste and pour over the chicken. Sprinkle over the almonds and serve hot.
Serves 4

Lamb and orange stew (page 123)

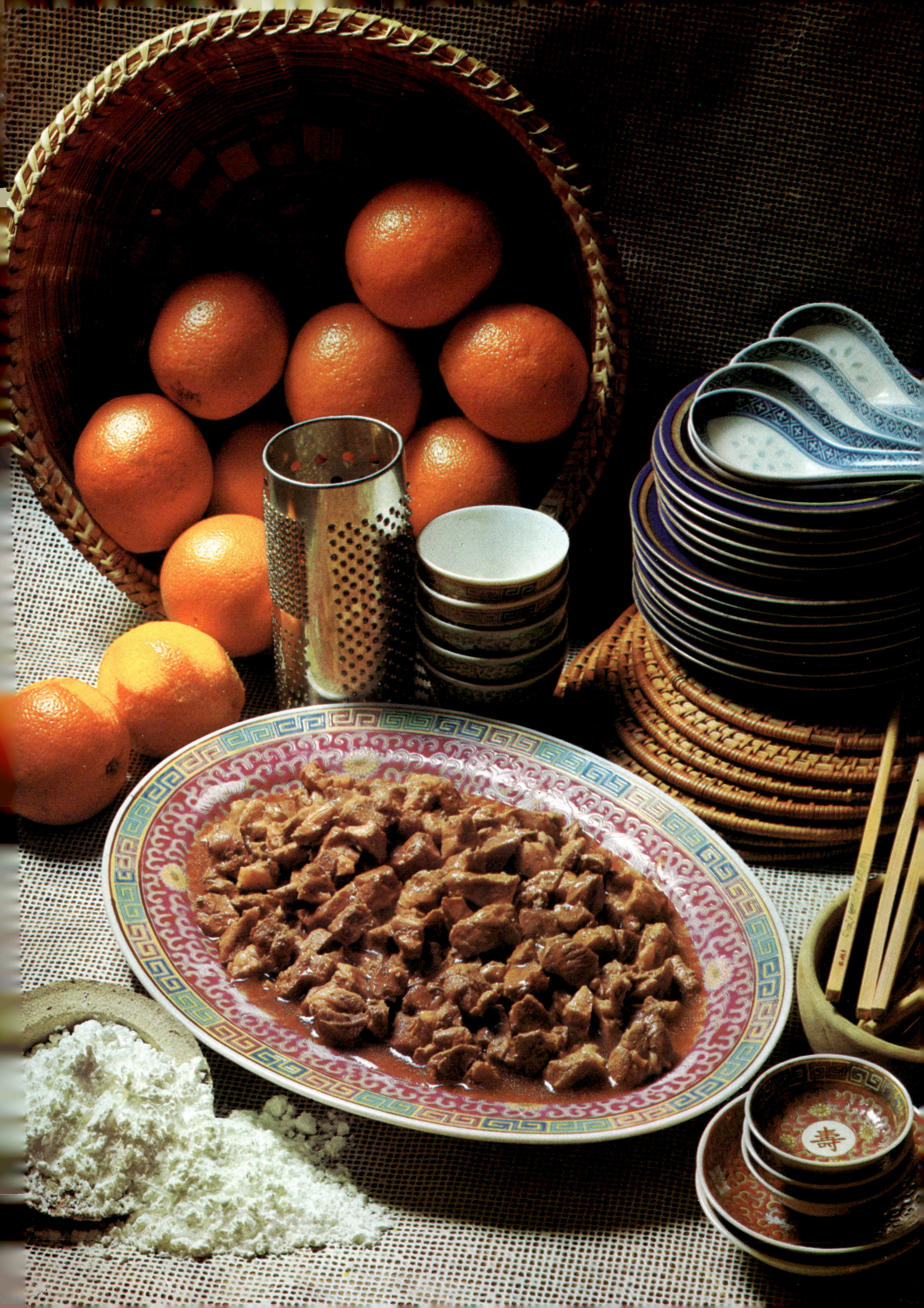

Glazed baked gammon (ham) (page 141); Pork fillets (tenderloin) in sherry sauce (page 370)

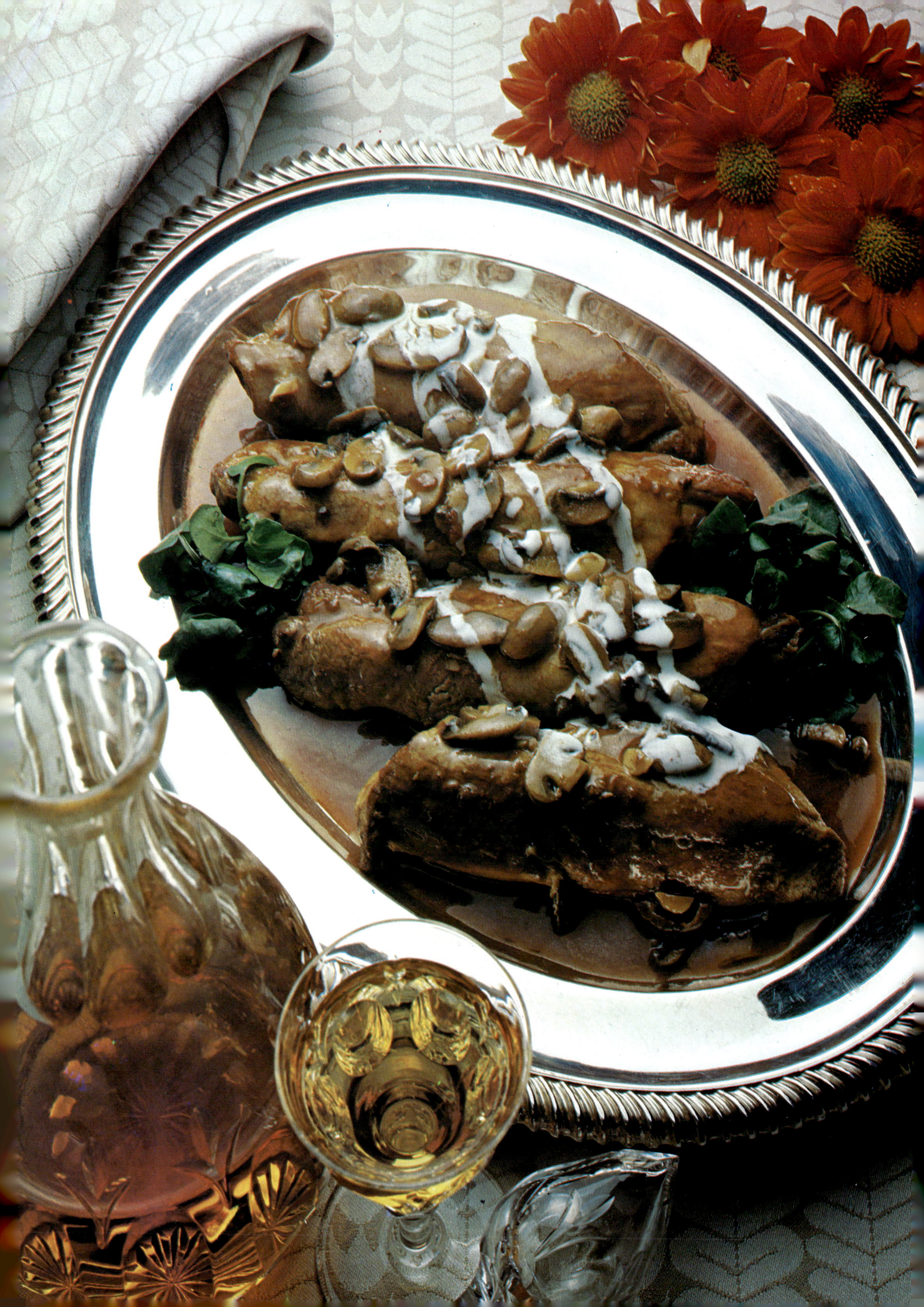

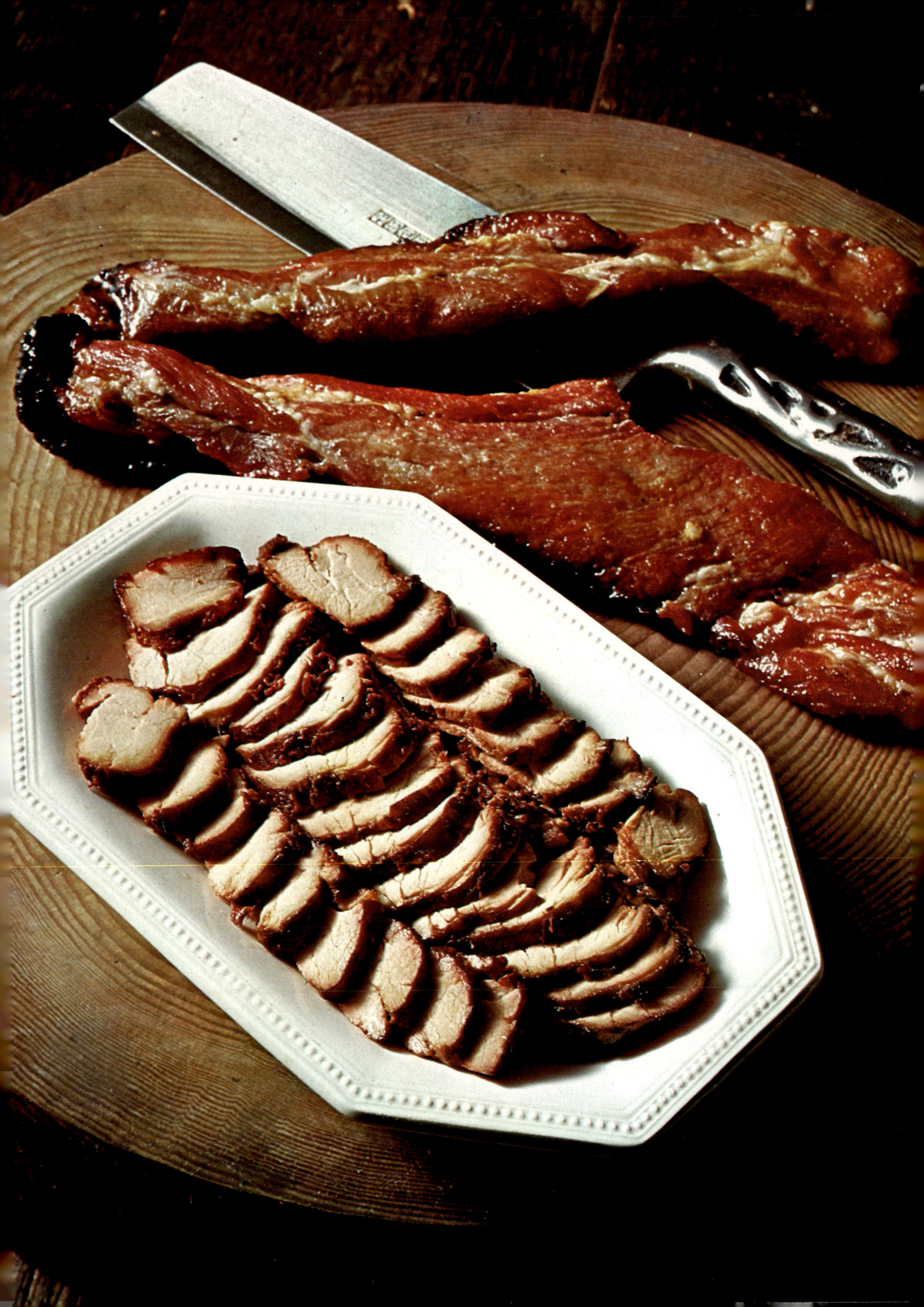

Crispy herb chicken

METRIC/IMPERIAL
4 chicken quarters, skinned
50g/2oz butter, melted
1 × 65g/2½oz packet plain crisps, crushed
100g/4oz Parmesan cheese, grated
1 × 15ml spoon/ 1 tablespoon chopped fresh chervil
pinch of garlic powder
1 × 15ml spoon/ 1 tablespoon chopped fresh tarragon
salt
freshly ground black pepper

AMERICAN
4 chicken quarters, skinned
¼ cup butter, melted
1 × 2½oz package plain potato chips, crushed (about 1¼ cups)
1 cup grated Parmesan cheese
1 tablespoon chopped fresh chervil
pinch of garlic powder
1 tablespoon chopped fresh tarragon
salt
freshly ground black pepper

Coat the chicken pieces with half the melted butter. Mix together the crisps (potato chips), cheese, chervil, garlic powder, tarragon and salt and pepper to taste. Press this mixture onto the chicken and arrange in a baking dish. Sprinkle over the remaining butter.

Bake in a preheated moderate oven (180°C/350°F, Gas Mark 4) for 45 minutes to 1 hour or until the chicken is cooked. Serve hot.
Serves 4

Chicken dhansak

METRIC/IMPERIAL
4 chicken quarters, skinned
175g/6oz dried brown lentils, soaked overnight and drained
2 onions, peeled and chopped
1 × 400g/14oz can tomatoes
2 medium potatoes, peeled and diced
1 × 2.5ml spoon/½ teaspoon mild chilli powder
1 × 5ml spoon/1 teaspoon turmeric
1 × 15ml spoon/ 1 tablespoon ground coriander
1 × 5ml spoon/1 teaspoon ground cumin
150ml/¼ pint chicken stock
salt
juice of 1 lemon
25g/1oz butter

AMERICAN
4 chicken quarters, skinned
¾ cup dried lentils, soaked overnight and drained
2 onions, peeled and chopped
1 × 14oz can tomatoes
2 medium potatoes, peeled and diced
½ teaspoon mild chili powder
1 teaspoon turmeric
1 tablespoon ground coriander
1 teaspoon ground cumin
⅔ cup chicken stock
salt
juice of 1 lemon
2 tablespoons butter

Put the chicken, lentils, onions, tomatoes with the can juice, potatoes, spices and stock in a saucepan. Add salt to taste and bring to the boil. Cover and simmer for 45 minutes or until all the ingredients are cooked and the liquid has been absorbed.

Remove the chicken from the pan and allow to cool slightly. Pour the lentil mixture into the goblet of an electric blender and blend until smooth. Return to the saucepan.

Remove the chicken meat from the bones and cut into bite-sized pieces. Add to the saucepan with the lemon juice and butter. Reheat gently, stirring. If the sauce is too thick, add a little stock. Serve hot.
Serves 4

Chinese quick-roast pork (page 139)

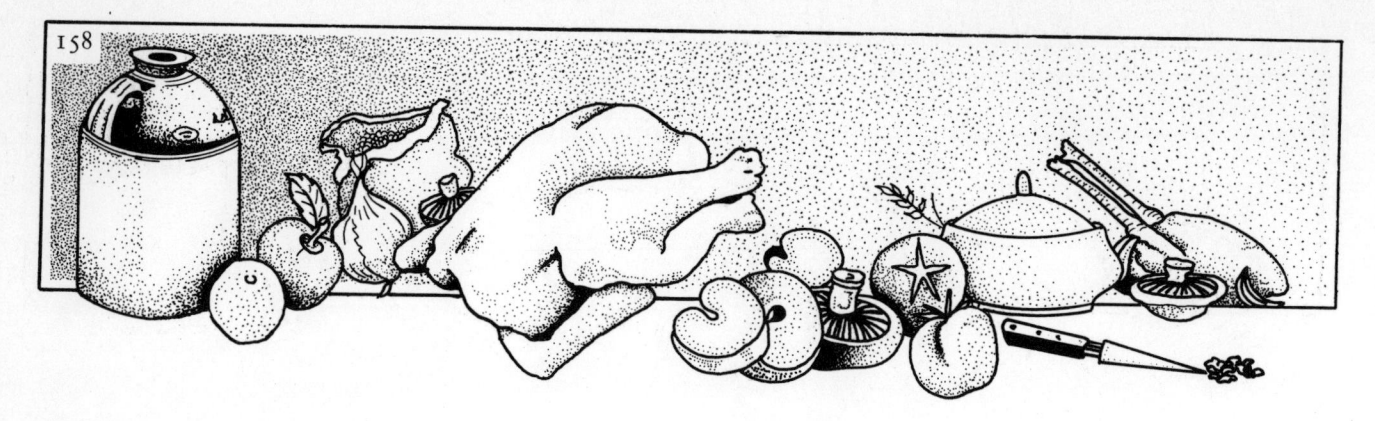

Italian chicken casserole

METRIC/IMPERIAL
25g/1oz plain flour
salt
freshly ground black pepper
4 chicken quarters
3 × 15ml spoons/
  3 tablespoons olive oil
2 onions, peeled and
  chopped
1 garlic clove, crushed
1 × 400g/14oz can
  tomatoes, drained
225g/8oz button
  mushrooms, sliced
100g/4oz stoned black
  olives
pinch of powdered saffron
300ml/½ pint dry white
  wine
juice of 1 lemon

AMERICAN
¼ cup all-purpose flour
salt
freshly ground black pepper
4 chicken quarters
3 tablespoons olive oil
2 onions, peeled and
  chopped
1 garlic clove, crushed
1 × 14oz can tomatoes,
  drained
2 cups sliced button
  mushrooms
¾ cup pitted black olives
pinch of powdered saffron
1¼ cups dry white wine
juice of 1 lemon

Mix the flour with salt and pepper and use to coat the chicken pieces. Heat the oil in a flameproof casserole. Add the chicken pieces and brown on all sides. Remove the chicken from the casserole.

Add the onions and garlic to the casserole and fry until the onions are soft but not brown. Stir in the tomatoes, mushrooms and olives and cook for 3 minutes. Dissolve the saffron in the wine and add to the casserole with the lemon juice. Bring to the boil.

Return the chicken pieces to the casserole and spoon the liquid over them. Cover and transfer to a preheated moderate oven (180°C/350°F, Gas Mark 4). Cook for 1 hour or until the chicken is tender.

Serve hot, from the casserole.

Serves 4

Paprika chicken

METRIC/IMPERIAL
50g/2oz butter
1 × 15ml spoon/
  1 tablespoon olive oil
4 chicken quarters
25g/1oz plain flour
2 × 15ml spoons/
  2 tablespoons paprika
600ml/1 pint chicken stock
2 × 15ml spoons/
  2 tablespoons redcurrant
  jelly
finely grated rind of ½ lemon
pinch of dried thyme
salt
freshly ground black pepper
100g/4oz button
  mushrooms
150ml/¼ pint sour cream

AMERICAN
¼ cup butter
1 tablespoon olive oil
4 chicken quarters
¼ cup all-purpose flour
2 tablespoons paprika
2½ cups chicken stock
2 tablespoons redcurrant
  jelly
finely grated rind of ½ lemon
pinch of dried thyme
salt
freshly ground black pepper
1 cup button mushrooms
⅔ cup sour cream

Melt the butter with the oil in a flameproof casserole. Add the chicken quarters and brown on all sides. Remove the chicken from the casserole.

Stir the flour and paprika into the fat in the casserole and cook, stirring, for 2 minutes. Gradually stir in the stock. Bring to the boil, stirring, and simmer until thickened and smooth. Stir in the jelly, lemon rind and thyme with salt and pepper to taste.

Return the chicken pieces to the casserole and spoon the sauce over them. Cover and transfer to a preheated moderate oven (180°C/350°F, Gas Mark 4). Cook for 1 hour.

Stir in the mushrooms and cook for a further 30 minutes or until the chicken is tender. Serve hot from the casserole, topped with the sour cream.

Serves 4

Chicken salad paradiso

METRIC/IMPERIAL
1 × 1.5kg/3lb chicken, roasted and cooled
1 small pineapple, skinned, cored, eyes removed and chopped
1 green pepper, pith and seeds removed and chopped
300ml/½ pint mayonnaise*
2 heads chicory, separated into leaves
1 small lettuce, separated into leaves
2 large tomatoes, quartered
50g/2oz blanched almonds, toasted

AMERICAN
1 × 3lb chicken, roasted and cooled
1 small pineapple, skinned, cored, eyes removed and chopped
1 green pepper, pith and seeds removed and chopped
1¼ cups mayonnaise*
2 heads French or Belgian endive, separated into leaves
1 small head lettuce, separated into leaves
2 large tomatoes, quartered
½ cup blanched almonds, toasted

Remove the chicken meat from the carcass and take off the skin. Cut the meat into bite-sized pieces. Put the chicken meat, pineapple, green pepper and mayonnaise in a mixing bowl and fold together gently.

Line a serving dish with the chicory (endive) and lettuce leaves. Pile the chicken mixture in the centre and surround with the tomato quarters. Sprinkle over the almonds and serve.
Serves 4

Chicken chop suey

METRIC/IMPERIAL
4 × 15ml spoons/ 4 tablespoons oil
4 dried Chinese mushrooms, soaked in water for 20 minutes, drained and sliced
1 canned bamboo shoot, thinly sliced
1 onion, peeled and thinly sliced
1 green pepper, pith and seeds removed and thinly sliced
225g/8oz bean sprouts
0.5kg/1lb cooked chicken meat, diced
150ml/¼ pint chicken stock
pinch of sugar
1 × 5ml spoon/1 teaspoon soy sauce
salt
freshly ground black pepper
1 × 5ml spoon/1 teaspoon cornflour
1 × 15ml spoon/ 1 tablespoon dry sherry

AMERICAN
4 tablespoons oil
4 dried Chinese mushrooms, soaked in water for 20 minutes, drained and sliced
1 canned bamboo shoot, thinly sliced
1 onion, peeled and thinly sliced
1 green pepper, pith and seeds removed and thinly sliced
½lb bean sprouts
2 cups diced cooked chicken meat
⅔ cup chicken stock
pinch of sugar
1 teaspoon soy sauce
salt
freshly ground black pepper
1 teaspoon cornstarch
1 tablespoon dry sherry

Heat the oil in a frying pan (skillet). Add the vegetables and stir-fry for 4 minutes. Add the chicken and fry for a further 3 minutes. Stir in the stock, sugar, soy sauce and salt and pepper to taste and bring to the boil. Simmer for 5 minutes.

Dissolve the cornflour (cornstarch) in the sherry and stir into the pan. Simmer, stirring, until the liquid thickens. Serve hot.
Serves 4

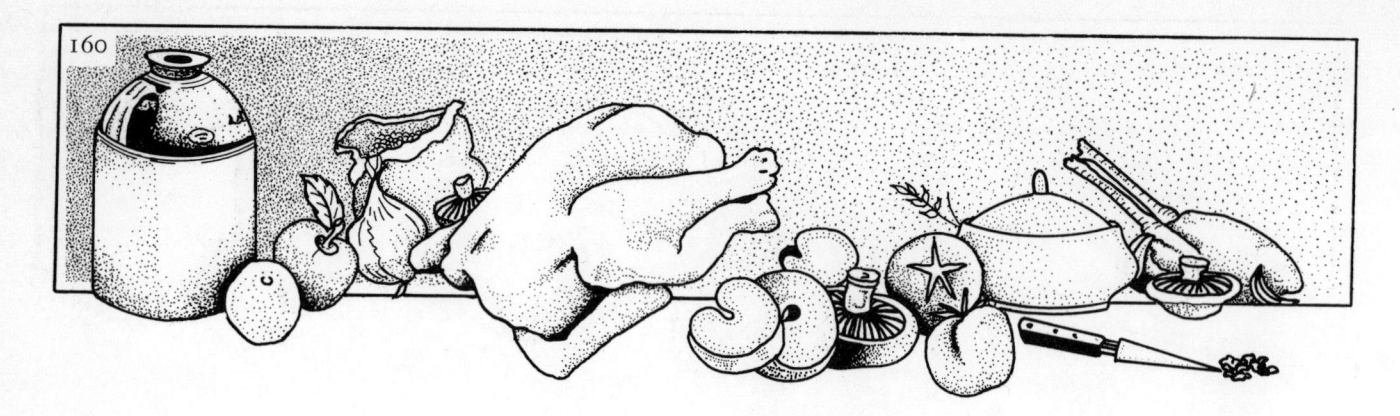

Chicken Kiev

METRIC/IMPERIAL
100g/4oz butter
finely grated rind and juice of ½ lemon
1 × 15ml spoon/ 1 tablespoon chopped fresh parsley
1 × 15ml spoon/ 1 tablespoon chopped fresh chives
1 garlic clove, crushed
salt
freshly ground black pepper
8 chicken breasts, boned, skinned and pounded thin
50g/2oz plain flour
2 eggs, lightly beaten
175g/6oz dry breadcrumbs
vegetable oil for deep frying
lemon wedges to garnish

AMERICAN
½ cup butter
finely grated rind and juice of ½ lemon
1 tablespoon chopped fresh parsley
1 tablespoon chopped fresh chives
1 garlic clove, crushed
salt
freshly ground black pepper
8 chicken breasts, boned, skinned and pounded thin
½ cup all-purpose flour
2 eggs, lightly beaten
1½ cups dry breadcrumbs
vegetable oil for deep frying
lemon wedges to garnish

Cream the butter until it is soft, then beat in the lemon rind and juice, parsley, chives, garlic and salt and pepper to taste. Divide into 8 portions and shape into small sausages. Refrigerate until firm.

Lay the chicken breasts flat and place a butter sausage on each. Roll up, making sure the butter sausage is completely enclosed. Mix the flour with salt and pepper and use to coat the chicken rolls. Dip in the beaten egg, then coat in the breadcrumbs. Chill for 1 hour.

Heat the oil in a deep frying pan (deep fat fryer) until it is 190°C/375°F. Lower the chicken rolls into the oil, in batches, and fry for 8 to 10 minutes or until crisp and golden brown. Drain on absorbent paper.

Serve hot, garnished with lemon wedges.
Serves 4

Chicken breasts with herbs

METRIC/IMPERIAL
25g/1oz butter
1 × 15ml spoon/ 1 tablespoon olive oil
4 chicken breasts, skinned
1 × 5ml spoon/1 teaspoon chopped fresh tarragon
1 × 5ml spoon/1 teaspoon chopped fresh chervil
1 × 5ml spoon/1 teaspoon chopped fresh thyme
salt
freshly ground black pepper
5 × 15ml spoons/ 5 tablespoons dry white wine

AMERICAN
2 tablespoons butter
1 tablespoon olive oil
4 chicken breasts, skinned
1 teaspoon chopped fresh tarragon
1 teaspoon chopped fresh chervil
1 teaspoon chopped fresh thyme
salt
freshly ground black pepper
⅓ cup dry white wine

Melt the butter with the oil in a frying pan (skillet). Add the chicken breasts and brown lightly on all sides. Sprinkle over the herbs, salt and pepper to taste and the wine. Bring to the boil, then cover and simmer for 20 minutes or until the chicken is cooked. Serve hot.
Serves 4

Chicken with apricots

METRIC/IMPERIAL
350g/12oz dried apricots
600ml/1 pint water
40g/1½oz plain flour
salt
freshly ground black pepper
4 chicken quarters
4 × 15ml spoons/
  4 tablespoons oil

AMERICAN
2 cups dried apricots
2½ cups water
6 tablespoons all-purpose
  flour
salt
freshly ground black pepper
4 chicken quarters
4 tablespoons oil

Soak the apricots in the water overnight. Drain the apricots, reserving the water.

Mix the flour with salt and pepper and use to coat the chicken pieces. Heat the oil in a saucepan. Add the chicken pieces and brown on all sides. Remove the chicken from the pan.

Add any remaining seasoned flour to the pan and cook, stirring, for 1 minute. Gradually stir in the reserved water and bring to the boil, stirring. Return the chicken pieces to the pan and add the apricots. Cover and simmer for 45 minutes or until the chicken is cooked. Serve hot.
Serves 4

Chicken Maryland

METRIC/IMPERIAL
25g/1oz plain flour
salt
freshly ground black pepper
4 chicken quarters
1 large egg, lightly beaten
100g/4oz dry breadcrumbs
50g/2oz butter
2 × 15ml spoons/
  2 tablespoons oil
4 bacon rashers, rinds
  removed
2 bananas, halved
  crossways
watercress to garnish

AMERICAN
¼ cup all-purpose flour
salt
freshly ground black pepper
4 chicken quarters
1 egg, lightly beaten
1 cup dry breadcrumbs
¼ cup butter
2 tablespoons oil
4 bacon slices
2 bananas, halved
  crosswise
watercress to garnish

Mix the flour with salt and pepper and use to coat the chicken pieces. Dip in the egg, then coat with the breadcrumbs. Melt the butter with the oil in a frying pan (skillet). Add the chicken pieces and brown on all sides. Transfer the chicken to a roasting tin and roast in a preheated moderate oven (180°C/350°F, Gas Mark 4) for 40 minutes or until cooked.

Cut the bacon rashers (slices) in half crossways and then in half lengthways. Roll up and secure with wooden cocktail sticks (toothpicks). Arrange the bacon rolls around the chicken and roast with it until crisp.

Heat the fat left in the frying pan (skillet). Add the banana halves and fry until lightly browned.

Arrange the chicken pieces on a warmed serving dish. Surround with the bacon rolls and banana halves and garnish with watercress. Serve hot.
Serves 4

Lemon chicken

METRIC/IMPERIAL
1 × 1.75kg/4lb chicken
salt
freshly ground black pepper
5 × 15ml spoons/
  5 tablespoons vegetable oil
6 medium dried Chinese mushrooms
15g/½oz butter
1 red pepper, pith and seeds removed and cut into matchstick strips
4 slices root ginger, peeled and chopped
finely pared rind of 2 medium lemons, cut into matchstick strips
5 spring onions, sliced
5 × 15ml spoons/
  5 tablespoons chicken stock
4 × 15ml spoons/
  4 tablespoons dry sherry
pinch of sugar
2 × 15ml spoons/
  2 tablespoons soy sauce
2 × 15ml spoons/
  2 tablespoons lemon juice
lemon slices to garnish

AMERICAN
1 × 4lb chicken
salt
freshly ground black pepper
⅓ cup vegetable oil
6 medium dried Chinese mushrooms
1 tablespoon butter
1 pimiento, pith and seeds removed and cut into matchstick strips
4 slices green ginger, peeled and chopped
finely pared rind of 2 medium lemons, cut into matchstick strips
5 scallions, sliced
⅓ cup chicken stock
4 tablespoons dry sherry
pinch of sugar
2 tablespoons soy sauce
2 tablespoons lemon juice
lemon slices to garnish

Remove the skin from the chicken and the meat from the carcass. Cut the meat into bite-sized pieces. Rub with salt, pepper and 1.5 × 15ml spoons/1½ tablespoons of the oil. Marinate for 30 minutes.

Meanwhile, soak the mushrooms in water to cover for 30 minutes. Drain and remove the stalks. Cut the caps into matchstick strips.

Heat the remaining oil in a frying pan (skillet). Add the chicken pieces and stir-fry for 2 minutes. Remove the chicken from the pan and keep warm. Add the butter to the pan. When it has melted, add the mushrooms, red pepper (pimiento) and ginger. Stir-fry for 1 minute. Add the lemon rind and spring onions (scallions) and continue to stir-fry for 30 seconds. Sprinkle over the stock, sherry, sugar and soy sauce and bring to the boil, stirring. Return the chicken to the pan and reheat for 2 minutes. Sprinkle with lemon juice and serve with lemon slices.
Serves 4 to 5

Paella

METRIC/IMPERIAL
4 × 15ml spoons/
  4 tablespoons olive oil
2 onions, peeled and chopped
1 garlic clove, crushed
2 dozen mussels, scrubbed and beards removed
salt
freshly ground black pepper
0.75kg/1½lb chicken meat, diced
200g/7oz long-grain rice
pinch of powdered saffron
900ml/1½ pints chicken stock
100g/4oz shelled peas
2 tomatoes, peeled and finely chopped
225g/8oz peeled prawns
parsley sprigs to garnish

AMERICAN
4 tablespoons olive oil
2 onions, peeled and chopped
1 garlic clove, crushed
2 dozen mussels, scrubbed and beards removed
salt
freshly ground black pepper
3 cups diced chicken meat
1 cup long-grain rice
pinch of powdered saffron
3¾ cups chicken stock
¾ cup shelled peas
2 tomatoes, peeled and finely chopped
1⅓ cups shelled shrimp
parsley sprigs to garnish

Heat the oil in a saucepan. Add the onions and garlic and fry until the onions are soft but not brown.

Meanwhile, put the mussels in another saucepan and cover with water. Add salt and pepper to taste and bring to the boil. Cover and cook for 10 minutes. Drain the mussels and discard any which are still closed. Remove half the mussels from the shells and leave the remainder on half shells. Keep hot.

Add the chicken and rice to the onions and stir well to coat with the oil. Dissolve the saffron in the stock and add to the saucepan. Bring to the boil, stirring, then simmer for about 25 minutes or until the rice is tender and the chicken is cooked.

Add the peas and tomatoes and continue simmering for about 5 minutes or until the peas are tender. Stir in the shelled mussels and prawns (shrimp) and heat through gently.

Spoon into a warmed serving dish and garnish with the mussels on half shells and parsley sprigs.
Serves 6

Chicken breasts Parmesan

METRIC/IMPERIAL
25g/1oz plain flour
salt
freshly ground black pepper
pinch of dried oregano
4 chicken breasts, boned and skinned
50g/2oz Parmesan cheese, grated
25g/1oz dry breadcrumbs
1 egg, lightly beaten
50g/2oz butter

AMERICAN
¼ cup all-purpose flour
salt
freshly ground black pepper
pinch of dried oregano
4 chicken breasts, boned and skinned
½ cup grated Parmesan cheese
¼ cup dry breadcrumbs
1 egg, lightly beaten
¼ cup butter

Mix the flour with salt, pepper and the oregano and use to coat the chicken pieces. Mix together the cheese and breadcrumbs. Dip the chicken pieces in the egg, then coat in the cheese mixture.

Melt the butter in a frying pan (skillet). Add the chicken pieces and brown on all sides. Reduce the heat and cook gently for 15 minutes or until tender. Serve hot.
Serves 4

Pâté-stuffed chicken

METRIC/IMPERIAL
8 chicken leg portions, skinned and boned
0.5kg/1lb liver pâté
2 large eggs, lightly beaten
2 × 15ml spoons/ 2 tablespoons water
350g/12oz fresh breadcrumbs
salt
freshly ground black pepper
75g/3oz butter, melted

AMERICAN
8 chicken leg portions, skinned and boned
2 cups liver sausage
2 eggs, lightly beaten
2 tablespoons water
6 cups fresh breadcrumbs
salt
freshly ground black pepper
⅓ cup butter, melted

Stuff the chicken legs with the pâté, being careful not to split the flesh. Reshape the legs and secure with wooden cocktail sticks (toothpicks). Chill for 1 hour.

Mix the eggs with the water and use to coat the chicken legs, then coat with half the breadcrumbs, seasoned with salt and pepper. Coat a second time with the egg mixture and the remaining breadcrumbs.

Pour the butter into a baking dish. Put the chicken legs in the dish and turn them over to coat with the butter. Bake in a preheated moderate oven (180°C/350°F, Gas Mark 4) for 1 hour, turning over halfway through the cooking.

Increase the temperature to moderately hot (200°C/400°F, Gas Mark 6) and bake for a further 20 minutes or until crisp and golden. Serve hot or cold.
Serves 4 to 8

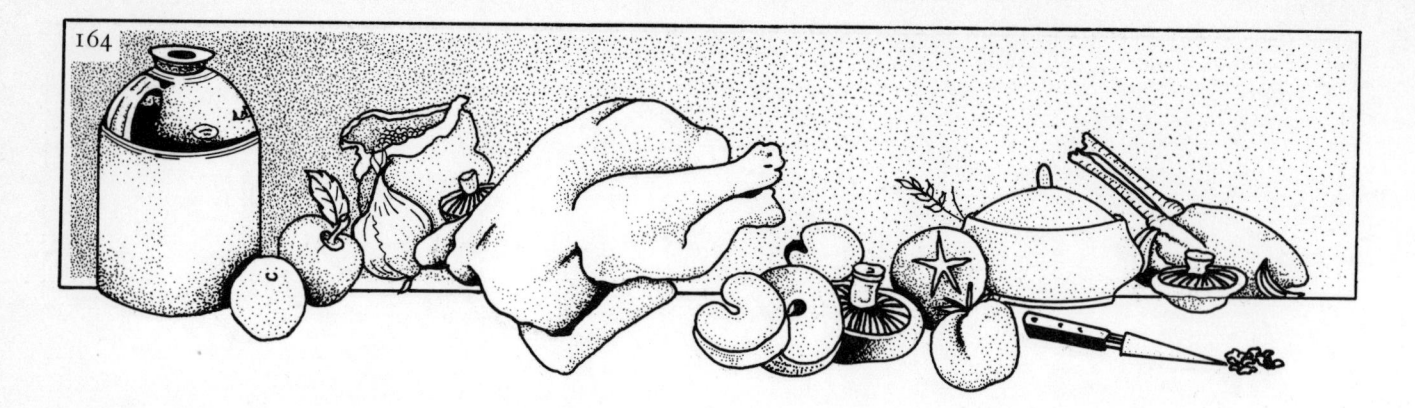

Chicken mille feuilles

METRIC/IMPERIAL
225g/8oz quantity flaky or puff pastry★
225g/8oz cream cheese
4 × 15ml spoons/ 4 tablespoons mayonnaise★
2 × 5ml spoons/2 teaspoons lemon juice
salt
freshly ground black pepper
350g/12oz cooked chicken meat, diced
4 lettuce leaves, shredded
4 tomatoes, peeled, thinly sliced and slices halved
chopped chives to garnish

AMERICAN
2 cup quantity flaky or puff pastry★
1 cup cream cheese
4 tablespoons mayonnaise★
2 teaspoons lemon juice
salt
freshly ground black pepper
1½ cups diced cooked chicken meat
4 lettuce leaves, shredded
4 tomatoes, peeled, thinly sliced and slices halved
chopped chives to garnish

Roll out the pastry dough to a rectangle about 30 × 28cm/12 × 11 inches and 5mm/¼ inch thick. Place on a dampened baking sheet and prick all over with a fork. Cut into 3, crosswise, and separate the 3 rectangles. Bake in a preheated moderately hot oven (200°C/400°F, Gas Mark 6) for 20 to 25 minutes or until well risen. Allow to cool on a wire rack.

Beat together the cream cheese, mayonnaise, lemon juice and salt and pepper to taste. Fold in the chicken.

Place one of the pastry rectangles on a serving plate. Spread with half the chicken mixture and cover with half the shredded lettuce and half the tomato slices. Add another pastry rectangle and cover with the remaining chicken mixture, lettuce and tomatoes. Put the last pastry rectangle on top. Sprinkle over chives and serve, cut in thick slices.
Serves 6

Cold chicken with sherry sauce

METRIC/IMPERIAL
2 egg yolks
250ml/8fl oz single cream
4 × 15ml spoons/ 4 tablespoons medium sherry
1 × 2.5ml spoon/½ teaspoon finely grated lemon rind
0.75kg/1½lb cooked chicken meat, thinly sliced

AMERICAN
2 egg yolks
1 cup light cream
4 tablespoons medium sherry
½ teaspoon finely grated lemon rind
1½lb cooked chicken meat, thinly sliced

Put the egg yolks in a heatproof mixing bowl over a pan of hot water. Beat together, then beat in the cream, sherry and lemon rind. Continue beating until the sauce thickens. Remove from the heat.

Arrange the chicken slices in a shallow serving dish. Pour over the sherry sauce and allow to cool, then chill for at least 30 minutes before serving.
Serves 4

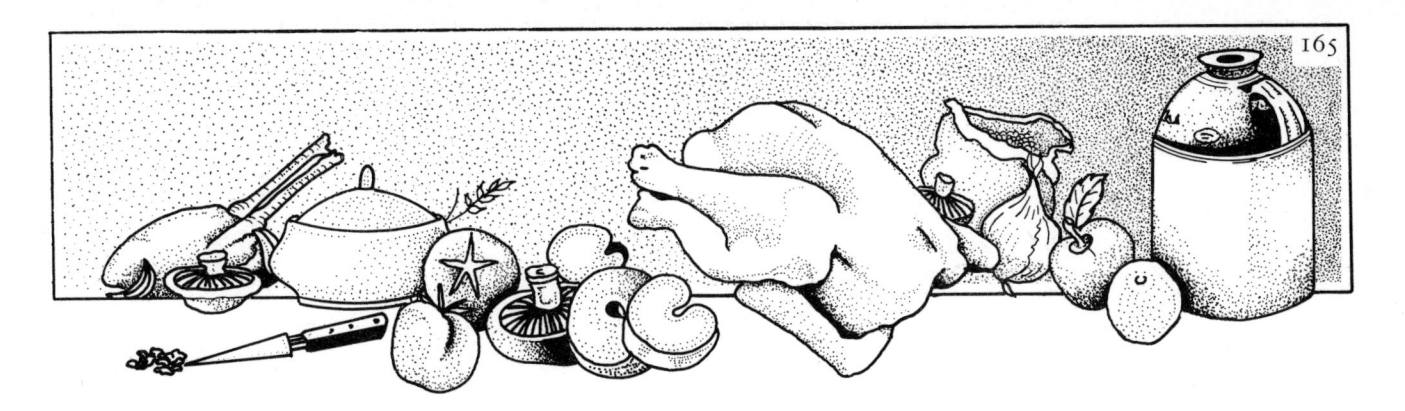

Turkey à la king

METRIC/IMPERIAL
50g/2oz butter
225g/8oz button mushrooms, sliced
1 small green pepper, pith and seeds removed and thinly sliced
40g/1½oz plain flour
150ml/¼ pint turkey stock
150ml/¼ pint milk
dash of Tabasco sauce
salt
freshly ground black pepper
350g/12oz cooked turkey meat, diced
1 × 175g/6oz can pimento, drained and diced
2 × 15ml spoons/ 2 tablespoons medium sherry

AMERICAN
¼ cup butter
2 cups sliced button mushrooms
1 small green pepper, pith and seeds removed and thinly sliced
6 tablespoons all-purpose flour
⅔ cup turkey stock
⅔ cup milk
dash of Tabasco sauce
salt
freshly ground black pepper
1½ cups diced cooked turkey meat
1 × 6oz can pimiento, drained and diced
2 tablespoons medium sherry

Melt the butter in a saucepan. Add the mushrooms and green pepper and fry for 8 minutes. Remove the vegetables from the pan with a slotted spoon.

Add the flour to the fat in the pan and cook, stirring, for 1 minute. Remove from the heat and gradually stir in the stock and milk. Return to the heat and bring to the boil, stirring. Simmer until thickened and smooth. Stir in the Tabasco and salt and pepper to taste.

Return the mushrooms and green pepper to the pan with the turkey, pimento and sherry. Heat through gently for about 15 minutes.

Serve hot with rice or over hot buttered toast.
Serves 4

Turkey suprême

METRIC/IMPERIAL
25g/1oz butter
1 small onion, peeled and grated
3 × 15ml spoons/ 3 tablespoons plain flour
300ml/½ pint turkey stock
1 × 5ml spoon/1 teaspoon lemon juice
100g/4oz mushrooms, sliced
0.5kg/1lb cooked turkey meat, diced
225g/8oz long-grain rice
salt
1 egg yolk
4 × 15ml spoons/ 4 tablespoons double cream
freshly ground black pepper
pinch of cayenne pepper

AMERICAN
2 tablespoons butter
1 small onion, peeled and grated
3 tablespoons all-purpose flour
1¼ cups turkey stock
1 teaspoon lemon juice
1 cup sliced mushrooms
2 cups diced cooked turkey meat
1⅓ cups long-grain rice
salt
1 egg yolk
4 tablespoons heavy cream
freshly ground black pepper
pinch of cayenne pepper

Melt the butter in a saucepan. Add the onion and fry until it is soft but not brown. Add the flour and cook, stirring, for 1 minute. Remove from the heat and gradually stir in the stock and lemon juice. Return to the heat and bring to the boil, stirring. Simmer until thickened.

Add the mushrooms and turkey and cook gently for 20 minutes.

Meanwhile, cook the rice in boiling salted water according to the directions on the package. Drain well and pile in a warmed serving dish. Keep hot.

Mix together the egg yolk, cream, salt and pepper to taste and the cayenne. Add a little of the hot turkey liquid, then stir into the saucepan. Heat through gently without boiling. Spoon the turkey mixture over the rice and serve hot.
Serves 4

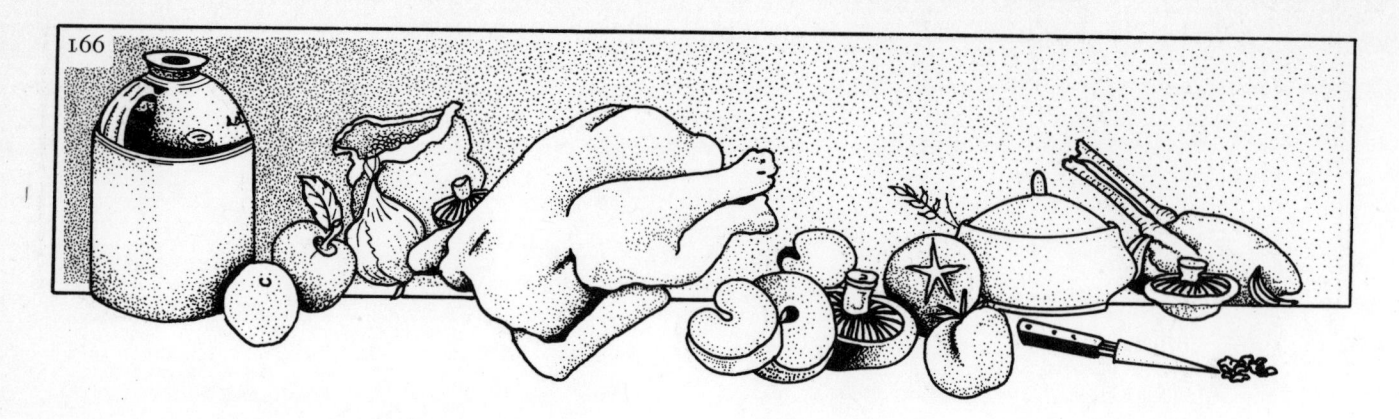

Curried turkey balls

METRIC/IMPERIAL
0.5kg/1lb cooked turkey meat, minced
2 onions, peeled and finely chopped
225g/8oz potatoes, peeled, cooked, drained and mashed
1 garlic clove, crushed
2 × 5ml spoons/2 teaspoons garam masala
salt
freshly ground black pepper
1 egg, lightly beaten
25g/1oz plain flour
5–6 × 15ml spoons/
5–6 tablespoons vegetable oil
1 × 5ml spoon/1 teaspoon ground ginger
1 × 5ml spoon/1 teaspoon ground coriander
1 × 5ml spoon/1 teaspoon ground cumin
1 × 5ml spoon/1 teaspoon turmeric
1 × 400g/14oz can tomatoes, sieved

AMERICAN
2 cups ground cooked turkey meat
2 onions, peeled and finely chopped
½lb potatoes, peeled, cooked, drained and mashed (about 1 cup)
1 garlic clove, crushed
2 teaspoons garam masala
salt
freshly ground black pepper
1 egg, lightly beaten
¼ cup all-purpose flour
5–6 tablespoons vegetable oil
1 teaspoon ground ginger
1 teaspoon ground coriander
1 teaspoon ground cumin
1 teaspoon turmeric
1 × 14oz can tomatoes, strained

Mix together the turkey, half the onions, the potatoes, garlic, garam masala, salt and pepper to taste and the egg. Use your fingertips to bind the mixture. Divide into 24 portions and shape into small balls. Coat in the flour.

Heat 3 × 15ml spoons/3 tablespoons of the oil in a frying pan (skillet). Add the meatballs, in batches, and brown on all sides. Add more oil if necessary. Remove the meatballs from the pan as they are browned.

When all the meatballs have been browned, add another 2 × 15ml spoons/2 tablespoons of oil to the pan. When it is hot, add the remaining onion. Fry until it is soft but not brown. Stir in the spices and cook for 2 minutes.

Add enough water to the tomatoes to make up to 600ml/1 pint/2½ cups. Add to the pan with salt and pepper to taste and stir well. Bring to the boil. Return the meatballs to the pan and spoon the sauce over them. Cover and simmer for 20 minutes. Serve hot.
Serves 4

Turkey croquettes

METRIC/IMPERIAL
25g/1oz butter
50g/2oz plain flour
150ml/¼ pint milk
salt
freshly ground black pepper
pinch of grated nutmeg
350g/12oz cooked turkey meat, diced
100g/4oz mushrooms, finely chopped
1 × 15ml spoon/
1 tablespoon chopped fresh parsley
1 egg, lightly beaten
175g/6oz dry breadcrumbs
vegetable oil for deep frying

AMERICAN
2 tablespoons butter
½ cup all-purpose flour
⅔ cup milk
salt
freshly ground black pepper
pinch of grated nutmeg
1½ cups diced cooked turkey meat
1 cup finely chopped mushrooms
1 tablespoon chopped fresh parsley
1 egg, lightly beaten
1½ cups dry breadcrumbs
vegetable oil for deep frying

Melt the butter in a saucepan. Add 25g/1oz/¼ cup of the flour and cook, stirring, for 1 minute. Remove from the heat and gradually stir in the milk. Return to the heat and bring to the boil, stirring. Simmer until thickened and smooth. Season to taste with salt and pepper and the nutmeg. Remove from the heat and allow to cool.

Stir the turkey, mushrooms and parsley into the sauce. Divide into 8 portions and shape each into a flat cake. Coat in the remaining flour, then dip in the egg and coat in the breadcrumbs. Chill for 1 hour.

Heat the oil in a deep frying pan (deep fat fryer) until it is 190°C/375°F. Fry the croquettes, in batches, for 10 minutes or until they are crisp and golden brown. Drain on absorbent paper and serve hot.
Serves 4

Duck with orange

METRIC/IMPERIAL
1 × 1.75kg/4lb duck
300ml/½ pint water
150ml/¼ pint dry white wine
salt
freshly ground black pepper
1 bay leaf
4 oranges
1 × 15ml spoon/
  1 tablespoon arrowroot

AMERICAN
1 × 4lb duck
1¼ cups water
⅔ cup dry white wine
salt
freshly ground black pepper
1 bay leaf
4 oranges
1 tablespoon arrowroot flour

Prick the duck all over and place on a rack in a roasting tin. Roast in a preheated moderately hot oven (190°C/375°F, Gas Mark 5) for 30 minutes.

Pour off all the fat from the roasting tin. Put the water, wine, salt and pepper and bay leaf in the tin. Pare the rind from one of the oranges and add to the tin. Return to a moderate oven (160°C/325°F, Gas Mark 3) and continue roasting the duck for 1¼ to 1½ hours. Transfer the duck to a warmed serving dish and keep hot.

Skim all the fat from the surface of the cooking liquid in the roasting tin, then strain into a measuring jug. Make up to 450ml/¾ pint/2 cups with water. Squeeze the juice from the peeled orange and 2 of the remaining oranges. Dissolve the arrowroot in the orange juice and mix with the cooking liquid in a saucepan. Bring to the boil, stirring, and simmer until thickened.

Slice the remaining orange and garnish the duck with the slices. Serve hot with the orange sauce.
Serves 4

Chinese duck casserole

METRIC/IMPERIAL
6 medium dried Chinese mushrooms
1.2 litres/2 pints water
5 × 15ml spoons/
  5 tablespoons vegetable oil
4 medium onions, peeled and halved
1 × 2.25kg/5lb duck
4 slices root ginger, peeled and chopped
1 × 5ml spoon/1 teaspoon salt
4 × 15ml spoons/
  4 tablespoons soy sauce
300ml/½ pint dry red wine
1 chicken stock cube
2 leeks, thoroughly cleaned and cut into 5cm/2 inch pieces

AMERICAN
6 medium dried Chinese mushrooms
5 cups water
⅓ cup vegetable oil
4 medium onions, peeled and halved
1 × 5lb duck
4 slices green ginger, peeled and chopped
1 teaspoon salt
4 tablespoons soy sauce
1¼ cups dry red wine
1 chicken bouillon cube
2 leeks, thoroughly cleaned and cut into 2 inch pieces

Soak the mushrooms in 300ml/½ pint/1¼ cups of the water for 30 minutes. Drain the mushrooms, reserving the water. Remove the stalks and slice the caps.

Heat the oil in a frying pan (skillet). Add the onions and fry for 5 minutes. Remove the onions from the pan and drain on absorbent paper. Add the duck to the pan and brown well on all sides. Remove from the heat. Stuff the cavity in the duck with the onions, ginger, salt and mushrooms.

Put the duck in a saucepan. Pour over the remaining water and half the soy sauce. Bring to the boil, then simmer gently for 45 minutes. Turn the duck over halfway through the cooking. Remove from the heat and allow to cool.

Remove the duck from the pan. Skim the fat from the cooking liquid. Discard all but 300ml/½ pint/1¼ cups. Add the wine, reserved mushroom soaking water, the remaining soy sauce and the stock (bouillon) cube. Bring to the boil, stirring.

Return the duck to the pan and simmer gently for 1 hour or until the liquid has reduced by half. Turn the duck twice during the cooking. Transfer the duck to a warmed serving dish. Keep hot.

Add the leeks to the cooking liquid in the pan and return to the boil. Boil rapidly until the liquid has reduced again by half. Arrange the leeks around the duck and pour over the liquid from the pan.
Serves 4 to 6

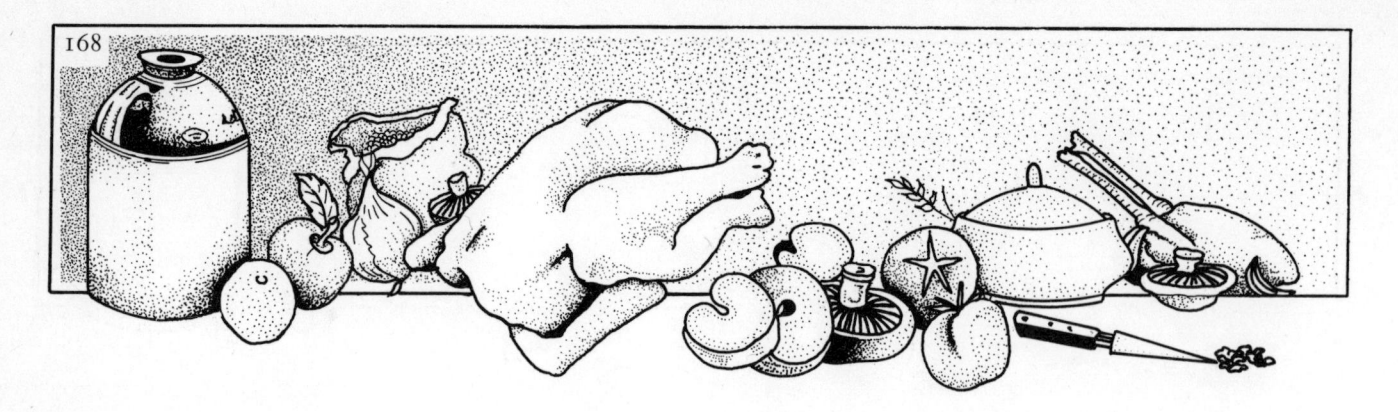

Duck with sweet and sour sauce

METRIC/IMPERIAL
3 × 15ml spoons/
  3 tablespoons soy sauce
1 × 15ml spoon/
  1 tablespoon sugar
1 × 2.5ml spoon/½ teaspoon
  ground ginger
1 garlic clove, crushed
4 duck quarters
25g/1oz butter
1 × 15ml spoon/
  1 tablespoon vegetable oil
300ml/½ pint duck or
  chicken stock
1 × 400g/14oz can
  pineapple chunks
salt
freshly ground black pepper
1 × 15ml spoon/
  1 tablespoon cornflour
2 × 15ml spoons/
  2 tablespoons vinegar

AMERICAN
3 tablespoons soy sauce
1 tablespoon sugar
½ teaspoon ground ginger
1 garlic clove, crushed
4 duck quarters
2 tablespoons butter
1 tablespoon vegetable oil
1¼ cups duck or chicken
  stock
1 × 14oz can pineapple
  chunks
salt
freshly ground black pepper
1 tablespoon cornstarch
2 tablespoons vinegar

Mix together the soy sauce, sugar, ginger and garlic in a shallow dish. Add the duck portions and turn to coat them with the marinade. Leave to marinate for 1 hour.

Melt the butter with the oil in a flameproof casserole. Add the duck portions and brown on all sides. Mix together the stock and syrup from the can of pineapple. Make up to 750ml/1¼ pints/3 cups with water if necessary. Add to the casserole with any remaining marinade and salt and pepper to taste. Cover and transfer to a preheated moderate oven (180°C/350°F, Gas Mark 4). Cook for 1 hour.

Remove the duck from the casserole and keep hot. Dissolve the cornflour (cornstarch) in the vinegar and add to the liquid in the casserole. Bring to the boil on top of the stove, stirring. Simmer until thickened. Stir in the pineapple chunks.

Return the duck portions to the casserole and spoon the sauce over them. Return to the oven, uncovered, and cook for a further 10 minutes. Serve hot, from the casserole.
Serves 4

Duck with turnips

METRIC/IMPERIAL
4 duck quarters
salt
freshly ground black pepper
2 large onions, peeled and
  chopped
0.5kg/1lb small turnips,
  peeled and quartered
2 celery sticks, chopped
1 × 5ml spoon/1 teaspoon
  dried thyme
600ml/1 pint duck or beef
  stock
1 × 15ml spoon/
  1 tablespoon cornflour
2 × 15ml spoons/
  2 tablespoons water

AMERICAN
4 duck quarters
salt
freshly ground black pepper
2 large onions, peeled and
  chopped
1lb small turnips, peeled
  and quartered
2 celery stalks, chopped
1 teaspoon dried thyme
2½ cups duck or beef stock
1 tablespoon cornstarch
2 tablespoons water

Rub the duck pieces with salt and pepper and prick all over. Place in a roasting tin and cook in a preheated moderately hot oven (200°C/400°F, Gas Mark 6) for 20 minutes or until well browned. Transfer the duck pieces to absorbent paper to drain.

Put the onions, turnips, celery and thyme in a casserole. Arrange the duck pieces on top and pour over the stock. Cover and cook in a moderately hot oven (190°C/375°F, Gas Mark 5) for 1 hour.

Transfer the duck and vegetables to a warmed serving plate. Keep hot.

Strain the cooking juices into a saucepan. Skim off all the fat. Dissolve the cornflour (cornstarch) in the water and add to the saucepan. Bring to the boil, stirring, and simmer until thickened and smooth. Pour this sauce over the duck and serve.
Serves 4

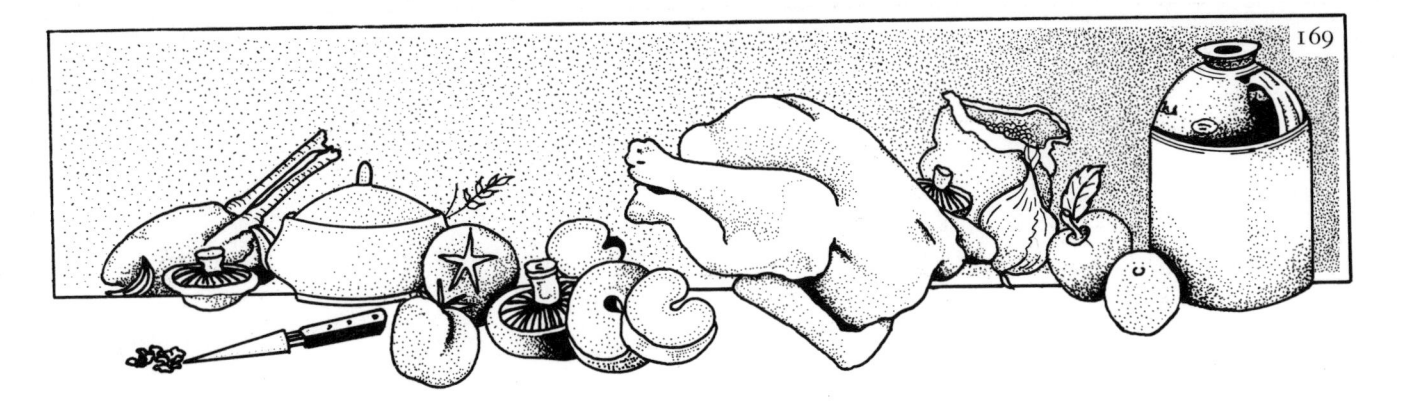

Rabbit in white wine

METRIC/IMPERIAL
25g/1oz plain flour
salt
freshly ground black pepper
1 young rabbit, cut into serving pieces
50g/2oz butter
1 × 15ml spoon/ 1 tablespoon olive oil
1 onion, peeled and finely chopped
1 garlic clove, crushed
2 medium carrots, peeled and grated
2 celery sticks, finely chopped
1 thick slice lean cooked ham, diced
juice of ½ lemon
225g/8oz mushrooms, sliced
300ml/½ pint dry white wine
150ml/¼ pint chicken stock
1 × 2.5ml spoon/½ teaspoon dried rosemary

AMERICAN
¼ cup all-purpose flour
salt
freshly ground black pepper
1 young rabbit, cut into serving pieces
¼ cup butter
1 tablespoon olive oil
1 onion, peeled and finely chopped
1 garlic clove, crushed
2 medium carrots, peeled and grated
2 celery stalks, finely chopped
1 thick slice lean cooked ham, diced
juice of ½ lemon
2 cups sliced mushrooms
1¼ cups dry white wine
⅔ cup chicken stock
½ teaspoon dried rosemary

Mix the flour with salt and pepper and use to coat the rabbit pieces. Melt the butter with the oil in a saucepan. Add the rabbit pieces and fry until they are golden brown. Remove the rabbit from the pan.

Add the onion, garlic, carrots and celery to the pan and fry until the onions are soft but not brown. Stir in the ham, lemon juice, mushrooms, wine, stock and rosemary and bring to the boil. Return the rabbit pieces to the pan with salt and pepper to taste and spoon the sauce over them. Cover and simmer for 45 minutes or until the rabbit is tender. Serve hot.
Serves 4

Rabbit stew

METRIC/IMPERIAL
25g/1oz plain flour
salt
freshly ground black pepper
1 young rabbit, cut into serving pieces
25g/1oz butter
1 × 15ml spoon/ 1 tablespoon olive oil
2 shallots, peeled and chopped
150ml/¼ pint dry red wine
150ml/¼ pint chicken stock
1 tomato, peeled, deseeded and chopped
1 garlic clove, crushed
1 bouquet garni
100g/4oz button mushrooms
fried bread croûtons to garnish

AMERICAN
¼ cup all-purpose flour
salt
freshly ground black pepper
1 young rabbit, cut into serving pieces
2 tablespoons butter
1 tablespoon olive oil
2 shallots, peeled and chopped
⅔ cup dry red wine
⅔ cup chicken stock
1 tomato, peeled, deseeded and chopped
1 garlic clove, crushed
1 bouquet garni
1 cup button mushrooms
fried bread croûtons to garnish

Mix the flour with salt and pepper and use to coat the rabbit pieces. Melt the butter with the oil in a saucepan. Add the rabbit pieces and fry until golden on all sides. Remove the rabbit from the pan. Add the shallots to the pan and fry until softened. Stir in any remaining seasoned flour, then stir in the wine and stock. Bring to the boil, stirring. Add the tomato, garlic, bouquet garni and salt and pepper to taste.

Return the rabbit pieces to the pan, cover and simmer for 30 minutes. Add the mushrooms and simmer for a further 10 minutes or until the rabbit is tender.

Remove the bouquet garni and transfer the rabbit mixture to a warmed serving dish. Serve hot, sprinkled with croûtons.
Serves 4

Rabbit with mustard cream sauce

METRIC/IMPERIAL
1 rabbit, cut into serving pieces
250ml/8fl oz dry white wine
5 × 15ml spoons/ 5 tablespoons oil
1 garlic clove, crushed
1 onion, peeled and chopped
1 × 5ml spoon/1 teaspoon dried rosemary
25g/1oz butter
3 × 15ml spoons/ 3 tablespoons plain flour
300ml/½ pint single cream
1 × 15ml spoon/ 1 tablespoon made French mustard
salt
freshly ground black pepper

AMERICAN
1 rabbit, cut into serving pieces
1 cup dry white wine
⅓ cup oil
1 garlic clove, crushed
1 onion, peeled and chopped
1 teaspoon dried rosemary
2 tablespoons butter
3 tablespoons all-purpose flour
1¼ cups light cream
1 tablespoon prepared French mustard
salt
freshly ground black pepper

Put the rabbit pieces in a shallow dish. Mix together the wine, 3 × 15ml spoons/3 tablespoons of the oil, the garlic, onion and rosemary and pour over the rabbit. Leave to marinate for 6 hours, turning occasionally.

Remove the rabbit pieces from the marinade and pat dry with absorbent paper. Reserve the marinade.

Heat the remaining oil in a saucepan. Add the rabbit pieces and brown on all sides. Pour in the marinade and bring to the boil. Cover and simmer for 1¼ hours or until the rabbit is tender.

Transfer the rabbit pieces to a warmed serving dish and keep hot. Strain the cooking liquid and reserve 150ml/¼ pint/⅔ cup.

Melt the butter in a saucepan. Add the flour and cook, stirring, for 1 minute. Gradually stir in the reserved cooking liquid and bring to the boil, stirring. Simmer until thickened and smooth.

Stir in the cream, mustard and salt and pepper to to taste and heat through gently. Pour the mustard sauce over the rabbit and serve hot.

Serves 4

Jugged hare

METRIC/IMPERIAL
25g/1oz plain flour
salt
freshly ground black pepper
1 hare, cut into serving pieces
40g/1½oz dripping
150ml/¼ pint dry cider
300–450ml/½–¾ pint chicken stock
2 medium onions, peeled and stuck with a few cloves
1 bouquet garni

AMERICAN
¼ cup all-purpose flour
salt
freshly ground black pepper
1 hare, cut into serving pieces
3 tablespoons drippings
⅔ cup hard cider
1¼–2 cups chicken stock
2 medium onions, peeled and stuck with a few cloves
1 bouquet garni

Mix the flour with salt and pepper and use to coat the hare pieces. Melt the dripping in a flameproof casserole. Add the hare pieces and brown on all sides. Stir in the cider and enough stock to cover and bring to the boil. Add the onions and bouquet garni.

Cover and transfer to a preheated moderate oven (160°C/325°F, Gas Mark 3). Cook for 3 to 4 hours or until the hare is tender.

Discard the bouquet garni. Remove the hare pieces and onions from the casserole. Take the meat from the bones and cut into smaller pieces. Return to the casserole.

Discard the cloves and break the onions into slices. Return to the casserole. Taste and add more salt and pepper if necessary. Reheat gently and serve hot, from the casserole. Serve with redcurrant jelly.

Serves 4 to 6

Note: If the hare's blood is available, add it with the cider and stock.

Hare in Madeira sauce

METRIC/IMPERIAL
50g/2oz plain flour
salt
freshly ground black pepper
1 × 5ml spoon/1 teaspoon dried sage
1 hare, cut into serving pieces
4 × 15ml spoons/4 tablespoons oil
4 streaky bacon rashers, rinds removed and diced
300ml/½ pint Madeira
150ml/¼ pint chicken or game stock
225g/8oz button mushrooms

AMERICAN
½ cup all-purpose flour
salt
freshly ground black pepper
1 teaspoon dried sage
1 hare, cut into serving pieces
4 tablespoons oil
4 bacon slices, diced
1¼ cups Madeira
⅔ cup chicken or game stock
2 cups button mushrooms

Mix the flour with salt and pepper and the sage and use to coat the hare pieces. Heat the oil in a flameproof casserole. Add the bacon and fry until it is crisp and has rendered most of its fat. Add the hare pieces and brown on all sides. Remove the hare from the pot.

Sprinkle over any remaining flour mixture and stir well. Gradually stir in the Madeira and stock and bring to the boil, stirring. Return the hare pieces to the casserole and spoon over the sauce. Cover and transfer to a preheated moderate oven (160°C/325°F, Gas Mark 3). Cook for 1½ hours.

Stir in the mushrooms and cook for a further 30 minutes or until the hare is tender. Serve hot, from the casserole.
Serves 6

Game pie

METRIC/IMPERIAL
25g/1oz plain flour
salt
freshly ground black pepper
1 × 2.5ml spoon/½ teaspoon ground cinnamon
0.5kg/1lb boneless venison, diced
120ml/4fl oz dry red wine or port
350g/12oz pork sausage meat
225g/8oz cooked ham, diced
175g/6oz quantity puff pastry★ (made with 175g/6oz flour, etc.)
1 egg, lightly beaten
150ml/¼ pint hot game or beef stock

AMERICAN
¼ cup all-purpose flour
salt
freshly ground black pepper
½ teaspoon ground cinnamon
1lb boneless venison, diced
½ cup dry red wine or port
1½ cups pork sausage meat
1 cup diced cooked ham
1½ cup quantity puff pastry★ (made with 1½ cups flour, etc.)
1 egg, lightly beaten
⅔ cup hot game or beef stock

Mix the flour with salt and pepper and the cinnamon. Use to coat the venison and put in a baking dish. Pour over the wine or port, cover and cook in a preheated moderate oven (180°C/350°F, Gas Mark 4) for 1½ to 2 hours or until the venison is tender.

Put half the sausage meat in the bottom of a 900ml/1½ pint/3¾ cup deep pie dish. Stir the ham into the venison mixture and pour over the sausage meat. Cover with the remaining sausage meat.

Roll out the pastry dough and use to cover the pie dish. Make a hole in the centre (use a pastry funnel if you like) and use the dough trimmings to decorate the top. Brush with the beaten egg.

Bake in a preheated moderately hot oven (200°C/400°F, Gas Mark 6) for 30 minutes or until the pastry is well risen and golden brown. Carefully pour the hot stock through the hole in the pastry lid. Serve hot or cold.
Serves 4 to 6

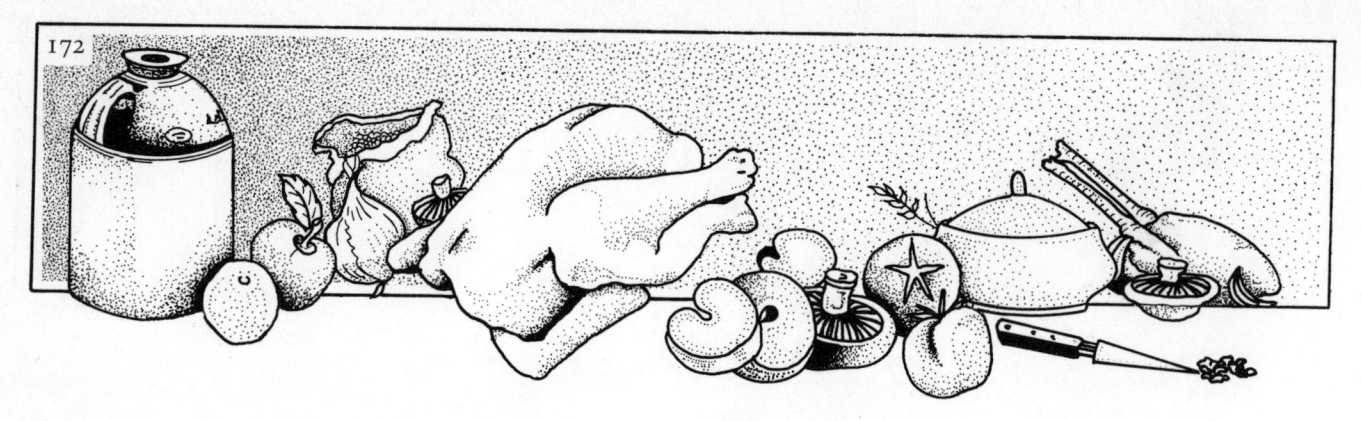

Casseroled pigeons with apples and cider sauce

METRIC/IMPERIAL
40g/1½oz butter
1 × 15ml spoon/
 1 tablespoon olive oil
4 small pigeons
1 onion, peeled and chopped
4 dessert apples
25g/1oz plain flour
450ml/¾ pint chicken stock
 or water
300ml/½ pint dry cider
salt
freshly ground black pepper
1 bouquet garni

AMERICAN
3 tablespoons butter
1 tablespoon olive oil
4 small pigeons
1 onion, peeled and chopped
4 dessert apples
¼ cup all-purpose flour
2 cups chicken stock or
 water
1¼ cups hard cider
salt
freshly ground black pepper
1 bouquet garni

Melt 25g/1oz/2 tablespoons of the butter with the oil in a flameproof casserole. Add the pigeons and fry until golden on all sides. Remove the pigeons from the casserole.

Add the onion and fry until it is soft. Peel, core and slice one of the apples and add to the casserole. Continue to fry the onion until it is golden. Stir in the flour and cook, stirring, for 2 minutes. Gradually stir in the stock or water and cider and bring to the boil, stirring. Simmer until thickened.

Add salt and pepper to taste and the bouquet garni. Return the pigeons to the casserole and spoon the sauce over them. Cover and transfer to a preheated moderate oven (180°C/350°F, Gas Mark 4). Cook for 1½ hours.

Ten minutes before the pigeons are cooked, prepare the garnish. Peel, core and slice the remaining apples into rings. Melt the remaining butter in a frying pan (skillet) and add the apple rings. Fry until they are golden. Remove from the heat and keep hot.

Transfer the pigeons to a warmed serving dish and keep hot. Strain the cooking liquid into a saucepan and boil until reduced and quite thick. Pour over the pigeons and garnish with apple rings.
Serves 4

Pheasant casserole

METRIC/IMPERIAL
25g/1oz butter
1 × 15ml spoon/
 1 tablespoon oil
1 large pheasant, cut into
 4 pieces
1 large onion, peeled and
 chopped
50g/2oz plain flour
600ml/1 pint chicken or
 game stock
finely grated rind and juice
 of 1 orange
1 × 15ml spoon/
 1 tablespoon redcurrant
 jelly
150ml/¼ pint port wine
1 bay leaf
salt
freshly ground black pepper

AMERICAN
2 tablespoons butter
1 tablespoon oil
1 large pheasant, cut into
 4 pieces
1 large onion, peeled and
 chopped
½ cup all-purpose flour
2½ cups chicken or game
 stock
finely grated rind and juice
 of 1 orange
1 tablespoon redcurrant
 jelly
⅔ cup port wine
1 bay leaf
salt
freshly ground black pepper

Melt the butter with the oil in a flameproof casserole. Add the pheasant pieces and fry until golden brown on all sides. Remove from the casserole.

Add the onion to the casserole and fry until it is soft but not brown. Stir in the flour and cook, stirring, for 2 minutes. Gradually stir in the stock and bring to the boil, stirring. Simmer until thickened. Stir in the orange rind and juice, redcurrant jelly, port, bay leaf and salt and pepper to taste.

Return the pheasant pieces to the casserole and spoon the liquid over them. Cover and transfer to a preheated moderate oven (160°C/325°F, Gas Mark 3). Cook for 2 to 4 hours depending on the age of the bird. Serve hot, from the casserole.
Serves 4

Crispy herb chicken (page 157)

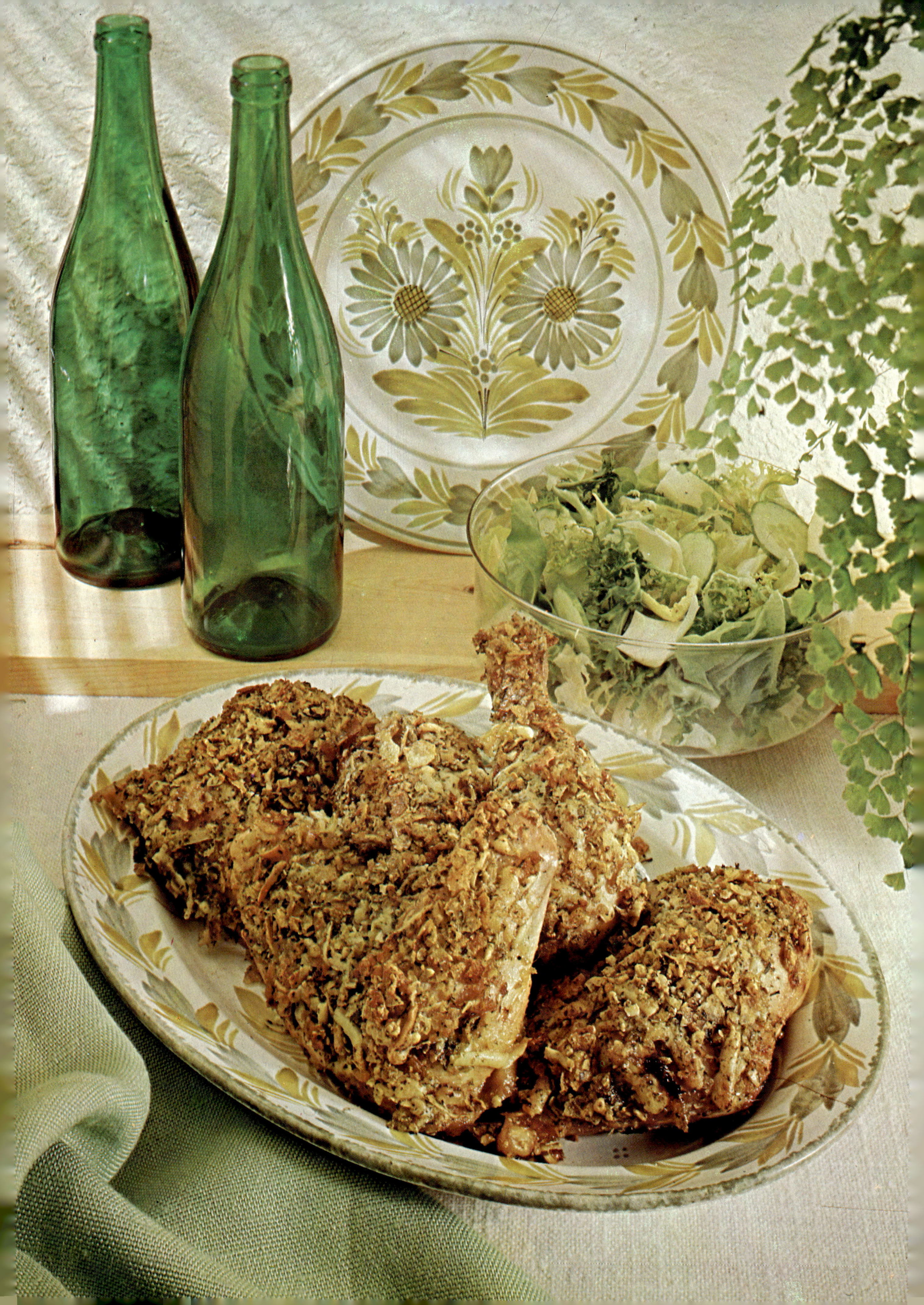

Lemon chicken (page 162); Chinese duck casserole (page 167)

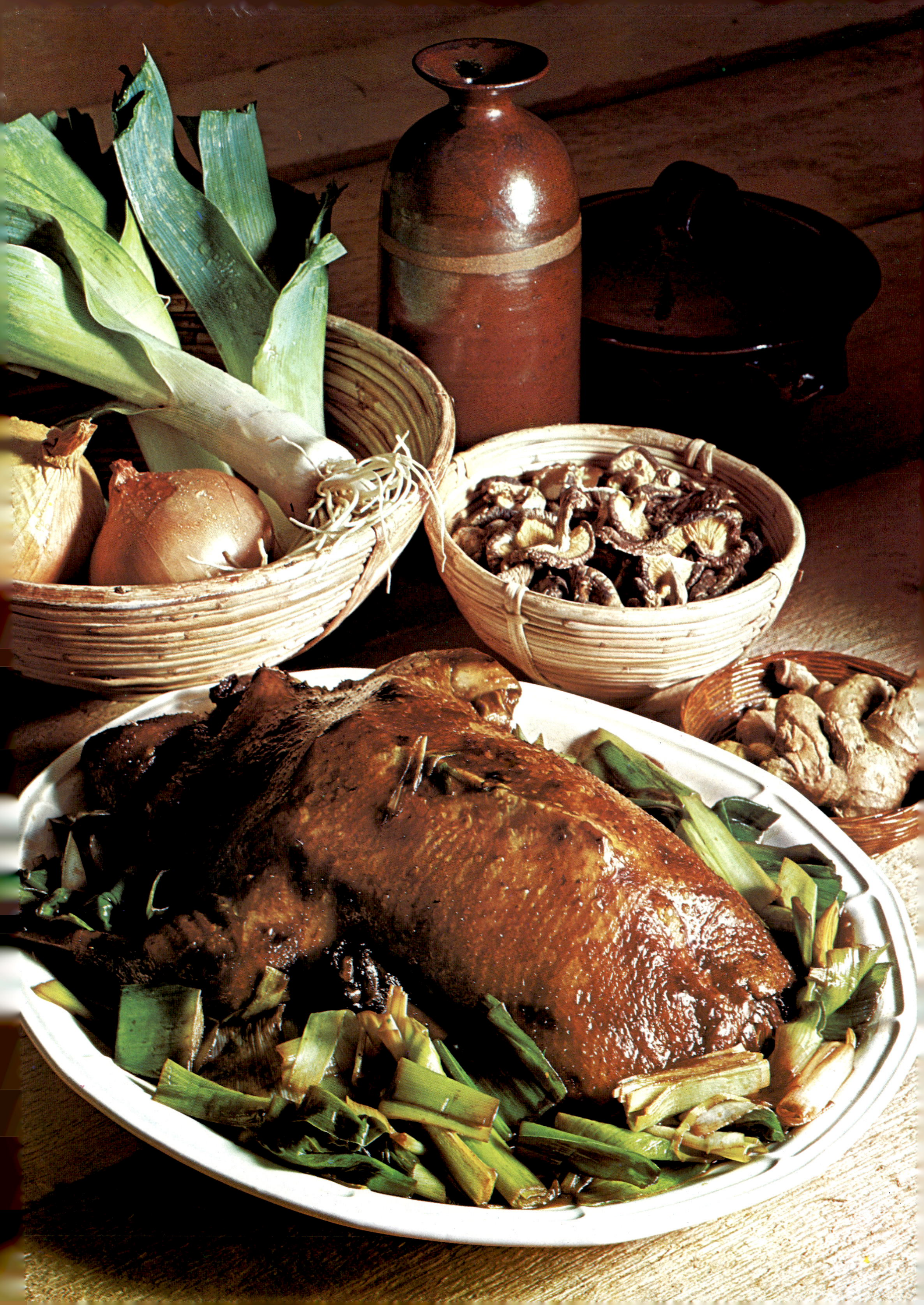

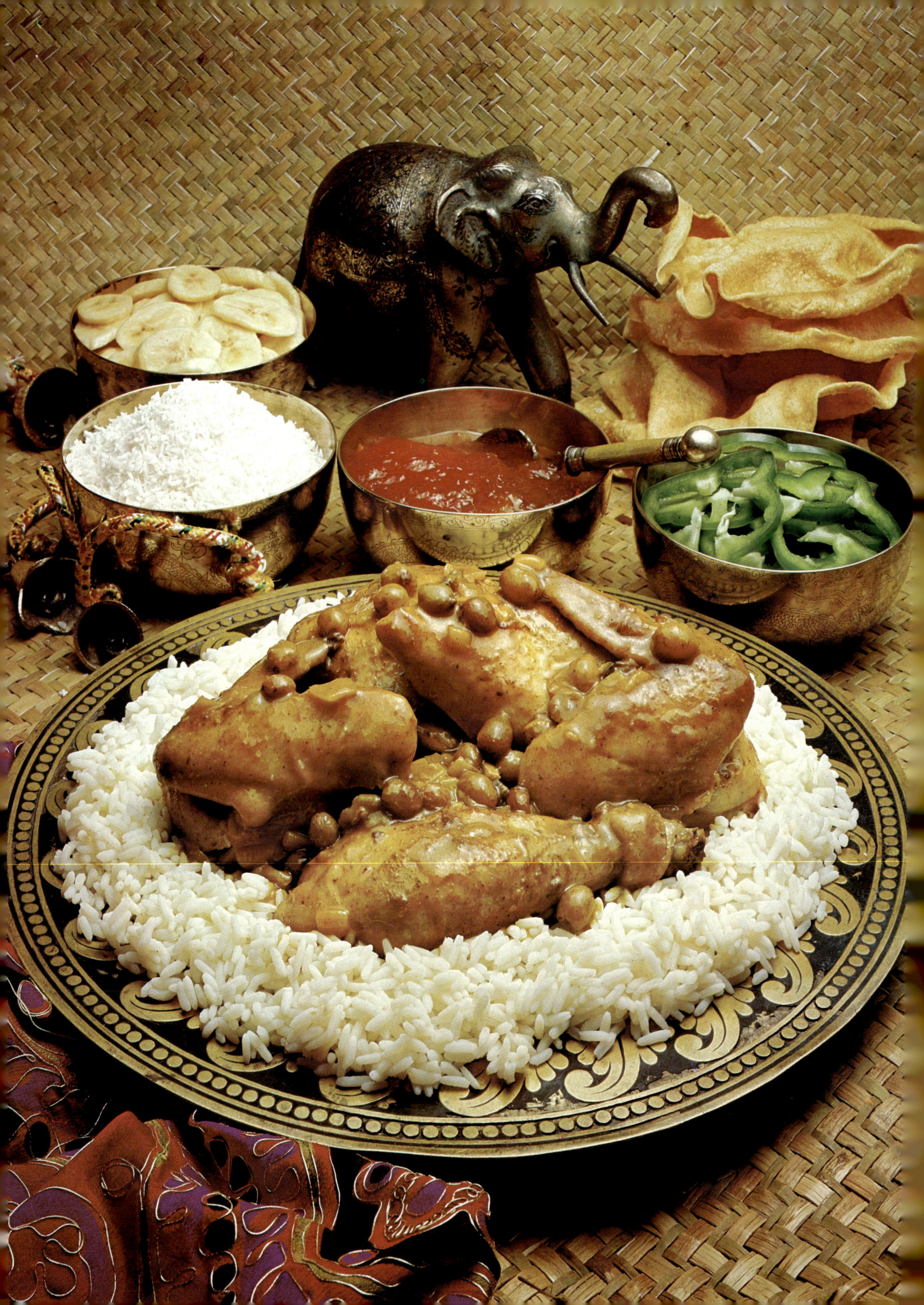

Partridge with cabbage

METRIC/IMPERIAL
2 large partridges
1 small, firm, green
  cabbage, cut into quarters
175g/6oz fat bacon, sliced
  thickly
4 carrots, peeled and sliced
2 onions, peeled and sliced
salt
freshly ground black pepper
6 juniper berries
2 cloves garlic, crushed
pinch of grated nutmeg
white stock
1 × 15ml spoon/
  1 tablespoon arrowroot

AMERICAN
2 large partridges
1 small, firm, green
  cabbage, cut into quarters
6oz bacon (in one piece),
  sliced thickly
4 carrots, peeled and sliced
2 onions, peeled and sliced
salt
freshly ground black pepper
6 juniper berries
2 cloves garlic, crushed
pinch of grated nutmeg
white stock
1 tablespoon arrowroot
  flour

Wipe the partridges. Blanch the cabbage in boiling salted water for 3 to 4 minutes then slice each quarter into thin slices. Fry a little of the bacon in a large saucepan, add the patridges and brown all over.

Put a layer of cabbage in the bottom of a large ovenproof dish, top with the remaining bacon slices, carrots, onions and the partridges. Season to taste with salt and pepper, add the juniper berries, garlic, nutmeg and enough stock to almost cover the vegetables. Cover with the remaining cabbage. Cover the dish with greased greaseproof paper (non-stick parchment) and then a light lid. Place in a preheated moderate oven (160°C/325°F, Gas Mark 3) and cook for about 2 hours. Remove the bacon after 45 minutes and return to the dish about 15 minutes before the end of the cooking time. Drain all the cooked ingredients and carve the partridges. Keep them hot.

Mix the arrowroot with a little of the stock and pour the remainder into a saucepan. Add the arrowroot, bring to the boil and simmer for 2 to 3 minutes. Arrange the cabbage and other vegetables on a warmed serving plate and place the carved partridge meat on top. Pour a little sauce over the cabbage. Serve the remainder separately in a sauce boat.
Serves 4

Game casserole

METRIC/IMPERIAL
25g/1oz butter
2 × 15ml spoons/
  2 tablespoons olive oil
2 partridges or pheasants
1 small onion, peeled and
  chopped
100g/4oz lean veal, minced
100g/4oz lean ham, minced
1 small cooking apple,
  peeled and sliced
1 garlic clove, crushed
salt
freshly ground black pepper
1 bay leaf
4 × 15ml spoons/
  4 tablespoons chicken stock
150ml/¼ pint single cream
2 × 15ml spoons/
  2 tablespoons brandy
watercress to garnish

AMERICAN
2 tablespoons butter
2 tablespoons olive oil
2 partridges or pheasants
1 small onion, peeled and
  chopped
½ cup ground lean veal
½ cup ground cooked ham
1 small baking apple,
  peeled and sliced
1 garlic clove, crushed
salt
freshly ground black pepper
1 bay leaf
4 tablespoons chicken stock
⅔ cup light cream
2 tablespoons brandy
watercress to garnish

Melt the butter with the oil in a flameproof casserole. Add the partridges or pheasants and brown on all sides. Remove from the casserole.

Add the onion, veal, ham, apple and garlic to the casserole and fry for 5 minutes. Add salt and pepper to taste and the bay leaf. Remove from the heat and place the birds on top, breasts down. Sprinkle with the stock.

Cook in a preheated moderate oven (160°C/325°F, Gas Mark 3) for 1 hour. Turn the birds over and pour the cream into the casserole. Warm the brandy and set alight. Pour while flaming into the casserole. When the flames have died away, cover the casserole and return to the oven. Cook for a further 45 minutes.

Transfer the birds to a carving board. Carve and arrange on a warmed serving dish. Keep hot.

Stir the mixture in the casserole and reheat if necessary. Pour over the birds and serve hot, garnished with watercress.
Serves 4

Curried chicken (page 147)

OFFAL
(variety meats)

Liver and bacon hotpot

METRIC/IMPERIAL
50g/2oz plain flour
salt
freshly ground black pepper
0.5kg/1lb lambs' liver, cut into long strips
25g/1oz butter
225g/8oz streaky bacon rashers, rinds removed and chopped
2 large onions, peeled and thinly sliced
1 × 400g/14oz can tomatoes
1 × 15ml spoon/
 1 tablespoon Worcestershire sauce
1 bay leaf
1 × 5ml spoon/1 teaspoon marjoram
300ml/½ pint beef stock

AMERICAN
½ cup all-purpose flour
salt
freshly ground black pepper
1lb lamb liver, cut into long strips
2 tablespoons butter
½lb bacon slices, chopped
2 large onions, peeled and thinly sliced
1 × 14oz can tomatoes
1 tablespoon Worcestershire sauce
1 bay leaf
1 teaspoon marjoram
1¼ cups beef stock

Mix the flour with salt and pepper and use to coat the liver strips. Melt the butter in a flameproof casserole. Add the liver strips and brown on all sides. Remove the liver from the casserole.

Add the bacon and onions to the casserole and fry until the bacon is crisp and the onions are soft but not brown. Stir in the tomatoes with the can juice, the Worcestershire sauce, bay leaf, marjoram and stock. Return the liver strips to the casserole and stir well to coat with the liquid. Cover tightly and transfer to a preheated cool oven (150°C/300°F, Gas Mark 2). Cook for 1½ hours. Discard the bay leaf.

Serve hot, from the casserole.
Serves 4

Liver and bacon rolls with Marsala sauce

METRIC/IMPERIAL
4 lean bacon rashers, rinds removed
4 slices of lamb's liver
salt
freshly ground black pepper
juice of ½ lemon
4 thyme sprigs
25g/1oz plain flour
25g/1oz butter
4 × 15ml spoons/
 4 tablespoons beef stock
4 × 15ml spoons/
 4 tablespoons Marsala
3 tomatoes, peeled and finely chopped

AMERICAN
4 Canadian bacon slices
4 slices of lamb liver
salt
freshly ground black pepper
juice of ½ lemon
4 thyme sprigs
¼ cup all-purpose flour
2 tablespoons butter
4 tablespoons beef stock
4 tablespoons Marsala
3 tomatoes, peeled and finely chopped

Put a bacon rasher (slice) on each slice of liver and sprinkle with salt and pepper and lemon juice. Put a thyme sprig on each and roll up. Secure with wooden cocktail sticks (toothpicks). Mix the flour with salt and pepper and use to coat the liver rolls.

Melt the butter in a frying pan (skillet). Add the liver rolls and brown on all sides. Add the stock, Marsala and tomatoes and bring to the boil. Cover and simmer for 10 minutes or until the liver rolls are cooked. Serve hot.
Serves 2

Liver, bacon and mushrooms

METRIC/IMPERIAL
25g/1oz plain flour
salt
freshly ground black pepper
0.75kg/1½lb lambs' liver, cut into strips
25g/1oz butter
4 lean bacon rashers, rinds removed and diced
2 onions, peeled and thinly sliced
100g/4oz mushrooms, sliced

AMERICAN
¼ cup all-purpose flour
salt
freshly ground black pepper
1½lb lamb liver, cut into strips
2 tablespoons butter
4 Canadian bacon slices, diced
2 onions, peeled and thinly sliced
1 cup sliced mushrooms

Mix the flour with salt and pepper and use to coat the liver strips. Melt the butter in a frying pan (skillet). Add the bacon and onions and fry until the onions are soft but not brown.

Add the liver strips, with more butter if necessary, and fry for about 5 minutes, stirring. Add the mushrooms and fry for a further 3 minutes, stirring, or until the liver is cooked. Serve hot.
Serves 4

Liver with orange

METRIC/IMPERIAL
25g/1oz plain flour
salt
freshly ground black pepper
0.75kg/1½lb lambs' liver, cut into thin slices
25g/1oz butter
1 × 15ml spoon/ 1 tablespoon olive oil
1 large onion, peeled and thinly sliced
300ml/½ pint chicken stock
2 × 5ml spoons/2 teaspoons brown sugar
4 × 15ml spoons/ 4 tablespoons orange juice
2 oranges, peeled and thinly sliced

AMERICAN
¼ cup all-purpose flour
salt
freshly ground black pepper
1½lb lamb liver, cut into thin slices
2 tablespoons butter
1 tablespoon olive oil
1 large onion, peeled and thinly sliced
1¼ cups chicken stock
2 teaspoons brown sugar
4 tablespoons orange juice
2 oranges, peeled and thinly sliced

Mix the flour with salt and pepper and use to coat the liver slices. Melt the butter with the oil in a frying pan (skillet). Add the onion and fry until it is soft but not brown. Add the liver and brown quickly on all sides.

Gradually stir in the stock, sugar and orange juice and bring to the boil. Simmer for 10 to 15 minutes or until the liver is cooked.

Add the orange slices and cook for a further 2 to 3 minutes. Serve hot.
Serves 4

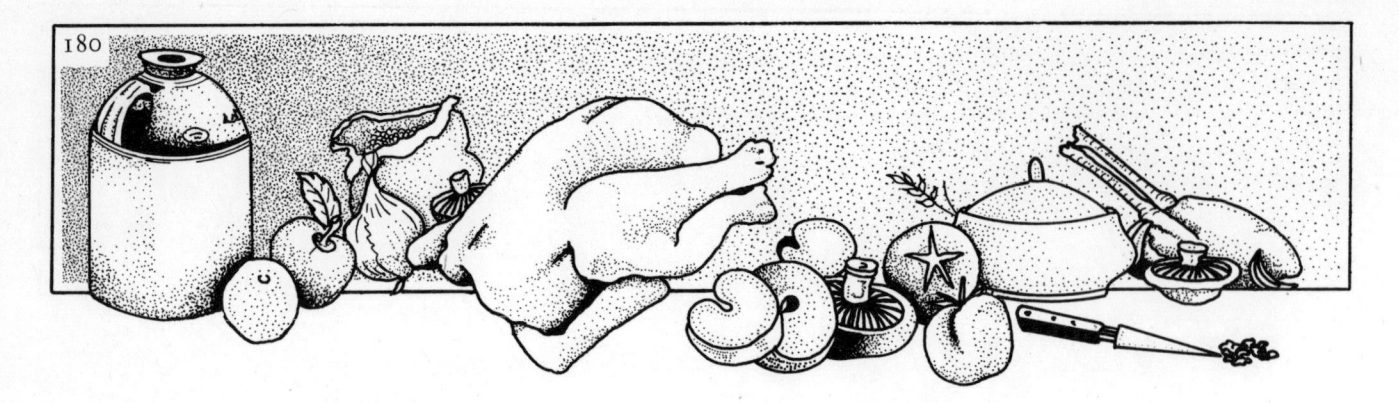

Liver soufflé

METRIC/IMPERIAL
25g/1oz butter
25g/1oz plain flour
150ml/¼ pint milk
350g/12oz lambs' or calves'
  liver, minced
salt
freshly ground black pepper
pinch of sugar
3 egg yolks
4 egg whites

AMERICAN
2 tablespoons butter
¼ cup all-purpose flour
⅔ cup milk
1½ cups ground lamb or calf
  liver
salt
freshly ground black pepper
pinch of sugar
3 egg yolks
4 egg whites

Melt the butter in a saucepan. Add the flour and cook, stirring, for 1 minute. Remove from the heat and gradually stir in the milk. Return to the heat and bring to the boil, stirring. Simmer until thickened and smooth. Remove from the heat and stir in the liver, salt and pepper to taste and the sugar. Allow to cool.

Beat in the egg yolks. Beat the egg whites until they are stiff, then fold into the liver mixture. Spoon into a greased 18cm/7 inch diameter soufflé dish.

Bake in a preheated moderate oven (180°C/350°F, Gas Mark 4) for 35 minutes or until lightly set. Serve immediately.
Serves 4

Chicken livers on toast

METRIC/IMPERIAL
50g/2oz plain flour
salt
freshly ground black pepper
350g/12oz chicken livers,
  cut into small pieces
50g/2oz butter
150ml/¼ pint Madeira
12 slices of hot buttered
  toast, crusts removed
parsley sprigs to garnish

AMERICAN
½ cup all-purpose flour
salt
freshly ground black pepper
¾lb chicken livers, cut into
  small pieces
¼ cup butter
⅔ cup Madeira
12 slices of hot buttered
  toast, crusts removed
parsley sprigs to garnish

Mix the flour with salt and pepper and use to coat the chicken livers. Melt the butter in a frying pan (skillet). Add the livers and fry, stirring, until browned. Stir in the Madeira and bring to the boil, stirring. Simmer gently for 15 minutes.

Spoon the chicken livers onto the hot toast and garnish with parsley sprigs.
Serves 4 to 6

Scrambled eggs with chicken livers

METRIC/IMPERIAL
40g/1½oz butter
1 small onion, peeled and finely chopped
225g/8oz chicken livers, chopped
4 large eggs
3 × 15ml spoons/ 3 tablespoons milk
salt
freshly ground black pepper
pinch of paprika

AMERICAN
3 tablespoons butter
1 small onion, peeled and finely chopped
½lb chicken livers, chopped
4 large eggs
3 tablespoons milk
salt
freshly ground black pepper
pinch of paprika

Melt the butter in a frying pan (skillet). Add the onion and fry until it is soft but not brown. Add the chicken livers and fry until they are lightly browned. Continue cooking for about 4 minutes or until they are tender.

Meanwhile, beat the eggs lightly with the milk, salt and pepper to taste and the paprika. Add to the pan and cook gently, stirring occasionally, until the eggs are lightly scrambled. Serve hot.
Serves 2 to 3

Italian-style liver

METRIC/IMPERIAL
25g/1oz plain flour
salt
freshly ground black pepper
0.75–1kg/1½–2lb lambs' liver, cut into strips
25g/1oz butter
1 × 15ml spoon/ 1 tablespoon olive oil
1 large onion, peeled and sliced
0.5kg/1lb pasta (bows, rings, etc.)
1 × 5ml spoon/1 teaspoon dried oregano
1 × 400g/14oz can tomatoes

AMERICAN
¼ cup all-purpose flour
salt
freshly ground black pepper
1½–2lb lamb liver, cut into strips
2 tablespoons butter
1 tablespoon olive oil
1 large onion, peeled and sliced
1lb pasta (bows, rings, etc.)
1 teaspoon dried oregano
1 × 14oz can tomatoes

Mix the flour with salt and pepper and use to coat the liver strips. Melt the butter with the oil in a frying pan (skillet). Add the onion and fry until it is soft but not brown.

Meanwhile, cook the pasta in boiling salted water for 12 to 15 minutes or until it is *al dente* (just tender to the bite).

Add the liver strips to the frying pan (skillet) and fry, stirring, until browned on all sides. Stir in the oregano and tomatoes with the can juice. Cover and simmer for 5 to 7 minutes or until the liver is cooked through and tender. Do not overcook or the liver will become tough.

Drain the pasta and arrange on a warmed serving dish. Spoon over the liver mixture and serve immediately.
Serves 4

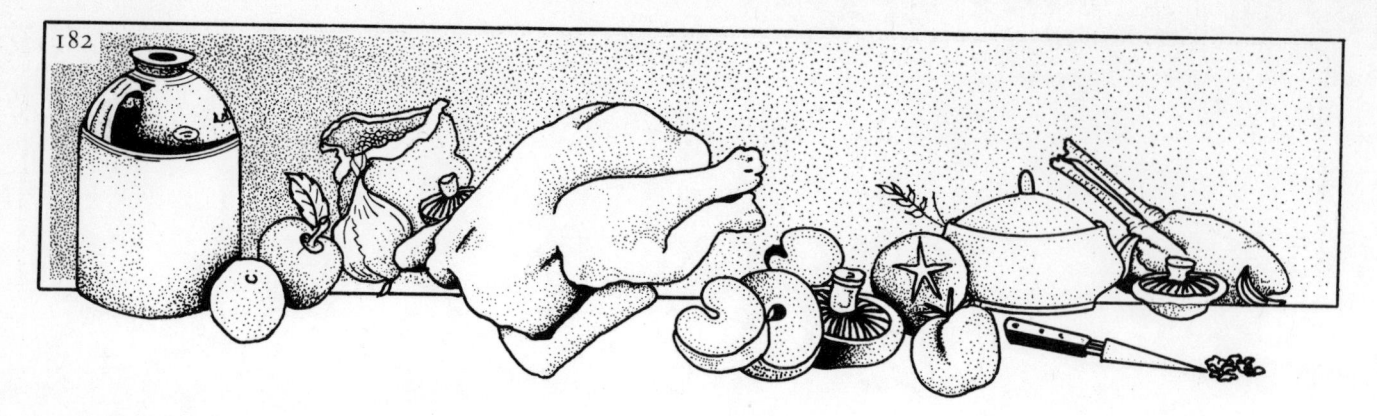

Kidneys in sour cream and whisky sauce

METRIC/IMPERIAL
40g/1½oz butter
1 onion, peeled and finely chopped
1 small red pepper, pith and seeds removed and diced
8 lambs' kidneys, skinned, cored and chopped
salt
freshly ground black pepper
2 × 15ml spoons/ 2 tablespoons whisky
4 × 15ml spoons/ 4 tablespoons sour cream

AMERICAN
3 tablespoons butter
1 onion, peeled and finely chopped
1 small pimiento, pith and seeds removed and diced
8 lamb kidneys, skinned, cored and chopped
salt
freshly ground black pepper
2 tablespoons whisky
4 tablespoons sour cream

Melt the butter in a frying pan (skillet). Add the onion and red pepper (pimiento) and fry until the onion is soft but not brown. Stir in the kidneys with salt and pepper to taste and fry for a further 15 minutes.

Warm the whisky and set alight. Pour flaming over the kidney mixture. Stir well and when the flames have died away, stir in the sour cream. Heat through gently and serve hot.
Serves 4

Kidneys milanaise

METRIC/IMPERIAL
25g/1oz butter
2 onions, peeled and thinly sliced
150ml/¼ pint beef stock
1 × 225g/8oz can tomatoes, drained and chopped
8 lambs' kidneys, skinned, cored and halved
salt
freshly ground black pepper
2 × 5ml spoons/2 teaspoons cornflour
2 × 15ml spoons/ 2 tablespoons Marsala

AMERICAN
2 tablespoons butter
2 onions, peeled and thinly sliced
⅔ cup beef stock
1 × ½lb can tomatoes, drained and chopped
8 lamb kidneys, skinned, cored and halved
salt
freshly ground black pepper
2 teaspoons cornstarch
2 tablespoons Marsala

Melt the butter in a saucepan. Add the onions and fry until they are soft but not brown. Stir in the stock and tomatoes, then add the kidneys with salt and pepper to taste. Bring to the boil, cover and simmer for 10 to 15 minutes.

Dissolve the cornflour (cornstarch) in the Marsala and add to the saucepan. Simmer, stirring, until thickened. Serve hot.
Serves 4

Sherried kidneys

METRIC/IMPERIAL
25g/1oz plain flour
salt
freshly ground black pepper
8 lambs' kidneys, skinned, cored and halved
25g/1oz butter
2 × 15ml spoons/ 2 tablespoons oil
1 red pepper, pith and seeds removed and thinly sliced
150ml/¼ pint single cream
3 × 15ml spoons/ 3 tablespoons medium sherry

AMERICAN
¼ cup all-purpose flour
salt
freshly ground black pepper
8 lamb kidneys, skinned, cored and halved
2 tablespoons butter
2 tablespoons oil
1 pimiento, pith and seeds removed and thinly sliced
⅔ cup light cream
3 tablespoons medium sherry

Mix the flour with salt and pepper and use to coat the kidney halves. Melt the butter with the oil in a frying pan (skillet). Add the kidney halves and fry until they are browned on all sides. Add the red pepper (pimiento) and fry for a further 20 minutes or until the kidneys are cooked.
    Stir in the cream and sherry and heat through gently. Serve hot.
Serves 4

Devilled kidneys

METRIC/IMPERIAL
25g/1oz butter
1 × 15ml spoon/ 1 tablespoon olive oil
1 onion, peeled and finely chopped
6 streaky bacon rashers, rinds removed and diced
8 lambs' kidneys, skinned, cored and chopped
1 × 225g/8oz can tomatoes
1 × 5ml spoon/1 teaspoon dried oregano
1 × 2.5ml spoon/½ teaspoon cayenne pepper
1 × 5ml spoon/1 teaspoon Worcestershire sauce
dash of Tabasco sauce
4 × 15ml spoons/ 4 tablespoons medium sherry

AMERICAN
2 tablespoons butter
1 tablespoon olive oil
1 onion, peeled and finely chopped
6 bacon slices, diced
8 lamb kidneys, skinned, cored and chopped
1 × ½lb can tomatoes
1 teaspoon dried oregano
½ teaspoon cayenne pepper
1 teaspoon Worcestershire sauce
dash of Tabasco sauce
4 tablespoons medium sherry

Melt the butter with the oil in a frying pan (skillet). Add the onion and bacon and fry until the onion is soft but not brown. Add the kidneys and brown on all sides.
    Stir in the tomatoes with the can juice, the oregano, cayenne, Worcestershire sauce, Tabasco and sherry. Bring to the boil, then simmer for 10 minutes. Taste and add salt if necessary. Serve hot.
Serves 4

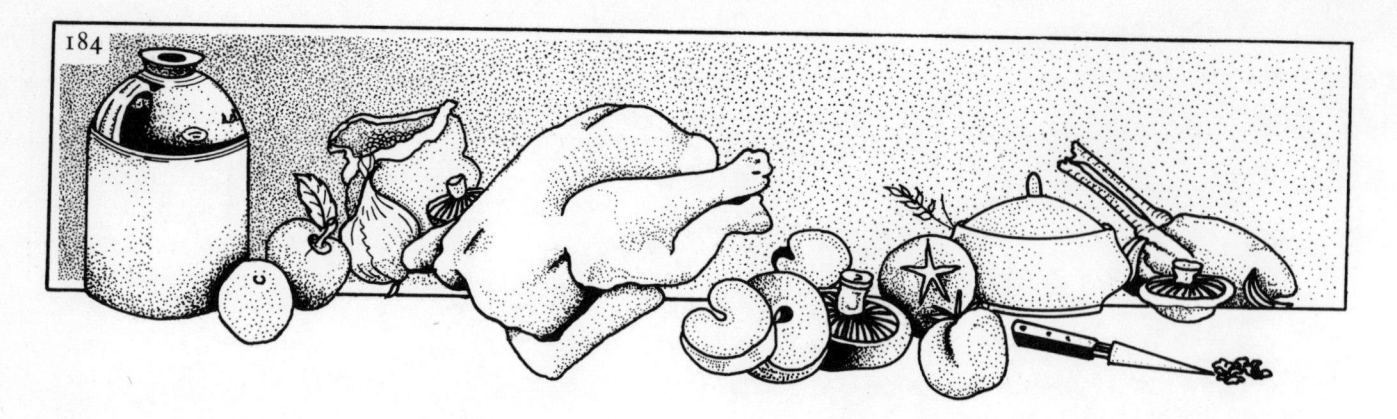

Kidneys in white wine

METRIC/IMPERIAL
25g/1oz butter
1 × 15ml spoon/
 1 tablespoon olive oil
4 veal kidneys, skinned,
 cored and thinly sliced
1 onion, peeled and thinly
 sliced
50g/2oz mushrooms, sliced
150ml/¼ pint dry white
 wine
300ml/½ pint beef stock
1 × 5ml spoon/1 teaspoon
 tomato purée
salt
freshly ground black pepper
1 × 15ml spoon/
 1 tablespoon arrowroot
1 × 15ml spoon/
 1 tablespoon water
chopped parsley to garnish

AMERICAN
2 tablespoons butter
1 tablespoon olive oil
4 veal kidneys, skinned,
 cored and thinly sliced
1 onion, peeled and thinly
 sliced
½ cup sliced mushrooms
⅔ cup dry white wine
1¼ cups beef stock
1 teaspoon tomato paste
salt
freshly ground black pepper
1 tablespoon arrowroot flour
1 tablespoon water
chopped parsley to garnish

Melt the butter with the oil in a saucepan. Add the kidneys and fry until they are well browned. Remove from the pan.

Add the onion to the pan and fry until it is soft but not brown. Add the mushrooms and fry for 2 minutes. Stir in the wine and stock and bring to the boil. Stir in the tomato purée (paste) and salt and pepper to taste and simmer for 5 minutes.

Add the kidneys and reheat gently. Dissolve the arrowroot in the water and stir into the saucepan. Simmer for 2 to 3 minutes or until thickened.

Serve hot, garnished with parsley.
Serves 4

Lemon garlic kidneys

METRIC/IMPERIAL
50g/2oz butter
2 garlic cloves, crushed
8 lambs' kidneys, skinned,
 cored and sliced
salt
freshly ground black pepper
juice of 1 large lemon

AMERICAN
¼ cup butter
2 garlic cloves, crushed
8 lamb kidneys, skinned,
 cored and sliced
salt
freshly ground black pepper
juice of 1 large lemon

Melt the butter in a frying pan (skillet). Add the garlic and fry for 3 minutes. Add the kidneys with salt and pepper to taste and brown on all sides. Sprinkle over the lemon juice and fry for a further 10 minutes or until cooked. Serve hot.
Serves 4

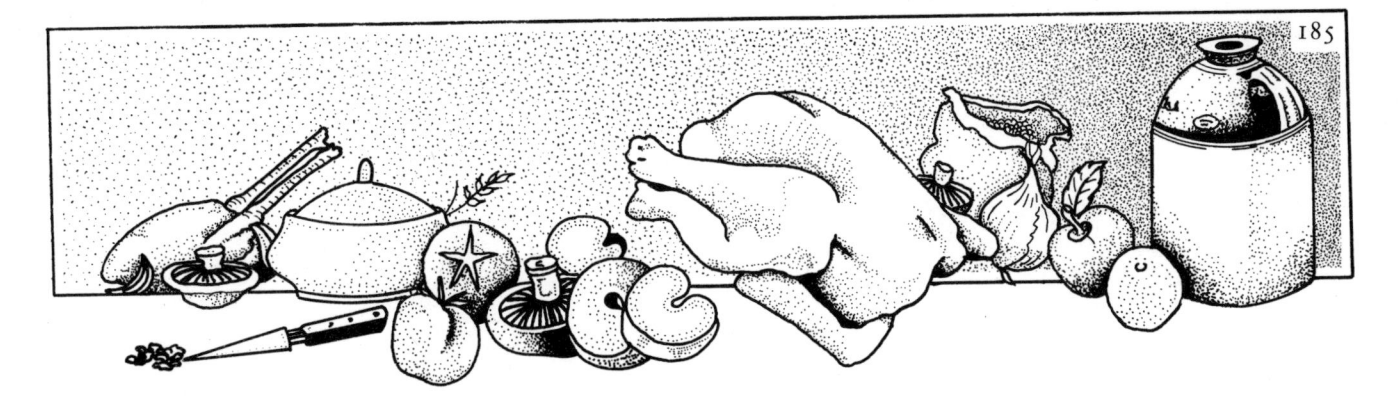

Oxtail stew

METRIC/IMPERIAL
75g/3oz plain flour
salt
freshly ground black pepper
1 medium oxtail, cut into pieces
2 streaky bacon rashers, rinds removed and diced
2 × 15ml spoons/ 2 tablespoons oil
2 onions, peeled and chopped
3 carrots, peeled and sliced
2 celery sticks, chopped
1 small turnip, peeled and chopped
600ml/1 pint beef stock
1 bouquet garni

AMERICAN
¾ cup all-purpose flour
salt
freshly ground black pepper
1 medium oxtail, cut into pieces
2 bacon slices, diced
2 tablespoons oil
2 onions, peeled and chopped
3 carrots, peeled and sliced
2 celery stalks, chopped
1 small turnip, peeled and chopped
2½ cups beef stock
1 bouquet garni

Mix the flour with salt and pepper and use to coat the pieces of oxtail. Put the bacon and oil in a saucepan and fry until the bacon is crisp and has rendered most of its fat. Add the oxtail pieces and brown on all sides. Remove the oxtail from the pan.

Add the vegetables and cook until they are soft but not brown. Return the oxtail pieces to the pan and stir in the stock. Add the bouquet garni and bring to the boil. Cover and simmer for 4 hours or until the meat is falling off the bones. Discard the bouquet garni and serve hot.
Serves 4 to 6

Oxtail and grape casserole

METRIC/IMPERIAL
5 streaky bacon rashers, rinds removed and diced
2 onions, peeled and chopped
1 garlic clove, crushed
4 large carrots, peeled and sliced
2 medium oxtails, cut into 5cm/2 inch pieces
1kg/2lb seedless green grapes
1 bouquet garni
salt
freshly ground black pepper

AMERICAN
5 bacon slices, diced
2 onions, peeled and chopped
1 garlic clove, crushed
4 large carrots, peeled and sliced
2 medium oxtails, cut into 2 inch pieces
2lb seedless green grapes
1 bouquet garni
salt
freshly ground black pepper

Fry the bacon in a flameproof casserole until it is crisp and has rendered most of its fat. Add the onions, garlic and carrots and fry until the onions are soft but not brown. Add the oxtail pieces and turn to brown on all sides.

Lightly crush the grapes and add to the casserole with the bouquet garni and salt and pepper to taste. Cover tightly and transfer to a preheated cool oven (150°C/300°F, Gas Mark 2). Cook for 4 hours.

Remove from the oven and allow to cool, then skim off the fat from the surface. Take the meat off the bones and put in another casserole with the carrots. Discard the bouquet garni and pour the grape mixture into the goblet of an electric blender. Blend until smooth. Pour the grape mixture over the oxtail meat and carrots and stir well.

Reheat in a preheated moderate oven (180°C/ 350°F, Gas Mark 4) for 35 minutes. Serve hot, from the casserole.
Serves 6 to 8

Stuffed lambs' hearts

METRIC/IMPERIAL
4 small lambs' hearts
25g/1oz plain flour
15g/½oz butter
1 × 15ml spoon/
  1 tablespoon oil
600ml/1 pint beef stock
1 onion, peeled and sliced
4 celery sticks, chopped
4 carrots, peeled and sliced
Stuffing:
100g/4oz fresh breadcrumbs
1 onion, peeled and finely
  chopped
40g/1½oz butter, melted
1 × 5ml spoon/1 teaspoon
  dried thyme
1 × 5ml spoon/1 teaspoon
  dried sage
salt
freshly ground black pepper

AMERICAN
4 small lamb hearts
¼ cup all-purpose flour
1 tablespoon butter
1 tablespoon oil
2½ cups beef stock
1 onion, peeled and sliced
4 celery stalks, chopped
4 carrots, peeled and sliced
Stuffing:
2 cups fresh breadcrumbs
1 onion, peeled and finely
  chopped
3 tablespoons butter, melted
1 teaspoon dried thyme
1 teaspoon dried sage
salt
freshly ground black pepper

Slit open the hearts and remove the tubes. Wash the hearts well. Mix together all the stuffing ingredients with salt and pepper to taste. Fill the hearts with the stuffing and tie into the original shapes with string. Mix the flour with salt and pepper and use to coat the hearts.

Melt the butter with the oil in a frying pan (skillet). Add the stuffed hearts and brown quickly on all sides. Remove from the heat.

Transfer the hearts to a casserole and pour over the stock. Cover and cook in a preheated moderate oven (180°C/350°F, Gas Mark 4) for 1¾ hours. Add the onion, celery and carrots and cook for a further 45 minutes. Serve hot, from the casserole.
Serves 4

Deep-fried sweetbreads

METRIC/IMPERIAL
0.5kg/1lb lambs' or calves'
  sweetbreads, soaked in cold
  water for 1 hour and
  drained
300ml/½ pint chicken stock
juice of ½ lemon
salt
freshly ground black pepper
25g/1oz plain flour
1 egg
2 × 15ml spoons/
  2 tablespoons water
75g/3oz dry breadcrumbs
vegetable oil for deep frying
lemon wedges to garnish

AMERICAN
1lb lamb or calf
  sweetbreads, soaked in cold
  water for 1 hour and
  drained
1¼ cups chicken stock
juice of ½ lemon
salt
freshly ground black pepper
¼ cup all-purpose flour
1 egg
2 tablespoons water
¾ cup dry breadcrumbs
vegetable oil for deep frying
lemon wedges to garnish

Put the sweetbreads in a saucepan and cover with fresh water. Bring to the boil, then drain well. Return the sweetbreads to the pan and add the stock, lemon juice and salt and pepper to taste. Bring to the boil and simmer for 10 to 15 minutes. Drain the sweetbreads and allow to cool.

Remove the skin and gristle from the sweetbreads. Mix the flour with salt and pepper and use to coat the sweetbreads. Beat the egg with the water. Dip the sweetbreads in this mixture, then coat with the breadcrumbs.

Heat the oil in a deep frying pan (deep fat fryer) until it is 190°C/375°F. Fry the sweetbreads for 5 to 6 minutes or until they are golden brown. Drain on absorbent paper and serve hot, garnished with lemon wedges.
Serves 4

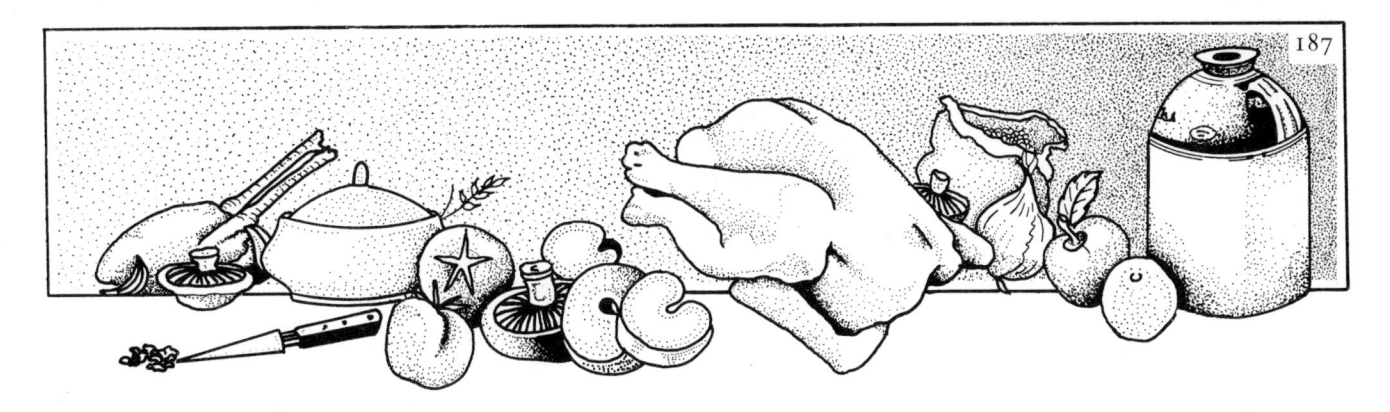

Tongue with raisin sauce

METRIC/IMPERIAL
25g/1oz butter
25g/1oz plain flour
450ml/¾ pint beef stock
salt
freshly ground black pepper
1 × 2.5ml spoon/½ teaspoon grated lemon rind
2 × 5ml spoons/2 teaspoons lemon juice
1 × 5ml spoon/1 teaspoon brown sugar
pinch of ground ginger
100g/4oz raisins
4–8 thick slices of cooked tongue

AMERICAN
2 tablespoons butter
¼ cup all-purpose flour
2 cups beef stock
salt
freshly ground black pepper
½ teaspoon grated lemon rind
2 teaspoons lemon juice
1 teaspoon brown sugar
pinch of ground ginger
⅔ cup raisins
4–8 thick slices of cooked tongue

Melt the butter in a saucepan. Add the flour and cook, stirring, for 1 minute. Remove from the heat and gradually stir in the stock. Return to the heat and bring to the boil, stirring. Simmer until thickened and smooth.

Add salt and pepper to taste, the lemon rind, lemon juice, sugar, ginger and raisins and simmer for 3 minutes. Put the tongue slices in the sauce and turn to coat. Cook gently for 5 to 10 minutes or until the tongue is heated through. Serve hot.
Serves 4

Brains in lemon sauce

METRIC/IMPERIAL
3 sets of calves' brains
salt
juice of ½ lemon
50g/2oz plain flour
freshly ground black pepper
2 eggs, lightly beaten
100g/4oz dry breadcrumbs
vegetable oil for deep frying
Sauce:
6 egg yolks
120ml/4fl oz lemon juice
5 × 15ml spoons/ 5 tablespoons chicken stock

AMERICAN
3 sets of calf brains
salt
juice of ½ lemon
½ cup all-purpose flour
freshly ground black pepper
2 eggs, lightly beaten
1 cup dry breadcrumbs
vegetable oil for deep frying
Sauce:
6 egg yolks
½ cup lemon juice
⅓ cup chicken stock

Soak the brains in salted water for 3 hours. Drain and skin, then wash to remove the blood. Blanch in boiling water to which the lemon juice has been added for 20 minutes. Drain again and cut into small pieces. Dry with absorbent paper.

Mix the flour with salt and pepper in a polythene (plastic) bag. Add the brain pieces and shake to coat with the seasoned flour. Dip in the eggs, then coat with the breadcrumbs.

Heat the oil in a deep frying pan (deep fat fryer) until it is 190°C/375°F. Fry the brain pieces until they are golden. Drain on absorbent paper and keep hot.

To make the sauce, put the egg yolks and lemon juice in a heatproof mixing bowl over a pan of hot water. Beat together, then beat in the stock. Continue beating until the sauce is thick and pale.

Serve the brains hot with the lemon sauce.
Serves 4

MEATLESS DISHES

Baked potatoes and eggs

METRIC/IMPERIAL
4 large potatoes, scrubbed
50g/2oz butter
2 × 15ml spoons/
  2 tablespoons top of the
  milk
salt
freshly ground black pepper
4 eggs

AMERICAN
4 large potatoes, scrubbed
¼ cup butter
2 tablespoons half-and-half
salt
freshly ground black pepper
4 eggs

Prick the potatoes and bake in a preheated moderately hot oven (200°C/400°F, Gas Mark 6) for 1 hour or until soft.
  Slice off the tops, lengthways. Scoop out the potato into a mixing bowl, being careful not to break the skins, and mash until smooth with the butter, milk (half-and-half) and salt and pepper to taste.
  Pile the mixture back into the potato skins and make a hollow in the centre of each. Break an egg into each hollow and sprinkle with salt and pepper. Return to the oven and bake for a further 10 to 15 minutes or until the eggs are just set. Serve hot.
Serves 4

Baked eggs in tomato shells

METRIC/IMPERIAL
4 large tomatoes
salt
freshly ground black pepper
4 eggs
4 × 15ml spoons/
  4 tablespoons double cream
4 × 5ml spoons/4 teaspoons
  grated Parmesan cheese

AMERICAN
4 large tomatoes
salt
freshly ground black pepper
4 eggs
4 tablespoons heavy cream
4 teaspoons grated Parmesan
  cheese

Cut the tops off the tomatoes and scoop out the insides. Turn upside-down on absorbent paper to drain, then season the insides with salt and pepper.
  Break an egg into each tomato shell. Top each with a spoonful of cream and a spoonful of cheese. Arrange in a baking dish.
  Bake in a preheated moderate oven (180°C/350°F, Gas Mark 4) for 15 to 20 minutes or until the eggs are set. Serve hot.
Serves 2 to 4

Aubergine (eggplant) and cheese casserole

METRIC/IMPERIAL
2 large aubergines, sliced
salt
50g/2oz plain flour
freshly ground black pepper
5 × 15ml spoons/
 5 tablespoons oil
225g/8oz Mozzarella
 cheese, thinly sliced
150ml/¼ pint tomato sauce★
50g/2oz Parmesan cheese,
 grated

AMERICAN
2 large eggplants, sliced
salt
½ cup all-purpose flour
freshly ground black pepper
⅓ cup oil
½lb Mozzarella cheese,
 thinly sliced
⅔ cup tomato sauce★
½ cup grated Parmesan
 cheese

Sprinkle the aubergine (eggplant) slices with salt and leave to drain for 20 minutes. Rinse well and pat dry with absorbent paper.

Mix the flour with salt and pepper. Coat the aubergine (eggplant) slices with the seasoned flour. Heat the oil in a frying pan (skillet). Add the aubergine (eggplant) slices in batches, and fry until lightly browned on both sides. Remove the slices from the pan as they brown and drain on absorbent paper.

Make alternate layers of aubergine (eggplant) slices, Mozzarella cheese and tomato sauce in a baking dish. Sprinkle over the Parmesan cheese. Bake in a preheated moderate oven (180°C/350°F, Gas Mark 4) for 25 minutes. Serve hot, from the dish.
Serves 4 to 6

Chick pea and vegetable casserole

METRIC/IMPERIAL
225g/8oz dried chick peas,
 soaked overnight and
 drained
salt
2 × 15ml spoons/
 2 tablespoons oil
1 onion, peeled and
 chopped
0.5kg/1lb tomatoes,
 peeled and chopped
225g/8oz cabbage, cored
 and shredded
1 green pepper, pith and
 seeds removed and diced
1 × 2.5ml spoon/½ teaspoon
 ground ginger
pinch of ground cloves
freshly ground black pepper

AMERICAN
1 cup dried chick peas
 (garbanzos), soaked
 overnight and drained
salt
2 tablespoons oil
1 onion, peeled and chopped
2 cups peeled and chopped
 tomatoes
½lb cabbage, shredded
1 green pepper, pith and
 seeds removed and diced
½ teaspoon ground ginger
pinch of ground cloves
freshly ground black pepper

Cook the chick peas in boiling salted water for about 2 hours or until tender. Drain, reserving the cooking liquid.

Heat the oil in a frying pan (skillet). Add the onion and fry until it is soft but not brown. Stir in the tomatoes, cabbage and green pepper and fry for a further 5 minutes. Add the ginger, cloves and salt and pepper to taste. Stir in the drained chick peas.

Pour the mixture into a casserole and stir in 300ml/½ pint/1¼ cups of the chick pea cooking liquid. Cover and cook in a preheated moderate oven (180°C/350°F, Gas Mark 4) for 1 hour. Serve hot, from the casserole.
Serves 4

Cauliflower cheese surprise

METRIC/IMPERIAL
50g/2oz butter
2 onions, peeled and chopped
100g/4oz mushrooms, chopped
4 tomatoes, peeled and chopped
1 × 200g/7oz can sweetcorn, drained
1 large cauliflower, broken into florets
salt
600ml/1 pint hot mornay sauce*
4 × 15ml spoons/ 4 tablespoons grated Parmesan cheese
4 × 15ml spoons/ 4 tablespoons dry breadcrumbs

AMERICAN
¼ cup butter
2 onions, peeled and chopped
1 cup chopped mushrooms
4 tomatoes, peeled and chopped
1 × 7oz can corn kernels, drained
1 large cauliflower, broken into florets
salt
2½ cups hot mornay sauce*
4 tablespoons grated Parmesan cheese
4 tablespoons dry breadcrumbs

Melt the butter in a saucepan. Add the onions and fry until they are soft but not brown. Stir in the mushrooms and cook for 2 minutes. Add the tomatoes and sweetcorn (corn kernels) and heat through gently.

Meanwhile, cook the cauliflower in boiling salted water until it is just tender. Drain well and keep hot.

Mix one-quarter of the mornay sauce into the vegetable mixture. Spoon into a warmed flameproof serving dish. Arrange the cauliflower florets on top and pour over the remaining sauce. Mix together the Parmesan and breadcrumbs and sprinkle over the top.

Grill (broil) for 3 to 4 minutes or until lightly browned. Serve hot.
Serves 4

Lentil and vegetable stew

METRIC/IMPERIAL
225g/8oz dried lentils, soaked overnight and drained
1.5 litres/2½ pints water
1 onion, peeled
4 whole cloves
1 bay leaf
2 potatoes, peeled and chopped
3 medium courgettes, sliced
2 leeks, thoroughly cleaned and sliced
1 celery stick, chopped
2 carrots, peeled and chopped
1 red pepper, pith and seeds removed and chopped
salt
freshly ground black pepper
1 × 15ml spoon/ 1 tablespoon lemon juice

AMERICAN
1 cup dried lentils, soaked overnight and drained
6¼ cups water
1 onion, peeled
4 whole cloves
1 bay leaf
2 potatoes, peeled and chopped
3 medium zucchini, sliced
2 leeks, thoroughly cleaned and sliced
1 celery stalk, chopped
2 carrots, peeled and chopped
1 pimiento, pith and seeds removed and chopped
salt
freshly ground black pepper
1 tablespoon lemon juice

Put the lentils in a casserole and add the water. Stick the onion with the cloves and add to the casserole with the bay leaf. Cover and cook in a preheated moderate oven (180°C/350°F, Gas Mark 4) for 1 hour.

Remove the onion, discard the cloves and roughly chop the onion. Return to the casserole and add the remaining vegetables with salt and pepper to taste. Cover and cook for a further 1 hour.

Stir in the lemon juice and serve hot, from the casserole.
Serves 4

Cheese and onion casserole

METRIC/IMPERIAL
0.5kg/1lb potatoes, peeled and thinly sliced
2 large onions, peeled and thinly sliced
225g/8oz Cheddar cheese, grated
salt
freshly ground black pepper
150ml/¼ pint milk
15g/½oz butter, melted

AMERICAN
1lb potatoes, peeled and thinly sliced
2 large onions, peeled and thinly sliced
2 cups grated Cheddar cheese
salt
freshly ground black pepper
⅔ cup milk
1 tablespoon butter, melted

Make layers of potatoes, onions and cheese in a casserole, beginning and ending with potatoes. Sprinkle each layer with salt and pepper. Pour in the milk. Brush the top layer of potatoes with the butter.

Bake in a preheated moderate oven (180°C/350°F, Gas Mark 4) for about 1¼ hours. Serve hot, from the casserole.
Serves 3 to 4

Marrow (squash) soufflé

METRIC/IMPERIAL
0.5kg/1lb marrow, peeled, deseeded and cut into thick slices
salt
50g/2oz butter
25g/1oz plain flour
300ml/½ pint milk
freshly ground black pepper
2 × 5ml spoons/2 teaspoons dried summer savory
3 eggs, separated
100g/4oz Cheddar cheese, grated

AMERICAN
1lb summer squash, peeled, deseeded and cut into thick slices
salt
¼ cup butter
¼ cup all-purpose flour
1¼ cups milk
freshly ground black pepper
2 teaspoons dried summer savory
3 eggs, separated
1 cup grated Cheddar cheese

Cook the marrow (squash) in boiling salted water until it is tender but still firm. Drain well and roughly chop.

Melt the butter in a saucepan. Stir in the flour and cook, stirring, for 1 minute. Remove from the heat and gradually stir in the milk. Return to the heat and bring to the boil, stirring. Simmer until thickened and smooth. Stir in salt and pepper to taste and remove from the heat.

Put the marrow (squash) in a greased 1.2 litre/ 2 pint/5 cup soufflé dish. Pour over half the sauce and sprinkle with the savory. Fold together gently.

Beat the egg yolks and cheese into the remaining sauce. Beat the egg whites until stiff and fold into the cheese mixture. Spoon over the marrow (squash) mixture in the soufflé dish. Bake in a preheated moderately hot oven (190°C/375°F, Gas Mark 5) for 30 minutes or until well risen. Serve immediately.
Serves 4

Vegetable curry

METRIC/IMPERIAL
1 cauliflower, broken into florets
6 tomatoes, peeled and sliced
8 small potatoes, peeled and quartered
100g/4oz shelled peas
100g/4oz French beans, sliced
1 × 15ml spoon/ 1 tablespoon turmeric
1.5 × 5ml spoons/ 1½ teaspoons mild curry powder
salt
50g/2oz butter
6 small onions, peeled
1 garlic clove, crushed
300ml/½ pint chicken stock

AMERICAN
1 cauliflower, broken into florets
6 tomatoes, peeled and sliced
8 small potatoes, peeled and quartered
¾ cup shelled peas
½ cup sliced green beans
1 tablespoon turmeric
1½ teaspoons mild curry powder
salt
¼ cup butter
6 small onions, peeled
1 garlic clove, crushed
1¼ cups chicken stock

Put the cauliflower, tomatoes, potatoes, peas and beans on a plate. Sprinkle with the turmeric, curry powder and salt to taste.

Melt the butter in a saucepan. Add the onions and garlic and fry until the onions are lightly browned. Add the spiced vegetables and stock and bring to the boil. Cover and simmer for 20 minutes or until all the vegetables are tender. Serve hot.
Serves 4

Baked stuffed onions with tomato sauce

METRIC/IMPERIAL
4 large onions, peeled
4 × 15ml spoons/ 4 tablespoons fresh breadcrumbs
salt
freshly ground black pepper
100g/4oz cheese, grated
25g/1oz butter, cut into small pieces
300ml/½ pint hot tomato sauce*

AMERICAN
4 large onions, peeled
4 tablespoons fresh breadcrumbs
salt
freshly ground black pepper
1 cup grated cheese
2 tablespoons butter, cut into small pieces
1¼ cups hot tomato sauce*

Cook the onions in boiling water for 15 minutes or until they are just tender but not soft. Drain well and allow to cool.

Scoop out the onion centres and chop finely. Mix with the breadcrumbs, salt and pepper to taste and the cheese. Spoon back into the onion shells, packing firmly and doming the tops. Arrange in a greased baking dish and dot the tops with pieces of butter. Bake in a preheated moderately hot oven (200°C/ 400°F, Gas Mark 6) for 20 to 30 minutes or until the onions are cooked and browned.

Transfer the onions to a warmed serving dish and pour around the tomato sauce. Serve hot.
Serves 4

Oxtail and grape casserole (page 185)

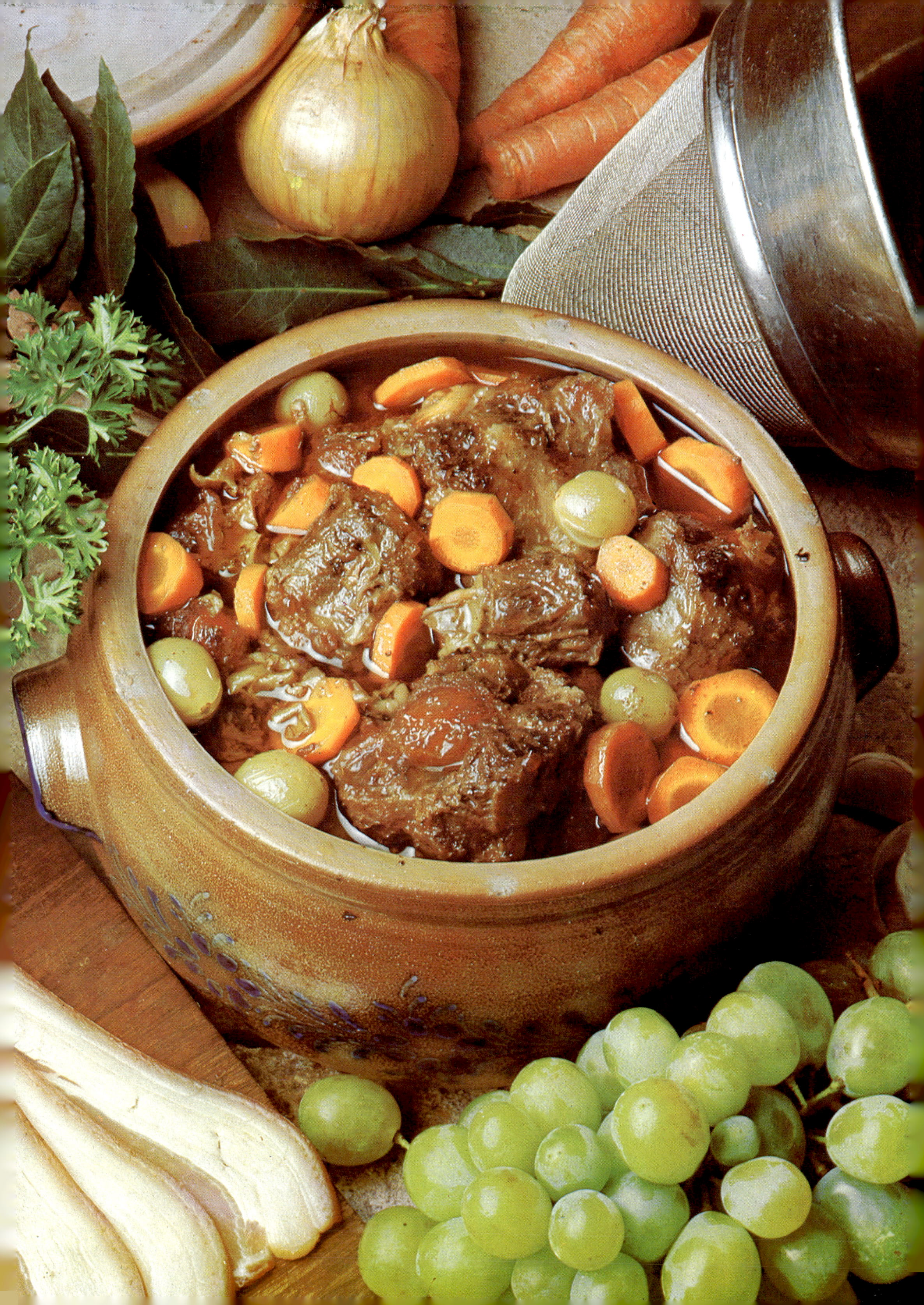

Italian-style liver (page 181); Jugged hare (page 170)

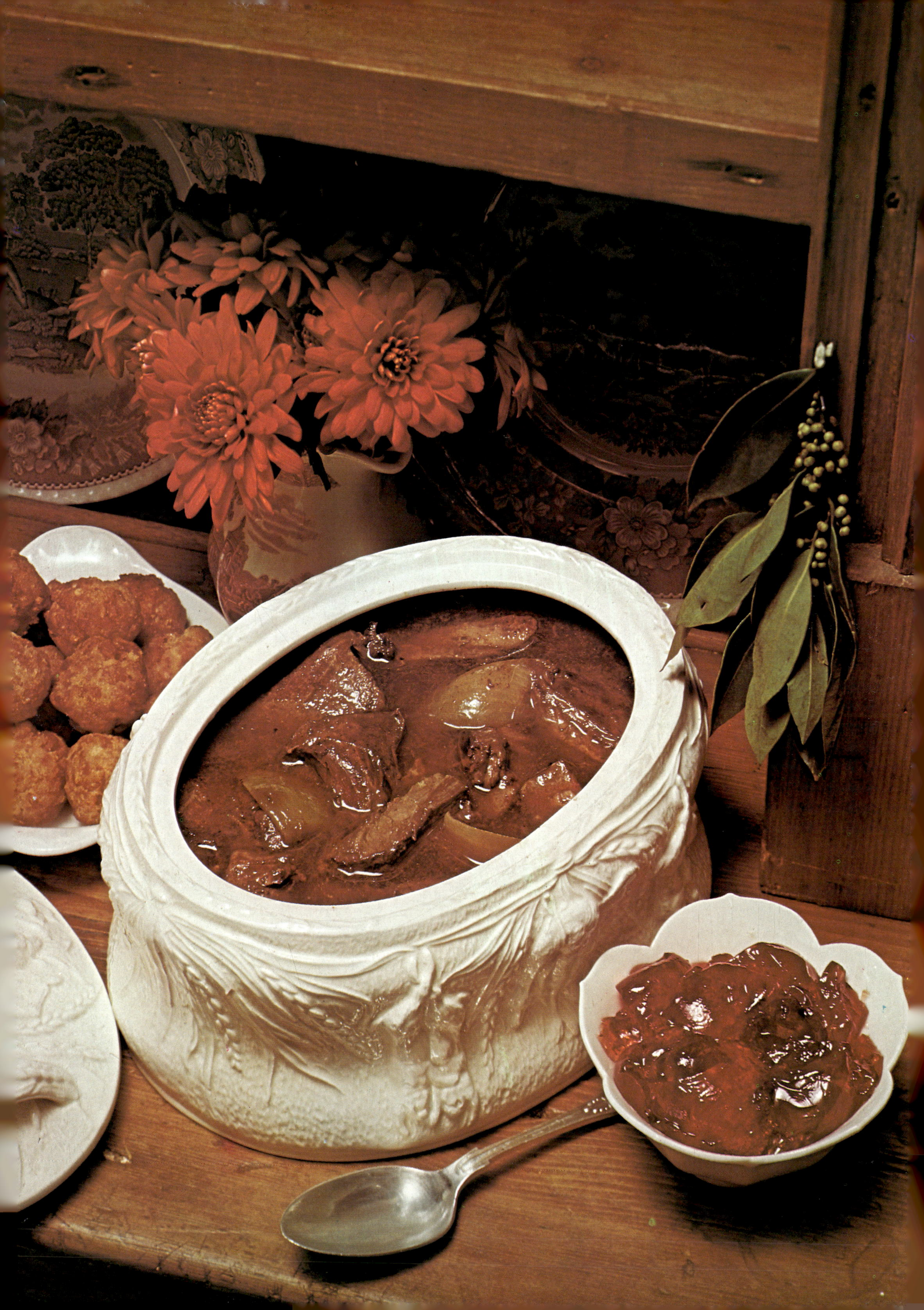

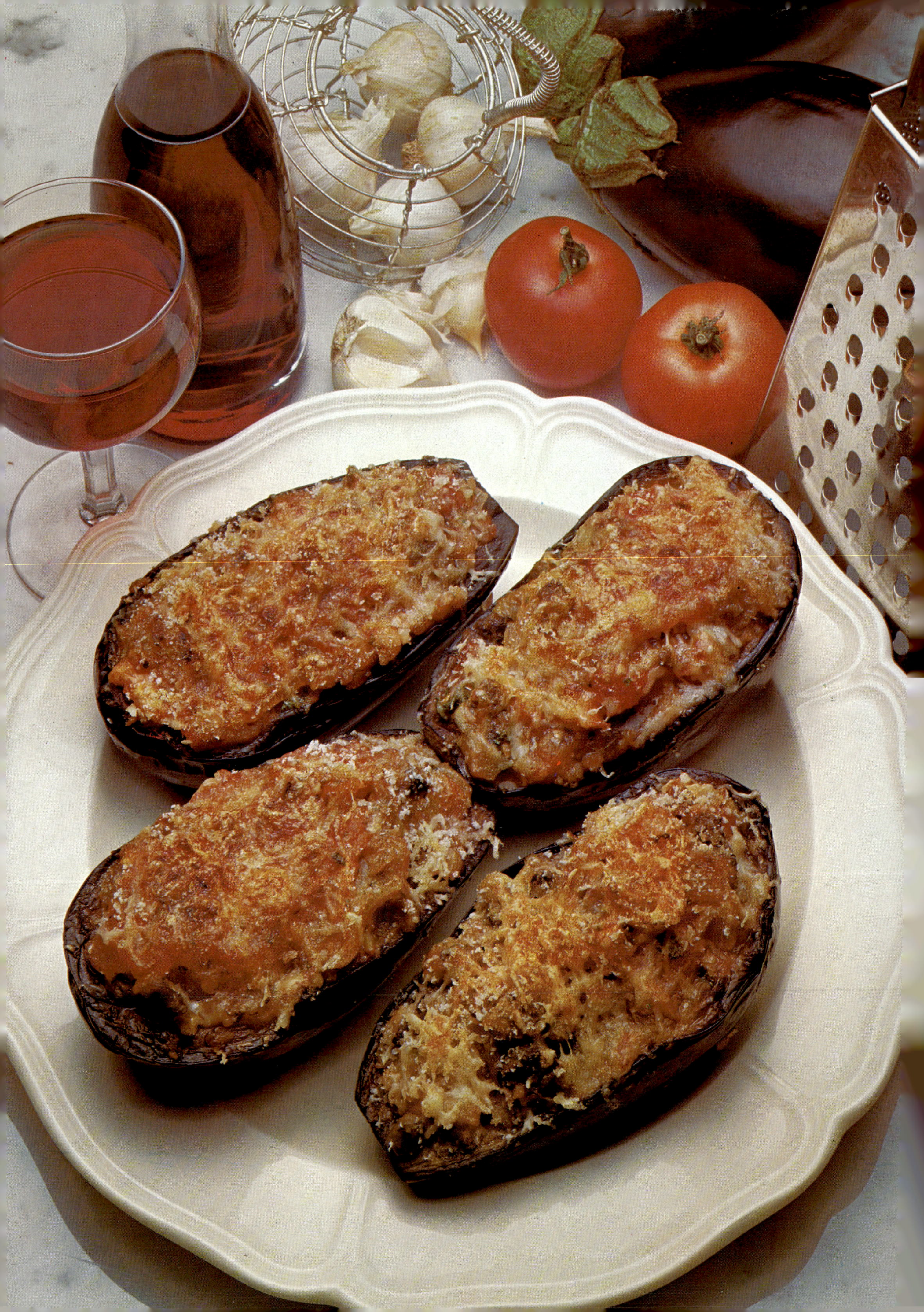

Spanish omelette

METRIC/IMPERIAL
25g/1oz butter
1 small onion, peeled and chopped
3 mushrooms, sliced
1 potato, peeled, cooked and diced
1 canned pimento, chopped
3 × 15ml spoons/ 3 tablespoons cooked peas
4 eggs
salt
freshly ground black pepper

AMERICAN
2 tablespoons butter
1 small onion, peeled and chopped
3 mushrooms, sliced
1 potato, peeled, cooked and diced
1 canned pimiento, chopped
3 tablespoons cooked peas
4 eggs
salt
freshly ground black pepper

Melt the butter in a 20cm/8 inch diameter frying pan (skillet). Add the onion and fry until it is soft but not brown. Stir in the mushrooms, potato, pimento and peas and cook gently for 3 to 4 minutes.

Beat the eggs with salt and pepper to taste. Pour over the vegetable mixture and cook, stirring gently with a fork. As the edges set, lift them to allow any liquid egg mixture to run onto the pan. As soon as the omelette is lightly set, turn out onto a warmed serving plate. Serve hot.
Serves 1 to 2

Quick courgette (zucchini) and tomato bake

METRIC/IMPERIAL
0.5kg/1lb courgettes, sliced
salt
0.5kg/1lb tomatoes, peeled and sliced
freshly ground black pepper
1 × 2.5ml spoon/½ teaspoon dried thyme
450ml/¾ pint hot mornay sauce★
25g/1oz butter
50g/2oz fresh breadcrumbs

AMERICAN
1lb zucchini, sliced
salt
2 cups peeled and sliced tomatoes
freshly ground black pepper
½ teaspoon dried thyme
2 cups hot mornay sauce★
2 tablespoons butter
1 cup fresh breadcrumbs

Blanch the courgettes (zucchini) in boiling salted water for 3 minutes. Drain well. Arrange the courgette (zucchini) and tomato slices, in alternating layers, in a greased baking dish. Sprinkle with salt and pepper to taste and the thyme. Cover with foil and bake in a preheated moderate oven (180°C/350°F, Gas Mark 4) for 10 minutes.

Pour the mornay sauce over the vegetables. Return to the oven and continue baking, uncovered, while you prepare the breadcrumbs.

Melt the butter in a frying pan (skillet). Add the breadcrumbs and fry until they are golden brown and crisp. Sprinkle the breadcrumbs over the cheese sauce and bake for a further 10 minutes. Serve hot, from the dish.
Serves 4

Stuffed aubergines (eggplants) (page 200)

Italian spinach and cheese crêpes

METRIC/IMPERIAL
12 cooked crêpes★
0.75kg/1½lb spinach
25g/1oz butter
salt
freshly ground black pepper
225g/8oz Ricotta or cottage cheese
1 egg
pinch of grated nutmeg
300ml/½ pint hot white sauce★
50g/2oz Parmesan cheese, grated
100g/4oz Mozzarella cheese, thinly sliced

AMERICAN
12 cooked crêpes★
1½lb spinach
2 tablespoons butter
salt
freshly ground black pepper
1 cup Ricotta or cottage cheese
1 egg
pinch of grated nutmeg
1¼ cups hot white sauce★
½ cup grated Parmesan cheese
¼lb Mozzarella cheese, thinly sliced

Keep the crêpes hot.

Cook the spinach for about 7 minutes or until it is tender. (Do not add any water: there should be enough left on the leaves after washing.) Drain the spinach, pressing out any excess moisture. Chop the spinach and put in the goblet of an electric blender with the butter and salt and pepper to taste. Blend to a smooth purée. Add the Ricotta or cottage cheese and blend until the mixture is smooth.

Stir the egg and nutmeg into the spinach mixture. Divide this filling between the crêpes and roll up. Arrange in a greased baking dish.

Mix the white sauce with the Parmesan cheese and pour over the crêpes. Cover with the slices of Mozzarella. Bake in a preheated hot oven (220°C/425°F, Gas Mark 7) for 15 to 20 minutes or until the cheese topping has melted and is lightly browned. Serve hot, from the dish.

Serves 4 to 6

Oeufs florentine

METRIC/IMPERIAL
0.5kg/1lb spinach
40g/1½oz butter
salt
freshly ground black pepper
pinch of grated nutmeg
2 × 15ml spoons/ 2 tablespoons oil
6 eggs
450ml/¾ pint hot mornay sauce★
4 × 15ml spoons/ 4 tablespoons grated Parmesan cheese

AMERICAN
1lb spinach
3 tablespoons butter
salt
freshly ground black pepper
pinch of grated nutmeg
2 tablespoons oil
6 eggs
2 cups hot mornay sauce★
4 tablespoons grated Parmesan cheese

Cook the spinach for about 7 minutes or until it is tender. (Do not add any water: there should be enough left on the leaves after washing.) Drain well, pressing out all the excess moisture. Chop the spinach and return to the saucepan. Add 15g/½oz/1 tablespoon of the butter, salt and pepper to taste and the nutmeg. Stir well. Spread the spinach out in the bottom of a warmed flameproof serving dish and keep hot.

Melt 15g/½oz/1 tablespoon of the remaining butter with 1 × 15ml spoon/1 tablespoon of the oil in a frying pan (skillet). Add three of the eggs and fry until they are just set. Remove the eggs from the pan and arrange on top of the spinach. Fry the remaining eggs in the remaining butter and oil and add to the spinach.

Pour over the sauce and sprinkle the top with the Parmesan cheese. Grill (broil) until the top is beginning to brown. Serve hot.

Serves 4

Mushroom soufflé

METRIC/IMPERIAL
50g/2oz butter
225g/8oz mushrooms, finely chopped
1 shallot, peeled and grated
40g/1½oz plain flour
300ml/½ pint milk
4 egg yolks
50g/2oz Parmesan cheese, grated
1 × 5ml spoon/1 teaspoon lemon juice
pinch of grated nutmeg
salt
freshly ground black pepper
5 egg whites

AMERICAN
¼ cup butter
2 cups finely chopped mushrooms
1 shallot, peeled and grated
6 tablespoons all-purpose flour
1¼ cups milk
4 egg yolks
½ cup grated Parmesan cheese
1 teaspoon lemon juice
pinch of grated nutmeg
salt
freshly ground black pepper
5 egg whites

Melt the butter in a saucepan. Add the mushrooms and shallot and fry for 4 minutes. Remove from the pan with a slotted spoon.

Stir the flour into the fat in the pan and cook, stirring, for 1 minute. Remove from the heat and gradually stir in the milk. Return to the heat and bring to the boil, stirring. Simmer until thickened. Remove from the heat and allow to cool slightly.

Stir in the egg yolks, cheese, lemon juice, nutmeg and salt and pepper to taste. Fold in the mushrooms and shallot. Beat the egg whites until stiff and fold into the mushroom mixture.

Spoon into a greased soufflé dish fitted with a paper collar. Bake in a preheated moderately hot oven (190°C/375°F, Gas Mark 5) for 35 to 40 minutes or until well risen and golden. Serve immediately.
Serves 4

Garbure

METRIC/IMPERIAL
25g/1oz butter
2 × 15ml spoons/2 tablespoons olive oil
2 carrots, peeled and thinly sliced
2 onions, peeled and thinly sliced
1 small turnip, peeled and thinly sliced
¼ cabbage, shredded
2 leeks, thoroughly cleaned and thinly sliced
4 celery sticks, thinly sliced
2 potatoes, peeled and diced
200g/7oz cooked haricot beans
2.25 litres/4 pints stock
salt
freshly ground black pepper
6 slices of French bread
50g/2oz Gruyère cheese, grated

AMERICAN
2 tablespoons butter
2 tablespoons olive oil
2 carrots, peeled and thinly sliced
2 onions, peeled and thinly sliced
1 small turnip, peeled and thinly sliced
¼ head cabbage, shredded
2 leeks, thoroughly cleaned and thinly sliced
4 celery stalks, thinly sliced
2 potatoes, peeled and diced
1 cup cooked navy beans
5 pints stock
salt
freshly ground black pepper
6 slices of French bread
½ cup grated Gruyère cheese

Melt the butter with 1 × 15ml spoon/1 tablespoon of the oil in a saucepan. Add the carrots, onions, turnip, cabbage, leeks, celery and potatoes. Cover and cook gently for 20 minutes.

Stir in the beans and stock and bring to the boil. Re-cover and simmer for 30 minutes.

Purée the soup in an electric blender or by pushing it through a sieve (strainer). Return the puréed soup to the saucepan and add salt and pepper to taste. Continue to simmer, uncovered, until the soup is very thick.

Heat the remaining oil in a frying pan (skillet). Add the bread slices and fry until golden on both sides. Remove from the heat. Spread each slice with a little soup, then sprinkle with cheese.

Ladle the soup into individual bowls and float a slice of bread on each.
Serves 6

Stuffed aubergines (eggplants)

METRIC/IMPERIAL
2 large aubergines
25g/1oz butter
2 onions, peeled and chopped
1 garlic clove, crushed
3 tomatoes, peeled, deseeded and chopped
1 × 2.5ml spoon/½ teaspoon dried thyme
pinch of dried oregano
salt
freshly ground black pepper
4 anchovy fillets, chopped
50g/2oz Parmesan or Cheddar cheese, grated
25g/1oz dry breadcrumbs
2 × 5ml spoons/2 teaspoons olive oil

AMERICAN
2 large eggplants
2 tablespoons butter
2 onions, peeled and chopped
1 garlic clove, crushed
3 tomatoes, peeled, deseeded and chopped
½ teaspoon dried thyme
pinch of dried oregano
salt
freshly ground black pepper
4 anchovy fillets, chopped
½ cup grated Parmesan or Cheddar cheese
¼ cup dry breadcrumbs
2 teaspoons olive oil

Blanch the aubergines (eggplants) in boiling water to cover for 10 minutes. Drain and allow to cool slightly. Cut the aubergines (eggplants) in half lengthways and scoop out the pulp, leaving a shell about 1cm/½ inch thick. Coarsely chop the pulp.

Melt the butter in a frying pan (skillet). Add the onions and garlic and fry until the onions are soft but not brown. Stir in the tomatoes, herbs, salt and pepper to taste and the aubergine (eggplant) pulp. Cover and cook gently for 5 minutes. Stir in the anchovies and remove from the heat.

Fill the aubergine (eggplant) shells with the tomato mixture. Mix together the cheese and breadcrumbs and sprinkle over the tops. Dribble over the oil. Arrange the stuffed aubergines (eggplants) in a grill (broiler) pan and grill (broil) until the tops are golden brown. Serve hot.

Serves 4

Artichoke omelette

METRIC/IMPERIAL
25g/1oz butter
2 canned or fresh artichoke hearts, cut into quarters
3 eggs, lightly beaten
1 × 15ml spoon/1 tablespoon water
salt
freshly ground black pepper
1 × 15ml spoon/1 tablespoon grated Parmesan cheese

AMERICAN
2 tablespoons butter
2 canned or fresh artichoke hearts, cut into quarters
3 eggs, lightly beaten
1 tablespoon water
salt
freshly ground black pepper
1 tablespoon grated Parmesan cheese

Melt half the butter in a saucepan. Add the artichoke hearts and allow to cook gently while you make the omelette.

Beat together the eggs, water and salt and pepper to taste. Melt the remaining butter in a 20cm/8 inch omelette pan or frying pan (skillet). Pour in the egg mixture and cook gently, lifting the set edges of the omelette to allow the liquid egg mixture to run onto the pan. When the omelette is almost cooked, add the artichoke hearts and sprinkle over the cheese. Cook for a further 1 minute, then slide the omelette onto a warmed serving dish. Serve hot.

Serves 1

Egg and cauliflower salad

METRIC/IMPERIAL
1 large cauliflower, broken into florets and cooked
4 eggs, hard-boiled and quartered
150ml/¼ pint mayonnaise★
salt
freshly ground black pepper
2 × 15ml spoons/ 2 tablespoons tomato purée
1 × 5ml spoon/1 teaspoon Worcestershire sauce
pinch of paprika

AMERICAN
1 large cauliflower, broken into florets and cooked
4 eggs, hard-cooked and quartered
⅔ cup mayonnaise★
salt
freshly ground black pepper
2 tablespoons tomato paste
1 teaspoon Worcestershire sauce
pinch of paprika

Gently fold together the cauliflower florets and egg quarters. Mix together the mayonnaise, salt and pepper to taste, the tomato purée (paste) and Worcestershire sauce. Pour this dressing over the egg and cauliflower mixture and sprinkle the top with paprika. Chill lightly before serving.
Serves 4

Vegetable hotpot

METRIC/IMPERIAL
0.75kg/1½lb potatoes, peeled
50g/2oz butter
6 medium courgettes, sliced
0.5kg/1lb tomatoes, peeled, deseeded and chopped
225g/8oz mushrooms, sliced
salt
freshly ground black pepper
250ml/8fl oz sour cream
50g/2oz Parmesan cheese, grated
1 × 5ml spoon/1 teaspoon dried thyme

AMERICAN
1½lb potatoes, peeled
¼ cup butter
6 medium zucchini, sliced
2 cups peeled, deseeded and chopped tomatoes
2 cups sliced mushrooms
salt
freshly ground black pepper
1 cup sour cream
½ cup grated Parmesan cheese
1 teaspoon dried thyme

Cook the potatoes in boiling water for 10 minutes or until they are half cooked.
 Meanwhile, melt half the butter in a saucepan. Add the courgettes (zucchini), cover and cook gently for 10 minutes or until they are just tender. Remove from the heat and stir in the tomatoes, mushrooms and salt and pepper to taste.
 Drain the potatoes and slice them. Arrange a layer of potatoes on the bottom of a baking dish. Cover with a layer of the courgette (zucchini) mixture. Mix together the sour cream, Parmesan cheese and thyme. Spoon a little into the baking dish. Continue making layers in this way, ending with a layer of potatoes. Dot with the remaining butter, cut into small pieces.
 Bake in a preheated moderate oven (180°C/350°F, Gas Mark 4) for 30 minutes or until the potatoes are tender. Serve hot, from the casserole.
Serves 4

BARBECUES & PICNICS

Tandoori chicken

METRIC/IMPERIAL
4 chicken quarters
salt
freshly ground black pepper
25g/1oz butter, melted
Marinade:
150ml/¼ pint natural yogurt
1 × 5ml spoon/1 teaspoon hot chilli powder
pinch of ground ginger
pinch of ground coriander
1 garlic clove, crushed
juice of 1 lemon

AMERICAN
4 chicken quarters
salt
freshly ground black pepper
2 tablespoons butter, melted
Marinade:
⅔ cup unflavored yogurt
1 teaspoon hot chili powder
pinch of ground ginger
pinch of ground coriander
1 garlic clove, crushed
juice of 1 lemon

Rub the chicken with salt and pepper. Mix together the yogurt, chilli powder, ginger, coriander, garlic, lemon juice and salt and pepper to taste in a shallow dish. Add the chicken pieces and turn over to coat with the yogurt marinade. Leave to marinate for 4 hours, turning occasionally.

Remove the chicken from the marinade, shaking off as much of the marinade as possible. Brush with the melted butter and place on the hot barbecue grid. Brown quickly on all sides.

Remove the chicken from the barbecue and place each piece on an individual square of foil. Wrap the chicken pieces securely in the foil and place on the barbecue grid. Cook for a further 20 minutes, turning once.

Heat the marinade gently and serve with the chicken.
Serves 4

Barbecued chicken drumsticks and sausages

METRIC/IMPERIAL
100g/4oz butter, melted
2 × 5ml spoons/2 teaspoons made mustard
2 × 15ml spoons/ 2 tablespoons Worcestershire sauce
salt
freshly ground black pepper
dash of Tabasco sauce (optional)
6 chicken drumsticks
6 large pork sausages

AMERICAN
½ cup butter, melted
2 teaspoons prepared mustard
2 tablespoons Worcestershire sauce
salt
freshly ground black pepper
dash of Tabasco sauce (optional)
6 chicken drumsticks
6 large pork sausages

Mix together the butter, mustard, Worcestershire sauce, salt and pepper to taste and the Tabasco sauce, if using. Brush the drumsticks and sausages with this mixture.

Prepare the barbecue, allowing the charcoal to burn down to fiercely glowing red coals before putting the meat on to cook. Cook the drumsticks and sausages, turning and brushing frequently with the sauce, for 10 to 15 minutes or until cooked through. Serve hot.
Serves 4 to 6

Hamburgers

METRIC/IMPERIAL
1kg/2lb lean beef, minced
25g/1oz fresh breadcrumbs
1 egg
1 × 2.5ml spoon/½ teaspoon dried thyme
salt
freshly ground black pepper
To serve:
6–8 soft baps or buns, split in half
sliced tomatoes
sliced onions
lettuce leaves
ketchup, mustard and relishes

AMERICAN
4 cups ground lean beef
½ cup fresh breadcrumbs
1 egg
½ teaspoon dried thyme
salt
freshly ground black pepper
To serve:
6–8 hamburger buns, split in half
sliced tomatoes
sliced onions
lettuce leaves
ketchup, mustard and relishes

Mix together the beef, breadcrumbs, egg, thyme and salt and pepper to taste, using your fingers to combine the ingredients thoroughly. Divide into 6 to 8 portions and shape into patties.

Place the patties on the barbecue grid and cook for 3 to 5 minutes on each side, or according to personal preference. If you like, toast the buns, cut sides down, on the barbecue.

Place a hamburger patty in each bun and serve hot with the tomatoes, onions, lettuce and condiments.
Serves 4 to 6

Barbecued leg of lamb

METRIC/IMPERIAL
1 × 1.5kg/3½lb leg of lamb, boned and trimmed of excess fat
1 × 5ml spoon/1 teaspoon dry mustard
1 × 5ml spoon/1 teaspoon ground ginger
salt
freshly ground black pepper
2 garlic cloves, cut into slivers
5 × 15ml spoons/ 5 tablespoons oil
Sauce:
4 × 15ml spoons/ 4 tablespoons Worcestershire sauce
4 × 15ml spoons/ 4 tablespoons mild chilli sauce or brown sauce
4 × 15ml spoons/ 4 tablespoons mushroom ketchup
2 × 5ml spoons/2 teaspoons sugar
1 × 15ml spoon/ 1 tablespoon vinegar
25g/1oz butter, melted
cayenne pepper
150ml/¼ pint water

AMERICAN
1 × 3½lb leg of lamb, boned and trimmed of excess fat
1 teaspoon dry mustard
1 teaspoon ground ginger
salt
freshly ground black pepper
2 garlic cloves, cut into slivers
⅓ cup oil
Sauce:
4 tablespoons Worcestershire sauce
4 tablespoons mild chili sauce
4 tablespoons mushroom ketchup
2 teaspoons sugar
1 tablespoon vinegar
2 tablespoons butter, melted
cayenne pepper
⅔ cup water

Impale the leg of lamb securely on a rotisserie skewer. Rub the lamb all over with the mustard, ginger and salt and pepper to taste. Make incisions in the meat and insert the garlic cloves. Brush the lamb generously with oil.

When the charcoal has burned down to glowing red coals, put the spit in place over the heat. Cook the lamb for about 1 hour, turning occasionally and basting with oil if necessary.

Alternatively, flatten the lamb and cook on the barbecue grid, turning every 20 minutes.

Twenty minutes before the lamb is cooked, mix together the ingredients for the sauce with cayenne and salt to taste. Brush the sauce over the lamb and continue basting occasionally until the lamb is cooked.

Serve the lamb hot with any remaining sauce.
Serves 4

Cheese kebabs

METRIC/IMPERIAL
4 streaky bacon rashers
0.5kg/1lb Edam or Gouda cheese, rind removed and cut into 2.5cm/1 inch cubes
8 button mushrooms
8 cocktail onions
8 small tomatoes
1 green pepper, pith and seeds removed and cut into cubes
2 bananas, thickly sliced
1 red-skinned apple, cored and sliced
1 large orange, peeled and segmented
lemon juice
melted butter

AMERICAN
8 bacon slices
1lb Edam or Gouda cheese, rind removed and cut into 1 inch cubes
8 button mushrooms
8 cocktail onions
8 small tomatoes
1 green pepper, pith and seeds removed and cut into cubes
2 bananas, thickly sliced
1 red-skinned apple, cored and sliced
1 large orange, peeled and segmented
lemon juice
melted butter

Halve the bacon rashers crossways (leave American bacon slices whole). Stretch the bacon with a flat-bladed knife and roll up each piece or slice.

Thread the ingredients onto skewers, first sprinkling the apple and banana slices with lemon juice to prevent discoloration. Suggested combinations are: cheese, bacon, mushroom and onion; cheese, tomato and green pepper; banana, apple, orange and cheese. Brush the kebabs with melted butter and place on the barbecue grid. Cook, turning the kebabs and brushing with melted butter, until the ingredients are cooked or softened.
Serves 6 to 8

Marinated pork chops

METRIC/IMPERIAL
4 large pork chops, trimmed of all fat
Marinade:
2 × 15ml spoons/ 2 tablespoons oil
2 × 15ml spoons/ 2 tablespoons mild chilli sauce
2 × 15ml spoons/ 2 tablespoons soy sauce
2 × 15ml spoons/ 2 tablespoons Worcestershire sauce
1 × 15ml spoon/ 1 tablespoon brown sugar
1 × 15ml spoon/ 1 tablespoon tomato purée
1 × 15ml spoon/ 1 tablespoon red wine vinegar
1 × 5ml spoon/1 teaspoon ground ginger
salt
freshly ground black pepper

AMERICAN
4 large pork chops, trimmed of all fat
Marinade:
2 tablespoons oil
2 tablespoons mild chili sauce
2 tablespoons soy sauce
2 tablespoons Worcestershire sauce
1 tablespoon brown sugar
1 tablespoon tomato paste
1 tablespoon red wine vinegar
1 teaspoon ground ginger
salt
freshly ground black pepper

Mix together the oil, chilli sauce, soy sauce, Worcestershire sauce, sugar, tomato purée (paste), vinegar, ginger and salt and pepper to taste in a shallow dish. Add the chops and turn to coat with the spicy mixture. Leave to marinate for at least 4 hours.

Lay the chops on the barbecue grid and cook for about 5 to 7 minutes on each side, basting with the leftover spicy mixture from time to time. Serve hot.
Serves 4

Liver kebabs

METRIC/IMPERIAL
0.75kg/1½lb calves' liver, cut into 2.5cm/1 inch cubes
4 lean bacon rashers, rinds removed and cut into 2.5cm/1 inch pieces
4 tomatoes, quartered
2 × 15ml spoons/ 2 tablespoons olive oil
juice of ½ lemon
salt
freshly ground black pepper
1 × 5ml spoon/1 teaspoon dried basil

AMERICAN
1½lb calf liver, cut into 1 inch cubes
4 Canadian bacon slices, cut into 1 inch pieces
4 tomatoes, quartered
2 tablespoons olive oil
juice of ½ lemon
salt
freshly ground black pepper
1 teaspoon dried basil

Thread the liver cubes, bacon pieces and tomato quarters onto 4 skewers. Mix together the oil, lemon juice, salt and pepper to taste and the basil and brush over the kebabs.
  Cook over the barbecue for about 8 minutes, turning and basting with the oil mixture. Serve hot.
Serves 4

Marinated lamb kebabs

METRIC/IMPERIAL
0.75kg/1½lb lean lamb (from the leg), cut into 2.5cm/1 inch cubes
4 small tomatoes, halved
8 streaky bacon rashers, rinds removed and rolled
8 button mushrooms
2 small onions, peeled and quartered
50g/2oz butter, melted
Marinade:
3 × 15ml spoons/ 3 tablespoons olive oil
1 × 15ml spoon/ 1 tablespoon lemon juice
salt
freshly ground black pepper
1 garlic clove, crushed

AMERICAN
1½lb lean lamb (from the leg), cut into 1 inch cubes
4 small tomatoes, halved
8 bacon slices, rolled
8 button mushrooms
2 small onions, peeled and quartered
¼ cup butter, melted
Marinade:
3 tablespoons olive oil
1 tablespoon lemon juice
salt
freshly ground black pepper
1 garlic clove, crushed

Mix together the oil, lemon juice, salt and pepper to taste and the garlic in a shallow dish. Add the lamb cubes and turn to coat with the marinade. Leave to marinate for at least 2 hours.
  Remove the lamb cubes from the marinade and thread onto skewers alternately with the tomato halves, bacon rolls, mushrooms and onion quarters. Brush the kebabs with the melted butter.
  Place the kebabs on the barbecue grid and cook for about 15 minutes, turning and basting with the melted butter. Serve hot.
Serves 4

Shashlik

METRIC/IMPERIAL
4 streaky bacon rashers, rinds removed
0.75kg/1½lb lean lamb, cut into cubes
12 large mushrooms
8 small tomatoes
1 large green pepper, pith and seeds removed and cut into squares
lemon wedges to serve
Marinade:
4 × 15ml spoons/ 4 tablespoons oil
4 × 15ml spoons/ 4 tablespoons lemon juice
1 × 2.5ml spoon/½ teaspoon dried thyme
1 × 2.5ml spoon/½ teaspoon dried rosemary
salt
freshly ground black pepper

AMERICAN
8 bacon slices
1½lb lean lamb, cut into cubes
12 large mushrooms
8 small tomatoes
1 large green pepper, pith and seeds removed and cut into squares
lemon wedges to serve
Marinade:
4 tablespoons oil
4 tablespoons lemon juice
½ teaspoon dried thyme
½ teaspoon dried rosemary
salt
freshly ground black pepper

Halve the bacon rashers crossways (leave American bacon slices whole). Stretch the bacon with a flat-bladed knife and roll up each piece or slice.

Mix together the ingredients for the marinade with salt and pepper to taste in a shallow dish. Add the lamb cubes and mushrooms and turn to coat with the marinade. Leave to marinate for 4 hours, turning occasionally.

Remove the lamb cubes and mushrooms from the marinade and thread onto skewers with the tomatoes, green pepper squares and bacon rolls. Place on the barbecue grid and cook for 10 to 15 minutes, turning and basting with the marinade from time to time. Serve with lemon wedges.
Serves 4

Fish and pepper kebabs

METRIC/IMPERIAL
0.75kg/1½lb firm-fleshed white fish, cut into cubes
1 red pepper, pith and seeds removed and cut into squares
1 green pepper, pith and seeds removed and cut into squares
about 24 small button mushrooms
100g/4oz butter
juice of 1 large lemon
salt
freshly ground black pepper
dash of Tabasco sauce

AMERICAN
1½lb firm-fleshed white fish, cut into cubes
1 pimiento, pith and seeds removed and cut into squares
1 green pepper, pith and seeds removed and cut into squares
about 24 small button mushrooms
½ cup butter
juice of 1 large lemon
salt
freshly ground black pepper
dash of Tabasco sauce

Thread the fish cubes, pepper (pimiento) and mushrooms onto skewers. Melt the butter in a saucepan and stir in the lemon juice, salt and pepper to taste and the Tabasco. Brush some of this seasoned butter over the kebabs.

Place the kebabs on the barbecue grid and cook, turning and basting with the seasoned butter, until the fish is tender. Serve hot.
Serves 4

Indonesian beef satay

METRIC/IMPERIAL
1kg/2lb rump steak, cut into cubes
Marinade:
1 × 15ml spoon/ 1 tablespoon clear honey
2 × 15ml spoons/ 2 tablespoons soy sauce
2 × 15ml spoons/ 2 tablespoons oil
1 garlic clove, crushed
1 × 5ml spoon/1 teaspoon ground coriander
pinch of chilli powder
1 × 5ml spoon/1 teaspoon caraway seeds

AMERICAN
2lb boneless sirloin steak, cut into cubes
Marinade:
1 tablespoon clear honey
2 tablespoons soy sauce
2 tablespoons oil
1 garlic clove, crushed
1 teaspoon ground coriander
pinch of chili powder
1 teaspoon caraway seeds

Mix together the ingredients for the marinade in a shallow dish. Add the steak cubes and turn to coat in the marinade. Leave to marinate for at least 1 hour, turning occasionally.

Thread the steak cubes onto skewers. Place on the barbecue grid and cook for about 10 minutes, turning and basting with the marinade from time to time. Serve hot.
Serves 6

Cheesy Scotch eggs

METRIC/IMPERIAL
4 eggs, hard-boiled and halved
75g/3oz Cheddar cheese, grated
25g/1oz butter
salt
freshly ground black pepper
350g/12oz pork sausage meat
25g/1oz plain flour
1 egg, lightly beaten
50g/2oz dry breadcrumbs
vegetable oil for deep frying

AMERICAN
4 eggs, hard-cooked and halved
¾ cup grated Cheddar cheese
2 tablespoons butter
salt
freshly ground black pepper
1½ cups pork sausage meat
¼ cup all-purpose flour
1 egg, lightly beaten
½ cup dry breadcrumbs
vegetable oil for deep frying

Remove the yolks from the eggs and mash with the cheese, butter and salt and pepper to taste. Fill the hollows in the egg white halves with the yolk mixture and reshape the eggs.

Divide the sausage meat into 4 portions and wrap 1 portion around each egg to cover completely. Coat with the flour, then with egg and finally with the breadcrumbs.

Heat the oil in a deep frying pan (deep fat fryer) until it is 180°C/350°F. Fry the eggs until they are crisp and brown. Drain well on absorbent paper and allow to cool.

Wrap in foil to take on a picnic.
Makes 4

Meat loaf

METRIC/IMPERIAL
0.5kg/1lb lean beef, minced
225g/8oz lean pork, minced
225g/8oz lean bacon, minced
50g/2oz fresh breadcrumbs
1 small onion, peeled and finely chopped
1 garlic clove, crushed
finely grated rind of ½ lemon
2 large eggs, lightly beaten
300ml/½ pint dry red wine
1 × 2.5ml spoon/½ teaspoon dried sage
1 × 2.5ml spoon/½ teaspoon dry mustard
1 × 5ml spoon/1 teaspoon Worcestershire sauce
1 × 15ml spoon/ 1 tablespoon chopped fresh parsley
salt
freshly ground black pepper

AMERICAN
2 cups ground lean beef
1 cup ground lean pork
1 cup ground Canadian bacon
1 cup fresh breadcrumbs
1 small onion, peeled and finely chopped
1 garlic clove, crushed
finely grated rind of ½ lemon
2 large eggs, lightly beaten
1¼ cups dry red wine
½ teaspoon dried sage
½ teaspoon dry mustard
1 teaspoon Worcestershire sauce
1 tablespoon chopped fresh parsley
salt
freshly ground black pepper

Mix together all the ingredients with salt and pepper to taste. Use your fingers to blend the mixture thoroughly. Spoon into a loaf tin and smooth the top. Cover with foil.

Bake in a preheated moderate oven (160°C/325°F, Gas Mark 3) for 1½ hours.

Pour off the fat from the tin and allow to cool. Wrap in foil and serve at a picnic in thick slices.
Serves 6 to 8

Cornish pasties

METRIC/IMPERIAL
350g/12oz quantity shortcrust pastry★ (made with 350g/12oz flour, etc.)
350g/12oz chuck steak, cut into small pieces
1 large potato, peeled and chopped
1 small onion, peeled and chopped
salt
freshly ground black pepper

AMERICAN
3 cup quantity pie pastry★ (made with 3 cups flour, etc.)
¾lb chuck steak, cut into small pieces
1 large potato, peeled and chopped
1 small onion, peeled and chopped
salt
freshly ground black pepper

Divide the dough into 4 portions and roll out each into a round about 20cm/8 inches in diameter. Mix together the steak, potato, onion and salt and pepper to taste. Divide between the dough rounds.

Dampen the edges of the dough and fold over to make a half-moon shape. Press the edges together to seal. Place on a baking sheet.

Bake in a preheated hot oven (220°C/425°F, Gas Mark 7) for 15 minutes, then reduce the temperature to moderate (160°C/325°F, Gas Mark 3). Bake for a further 1 hour.

Remove from the oven and allow to cool before wrapping in foil.
Makes 4

Leek and tomato salad

METRIC/IMPERIAL
4 medium leeks, thoroughly cleaned
4 tomatoes, peeled and quartered
1 lettuce, torn into small pieces
1 × 5ml spoon/1 teaspoon chopped fresh basil
2 × 5ml spoons/2 teaspoons chopped fresh chervil
4 × 15ml spoons/ 4 tablespoons French dressing★

AMERICAN
4 medium leeks, thoroughly cleaned
4 tomatoes, peeled and quartered
1 head lettuce, torn into small pieces
1 teaspoon chopped fresh basil
2 teaspoons chopped fresh chervil
4 tablespoons French dressing★

Blanch the leeks in boiling water for 5 minutes. Drain well and allow to cool, then cut into thin slices.

Mix together the leeks, tomatoes and lettuce and pack into a rigid plastic container. Sprinkle with the basil and chervil. Carry the dressing in a separate container and pour over the salad at the picnic.
Serves 4 to 6

Pork and ham loaf

METRIC/IMPERIAL
0.5kg/1lb lean pork, minced
0.5kg/1lb lean cooked ham, minced
½ small onion, peeled and finely chopped
150ml/¼ pint white sauce★
1 egg, lightly beaten
salt
freshly ground black pepper
pinch of dried rosemary
6–8 lean bacon rashers, rinds removed
1 × 5ml spoon/1 teaspoon vinegar

AMERICAN
2 cups ground lean pork
2 cups ground lean cooked ham
½ small onion, peeled and finely chopped
⅔ cup white sauce★
1 egg, lightly beaten
salt
freshly ground black pepper
pinch of dried rosemary
6–8 Canadian bacon slices
1 teaspoon vinegar

Mix together the pork, ham, onion, sauce, egg, salt and pepper to taste and the rosemary. Form into a loaf shape and place in the centre of a sheet of foil. Cover the loaf with the bacon rashers (slices) and wrap the foil around the loaf to enclose completely. Seal tightly.

Place the loaf in a saucepan of boiling water to which the vinegar has been added. Simmer for 2½ hours.

Remove from the pan and allow to cool. Replace the foil for the picnic.
Serves 4 to 6

Chef's salad

METRIC/IMPERIAL
1 lettuce, shredded
175g/6oz cooked ham, cut into matchsticks
175g/6oz cooked tongue, cut into matchsticks
350g/12oz cooked chicken meat, cut into matchsticks
175g/6oz Gruyère cheese, cut into matchsticks
4 tomatoes, quartered
3 eggs, hard-boiled and quartered
400ml/14fl oz thousand island dressing★

AMERICAN
1 head lettuce, shredded
6oz cooked ham, cut into matchsticks
6oz cooked tongue, cut into matchsticks
¾lb cooked chicken meat, cut into matchsticks
6oz Gruyère cheese, cut into matchsticks
4 tomatoes, quartered
3 eggs, hard-cooked and quartered
1¾ cups thousand island dressing★

Put the lettuce in a large rigid plastic container. Cover with layers of ham, tongue, chicken and cheese. Top with the tomatoes and eggs. Carry the dressing in a separate container and serve with the salad at the picnic.
Serves 6

Stuffed French loaf

METRIC/IMPERIAL
1 French loaf, split lengthways
100g/4oz butter
2 × 5ml spoons/2 teaspoons made mustard
2 × 15ml spoons/ 2 tablespoons tomato ketchup
1 × 15ml spoon/ 1 tablespoon chopped gherkins
2 × 15ml spoons/ 2 tablespoons chopped spring onions
350g/12oz liver pâté
3 tomatoes, peeled and chopped

AMERICAN
1 French loaf, split lengthwise
½ cup butter
2 teaspoons prepared mustard
2 tablespoons tomato ketchup
1 tablespoon chopped dill pickle
2 tablespoons chopped scallions
1½ cups liver sausage
3 tomatoes, peeled and chopped

Spread the inside of the loaf with half the butter. Cream the remaining butter with the mustard and ketchup. Stir in the gherkins (pickle), spring onions (scallions) and liver pâté (sausage). Spread this mixture inside the loaf. Cover with the chopped tomato.
　Close the loaf and wrap in foil. Serve at a picnic cut into slices.
Serves 4 to 6

Sandwich cake

METRIC/IMPERIAL
1 small white or brown loaf of bread, crusts removed
75g/3oz butter
350g/12oz cream cheese
4 tomatoes, peeled and sliced
¼ cucumber, peeled and sliced
1 × 100g/4oz can salmon, drained and flaked
4 eggs, hard-boiled and chopped
4 × 15ml spoons/ 4 tablespoons mayonnaise★
2 × 15ml spoons/ 2 tablespoons chopped fresh chives

AMERICAN
1 small white or brown loaf of bread, crusts removed
⅓ cup butter
1½ cups cream cheese
4 tomatoes, peeled and sliced
¼ cucumber, peeled and sliced
1 × ¼lb can salmon, drained and flaked
4 eggs, hard-cooked and chopped
4 tablespoons mayonnaise★
2 tablespoons chopped fresh chives

Cut the loaf into 4 slices lengthways. Spread each of these layers with butter.

Place one layer, buttered side up, on a large sheet of foil. Spread with about one-third of the cream cheese, then cover with the tomato slices. Put another bread layer on top. Cover with cucumber slices, then with salmon.

Put another bread layer on top. Mix together the eggs, mayonnaise and chives and spread over the bread. Put the last bread layer on top, to reshape the loaf, buttered side down.

Spread the remaining cream cheese over the top and sides of the loaf to cover completely. Wrap loosely in the foil and chill for at least 1 hour.

To serve at the picnic, cut into slices as you would a loaf of bread.
Serves 6

Gingerbread

METRIC/IMPERIAL
275g/10oz plain flour
50g/2oz cornflour
1 × 5ml spoon/1 teaspoon bicarbonate of soda
1 × 5ml spoon/1 teaspoon ground mixed spice
1 × 15ml spoon/ 1 tablespoon ground ginger
100g/4oz brown sugar
75g/3oz chopped mixed candied peel
50g/2oz crystallized ginger, chopped
2 × 15ml spoons/ 2 tablespoons treacle
150ml/¼ pint milk
150ml/¼ pint corn oil
1 egg, lightly beaten

AMERICAN
2½ cups all-purpose flour
½ cup cornstarch
1 teaspoon baking soda
½ teaspoon grated nutmeg
½ teaspoon ground cinnamon
1 tablespoon ground ginger
⅔ cup brown sugar
½ cup chopped mixed candied peel
⅓ cup chopped candied ginger
2 tablespoons molasses
⅔ cup milk
⅔ cup corn oil
1 egg, lightly beaten

Sift the flour, cornflour (cornstarch), soda, spices and sugar into a mixing bowl. Stir in the candied peel and ginger. Mix together the treacle (molasses), milk, oil and egg and add to the dry ingredients. Mix well together.

Pour into a greased cake tin, 25 × 15cm/10 × 6 inches, and 6cm/2½ inches deep. Bake in a preheated moderate oven (180°C/350°F, Gas Mark 4) for 1¼ hours or until well risen and spongy to the touch.

Allow to cool on a wire rack. Pack in an airtight tin and serve cut into slices.
Serves 8

BUDGET DISHES

Stuffed onion casserole

METRIC/IMPERIAL
4 large onions, peeled
salt
75g/3oz fresh breadcrumbs
225g/8oz cooked meat, minced
25g/1oz butter
pinch of dried sage
freshly ground black pepper
1 small packet frozen French beans
Sauce:
25g/1oz butter
25g/1oz plain flour
300ml/½ pint beef stock
1 × 5ml spoon/1 teaspoon beef or yeast extract

AMERICAN
4 large onions, peeled
salt
1½ cups fresh breadcrumbs
1 cup ground cooked meat
2 tablespoons butter
pinch of dried sage
freshly ground black pepper
1 small package frozen green beans
Sauce:
2 tablespoons butter
¼ cup all-purpose flour
1¼ cups beef stock
1 teaspoon beef or yeast extract

Cook the onions in boiling salted water until they are almost soft. Drain well and allow to cool slightly. Scoop out the centre of each onion and chop finely. Mix with the breadcrumbs, meat, butter, sage and salt and pepper to taste. Pack into the onion shells. Arrange the stuffed onions in a casserole.

To make the sauce, melt the butter in a saucepan. Add the flour and cook, stirring, for 2 to 3 minutes or until it is lightly browned. Remove from the heat and gradually stir in the stock. Return to the heat and bring to the boil, stirring. Simmer until thickened and smooth. Stir in the beef or yeast extract and salt and pepper to taste.

Pour the sauce around the onions and add the beans to the casserole. Cover and bake in a moderately hot oven (190°C/375°F, Gas Mark 5) for 45 minutes. Serve hot, from the casserole.
Serves 4

Cabbage rolls

METRIC/IMPERIAL
12 large cabbage leaves
350g/12oz beef, minced
1 small onion, peeled and grated
1 × 15ml spoon/ 1 tablespoon chopped fresh parsley
salt
freshly ground black pepper
1 × 5ml spoon/1 teaspoon dried thyme
2 × 15ml spoons/ 2 tablespoons brown sugar
1 × 400g/14oz can tomatoes, chopped

AMERICAN
12 large cabbage leaves
1½ cups ground beef
1 small onion, peeled and grated
1 tablespoon chopped fresh parsley
salt
freshly ground black pepper
1 teaspoon dried thyme
2 tablespoons brown sugar
1 × 14oz can tomatoes, chopped

Blanch the cabbage leaves in boiling water for 1 minute. Drain well. Mix together the beef, onion, parsley, salt and pepper to taste and the thyme. Divide into 12 portions and shape each into a fat rectangle. Place one portion on each cabbage leaf, near the stalk end, and roll up to enclose completely.

Arrange the cabbage rolls in a greased baking dish or casserole and sprinkle with the sugar. Pour over the tomatoes with the can juice. Cover with a lid or foil and bake in a preheated moderately hot oven (190°C/375°F, Gas Mark 5) for 1 hour or until tender. Serve hot.
Serves 4

Moussaka (page 219)

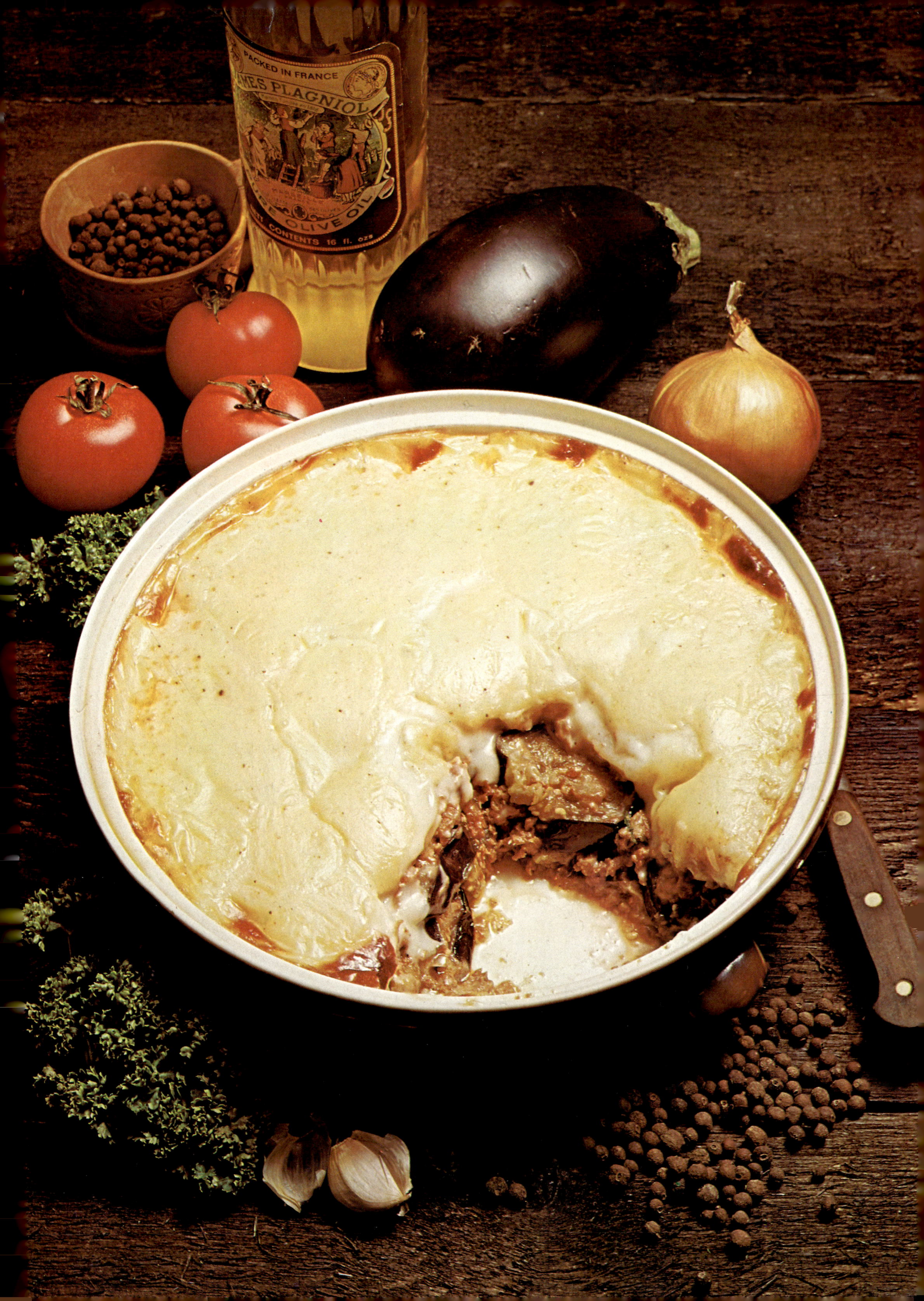
PACKED IN FRANCE
PLAGNIOL
OLIVE OIL
CONTENTS 16 fl. ozs

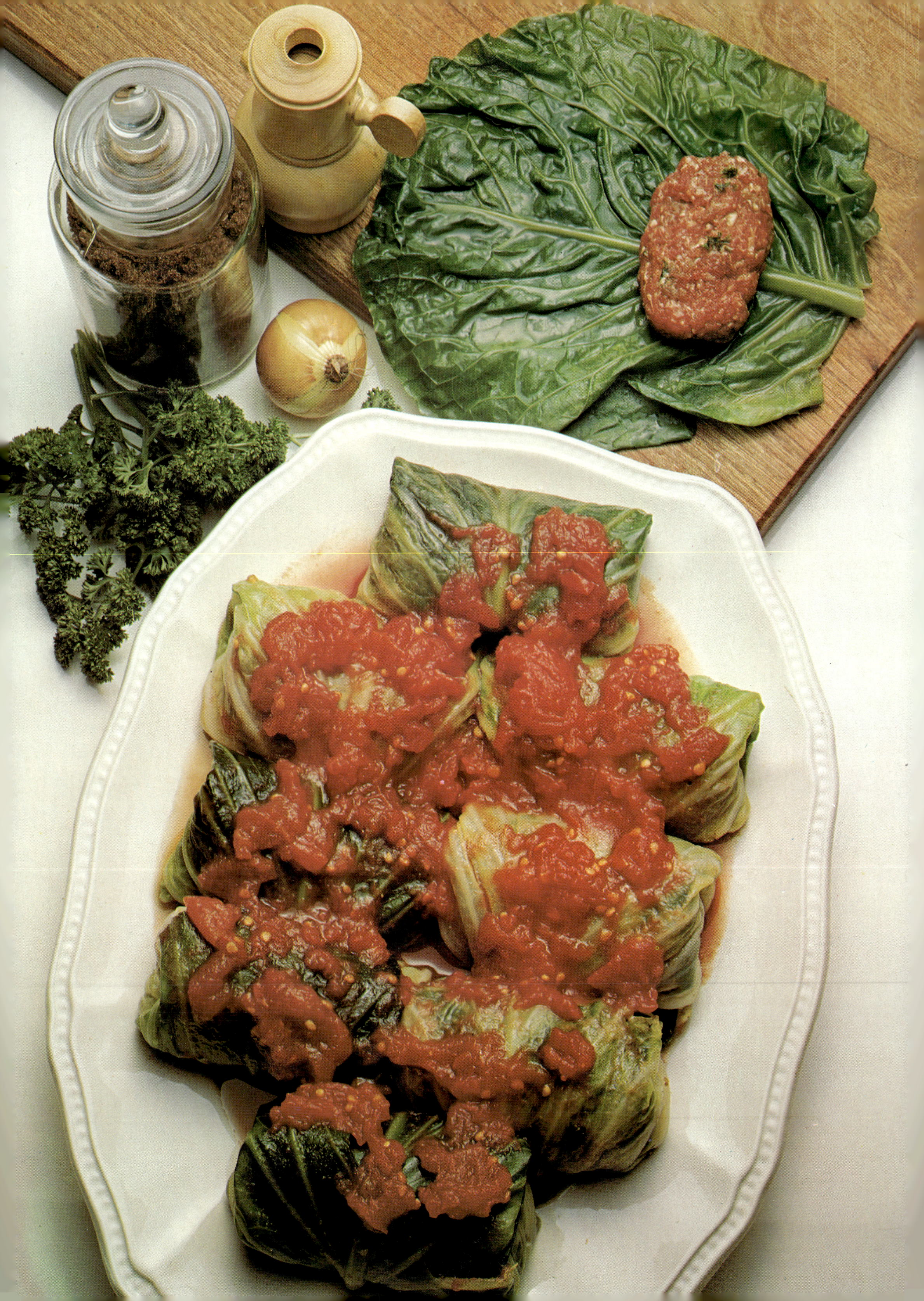

Cabbage rolls (page 212); Cheese soufflé (page 244)

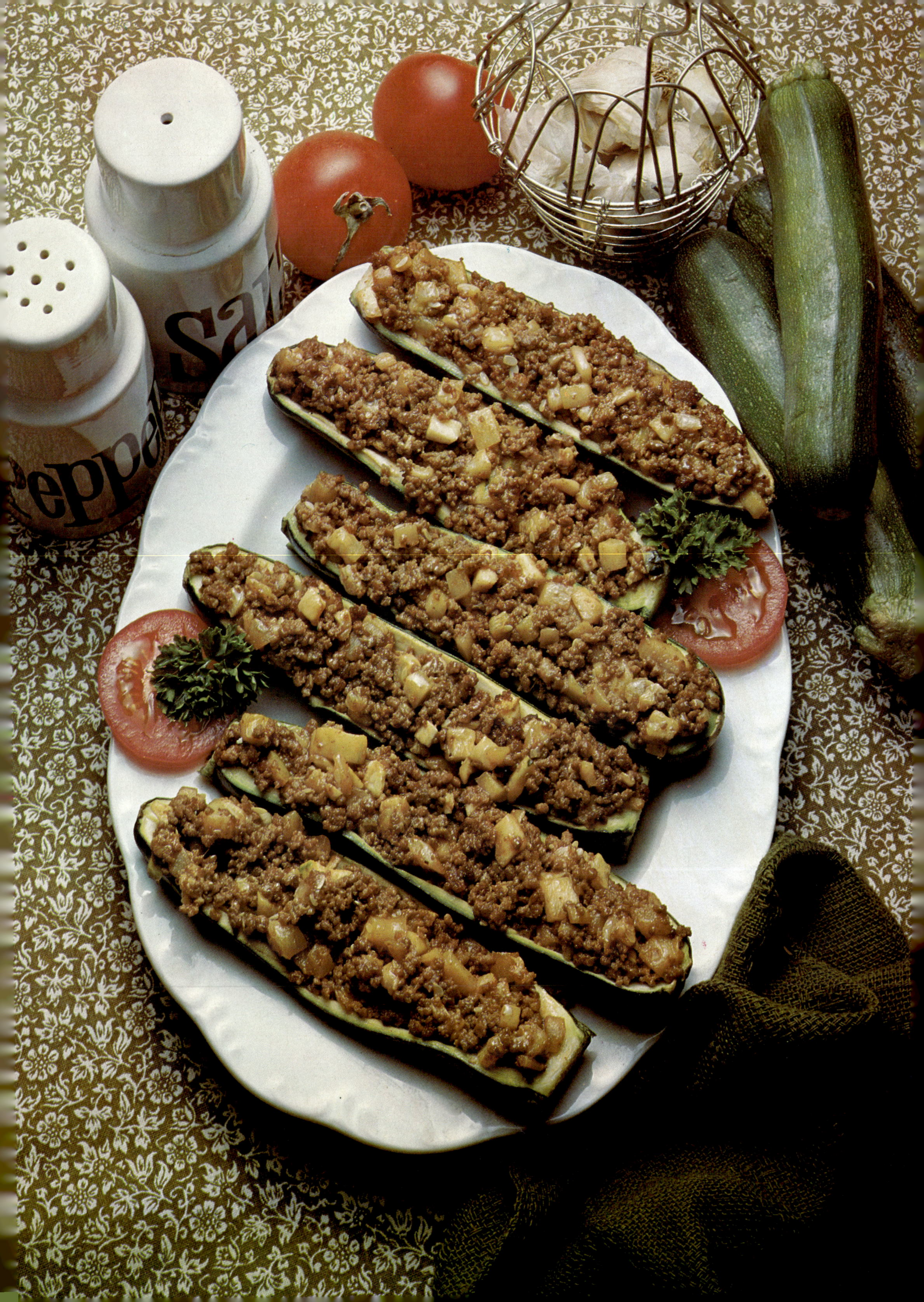
Salt
Pepper

Shepherd's pie

METRIC/IMPERIAL
0.75kg/1½lb potatoes, peeled
salt
freshly ground black pepper
75g/3oz butter
2–3 × 15ml spoons/
  2–3 tablespoons milk
2 onions, peeled and
  chopped
1 × 15ml spoon/
  1 tablespoon plain flour
150ml/¼ pint chicken stock
0.5kg/1lb cooked lamb,
  minced or diced
3 tomatoes, peeled and
  chopped
pinch of dried thyme

AMERICAN
1½lb potatoes, peeled
salt
freshly ground black pepper
⅓ cup butter
2–3 tablespoons milk
2 onions, peeled and
  chopped
1 tablespoon all-purpose
  flour
⅔ cup chicken stock
2 cups ground or diced
  cooked lamb
3 tomatoes, peeled and
  chopped
pinch of dried thyme

Cook the potatoes in boiling salted water until they are tender. Drain well and mash until smooth. Beat in salt and pepper to taste, 25g/1oz/2 tablespoons of the butter and the milk.

Melt 40g/1½oz/3 tablespoons of the remaining butter in a frying pan (skillet). Add the onions and fry until they are soft but not brown. Sprinkle over the flour and stir in well. Gradually stir in the stock and bring to the boil, stirring. Simmer until thickened.

Add the lamb, tomatoes, thyme and salt and pepper to taste. Pour the lamb mixture into a baking dish. Spread the mashed potatoes over the top and dot with the remaining butter, cut into small pieces. Bake in a preheated moderately hot oven (190°C/375°F, Gas Mark 5) for 25 to 30 minutes. Serve hot, from the dish.
Serves 4

Cottage crêpes

METRIC/IMPERIAL
8 cooked crêpes★
25g/1oz dripping
1 onion, peeled and chopped
2 carrots, peeled and grated
0.5kg/1lb beef, minced
300ml/½ pint beef stock
1 × 15ml spoon/
  1 tablespoon tomato purée
salt
freshly ground black pepper
1 × 15ml spoon/
  1 tablespoon plain flour

AMERICAN
8 cooked crêpes★
2 tablespoons drippings
1 onion, peeled and chopped
2 carrots, peeled and grated
2 cups ground beef
1¼ cups beef stock
1 tablespoon tomato paste
salt
freshly ground black pepper
1 tablespoon all-purpose
  flour

Keep the crêpes hot.

Heat the dripping in a frying pan (skillet). Add the onion and carrots and fry until the onion is soft but not brown. Add the meat and brown well. Stir in all but 2 × 15ml spoons/2 tablespoons of the stock, the tomato purée (paste) and salt and pepper to taste. Bring to the boil and simmer for 30 minutes.

Skim off the fat from the surface. Dissolve the flour in the reserved stock and stir into the beef mixture. Simmer, stirring, until thickened.

Divide the beef filling between the crêpes and roll up. Arrange in a baking dish. Reheat in a preheated moderately hot oven (190°C/375°F, Gas Mark 5) for 15 minutes. Serve hot.
Serves 4

Beef-stuffed courgettes (zucchini) (page 223)

Stuffed baked marrow (squash)

METRIC/IMPERIAL
1 large vegetable marrow
2 × 15ml spoons/
  2 tablespoons oil
1 small onion, peeled and chopped
0.5kg/1lb beef, minced
salt
freshly ground black pepper
2 × 5ml spoons/2 teaspoons
  Worcestershire sauce
2 × 15ml spoons/
  2 tablespoons tomato purée
225g/8oz tomatoes, peeled and chopped
25g/1oz fresh breadcrumbs
1 × 5ml spoon/½ teaspoon dried oregano
300ml/½ pint hot mornay sauce★
4 × 15ml spoons/
  4 tablespoons grated Parmesan cheese

AMERICAN
1 large summer squash
2 tablespoons oil
1 small onion, peeled and chopped
2 cups ground beef
salt
freshly ground black pepper
2 teaspoons Worcestershire sauce
2 tablespoons tomato paste
1 cup peeled and chopped tomatoes
½ cup fresh breadcrumbs
½ teaspoon dried oregano
1¼ cups hot mornay sauce★
4 tablespoons grated Parmesan cheese

Put the marrow (squash) in a large saucepan and add a little water. Cover and steam for 10 minutes.

Meanwhile, heat the oil in a frying pan (skillet). Add the onion and fry until it is soft but not brown. Stir in the beef and brown well. Pour off all the fat from the pan. Add salt and pepper to taste, the Worcestershire sauce, tomato purée (paste) and tomatoes and cook for a further 5 minutes. Remove from the heat and stir in the breadcrumbs and oregano.

Halve the marrow (squash) lengthways and scoop out the seeds. Arrange the halves, cut sides up, in a baking dish. Fill the hollows with the beef mixture. Cover with foil and bake in a preheated moderate oven (180°C/350°F, Gas Mark 4) for 45 minutes.

Pour over the mornay sauce and sprinkle with the Parmesan cheese. Bake for a further 30 minutes or until the marrow (squash) is tender and the top is lightly browned. Serve hot.
Serves 4 to 6

Cassoulet

METRIC/IMPERIAL
100g/4oz salt pork
100g/4oz lean lamb, in one piece
2 garlic cloves, crushed
2 × 15ml spoons/
  2 tablespoons olive oil
1 onion, peeled and sliced
225g/8oz dried haricot beans, soaked overnight and drained
1 bouquet garni
salt
freshly ground black pepper
50g/2oz garlic sausage, sliced
2 large tomatoes, peeled, deseeded and chopped

AMERICAN
¼lb salt or pickled pork
¼lb lean lamb, in one piece
2 garlic cloves, crushed
2 tablespoons olive oil
1 onion, peeled and sliced
1 cup dried navy beans, soaked overnight and drained
1 bouquet garni
salt
freshly ground black pepper
¼ cup sliced garlic sausage
2 large tomatoes, peeled, deseeded and chopped

Put the pork, lamb and garlic in a saucepan and cover with water. Bring to the boil and simmer for 5 minutes. Drain the meat and slice.

Heat the oil in a flameproof casserole. Add the pork, lamb and onion and fry until the onion is golden. Stir in the beans and add the bouquet garni with salt and pepper to taste. Pour in enough boiling water to cover the mixture. Cover tightly and transfer to a preheated cool oven (150°C/300°F, Gas Mark 2). Cook for 2 hours.

Stir in the sausage slices and tomatoes and continue cooking for 1 hour. Discard the bouquet garni and serve hot, from the casserole.
Serves 4

Dolmades

METRIC/IMPERIAL
1 × 425g/15oz can vine
  leaves, drained
3 × 15ml spoons/
  3 tablespoons olive oil
2 medium onions, peeled
  and chopped
0.5kg/1lb cooked lamb,
  minced
4 × 15ml spoons/
  4 tablespoons cooked
  long-grain rice
1 × 15ml spoon/
  1 tablespoon chopped fresh
  parsley
2 × 15ml spoons/
  2 tablespoons tomato purée
juice of 1 lemon
salt
freshly ground black pepper
4 × 15ml spoons/
  4 tablespoons water

AMERICAN
1 × 15oz can vine leaves,
  drained
3 tablespoons olive oil
2 medium onions, peeled
  and chopped
2 cups ground cooked lamb
4 tablespoons cooked
  long-grain rice
1 tablespoon chopped fresh
  parsley
2 tablespoons tomato paste
juice of 1 lemon
salt
freshly ground black pepper
4 tablespoons water

Soak the vine leaves in boiling water for 2 minutes, then drain carefully and leave to dry.

Heat 2 × 15ml spoons/2 tablespoons of the oil in a frying pan (skillet). Add the onions and fry until they are soft but not brown. Stir in the lamb, rice, parsley, 1 × 15ml spoon/1 tablespoon of the tomato purée (paste), the lemon juice and salt and pepper to taste. Remove from the heat.

Lay the vine leaves flat and divide the stuffing between them. Roll up the leaves, tucking in the sides to make neat parcels. Arrange in a baking dish.

Mix together the remaining oil, tomato purée (paste) and water and pour over the rolls. Cover and cook in a preheated moderate oven (180°C/350°F, Gas Mark 4) for 45 minutes. Serve hot.
Serves 4

Moussaka

METRIC/IMPERIAL
2 medium aubergines, sliced
salt
25g/1oz butter
1 large onion, peeled and
  chopped
1 garlic clove, crushed
0.5kg/1lb cooked lamb,
  minced or finely chopped
1 × 2.5ml spoon/½ teaspoon
  ground cinnamon
freshly ground black pepper
4 × 15ml spoons/
  4 tablespoons tomato purée
4–6 × 15ml spoons/
  4–6 tablespoons olive oil
0.5kg/1lb potatoes, peeled,
  parboiled and thinly sliced
pinch of ground allspice
1 egg yolk
450ml/¾ pint hot béchamel
  sauce*

AMERICAN
2 medium eggplants, sliced
salt
2 tablespoons butter
1 large onion, peeled and
  chopped
1 garlic clove, crushed
2 cups ground or finely
  chopped cooked lamb
½ teaspoon ground cinnamon
freshly ground black pepper
4 tablespoons tomato paste
4–6 tablespoons olive oil
1lb potatoes, peeled,
  parboiled and thinly sliced
pinch of ground allspice
1 egg yolk
1 pint hot béchamel sauce*

Sprinkle the aubergine (eggplant) slices with salt and leave for 20 minutes.

Meanwhile, melt the butter in a frying pan (skillet). Add the onion and garlic and fry until the onion is soft but not brown. Stir in the lamb, cinnamon, salt and pepper to taste and the tomato purée (paste). Cook for a further 5 minutes. Remove from the heat and keep hot.

Rinse the aubergine (eggplant) slices and pat dry with absorbent paper. Heat a little of the oil in another frying pan (skillet) Add the aubergine (eggplant) slices, in batches, and fry until lightly browned on both sides. Add more oil to the pan when necessary, but remember that the aubergines (eggplants) will soak up as much as you add and the finished dish may be too greasy. Remove from the heat.

Make alternating layers of the lamb mixture and aubergine (eggplant) slices in a baking dish. Cover with the potato slices. Beat the allspice and egg yolk into the béchamel sauce and pour over the top.

Bake in a preheated moderately hot oven (190°C/375°F, Gas Mark 5) for 25 to 30 minutes or until the sauce topping is golden brown. Serve hot.
Serves 4

Stuffed baked potatoes with bacon filling

METRIC/IMPERIAL
6 large potatoes
25g/1oz butter
1 small onion, peeled and chopped
175g/6oz lean bacon rashers, rinds removed and diced
1 × 2.5ml spoon/½ teaspoon dried marjoram
1 × 15ml spoon/ 1 tablespoon milk
salt
freshly ground black pepper
100g/4oz Cheddar cheese, grated

AMERICAN
6 large potatoes
2 tablespoons butter
1 small onion, peeled and chopped
6oz Canadian bacon slices, diced
½ teaspoon dried marjoram
1 tablespoon milk
salt
freshly ground black pepper
1 cup grated Cheddar cheese

Prick the potatoes with a fork, then bake in a preheated moderate oven (180°C/350°F, Gas Mark 4) for 1½ hours or until tender.

Ten minutes before the potatoes are ready, melt the butter in a saucepan. Add the onion and fry until it is soft but not brown. Add the bacon and fry until it is cooked. Stir in the marjoram and remove from the heat. Keep hot.

Cut a slice off the potatoes and scoop out the centres. Add to the bacon and onion mixture, with the milk and salt and pepper to taste. Mix well together. Spoon back into the potato cases, doming the tops.

Arrange the potatoes in a grill (broiler) pan and sprinkle with the cheese. Grill (broil) slowly until the cheese melts and is lightly browned. Serve hot.
Serves 6

Sausage and bean salad

METRIC/IMPERIAL
0.5kg/1lb cold cooked pork sausages, sliced
1 × 200g/7oz can red kidney beans, drained
2 large potatoes, peeled, cooked and diced
2 dessert apples, cored and diced
2 tomatoes, peeled, deseeded and chopped
Dressing:
4 × 15ml spoons/ 4 tablespoons vegetable oil
2 × 15ml spoons/ 2 tablespoons tarragon vinegar
1 small onion, peeled and very finely chopped
2 × 15ml spoons/ 2 tablespoons chopped fresh parsley
1 × 5ml spoon/1 teaspoon dry mustard
1 × 5ml spoon/1 teaspoon made French mustard
1 × 5ml spoon/1 teaspoon paprika
pinch of grated nutmeg
2 × 5ml spoons/2 teaspoons sugar
juice of 1 orange
salt
freshly ground black pepper

AMERICAN
1lb cold cooked pork sausages, sliced
1 × 7oz can red kidney beans, drained
2 large potatoes, peeled, cooked and diced
2 dessert apples, cored and diced
2 tomatoes, peeled, deseeded and chopped
Dressing:
4 tablespoons vegetable oil
2 tablespoons tarragon vinegar
1 small onion, peeled and very finely chopped
2 tablespoons chopped fresh parsley
1 teaspoon dry mustard
1 teaspoon prepared French mustard
1 teaspoon paprika
pinch of grated nutmeg
2 teaspoons sugar
juice of 1 orange
salt
freshly ground black pepper

Put the sausages, beans, potatoes, apples and tomatoes in a mixing bowl. Mix together the ingredients for the dressing, with salt and pepper to taste, in a screwtop jar. Pour over the sausage mixture and toss well together. Leave to marinate for at least 30 minutes.

Spoon into a salad bowl to serve.
Serves 4

Stuffed globe artichokes

METRIC/IMPERIAL
4 globe artichokes, tips of leaves trimmed
15g/½oz butter
½ small onion, peeled and finely chopped
50g/2oz mushrooms, finely chopped
50g/2oz cooked ham, finely chopped
1 × 15ml spoon/
1 tablespoon fresh breadcrumbs
salt
freshly ground black pepper
1 small egg, lightly beaten

AMERICAN
4 globe artichokes, tips of leaves trimmed
1 tablespoon butter
½ small onion, peeled and finely chopped
½ cup finely chopped mushrooms
¼ cup finely chopped cooked ham
1 tablespoon fresh breadcrumbs
salt
freshly ground black pepper
1 egg, lightly beaten

Cook the artichokes in boiling water for 20 minutes or until the leaves will pull out easily. Drain and allow to cool slightly, then remove the inner leaves and hairy choke.

Melt the butter in a saucepan. Add the onion and mushrooms and fry until the onion is soft but not brown. Remove from the heat and stir in the ham, breadcrumbs, salt and pepper to taste and enough egg to bind the mixture.

Divide the stuffing between the artichokes and pack into the centre cavities. Arrange in a greased baking dish and cover with foil. Bake in a preheated moderately hot oven (190°C/375°F, Gas Mark 5) for 15 minutes. Serve hot.

Serves 2 to 4

Bacon and green bean quiche

METRIC/IMPERIAL
Pastry:
100g/4oz self-raising flour
salt
50g/2oz butter
50g/2oz Cheddar cheese, grated
2–3 × 15ml spoons/
2–3 tablespoons water
Filling:
6 streaky bacon rashers, rinds removed and diced
100g/4oz French beans, cooked and diced
4 eggs, lightly beaten
4 × 15ml spoons/
4 tablespoons single cream
50g/2oz Cheddar cheese, grated
freshly ground black pepper

AMERICAN
Pastry:
1 cup self-rising flour
salt
¼ cup butter
½ cup grated Cheddar cheese
2–3 tablespoons water
Filling:
6 bacon slices, diced
½ cup diced cooked green beans
4 eggs, lightly beaten
4 tablespoons light cream
½ cup grated Cheddar cheese
freshly ground black pepper

Sift the flour and salt into a mixing bowl. Rub in the butter until the mixture resembles breadcrumbs. Stir in the cheese, then bind to a dough with the water. Roll out the dough and use to line a 20cm/8 inch diameter flan ring (pie pan).

Bake the pastry case (pie shell) blind in a preheated moderately hot oven (200°C/400°F, Gas Mark 6) for 10 minutes. Remove from the oven.

Grill (broil) or fry the bacon until it is crisp. Drain on absorbent paper, then spread out in the pastry case (pie shell). Cover with the beans.

Mix together the eggs, cream, cheese and salt and pepper to taste. Pour into the pastry case (pie shell). Bake in a moderately hot oven (190°C/375°F, Gas Mark 5) for 30 minutes or until firm. Serve warm or cold.

Serves 4

Pork-stuffed peppers

METRIC/IMPERIAL
4 large green peppers
50g/2oz butter
1 onion, peeled and finely chopped
50g/2oz long-grain rice
450ml/¾ pint beef stock
0.5kg/1lb lean pork, minced
2 × 15ml spoons/ 2 tablespoons chopped fresh parsley
salt
freshly ground black pepper
0.5kg/1lb tomatoes, peeled, deseeded and chopped
1 × 15ml spoon/ 1 tablespoon plain flour
pinch of sugar

AMERICAN
4 large green peppers
¼ cup butter
1 onion, peeled and finely chopped
⅓ cup long-grain rice
2 cups beef stock
2 cups ground lean pork
2 tablespoons chopped fresh parsley
salt
freshly ground black pepper
2 cups peeled, deseeded and chopped tomatoes
1 tablespoon all-purpose flour
pinch of sugar

Cut the tops off the peppers and scoop out the seeds and white pith. Blanch the peppers and tops in boiling water for 2 minutes. Drain well and allow to cool.

Melt 25g/1oz/2 tablespoons of the butter in a saucepan. Add the onion and fry until it is soft but not brown. Stir in the rice and cook until it is opaque.

Add 250ml/8fl oz/1 cup of the stock and bring to the boil. Cover and simmer for 12 minutes or until the liquid has been absorbed.

Meanwhile, fry the pork in a frying pan (skillet) until it is well browned. If necessary, add a little butter or oil. Drain the pork well and stir in the rice mixture with the parsley and salt and pepper to taste. Stuff the peppers with this mixture and replace the tops. Arrange in a baking dish.

Melt the remaining butter in another saucepan. Add the tomatoes and cook to a pulp. Stir in the flour, then the remaining stock. Bring to the boil, stirring, and simmer until thickened. Add salt and pepper to taste and the sugar and pour over the stuffed peppers.

Cover the dish and bake in a preheated moderately hot oven (190°C/375°F, Gas Mark 5) for 30 minutes. Serve hot.
Serves 4

Ham and mushroom crêpes

METRIC/IMPERIAL
12 cooked crêpes★
25g/1oz butter
1 onion, peeled and finely chopped
225g/8oz mushrooms, finely chopped
3 tomatoes, peeled, deseeded and chopped
100g/4oz cooked ham, diced
pinch of dried marjoram
salt
freshly ground black pepper
300ml/½ pint hot mornay sauce★
25g/1oz Parmesan cheese, grated

AMERICAN
12 cooked crêpes★
2 tablespoons butter
1 onion, peeled and finely chopped
2 cups finely chopped mushrooms
3 tomatoes, peeled, deseeded and chopped
½ cup diced cooked ham
pinch of dried marjoram
salt
freshly ground black pepper
1¼ cups hot mornay sauce★
¼ cup grated Parmesan cheese

Keep the crêpes hot.

Melt the butter in a frying pan (skillet). Add the onion and fry until it is soft but not brown. Add the mushrooms and fry for 2 minutes. Stir in the tomatoes, ham, marjoram and salt and pepper to taste and heat through for about 5 minutes.

Divide the filling between the crêpes and roll up. Arrange in a warmed flameproof serving dish. Pour over the mornay sauce and sprinkle the cheese over the top. Grill (broil) for 3 to 4 minutes or until the top is lightly browned and bubbling. Serve hot, from the dish.
Serves 4

Beef-stuffed courgettes (zucchini)

METRIC/IMPERIAL
3 large courgettes
25g/1oz lard
225g/8oz beef, minced
1 garlic clove, crushed
1 × 15ml spoon/
  1 tablespoon tomato purée
2 × 5ml spoons/
  2 teaspoons soy sauce
salt
freshly ground black pepper
150ml/¼ pint stock
To garnish:
tomato slices
parsley sprigs

AMERICAN
3 large zucchini
2 tablespoons lard
1 cup ground beef
1 garlic clove, crushed
1 tablespoon tomato paste
2 teaspoons soy sauce
salt
freshly ground black pepper
⅔ cup stock
To garnish:
tomato slices
parsley sprigs

Cut the courgettes (zucchini) in half lengthways and scoop out the centre. Chop the flesh. Heat the lard in a frying pan (skillet) and brown the meat well, with the garlic. Stir in the tomato purée (paste), soy sauce and chopped flesh and season to taste with salt and pepper. Spoon this mixture back into the courgette (zucchini) shells. Place in a shallow baking dish and pour round the stock. Cover and place in a preheated moderate oven (180°C/350°F, Gas Mark 4) and bake for about 45 minutes or until tender. Serve garnished with tomato slices and parsley sprigs.
Serves 3

Kidney crêpes

METRIC/IMPERIAL
12 cooked crêpes★
6 streaky bacon rashers, rinds removed and diced
6 lambs' kidneys, skinned, cored and thinly sliced
15g/½oz butter
1 onion, peeled and chopped
25g/1oz plain flour
300ml/½ pint chicken stock
salt
freshly ground black pepper
1 × 15ml spoon/
  1 tablespoon tomato purée
2 × 15ml spoons/
  2 tablespoons sherry
chopped fresh parsley
  to garnish

AMERICAN
12 cooked crêpes★
6 bacon slices, diced
6 lamb kidneys, skinned, cored and thinly sliced
1 tablespoon butter
1 onion, peeled and chopped
¼ cup all-purpose flour
1¼ cups chicken stock
salt
freshly ground black pepper
1 tablespoon tomato paste
2 tablespoons sherry
chopped fresh parsley
  to garnish

Keep the crêpes hot.
  Fry the bacon in a saucepan until it is crisp. Remove from the pan. Add the kidneys to the pan and fry for 3 minutes. Remove from the pan. Add the butter to the pan and when it has melted add the onion. Fry until it is soft but not brown. Stir in the flour and cook, stirring, for 1 minute. Gradually stir in the stock and bring to the boil, stirring. Simmer until thickened.
  Return the bacon and kidneys to the saucepan with salt and pepper to taste, the tomato purée (paste) and sherry. Cover and simmer for 20 minutes.
  Divide the filling between the crêpes and roll up. Arrange in a baking dish and cover with foil. Reheat in a preheated moderate oven (180°C/350°F, Gas Mark 4) for 15 minutes.
  Serve hot, garnished with parsley.
Serves 4 to 6

Chicken and ham gougère

METRIC/IMPERIAL
50g/2oz Gruyère cheese, grated
65g/2½oz quantity warm choux pastry★
1.5 × 15ml spoons/ 1½ tablespoons olive oil
2 shallots, peeled and chopped
4 mushrooms, chopped
2 × 5ml spoons/2 teaspoons plain flour
150ml/¼ pint chicken stock
100g/4oz cooked chicken meat, chopped
50g/2oz cooked ham, chopped
1 tomato, peeled and chopped
salt
freshly ground black pepper
1 × 15ml spoon/ 1 tablespoon grated Parmesan cheese
1 × 15ml spoon/ 1 tablespoon dry breadcrumbs

AMERICAN
½ cup grated Gruyère cheese
10 tablespoon quantity warm choux pastry★
1½ tablespoons olive oil
2 shallots, peeled and chopped
4 mushrooms, chopped
2 teaspoons all-purpose flour
⅔ cup chicken stock
½ cup chopped cooked chicken meat
¼ cup chopped cooked ham
1 tomato, peeled and chopped
salt
freshly ground black pepper
1 tablespoon grated Parmesan cheese
1 tablespoon dry breadcrumbs

Beat the Gruyère cheese into the choux pastry until the mixture is smooth. Keep warm.

Heat the oil in a saucepan. Add the shallots and fry for 2 minutes. Add the mushrooms and fry for 2 minutes. Stir in the flour and cook, stirring, for 1 minute. Gradually stir in the stock and bring to the boil, stirring. Simmer until thickened. Remove from the heat. Add the chicken, ham, tomato and salt and pepper to taste.

Arrange the cheese choux pastry in spoonful in a ring in a greased baking dish. Pile the cheese and ham mixture in the centre. Mix together the Parmesan and breadcrumbs and sprinkle over the top. Bake in a preheated moderately hot oven (200°C/400°F, Gas Mark 6) for 30 to 40 minutes or until well risen and golden. Serve hot.
Serves 4 to 6

Toad in the hole

METRIC/IMPERIAL
25g/1oz dripping
8 large pork or beef sausages
100g/4oz plain flour
pinch of salt
2 eggs, lightly beaten
300ml/½ pint milk
1 × 5ml spoon/1 teaspoon dried thyme
freshly ground black pepper

AMERICAN
2 tablespoons drippings
8 large pork or beef sausages
1 cup all-purpose flour
pinch of salt
2 eggs, lightly beaten
1¼ cups milk
1 teaspoon dried thyme
freshly ground black pepper

Melt the dripping in a shallow rectangular baking dish. Put the sausages in the dish and bake in a preheated hot oven (220°C/425°F, Gas Mark 7) for 10 minutes, turning to brown evenly.

Meanwhile, sift the flour and salt into a mixing bowl. Beat in the eggs, then gradually beat in the milk until the batter is smooth. Stir in the thyme and pepper to taste.

Pour off most of the fat from the baking dish. Pour the batter into the dish around the sausages. Bake for a further 40 to 45 minutes or until the batter has risen and is lightly browned and crisp. Serve hot, from the dish.
Serves 4

Smoked haddock kedgeree

METRIC/IMPERIAL
100g/4oz butter
0.5kg/1lb cooked rice
0.75kg/1½lb cooked smoked haddock, skinned and flaked
150ml/¼ pint single cream
4 eggs, hard-boiled and chopped
salt
freshly ground black pepper

AMERICAN
½ cup butter
3 cups cooked rice
1½lb cooked smoked haddock, skinned and flaked
⅔ cup light cream
4 eggs, hard-cooked and chopped
salt
freshly ground black pepper

Melt the butter in a saucepan. Add the rice, haddock and cream and heat through gently, stirring occasionally. Stir in the eggs and salt and pepper to taste. Cook gently for a further 3 to 4 minutes, then serve hot.
Serves 4

Cod and bean pie

METRIC/IMPERIAL
175g/6oz haricot beans, soaked overnight in cold water and drained
2 onions, peeled and chopped
1kg/2lb cod or other white fish fillet, skinned and cut into small pieces
4 streaky bacon rashers, rinds removed and chopped
salt
freshly ground black pepper
1 × 15ml spoon/ 1 tablespoon chopped fresh parsley
600ml/1 pint milk
0.5kg/1lb potatoes, peeled and thinly sliced
25g/1oz butter

AMERICAN
1 cup navy beans, soaked overnight in cold water and drained
2 onions, peeled and chopped
2lb cod or other white fish fillet, skinned and cut into small pieces
4 bacon slices, chopped
salt
freshly ground black pepper
1 tablespoon chopped fresh parsley
2½ cups milk
1lb potatoes, peeled and thinly sliced
2 tablespoons butter

Cover the beans with fresh cold water, bring to the boil and simmer for 1½ hours or until tender. Drain.
 Put the onions into a greased casserole and cover with the fish and bacon. Add salt and pepper to taste and sprinkle with parsley. Add a layer of beans and pour over the milk. Arrange the potato slices on top.
 Dot the pie with butter and place in a preheated moderate oven (180°C/350°F, Gas Mark 4) and cook for 40 minutes or until the potatoes are cooked and golden. Serve very hot.
Serves 6

Tuna crêpe cake

METRIC/IMPERIAL
8 cooked crêpes★
1 × 425g/15oz can tuna fish, drained and flaked
300ml/½ pint hot white sauce★
2 spring onions, chopped
2 eggs, hard-boiled and chopped
1 × 15ml spoon/ 1 tablespoon chopped fresh parsley

AMERICAN
8 cooked crêpes★
1 × 15oz can tuna fish, drained and flaked
1¼ cups hot white sauce★
2 scallions, chopped
2 eggs, hard-cooked and chopped
1 tablespoon chopped fresh parsley

Keep the crêpes hot.
   Mix together the remaining ingredients. Lay a crêpe flat on an ovenproof serving dish. Cover with a little of the tuna mixture, then put another crêpe on top. Continue making layers in this way, ending with a crêpe.
   Cover the crêpe cake with foil and reheat in a preheated moderately hot oven (190°C/375°F, Gas Mark 5) for 15 minutes. Serve hot.
Serves 4

Leek and bacon cheese

METRIC/IMPERIAL
8 leeks, thoroughly cleaned and sliced
2 carrots, peeled and sliced
12 streaky bacon rashers, rinds removed
Sauce:
25g/1oz butter
25g/1oz flour
450ml/¾ pint milk
salt
freshly ground black pepper
75g/3oz grated Parmesan cheese

AMERICAN
8 leeks, thoroughly cleaned and sliced
2 carrots, peeled and sliced
12 bacon slices
Sauce:
2 tablespoons butter
¼ cup flour
2 cups milk
salt
freshly ground black pepper
¾ cup grated Parmesan cheese

Put the leeks and carrots in boiling, salted water and cook for 10 to 15 minutes, or until tender. Drain well and arrange in a buttered flameproof serving dish.
   Meanwhile make the sauce. Melt the butter in a saucepan, add the flour and cook for 2 minutes, stirring constantly. Remove the pan from the heat and gradually add the milk, stirring constantly. Return the pan to the heat and bring to the boil. Lower the heat and simmer until thickened and smooth. Add salt and pepper to taste and 50g/2oz/ ½ cup of the cheese.
   Grill (broil) the bacon and arrange on top of the leeks and carrots. Pour over the sauce and sprinkle with the remaining cheese. Grill (broil) until golden brown and bubbling. Serve at once.
Serves 4

Egg croquettes

METRIC/IMPERIAL	AMERICAN
4 hard-boiled eggs, shelled and chopped	4 hard-cooked eggs, shelled and chopped
1 egg yolk	1 egg yolk
salt	salt
freshly ground black pepper	freshly ground black pepper
Panada:	**Panada:**
250ml/8 fl oz milk	1 cup milk
large slice of onion	large slice of onion
6 peppercorns	6 peppercorns
1 mace blade	1 mace blade
1 bay leaf	1 bay leaf
pinch of grated nutmeg	pinch of grated nutmeg
50g/2oz butter	¼ cup butter
50g/2oz flour	½ cup flour
Coating:	**Coating:**
seasoned flour	seasoned flour
1 egg, beaten	1 egg, beaten
dry white breadcrumbs	dry white breadcrumbs
vegetable oil for frying	vegetable oil for frying

To make the panada, put the milk into a saucepan and add the onion, peppercorns, mace, bay leaf and nutmeg. Bring slowly to the boil, then remove from the heat, cover and leave to stand for 15 minutes.

Melt the butter in another saucepan, add the flour and cook, stirring for 2 minutes. Gradually add the strained milk and bring to the boil, stirring constantly. When the mixture is very thick and smooth, remove from the heat and add the hard-boiled (hard-cooked) eggs, egg yolk and salt and pepper to taste. Turn the mixture onto a plate to cool, then chill in the refrigerator.

Shape the mixture into 8 croquettes. Coat with seasoned flour, then dip in the beaten egg and finally coat thoroughly with breadcrumbs.

Heat the oil in a deep frying pan (deep fat fryer). Fry the croquettes, 4 at a time, until golden brown and crisp. Drain on absorbent paper and serve with tomato sauce* and salad.

Makes 8

Beef and kidney pie

METRIC/IMPERIAL	AMERICAN
Pastry:	**Pastry:**
225g/8oz flour	2 cups flour
pinch of salt	pinch of salt
100g/4oz lard	½ cup lard
2–3 × 15ml spoons/ 2–3 tablespoons cold water	2–3 tablespoons cold water
Filling:	**Filling:**
25g/1oz dripping	2 tablespoons drippings
1 onion, peeled and chopped	1 onion, peeled and chopped
0.5kg/1lb beef, minced	2 cups ground beef
100g/4oz ox kidney, skinned, cored and finely chopped	¼ lb beef kidney, skinned, cored and finely chopped
300ml/½ pint beef stock	1¼ cups beef stock
1 × 5ml spoon/ 1 teaspoon dried marjoram	1 teaspoon dried marjoram
salt	salt
freshly ground black pepper	freshly ground black pepper
1 × 15ml spoon/ 1 tablespoon cornflour	1 tablespoon cornstarch
milk to glaze	milk to glaze

Sift the flour and salt into a bowl. Cut the lard into small pieces and rub into the flour until the mixture resembles breadcrumbs. Stir in enough water to bind the mixture and knead lightly until smooth. Wrap in foil and chill in the refrigerator for at least 30 minutes.

Melt the dripping in a large frying pan (skillet), add the onion and fry for 3 to 4 minutes until soft but not brown. Add the minced (ground) beef and kidney and continue to fry until the meat is browned, stirring constantly. Add the stock, marjoram and salt and pepper to taste. Bring to the boil and stir well. Cover and simmer for 1 hour.

Blend the cornflour (cornstarch) with a little cold water. Stir into the meat mixture and stir constantly until thickened. Cool.

Divide the pastry in half and roll out one half on a floured surface to fit a 20cm/8 inch pie dish. Line the pie dish with the pastry and spoon in the meat mixture. Roll out the remaining pastry to make a lid. Lay over the filling and seal the edges. Use the pastry trimmings to decorate the top of the pie. Cut an air vent in the centre and brush the top with milk.

Place on a baking sheet and bake in a preheated moderately hot oven (200°C/400°F, Gas Mark 6) for 20 minutes or until golden brown.

Serves 4

PASTA & RICE

Spaghetti bolognese

METRIC/IMPERIAL
2 × 15ml spoons/
  2 tablespoons olive oil
1 onion, peeled and finely
  chopped
2 garlic cloves, crushed
3 lean bacon rashers, rinds
  removed and diced
1 celery stick, finely
  chopped
1 carrot, peeled and grated
225g/8oz beef, minced
4 tomatoes, peeled and
  chopped
4 × 15ml spoons/
  4 tablespoons tomato purée
120ml/4 fl oz dry white or
  red wine
300ml/½ pint beef stock
2 × 5ml spoons/2 teaspoons
  brown sugar
pinch of grated nutmeg
salt
freshly ground black pepper
100g/4oz mushrooms, sliced
0.5kg/1lb spaghetti
grated Parmesan cheese

AMERICAN
2 tablespoons olive oil
1 onion, peeled and finely
  chopped
2 garlic cloves, crushed
3 Canadian bacon slices,
  diced
1 celery stalk, finely
  chopped
1 carrot, peeled and grated
1 cup ground beef
4 tomatoes, peeled and
  chopped
4 tablespoons tomato paste
½ cup dry white or red wine
1¼ cups beef stock
2 teaspoons brown sugar
pinch of grated nutmeg
salt
freshly ground black pepper
1 cup sliced mushrooms
1lb spaghetti
grated Parmesan cheese

Heat the oil in a saucepan. Add the onion, garlic and bacon and fry until the onion is soft but not brown and the bacon is crisp. Add the celery and carrot and cook for 3 minutes. Add the beef and fry until it is browned.

Stir in the tomatoes, tomato purée (paste), wine, stock, sugar, nutmeg and salt and pepper to taste and bring to the boil. Cover and simmer for 30 minutes. Add the mushrooms and simmer for a further 15 minutes.

Meanwhile, cook the spaghetti in boiling salted water until it is *al dente* (just tender to the bite). Drain well and add to the saucepan. Toss gently to mix with the sauce and serve sprinkled with Parmesan cheese.
Serves 4

Spaghetti with bacon and onion

METRIC/IMPERIAL
0.5kg/1lb spaghetti
salt
225g/8oz streaky bacon
  rashers, rinds removed and
  chopped
3 large onions, peeled and
  chopped
freshly ground black pepper
2 × 15ml spoons/
  2 tablespoons chopped
  fresh parsley
25g/1oz Parmesan cheese,
  grated

AMERICAN
1lb spaghetti
salt
½lb bacon slices, chopped
3 large onions, peeled and
  chopped
freshly ground black pepper
2 tablespoons chopped fresh
  parsley
¼ cup grated Parmesan
  cheese

Cook the spaghetti in boiling salted water until it is *al dente* (just tender to the bite).

Meanwhile, fry the bacon in a frying pan (skillet) until it has rendered most of its fat. Add the onions and fry until they are soft but not brown. Stir in salt and pepper to taste.

Drain the spaghetti and return to the saucepan. Add the bacon and onion mixture with the parsley and cheese and toss well together. Serve hot.
Serves 4

Spaghetti with ham and tomato sauce

METRIC/IMPERIAL
0.5kg/1lb spaghetti
salt
1 × 400g/14oz can tomatoes
1 × 15ml spoon/
　1 tablespoon tomato purée
225g/8oz cooked ham,
　diced
1 × 5ml spoon/1 teaspoon
　dried oregano
freshly ground black pepper
25g/1oz butter
50g/2oz Parmesan cheese,
　grated

AMERICAN
1lb spaghetti
salt
1 × 14oz can tomatoes
1 tablespoon tomato paste
1 cup diced cooked ham
1 teaspoon dried oregano
freshly ground black pepper
2 tablespoons butter
½ cup grated Parmesan
　cheese

Cook the spaghetti in boiling salted water until it is *al dente* (just tender to the bite).

Meanwhile, push the tomatoes and their juice through a sieve (strainer) into a saucepan. Stir in the tomato purée (paste), ham, oregano and salt and pepper to taste. Heat through gently, stirring occasionally.

Drain the spaghetti and return to the saucepan. Add the butter and 2 × 15ml spoons/2 tablespoons of the cheese. Toss together until the spaghetti strands are well coated. Pile onto a hot serving dish. Pour over the hot tomato and ham sauce and sprinkle the remaining cheese on top. Serve hot.

Serves 4

Tagliatelle Riviera

METRIC/IMPERIAL
0.5kg/1lb tagliatelle
salt
3 × 15ml spoons/
　3 tablespoons olive oil
2 onions, peeled and thinly
　sliced
2 garlic cloves, crushed
3 lean bacon rashers, rinds
　removed and chopped
225g/8oz mushrooms, sliced
5 anchovy fillets, chopped
6 black olives, halved and
　stoned
freshly ground black pepper
25g/1oz Parmesan cheese,
　grated

AMERICAN
1lb tagliatelle
salt
3 tablespoons olive oil
2 onions, peeled and thinly
　sliced
2 garlic cloves, crushed
3 Canadian bacon slices,
　chopped
2 cups sliced mushrooms
5 anchovy fillets, chopped
6 black olives, halved and
　pitted
freshly ground black pepper
¼ cup grated Parmesan
　cheese

Cook the tagliatelle in boiling salted water until it is *al dente* (just tender to the bite).

Meanwhile, heat the oil in a frying pan (skillet). Add the onions, garlic and bacon and fry until the onions are soft but not brown. Stir in the mushrooms, anchovy fillets, olives and salt and pepper to taste and cook for a further 4 to 5 minutes or until very hot.

Drain the tagliatelle and arrange in a warmed serving dish. Spoon over the sauce and sprinkle with the Parmesan. Serve hot.

Serves 4

Tagliatelle with chicken liver sauce

METRIC/IMPERIAL
225g/8oz chicken livers, cut into small pieces
25g/1oz plain flour
25g/1oz butter
1 × 15ml spoon/ 1 tablespoon olive oil
1 small onion, peeled and finely chopped
1 garlic clove, crushed
100g/4oz mushrooms, sliced
150ml/¼ pint chicken stock
150ml/¼ pint dry white wine
salt
freshly ground black pepper
0.5kg/1lb tagliatelle

AMERICAN
½lb chicken livers, cut into small pieces
¼ cup all-purpose flour
2 tablespoons butter
1 tablespoon olive oil
1 small onion, peeled and finely chopped
1 garlic clove, crushed
1 cup sliced mushrooms
⅔ cup chicken stock
⅔ cup dry white wine
salt
freshly ground black pepper
1lb tagliatelle

Coat the chicken liver pieces with the flour. Melt the butter with the oil in a saucepan. Add the onion and garlic and fry until the onion is soft but not brown. Add the chicken livers and mushrooms and fry until the livers are lightly browned.

Stir in the stock, wine and salt and pepper to taste and bring to the boil. Cover and simmer for 15 minutes.

Meanwhile, cook the tagliatelle in boiling salted water until it is *al dente* (just tender to the bite). Drain well and arrange on a warmed serving dish. Pile the liver sauce in the centre and serve hot.

Serves 4

Macaroni cheese

METRIC/IMPERIAL
225g/8oz elbow macaroni
salt
450ml/¾ pint hot white sauce★
100g/4oz Parmesan cheese, grated
25g/1oz butter, cut into small pieces

AMERICAN
½lb elbow macaroni
salt
2 cups hot white sauce★
1 cup grated Parmesan cheese
2 tablespoons butter, cut into small pieces

Cook the macaroni in boiling salted water until it is *al dente* (just tender to the bite). Drain well.

Mix the white sauce with 75g/3oz/¾ cup of the cheese. Stir in the macaroni and mix well. Spoon into a baking dish and sprinkle with the remaining cheese. Dot the top with the pieces of butter.

Bake in a preheated moderate oven (180°C/350°F, Gas Mark 4) for 30 minutes.

Serve hot, from the dish.

Serves 4

Frankfurter macaroni

METRIC/IMPERIAL
225g/8oz macaroni
salt
8 frankfurter sausages
1 × 200g/7oz can sweetcorn, drained
450ml/¾ pint hot mornay sauce★
3 spring onions, chopped
25g/1oz Cheddar cheese, grated

AMERICAN
½lb macaroni
salt
8 frankfurters
1 × 7oz can corn kernels, drained
2 cups hot mornay sauce★
3 scallions, chopped
¼ cup grated Cheddar cheese

Cook the macaroni in boiling salted water until it is *al dente* (just tender to the bite).

Meanwhile, cook the frankfurters in boiling water according to the instructions on the packet. Drain the frankfurters and cut into 2.5cm/1 inch pieces. Keep hot.

Drain the macaroni and return to the saucepan. Stir in the frankfurter pieces and corn, then fold in the sauce and spring onions (scallions). Spoon into a flameproof serving dish. Sprinkle the cheese on top and grill (broil) until the top is lightly browned and bubbling. Serve hot.

Serves 4

Macaroni and mushroom salad

METRIC/IMPERIAL
0.5kg/1lb macaroni
salt
225g/8oz button mushrooms, sliced
4 × 15ml spoons/ 4 tablespoons lemon juice
2 × 15ml spoons/ 2 tablespoons wine vinegar
1 garlic clove, crushed
freshly ground black pepper
1 large red pepper, pith and seeds removed and diced
1 large green pepper, pith and seeds removed and diced
150ml/¼ pint mayonnaise★
150ml/¼ pint natural yogurt
parsley sprigs to garnish

AMERICAN
1lb macaroni
salt
2 cups sliced button mushrooms
4 tablespoons lemon juice
2 tablespoons wine vinegar
1 garlic clove, crushed
freshly ground black pepper
1 large pimiento, pith and seeds removed and diced
1 large green pepper, pith and seeds removed and diced
⅔ cup mayonnaise★
⅔ cup unflavored yogurt
parsley sprigs to garnish

Cook the macaroni in boiling salted water until it is *al dente* (just tender to the bite).

Meanwhile, put the mushrooms in a shallow dish. Sprinkle over the lemon juice, vinegar, garlic and salt and pepper to taste and fold gently together. Leave to marinate for 30 minutes.

Drain the macaroni and allow to cool.

Stir the diced peppers into the mushroom mixture. Mix together the mayonnaise and yogurt and add to the mushroom mixture with the macaroni. Fold together until well mixed. Chill lightly before serving, garnished with parsley.

Serves 6

Lasagne al forno

METRIC/IMPERIAL
3 × 15ml spoons/
3 tablespoons olive oil
2 streaky bacon rashers,
rinds removed and
chopped
1 large onion, peeled and
chopped
1 garlic clove, crushed
225g/8oz beef, minced
2 celery sticks, chopped
1 large carrot, peeled and
diced
pinch of sugar
1 × 2.5ml spoon/½ teaspoon
dried oregano
salt
freshly ground black pepper
1 × 400g/14oz can
tomatoes
225g/8oz lasagne sheets
100g/4oz Parmesan cheese,
grated
300ml/½ pint hot mornay
sauce★

AMERICAN
3 tablespoons olive oil
2 bacon slices, chopped
1 large onion, peeled and
chopped
1 garlic clove, crushed
1 cup ground beef
2 celery stalks, chopped
1 large carrot, peeled and
diced
pinch of sugar
½ teaspoon dried oregano
salt
freshly ground black pepper
1 × 14oz can tomatoes
½lb lasagne sheets
1 cup grated Parmesan
cheese
1¼ cups hot mornay sauce★

Heat 2 × 15ml spoons/2 tablespoons of the oil in a saucepan. Add the bacon and fry until it has rendered most of its fat. Add the onion and garlic and fry until the onion is soft but not brown. Add the meat and brown well.

Stir in the celery and carrot and cook for 5 minutes. Add the sugar, oregano, salt and pepper to taste and the tomatoes with the can juice. Bring to the boil, stirring well, and simmer for 30 minutes.

Cook the lasagne, in batches, in boiling salted water to which the remaining oil has been added. Cook until *al dente* (just tender to the bite) then drain on absorbent paper.

Make alternate layers of meat sauce, lasagne and Parmesan cheese in a baking dish, reserving a little cheese for the topping. Pour over the mornay sauce and sprinkle with the reserved cheese.

Bake in a preheated moderately hot oven (190°C/375°F, Gas Mark 5) for 30 minutes or until very hot and the top is golden brown. Serve hot, from the dish.
Serves 4 to 6

Cannelloni with tomato stuffing

METRIC/IMPERIAL
12 cannelloni tubes or sheets
salt
225g/8oz tomatoes, peeled
and chopped
100g/4oz cheese, grated
(preferably a mixture of
Cheddar and Parmesan)
100g/4oz fresh breadcrumbs
freshly ground black pepper
1 egg, lightly beaten
1 × 400g/14oz can tomatoes
1 × 5ml spoon/1 teaspoon
dried oregano

AMERICAN
12 cannelloni tubes or sheets
salt
1 cup peeled and chopped
tomatoes
1 cup grated cheese
(preferably a mixture of
Cheddar and Parmesan)
2 cups fresh breadcrumbs
freshly ground black pepper
1 egg, lightly beaten
1 × 14oz can tomatoes
1 teaspoon dried oregano

Cook the cannelloni tubes or sheets in boiling salted water for 12 to 15 minutes or until they are *al dente* (just tender to the bite). Drain well.

Mix together the tomatoes, cheese, breadcrumbs, salt and pepper to taste and the egg. Fill the cannelloni tubes with this mixture or divide between the cannelloni sheets and roll up. Place the filled cannelloni in a greased baking dish. Mix together the canned tomatoes, with the can juice, and oregano, stirring to break up the tomatoes. Pour over the cannelloni.

Bake in a preheated moderate oven (180°C/350°F, Gas Mark 4) for 1 hour. Serve hot.
Serves 4

Gnocchi alla romana

METRIC/IMPERIAL
600ml/1 pint milk
150g/5oz coarse semolina
1 × 5ml spoon/1 teaspoon salt
freshly ground black pepper
75g/3oz butter
75g/3oz Parmesan cheese, grated
pinch of grated nutmeg
1 large egg, lightly beaten

AMERICAN
2½ cups milk
1 cup cream of wheat
1 teaspoon salt
freshly ground black pepper
⅓ cup butter
¾ cup grated Parmesan cheese
pinch of grated nutmeg
1 egg, lightly beaten

Put the milk, semolina (cream of wheat), salt, pepper to taste and 50g/2oz/¼ cup of the butter in a saucepan. Bring to the boil, stirring, and simmer for 5 to 7 minutes or until the mixture is very thick.

Remove from the heat and beat in 50g/2oz/½ cup of the cheese, the nutmeg and egg. Spread out on a baking sheet to about 5mm/¼ inch thick. Allow to cool until set.

Cut the semolina (cream of wheat) mixture into 3.5cm/1½ inch squares or rounds and arrange in a buttered baking dish in overlapping circles. Sprinkle with the remaining cheese, then dot with the remaining butter, cut into small pieces. Bake in a preheated hot oven (220°C/425°F, Gas Mark 7) for 15 minutes. Serve hot.
Serves 4

Neapolitan pizza

METRIC/IMPERIAL
Dough base:
7g/¼oz fresh yeast
150ml/¼ pint lukewarm water
225g/8oz plain flour
1 × 5ml spoon/1 teaspoon salt
15g/½oz butter
Topping:
1 × 15ml spoon/ 1 tablespoon olive oil
6 tomatoes, peeled and sliced
1 garlic clove, finely chopped
12 anchovy fillets
100g/4oz Mozzarella cheese, thinly sliced
6 black olives, stoned
dried oregano
freshly ground black pepper

AMERICAN
Dough base:
¼ cake compressed yeast
⅔ cup lukewarm water
2 cups all-purpose flour
1 teaspoon salt
1 tablespoon butter
Topping:
1 tablespoon olive oil
6 tomatoes, peeled and sliced
1 garlic clove, finely chopped
12 anchovy fillets
¼lb Mozzarella cheese, thinly sliced
6 black olives, pitted
dried oregano
freshly ground black pepper

Blend the yeast with the lukewarm water. Sift the flour and salt into a mixing bowl. Rub in the butter, then stir in the yeast liquid to make a soft dough. Knead for 10 minutes or until the dough is smooth and elastic. Put into an oiled polythene (plastic) bag and leave to rise in a warm place for 1 to 1½ hours.

Roll out the dough to a circle or oblong on a baking sheet. Brush with the olive oil, then arrange the tomato slices on top to cover. Sprinkle with the garlic. Top with the anchovies, cheese slices and olives, then sprinkle liberally with oregano and pepper.

Bake in a preheated hot oven (230°C/450°F, Gas Mark 8) for 25 to 30 minutes or until the cheese has melted and the dough base is cooked. Serve hot.
Serves 2

Seafood risotto

METRIC/IMPERIAL
100g/4oz butter
1 × 15ml spoon/
 1 tablespoon olive oil
1 small onion, finely
 chopped
350g/12oz avorio (Italian
 rice)
120ml/4 fl oz dry white
 wine
600ml/1 pint boiling fish
 stock★
600ml/1 pint boiling water
salt
freshly ground black pepper
225g/8oz shelled seafood
 (lobster, shrimps, etc.)
4 × 15ml spoons/
 4 tablespoons Marsala
4 × 15ml spoons/
 4 tablespoons grated
 Parmesan cheese

AMERICAN
½ cup butter
1 tablespoon olive oil
1 small onion, finely
 chopped
2 cups avorio (Italian rice)
½ cup dry white wine
2½ cups boiling fish stock★
2½ cups boiling water
salt
freshly ground black pepper
1 cup shelled seafood
 (lobster, shrimp, etc.)
4 tablespoons Marsala
4 tablespoons grated
 Parmesan cheese

Melt 25g/1oz/2 tablespoons of the butter with the oil in a saucepan. Add the onion and fry until it is soft but not brown. Add the rice and cook gently for 3 minutes, stirring to coat with the fat in the pan. Stir in the wine and bring to the boil. Simmer until it has been absorbed.

Gradually stir in the stock and water, waiting for each addition to be absorbed before adding the next. Stir frequently and allow 20 to 30 minutes cooking time, by which time the rice should be creamy but still firm. Add salt and pepper to taste.

Five minutes before the rice is ready, melt 50g/2oz/¼ cup of the remaining butter in a frying pan (skillet). Add the seafood and fry for 2 to 3 minutes. Stir in the Marsala and bring to the boil. Simmer until the Marsala has evaporated.

Stir the seafood into the rice mixture, then add the remaining butter and cheese. Stir well and serve hot.
Serves 4

Chicken liver and mushroom risotto

METRIC/IMPERIAL
2 × 15ml spoons/
 2 tablespoons olive oil
2 onions, peeled and thinly
 sliced
1 garlic clove, crushed
1 green pepper, pith and
 seeds removed and diced
100g/4oz mushrooms,
 sliced
225g/8oz long-grain rice
750ml/1¼ pints chicken
 stock
salt
freshly ground black pepper
225g/8oz chicken livers,
 diced

AMERICAN
2 tablespoons olive oil
2 onions, peeled and thinly
 sliced
1 garlic clove, crushed
1 green pepper, pith and
 seeds removed and diced
1 cup sliced mushrooms
1⅓ cups long-grain rice
3 cups chicken stock
salt
freshly ground black pepper
½lb chicken livers, diced

Heat the oil in a flameproof casserole. Add the onions and garlic and fry until the onions are soft but not brown. Add the green pepper and mushrooms and fry for a further 3 to 4 minutes. Stir in the rice, then add the stock with salt and pepper to taste. Bring to the boil and stir in the chicken livers.

Cover the casserole tightly and transfer to a preheated moderate oven (180°C/350°F, Gas Mark 4). Cook for 1 hour or until the rice is tender and all the liquid has been absorbed. Serve hot, from the casserole.
Serves 4

Risi e bisi (green pea risotto)

METRIC/IMPERIAL
50g/2oz butter
1 small onion, peeled and finely chopped
2 streaky bacon rashers, rinds removed and diced
350g/12oz shelled peas
1.75 litres/3 pints chicken stock
350g/12oz avorio (Italian rice)
2 × 15ml spoons/ 2 tablespoons chopped fresh parsley
salt
freshly ground black pepper
75g/3oz Parmesan cheese, grated

AMERICAN
¼ cup butter
1 small onion, peeled and finely chopped
2 bacon slices, diced
2¼ cups shelled peas
7½ cups chicken stock
2 cups avorio (Italian rice)
2 tablespoons chopped fresh parsley
salt
freshly ground black pepper
¾ cup grated Parmesan cheese

Melt the butter in a saucepan. Add the onion and bacon and fry until the onion is soft but not brown. Stir in the peas with 600ml/1 pint/2½ cups of the stock and bring to the boil. Cover and simmer for 10 minutes.

Add the rice and simmer until the stock has been absorbed. Gradually stir in the remaining stock, waiting for each addition to be absorbed before adding the next. Stir frequently and allow 20 to 25 minutes cooking time, by which time the rice should be tender and most of the liquid absorbed.

Stir in the parsley, salt and pepper to taste and the cheese. Serve hot.

Serves 4

Hungarian veal risotto

METRIC/IMPERIAL
25g/1oz butter
0.5kg/1lb pie veal, cut into small pieces
1 large onion, peeled and thinly sliced
1 × 5ml spoon/1 teaspoon paprika
1 × 15ml spoon/ 1 tablespoon tomato purée
450ml/¾ pint beef stock
175g/6oz long-grain rice
150ml/¼ pint sour cream
salt
freshly ground black pepper

AMERICAN
2 tablespoons butter
1lb stewing veal, cut into small pieces
1 large onion, peeled and thinly sliced
1 teaspoon paprika
1 tablespoon tomato paste
2 cups beef stock
1 cup long-grain rice
⅔ cup sour cream
salt
freshly ground black pepper

Melt the butter in a flameproof casserole. Add the veal and brown on all sides. Remove the veal from the pot.

Add the onion to the casserole and fry until it is soft but not brown. Stir in the paprika, tomato purée (paste) and stock. Return the veal to the pot, cover and transfer to a preheated moderate oven (160°C/325°F, Gas Mark 3). Cook for 1 hour or until the veal is tender.

Stir in the rice, re-cover and cook for a further 30 minutes.

Mix the sour cream with salt and pepper to taste and heat gently. Remove the casserole from the oven and stir the sour cream mixture into the risotto. Serve hot.

Serves 4

Chicken pilau

METRIC/IMPERIAL
2 × 15ml spoons/
  2 tablespoons oil
2 onions, peeled and
  chopped
225g/8oz long-grain rice
600ml/1 pint chicken stock
50g/2oz sultanas
350g/12oz cooked chicken
  meat, diced
salt
freshly ground black pepper
50g/2oz cashew nuts,
  chopped

AMERICAN
2 tablespoons oil
2 onions, peeled and
  chopped
1⅓ cups long-grain rice
2½ cups chicken stock
⅓ cup seedless white raisins
1½ cups diced cooked
  chicken meat
salt
freshly ground black pepper
½ cup chopped cashew nuts

Heat the oil in a saucepan. Add the onions and fry until they are soft but not brown. Stir in the rice, then stir in the stock and bring to the boil. Simmer for 10 minutes.

Stir in the sultanas (raisins), chicken and salt and pepper to taste. Simmer for a further 10 to 15 minutes or until the rice is tender and the liquid has been absorbed.

Stir in the nuts and cook for a further 2 to 3 minutes. Serve hot.
Serves 4

Vegetable pilaff

METRIC/IMPERIAL
2 × 15ml spoons/
  2 tablespoons oil
2 large onions, peeled and
  thinly sliced into rings
175g/6oz long-grain rice
600ml/1 pint stock
2 large carrots, peeled and
  grated
100g/4oz shelled peas
50g/2oz mushrooms, sliced
0.5kg/1lb tomatoes, peeled
  and chopped
salt
freshly ground black pepper
175g/6oz Gruyère cheese,
  grated

AMERICAN
2 tablespoons oil
2 large onions, peeled and
  thinly sliced into rings
1 cup long-grain rice
2½ cups stock
2 large carrots, peeled and
  grated
¾ cup shelled peas
½ cup sliced mushrooms
2 cups peeled and chopped
  tomatoes
salt
freshly ground black pepper
1½ cups grated Gruyère
  cheese

Heat the oil in a saucepan. Add the onions and fry until they are soft but not brown. Stir in the rice, then stir in the stock and bring to the boil.

Stir in the carrots and peas and simmer for 10 minutes. Add the mushrooms and tomatoes with salt and pepper to taste and simmer until the rice is tender and most of the liquid has been absorbed.

Stir in most of the cheese and heat gently for 2 to 3 minutes. Pile into a warmed serving dish and sprinkle over the remaining cheese. Serve hot.
Serves 4

Rice and bean casserole

METRIC/IMPERIAL
3 × 15ml spoons
  3 tablespoons oil
1 onion, peeled and
  chopped
1 garlic clove, crushed
0.5kg/1lb long-grain rice
pinch of powdered saffron
pinch of turmeric
pinch of ground coriander
1.2 litres/2 pints stock
1 green pepper, pith and
  seeds removed and diced
3 carrots, peeled and diced
225g/8oz French beans,
  chopped
1 × 400g/14oz can red
  kidney beans, drained
salt
freshly ground black pepper

AMERICAN
3 tablespoons oil
1 onion, peeled and
  chopped
1 garlic clove, crushed
2⅔ cups long-grain rice
pinch of powdered saffron
pinch of turmeric
pinch of ground coriander
5 cups stock
1 green pepper, pith and
  seeds removed and diced
3 carrots, peeled and diced
1 cup chopped green beans
1 × 14oz can red kidney
  beans, drained
salt
freshly ground black pepper

Heat the oil in a flameproof casserole. Add the onion and garlic and fry until the onion is soft but not brown. Stir in the rice and fry for 2 minutes, stirring.

Mix the saffron, turmeric and coriander with the stock and stir into the casserole. Bring to the boil, stirring. Add the green pepper, carrots and French (green) beans. Cover and transfer to a preheated moderate oven (180°C/350°F, Gas Mark 4). Cook for 1 hour.

Stir in the red kidney beans with salt and pepper to taste. Cook for a further 15 minutes or until all the vegetables and rice are tender. Serve hot.
Serves 6

Salmon rice salad

METRIC/IMPERIAL
225g/8oz long-grain rice
salt
1 × 50g/2oz can anchovy
  fillets, drained
3 × 15ml spoons/
  3 tablespoons milk
5 × 15ml spoons/
  5 tablespoons French
  dressing★
1 small onion, peeled and
  finely chopped
2 × 15ml spoons/
  2 tablespoons chopped
  fresh parsley
1 × 200g/7oz can pink
  salmon, drained and flaked
6 black olives, halved and
  stoned

AMERICAN
1⅓ cups long-grain rice
salt
1 × 2oz can anchovy fillets,
  drained
3 tablespoons milk
⅓ cup French dressing★
1 small onion, peeled and
  finely chopped
2 tablespoons chopped fresh
  parsley
1 × 7oz can pink salmon,
  drained and flaked
6 black olives, halved and
  pitted

Cook the rice in boiling salted water according to the directions on the packet. Allow to cool.

Separate the anchovies and place on a saucer. Cover with the milk and leave to soak for 10 minutes. Drain and chop.

Toss the dressing into the rice, then fold in the anchovies, onion, parsley and salmon, mixing well. Spoon into a salad bowl and chill for 20 minutes.

Serve garnished with the olives.
Serves 4 to 6

EGGS & CHEESE

Cheese omelette

METRIC/IMPERIAL
2 eggs
1 × 15ml spoon/
 1 tablespoon water
salt
freshly ground black pepper
dash of Tabasco sauce
15g/½oz butter
25g/1oz Cheddar or
 Gruyère cheese, grated

AMERICAN
2 eggs
1 tablespoon water
salt
freshly ground black pepper
dash of Tabasco sauce
1 tablespoon butter
¼ cup grated Cheddar or
 Gruyère cheese

Beat the eggs lightly until well mixed but not frothy. Add the water, salt and pepper to taste and the Tabasco and stir well. Melt the butter in a 15cm/6 inch diameter omelette pan or frying pan (skillet). Pour in the egg mixture and cook quickly, stirring with a fork. As the mixture sets, lift the edges to allow the liquid egg mixture to run onto the pan. Cook until the top is lightly set and the bottom is golden brown.

Sprinkle over the cheese and fold the omelette in half. Slide onto a warmed serving plate and serve hot.
Serves 1

Omelette aux fines herbes

METRIC/IMPERIAL
2 eggs
1 × 15ml spoon/
 1 tablespoon water
salt
freshly ground black pepper
1 × 5ml spoon/1 teaspoon
 chopped fresh chervil
1 × 5ml spoon/1 teaspoon
 chopped fresh tarragon
1 × 5ml spoon/1 teaspoon
 chopped fresh chives
15g/½oz butter

AMERICAN
2 eggs
1 tablespoon water
salt
freshly ground black pepper
1 teaspoon chopped fresh
 chervil
1 teaspoon chopped fresh
 tarragon
1 teaspoon chopped fresh
 chives
1 tablespoon butter

Beat the eggs lightly until well mixed but not frothy. Add the water, salt and pepper to taste and the herbs and stir well.

Melt the butter in a 15cm/6 inch diameter omelette pan or frying pan (skillet). Pour in the egg mixture and cook quickly, stirring with a fork. As the mixture sets, lift the edges to allow the liquid egg mixture to run onto the pan. Cook until the top is lightly set and the bottom is golden brown. Fold the omelette in half and slide onto a warmed serving plate. Serve hot.
Serves 1

Potato omelette

METRIC/IMPERIAL
40g/1½oz butter
1 medium potato, peeled, cooked and thinly sliced
pinch of dried rosemary
2 eggs
1 × 15ml spoon/ 1 tablespoon water
salt
freshly ground black pepper

AMERICAN
3 tablespoons butter
1 medium potato, peeled, cooked and thinly sliced
pinch of dried rosemary
2 eggs
1 tablespoon water
salt
freshly ground black pepper

Melt 25g/1oz/2 tablespoons of the butter in a frying pan (skillet). Add the potato slices and fry quickly until crisp and golden brown. Sprinkle with the rosemary. Remove from the heat and keep hot.

Beat the eggs lightly until well mixed but not frothy. Add the water and salt and pepper to taste and stir well.

Melt the remaining butter in a 15cm/6 inch diameter omelette pan or frying pan (skillet). Pour in the egg mixture and cook quickly, stirring with a fork. As the mixture sets, lift the edges to allow the liquid egg mixture to run onto the pan. Cook until the top is lightly set and the bottom is golden brown.

Spoon the potato mixture onto one half of the omelette and fold over the other half. Slide the omelette onto a warmed serving plate and serve hot.
Serves 1

Eggs Lorraine

METRIC/IMPERIAL
4 bacon rashers, rinds removed and diced
25g/1oz butter, melted
25g/1oz Gruyère cheese, grated
4 eggs
salt
freshly ground black pepper
4 × 15ml spoons/ 4 tablespoons single cream

AMERICAN
4 bacon slices, diced
2 tablespoons butter, melted
¼ cup grated Gruyère cheese
4 eggs
salt
freshly ground black pepper
4 tablespoons light cream

Blanch the bacon in boiling water for 3 minutes. Drain well.

Pour the butter into a small baking dish and tilt to coat the bottom. Cover with the bacon and then with the cheese. Break the eggs into the dish and season with salt and pepper to taste. Pour over the cream.

Bake in a preheated moderate oven (180°C/350°F, Gas Mark 4) for 5 to 7 minutes or until the eggs are set. Serve hot, from the dish.
Serves 2 to 4

Stuffed baked eggs

METRIC/IMPERIAL
4 streaky bacon rashers, rinds removed
4 eggs, hard-boiled and halved
1 × 425g/15oz can celery hearts, drained and sliced
450ml/¾ pint hot white sauce★
100g/4oz Cheddar cheese, grated
1 × 5ml spoon/1 teaspoon made mustard

AMERICAN
4 bacon slices
4 eggs, hard-cooked and halved
1 × 15oz can celery hearts, drained and sliced
2 cups hot white sauce★
1 cup grated Cheddar cheese
1 teaspoon prepared mustard

Grill (broil) or fry the bacon until it is crisp. Drain on absorbent paper and crumble finely. Remove the yolks from the eggs and mash together with the crumbled bacon. Fill the whites with this mixture and reshape the eggs.

Put the celery heart slices in a baking dish and arrange the stuffed eggs on top. Mix the sauce with all but 3 × 15ml spoons/3 tablespoons of the cheese and the mustard and pour over the eggs. Sprinkle over the reserved cheese.

Bake in a preheated moderate oven (180°C/350°F, Gas Mark 4) for 20 minutes or until heated through and lightly browned on top. Serve hot.
Serves 2 to 4

Convent eggs

METRIC/IMPERIAL
4 eggs
salt
freshly ground black pepper
4 × 15ml spoons/ 4 tablespoons double cream

AMERICAN
4 eggs
salt
freshly ground black pepper
4 tablespoons heavy cream

Break the eggs into 4 greased ramekin dishes or cocottes. Season with salt and pepper and top each with 1 × 15ml spoon/1 tablespoon of cream. Arrange the dishes in a roasting tin and add a little hot water to the tin.

Bake in a preheated moderate oven (180°C/350°F, Gas Mark 4) for 10 to 15 minutes or until the eggs are set. Serve hot.
Serves 4

Pipérade

METRIC/IMPERIAL
25g/1oz butter
1 × 15ml spoon/
  1 tablespoon olive oil
2 onions, peeled and
  chopped
1 garlic clove, crushed
1 green pepper, pith and
  seeds removed and diced
2 tomatoes, peeled and
  chopped
4 eggs
salt
freshly ground black pepper

AMERICAN
2 tablespoons butter
1 tablespoon olive oil
2 onions, peeled and
  chopped
1 garlic clove, crushed
1 green pepper, pith and
  seeds removed and diced
2 tomatoes, peeled and
  chopped
4 eggs
salt
freshly ground black pepper

Melt the butter with the oil in a frying pan (skillet). Add the onions and garlic and fry until the onions are soft but not brown. Stir in the green pepper and tomatoes and cook for a further 5 minutes.
  Beat the eggs with salt and pepper to taste and pour into the pan. Cook gently, stirring, until the eggs are scrambled and just set. Serve hot.
Serves 2

Egg salad with yogurt dressing

METRIC/IMPERIAL
6 celery sticks, thinly sliced
4 eggs, hard-boiled and
  halved
4 carrots, peeled and grated
4 large radishes, sliced
½ cucumber, peeled and
  sliced
Dressing:
300ml/½ pint natural yogurt
1 × 5ml spoon/1 teaspoon
  paprika
1 × 5ml spoon/1 teaspoon
  sugar
1 × 15ml spoon/
  1 tablespoon lemon juice
1 × 15ml spoon/
  1 tablespoon orange juice
freshly ground black pepper

AMERICAN
6 celery stalks, thinly sliced
4 eggs, hard-cooked and
  halved
4 carrots, peeled and grated
4 large radishes, sliced
½ cucumber, peeled and
  sliced
Dressing:
1¼ cups unflavored yogurt
1 teaspoon paprika
1 teaspoon sugar
1 tablespoon lemon juice
1 tablespoon orange juice
freshly ground black pepper

Mix together the ingredients for the dressing with pepper to taste. Pour half the dressing into a salad bowl. Fold in the celery. Arrange the egg halves on top and cover with the carrots, radishes and cucumber. Pour over the remaining dressing and serve lightly chilled.
Serves 4

Baked eggs and tomatoes

METRIC/IMPERIAL
50g/2oz butter
2 large onions, peeled and thinly sliced
0.5kg/1lb tomatoes, peeled and sliced
100g/4oz fresh breadcrumbs
salt
freshly ground black pepper
4 eggs

AMERICAN
¼ cup butter
2 large onions, peeled and thinly sliced
2 cups peeled and sliced tomatoes
2 cups fresh breadcrumbs
salt
freshly ground black pepper
4 eggs

Melt 40g/1½oz/3 tablespoons of the butter in a frying pan (skillet). Add the onions and fry until they are soft but not brown. Remove from the heat.

Make alternate layers of onions, tomato slices and breadcrumbs in a greased baking dish. Season each layer with salt and pepper and dot the top with the remaining butter. Bake in a preheated moderate oven (180°C/350°F, Gas Mark 4) for 40 minutes.

Make 4 hollows in the tomato mixture and break an egg into each. Bake for a further 15 minutes or until the eggs are just set. Serve hot, from the dish.
Serves 4

Curried scrambled eggs

METRIC/IMPERIAL
25g/1oz butter
1 onion, peeled and finely chopped
1 × 15ml spoon/
1 tablespoon mild curry powder
8 eggs
6 × 15ml spoons/
6 tablespoons milk
salt
freshly ground black pepper
2 × 5ml spoons/2 teaspoons chopped fresh parsley

AMERICAN
2 tablespoons butter
1 onion, peeled and finely chopped
1 tablespoon mild curry powder
8 eggs
6 tablespoons milk
salt
freshly ground black pepper
2 teaspoons chopped fresh parsley

Melt the butter in a frying pan (skillet). Add the onion and fry until it is soft but not brown. Stir in the curry powder and cook gently for 5 minutes.

Meanwhile, beat together the eggs, milk, salt and pepper to taste and the parsley. Pour into the pan and cook gently, stirring occasionally, until the eggs are lightly scrambled.

Serve hot, on buttered toast.
Serves 4

Curried eggs

METRIC/IMPERIAL
shredded lettuce
6 eggs, hard-boiled and halved
Sauce:
300ml/½ pint mayonnaise★
2 × 5ml spoons/2 teaspoons lemon juice
1 × 5ml spoon/1 teaspoon mild curry powder
1 × 15ml spoon/ 1 tablespoon chutney
pinch of chilli powder
salt
freshly ground black pepper

AMERICAN
shredded lettuce
6 eggs, hard-cooked and halved
Sauce:
1¼ cups mayonnaise★
2 teaspoons lemon juice
1 teaspoon mild curry powder
1 tablespoon chutney
pinch of chili powder
salt
freshly ground black pepper

Make a bed of shredded lettuce on 6 serving plates. Arrange 2 egg halves, cut sides down, on each plate.

Mix together the ingredients for the sauce with salt and pepper to taste. Spoon over the eggs and chill lightly before serving.
Serves 6

Egg mousse

METRIC/IMPERIAL
6 eggs, hard-boiled and finely chopped
1 × 15ml spoon/ 1 tablespoon grated onion
1 × 15ml spoon/ 1 tablespoon chopped fresh parsley
1 × 2.5ml spoon/½ teaspoon anchovy essence
120ml/4fl oz mayonnaise★
150ml/¼ pint sour cream
1 × 275g/10oz can consommé
2 × 5ml spoons/2 teaspoons gelatine
2 × 15ml spoons/ 2 tablespoons water
salt
freshly ground black pepper
watercress to garnish

AMERICAN
6 eggs, hard-cooked and finely chopped
1 tablespoon grated onion
1 tablespoon chopped fresh parsley
½ teaspoon anchovy paste
½ cup mayonnaise★
⅔ cup sour cream
1 × 10oz can consommé
2 teaspoons unflavored gelatin
2 tablespoons water
salt
freshly ground black pepper
watercress to garnish

Mix together the eggs, onion, parsley and anchovy essence (paste). Add the mayonnaise, sour cream and consommé and mix well. Dissolve the gelatine in the water and strain into the egg mixture.

Add salt and pepper to taste and mix well. Spoon into a decorative mould and chill until set. Serve cold, garnished with watercress.
Serves 6

Smoked haddock and cheese flan

METRIC/IMPERIAL
175g/6oz quantity rich
  shortcrust pastry★
225g/8oz smoked haddock
150ml/¼ pint water
1 × 15ml spoon/
  1 tablespoon lemon juice
25g/1oz butter
1 small onion, peeled and
  finely chopped
50g/2oz mushrooms,
  chopped
2 eggs
3 × 15ml spoons/
  3 tablespoons single cream
100g/4oz cottage cheese
salt
freshly ground black pepper

AMERICAN
1½ cup quantity rich pie
  pastry★
½lb smoked haddock
⅔ cup water
1 tablespoon lemon juice
2 tablespoons butter
1 small onion, peeled and
  finely chopped
½ cup chopped mushrooms
2 eggs
3 tablespoons light cream
½ cup cottage cheese
salt
freshly ground black pepper

Roll out the pastry dough and use to line a 20cm/ 8 inch diameter flan ring (pie pan). Prick the base and bake blind in a preheated moderately hot oven (200°C/400°F, Gas Mark 6) for about 20 minutes or until the pastry is lightly browned and set. Remove from the oven and allow to cool.

Put the haddock, water and lemon juice in a saucepan and bring to the boil. Simmer gently for 10 minutes, then drain well. Remove the skin and bones and flake the fish.

Melt the butter in a saucepan. Add the onion and fry until it is soft but not brown. Add the mushrooms and fry for a further 2 minutes. Remove from the heat and stir in the flaked fish. Spread this mixture over the bottom of the pastry case (pie shell).

Mix together the eggs, cream, cottage cheese and salt and pepper to taste. Pour over the fish mixture in the pastry case (pie shell). Bake in a preheated moderately hot oven (190°C/375°F, Gas Mark 5) for 35 minutes or until the filling is set and golden. Serve warm or cold.
Serves 6 to 8

Cheese soufflé

METRIC/IMPERIAL
40g/1½oz butter
25g/1oz plain flour
300ml/½ pint milk
4 large eggs, separated
175g/6oz cheese, grated
  (preferably a mixture of
  Cheddar and Gruyère)
salt
freshly ground black pepper

AMERICAN
3 tablespoons butter
¼ cup all-purpose flour
1¼ cups milk
4 large eggs, separated
1½ cups grated cheese
  (preferably a mixture of
  Cheddar and Gruyère)
salt
freshly ground black pepper

Melt the butter in a saucepan. Add the flour and cook, stirring, for 1 minute. Remove from the heat and gradually stir in the milk. Return to the heat and bring to the boil, stirring. Simmer until thickened and smooth. Remove from the heat and allow to cool slightly.

Beat the egg yolks and cheese into the sauce, then add salt and pepper to taste. Beat the egg whites until stiff and fold into the cheese mixture. Spoon into a greased 1.2 litre/2 pint/5 cup soufflé dish.

Bake in a preheated moderate oven (180°C/350°F, Gas Mark 4) for 45 minutes or until well risen and lightly browned. Serve immediately.
Serves 4

Cheese charlotte

METRIC/IMPERIAL
100g/4oz fresh breadcrumbs
450ml/¾ pint milk
25g/1oz butter
175g/6oz Cheddar cheese, grated
3 eggs, lightly beaten
salt
freshly ground black pepper

AMERICAN
2 cups fresh breadcrumbs
2 cups milk
2 tablespoons butter
1½ cups grated Cheddar cheese
3 eggs, lightly beaten
salt
freshly ground black pepper

Put the breadcrumbs in a mixing bowl. Put the milk and butter in a saucepan and heat gently, stirring to melt the butter. Pour the hot milk mixture over the breadcrumbs and leave to soak for 10 minutes.

Stir in the cheese, eggs and salt and pepper to taste. Pour into a 1.2 litre/2 pint/5 cup baking dish. Bake in a preheated moderately hot oven (200°C/400°F, Gas Mark 6) for 30 to 35 minutes or until well risen and golden brown. Serve hot, from the dish.
Serves 4

Cottage cheese and nut salad

METRIC/IMPERIAL
350g/12oz cottage cheese
2 × 15ml spoons/ 2 tablespoons chopped fresh mint
6 lettuce leaves, shredded
1 small bunch of watercress
100g/4 oz cashew nuts, chopped
2 red-skinned dessert apples, cored and sliced into rings
2 × 15ml spoons/ 2 tablespoons lemon juice
mayonnaise★

AMERICAN
1½ cups cottage cheese
2 tablespoons chopped fresh mint
6 lettuce leaves, shredded
1 small bunch of watercress
1 cup chopped cashew nuts
2 red-skinned dessert apples, cored and sliced into rings
2 tablespoons lemon juice
mayonnaise★

Mix the cottage cheese and mint together. Arrange the lettuce and watercress on a serving dish and pile the cottage cheese mixture in the centre. Sprinkle with the nuts.

Dip the apple rings in lemon juice to prevent discoloration. Arrange the apple rings around the cottage cheese mixture. Serve with mayonnaise.
Serves 2 to 4

Herb cheese fondue

METRIC/IMPERIAL
1 garlic clove, halved
150ml/¼ pint dry white wine
0.5kg/1lb Gouda cheese, rind removed and grated
1 × 15ml spoon/ 1 tablespoon cornflour
2 × 15ml spoons/ 2 tablespoons Kirsch
1 × 5ml spoon/1 teaspoon chopped fresh thyme
1 × 5ml spoon/1 teaspoon chopped fresh tarragon
2 × 5ml spoons/2 teaspoons chopped fresh chervil
freshly ground black pepper
pinch of grated nutmeg
French bread, cut into cubes, to serve

AMERICAN
1 garlic clove, halved
⅔ cup dry white wine
1lb Gouda cheese, rind removed and grated
1 tablespoon cornstarch
2 tablespoons Kirsch
1 teaspoon chopped fresh thyme
1 teaspoon chopped fresh tarragon
2 teaspoons chopped fresh chervil
freshly ground black pepper
pinch of grated nutmeg
French bread, cut into cubes, to serve

Rub the inside of a cheese fondue pot with the cut sides of the garlic. Discard the garlic. Put the wine in the pan and heat gently. Gradually stir in the cheese and continue stirring until the cheese has melted and the mixture is bubbling.

Dissolve the cornflour (cornstarch) in the liqueur and add to the pot with the herbs, pepper to taste and the nutmeg. Stir well and allow to bubble for 1 to 2 minutes before serving.

Place the pot over a lighted spirit burner and serve with the cubes of bread.
Serves 4

Cheese fondue

METRIC/IMPERIAL
1 garlic clove, halved
350g/12oz Emmenthal cheese, grated
350g/12oz Gruyère cheese, grated
2 × 5ml spoons/2 teaspoons plain flour
450ml/¾ pint dry white wine
1 × 5ml spoon/1 teaspoon lemon juice
2 × 15ml spoons/ 2 tablespoons Kirsch
pinch of grated nutmeg
freshly ground black pepper
French bread, cut into cubes, to serve

AMERICAN
1 garlic clove, halved
3 cups grated Emmenthal cheese
3 cups grated Gruyère cheese
2 teaspoons all-purpose flour
2 cups dry white wine
1 teaspoon lemon juice
2 tablespoons Kirsch
pinch of grated nutmeg
freshly ground black pepper
French bread, cut into cubes, to serve

Rub the inside of a cheese fondue pot with the cut sides of the garlic. Discard the garlic. Put the cheeses and flour in the pot and mix well together. Stir in the wine, lemon juice, Kirsch, nutmeg and pepper to taste. Heat gently, on top of the stove, stirring to melt the cheeses. When the fondue is creamy, transfer the pot to a spirit burner and keep warm. Serve with the bread, stirring frequently to prevent the fondue from sticking.
Serves 8

Cream cheese fritters

METRIC/IMPERIAL
225g/8oz cream cheese
50g/2oz plain flour
2 large potatoes, peeled and grated
1 egg, lightly beaten
salt
freshly ground black pepper
milk
vegetable oil

AMERICAN
1 cup cream cheese
½ cup all-purpose flour
2 large potatoes, peeled and grated
1 egg, lightly beaten
salt
freshly ground black pepper
milk
vegetable oil

Cream the cheese until it is soft. Sift in the flour and fold into the cheese. Beat in the potatoes, egg, salt and pepper to taste and enough milk to make a smooth thick batter.

Put enough oil in a frying pan (skillet) to make a 2.5cm/1 inch layer. Heat the oil. Drop spoonsful of batter into the pan, well spaced apart, and fry for 2 to 3 minutes on each side, or until golden brown. Drain on absorbent paper and serve hot.

Serves 4

Cheese and courgette (zucchini) quiche

METRIC/IMPERIAL
175g/6oz quantity shortcrust pastry★ (made with 175g/6oz flour, etc.)
25g/1oz butter
1 × 15ml spoon/ 1 tablespoon olive oil
6 medium courgettes, sliced
100g/4oz Gruyère cheese, grated
3 eggs
150ml/¼ pint single cream
salt
freshly ground black pepper

AMERICAN
1½ cup quantity pie pastry★ (made with 1½ cups flour, etc.)
2 tablespoons butter
1 tablespoon olive oil
6 medium zucchini, sliced
1 cup grated Gruyère cheese
3 eggs
⅔ cup light cream
salt
freshly ground black pepper

Roll out the pastry dough and use to line a 20cm/ 8 inch flan ring (pie pan).

Melt the butter with the oil in a saucepan. Add the courgettes (zucchini) and shake to coat them with the butter and oil. Cover and cook gently until just tender, shaking the pan occasionally. Remove from the heat and allow to cool slightly.

Arrange the courgette (zucchini) slices in the pastry case (pie shell). Sprinkle over the cheese.

Mix together the eggs, cream and salt and pepper to taste and pour into the pastry case (pie shell). Place on a baking sheet and bake in a preheated moderately hot oven (190°C/375°F, Gas Mark 5) for 25 to 30 minutes or until the pastry is golden and the filling is set and lightly browned.

Serve warm or cold.

Serves 4 to 6

VEGETABLES & SALADS

Celery with cheese sauce

METRIC/IMPERIAL
1 large head of celery, cut into 2.5cm/1 inch pieces
salt
300ml/½ pint hot mornay sauce★
3 × 15ml spoons/ 3 tablespoons grated Parmesan cheese
15g/½oz butter, cut into small pieces

AMERICAN
1 large head of celery, cut into 1 inch pieces
salt
1¼ cups hot mornay sauce★
3 tablespoons grated Parmesan cheese
1 tablespoon butter, cut into small pieces

Cook the celery in boiling salted water until it is tender but still firm. Drain well and transfer to a greased flameproof serving dish.
 Pour the mornay sauce over the celery and sprinkle with the Parmesan cheese. Dot the top with the pieces of butter. Grill (broil) until the top is lightly browned and serve hot.
Serves 4

Leeks mornay

METRIC/IMPERIAL
4 medium leeks, thoroughly cleaned
salt
300ml/½ pint hot mornay sauce★
2 × 15ml spoons/ 2 tablespoons grated Cheddar cheese

AMERICAN
4 medium leeks, thoroughly cleaned
salt
1¼ cups hot mornay sauce★
2 tablespoons grated Cheddar cheese

Cook the leeks in boiling salted water for 15 minutes or until they are tender. Drain well and arrange in a warmed flameproof serving dish.
 Pour over the sauce and sprinkle the top with the cheese. Grill (broil) until the top is lightly browned and bubbling. Serve hot.
Serves 4

Aubergines (eggplants) with tomato sauce

METRIC/IMPERIAL
2 medium aubergines, sliced
salt
300ml/½ pint tomato sauce★
chopped fresh parsley to garnish

AMERICAN
2 medium eggplants, sliced
salt
1¼ cups tomato sauce★
chopped fresh parsley to garnish

Sprinkle the aubergine (eggplant) slices with salt and leave for 20 minutes. Rinse and pat dry with absorbent paper.
 Put the tomato sauce in a saucepan and add the aubergine (eggplant) slices. Mix well, then cover and simmer for 45 minutes.
 Serve hot, sprinkled with parsley.
Serves 4

Carrots Vichy

METRIC/IMPERIAL
0.5kg/1lb small new carrots, peeled
25g/1oz butter
salt
2 × 5ml spoons/2 teaspoons sugar
450ml/¾ pint water
chopped fresh parsley to garnish

AMERICAN
1lb small new carrots, peeled
2 tablespoons butter
salt
2 teaspoons sugar
2 cups water
chopped fresh parsley to garnish

Put the carrots in a saucepan with half the butter, salt to taste, the sugar and water. Bring to the boil and simmer for 8 to 10 minutes or until the carrots are tender and most of the water has evaporated.
 Drain the carrots and return to the saucepan. Add the remaining butter and the parsley and shake to coat the carrots. Serve hot.
Serves 4

Smoked haddock and cheese flan (page 244)

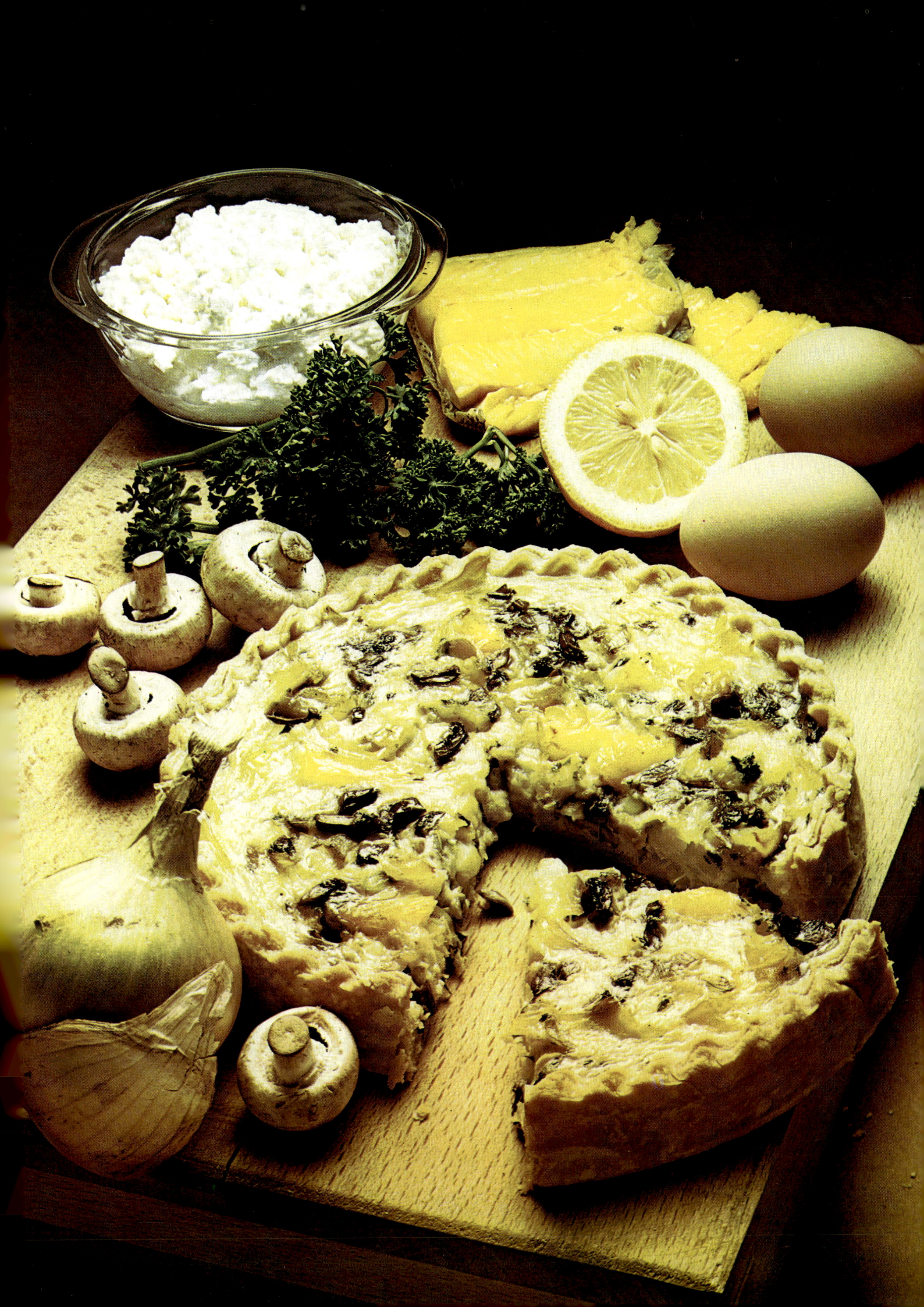

Corn-on-the-cob (page 260); Cheese fondue (page 246)

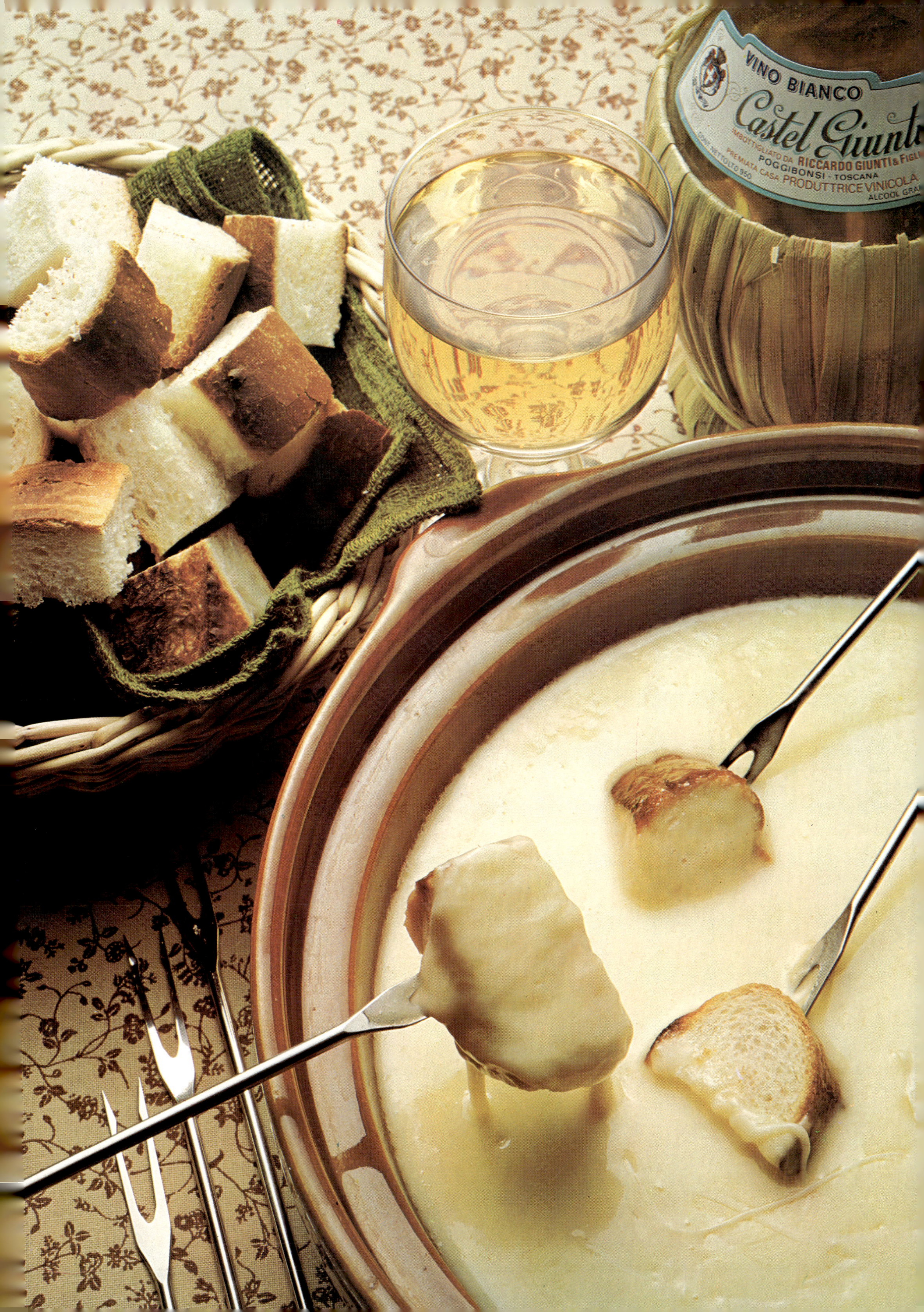
VINO BIANCO
POGGIBONSI - TOSCANA
PRODUTTRICE VINICOLA

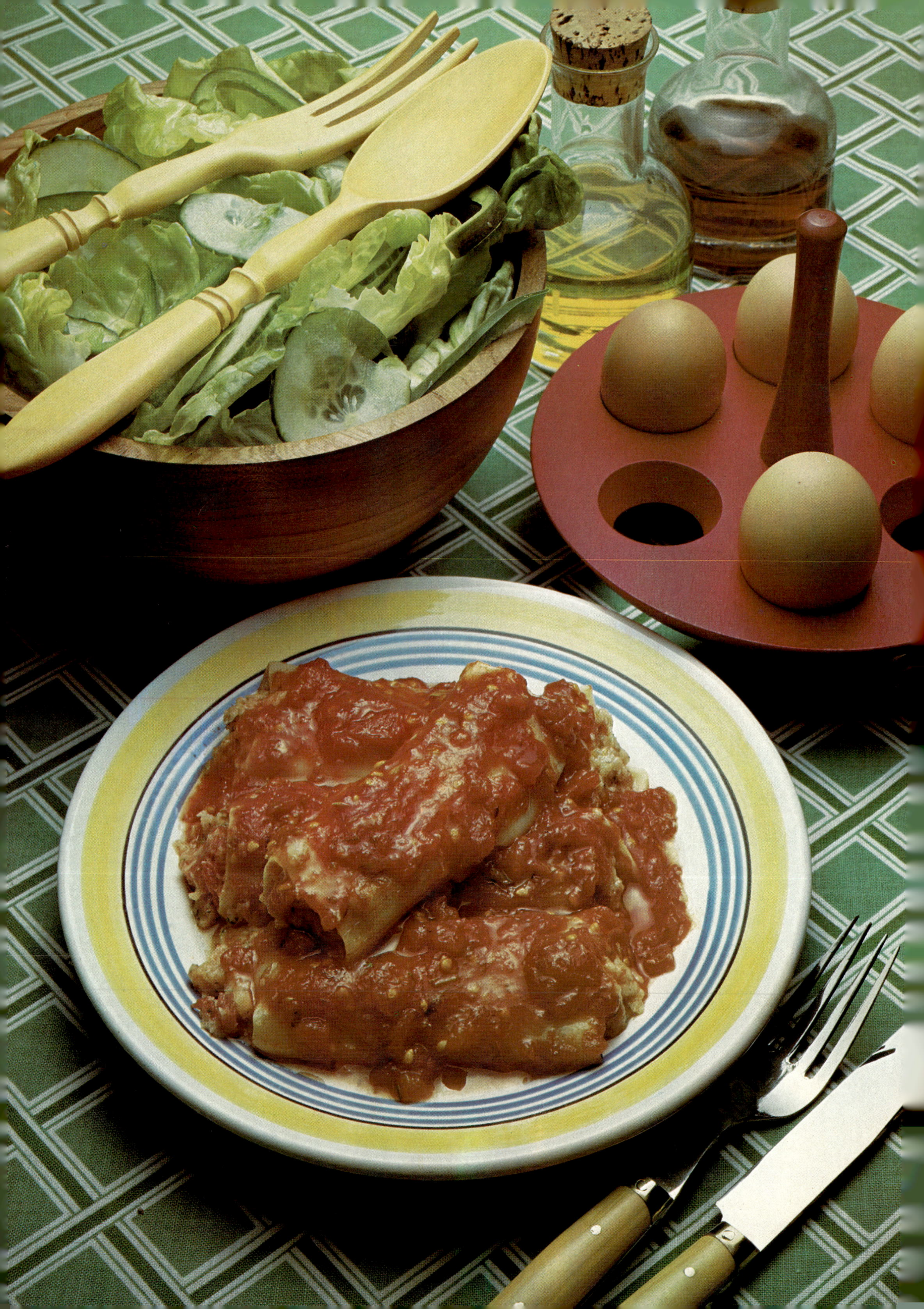

Tomatoes baked with herbs

METRIC/IMPERIAL
4–6 large tomatoes, halved
salt
freshly ground black pepper
1 × 15ml spoon/
  1 tablespoon minced onion
1 × 15ml spoon/
  1 tablespoon chopped fresh basil
1 × 15ml spoon/
  1 tablespoon chopped fresh dill
1 × 5ml spoon/1 teaspoon celery seed
50g/2oz dry breadcrumbs
25g/1oz butter, cut into small pieces

AMERICAN
4–6 large tomatoes, halved
salt
freshly ground black pepper
1 tablespoon ground onion
1 tablespoon chopped fresh basil
1 tablespoon chopped fresh dill
1 teaspoon celery seed
½ cup dry breadcrumbs
2 tablespoons butter, cut into small pieces

Arrange the tomatoes in a baking dish, cut sides up. Season with salt and pepper. Mix together the onion, basil, dill, celery seed and breadcrumbs. Sprinkle over the tomatoes. Dot the top with the pieces of butter.
　Bake in a preheated moderately hot oven (200°C/400°F, Gas Mark 6) for 15 minutes. Serve hot, from the dish.
Serves 4

Broccoli ring

METRIC/IMPERIAL
0.75kg/1½lb broccoli
salt
225g/8oz potatoes, peeled, cooked, drained and mashed
25g/1oz butter
1 egg, lightly beaten
2 × 15ml spoons/
  2 tablespoons single cream
pinch of grated nutmeg
freshly ground black pepper

AMERICAN
1½lb broccoli
salt
½lb potatoes, peeled, cooked, drained and mashed (about 1 cup)
2 tablespoons butter
1 egg, lightly beaten
2 tablespoons light cream
pinch of grated nutmeg
freshly ground black pepper

Cook the broccoli in boiling salted water for about 8 minutes or until it is tender. Drain well and purée in an electric blender.
　Add the remaining ingredients, with salt and pepper to taste, to the broccoli purée. Spoon into a greased 18cm/7 inch diameter ring mould. Place the mould in a roasting tin and add a little hot water to the tin.
　Bake in a preheated moderately hot oven (190°C/375°F, Gas Mark 5) for 45 minutes or until a knife inserted into the centre comes out clean.
　Turn out onto a warmed serving plate and serve hot.
Serves 4

Cannelloni with tomato stuffing (page 232)

Sweet and sour beetroot (beet) and onions

METRIC/IMPERIAL
2 × 5ml spoons/2 teaspoons cornflour
150ml/¼ pint white wine vinegar
2 × 15ml spoons/ 2 tablespoons clear honey
3 × 15ml spoons/ 3 tablespoons tomato chutney
150ml/¼ pint chicken stock
salt
freshly ground black pepper
1 large beetroot, cooked, peeled and diced
12 pickled onions

AMERICAN
2 teaspoons cornstarch
⅔ cup white wine vinegar
2 tablespoons clear honey
3 tablespoons tomato chutney
⅔ cup chicken stock
salt
freshly ground black pepper
1 large beet, cooked, peeled and diced
12 pickled onions

Mix together the cornflour (cornstarch), vinegar, honey, chutney, stock and salt and pepper to taste in a saucepan. Bring to the boil and simmer until thickened. Stir in the beetroot (beet) and remove from the heat. Allow to cool.

Put the onions in a mixing bowl and pour over the beetroot (beet) mixture. Leave to marinate for several hours before serving.
Serves 4

Ratatouille

METRIC/IMPERIAL
3 aubergines, sliced
salt
150ml/¼ pint olive oil
3 onions, peeled and sliced
2 garlic cloves, crushed
3 courgettes, sliced
3 red peppers, pith and seeds removed and thinly sliced
5 tomatoes, peeled and sliced
1 × 5ml spoon/1 teaspoon dried basil
freshly ground black pepper

AMERICAN
3 eggplants, sliced
salt
⅔ cup olive oil
3 onions, peeled and sliced
2 garlic cloves, crushed
3 zucchini, sliced
3 pimientos, pith and seeds removed and thinly sliced
5 tomatoes, peeled and sliced
1 teaspoon dried basil
freshly ground black pepper

Sprinkle the aubergine (eggplant) slices with salt and leave to drain for 20 minutes. Rinse and pat dry with absorbent paper.

Heat the oil in a saucepan. Add the onions and garlic and fry until the onions are soft but not brown. Add the remaining ingredients with salt and pepper to taste. Cover and cook gently for about 1 hour or until the vegetables are soft but not mushy.

Serve hot or chilled.
Serves 6 to 8

Peperonata

METRIC/IMPERIAL
5 × 15ml spoons/
  5 tablespoons olive oil
2 large onions, peeled and
  thinly sliced
1 garlic clove, crushed
6 medium red peppers, pith
  and seeds removed and cut
  into strips
12 medium tomatoes, peeled
  and chopped
salt

AMERICAN
⅓ cup olive oil
2 large onions, peeled and
  thinly sliced
1 garlic clove, crushed
6 medium pimientos, pith
  and seeds removed and cut
  into strips
12 medium tomatoes, peeled
  and chopped
salt

Heat the oil in a saucepan. Add the onions, garlic and red peppers (pimientos) and fry gently for 15 minutes. Stir in the tomatoes and salt to taste. Cover and simmer for 30 minutes.
  Serve hot.
Serves 4 to 6

Courgettes (zucchini) à la grecque

METRIC/IMPERIAL
3 × 15ml spoons/
  3 tablespoons olive oil
2 small onions, peeled and
  thinly sliced
1 garlic clove, crushed
150ml/¼ pint dry white
  wine
salt
freshly ground black pepper
0.75kg/1½lb courgettes,
  sliced
0.5kg/1lb tomatoes, peeled,
  deseeded and quartered
chopped fresh chervil to
  garnish

AMERICAN
3 tablespoons olive oil
2 small onions, peeled and
  thinly sliced
1 garlic clove, crushed
⅔ cup dry white wine
salt
freshly ground black pepper
1½lb zucchini, sliced
1lb tomatoes, peeled,
  deseeded and quartered
chopped fresh chervil to
  garnish

Heat the oil in a saucepan. Add the onions and garlic and fry until the onions are soft but not brown. Stir in the wine with salt and pepper to taste, then add the courgettes (zucchini) and tomatoes. Simmer for 10 minutes or until the courgettes (zucchini) are just tender.
  Remove from the heat and allow to cool. Transfer to a serving dish and chill lightly. Serve cold, sprinkled with chopped chervil.
Serves 4
Note: This dish may also be served warm.

Braised chicory (endive)

METRIC/IMPERIAL
0.75kg/1½lb chicory
25g/1oz butter, cut into small pieces
pinch of grated nutmeg
juice of ½ lemon
150ml/¼ pint chicken stock
1.5 × 5ml spoons/
  1½ teaspoons cornflour
1 × 15ml spoon/
  1 tablespoon water
salt
freshly ground black pepper

AMERICAN
1½lb French or Belgian endive
2 tablespoons butter, cut into small pieces
pinch of grated nutmeg
juice of ½ lemon
⅔ cup chicken stock
1½ teaspoons cornstarch
1 tablespoon water
salt
freshly ground black pepper

Blanch the chicory (endive) in boiling water for 1 minute. Drain and refresh under cold running water. Put half the butter pieces on the bottom of a casserole. Arrange the chicory (endive) on top and dot with the remaining butter. Sprinkle over the nutmeg and lemon juice and pour in the stock. Cover and braise in a preheated moderate oven (160°C/325°F, Gas Mark 3) for 1½ hours.

Transfer the chicory (endive) to a warmed serving dish. Keep hot.

Pour the cooking liquid into a saucepan. Dissolve the cornflour (cornstarch) in the water and add to the saucepan. Bring to the boil, stirring, and simmer until thickened and smooth. Season to taste with salt and pepper. Pour this sauce over the chicory (endive) and serve hot.
Serves 4

Green beans with almonds

METRIC/IMPERIAL
0.5kg/1lb French beans, sliced
salt
50g/2oz butter
25g/1oz blanched almonds, flaked
2 × 5ml spoons/2 teaspoons lemon juice

AMERICAN
2 cups sliced green beans
salt
¼ cup butter
¼ cup blanched slivered almonds
2 teaspoons lemon juice

Cook the beans in boiling salted water for 10 minutes or until just tender.

Meanwhile, melt the butter in a frying pan (skillet). Add the almonds and fry until they are golden brown. Stir in the lemon juice and a pinch of salt. Remove from the heat and keep hot.

Drain the beans. Add to the frying pan (skillet) and toss together with the almond mixture. Spoon into a warmed serving dish and serve hot.
Serves 4

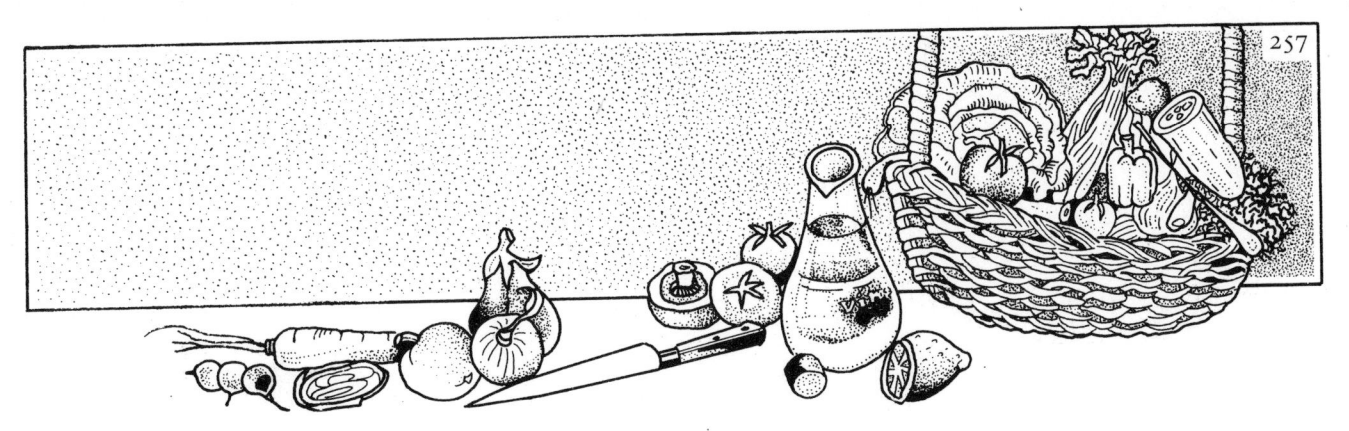

Spinach niçoise

METRIC/IMPERIAL
1kg/2lb spinach
75g/3oz butter
salt
freshly ground black pepper
3 × 15ml spoons/
  3 tablespoons double cream
pinch of grated nutmeg
2 onions, peeled and
  chopped
4 large tomatoes, peeled and
  chopped
100g/4oz Cheddar or
  Gruyère cheese, grated

AMERICAN
2lb spinach
⅓ cup butter
salt
freshly ground black pepper
3 tablespoons heavy cream
pinch of grated nutmeg
2 onions, peeled and
  chopped
4 large tomatoes, peeled and
  chopped
1 cup grated Cheddar or
  Gruyère cheese

Cook the spinach for about 7 minutes or until it is tender. (Do not add any water: there should be enough left on the leaves after washing.) Drain well, pressing out excess moisture. Chop finely and stir in 40g/1½oz/3 tablespoons of the butter, salt and pepper to taste, the cream and nutmeg. Put into a warmed flameproof serving dish and keep hot.

Melt the remaining butter in a frying pan (skillet). Add the onions and fry until they are soft but not brown. Stir in the tomatoes and cook for 5 minutes or until the mixture is very soft.

Spoon the onion and tomato mixture over the spinach and sprinkle with the cheese. Grill (broil) slowly until the cheese has melted and the top is golden brown and bubbling. Serve hot.

Serves 4 to 6

Cauliflower fritters

METRIC/IMPERIAL
1 large cauliflower, broken
  into florets
vegetable oil for deep frying
Batter:
100g/4oz plain flour
pinch of salt
pinch of mild curry powder
2 eggs, separated
150ml/¼ pint water
4 × 15ml spoons/
  4 tablespoons milk

AMERICAN
1 large cauliflower, broken
  into florets
vegetable oil for deep frying
Batter:
1 cup all-purpose flour
pinch of salt
pinch of mild curry powder
2 eggs, separated
⅔ cup water
4 tablespoons milk

Blanch the cauliflower florets in boiling water for 5 minutes. Drain and pat dry with absorbent paper.

To make the batter, sift the flour, salt and curry powder into a mixing bowl. Add the egg yolks and water and beat until smooth. Beat in the milk. Beat the egg whites until stiff and fold into the batter.

Coat the cauliflower florets with the batter.

Heat the oil in a deep frying pan (deep fat fryer) until it is 190°C/375°F. Fry the florets, in batches, until they are golden brown. Drain on absorbent paper and serve hot.

Serves 4

Boston baked beans

METRIC/IMPERIAL
0.5kg/1lb dried white haricot beans, soaked overnight and drained
2 large tomatoes, peeled and chopped
2 × 15ml spoons/ 2 tablespoons treacle
2 × 5ml spoons/2 teaspoons made mustard
salt
freshly ground black pepper
350g/12oz fat salt pork, diced
2 onions, peeled and chopped

AMERICAN
2⅓ cups dried navy beans, soaked overnight and drained
2 large tomatoes, peeled and chopped
2 tablespoons molasses
2 teaspoons prepared mustard
salt
freshly ground black pepper
¾lb salt pork, diced
2 onions, peeled and chopped

Put the beans in a saucepan and cover with fresh water. Bring to the boil and simmer for 15 minutes. Drain the beans, reserving 300ml/½ pint/1¼ cups of the liquid.

Return the cooking liquid to the saucepan and add the tomatoes. Bring to the boil and simmer for 10 minutes. Remove from the heat and stir in the treacle (molasses), mustard and salt and pepper to taste.

Put the beans, salt pork and onions in a deep heavy casserole, filling it only half full. Pour over the tomato mixture. Cover and bake in a preheated cool oven (140°C/275°F, Gas Mark 1) for 5 hours. Serve hot.
Serves 8

Rosemary potatoes

METRIC/IMPERIAL
50g/2oz butter
2 × 15ml spoons/ 2 tablespoons olive oil
6 medium potatoes, peeled, cooked and thinly sliced
1 × 5ml spoon/1 teaspoon dried rosemary

AMERICAN
¼ cup butter
2 tablespoons olive oil
6 medium potatoes, peeled, cooked and thinly sliced
1 teaspoon dried rosemary

Melt the butter with the oil in a frying pan (skillet). Add the potato slices and sprinkle over the rosemary. Fry until the potatoes are golden brown, turning frequently. Serve hot.
Serves 4

Scalloped herb potatoes

METRIC/IMPERIAL
0.5kg/1lb potatoes, peeled and very thinly sliced
1 × 15ml spoon/ 1 tablespoon chopped fresh parsley
1 × 5ml spoon/1 teaspoon chopped fresh sage
1 × 5ml spoon/1 teaspoon chopped fresh rosemary
1 × 5ml spoon/1 teaspoon chopped fresh thyme
450ml/¾ pint milk
50g/2oz butter
salt
freshly ground black pepper

AMERICAN
1lb potatoes, peeled and very thinly sliced
1 tablespoon chopped fresh parsley
1 teaspoon chopped fresh sage
1 teaspoon chopped fresh rosemary
1 teaspoon chopped fresh thyme
2 cups milk
¼ cup butter
salt
freshly ground black pepper

Make layers of the potatoes in a baking dish, sprinkling each layer with herbs. Put the milk, butter and salt and pepper to taste in a saucepan and heat, stirring to melt the butter. Pour the milk mixture over the potatoes.

Bake in a preheated moderate oven (180°C/350°F, Gas Mark 4) for 1¼ hours. Serve hot, from the dish.
Serves 4

Savoyarde potatoes

METRIC/IMPERIAL
0.5kg/1lb potatoes, peeled and thinly sliced
300ml/½ pint chicken stock
1 egg, lightly beaten
salt
freshly ground black pepper
pinch of grated nutmeg
50g/2oz Gruyère cheese, grated
1 garlic clove, halved
25g/1oz butter, cut into small pieces

AMERICAN
1lb potatoes, peeled and thinly sliced
1¼ cups chicken stock
1 egg, lightly beaten
salt
freshly ground black pepper
pinch of grated nutmeg
½ cup grated Gruyère cheese
1 garlic clove, halved
2 tablespoons butter, cut into small pieces

Mix together the potatoes, stock, egg, salt and pepper to taste, the nutmeg and cheese. Fold together gently to mix well.

Rub the inside of a baking dish with the cut sides of the garlic. Discard the garlic. Spoon the potato mixture into the dish and dot the top with the butter pieces.

Bake in a preheated moderate oven (160°C/325°F, Gas Mark 3) for 35 to 40 minutes or until the potatoes are tender and the top is lightly browned.

Serve hot, from the baking dish.
Serves 4

Asparagus hollandaise

METRIC/IMPERIAL
24–32 fresh asparagus
 spears
salt
300ml/½ pint warm
 hollandaise sauce★

AMERICAN
24–32 fresh asparagus
 spears
salt
1¼ cups warm hollandaise
 sauce★

Tie the asparagus in 4 bunches of 6 to 8 spears each. Stand in a tall saucepan of boiling salted water, keeping the tips above the water level, and simmer gently for 10 to 15 minutes or until tender. Drain well.
    Arrange the asparagus on 4 warmed serving plates and spoon over the sauce. Serve hot.
Serves 4

Corn-on-the-cob

METRIC/IMPERIAL
1–2 corn cobs per person
To serve:
melted butter
salt
freshly ground black pepper

AMERICAN
1–2 corn cobs per person
To serve:
melted butter
salt
freshly ground black pepper

Remove the outer leaves and 'silk' from the corn and wash thoroughly. Put the cobs into boiling unsalted water (salt toughens the corn) and cook for about 15 minutes, depending on size. Drain well and serve with melted butter, salt and pepper.

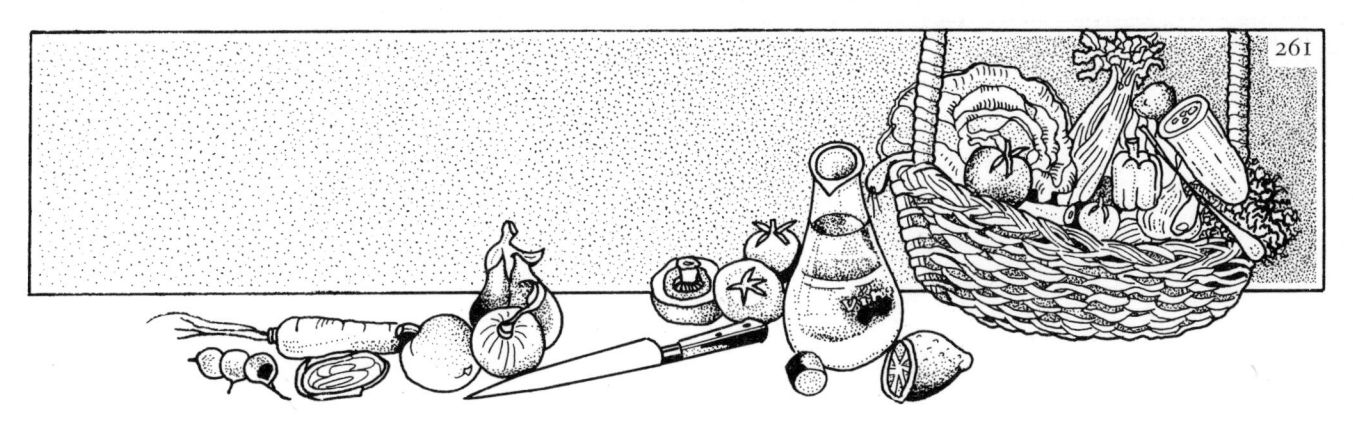

Red cabbage with apples

METRIC/IMPERIAL
50g/2oz butter
1 red cabbage, cored and shredded
2 dessert apples, peeled, cored and chopped
1 small onion, peeled and chopped
salt
freshly ground black pepper
pinch of grated nutmeg
175ml/6fl oz dry red wine

AMERICAN
¼ cup butter
1 head red cabbage, cored and shredded
2 dessert apples, peeled, cored and chopped
1 small onion, peeled and chopped
salt
freshly ground black pepper
pinch of grated nutmeg
¾ cup dry red wine

Melt the butter in a saucepan. Add the cabbage, apples and onion and cook, turning in the butter, for 5 minutes. Stir in salt and pepper to taste, the nutmeg and wine.
   Cover and simmer for 35 minutes or until the cabbage is tender and the liquid has evaporated. Serve hot.
Serves 4 to 6

Sweet and sour Chinese cabbage

METRIC/IMPERIAL
2 × 15ml spoons/ 2 tablespoons vegetable oil
1 Chinese cabbage, shredded
2 × 15ml spoons/ 2 tablespoons dry sherry
Sauce:
1 × 15ml spoon/ 1 tablespoon vegetable oil
1 large carrot, peeled and grated
3 tomatoes, peeled and chopped
1 × 15ml spoon/ 1 tablespoon cornflour
150ml/¼ pint chicken stock or water
2 × 15ml spoons/ 2 tablespoons soy sauce
1 × 5ml spoon/1 teaspoon salt
1 × 15ml spoon/ 1 tablespoon brown sugar
2 × 15ml spoons/ 2 tablespoons wine vinegar

AMERICAN
2 tablespoons vegetable oil
1 head Chinese cabbage, shredded
2 tablespoons dry sherry
Sauce:
1 tablespoon vegetable oil
1 large carrot, peeled and grated
3 tomatoes, peeled and chopped
1 tablespoon cornstarch
⅔ cup chicken stock or water
2 tablespoons soy sauce
1 teaspoon salt
1 tablespoon brown sugar
2 tablespoons wine vinegar

First make the sauce. Heat the oil in a saucepan. Add the carrot and tomatoes and cook for 2 to 3 minutes, stirring. Dissolve the cornflour (cornstarch) in the stock or water and add to the saucepan with the remaining sauce ingredients. Bring to the boil, stirring, and simmer until thickened. Allow to simmer gently while cooking the cabbage.
   Heat the oil in another saucepan and add the cabbage. Stir-fry for 3 to 4 minutes. Add the sherry and continue to stir-fry for 2 minutes. Transfer the cabbage to a warmed serving dish and pour over the sauce. Serve hot.
Serves 4

Petits pois à la française

METRIC/IMPERIAL
0.5kg/1lb shelled peas
6 lettuce leaves, shredded
8 spring onions, chopped
1 × 5ml spoon/1 teaspoon sugar
salt
freshly ground black pepper
15g/½oz butter
1 × 15ml spoon/
 1 tablespoon chopped fresh mint

AMERICAN
3 cups shelled peas
6 lettuce leaves, shredded
8 scallions, chopped
1 teaspoon sugar
salt
freshly ground black pepper
1 tablespoon butter
1 tablespoon chopped fresh mint

Put the peas, lettuce, spring onions (scallions), sugar and salt and pepper to taste in a saucepan. Add just enough water to cover the bottom of the pan and bring to the boil. Simmer gently for 20 minutes or until the peas are tender.

If there is any liquid left in the pan, drain it away. Add the butter and mint and fold through the pea mixture. Serve hot.
Serves 4

Braised peas

METRIC/IMPERIAL
25g/1oz butter
1 onion, peeled and finely chopped
4 × 15ml spoons/
 4 tablespoons finely chopped cooked ham
350g/12oz shelled peas
4 × 15ml spoons/
 4 tablespoons water
salt
freshly ground black pepper

AMERICAN
2 tablespoons butter
1 onion, peeled and finely chopped
4 tablespoons finely chopped cooked ham
2¼ cups shelled peas
4 tablespoons water
salt
freshly ground black pepper

Melt the butter in a saucepan. Add the onion and fry until it is soft but not brown. Stir in the ham, peas, water and salt and pepper to taste. Cover tightly and cook gently for 15 minutes.

Uncover and simmer for a further 15 minutes or until most of the liquid has evaporated. Serve hot.
Serves 4

Chinese rice and vegetable salad

METRIC/IMPERIAL
25g/1oz butter
4 × 15ml spoons/
 4 tablespoons vegetable oil
1 large onion, peeled and
 thinly sliced
4 streaky bacon rashers,
 rinds removed and cut into
 strips
4 eggs, lightly beaten
100g/4oz shelled peas
175g/6oz long-grain rice,
 cooked and kept hot
1.5 × 15ml spoons/
 1½ tablespoons soy sauce
1 cos lettuce, torn into
 small pieces
100g/4oz bean sprouts
2 tomatoes, roughly
 chopped
2 celery sticks, chopped
½ bunch of watercress
Dressing:
2 × 15ml spoons/
 2 tablespoons wine
 vinegar
1.5 × 15ml spoons/
 1½ tablespoons soy sauce
2 × 15ml spoons/
 2 tablespoons chicken stock
2 × 15ml spoons/
 2 tablespoons sesame or
 olive oil
1.5 × 5ml spoons/
 1½ teaspoons sugar
1 garlic clove, crushed
2 slices root ginger, peeled
 and grated
2 spring onions, thinly
 sliced

AMERICAN
2 tablespoons butter
4 tablespoons vegetable oil
1 large onion, peeled and
 thinly sliced
4 bacon slices, cut into
 strips
4 eggs, lightly beaten
¾ cup shelled peas
1 cup long-grain rice,
 cooked and kept hot
1½ tablespoons soy sauce
1 head romaine lettuce, torn
 into small pieces
¼lb bean sprouts
2 tomatoes, roughly
 chopped
2 celery stalks, chopped
½ bunch of watercress
Dressing:
2 tablespoons wine vinegar
1½ tablespoons soy sauce
2 tablespoons chicken stock
2 tablespoons sesame or
 olive oil
1½ teaspoons sugar
1 garlic clove, crushed
2 slices green ginger, peeled
 and grated
2 scallions, thinly sliced

Melt the butter with the oil in a saucepan. Add the onion and bacon and fry until the onion is soft but not brown and the bacon is crisp. Pour the eggs onto one half of the pan and put the peas on the other half. Cook without stirring for 1 minute, then remove from the heat. Leave until the eggs are almost set, then stir all the ingredients in the pan together. Return to the heat and stir in the cooked rice and soy sauce. Keep hot.

Put the lettuce, bean sprouts, tomatoes, celery and watercress in a mixing bowl. Mix together all the ingredients for the dressing. Add to the vegetables and toss well to mix.

Pile the rice mixture in a serving bowl and spoon over the vegetable mixture. Serve immediately.
Serves 6

Tomato and mushroom salad

METRIC/IMPERIAL
6 tomatoes, peeled and sliced
120ml/4 fl oz French dressing★
100g/4oz button mushrooms, sliced
chopped fresh parsley to garnish

AMERICAN
6 tomatoes, peeled and sliced
½ cup French dressing★
1 cup sliced button mushrooms
chopped fresh parsley to garnish

Arrange the tomato slices in a shallow serving dish or in individual serving dishes. Sprinkle over most of the dressing. Place the mushroom slices on top in rows, slightly overlapping. Sprinkle with the remaining dressing. Allow to marinate for 20 minutes.
 Sprinkle with parsley just before serving.
Serves 4

Broad (lima) bean and ham salad

METRIC/IMPERIAL
350g/12oz shelled broad beans
salt
1 garlic clove, halved
75g/3oz lean cooked ham, finely chopped
3 × 15ml spoons/ 3 tablespoons olive oil
2 × 15ml spoons/ 2 tablespoons lemon juice
freshly ground black pepper
1 × 5ml spoon/1 teaspoon chopped fresh basil to garnish

AMERICAN
2 cups shelled lima beans
salt
1 garlic clove, halved
⅓ cup finely chopped lean cooked ham
3 tablespoons olive oil
2 tablespoons lemon juice
freshly ground black pepper
1 teaspoon chopped fresh basil to garnish

Cook the beans in boiling salted water until they are just tender. Drain well and allow to cool.
 Rub the inside of a salad bowl with the cut sides of the garlic. Discard the garlic. Put the beans and ham in the bowl.
 Mix together the oil, lemon juice and salt and pepper to taste. Pour this dressing over the beans and ham and toss well. Chill for 20 minutes. Sprinkle over the basil and serve.
Serves 4

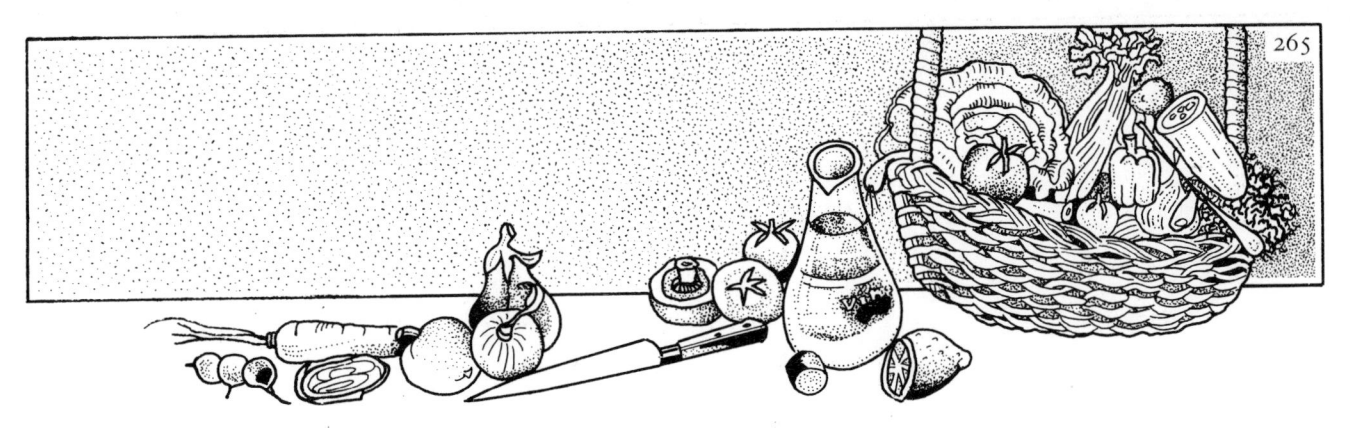

Italian cauliflower salad

METRIC/IMPERIAL
1 medium cauliflower, broken into florets
salt
8 anchovy fillets, finely chopped
20 black olives, halved and stoned
1 small onion, peeled and grated
1 × 15ml spoon/ 1 tablespoon capers
150ml/¼ pint French dressing★

AMERICAN
1 medium cauliflower, broken into florets
salt
8 anchovy fillets, finely chopped
20 black olives, halved and pitted
1 small onion, peeled and grated
1 tablespoon capers
⅔ cup French dressing★

Cook the cauliflower in boiling salted water until it is just tender. Drain well and allow to cool, then chill for 30 minutes.
 Put the cauliflower, anchovies, olives, onion and capers in a salad bowl. Pour over the dressing and toss to coat the ingredients. Chill for 20 minutes before serving.
Serves 4

Cheese slaw

METRIC/IMPERIAL
1 small green cabbage, cored and shredded
100g/4oz Gruyère cheese, cut into thin strips
150ml/¼ pint mayonnaise★
1 × 15ml spoon/ 1 tablespoon made mustard
1 × 5ml spoon/1 teaspoon sugar
3 red-skinned dessert apples, cored and diced

AMERICAN
1 small head green cabbage, cored and shredded
¼lb Gruyère cheese, cut into thin strips
⅔ cup mayonnaise★
1 tablespoon prepared mustard
1 teaspoon sugar
3 red-skinned dessert apples, cored and diced

Put the cabbage and cheese in a mixing bowl. Mix together the mayonnaise, mustard and sugar and fold into the cabbage mixture. Spoon into a salad bowl and chill lightly. Add the diced apple just before serving.
Serves 6 to 8

Coleslaw

METRIC/IMPERIAL
½ white cabbage, shredded
4 celery sticks, chopped
1 medium onion, peeled and chopped
4 large carrots, peeled and grated
25g/1oz walnuts, chopped
salt
freshly ground black pepper
4 × 15ml spoons/
 4 tablespoons mayonnaise★
squeeze of lemon juice
2 red-skinned apples, cored and chopped

AMERICAN
½ head white cabbage, shredded
4 celery stalks, chopped
1 medium onion, peeled and chopped
4 large carrots, peeled and grated
¼ cup chopped walnuts
salt
freshly ground black pepper
4 tablespoons mayonnaise★
squeeze of lemon juice
2 red-skinned apples, cored and chopped

Mix the cabbage, celery and onion together in a large bowl. Add the carrots, walnuts and salt and pepper to taste. Stir in the mayonnaise and lemon juice and mix well. Add the chopped apple just before serving. If liked, add orange segments in place of the apple slices.
Serves 6 to 8

Waldorf salad

METRIC/IMPERIAL
4 red-skinned dessert apples, cored and sliced
50g/2oz walnuts, chopped
4 celery sticks, finely chopped
120ml/4fl oz double cream
4 × 15ml spoons/
 4 tablespoons mayonnaise★
1 × 5ml spoon/1 teaspoon caster sugar
2 × 5ml spoons/2 teaspoons lemon juice
lettuce leaves

AMERICAN
4 red-skinned dessert apples, cored and sliced
½ cup chopped walnuts
4 celery stalks, finely chopped
½ cup heavy cream
4 tablespoons mayonnaise★
1 teaspoon sugar
2 teaspoons lemon juice
lettuce leaves

Put the apples, walnuts and celery in a mixing bowl. Lightly whip the cream and stir in the mayonnaise, sugar and lemon juice. Fold into the apple mixture.
 Line a salad bowl with lettuce leaves and pile in the apple mixture. Serve at room temperature.
Serves 4 to 6

Corn and cabbage salad

METRIC/IMPERIAL
0.75kg/1½lb red cabbage, cored and finely shredded
6 × 15ml spoons/6 tablespoons French dressing★
½ cucumber, diced
salt
freshly ground black pepper
1 × 300g/11oz can sweetcorn, drained
0.5 × 2.5ml spoon/¼ teaspoon finely grated lemon rind
2 × 5ml spoons/2 teaspoons clear honey

AMERICAN
1½lb red cabbage, cored and finely shredded
6 tablespoons French dressing★
½ cucumber, diced
salt
freshly ground black pepper
1 × 11oz can corn kernels, drained
¼ teaspoon finely grated lemon rind
2 teaspoons clear honey

Put the cabbage in a mixing bowl. Add the dressing and fold together. Leave for 2 hours.

Meanwhile, put the cucumber in another bowl and sprinkle with salt and pepper. Leave for 2 hours, then drain off the excess moisture.

Add the cucumber to the cabbage with the corn, lemon rind and honey. Toss well together and serve lightly chilled.
Serves 8

Pineapple and cabbage salad

METRIC/IMPERIAL
½ firm cabbage, cored and shredded
1 × 200g/7oz can pineapple chunks, drained
2 dessert apples, cored and diced
2 celery sticks, finely chopped
150ml/¼ pint mayonnaise★
chopped fresh chives to garnish

AMERICAN
½ firm head cabbage, cored and shredded
1 × 7oz can pineapple chunks, drained
2 dessert apples, cored and diced
2 celery stalks, finely chopped
⅔ cup mayonnaise★
chopped fresh chives to garnish

Mix together the cabbage, pineapple, apples and celery. Fold in the mayonnaise until all the ingredients are coated. Serve lightly chilled, sprinkled with chives.
Serves 6

Tomato and endive salad

METRIC/IMPERIAL
1 endive, torn into small pieces
3 tomatoes, peeled and quartered
4–6 spring onions, chopped
4 × 15ml spoons/
4 tablespoons French dressing★

AMERICAN
1 head curly endive, torn into small pieces
3 tomatoes, peeled and quartered
4–6 scallions, chopped
4 tablespoons French dressing★

Put the endive, tomatoes and spring onions (scallions) in a salad bowl. Pour over the dressing and toss together gently. Serve immediately.
Serves 4 to 6

Pineapple salad

METRIC/IMPERIAL
2 × 400g/14oz cans pineapple chunks
¼ cucumber, peeled and diced
1 green pepper, pith and seeds removed and diced
2 celery sticks, finely chopped
4 × 15ml spoons/
4 tablespoons French dressing★
2 × 15ml spoons/
2 tablespoons mayonnaise★
1 small lettuce, shredded

AMERICAN
2 × 14oz cans pineapple chunks
¼ cucumber, peeled and diced
1 green pepper, pith and seeds removed and diced
2 celery stalks, finely chopped
4 tablespoons French dressing★
2 tablespoons mayonnaise★
1 small head lettuce, shredded

Drain the pineapple, reserving 2 × 15ml spoons/ 2 tablespoons of the syrup. Mix together the pineapple, cucumber, green pepper and celery. Put the dressing, mayonnaise and reserved pineapple syrup in a screwtop jar and shake until well mixed. Fold into the pineapple mixture.
  Line a salad bowl with the lettuce. Pile the pineapple mixture on top and serve.
Serves 8

Coleslaw (page 266)

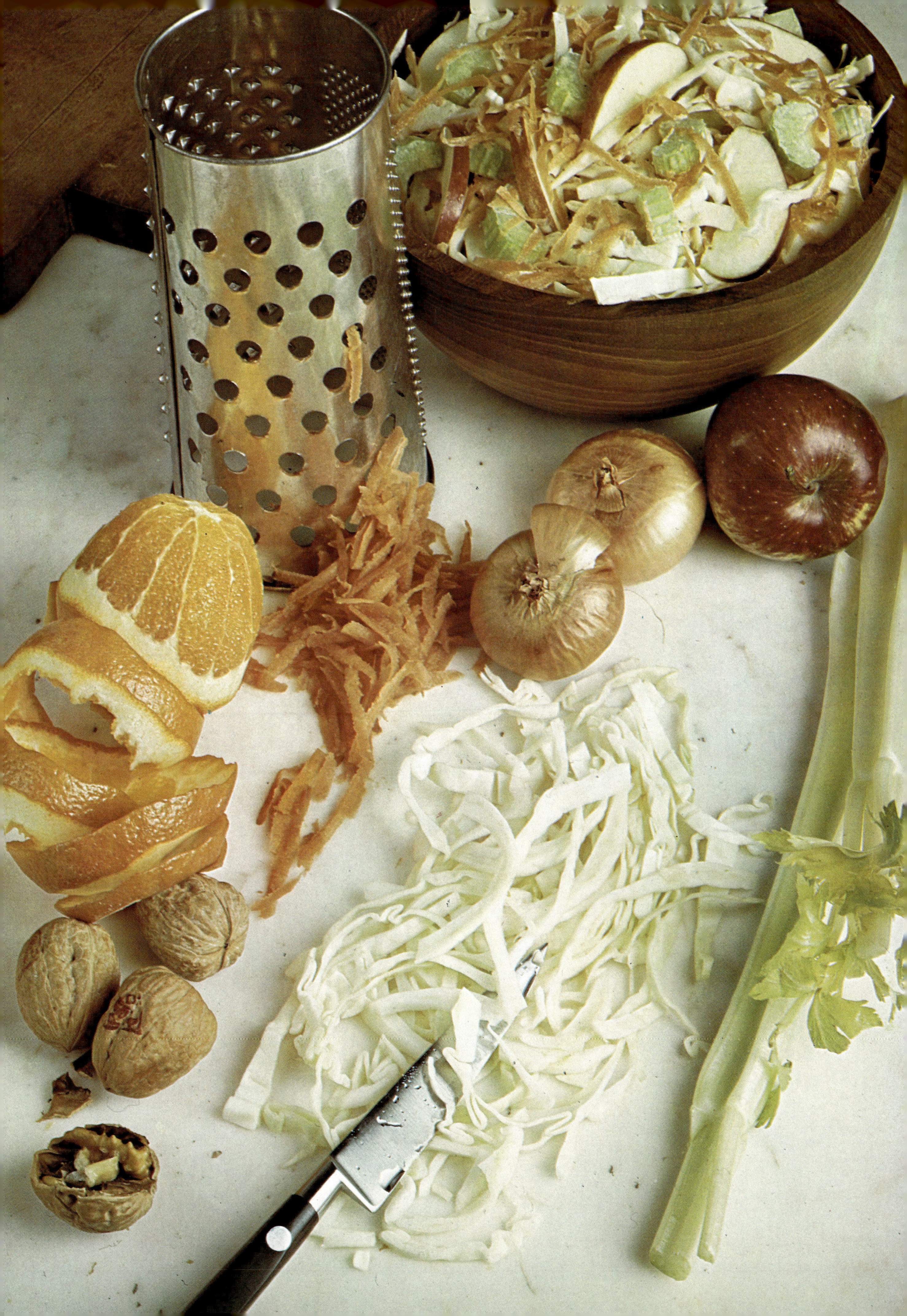

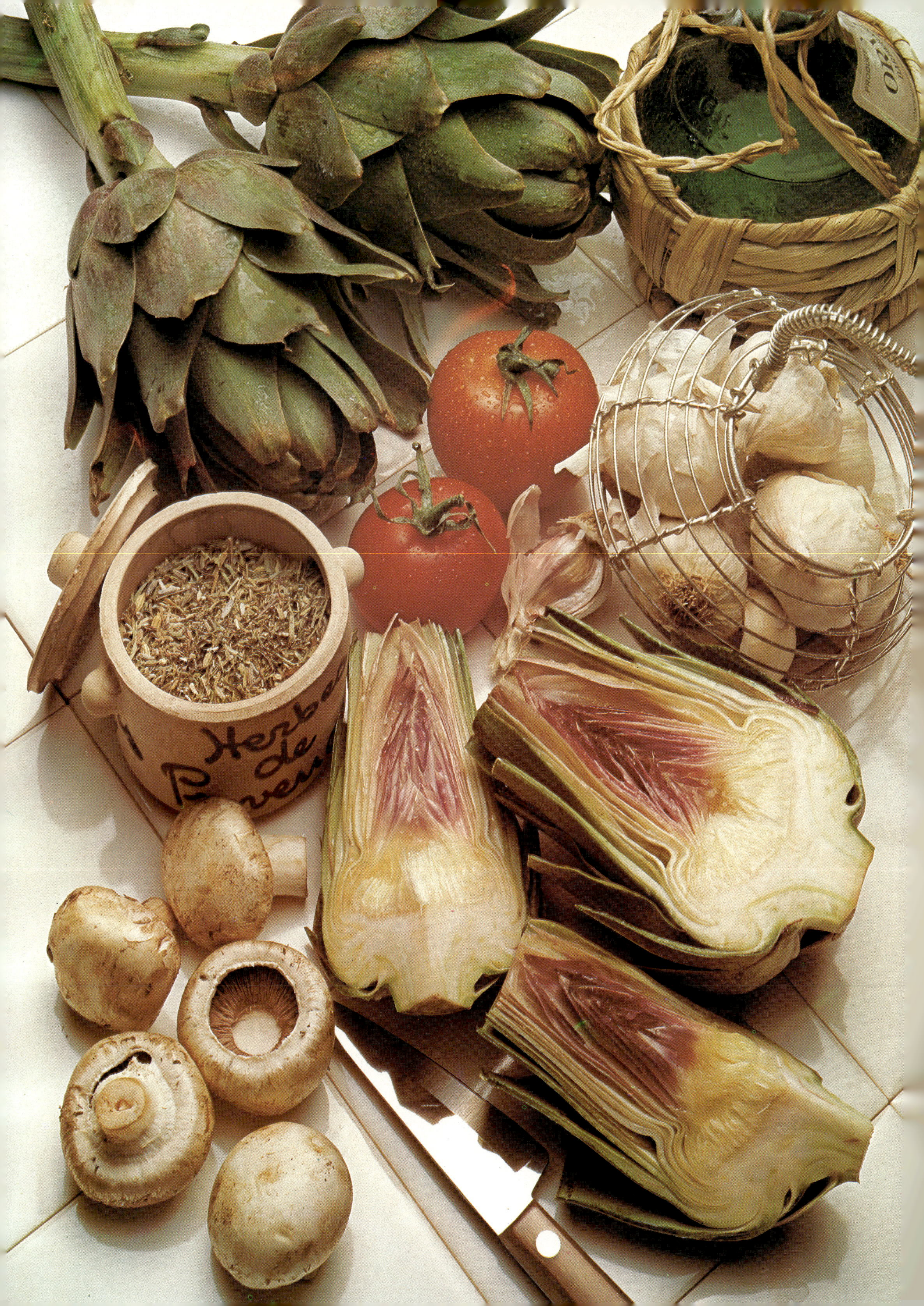

Mediterranean artichokes (page 369); Sweet and sour Chinese cabbage (page 261)

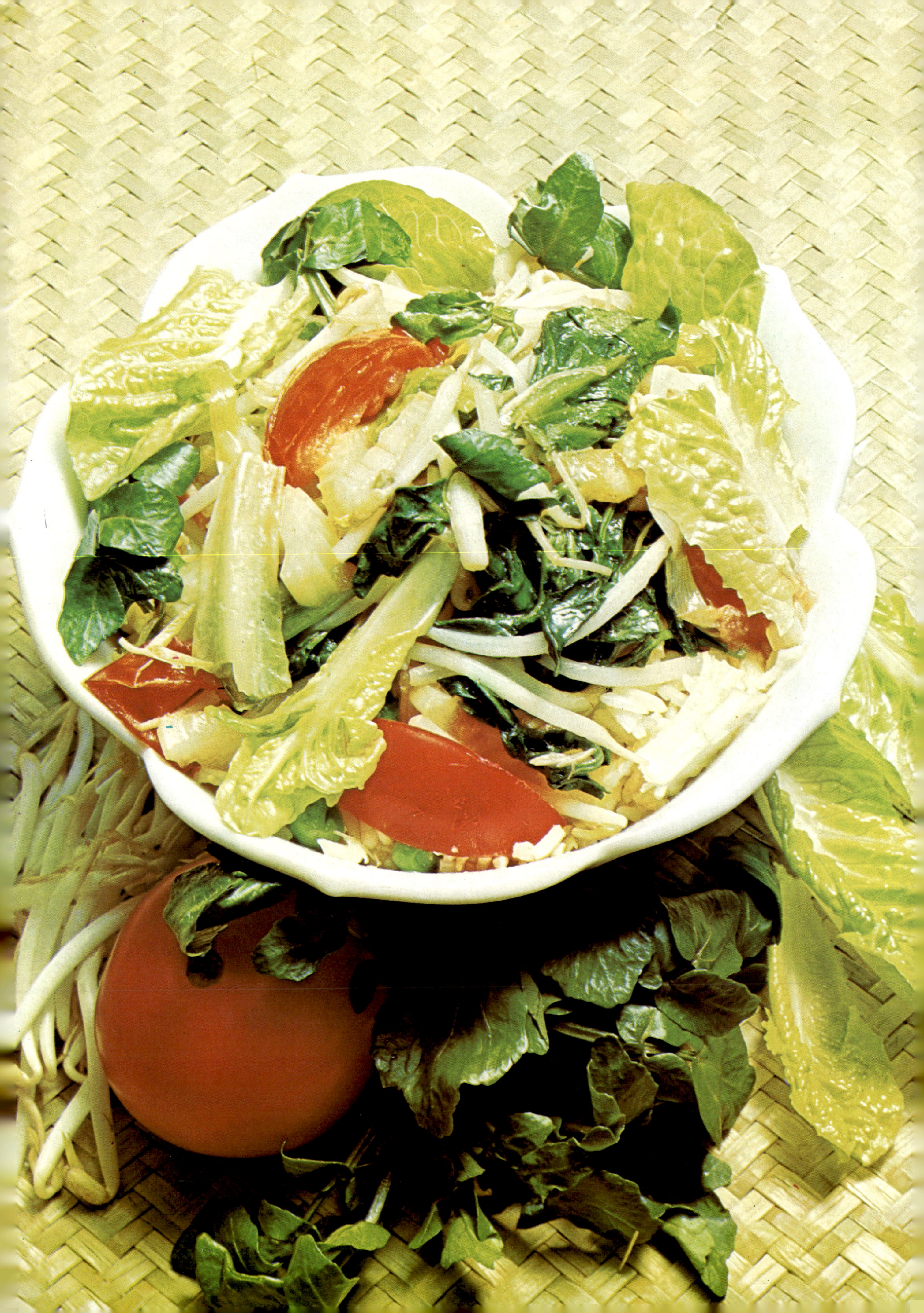

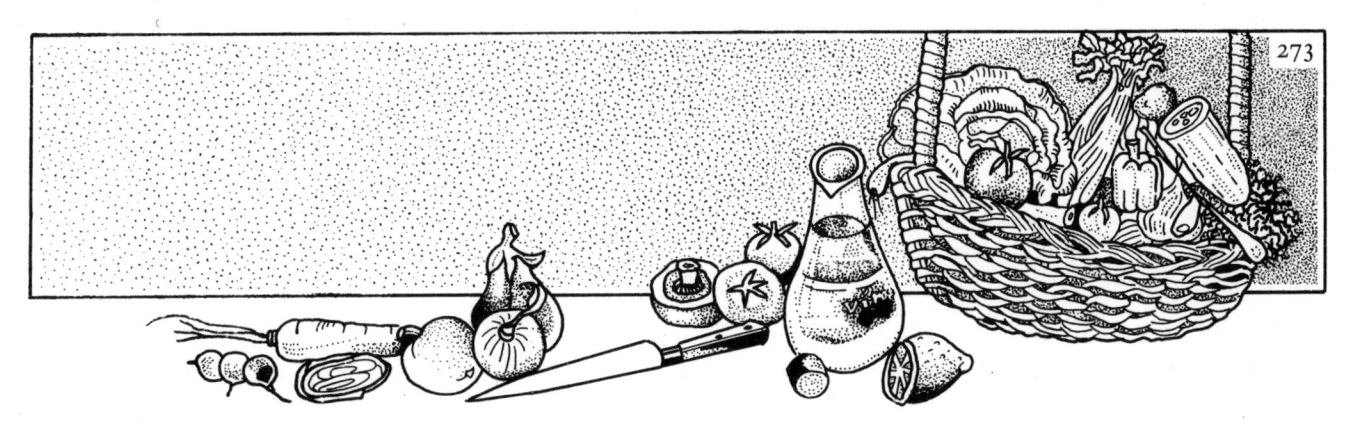

Portuguese-style cucumber

METRIC/IMPERIAL
2 large cucumbers, peeled, halved lengthways and deseeded
salt
4 × 15ml spoons/ 4 tablespoons olive oil
1 onion, peeled and finely chopped
1 garlic clove, crushed
4 tomatoes, peeled, deseeded and diced
1 × 15ml spoon/ 1 tablespoon tomato purée
2 × 15ml spoons/ 2 tablespoons red wine vinegar
freshly ground black pepper

AMERICAN
2 large cucumbers, peeled, halved lengthwise and deseeded
salt
4 tablespoons olive oil
1 onion, peeled and finely chopped
1 garlic clove, crushed
4 tomatoes, peeled, deseeded and diced
1 tablespoon tomato paste
2 tablespoons red wine vinegar
freshly ground black pepper

Cut the cucumber halves in half lengthways and then crossways into 2.5cm/1 inch pieces. Blanch in boiling salted water for 5 minutes. Drain well and refresh under cold running water.

Heat the oil in a frying pan (skillet). Add the onion and garlic and fry until the onion is soft but not brown. Stir in the tomatoes, tomato purée (paste), vinegar and salt and pepper to taste. Remove from the heat and stir in the cucumber.

Spoon into a serving bowl and chill thoroughly.
Serves 4 to 6

Beetroot (beet) and apple moulded salad

METRIC/IMPERIAL
1 packet red fruit-flavoured jelly
300ml/½ pint boiling water
150ml/¼ pint vinegar
2 × 15ml spoons/ 2 tablespoons lemon juice
50g/2oz walnut halves
0.5kg/1lb beetroot, cooked, peeled and diced
2 dessert apples, peeled, cored and sliced

AMERICAN
1 package red fruit-flavored gelatin
1¼ cups boiling water
⅔ cup vinegar
2 tablespoons lemon juice
½ cup walnut halves
2⅔ cups diced, cooked beets
2 dessert apples, peeled, cored and sliced

Dissolve the jelly (gelatin) in the boiling water, then stir in the vinegar and lemon juice.

Put the walnuts in the bottom of a plain 1.2 litre/ 2 pint/5 cup mould. Arrange the beetroot (beets) and apples on top in alternating layers. Carefully pour in the jelly (gelatin).

Leave in the refrigerator until set, then turn out of the mould onto a serving plate.
Serves 6

Chinese rice and vegetable salad (page 263)

Bean salad

METRIC/IMPERIAL
225g/8oz French beans
salt
1 × 200g/7oz can butter beans, drained
3 celery sticks, finely chopped
1 small dill pickled cucumber, finely chopped
4 × 15ml spoons/ 4 tablespoons French dressing★
chopped fresh chives to garnish

AMERICAN
½lb green beans
salt
1 × 7oz can wax beans, drained
3 celery stalks, finely chopped
1 small dill pickle, finely chopped
4 tablespoons French dressing★
chopped fresh chives to garnish

Cook the French (green) beans in boiling salted water for 5 minutes or until just tender. Drain well and allow to cool.

Add the butter (wax) beans, celery and cucumber (pickle) to the French (green) beans and stir to mix. Fold in the dressing. Spoon into a salad bowl and chill for 20 minutes.

Sprinkle with chopped chives and serve.
Serves 4

Spinach slaw

METRIC/IMPERIAL
225g/8oz spinach, shredded
175g/6oz white cabbage, cored and shredded
50g/2oz raisins
4 × 15ml spoons/ 4 tablespoons lemon juice
3 × 15ml spoons/ 3 tablespoons olive oil
salt
freshly ground black pepper
pinch of sugar
1 dessert apple, cored and chopped

AMERICAN
½lb spinach, shredded
6oz white cabbage, cored and shredded
⅓ cup raisins
4 tablespoons lemon juice
3 tablespoons olive oil
salt
freshly ground black pepper
pinch of sugar
1 dessert apple, cored and chopped

Mix together the spinach and cabbage in a mixing bowl. Soak the raisins in half the lemon juice until soft, then add to the spinach mixture.

Mix together the remaining lemon juice, the oil, salt and pepper to taste and the sugar. Pour over the spinach mixture and toss well. Fold in the apple and serve.
Serves 4

Chicory (endive) and orange salad

METRIC/IMPERIAL
4 heads chicory,
　separated into leaves
salt
freshly ground black pepper
2 large oranges, peeled and
　thinly sliced
50g/2oz walnuts, chopped
150ml/¼ pint French
　dressing★

AMERICAN
4 heads French or Belgian
　endive, separated into
　leaves
salt
freshly ground black pepper
2 large oranges, peeled and
　thinly sliced
½ cup chopped walnuts
⅔ cup French dressing★

Put the chicory (endive) in a salad bowl and sprinkle with salt and pepper. Pile the orange slices in the centre and sprinkle over the walnuts. Pour over the dressing and toss well before serving.
Serves 4

Mixed salad

METRIC/IMPERIAL
1 medium crisp lettuce, torn
　into small pieces
½ small cucumber, peeled
　and chopped
3 celery sticks, chopped
4 spring onions, chopped
4 tomatoes, quartered
1 large carrot, peeled and
　grated
2 × 15ml spoons/
　2 tablespoons chopped
　mustard and cress
salad dressing of your choice

AMERICAN
1 medium head crisp
　lettuce, torn into small
　pieces
½ small cucumber, peeled
　and chopped
3 celery stalks, chopped
4 scallions, chopped
4 tomatoes, quartered
1 large carrot, peeled and
　grated
2 tablespoons chopped
　garden cress
salad dressing of your choice

Put the lettuce in a salad bowl and add the cucumber, celery, spring onions (scallions) and tomatoes. Toss well together. Sprinkle the grated carrot and cress on top.
　Toss with the dressing just before serving.
Serves 4

DESSERTS

Bananas baked with rum

METRIC/IMPERIAL
6 bananas, peeled
6 × 15ml spoons/
 6 tablespoons dark rum
2 × 15ml spoons/
 2 tablespoons orange juice
50g/2oz dark brown sugar
25g/1oz desiccated coconut
15g/½oz butter, cut into
 small pieces
orange 'wings' to decorate

AMERICAN
6 bananas, peeled
6 tablespoons dark rum
2 tablespoons orange juice
⅓ cup dark brown sugar
⅓ cup shredded coconut
1 tablespoon butter, cut into
 small pieces
orange 'wings' to decorate

Slice the bananas in half lengthways and arrange in a greased baking dish. Sprinkle with the rum and orange juice, then with the sugar and coconut. Dot the pieces of butter over the top. Bake in a preheated moderately hot oven (190°C/375°F, Gas Mark 5) for 30 minutes.
 Serve hot, decorated with orange 'wings'.
Serves 4

Plums baked with port

METRIC/IMPERIAL
1kg/2lb plums, halved and
 stoned
100g/4oz brown sugar
150ml/¼ pint port wine

AMERICAN
2lb plums, halved and
 pitted
⅔ cup brown sugar
⅔ cup port wine

Put the plums in a baking dish and sprinkle over the sugar and port. Cover and bake in a cool oven (150°C/300°F, Gas Mark 2) for 45 minutes to 1 hour or until the plums are tender.
 Serve warm or lightly chilled.
Serves 4 to 6

Orange ice cream

METRIC/IMPERIAL
300ml/½ pint double cream
300ml/½ pint orange juice
caster sugar to taste

AMERICAN
1¼ cups heavy cream
1¼ cups orange juice
sugar to taste

Whip the cream until it is thick. Beat in half the orange juice, then gradually stir in the remainder. Add enough sugar to make the mixture taste slightly over-sweet.
 Pour into a freezerproof container and freeze until mushy.
 Turn out into a mixing bowl and beat for 1 minute. Return to the freezerproof container and freeze again until hard.
 To serve, allow to soften slightly.
Serves 4

Baked orange rhubarb

METRIC/IMPERIAL
0.75kg/1½lb rhubarb, cut
 into 2.5cm/1 inch pieces
finely grated rind and juice
 of 1 large orange
4 × 15ml spoons/
 4 tablespoons clear honey

AMERICAN
1½lb rhubarb, cut into
 1 inch pieces
finely grated rind and juice
 of 1 large orange
4 tablespoons clear honey

Put the rhubarb in a baking dish and sprinkle over the orange rind and juice and honey. Cover and bake in a preheated moderate oven (160°C/325°F, Gas Mark 3) for 45 minutes to 1 hour or until the rhubarb is soft.
 Serve hot.
Serves 4

Orange baked apples

METRIC/IMPERIAL
4 large cooking apples, cored
50g/2oz butter
50g/2oz brown sugar
finely grated rind and juice of 1 orange
whipped cream to serve

AMERICAN
4 large baking apples, cored
¼ cup butter
⅓ cup brown sugar
finely grated rind and juice of 1 orange
whipped cream to serve

Make a shallow cut around the centre of each apple. Mix together the butter, sugar and orange rind. Pile into the cavities in the apples and arrange in a baking dish. Pour over the orange juice.
    Bake in a preheated moderate oven (180°C/350°F, Gas Mark 4) for 30 minutes or until soft. Serve hot with cream.
Serves 4

Pears poached in red wine

METRIC/IMPERIAL
225g/8oz sugar
150ml/¼ pint water
4 large pears, peeled
150ml/¼ pint dry red wine

AMERICAN
1 cup sugar
⅔ cup water
4 large pears, peeled
⅔ cup dry red wine

Put the sugar and water in a saucepan and heat gently, stirring to dissolve the sugar. Add the pears, cover and simmer for 15 minutes.
    Stir in the wine and continue simmering, uncovered, for 15 minutes.
    Remove the pears from the pan and arrange in a serving dish. Bring the wine syrup back to the boil and boil rapidly until thick. Pour over the pears and allow to cool. Serve chilled.
Serves 4

Queen of puddings

METRIC/IMPERIAL
75g/3oz jam
50g/2oz fresh breadcrumbs
2 eggs, separated
75g/3oz caster sugar
450ml/¾ pint milk, scalded

AMERICAN
¼ cup jam
1 cup fresh breadcrumbs
2 eggs, separated
⅓ cup sugar
2 cups milk, scalded

Spread half the jam over the bottom of a baking dish. Cover with the breadcrumbs. Beat the egg yolks and sugar together, then stir in the milk. Strain into the baking dish.
    Bake in a preheated cool oven (150°C/300°F, Gas Mark 2) for 1 hour or until the custard is set.
    Beat the egg whites until stiff. Spread the remaining jam over the custard and cover with the egg whites. Return to a moderately hot oven (190°C/375°F, Gas Mark 5) and bake for 15 minutes or until the meringue topping is set and lightly browned. Serve hot.
Serves 4

Rice pudding

METRIC/IMPERIAL
5 × 15ml spoons/ 5 tablespoons pudding rice
50g/2oz sugar
600ml/1 pint milk
1 × 2.5ml spoon/½ teaspoon grated nutmeg
15g/½oz butter

AMERICAN
⅓ cup short-grain rice
¼ cup sugar
2½ cups milk
½ teaspoon grated nutmeg
1 tablespoon butter

Put the rice and sugar in a baking dish and stir in the milk and nutmeg. Put the butter in the centre.
    Bake in a hot oven (230°C/450°F, Gas Mark 8) for 15 minutes, then reduce the temperature to cool (140°C/275°F, Gas Mark 1). Continue baking for 1 hour or until the pudding is soft and creamy. Serve hot, from the dish.
Serves 4

Apple dumplings with walnut sauce

METRIC/IMPERIAL
350g/12oz quantity shortcrust pastry★ (made with 350g/12oz flour, etc.)
4 large cooking apples, cored
6 × 15ml spoons/ 6 tablespoons mincemeat★
1 egg, lightly beaten
Sauce:
50g/2oz butter
50g/2oz light brown sugar
1.5 × 15ml spoons/ 1½ tablespoons double cream
50g/2oz walnuts, chopped

AMERICAN
3 cup quantity pie pastry★ (made with 3 cups flour, etc.)
4 large baking apples, cored
6 tablespoons mincemeat★
1 egg, lightly beaten
Sauce:
¼ cup butter
⅓ cup brown sugar
1½ tablespoons heavy cream
½ cup chopped walnuts

Divide the dough into 4 portions. Roll out each portion into a round large enough to enclose an apple. Place the apples in the centre of the dough rounds and fill the cavities with mincemeat. Wrap the dough around the apples and moisten the edges with beaten egg. Press together to seal.

Place the dumplings on a baking sheet and brush all over with beaten egg. Bake in a preheated moderately hot oven (200°C/400°F, Gas Mark 6) for 35 minutes or until golden brown.

Meanwhile, make the sauce. Melt the butter in a saucepan and stir in the sugar. When the sugar has dissolved, stir in the cream and walnuts. Heat through gently.

Serve the dumplings hot with the walnut sauce.
Serves 4

Pineapple liqueur fritters

METRIC/IMPERIAL
8 canned or fresh pineapple rings
2 × 15ml spoons/ 2 tablespoons Kirsch
100g/4oz plain flour
pinch of salt
1 egg
150ml/¼ pint milk
vegetable oil for deep frying
3 × 15ml spoons/ 3 tablespoons caster sugar
1 × 5ml spoon/1 teaspoon ground cinnamon

AMERICAN
8 canned or fresh pineapple rings
2 tablespoons Kirsch
1 cup all-purpose flour
pinch of salt
1 egg
⅔ cup milk
vegetable oil for deep frying
3 tablespoons sugar
1 teaspoon ground cinnamon

Put the pineapple rings in a shallow dish and sprinkle over the liqueur. Leave to marinate.

Sift the flour and salt into a mixing bowl. Make a well in the centre and add the egg and half the milk. Gradually draw the flour into the liquid and mix until smooth. Beat in the remaining milk.

Heat the oil in a deep frying pan (deep fat fryer) until it is 190°C/375°F. Pat the pineapple rings dry with absorbent paper and dip in the batter to coat well. Fry until golden and drain on absorbent paper.

Mix together the sugar and cinnamon. Roll the fritters in this mixture and serve hot.
Serves 4

Rhubarb crumble

METRIC/IMPERIAL
0.75kg/1½lb rhubarb, cut
  into 2.5cm/1 inch pieces
100g/4oz brown sugar
finely grated rind and juice
  of 1 orange
1 × 5ml spoon/1 teaspoon
  ground ginger
Topping:
175g/6oz plain flour
75g/3oz butter
75g/3oz sugar

AMERICAN
1½lb rhubarb, cut into
  1 inch pieces
⅔ cup brown sugar
finely grated rind and juice
  of 1 orange
1 teaspoon ground ginger
Topping:
1½ cups all-purpose flour
⅓ cup butter
⅓ cup sugar

Put the rhubarb in a baking dish and stir in the brown sugar, orange rind and juice and ginger.

Sift the flour into a mixing bowl. Rub in the butter until the mixture resembles breadcrumbs. Stir in the sugar. Sprinkle this topping over the rhubarb mixture.

Bake in a preheated moderately hot oven (200°C/400°F, Gas Mark 6) for 30 minutes or until the topping is golden brown. Serve hot, from the dish.
Serves 4

English apple pie

METRIC/IMPERIAL
225g/8oz quantity rich
  shortcrust pastry★
  (made with 225g/8oz
  flour, etc.)
0.75g/1½lb cooking apples,
  peeled, cored and sliced
4 × 15ml spoons/
  4 tablespoons raisins
175g/6oz brown sugar
1 × 2.5ml spoon/½ teaspoon
  ground cinnamon
1 × 2.5ml spoon/½ teaspoon
  grated nutmeg
finely grated rind and juice
  of ½ lemon
1 × 15ml spoon/
  1 tablespoon milk
1 × 15ml spoon/
  1 tablespoon caster sugar

AMERICAN
2 cup quantity rich pie
  pastry★ (made with
  2 cups flour, etc.)
1½lb baking apples, peeled,
  cored and sliced
4 tablespoons raisins
1 cup brown sugar
½ teaspoon ground cinnamon
½ teaspoon grated nutmeg
finely grated rind and juice
  of ½ lemon
1 tablespoon milk
1 tablespoon sugar

Divide the pastry dough in two and roll out one half. Use to line a 20cm/8 inch diameter pie dish (pan).

Mix together the apples, raisins, sugar, spices and lemon rind and juice. Turn the mixture into the pastry case (pie shell) and spread evenly. Roll out the remaining dough and use to cover the apple filling. Dampen the dough edges with a little of the milk and press together to seal. Crimp or flute the edge for a decorative effect. Make a slit in the centre of the dough lid.

Place the pie on a baking sheet. Brush the top of the dough with the remaining milk and sprinkle with the sugar. Bake in a preheated moderately hot oven (200°C/400°F, Gas Mark 6) for 15 minutes, then reduce the temperature to moderate (180°C/350°F, Gas Mark 4). Continue baking for 20 minutes. Allow to cool for 5 minutes before serving.
Serves 4 to 6

Jam roly-poly

METRIC/IMPERIAL
100g/4oz self-raising flour
pinch of salt
50g/2oz shredded suet
4 × 15ml spoons/
  4 tablespoons hot water
4 × 15ml spoons/
  4 tablespoons jam

AMERICAN
1 cup self-rising flour
pinch of salt
½ cup shredded suet
4 tablespoons hot water
4 tablespoons jam

Sift the flour and salt into a mixing bowl. Add the suet, then gradually stir in enough of the water to make a soft dough. Knead until smooth.

Roll out the dough to an oblong about 5mm/¼ inch thick. Spread over the jam, then roll up. Pinch and seal the edges together. Wrap loosely in foil, sealing well.

Steam for 1½ to 2 hours. Serve hot.
Serves 3 to 4

Brigade pudding

METRIC/IMPERIAL
225g/8oz quantity suet
  crust pastry★
2 × 15ml spoons/
  2 tablespoons golden
  syrup
225g/8oz mincemeat★
3 large cooking apples,
  peeled, cored and grated

AMERICAN
2 cup quantity suet crust
  pastry★
2 tablespoons light corn
  syrup
1 cup mincemeat★
3 large baking apples,
  peeled, cored and grated

Roll out the pastry dough and cut into 4 rounds of graduating sizes – one small to fit the bottom of a 1.2 litre/2 pint/5 cup pudding basin (steaming mold); one a little larger; one even larger; and one as large as the top of the basin (mold).

Put the syrup in the bottom of the basin (mold) and place the smallest dough round on it. Mix together the mincemeat and apples and spoon one-third of the mixture into the basin (mold). Cover with the next dough round and another one-third of the mincemeat mixture. Add the third dough round and the remaining mincemeat mixture. Cover with the final dough round.

Cover the basin (mold) with a lid of foil, tied on securely with string. Steam for 2½ hours, replenishing the boiling water when necessary.

Turn out of the basin (mold) and serve hot, with cream or custard sauce.
Serves 6

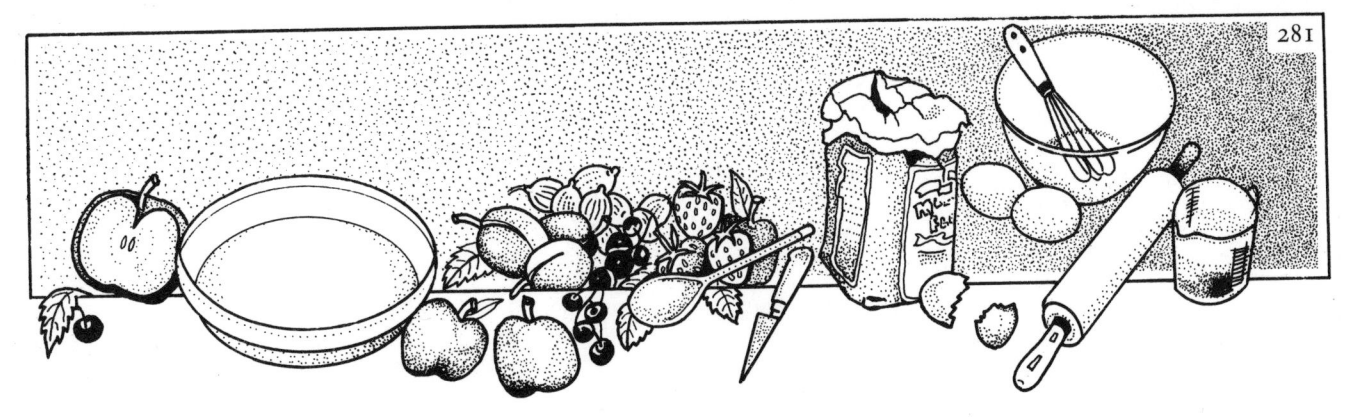

Steamed chocolate pudding with rum sauce

METRIC/IMPERIAL
50g/2oz plain cooking chocolate
few drops of vanilla essence
50g/2oz butter
100g/4oz caster sugar
2 eggs
175g/6oz self-raising flour
5 × 15ml spoons/ 5 tablespoons milk
Sauce:
2 × 15ml spoons/ 2 tablespoons cornflour
300ml/½ pint milk
2 × 15ml spoons/ 2 tablespoons sugar
2 × 15ml spoons/ 2 tablespoons dark rum

AMERICAN
2 squares semisweet chocolate
few drops of vanilla extract
¼ cup butter
½ cup sugar
2 eggs
1½ cups self-rising flour
⅓ cup milk
Sauce:
2 tablespoons cornstarch
1¼ cups milk
2 tablespoons sugar
2 tablespoons dark rum

Put the chocolate, vanilla and butter in a heatproof bowl placed over a pan of hot water. Heat gently, stirring to melt the chocolate and butter. Remove from the heat and allow to cool slightly.

Stir the sugar into the chocolate mixture, then beat in the eggs. Sift in the flour and mix well. Stir in the milk. Pour into a greased and floured 1.2 litre/2 pint/ 5 cup pudding basin (steaming mold). Cover with a foil lid tied on securely with string. Steam the pudding for 1 hour.

Just before the pudding is ready, make the sauce. Dissolve the cornflour (cornstarch) in the milk in a saucepan. Stir in the sugar and heat gently, stirring. Bring to the boil and simmer until thickened and smooth. Stir in the rum.

Turn out the pudding and serve hot with the sauce.
Serves 4

Yorkshire apple tart

METRIC/IMPERIAL
275g/10oz quantity shortcrust pastry★ (made with 275g/10oz plain flour, etc.)
350g/12oz cooking apples, peeled, cored and sliced
2 × 15ml spoons/ 2 tablespoons sugar
1 × 15ml spoon/ 1 tablespoon water
little milk and sugar to glaze
100g/4oz strong cheese, sliced

AMERICAN
2½ cup quantity pie pastry★ (made with 2½ cups all-purpose flour, etc.)
¾ lb baking apples, peeled, cored and sliced
2 tablespoons sugar
1 tablespoon water
little milk and sugar to glaze
¼ lb strong cheese, sliced

Roll out the pastry and use two-thirds to line a 20cm/8 inch flan ring (tart pan). Fill the centre with the sliced apples, sprinkle over the sugar and water. Roll out the remaining pastry and use to cover the tart. Seal the edges. Brush the top with a little milk and sprinkle with sugar.

Place in a preheated moderately hot oven (190°C/375°F, Gas Mark 5) and bake for 20 to 25 minutes, until the crust is firm and lightly browned. Leave to cool, then carefully remove the top crust using a sharp knife. Place the cheese on top of the apples. Replace the crust. Return to the oven and bake for a further 10 to 15 minutes until the cheese has melted. Serve hot with whipped cream.
Serves 4 to 6

Blackberry (bramble) and apple sponge

METRIC/IMPERIAL
100g/4oz butter
225g/8oz caster sugar
2 eggs, beaten
few drops of vanilla essence
175g/6oz self-raising flour, sifted
0.5kg/1lb cooking apples, peeled, cored, sliced and cooked
225g/8oz blackberries, cooked
juice of ½ lemon

AMERICAN
½ cup butter
1 cup sugar
2 eggs, beaten
few drops of vanilla extract
1½ cups self-rising flour, sifted
1lb baking apples, peeled, cored, sliced and cooked
½lb brambles, cooked
juice of ½ lemon

Beat together the butter and half the sugar until pale and fluffy. Gradually beat in the eggs and vanilla, beating well between each addition. Fold in the flour.

Mix together the fruit, lemon juice and remaining sugar. Grease a 0.75kg/1½lb pudding basin (steaming mold). Put 4 × 15ml spoons/4 tablespoons of the fruit mixture in the bottom of the basin (mold). Spoon in the sponge mixture. Cover the basin (mold) with greased greaseproof paper or foil, leaving a pleat in the centre to allow for expansion. Secure the paper or foil with string. Steam for 1½ hours.

Reheat the remaining fruit mixture and serve with the hot pudding.
Serves 4

Plum slices

METRIC/IMPERIAL
175g/6oz quantity shortcrust pastry★ (made with 175g/6oz flour, etc.)
0.5kg/1lb ripe plums, halved and stoned
2 eggs, separated
65g/2½oz caster sugar
50g/2oz self-raising flour
pinch of salt
few drops of vanilla essence
icing sugar to decorate

AMERICAN
1½ cup quantity pie pastry★ (made with 1½ cups flour, etc.)
1lb ripe plums, halved and pitted
2 eggs, separated
5 tablespoons sugar
½ cup self-rising flour
pinch of salt
few drops of vanilla extract
confectioners' sugar to decorate

Roll out the pastry on a lightly floured surface and use to line an 18 × 23cm/7 × 8 inch cake tin. Prick the base. Place in a preheated moderately hot oven (200°C/400°F, Gas Mark 6) and bake blind for 15 minutes. Arrange the plum halves on the pastry with the cut sides uppermost. (If they are not sweet enough, dip them in sugar first.) Whisk the egg whites until very stiff, whisk in the yolks, one at a time, and then the sugar, keeping the mixture as stiff as possible. Sift the flour with the salt and fold into the mixture with the vanilla. Spread evenly over the plums and bake for 35 to 40 minutes, or until the sponge is well risen and golden brown. Turn out onto a wire tray and allow to cool. Sprinkle with sifted icing (confectioners') sugar and serve cut into slices with cream or custard.
Serves 6

Pear and almond crêpes

METRIC/IMPERIAL
8 cooked crêpes★
100g/4oz butter
50g/2oz icing sugar
50g/2oz ground almonds
few drops of almond essence
grated rind of 1 lemon
1 × 425g/15oz can pears, drained and diced

AMERICAN
8 cooked crêpes★
½ cup butter
½ cup confectioners' sugar
½ cup ground almonds
few drops of almond extract
grated rind of 1 lemon
1 × 15oz can pears, drained and diced

Keep the crêpes warm.
    Cream the butter and sugar together until the mixture is light and fluffy. Beat in the ground almonds, almond essence (extract) and lemon rind. Fold in the pears.
    Divide the filling between the crêpes and roll up. Arrange in an ovenproof serving dish. Reheat in a preheated moderate oven (180°C/350°F, Gas Mark 4) for 15 minutes. Serve hot.
Serves 4

Crêpes Suzette

METRIC/IMPERIAL
8 cooked crêpes★
2 sugar lumps
2 oranges
25g/1oz butter
25g/1oz sugar
2 × 15ml spoons/
  2 tablespoons orange-
  flavoured liqueur
2 × 15ml spoons/
  2 tablespoons brandy

AMERICAN
8 cooked crêpes★
2 sugar lumps
2 oranges
2 tablespoons butter
2 tablespoons sugar
2 tablespoons orange-
  flavored liqueur
2 tablespoons brandy

Keep the crêpes warm.
    Rub the sugar lumps all over the oranges to extract the zest (oil from the skin). Put the sugar lumps in a mixing bowl and crush them. Beat in the butter, sugar, orange-flavoured liqueur and 1 × 15ml spoon/ 1 tablespoon of the juice from one of the oranges.
    Pour the orange mixture into a frying pan (skillet) and heat gently until it is very hot. Dip the crêpes into the orange mixture, one by one, and fold into quarters. Arrange the crêpes in a warmed serving dish, slightly overlapping. Pour over any remaining orange mixture.
    Heat the brandy and pour over the crêpes. Set alight and serve while still flaming.
Serves 4

Orange and gooseberry crêpes

METRIC/IMPERIAL
8 cooked crêpes★
0.5kg/1lb fresh or frozen and thawed gooseberries
grated rind and juice of 1 orange
75–100g/3–4oz sugar
icing sugar

AMERICAN
8 cooked crêpes★
1lb fresh or frozen and thawed gooseberries
grated rind and juice of 1 orange
$\frac{1}{3}$–$\frac{1}{2}$ cup sugar
confectioners' sugar

Keep the crêpes warm.
  To prepare the filling, put the gooseberries, orange rind and juice in a pan, heat gently and simmer for 5 to 7 minutes until the gooseberries are tender but still hold their shape. Stir in sufficient sugar to taste.
  Divide the hot filling between the crêpes and fold into 3. Serve at once, sprinkled generously with icing (confectioners') sugar.
  Serve with extra filling, passed separately.
Serves 4

Marinated fruit salad with vanilla ice cream

METRIC/IMPERIAL
25g/1oz sugar
150ml/$\frac{1}{4}$ pint water
3–4 × 15ml spoons/3–4 tablespoons sherry, or cherry- or orange-flavoured liqueur
1 small cantaloup or honeydew melon, halved, deseeded and cut into balls
2 crisp dessert apples, peeled, cored and chopped
2 juicy oranges, peeled, deseeded and chopped
2 large bananas, peeled and sliced
2 pears, peeled, cored and chopped
100g/4oz strawberries, hulled
50g/2oz black cherries, stoned
vanilla ice cream

AMERICAN
2 tablespoons sugar
$\frac{2}{3}$ cup water
3–4 tablespoons sherry, or cherry- or orange-flavored liqueur
1 small cantaloup or honeydew melon, halved, deseeded and cut into balls
2 crisp dessert apples, peeled, cored and chopped
2 juicy oranges, peeled, deseeded and chopped
2 large bananas, peeled and sliced
2 pears, peeled, cored and chopped
$\frac{1}{4}$lb strawberries, hulled
$\frac{1}{2}$ cup Bing cherries, pitted
vanilla ice cream

Dissolve the sugar in the water, then bring to the boil. Simmer for 1 minute. Remove from the heat and stir in the sherry or liqueur. Allow to cool, then pour the syrup into a glass serving bowl. Add all the fruit and stir well. The fruit should be well covered with syrup so it may be necessary to make more. Set aside to marinate for at least 2 hours. If you like, chill the fruit salad.
  Just before serving, top with 6 scoops of vanilla ice cream.
Serves 6

Redcurrant compote

METRIC/IMPERIAL
0.75kg/1½lb redcurrants
275g/10oz sugar
1 × 15ml spoon/
 1 tablespoon water
2 × 15ml spoons/
 2 tablespoons gin or brandy
To serve:
whipped cream
sponge finger biscuits

AMERICAN
1½lb redcurrants
1¼ cups sugar
1 tablespoon water
2 tablespoons gin or brandy
To serve:
whipped cream
ladyfingers

Put the redcurrants, sugar and water in a saucepan. Shake over a gentle heat until the sugar has dissolved. Remove from the heat and stir in the gin or brandy. Allow to cool.

Spoon the compote into a serving bowl and chill for 2 to 3 hours. Serve with whipped cream and sponge fingers (ladyfingers).
Serves 6

Chocolate and orange mousses

METRIC/IMPERIAL
1 small orange
1 × 15ml spoon/
 1 tablespoon orange-
 flavoured liqueur
225g/8oz plain chocolate,
 broken into small pieces
50g/2oz butter, cut into
 small pieces
3 large eggs, separated
50g/2oz sugar

AMERICAN
1 small orange
1 tablespoon orange-
 flavored liqueur
8 squares semisweet
 chocolate, broken into
 small pieces
¼ cup butter, cut into small
 pieces
3 large eggs, separated
¼ cup sugar

Pare the rind from half the orange, being careful not to take any of the white pith. Cut the pared rind into thin slivers. Finely grate the rind from the other half of the orange. Blanch the rind slivers in boiling water for 5 minutes. Drain well and transfer to a cup. Sprinkle over the liqueur and leave to marinate.

Melt 175g/6oz/6 squares of the chocolate very gently. Remove from the heat and stir in the butter until it has melted and the mixture is smooth.

Beat the egg yolks and sugar together until the mixture is pale and thick. Stir in the grated orange rind, 1 × 15ml spoon/1 tablespoon of juice from the orange and the chocolate mixture. Beat the egg whites until stiff and fold into the chocolate mixture. Spoon into individual glasses and chill until set (at least 4 hours).

Grate the remaining chocolate and sprinkle over each serving of mousse. Decorate with the orange rind slivers.
Serves 6

Poached minty pears

METRIC/IMPERIAL
4 large pears, peeled
4 × 15ml spoons/
 4 tablespoons sugar
4 × 15ml spoons/
 4 tablespoons clear honey
2 × 15ml spoons/
 2 tablespoons Crème de Menthe liqueur

AMERICAN
4 large pears, peeled
4 tablespoons sugar
4 tablespoons clear honey
2 tablespoons Crème de Menthe liqueur

Put the pears in a saucepan, standing upright, and pour over water to cover. Bring to the boil, then cover and simmer for 30 minutes.

Pour off half the water and sprinkle over the sugar. Simmer for a further 10 minutes. Transfer the pears to a bowl.

Pour off all but 150ml/¼ pint/⅔ cup of the water from the pan. Stir in the honey and liqueur. Pour this mixture over the pears. Allow to cool, then cover and chill for 2 hours.

To serve, stand each pear in an individual serving dish. Spoon over the mint sauce and serve.
Serves 4

Strawberry choux puffs

METRIC/IMPERIAL
65g/2½oz quantity choux pastry★
300ml/½ pint double cream
0.5kg/1lb strawberries, hulled and sliced
icing sugar

AMERICAN
10 tablespoon quantity choux pastry★
1¼ cups whipping cream
1lb strawberries, hulled and sliced
confectioners' sugar

Pipe the choux pastry dough in mounds on a baking sheet that has been sprinkled with water. (Alternatively, spoon the dough onto the baking sheet.) Bake in a preheated moderately hot oven (200°C/400°F, Gas Mark 6) for 30 to 35 minutes or until well risen and golden brown.

Remove from the oven and split each puff down one side. Allow to cool on a wire rack.

Whip the cream until it is thick. Fold in half the strawberries.

Fill the choux puffs with the cream mixture. Arrange around the edge of a serving plate. Pile the remaining strawberries in the centre. Sprinkle the choux puffs liberally with icing (confectioners') sugar and serve.
Makes about 8

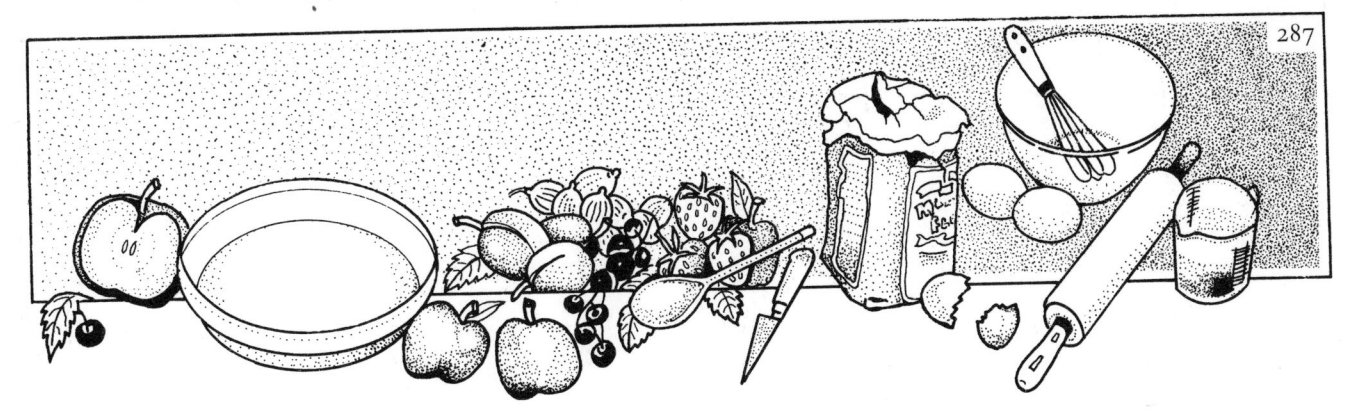

Syllabub

METRIC/IMPERIAL
thinly pared rind of 1 lemon
4 × 15ml spoons/
  4 tablespoons lemon juice
6 × 15ml spoons/
  6 tablespoons sweet white
  wine or sherry
2 × 15ml spoons/
  2 tablespoons brandy
50g/2oz sugar
300ml/½ pint double cream
grated nutmeg

AMERICAN
thinly pared rind of 1 lemon
4 tablespoons lemon juice
6 tablespoons sweet white
  wine or sherry
2 tablespoons brandy
¼ cup sugar
1¼ cups heavy cream
grated nutmeg

Put the lemon rind and juice, wine or sherry and brandy in a mixing bowl. Allow to soak overnight.

Remove the lemon rind. Stir the sugar into the lemon mixture until it has dissolved. Gradually stir in the cream, then beat the mixture until it will form soft peaks.

Spoon into 4 glasses and sprinkle over a little grated nutmeg.

Serves 4

Crème caramel

METRIC/IMPERIAL
75g/3oz sugar
3 × 15ml spoons/
  3 tablespoons water
2 eggs
2 egg yolks
450ml/¾ pint milk
few drops of vanilla essence

AMERICAN
⅓ cup sugar
3 tablespoons water
2 eggs
2 egg yolks
2 cups milk
few drops of vanilla extract

Put 50g/2oz/¼ cup of the sugar and the water in a saucepan. Heat gently, stirring to dissolve the sugar, then bring to the boil. Boil without stirring until golden brown. Remove from the heat and pour into a 600ml/1 pint/2½ cup baking dish or mould. Tilt the dish so the bottom is completely covered with the caramel.

Mix together the eggs, egg yolks, milk, vanilla and remaining sugar. Strain into the baking dish. Place the dish in a roasting tin and pour in enough boiling water to come halfway up the sides of the dish.

Bake in a preheated moderate oven (160°C/325°F, Gas Mark 3) for 50 minutes or until the custard is firm and set. Remove from the oven and allow to cool.

Chill, then turn the crème caramel out of the dish to serve.

Serves 4 to 6

Apricot fool

METRIC/IMPERIAL
0.5kg/1lb apricots, halved and stoned
2 × 15ml spoons/2 tablespoons water
150ml/¼ pint cold custard sauce★
sugar (optional)
450ml/¾ pint double cream
toasted flaked almonds to decorate

AMERICAN
1lb apricots, halved and pitted
2 tablespoons water
⅔ cup cold custard sauce★
sugar (optional)
2 cups heavy cream
toasted slivered almonds to decorate

Put the apricots in a saucepan with the water and cook gently until very soft. Pour into the goblet of an electric blender and add the custard. Blend to a smooth purée. Taste and add sugar if necessary.

Whip the cream until it is thick. Fold into the apricot mixture. Spoon into 4 glasses and chill lightly. Serve decorated with toasted flaked (slivered) almonds.
Serves 4

Stuffed baked peaches

METRIC/IMPERIAL
4 large peaches, peeled, halved and stoned
40g/1½oz crushed macaroons
25g/1oz ground almonds
1 × 2.5ml spoon/½ teaspoon finely grated orange rind
1 egg yolk
25g/1oz butter, cut into small pieces
150ml/¼ pint sweet white wine

AMERICAN
4 large peaches, peeled, halved and pitted
½ cup crushed macaroons
¼ cup ground almonds
½ teaspoon finely grated orange rind
1 egg yolk
2 tablespoons butter, cut into small pieces
⅔ cup sweet white wine

Put the peaches in a baking dish, cut sides up. Mix together the macaroons, almonds, orange rind and egg yolk. Divide between the peach halves, filling the hollows. Dot the pieces of butter over the top.

Pour the wine into the dish. Bake in a preheated moderate oven (180°C/350°F, Gas Mark 4) for 30 minutes. Serve warm.
Serves 4

Sherry trifle

METRIC/IMPERIAL
4 trifle sponge cakes
4 × 15ml spoons/
 4 tablespoons sweet or
 medium sherry
1 × 200g/7oz can peach
 slices, drained
3 bananas, peeled and sliced
25g/1oz blanched almonds,
 flaked
450ml/¾ pint cold custard
 sauce★
150ml/¼ pint double cream
To decorate:
small macaroons
chopped walnuts

AMERICAN
4 thick slices pound cake
4 tablespoons sweet or
 medium sherry
1 × 7oz can peach slices,
 drained
3 bananas, peeled and sliced
¼ cup blanched slivered
 almonds
2 cups cold custard sauce★
⅔ cup heavy cream
To decorate:
small macaroons
chopped walnuts

Arrange the cake in the bottom of a serving bowl, cutting it to fit. Sprinkle with the sherry. Arrange the peaches and bananas on the cake and sprinkle with the almonds. Pour over the custard.

Whip the cream until it is thick and spread over the custard. Decorate with macaroons and chopped walnuts.
Serves 4

Frozen almond meringue desserts

METRIC/IMPERIAL
2 egg whites
100g/4oz caster sugar
100g/4oz blanched
 almonds, toasted and
 chopped
300ml/½ pint double cream
2 × 15ml spoons/
 2 tablespoons brandy

AMERICAN
2 egg whites
½ cup sugar
1 cup chopped toasted
 blanched almonds
1¼ cups heavy cream
2 tablespoons brandy

Beat the egg whites until they are stiff. Add 4 × 5ml spoons/4 teaspoons of the sugar and continue beating for 1 minute or until the mixture is stiff and glossy. Fold in the remaining sugar and all but 2 × 15ml spoons/2 tablespoons of the almonds.

Beat the cream with the brandy until thick and fold into the almond mixture. Spoon into 6 individual freezerproof moulds and sprinkle over the reserved almonds. Freeze until set.
Serves 6

Raspberry and honey ice cream

METRIC/IMPERIAL
0.5kg/1lb raspberries
150ml/¼ pint double cream
150ml/¼ pint natural yogurt
2 × 15ml spoons/
  2 tablespoons lemon juice
150ml/¼ pint clear honey
pinch of salt
3 egg whites

AMERICAN
1lb raspberries
⅔ cup heavy cream
⅔ cup unflavored yogurt
2 tablespoons lemon juice
⅔ cup clear honey
pinch of salt
3 egg whites

Push the raspberries through a sieve (strainer) to make a purée. (There should be 300ml/½ pint/1¼ cups purée.) Alternatively, purée in an electric blender. Mix together the raspberry purée, cream, yogurt, lemon juice, honey and salt. Pour into a freezerproof container and freeze until firm.

Turn into a mixing bowl and beat until smooth. Beat the egg whites until stiff and fold into the raspberry mixture. Return to the freezerproof container and freeze again until hard.

To serve, allow to soften slightly.
Serves 8

Charlotte russe

METRIC/IMPERIAL
150ml/¼ pint lemon jelly,
  cool but not set
1 tangerine, skinned and
  segmented
angelica, cut into leaves
22 sponge finger biscuits
1 egg white, beaten
15g/½oz gelatine
2 × 15ml spoons/
  2 tablespoons water
600ml/1 pint double cream,
  lightly whipped
300ml/½ pint made custard,
  cooled
2 × 15ml spoons/
  2 tablespoons dry white
  wine
grated rind and juice of
  3 lemons
50–75g/2–3oz caster sugar

AMERICAN
⅔ cup lemon jello, cool but
  not set
1 tangerine, skinned and
  segmented
candied angelica, cut into
  leaves
22 ladyfingers
1 egg white, beaten
2 envelopes unflavored
  gelatine
2 tablespoons water
2½ cups heavy cream,
  lightly whipped
1¼ cups prepared custard,
  cooled
2 tablespoons dry white
  wine
grated rind and juice of
  3 lemons
¼–⅓ cup sugar

Line the bottom of a 1.2 litre/2 pint/5 cup tin with half the jelly (jello) and allow to set. Arrange the tangerine segments and angelica 'leaves' in an attractive pattern on the jelly (jello). Spoon over the remaining jelly (jello), and allow to set.

Trim the sponge biscuits (ladyfingers), brush them with the beaten egg white and arrange round the sides of the tin. Put the gelatine and water in a bowl over a pan of hot water, and dissolve. Mix the whipped cream, custard, wine, lemon rind and juice together, and stir in the gelatine. Stir in the sugar to taste, and pour the mixture into the prepared tin. Chill until set.

Turn out onto a plate and decorate by tying round a ribbon.
Serves 4 to 6

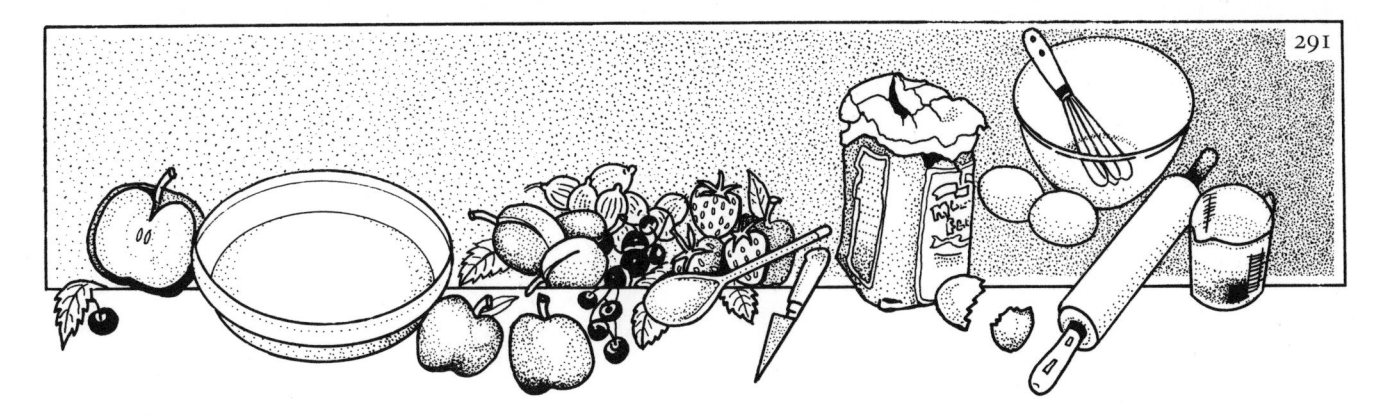

Stuffed apple jelly

METRIC/IMPERIAL
600ml/1 pint water
50g/2oz sugar
6 small sweet dessert apples
15g/½oz angelica, chopped
25g/1oz glacé cherries, chopped
25g/1oz nuts, chopped
honey
1 packet orange jelly
150ml/¼ pint double cream to decorate

AMERICAN
2½ cups water
¼ cup sugar
6 small sweet dessert apples
1½ tablespoons chopped candied angelica
2 tablespoons chopped candied cherries
¼ cup chopped nuts
honey
1 package orange-flavored jello
⅔ cup heavy cream to decorate

Put the water and sugar in a saucepan and bring to simmering point. Peel and core the apples and put at once into the simmering water. Cover the pan and simmer carefully for about 10 minutes, then remove from the heat and leave until the apples are soft but still whole. This will take a further 10 to 15 minutes. Lift out and arrange in a serving dish.

Mix the angelica, cherries and nuts with a little honey and use to stuff the apples. Make up the jelly (jello) according to the directions on the packet, using the syrup in which the apples were cooked. When almost set, spoon over the apples until each is completely coated. Pour any remaining jelly (jello) into the dish. Whisk the cream until stiff and sweeten to taste with a little sugar. Use the cream to decorate the top of the apples.

For a more substantial dessert, put a layer of sponge or plain cake in the bottom of the dish.
Serves 6

Coffee cream mousse

METRIC/IMPERIAL
175g/6oz cream cheese
4 large eggs, separated
150ml/¼ pint double cream
3 × 15ml spoons/ 3 tablespoons coffee essence
75g/3oz caster sugar

AMERICAN
¾ cup cream cheese
4 eggs, separated
⅔ cup heavy cream
3 tablespoons coffee flavoring
⅓ cup sugar

Beat the cream cheese and egg yolks together until well mixed. Beat in the cream until the mixture is thick. Stir in the coffee essence (flavoring).

Beat the egg whites until stiff, then gradually beat in the sugar until the mixture is stiff and glossy. Fold in the coffee mixture. Spoon into 6 glasses and chill until set.

If you like, serve decorated with curls of grated chocolate.
Serves 6

Rum bavarois

METRIC/IMPERIAL
600ml/1 pint milk
1 egg
1 egg yolk
50g/2oz sugar
2 × 15ml spoons/
  2 tablespoons light rum
15g/½oz gelatine
3 × 15ml spoons/
  3 tablespoons water
150ml/¼ pint double cream

AMERICAN
2½ cups milk
1 egg
1 egg yolk
¼ cup sugar
2 tablespoons light rum
2 envelopes unflavored
  gelatin
3 tablespoons water
⅔ cup heavy cream

Put the milk, egg and egg yolk in the top of a double boiler or in a heatproof bowl over a pan of hot water. Cook, stirring, until the custard is thick enough to coat the back of a wooden spoon. Remove from the heat and stir in the sugar and rum.

Dissolve the gelatine in the water and strain into the rum mixture. Stir well, then strain into a mixing bowl. Allow to cool.

Whip the cream until it is thick. Fold into the rum mixture. Spoon into a dampened 600ml/1 pint/2½ cup mould and chill until set.

Turn out of the mould to serve.
Serves 4

Cherries jubilee

METRIC/IMPERIAL
1 × 0.5kg/1lb can black
  cherries
1 × 15ml spoon/
  1 tablespoon finely grated
  lemon rind
2 × 5ml spoons/2 teaspoons
  cornflour
4 × 15ml spoons/
  4 tablespoons brandy
vanilla ice cream

AMERICAN
1 × 1lb can Bing cherries
1 tablespoon finely grated
  lemon rind
2 teaspoons cornstarch
4 tablespoons brandy
vanilla ice cream

Drain the cherries, reserving the can juice. Set aside 1 × 15ml spoon/1 tablespoon of the can juice and put the remainder in a saucepan. Add the lemon rind and bring to the boil. Simmer for 2 minutes, then strain the juice. Return the juice to the saucepan and add the cherries.

Dissolve the cornflour (cornstarch) in the reserved can juice and add to the saucepan. Simmer, stirring, until thickened.

Warm the brandy and set alight. Pour flaming into the cherry mixture and cook, stirring, until the flames have died away. Serve hot, poured over vanilla ice cream.
Serves 4

Floating islands

METRIC/IMPERIAL
900ml/1½ pints milk
1 × 5ml spoon/1 teaspoon vanilla essence
3 eggs, separated
150g/5oz caster sugar
4 × 15ml spoons/
  4 tablespoons chocolate sauce★

AMERICAN
3¾ cups milk
1 teaspoon vanilla extract
3 eggs, separated
⅔ cup sugar
4 tablespoons chocolate sauce★

Put the milk in a saucepan and scald (bring to just below boiling point). Stir in the vanilla.

Beat 2 of the egg whites until stiff. Add 4 × 5ml spoons/4 teaspoons of the sugar and continue beating for 1 minute or until the mixture is stiff and glossy. Fold in all but 25g/1oz/2 tablespoons of the remaining sugar.

Drop spoonsful of the meringue mixture onto the hot milk and poach gently for 10 minutes or until set. Carefully remove the meringues from the milk and allow to cool.

Mix together the egg yolks, remaining egg white and remaining sugar. Stir in a little of the milk, then add to the remaining milk in the saucepan. Heat gently, stirring, until this custard is thick and smooth. Remove from the heat and pour into a serving dish. Allow to cool.

Arrange the meringues on top of the custard and pour over the chocolate sauce in a thin stream.
Serves 4

Apricot sherbet

METRIC/IMPERIAL
1 × 0.5kg/1lb can apricots, drained
2 eggs, separated
pinch of grated nutmeg
4 × 15ml spoons/
  4 tablespoons single cream
25g/1oz caster sugar

AMERICAN
1 × 1lb can apricots, drained
2 eggs, separated
pinch of grated nutmeg
4 tablespoons light cream
2 tablespoons sugar

Push the apricots through a sieve (strainer) to make a purée. Alternatively, purée in an electric blender. Mix the egg yolks, nutmeg and cream with the apricot purée.

Beat the egg whites until stiff. Add half the sugar and continue beating for 1 minute. Fold in the remaining sugar, then fold into the apricot mixture.

Pour into a freezerproof container and freeze for 3 to 4 hours or until firm.
Serves 4 to 6

Orange yogurt sorbet

METRIC/IMPERIAL
300ml/½ pint natural yogurt
1 × 175g/6oz can concentrated frozen orange juice, thawed
2 oranges
sugar
15g/½oz gelatine
3 × 15ml spoons/ 3 tablespoons water
2 egg whites
mint sprigs to decorate

AMERICAN
1¼ cups unflavored yogurt
1 × 6oz can concentrated frozen orange juice, thawed
2 oranges
sugar
2 envelopes unflavored gelatin
3 tablespoons water
2 egg whites
mint sprigs to decorate

Mix together the yogurt and orange juice. Grate the rind from the oranges and add to the yogurt mixture with sugar to taste.

Dissolve the gelatine in the water and strain into the orange mixture. Stir well, then leave until beginning to set.

Beat the egg whites until stiff and fold into the orange mixture. Spoon into a freezerproof dish and freeze until firm.

Peel the oranges and separate into segments. Remove all the skin from the segments.

To serve, put a scoop of sorbet in a dessert glass and top with some orange segments. Add another scoop of sorbet and decorate with a mint sprig. Fill 3 to 5 more glasses in the same way.
Serves 4 to 6

Apricot and apple soufflé

METRIC/IMPERIAL
0.75kg/1½lb cooking apples, peeled, cored and sliced
150ml/¼ pint water
6 fresh ripe apricots, halved and stoned
6 eggs, separated
275g/10oz caster sugar
2 × 15ml spoons/ 2 tablespoons lemon juice
5 × 5ml spoons/ 5 teaspoons gelatine
2 × 15ml spoons/ 2 tablespoons apricot liqueur
150ml/¼ pint single cream, whipped
grapes, halved and deseeded, to decorate

AMERICAN
1½lb baking apples, peeled, cored and sliced
⅔ cup water
6 fresh ripe apricots, halved and pitted
6 eggs, separated
1¼ cups sugar
2 tablespoons lemon juice
5 teaspoons unflavored gelatin
2 tablespoons apricot-flavored liqueur
⅔ cup light cream, whipped
grapes, halved and deseeded, to decorate

Prepare a 1.5 litre/2½ pint/6¼ cup soufflé dish, by tying a double band of greaseproof paper or non-stick parchment round the outside of the dish, to stand 7.5cm/3 inches above the rim.

Stew the apples and apricots in 6 × 15ml spoons/ 6 tablespoons of the water until soft. Cool, then push the apples and apricots through a sieve (strainer) or purée in a blender. Put the egg yolks, sugar and lemon juice in a bowl set over a pan of hot water, and whisk until very thick and creamy. Remove from the heat and whisk until cool. Dissolve the gelatine in the remaining water, in a bowl over hot water. Whisk the fruit purée, gelatine and apricot liqueur into the egg mixture. Fold the whipped cream into the mixture. Finally, stiffly beat the egg whites and fold in.

Turn the mixture into the prepared dish and chill until set. Using a knife, remove the paper collar from the soufflé. Decorate with grapes and extra whipped cream, if liked.
Serves 6 to 8

Hazelnut and chestnut meringue

METRIC/IMPERIAL
0.5kg/1lb chestnuts
175g/6oz sugar
2 × 15ml spoons
  2 tablespoons rum
150ml/¼ pint double cream,
  lightly whipped
5 egg whites
275g/10oz caster sugar
100g/4oz hazelnuts, finely
  chopped
50g/2oz hazelnuts, chopped
chocolate leaves to decorate

AMERICAN
1lb chestnuts
¾ cup sugar
2 tablespoons rum
⅔ cup heavy cream, lightly
  whipped
5 egg whites
1¼ cups superfine sugar
1 cup finely chopped
  hazelnuts
½ cup chopped hazelnuts
chocolate leaves to decorate

Cut a cross into the top of each chestnut. Drop into boiling water and boil for 5 minutes. Drain and remove both the outer shells and inner skins. Put the peeled chestnuts into a pan of cold water, cover and bring to the boil. Simmer until tender, then drain and mash. While still hot, stir in the rum and sugar. When cold, fold in the cream.

Draw a 20cm/8 inch circle on a sheet of non-stick parchment, and place the paper on a baking sheet. Whisk the egg whites until very stiff, then whisk in half the caster (superfine) sugar, keeping the mixture stiff. Fold in the remaining sugar and the finely chopped hazelnuts. Spread some of the meringue over the circle to form the base of the flan. Using a large star nozzle (tube), pipe the remaining meringue round the edge of the flan to form an edge made of rosettes.

Place on a low shelf in a preheated very cool oven (120°C/250°F, Gas Mark ½) for 1½ to 2 hours until firm and just beginning to colour. Allow to cool, remove the paper and place the meringue on a serving dish. Add the chopped hazelnuts to the chestnut mixture, and pile into the centre of the basket.

Serve decorated with chocolate leaves.
Serves 6 to 8

Lemon meringue pie

METRIC/IMPERIAL
175g/6oz quantity rich
  shortcrust pastry★
Filling:
300ml/½ pint water
grated rind and juice of 1
  large lemon
50g/2oz sugar
2 × 15ml spoons/
  2 tablespoons cornflour
2 large egg yolks
15g/½oz butter
Topping:
2 large egg whites
100g/4oz caster sugar

AMERICAN
1½ cup quantity rich pie
  pastry★
Filling:
1¼ cups water
grated rind and juice of 1
  large lemon
¼ cup sugar
2 tablespoons cornstarch
2 large egg yolks
1 tablespoon butter
Topping:
2 large egg whites
½ cup sugar

Roll out the pastry dough and use to line a 20cm/8 inch diameter flan ring (pie pan). Bake blind in a preheated moderately hot oven (200°C/400°F, Gas Mark 6) for 15 minutes.

To make the filling, put the water, lemon rind and sugar in a saucepan. Heat gently, stirring to dissolve the sugar. Dissolve the cornflour (cornstarch) in the lemon juice. Stir into the hot syrup and bring to the boil, stirring. Simmer until thickened and smooth. Remove from the heat and beat in the egg yolks and butter. Allow to cool.

Beat the egg whites until stiff. Add half the sugar and beat again for 1 minute. Fold in 40g/1½oz/3 tablespoons of the remaining sugar.

Pour the lemon filling into the pastry case (pie shell). Pile the meringue on top and spread to the edges. Sprinkle over the remaining sugar. Bake in a preheated cool oven (150°C/300°F, Gas Mark 2) for 30 minutes or until the meringue is crisp and lightly browned. Serve warm or cold.
Serves 4 to 6

Strawberry meringue gâteau

METRIC/IMPERIAL
6 large egg whites
350g/12oz caster sugar
450ml/¾ pint double cream
0.5kg/1lb strawberries

AMERICAN
6 large egg whites
1½ cups sugar
2 cups whipping cream
1lb strawberries

Line 3 baking sheets with lightly oiled greaseproof paper or non-stick parchment. Mark a circle 20cm/8 inches in diameter on each sheet of paper.

Beat the egg whites until they are stiff. Add 4 × 15ml spoons/4 tablespoons of the sugar and continue beating for 1 minute or until the meringue mixture is very stiff and glossy. Carefully fold in all but 3 × 15ml spoons/3 tablespoons of the remaining sugar.

Divide the meringue between the 3 baking sheets, spreading it over the marked-out circles. Bake the meringue rounds in a preheated cool oven (140°C/275°F, Gas Mark 1) for 3 hours or until set. Remove from the oven and allow to cool.

Beat the cream until it is thick. Slice half the strawberries. Fold the sliced strawberries into the cream with the remaining sugar.

Peel the paper from the meringue rounds. Place one round on a serving plate and cover with half the cream mixture. Place another meringue round on top and cover with the remaining cream mixture. Add the remaining meringue round. Decorate the top and around the base with the whole strawberries. Serve immediately.
Serves 6

Sour cream peaches

METRIC/IMPERIAL
4 large peaches, peeled, stoned and sliced
2 × 15ml spoons/ 2 tablespoons brown sugar
1 × 2.5ml spoon/½ teaspoon ground cinnamon
300ml/½ pint sour cream
4 × 15ml spoons/ 4 tablespoons sugar

AMERICAN
4 large peaches, peeled, pitted and sliced
2 tablespoons brown sugar
½ teaspoon ground cinnamon
1¼ cups sour cream
4 tablespoons sugar

Divide the peach slices between 4 flameproof serving dishes. Mix together the brown sugar and cinnamon and sprinkle over the peaches. Spoon the sour cream over the top and sprinkle 1 × 15ml spoon/1 tablespoon of sugar over each serving.

Grill (broil) quickly until the sugar melts and caramelizes. Serve hot or cold.
Serves 4

Custard tart

METRIC/IMPERIAL
100g/4oz quantity
  shortcrust pastry*
2 eggs, lightly beaten
25g/1oz caster sugar
300ml/½ pint milk, scalded
1 × 2.5ml spoon/½ teaspoon
  grated nutmeg

AMERICAN
1 cup quantity pie pastry*
2 eggs, lightly beaten
2 tablespoons sugar
1¼ cups milk, scalded
½ teaspoon grated nutmeg

Roll out the pastry dough and use to line an 18cm/7 inch diameter flan ring (pie pan).

Put the eggs and sugar in a mixing bowl and beat together. Gradually beat in the milk. Strain the egg mixture into the pastry case (pie shell). Sprinkle over the nutmeg.

Bake in a preheated moderately hot oven (200°C/400°F, Gas Mark 6) for 10 minutes, then reduce the temperature to moderate (180°C/350°F, Gas Mark 4). Continue baking for 20 to 25 minutes or until the custard filling is just set and the pastry is golden.

Serve warm or cold.
Serves 4

French apple tart

METRIC/IMPERIAL
100g/4oz quantity French
  flan pastry*
1kg/2lb cooking apples,
  peeled, cored and
  quartered
150ml/¼ pint fruity white
  wine
strip of lemon rind
50g/2oz butter
100g/4oz sugar
4 dessert apples, peeled,
  cored and thinly sliced
3 × 15ml spoons/
  3 tablespoons apricot jam
1 × 15ml spoon/
  1 tablespoon lemon juice

AMERICAN
1 cup quantity French flan
  pastry*
2lb baking apples, peeled,
  cored and quartered
⅔ cup fruity white wine
strip of lemon rind
¼ cup butter
½ cup sugar
4 dessert apples, peeled,
  cored and thinly sliced
3 tablespoons apricot jam
1 tablespoon lemon juice

Roll out the pastry dough and use to line a 20cm/8 inch diameter flan ring (pie pan).

Put the cooking apples in a saucepan with the wine, lemon rind, butter and 50g/2oz/¼ cup of the sugar. Cover and cook gently until the apples are very tender. Remove from the heat and discard the lemon rind. Purée the apple mixture in an electric blender or by pushing it through a sieve (strainer).

Fill the pastry case (pie shell) with the apple mixture and smooth the top. Arrange the dessert apple slices on top in a ring, slightly overlapping. Sprinkle with the remaining sugar. Bake in a preheated moderately hot oven (190°C/375°F, Gas Mark 5) for 25 to 30 minutes or until the pastry is set and golden.

Meanwhile, heat the jam and lemon juice in a saucepan, stirring until well mixed. Remove from the heat and strain the mixture. Glaze the top of the tart with the apricot mixture. Serve warm or cold.
Serves 6

Orange refrigerator cheesecake

METRIC/IMPERIAL	AMERICAN
finely grated rind and juice of 3 oranges	finely grated rind and juice of 3 oranges
juice of 1 lemon	juice of 1 lemon
2 × 15ml spoons/ 2 tablespoons gelatine	2 tablespoons unflavored gelatin
2 eggs, separated	2 eggs, separated
300ml/½ pint milk	1¼ cups milk
75g/3oz sugar	⅓ cup sugar
0.5kg/1¼lb cottage cheese	2½ cups cottage cheese
150ml/¼ pint double cream	⅔ cup heavy cream
100g/4oz digestive biscuits, crushed	1 cup crushed graham crackers
50g/2oz sugar	¼ cup sugar
50g/2oz butter, melted	¼ cup butter, melted

Mix together the orange and lemon juices. Put 4 × 15ml spoons/4 tablespoons of the mixed juices in a small bowl. Sprinkle over the gelatine and leave to soak.

Put the egg yolks, milk and 50g/2oz/¼ cup of the sugar in a saucepan. Mix well together and cook gently without boiling for 3 minutes. Stir in the soaked gelatine mixture and stir until dissolved. Remove from the heat and allow to cool.

When the orange mixture is starting to set, stir in the grated orange rind and 6 × 15ml spoons/ 6 tablespoons of the mixed orange and lemon juices.

Push the cheese through a sieve (strainer) until it is smooth and beat into the orange mixture. Whip the cream until it is thick and fold into the orange mixture. Beat the egg whites until stiff. Add the remaining sugar and continue beating until stiff and glossy. Fold into the orange mixture.

Spoon into a 1.75 litre/3 pint/7½ cup deep cake tin with sloping sides that has been lined with greaseproof (waxed) paper or non-stick parchment. Mix together the remaining ingredients and sprinkle over the cheesecake mixture. Smooth the top. Chill until set.

To serve, turn out onto a serving plate and peel off the paper. If you like, decorate with crystallized (candied) orange slices.
Serves 6 to 8

Loganberry cheesecake

METRIC/IMPERIAL	AMERICAN
100g/4oz digestive biscuit, crushed	1 cup crushed graham crackers
25g/1oz demerara sugar	3 tablespoons raw brown sugar
25g/1oz nuts, chopped	¼ cup chopped nuts
50g/2oz butter, melted	¼ cup butter, melted
2 eggs, separated	2 eggs, separated
75g/3oz sugar	⅓ cup sugar
pinch of salt	pinch of salt
225g/8oz loganberries	½lb loganberries
15g/½oz gelatine	2 envelopes unflavored gelatin
3 × 15ml spoons/ 3 tablespoons water	3 tablespoons water
350g/12oz cottage cheese, sieved	1½ cups cottage cheese, strained
150ml/¼ pint double cream, whipped	⅔ cup heavy cream, whipped

Mix the biscuit (cracker) crumbs, demerara (raw brown) sugar, nuts and butter together. Press the mixture firmly into the base of a 20cm/8 inch springform or loose-bottomed tin, which has been lined with a circle of foil. Whisk the egg yolks, sugar and salt in a bowl over a pan of hot, but not boiling, water until thick and creamy and the whisk leaves a trail when lifted. Cool, whisking occasionally.

Rub the loganberries through a sieve (strainer). Sprinkle the gelatine over the water in a bowl set over a pan of hot water. Dissolve the gelatine. Whisk the egg whites until stiff. Mix the yolks, fruit, gelatine and cottage cheese together and fold in the egg whites and half the cream. Pour into the prepared tin and smooth over the top. When set, decorate with the reserved cream and decorate with extra fruit.
Serves 8 to 10

Fruit savarin

METRIC/IMPERIAL
225g/8oz plain flour
25g/1oz fresh yeast
6 × 15ml spoons/
 6 tablespoons lukewarm milk
1 × 2.5ml spoon/½ teaspoon salt
25g/1oz sugar
4 eggs, lightly beaten
100g/4oz butter, softened
Syrup:
100g/4oz sugar
150ml/¼ pint water
3 × 15ml spoons/
 3 tablespoons rum or sherry
3 × 15ml spoons/
 3 tablespoons apricot jam
To decorate:
fresh fruit (cherries, grapes, orange segments, apple slices, etc.)

AMERICAN
2 cups all-purpose flour
1 cake compressed yeast
6 tablespoons lukewarm milk
½ teaspoon salt
2 tablespoons sugar
4 eggs, lightly beaten
½ cup butter, softened
Syrup:
½ cup sugar
⅔ cup water
3 tablespoons rum or sherry
3 tablespoons apricot jam
To decorate:
fresh fruit (cherries, grapes, orange segments, apple slices, etc.)

Sift 50g/2oz/½ cup of the flour into a mixing bowl. Cream the yeast with the milk and beat into the flour to form a smooth batter. Leave in a warm place for 15 to 20 minutes or until frothy.

Sift the remaining flour into another mixing bowl and add the salt, sugar, eggs and butter. Beat together with your hand, then beat in the yeast mixture to mix well. Turn the dough into a greased 20cm/8 inch diameter ring mould. Cover and allow to rise in a warm place for about 1½ hours or until the dough has risen to two-thirds fill the mould.

Bake in a preheated moderately hot oven (200°C/400°F, Gas Mark 6) for 20 minutes.

Turn the savarin out of the mould onto a serving plate.

To make the syrup, dissolve the sugar in the water over a gentle heat. Stir in the rum or sherry and heat through. Remove from the heat. Prick the savarin all over with a skewer and pour over most of the syrup. Allow the savarin to cool.

Stir the jam into the remaining syrup and heat through gently. Fill the centre of the savarin with fruit and pour over the jam mixture to glaze. Allow to set before serving. Decorate with whipped cream, if liked.
Serves 6.

Crème brûlée

METRIC/IMPERIAL
300ml/½ pint double cream
4 egg yolks, lightly beaten
3 × 15ml spoons/
 3 tablespoons icing sugar
1 × 2.5ml spoon/½ teaspoon vanilla essence
caster sugar

AMERICAN
1¼ cups heavy cream
4 egg yolks, lightly beaten
3 tablespoons confectioners' sugar
½ teaspoon vanilla extract
granulated sugar

Put the cream in the top of a double boiler or in a heatproof bowl placed over a pan of hot water. Heat gently until the cream is hot. Pour the cream onto the egg yolks, beating constantly. Return the mixture to the pan or bowl and stir in the icing (confectioners') sugar and vanilla. Cook gently, stirring, until the mixture thickens.

Pour into a 600ml/1 pint/2½ cup flameproof serving dish. Allow to cool, then chill overnight.

Sprinkle the top of the custard liberally with sugar. Grill (broil) until the sugar caramelizes to a deep golden brown. Allow to cool, then chill again before serving.
Serves 4

Coeur à la crème

METRIC/IMPERIAL
225g/8oz cottage cheese
300ml/½ pint double cream
2 × 5ml spoons/2 teaspoons icing sugar

AMERICAN
1 cup cottage cheese
1¼ cups heavy cream
2 teaspoons confectioners' sugar

Push the cottage cheese through a sieve (strainer) until it is smooth. Beat in the cream and sugar. Press the cheese mixture into 6 individual coeur à la crème moulds or into a muslin- (cheesecloth-) lined sieve (strainer). Allow to drain overnight.

Turn the cream out of the moulds or sieve (strainer) onto a plate. Serve with berries, such as strawberries or raspberries.
Serves 6

Summer pudding

METRIC/IMPERIAL
0.75kg/1½lb mixed soft fruits (raspberries, blackberries, cherries, blackcurrants, etc.)
100g/4oz caster sugar
6–8 slices stale white bread, crusts removed

AMERICAN
1½lb mixed soft fruits (raspberries, blackberries, cherries, blackcurrants, etc.)
½ cup sugar
6–8 slices stale white bread, crusts removed

Put the fruit in a saucepan with the sugar and cook gently for 5 minutes or until the fruit begins to soften. Remove from the heat.

Line a 900ml/1½ pint/3¾ cup pudding basin (slope-sided mold) with bread slices, being sure there are no gaps and reserving 2 slices for the top. Pour in the fruit mixture and cover with the reserved bread slices.

Put a small plate on top of the bread and add a small weight. Chill overnight.

Invert the pudding onto a serving plate to serve.
Serves 4

Zabaglione

METRIC/IMPERIAL
6 egg yolks
4 × 15ml spoons/
    4 tablespoons caster sugar
150ml/¼ pint Marsala

AMERICAN
6 egg yolks
4 tablespoons sugar
⅔ cup Marsala

Put the egg yolks and sugar in a large heatproof bowl placed over a pan of hot water. Beat until the mixture is thick and pale. Gradually beat in the Marsala and continue beating until light and foamy. Do not let the bowl become too hot or the egg yolks will scramble.
    Pour into 4 glasses and serve.
Serves 4

Strawberry ice cream cake

METRIC/IMPERIAL
3 eggs, separated
4 × 15ml spoons/
    4 tablespoons hot water
175g/6oz caster sugar
few drops of vanilla essence
175g/6oz plain flour
50g/2oz cornflour
3 × 5ml spoons/
    3 teaspoons baking powder
Filling:
1 litre/2 pints vanilla ice cream
225g/8oz fresh strawberries, hulled and sliced
caster sugar for sprinkling

AMERICAN
3 eggs, separated
4 tablespoons hot water
¾ cup sugar
few drops of vanilla extract
1½ cups all-purpose flour
½ cup cornstarch
3 teaspoons baking powder
Filling:
5 cups vanilla ice cream
½lb fresh strawberries, hulled and sliced
superfine sugar for sprinkling

Line the base of a greased 23cm/9 inch cake tin with greased greaseproof paper or non-stick parchment. Whisk the egg yolks with the hot water, sugar and vanilla until the mixture is thick and creamy. Sift together the flour, cornflour (cornstarch) and baking powder. Whisk the egg whites until stiff. Fold the flours into the egg yolk mixture, then fold in the egg whites. Turn into the prepared cake tin and bake in a preheated moderately hot oven (200°C/400°F, Gas Mark 6) for 25 minutes or until well risen and golden. Leave in the tin for a few minutes then turn out onto a wire rack to cool completely.
    To serve, split the cake in half and cover one layer with ice cream. Cover the ice cream with a layer of strawberries, then replace the top layer of the cake. Sprinkle the top with sugar and serve with extra strawberries, if liked.
Serves 8

CAKES & COOKIES

Victoria sandwich (layer) cake

METRIC/IMPERIAL
100g/4oz butter
100g/4oz sugar
2 large eggs
100g/4oz self-raising flour
grated rind of 1 lemon
4–6 × 15ml spoons/
 4–6 tablespoons raspberry jam
4 × 15ml spoons/
 4 tablespoons icing sugar

AMERICAN
½ cup butter
½ cup sugar
2 large eggs
1 cup self-rising flour
grated rind of 1 lemon
4–6 tablespoons raspberry jam
4 tablespoons confectioners' sugar

Cream the butter and sugar together until the mixture is light and fluffy. Beat in the eggs one at a time. Sift in the flour and fold in with the lemon rind.

Divide the cake batter between 2 greased and lined 18cm/7 inch diameter sandwich (layer) cake tins. Bake in a preheated moderate oven (180°C/350°F, Gas Mark 4) for 25 minutes or until the cakes spring back when lightly pressed in the centre. Cool on a wire rack.

Place one cake layer on a serving plate and spread with the jam. Place the other cake layer on top and sift over the icing (confectioners') sugar.
Makes one 18cm/7 inch round cake

Lemon chiffon (angel food) cake

METRIC/IMPERIAL
100g/4oz self-raising flour
1 × 2.5ml spoon/½ teaspoon salt
150g/5oz caster sugar
4 × 15ml spoons/
 4 tablespoons corn oil
3 eggs, separated
5 × 15ml spoons/
 5 tablespoons water
1 × 2.5ml spoon/½ teaspoon vanilla essence
finely grated rind of ½ lemon
1 × 2.5ml spoon/½ teaspoon cream of tartar

AMERICAN
1 cup self-rising flour
½ teaspoon salt
⅔ cup sugar
4 tablespoons corn oil
3 eggs, separated
⅓ cup water
½ teaspoon vanilla extract
finely grated rind of ½ lemon
½ teaspoon cream of tartar

Sift the flour and salt into a mixing bowl. Stir in the sugar. Add the oil, egg yolks, water, vanilla and lemon rind and stir until the batter is smooth.

Beat the egg whites with the cream of tartar until stiff. Fold into the lemon batter. Spoon into a 20cm/8 inch diameter deep ring tin (tube pan) with sloping sides.

Bake in a preheated moderate oven (160°C/325°F, Gas Mark 3) for 1¼ hours.

Invert the cake tin and leave until cool. When cool, turn out of the tin.
Makes one 20cm/8 inch ring cake

Walnut spice cake

METRIC/IMPERIAL
75g/3oz plain flour
pinch of salt
1 × 5ml spoon/1 teaspoon ground cinnamon
3 eggs
75g/3oz sugar
25g/1oz walnuts, finely chopped
250ml/8 fl oz double cream
12 walnut halves to decorate

AMERICAN
¾ cup all-purpose flour
pinch of salt
1 teaspoon ground cinnamon
3 eggs
⅓ cup sugar
¼ cup finely chopped walnuts
1 cup whipping cream
12 walnut halves to decorate

Sift the flour, salt and cinnamon into a mixing bowl. Put the eggs and sugar in the top of a double boiler or in a heatproof bowl placed over a pan of hot water. Beat until the mixture is pale and thick and will make a ribbon trail on itself when the beater is lifted. (If using an electric mixer, no heat is needed.)

Add the flour mixture and chopped walnuts and fold gently into the egg mixture. Pour into 2 greased and lined 18cm/7 inch sandwich (layer) cake tins. Bake in a preheated moderate oven (180°C/350°F, Gas Mark 4) for 15 to 20 minutes or until well risen and golden.

Turn the cakes out of the tins and allow to cool on a wire rack.

Whip the cream until it is thick. Use to sandwich the cake layers together. Decorate the top of the cake with the walnut halves and serve immediately.
Makes one 18cm/7 inch round cake

German apple cake

METRIC/IMPERIAL
0.5kg/1lb quantity flaky or puff pastry★ (made with 0.5kg/1lb flour, etc.)
4 large cooking apples, peeled, cored and sliced
sugar
2 × 15ml spoons/ 2 tablespoons light rum
1 egg, lightly beaten

AMERICAN
4 cup quantity flaky or puff pastry★ (made with 4 cups flour, etc.)
4 large baking apples, peeled, cored and sliced
sugar
2 tablespoons light rum
1 egg, lightly beaten

Roll out half the pastry dough and use to line a 20cm/8 inch diameter springform pan. Stand the pan on a baking sheet.

Put the apples in a saucepan and cook gently, stirring occasionally, until they are pulpy. Remove from the heat and beat until smooth. Stir in sugar to taste and the rum. Fill the pastry case (shell) with the apple mixture.

Roll out the remaining dough and use to cover the pan, pressing the edges together to seal. Mark into wedges with the back of a knife. Brush with the beaten egg. Bake in a preheated hot oven (220°C/425°F, Gas Mark 7) for 20 to 30 minutes or until the pastry is puffed up and golden brown.

Unclip the sides of the pan and carefully remove the cake. Allow to cool and cut into wedges when cold.
Serves 6 to 8

Coffee brandy cake

METRIC/IMPERIAL
175g/6oz butter
175g/6oz sugar
3 large eggs
2 × 15ml spoons/
 2 tablespoons coffee
 essence
1 × 15ml spoon/
 1 tablespoon brandy
24 sponge finger biscuits
150ml/¼ pint double cream
chopped walnuts to decorate

AMERICAN
¾ cup butter
¾ cup sugar
3 large eggs
2 tablespoons coffee
 flavoring
1 tablespoon brandy
24 ladyfingers
⅔ cup whipping cream
chopped walnuts to decorate

Cream the butter and sugar together until the mixture is light and fluffy. Beat in the eggs, then the coffee essence (flavoring) and brandy.

Line a small rectangular cake tin with greaseproof paper or non-stick parchment. Place 8 of the sponge fingers (ladyfingers) on the bottom of the tin. Cover with half the coffee mixture. Make another layer of 8 sponge fingers (ladyfingers) and pour in the remaining coffee mixture. Cover with the remaining sponge fingers (ladyfingers).

Press down well and cover with a lid. Put a small weight on top and chill for 3 hours or until set.

Whip the cream until it is thick. Turn the cake out of the tin and peel off the paper. Cover the top and sides of the cake with whipped cream and decorate with walnuts.
Serves 6

Strawberry shortcake

METRIC/IMPERIAL
225g/8oz plain flour
2 × 5ml spoons/2 teaspoons
 baking powder
50g/2oz butter
25g/1oz sugar
1 egg, lightly beaten
milk
350g/12oz strawberries,
 hulled
300ml/½ pint double cream

AMERICAN
2 cups all-purpose flour
2 teaspoons baking powder
¼ cup butter
2 tablespoons sugar
1 egg, lightly beaten
milk
¾lb strawberries, hulled
1¼ cups whipping cream

Sift the flour and baking powder into a mixing bowl. Rub in the butter until the mixture resembles breadcrumbs, then stir in the sugar. Add the egg and enough milk to bind the mixture to a stiff scone (biscuit) dough.

Roll out the dough to about 1cm/¾ inch and cut out 12 rounds, using a 7.5cm/3 inch cutter. Place the rounds on a baking sheet and bake in a preheated hot oven (230°C/450°F, Gas Mark 8) for 7 to 10 minutes or until well risen and golden brown. Cool on a wire rack.

Crush 225g/8oz of the strawberries very lightly. Whip the cream until it is thick. Fold the crushed berries into half the cream. Split the still warm shortcakes in half and sandwich together with the strawberry and cream mixture. Top each shortcake with a swirl of cream and a whole berry.
Makes 12

Chocolate and orange mousses (page 285)

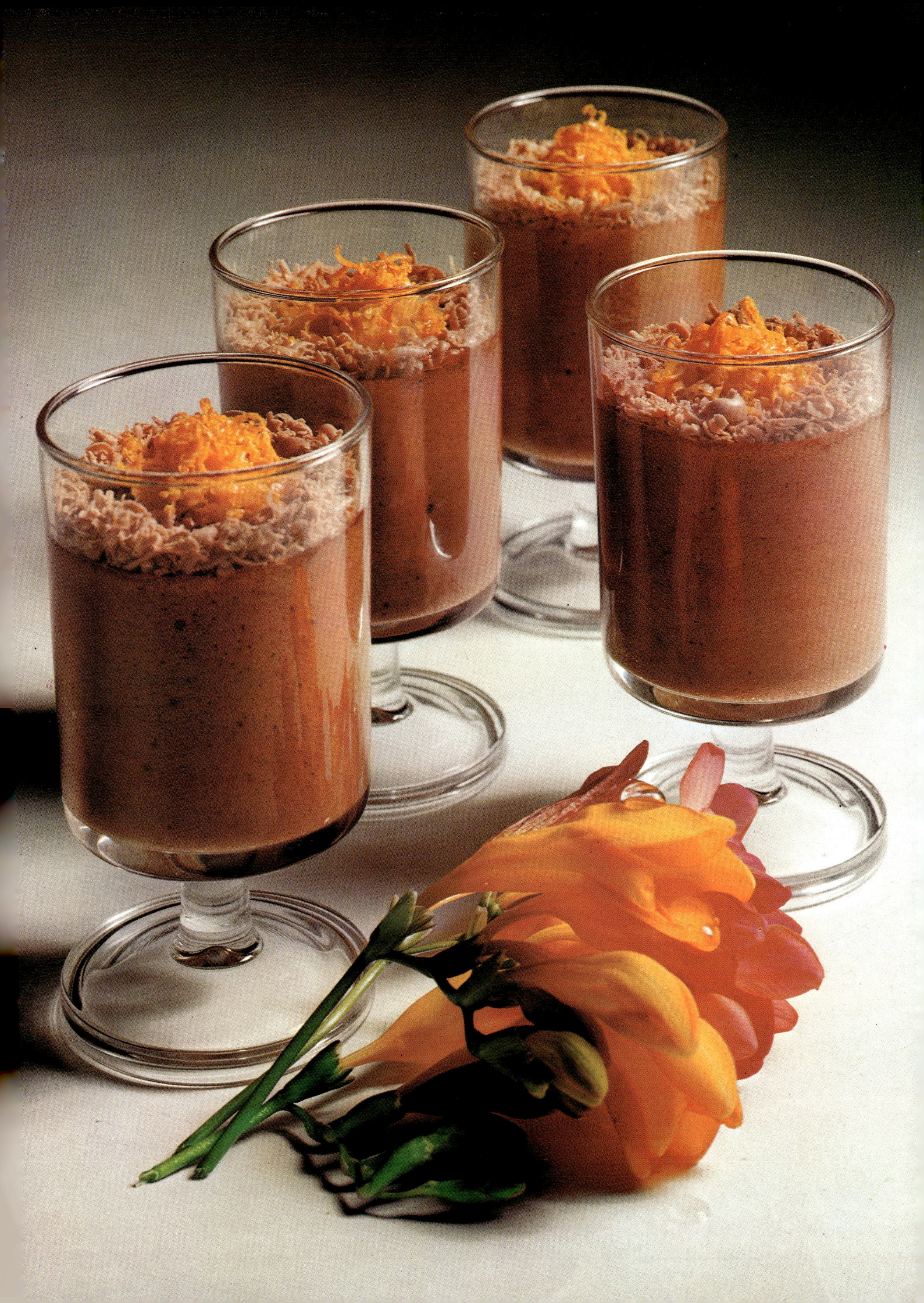

Redcurrant compote (page 285); Blackberry (bramble) and apple sponge (page 282)

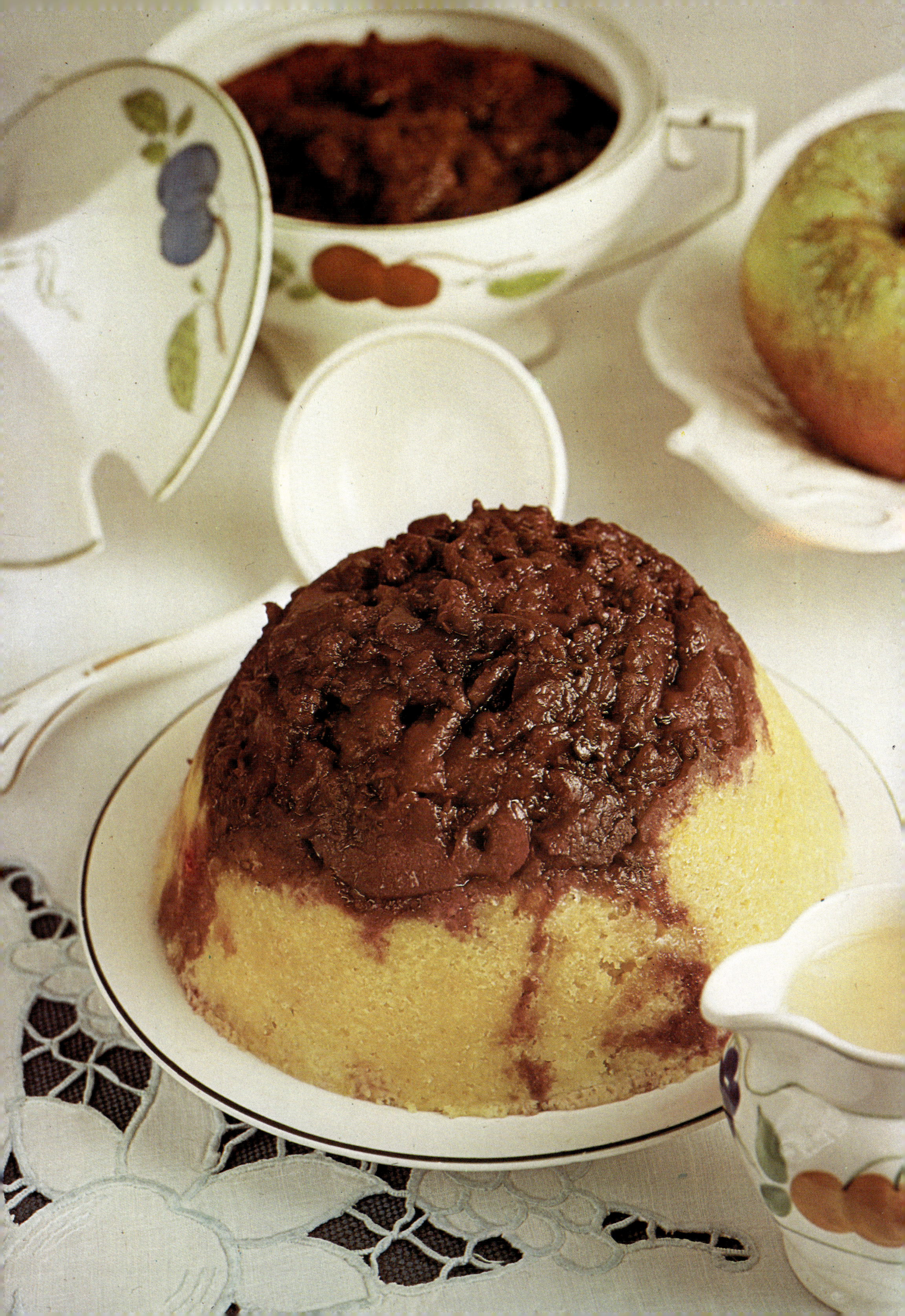

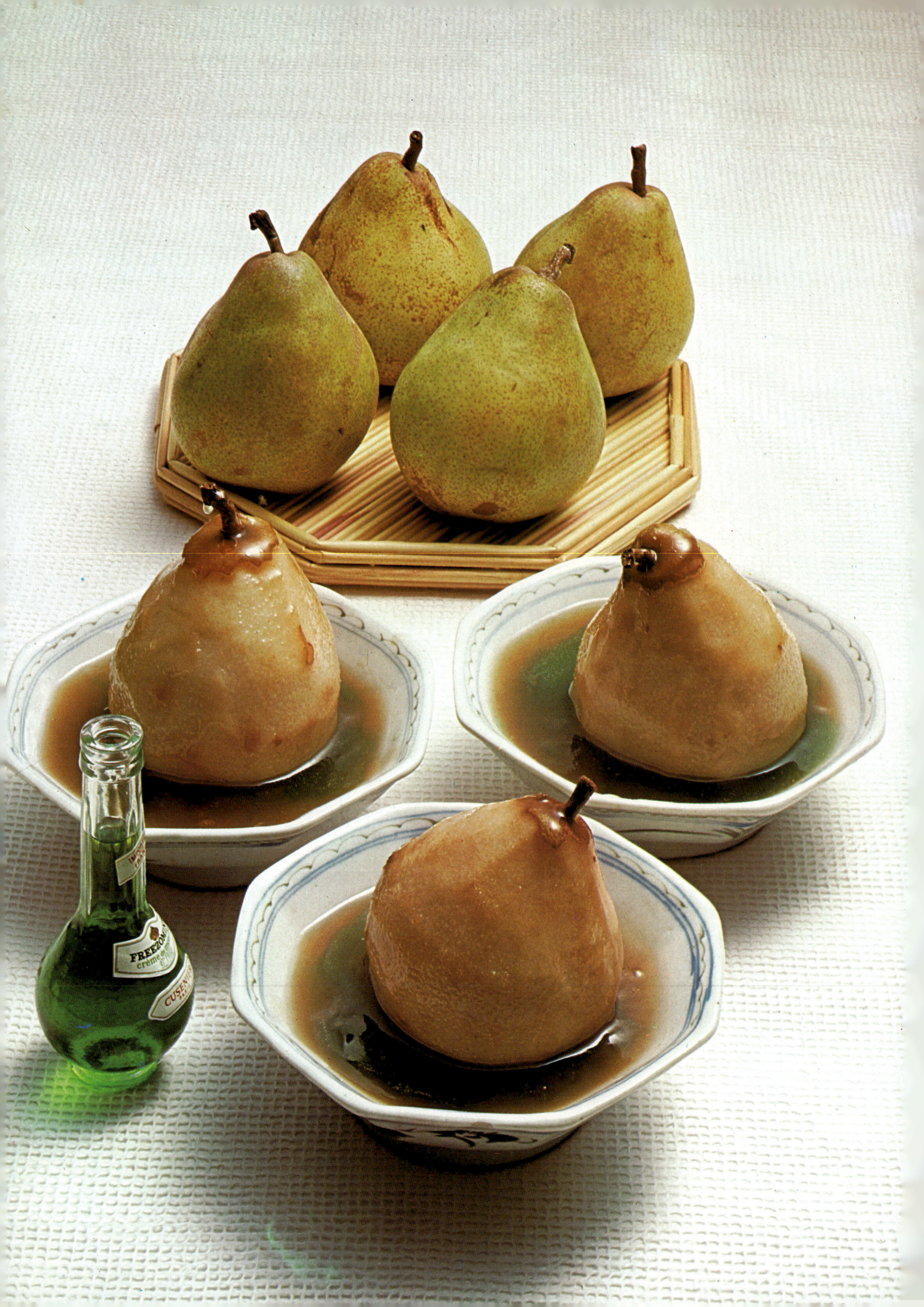

Pineapple gâteau

METRIC/IMPERIAL
4 eggs
225g/8oz caster sugar
50g/2oz plain flour
50g/2oz cornflour
2 × 5ml spoons/
  2 teaspoons baking powder
1 large can pineapple or
  6–8 slices
300ml/½ pint double cream
angelica, cut into leaves, to
  decorate

AMERICAN
4 eggs
1 cup sugar
½ cup all-purpose flour
½ cup cornstarch
2 teaspoons baking powder
1 large can pineapple or
  6–8 slices
1¼ cups heavy cream
candied angelica, cut into
  leaves, to decorate

Whisk the eggs and sugar together until the mixture falls in ribbons when the whisk is lifted. Sift together the flour, cornflour (cornstarch) and baking powder. Fold a little at a time into the whisked mixture. Turn into a 20cm/8 inch greased cake tin. Place in a preheated moderately hot oven (200°C/400°F, Gas Mark 6) and bake for 20 to 30 minutes until well risen and springy to the touch. Allow to cool slightly in the tin then turn out onto a wire rack.

Meanwhile drain the pineapple slices, reserving the syrup. Cut half the slices into wedges and halve the remainder. Whip the cream until stiff. When the sponge is cold, split in half. Put one half on a serving plate and spoon over 4 × 15ml spoons/4 tablespoons pineapple syrup. Arrange the pineapple wedges on top and spread with whipped cream. Cover with the top half of the sponge. Arrange the pineapple half slices on top in a circle, pipe on the remaining cream and decorate with angelica 'leaves'.

Serves 6 to 8

Bakewell tart

METRIC/IMPERIAL
100g/4oz quantity flaky or
  rough puff pastry★ (made
  with 100g/4oz flour, etc.)
2 × 15ml spoons/
  2 tablespoons raspberry
  jam
50g/2oz butter
50g/2oz caster sugar
grated rind and juice of
  ½ lemon
1 egg, beaten
75g/3oz cake crumbs
75g/3oz ground almonds

AMERICAN
1 cup quantity flaky or
  rough puff pastry★ (made
  with 1 cup flour, etc.)
2 tablespoons raspberry jam
¼ cup butter
¼ cup sugar
grated rind and juice of
  ½ lemon
1 egg, beaten
1½ cups cake crumbs
¾ cup ground almonds

Roll out the pastry dough and use to line a 20cm/8 inch diameter flan tin (tart pan). Spread the jam over the bottom of the pastry case (tart shell).

Cream the butter, sugar and lemon rind together until the mixture is light and fluffy. Beat in the egg. Mix together the cake crumbs and ground almonds and fold into the creamed mixture. Add a little lemon juice, if necessary, to give a dropping consistency.

Pour the almond mixture into the pastry case (tart shell) and smooth the top. Bake in a preheated hot oven (220°C/425°F, Gas Mark 7) for 15 minutes, then reduce the temperature to moderate (180°C/350°F, Gas Mark 4). Continue baking for 20 to 30 minutes or until the pastry is cooked and the filling feels firm to the touch.

Serve warm or cold.
Serves 4

Poached minty pears (page 286)

Chocolate Swiss (jelly) roll

METRIC/IMPERIAL
75g/3oz plain flour
pinch of salt
1 × 15ml spoon/
 1 tablespoon cocoa powder
75g/3oz sugar
3 eggs
150ml/¼ pint double cream
1 × 15ml spoon/
 1 tablespoon icing sugar

AMERICAN
¾ cup all-purpose flour
pinch of salt
1 tablespoon unsweetened
 cocoa powder
⅓ cup sugar
3 eggs
⅔ cup whipping cream
1 tablespoon confectioners'
 sugar

Sift the flour, salt and cocoa powder into a mixing bowl. Put the sugar and eggs in a heatproof bowl over a pan of hot water. Beat until the mixture is thick and pale and will make a ribbon trail on itself when the beater is lifted. (If using an electric beater, no heat is needed.)

Remove from the heat and fold in the flour mixture. Spoon into a greased and lined 30 × 20cm/ 12 × 8 inch Swiss (jelly) roll tin. Bake in a preheated moderately hot oven (200°C/400°F, Gas Mark 6) for 10 to 12 minutes or until well risen.

Turn out the cake onto a sheet of greaseproof (waxed) paper that has been sprinkled with sugar. Peel away the paper used to line the tin and trim away any crusty edges. Roll up loosely with the paper inside and cover with a damp cloth. Leave to cool.

Whip the cream with 1 × 5ml spoon/1 teaspoon of the icing (confectioners') sugar until thick.

Unroll the cake and remove the paper. Spread the cake with the whipped cream and roll up again. Sprinkle with the remaining sugar and serve.
Serves 4 to 6

Vanilla mille feuilles

METRIC/IMPERIAL
225g/8oz quantity puff
 pastry★
300ml/½ pint double cream
2 × 15ml spoons/
 2 tablespoons icing sugar
few drops of vanilla essence
jam

AMERICAN
2 cup quantity puff pastry★
1¼ cups whipping cream
2 tablespoons confectioners'
 sugar
few drops of vanilla extract
jam or jelly

Roll out the pastry dough until it is wafer thin. Cut into 15 fingers 10 × 3.5cm/4 × 1½ inches. Transfer to baking sheets. Bake in a preheated very hot oven (240°C/475°F, Gas Mark 9) for 10 minutes or until well risen and golden. Reduce the temperature to moderate (180°C/350°F, Gas Mark 4) and bake for a further 5 minutes. Cool on a wire rack.

Whip the cream, adding 2 × 5ml spoons/ 2 teaspoons of the sugar and the vanilla, until it is thick. Spread one-third of the pastry fingers with the cream mixture. Top each with another pastry finger and spread these with jam (or jelly). Put the remaining pastry fingers on top and sprinkle over the remaining icing (confectioners') sugar.
Makes 5

Orange yogurt cake

METRIC/IMPERIAL
100g/4oz butter
175g/6oz sugar
2 eggs
175g/6oz self-raising flour
pinch of salt
5 × 15ml spoons/
  5 tablespoons orange juice
150ml/¼ pint natural yogurt
Icing:
50g/2oz butter
175g/6oz icing sugar
2 × 15ml spoons/
  2 tablespoons orange juice
1 × 5ml spoon/1 teaspoon
  finely grated orange rind

AMERICAN
½ cup butter
¾ cup sugar
2 eggs
1½ cups self-rising flour
pinch of salt
⅓ cup orange juice
⅔ cup unflavored yogurt
Icing:
¼ cup butter
1⅓ cups confectioners' sugar
2 tablespoons orange juice
1 teaspoon finely grated orange rind

Cream the butter and sugar together until the mixture is light and fluffy. Beat in the eggs. Sift in the flour and salt and fold together. Beat in the orange juice and yogurt.

Spoon into 2 greased 20cm/8 inch diameter sandwich (layer) cake tins. Bake in a preheated moderately hot oven (190°C/375°F, Gas Mark 5) for 30 to 35 minutes or until a skewer inserted into the centres of the cakes comes out clean. Remove from the oven and allow to cool.

To make the icing, cream the butter and half the sugar together, then beat in the remaining sugar. Beat in the orange juice and rind.

Remove the cakes from the tins and place one on a serving plate. Spread with half the icing. Put the other cake on top and cover with the remaining icing.
Makes one 20cm/8 inch round cake

Pineapple upside-down cake

METRIC/IMPERIAL
175g/6oz butter
175g/6oz brown sugar
1 × 400g/14oz can
  pineapple rings, drained
225g/8oz self-raising flour
1 × 5ml spoon/1 teaspoon
  ground cinnamon
1 × 2.5ml spoon/½ teaspoon
  grated nutmeg
2 eggs, beaten
120ml/4 fl oz milk

AMERICAN
¾ cup butter
1 cup brown sugar
1 × 14oz can pineapple
  rings, drained
2 cups self-rising flour
1 teaspoon ground cinnamon
½ teaspoon grated nutmeg
2 eggs, beaten
½ cup milk

Put 50g/2oz/¼ cup of the butter and 50g/2oz/⅓ cup of the brown sugar in a saucepan. Heat gently, stirring to dissolve the sugar, then pour into a greased 25 × 15cm/10 × 6 inch rectangular cake tin. Arrange the pineapple rings in the tin to cover the bottom.

Sift the flour and spices into a mixing bowl and rub in the remaining butter. Stir in the remaining sugar and beat in the eggs and milk to form a stiff batter. Pour into the tin on top of the pineapple.

Bake in a preheated moderate oven (180°C/350°F, Gas Mark 4) for 50 minutes.

To serve, invert the cake onto a serving plate.
Makes one 25 × 15cm/10 × 6 inch cake

Devil's food cake

METRIC/IMPERIAL
50g/2oz butter
225g/8oz sugar
2 eggs
175g/6oz self-raising flour
1 × 5ml spoon/1 teaspoon bicarbonate of soda
4 × 15ml spoons/ 4 tablespoons buttermilk
5 × 15ml spoons/ 5 tablespoons strong black coffee
50g/2oz plain cooking chocolate
1 × 5ml spoon/1 teaspoon vanilla essence
Filling:
1 egg white
2.5 × 15ml spoons 2½ tablespoons cold water
200g/7oz sugar
pinch of cream of tartar
1 × 2.5ml spoon/½ teaspoon vanilla essence
Icing:
100g/4oz butter
225g/8oz icing sugar
100g/4oz plain cooking chocolate
1 × 15ml spoon/ 1 tablespoon milk

AMERICAN
¼ cup butter
1 cup sugar
2 eggs
1½ cups self-rising flour
1 teaspoon baking soda
4 tablespoons buttermilk
⅓ cup strong black liquid coffee
2 squares semisweet chocolate
1 teaspoon vanilla extract
Filling:
1 egg white
2½ tablespoons cold water
¾ cup plus 2 tablespoons sugar
pinch of cream of tartar
½ teaspoon vanilla extract
Icing:
½ cup butter
1¾ cups confectioners' sugar
4 squares semisweet chocolate
1 tablespoon milk

Cream the butter and sugar together until the mixture is light and fluffy. Beat in the eggs. Sift in the flour and soda and fold together. Stir in the buttermilk.

Put the coffee and chocolate in a saucepan and heat gently to melt the chocolate. Remove from the heat and allow to cool slightly, then stir into the creamed mixture with the vanilla. Spoon into 2 greased 23cm/9 inch diameter sandwich (layer) cake tins.

Bake in a preheated moderately hot oven (190°C/375°F, Gas Mark 5) for 25 to 30 minutes or until a skewer inserted into the centres of the cakes comes out clean. Remove from the oven and allow to cool.

To make the filling, put all the ingredients except the vanilla in a heatproof bowl over a pan of hot water. Beat until the mixture is stiff. Remove from the heat and stir in the vanilla.

Remove the cakes from the tins and place one on a serving plate. Spread with the filling and place the other cake on top.

To make the icing, cream the butter and half the icing (confectioners') sugar together. Gradually beat in the remaining icing (confectioners') sugar. Melt the chocolate with the milk, then stir into the creamed mixture. Spread the frosting over the top and sides of the cake.

Makes one 23cm/9 inch round cake

Coffee ginger cake

METRIC/IMPERIAL
3 large eggs, separated
75g/3oz sugar
75g/3oz self-raising flour
1 × 5ml spoon/1 teaspoon instant coffee powder
pinch of ground ginger
Icing:
175g/6oz butter
350g/12oz icing sugar
2 × 15ml spoons/ 2 tablespoons strong black coffee
2 × 15ml spoons/ 2 tablespoons rum
2 × 15ml spoons/ 2 tablespoons chopped crystallized ginger

AMERICAN
3 eggs, separated
⅓ cup sugar
¾ cup self-rising flour
1 teaspoon instant coffee powder
pinch of ground ginger
Icing:
¾ cup butter
2⅔ cups confectioners' sugar
2 tablespoons strong black liquid coffee
2 tablespoons rum
2 tablespoons chopped candied ginger

Put the egg yolks and sugar in the top of a double boiler or in a heatproof bowl placed over a pan of hot water. Beat until the mixture is thick and pale and will make a ribbon trail on itself when the beater is lifted. (If using an electric mixer, no heat is needed.) Remove from the heat and sift in the flour, coffee powder and ginger. Fold in gently.

Beat the egg whites until stiff and fold into the coffee mixture. Spoon into 2 greased 18cm/7 inch diameter sandwich (layer) cake tins. Bake in a preheated moderately hot oven (190°C/375°F, Gas Mark 5) for 20 to 25 minutes or until the cakes spring back when lightly pressed in the centre. Remove from the oven and allow to cool.

To make the icing, cream the butter and half the icing (confectioners') sugar together, then gradually beat in the remaining sugar. Beat in the coffee and rum. Fold in the ginger.

Remove the cakes from the tins and place one on a serving plate. Cover with half the icing. Place the other cake on top and spread with the remaining icing.

Makes one 18 cm/7 inch round cake

Marble cake

METRIC/IMPERIAL
100g/4oz butter
175g/6oz sugar
1 × 5ml spoon/1 teaspoon vanilla essence
2 eggs
225g/8oz self-raising flour
pinch of salt
3–4 × 15ml spoons/ 3–4 tablespoons milk
2 × 15ml spoons/ 2 tablespoons cocoa powder
2 × 15ml spoons/ 2 tablespoons water

AMERICAN
½ cup butter
¾ cup sugar
1 teaspoon vanilla extract
2 eggs
2 cups self-rising flour
pinch of salt
3–4 tablespoons milk
2 tablespoons unsweetened cocoa powder
2 tablespoons water

Cream the butter and sugar together until the mixture is light and fluffy. Beat in the vanilla and eggs. Sift in the flour and salt and fold together. Beat in enough of the milk to make a smooth dropping consistency.

Divide the batter into 2 portions. Dissolve the cocoa in the water and add to 1 portion. Pour the plain batter into a greased 18cm/7 inch diameter deep cake tin. Pour the cocoa batter on top and swirl the two together with a knife.

Bake in a preheated moderate oven (180°C/350°F, Gas Mark 4) for 50 minutes to 1 hour or until a skewer inserted into the centre of the cake comes out clean.

Makes one 18cm/7 inch round cake

Mocha chestnut cake

METRIC/IMPERIAL
4 eggs, separated
225g/8oz sugar
75g/3oz plain cooking chocolate
2 × 15ml spoons/ 2 tablespoons strong black coffee
1 × 225g/8oz can unsweetened chestnut purée
Icing:
75g/3oz plain cooking chocolate
2 × 15ml spoons/ 2 tablespoons strong black coffee
2 egg yolks
2 × 15ml spoons/ 2 tablespoons sugar
150ml/¼ pint double cream

AMERICAN
4 eggs, separated
1 cup sugar
3 squares semisweet chocolate
2 tablespoons strong black liquid coffee
1 × ½lb can unsweetened chestnut paste
Icing:
3 squares semisweet chocolate
2 tablespoons strong black liquid coffee
2 egg yolks
2 tablespoons sugar
⅔ cup heavy cream

Put the egg yolks and sugar in the top of a double boiler or in a heatproof bowl placed over a pan of hot water. Beat until the mixture is thick and pale and will make a ribbon trail on itself when the beater is lifted. (If using an electric mixer, no heat is needed.)

Remove from the heat and allow to cool, beating frequently. Melt the chocolate with the coffee and stir into the egg yolk mixture. Fold in the chestnut purée (paste).

Beat the egg whites until stiff and fold into the chestnut mixture. Spoon into 2 greased 15cm/6 inch diameter sandwich (layer) cake tins. Bake in a preheated moderate oven (180°C/350°F, Gas Mark 4) for 35 minutes or until the cakes spring back when lightly pressed in the centres. Remove from the oven and allow to cool.

To make the icing, melt the chocolate in the coffee. Stir in the egg yolks and sugar and cook gently, stirring to dissolve the sugar. Remove from the heat and allow to cool, then stir in the cream.

Remove the cakes from the tins and place one on a serving plate. Spread with half the icing. Place the other cake on top and cover with the remaining icing. Allow the icing to set before serving.
Makes one 15cm/6 inch round cake

Caramel cake

METRIC/IMPERIAL
100g/4oz butter
100g/4oz brown sugar
2 eggs
100g/4oz self-raising flour
1 × 2.5ml spoon/½ teaspoon mixed spice
2 × 15ml spoons/ 2 tablespoons milk
Icing:
50g/2oz butter
100g/4oz brown sugar
2 × 15ml spoons/ 2 tablespoons milk
225g/8oz icing sugar

AMERICAN
½ cup butter
⅔ cup brown sugar
2 eggs
1 cup self-rising flour
½ teaspoon apple pie spice
2 tablespoons milk
Icing:
¼ cup butter
⅔ cup brown sugar
2 tablespoons milk
1¾ cups confectioners' sugar

Cream the butter and sugar together until the mixture is light and fluffy. Beat in the eggs, then sift in the flour and spice. Fold together and stir in the milk. Spoon into a greased 23cm/9 inch square cake tin.

Bake in a preheated moderately hot oven (190°C/375°F, Gas Mark 5) for 20 to 25 minutes or until the cake springs back when lightly pressed in the centre. Remove from the oven and allow to cool.

To make the icing, melt the butter in a saucepan. Add the sugar and cook gently, stirring until dissolved. Remove from the heat and stir in the milk and half the icing (confectioners') sugar. Gradually beat in the remaining icing (confectioners') sugar.

Remove the cake from the tin and place on a serving plate. Cover the top and sides with the icing and allow to set before serving.
Makes one 23cm/9 inch square cake

Cut and keep cake

METRIC/IMPERIAL
350g/12oz plain flour
1.5 × 5ml spoons/
 1½ teaspoons bicarbonate
 of soda
1 × 5ml spoon/1 teaspoon
 mixed spice
175g/6oz butter
175g/6oz light brown sugar
175g/6oz currants
75g/3oz raisins
300ml/½ pint buttermilk

AMERICAN
3 cups all-purpose flour
1½ teaspoons baking soda
½ teaspoon ground cinnamon
½ teaspoon ground cloves
¾ cup butter
1 cup brown sugar
1 cup currants
½ cup raisins
1¼ cups buttermilk

Sift the flour, soda and spices into a mixing bowl. Rub in the butter until the mixture resembles breadcrumbs. Stir in the sugar, currants and raisins. Gradually stir in the buttermilk. Cover the bowl and leave overnight.

Pour into a greased and lined 1kg/2lb/9 × 5 × 3 inch loaf tin and bake in a preheated moderate oven (160°C/325°F, Gas Mark 3) for 1½ hours. Cool on a wire rack.

Wrap in foil and store in an airtight tin. The cake will keep for about 1 week.
Makes one 1kg/2lb/9 × 5 × 3 inch cake

Applesauce spice cake

METRIC/IMPERIAL
50g/2oz butter
175g/6oz brown sugar
1 × 5ml spoon/1 teaspoon
 ground allspice
1 × 2.5ml spoon/½ teaspoon
 grated nutmeg
1 × 2.5ml spoon/½ teaspoon
 ground ginger
275g/10oz thick apple
 purée
225g/8oz plain flour
1 × 5ml spoon/1 teaspoon
 baking powder
75g/3oz raisins
25g/1oz walnuts, chopped

AMERICAN
¼ cup butter
1 cup brown sugar
1 teaspoon ground allspice
½ teaspoon grated nutmeg
½ teaspoon ground ginger
1¼ cups thick applesauce
2 cups all-purpose flour
1 teaspoon baking powder
½ cup raisins
¼ cup chopped walnuts

Cream the butter and sugar together until the mixture is light and fluffy. Beat in the spices and apple purée (applesauce). Sift in the flour and baking powder and fold together well. Stir in the raisins and walnuts.

Spoon into a greased 18cm/7 inch diameter deep cake tin. Bake in a preheated moderate oven (180°C/350°F, Gas Mark 4) for 1 hour or until a skewer inserted into the centre comes out clean.
Makes one 18cm/7 inch round cake

Brandy, orange and raisin cake

METRIC/IMPERIAL
0.75kg/1½lb raisins
150ml/¼ pint brandy
grated rind and juice of 2 large oranges
225g/8oz butter
225g/8oz sugar
4 large eggs
225g/8oz plain flour
50g/2oz self-raising flour

AMERICAN
1½lb (4 cups) raisins
⅔ cup brandy
grated rind and juice of 2 large oranges
1 cup butter
1 cup sugar
4 eggs
2 cups all-purpose flour
½ cup self-rising flour

Put the raisins in a mixing bowl and pour over the brandy, orange rind and juice. Stir well. Allow to soak for at least 12 hours, stirring occasionally.

Cream the butter and sugar together until the mixture is light and fluffy. Gradually beat in the eggs. Sift in the flours and fold into the creamed mixture. Stir in the raisin mixture and mix well. Pour into a greased and lined 20cm/8 inch diameter deep cake tin.

Bake in a preheated moderate oven (160°C/325°F, Gas Mark 3) for 3 hours or until a skewer inserted into the centre of the cake comes out clean. If the cake appears to be browning too quickly, cover with foil.

Cool the cake on a wire rack, then store in an airtight tin. It will keep for 2 to 3 weeks.
Makes one 20cm/8 inch round cake

Madeira cake

METRIC/IMPERIAL
175g/6oz butter
175g/6oz sugar
225g/8oz plain flour
2 × 5ml spoons/2 teaspoons baking powder
3 eggs, lightly beaten
1 × 5ml spoon/1 teaspoon grated lemon rind
milk
sugar for sprinkling

AMERICAN
¾ cup butter
¾ cup sugar
2 cups all-purpose flour
2 teaspoons baking powder
3 eggs, lightly beaten
1 teaspoon grated lemon rind
milk
sugar for sprinkling

Cream the butter and sugar together until the mixture is light and fluffy. Sift in the flour and baking powder and fold into the creamed mixture. Gradually beat in the eggs and lemon rind, then add just enough milk to give a soft batter.

Pour into a greased and floured 18cm/7 inch diameter deep cake tin. Bake in a preheated moderate oven (160°C/325°F, Gas Mark 3) for 1½ hours. Sprinkle the top with a little sugar halfway through baking.
Makes one 18cm/7 inch round cake

Boiled fruit cake

METRIC/IMPERIAL
150ml/¼ pint tea
100g/4oz butter or margarine
150g/5oz soft brown sugar
175g/6oz currants
175g/6oz sultanas
1 × 15ml spoon/
 1 tablespoon mixed spice
275g/10oz plain flour
2 × 5ml spoons/2 teaspoons bicarbonate of soda
1 large egg, lightly beaten

AMERICAN
⅔ cup tea
½ cup butter or margarine
¾ cup brown sugar
1 cup currants
1 cup seedless white raisins
1 tablespoon apple pie spice
2½ cups all-purpose flour
2 teaspoons baking soda
1 egg, lightly beaten

Put the tea, butter or margarine, sugar, dried fruit and spice in a saucepan and bring to the boil, stirring to dissolve the sugar. Simmer for 20 minutes. Remove from the heat and allow to cool.

Sift the flour and soda into a mixing bowl. Beat in the dried fruit mixture and the egg. Pour into a greased 18cm/7 inch diameter deep cake tin.

Bake in a preheated moderate oven (180°C/350°F, Gas Mark 4) for 1 hour. Cool on a wire rack.
Makes one 18cm/7 inch round cake

Cider crumble cake

METRIC/IMPERIAL
0.5kg/1lb 2oz self-raising flour
100g/4oz brown sugar
75g/3oz stoned dates, chopped
3 × 15ml spoons/
 3 tablespoons treacle
300ml/½ pint cider
2 eggs, lightly beaten
Topping:
40g/1½oz plain flour
40g/1½oz sugar
40g/1½oz butter
40g/1½oz walnuts, chopped
1 × 2.5ml spoon/½ teaspoon ground cinnamon
3 × 15ml spoons/
 3 tablespoons apricot or plum jam

AMERICAN
4½ cups self-rising flour
⅔ cup brown sugar
½ cup chopped pitted dates
3 tablespoons molasses
1¼ cups hard cider
2 eggs, lightly beaten
Topping:
6 tablespoons all-purpose flour
3 tablespoons sugar
3 tablespoons butter
⅓ cup chopped walnuts
½ teaspoon ground cinnamon
3 tablespoons apricot or plum jam

Sift the flour into a mixing bowl. Stir in the sugar and dates. Put the treacle (molasses) and cider in a saucepan and heat gently, stirring until the mixture is well blended. Add to the date mixture and stir well. Stir in the eggs. Pour into a greased and lined 23cm/9 inch square cake tin.

Bake in a preheated moderate oven (160°C/325°F, Gas Mark 3) for 30 minutes.

Meanwhile, prepare the topping. Sift the flour into a mixing bowl. Add the sugar and butter and rub together until the mixture resembles breadcrumbs. Stir in the walnuts and cinnamon.

Remove the cake from the oven and spread the top with the jam. Sprinkle over the crumble topping and return to the oven. Bake for a further 20 minutes, or until a skewer inserted into the centre comes out clean. Cool in the tin.
Makes one 23cm/9 inch square cake

Walnut ring

METRIC/IMPERIAL
225g/8oz self-raising flour
pinch of salt
100g/4oz butter or margarine
100g/4oz walnuts, chopped
100g/4oz sugar
1 egg, lightly beaten
1 × 5ml spoon/1 teaspoon vanilla essence
6–7 × 15ml spoons/ 6–7 tablespoons milk
Icing:
100g/4oz icing sugar
3–4 × 15ml spoons/ 3–4 tablespoons orange juice
walnut halves to decorate

AMERICAN
2 cups self-rising flour
pinch of salt
½ cup butter or margarine
1 cup chopped walnuts
½ cup sugar
1 egg, lightly beaten
1 teaspoon vanilla extract
6–7 tablespoons milk
Icing:
¾ cup confectioners' sugar
3–4 tablespoons orange juice
walnut halves to decorate

Sift the flour and salt into a mixing bowl. Rub in the butter or margarine until the mixture resembles breadcrumbs. Stir in the walnuts and sugar. Add the egg, vanilla and enough milk to bind the mixture to a semi-stiff batter.

Pour into a greased 18cm/7 inch diameter ring tin (tube pan). Bake in a preheated moderate oven (180°C/350°F, Gas Mark 4) for 1 to 1¼ hours or until well risen and firm to the touch.

Allow to cool slightly in the tin, then turn out onto a wire rack to cool completely.

To make the icing, mix together the sugar and enough of the orange juice to make a thin but smooth mixture. Pour over the cooled cake and allow to set. Decorate with walnut halves.
Makes one 18cm/7 inch ring cake

Cherry cake

METRIC/IMPERIAL
175g/6oz plain flour
1 × 5ml spoon/1 teaspoon baking powder
pinch of salt
2 × 15ml spoons/ 2 tablespoons semolina
25g/1oz ground almonds
100g/4oz butter or margarine
100g/4oz sugar
1 × 5ml spoon/1 teaspoon vanilla or almond essence
2 eggs
3 × 15ml spoons/ 3 tablespoons halved glacé cherries
3 × 15ml spoons/ 3 tablespoons milk

AMERICAN
1½ cups all-purpose flour
1 teaspoon baking powder
pinch of salt
2 tablespoons cream of wheat
¼ cup ground almonds
½ cup butter or margarine
½ cup sugar
1 teaspoon vanilla or almond extract
2 eggs
3 tablespoons halved candied cherries
3 tablespoons milk

Sift the flour, baking powder and salt into a mixing bowl. Stir in the semolina (cream of wheat) and almonds. Cream the butter or margarine with the sugar until the mixture is light and fluffy. Beat in the vanilla or almond essence (extract) and eggs, then fold in the dry ingredients. Stir in the cherries and milk.

Pour into a greased and lined 18cm/7 inch diameter deep cake tin. Bake in a preheated moderate oven (180°C/350°F, Gas Mark 4) for 1½ to 1¾ hours or until a skewer inserted into the centre comes out clean.

Cool slightly in the tin before turning out onto a wire rack to cool completely.
Makes one 18cm/7 inch round cake

Parkin

METRIC/IMPERIAL
225g/8oz plain flour
1 × 2.5ml spoon/½ teaspoon salt
1 × 5ml spoon/1 teaspoon ground cinnamon
1 × 5ml spoon/1 teaspoon mixed spice
1 × 2.5ml spoon/½ teaspoon ground ginger
225g/8oz oatmeal
150g/5oz butter or margarine
100g/4oz soft brown sugar
5 × 15ml spoons/
 5 tablespoons golden syrup
5 × 15ml spoons/
 5 tablespoons treacle
1 egg, lightly beaten
150ml/¼ pint milk

AMERICAN
2 cups all-purpose flour
½ teaspoon salt
1 teaspoon ground cinnamon
1 teaspoon apple pie spice
½ teaspoon ground ginger
1⅓ cups oatmeal
⅔ cup butter or margarine
⅔ cup brown sugar
⅓ cup light corn syrup
⅓ cup molasses
1 egg, lightly beaten
⅔ cup milk

Sift the flour, salt and spices into a mixing bowl. Stir in the oatmeal. Put the butter or margarine, sugar, syrup and treacle (molasses) in a saucepan and heat gently, stirring to melt the butter and dissolve the sugar. Stir into the dry ingredients with the egg and milk.

Pour into a greased and lined 23cm/9 inch square cake tin. Bake in a preheated moderate oven (160°C/325°F, Gas Mark 3) for 1½ to 1¾ hours or until a skewer inserted into the centre comes out clean.

Leave to cool slightly in the tin, then turn out and cool completely on a wire rack. Store in an airtight container for at least 1 day before cutting into squares and serving.
Makes about 16 squares

Pineapple and walnut cake

METRIC/IMPERIAL
350g/12oz self-raising flour
pinch of salt
75g/3oz sugar
1 × 225g/8oz can pineapple rings, drained
50g/2oz walnuts, chopped
2 eggs, lightly beaten
150ml/¼ pint milk
50g/2oz butter, melted
Icing:
175g/6oz icing sugar
4 × 15ml spoons/
 4 tablespoons warm water
walnut halves to decorate

AMERICAN
3 cups self-rising flour
pinch of salt
⅓ cup sugar
1 × ½lb can pineapple rings, drained
½ cup chopped walnuts
2 eggs, lightly beaten
⅔ cup milk
¼ cup butter, melted
Icing:
1⅓ cups confectioners' sugar
4 tablespoons warm water
walnut halves to decorate

Sift the flour and salt into a mixing bowl. Stir in the sugar. Reserve 2 pineapple rings for the decoration and chop the remainder. Add to the flour mixture with the walnuts. Mix together the eggs, milk and melted butter and add to the pineapple mixture.

Spoon into a greased 1kg/2lb/9 × 5 × 3 inch loaf tin. Bake in a preheated moderate oven (160°C/325°F, Gas Mark 3) for 1¼ to 1½ hours or until a skewer inserted into the centre of the cake comes out clean. Cool in the tin.

Remove the cake from the tin and place on a serving plate.

Mix the icing (confectioners') sugar with the water, adding more if necessary to make a thick, spreading icing. Cover the top of the cake with the icing. Decorate with walnut halves and the reserved pineapple rings, either halved or chopped.
Makes one 1kg/2lb/9 × 5 × 3 inch cake

Danish layer cake

METRIC/IMPERIAL
4 eggs, separated
2 × 15ml spoons/
  2 tablespoons lemon juice
150g/5oz icing sugar, sifted
75g/3oz plain flour
25g/1oz cornflour
1 × 2.5ml spoon/
  ½ teaspoon baking powder
Filling:
2 × 5ml spoons/
  2 teaspoons gelatine
2 × 15ml spoons/
  2 tablespoons water
350ml/12 fl oz double
  cream, lightly whipped
2 × 15ml spoons/
  2 tablespoons caster sugar
1 × 400g/14oz can
  pineapple, drained and
  chopped
150g/5oz plain chocolate,
  grated

AMERICAN
4 eggs, separated
2 tablespoons lemon juice
1 cup plus 1 tablespoon
  confectioners' sugar, sifted
¾ cup all-purpose flour
¼ cup cornstarch
½ teaspoon baking powder
Filling:
2 teaspoons unflavored
  gelatin
2 tablespoons water
1½ cups heavy cream,
  lightly whipped
2 tablespoons sugar
1 × 14oz can pineapple,
  drained and chopped
5 squares semisweet
  chocolate, grated

Grease a 20cm/8 inch cake tin and line the base with greased greaseproof paper or non-stick parchment. Put the egg yolks, lemon juice and icing (confectioner's) sugar in a bowl and whisk together until light and creamy. Beat the egg whites until stiff then fold into the egg yolk mixture. Sift together the flour, cornflour (cornstarch) and baking powder and fold into the egg mixture. Turn into the prepared tin, place in a preheated moderate oven (180°C/350°F, Gas Mark 4) and bake for 30 minutes. Leave in the tin for a few minutes then turn out onto a wire rack to cool completely. When cold, slice the cake into 3 rounds.

Sprinkle the gelatine over the water in a small bowl. Leave for 5 minutes then stand the bowl over a pan of hot water. When the gelatine has dissolved, remove from the heat and allow to cool slightly. Beat the gelatine into the cream with the sugar. Fold in the pineapple and all but 50g/2oz/2 squares of the grated chocolate.

Leave until set, then spread each layer of the cake with the filling. Reassemble the cake and decorate the top with the remaining grated chocolate and extra pineapple pieces, if liked.
Makes one 20cm/8 inch round cake

Dundee cake

METRIC/IMPERIAL
175g/6oz butter
175g/6oz sugar
3 large eggs
225g/8oz plain flour
1.5 × 5ml spoons/
  1½ teaspoons baking
  powder
0.5kg/1lb mixed dried fruit
50g/2oz glacé cherries
50g/2oz mixed candied
  peel, chopped
milk
50g/2oz blanched almonds

AMERICAN
¾ cup butter
¾ cup sugar
3 eggs
2 cups all-purpose flour
1½ teaspoons baking powder
2⅔ cups mixed dried fruit
¼ cup candied cherries
⅓ cup chopped mixed
  candied peel
milk
½ cup blanched almonds

Cream the butter and sugar together until the mixture is light and fluffy. Gradually beat in the eggs. Sift in the flour and baking powder and fold into the creamed mixture. Stir in the dried fruit, cherries and peel, then add just enough milk to make a soft batter.

Pour into a greased and floured 20cm/8 inch diameter deep cake tin. Arrange the almonds on top in concentric circles. Brush the almonds with a little egg white (there should be enough left in the egg shells).

Bake in a preheated moderate oven (160°C/325°F, Gas Mark 3) for 1½ hours. Reduce the temperature to cool (150°C/300°F, Gas Mark 2) and continue baking for 30 to 45 minutes. Cool in the tin before turning out.
Makes one 20cm/8 inch round cake

Almond macaroons

METRIC/IMPERIAL
175g/6oz caster sugar
75g/3oz ground almonds
3 egg whites
8 blanched almonds, halved
sugar for sprinkling

AMERICAN
¾ cup sugar
¾ cup ground almonds
3 egg whites
8 blanched almonds, halved
sugar for sprinkling

Mix together the sugar and ground almonds. Beat the egg whites until stiff and use to bind together the sugar and ground almonds to make a soft dough.

Pipe the mixture onto a baking sheet lined with rice paper in 5cm/2 inch diameter rounds. Place an almond half in the centre of each round and sprinkle with sugar.

Bake in a preheated moderate oven (160°C/325°F, Gas Mark 3) for 40 minutes or until set and pale golden. Cool on a wire rack.
Makes about 16

Almond spice bars

METRIC/IMPERIAL
225g/8oz self-raising flour
1 × 5ml spoon/1 teaspoon ground cinnamon
1 × 2.5ml spoon/½ teaspoon ground ginger
1 × 2.5ml spoon/½ teaspoon ground cloves
150g/5oz butter
75g/3oz dark brown sugar
50g/2oz blanched almonds, flaked and toasted
2 egg yolks
milk
4 × 15ml spoons/ 4 tablespoons apricot jam
1 egg white, lightly beaten

AMERICAN
2 cups self-rising flour
1 teaspoon ground cinnamon
½ teaspoon ground ginger
½ teaspoon ground cloves
⅔ cup butter
½ cup brown sugar
½ cup blanched slivered almonds, toasted
2 egg yolks
milk
4 tablespoons apricot jam
1 egg white, lightly beaten

Sift the flour, cinnamon, ginger and cloves into a mixing bowl. Add the butter and cut into small pieces, then rub into the flour until the mixture resembles breadcrumbs. Stir in the sugar and almonds. Add the egg yolks and enough milk to bind the mixture to a stiff but pliable dough. Knead the dough lightly until smooth.

Divide the dough in half. Roll out each half into a 20cm/8 inch square and trim the edges. Place one dough square on a greased baking sheet and spread with the jam. Place the other dough square on top and brush with the egg white.

Bake in a preheated moderately hot oven (190°C/375°F, Gas Mark 5) for 30 to 40 minutes or until golden brown. Allow to cool, then cut into rectangular bars.
Makes about 16

Rock cakes

METRIC/IMPERIAL
225g/8oz plain flour
pinch of salt
2 × 5ml spoons/2 teaspoons
  baking powder
1 × 2.5ml spoon/½ teaspoon
  mixed spice
1 × 2.5ml spoon/½ teaspoon
  grated nutmeg
50g/2oz butter
50g/2oz lard
100g/4oz mixed dried fruit
100g/4oz light brown sugar
grated rind of ½ lemon
1 large egg, lightly beaten
milk

AMERICAN
2 cups all-purpose flour
pinch of salt
2 teaspoons baking powder
¼ teaspoon ground cinnamon
¼ teaspoon ground cloves
½ teaspoon grated nutmeg
¼ cup butter
¼ cup shortening
⅔ cup mixed dried fruit
⅔ cup brown sugar
grated rind of ½ lemon
1 egg, lightly beaten
milk

Sift the flour, salt, baking powder and spices into a mixing bowl. Add the butter and lard (shortening) and rub in until the mixture resembles breadcrumbs. Stir in the dried fruit, sugar and lemon rind, then add the egg and enough milk to bind the mixture to a stiff dough.

Using 2 forks, make small rough piles of the dough on greased baking sheets. Bake in a preheated moderately hot oven (200°C/400°F, Gas Mark 6) for 15 to 20 minutes. Cool on a wire rack.
Makes 12

Flapjacks

METRIC/IMPERIAL
100g/4oz butter or
  margarine
25g/1oz brown sugar
4 × 15ml spoons/
  4 tablespoons golden
  syrup
225g/8oz rolled oats

AMERICAN
½ cup butter or margarine
3 × 15ml spoons/
  3 tablespoons brown sugar
4 tablespoons light corn
  syrup
2¼ cups rolled oats

Melt the butter or margarine with the sugar and syrup in a saucepan, stirring to dissolve the sugar. Stir in the oats and mix well. Remove from the heat. Spread out the mixture in a 20 × 30cm/8 × 12 inch tin and bake in a preheated moderate oven (180°C/350°F, Gas Mark 4) for 15 to 20 minutes or until golden brown and firm to the touch.

Mark into fingers (bars) or squares and allow to cool in the tin. When cold, remove from the tin and break into the fingers (bars) or squares.
Makes 18 to 24

Cigarettes russe

METRIC/IMPERIAL
2 egg whites
90g/3½oz caster sugar
40g/1½oz plain flour, sifted
40g/1½oz butter, melted
50g/2oz plain chocolate, melted

AMERICAN
2 egg whites
7 tablespoons sugar
6 tablespoons all-purpose flour, sifted
3 tablespoons butter, melted
2 squares semisweet chocolate, melted

Beat the egg whites until they are stiff. Add the sugar and flour and fold in carefully. Fold in the butter. Spread the mixture thinly on a greased and floured baking sheet in rectangles about the size of a cigarette paper.
 Bake in a preheated moderately hot oven (200°C/400°F, Gas Mark 6) for 5 to 6 minutes or until golden brown.
 Remove the rectangles from the baking sheet and quickly roll around a pencil. Slide off and allow to cool on a wire rack. When cool, dip the ends in the melted chocolate and allow to set before serving.
Makes about 16

English madeleines

METRIC/IMPERIAL
100g/4oz butter
100g/4oz caster sugar
few drops of vanilla essence
2 eggs, beaten
100g/4oz self-raising flour
pinch of salt
about 1 × 15ml spoon/ 1 tablespoon milk
To finish:
4–6 × 15ml spoons/ 4–6 tablespoons raspberry jam, sieved
4 × 15ml spoons/ 4 tablespoons desiccated coconut
about 6 glacé cherries, halved
few pieces of candied angelica

AMERICAN
½ cup butter
½ cup sugar
few drops of vanilla extract
2 eggs, beaten
1 cup self-rising flour
pinch of salt
about 1 tablespoon milk
To finish:
4–6 tablespoons raspberry jam, strained
4 tablespoons shredded coconut
about 6 candied cherries, halved
few pieces of candied angelica

Soften the butter in a bowl, add the sugar and vanilla and cream together until pale and fluffy. Beat in the eggs, a little at a time. Sift the flour with the salt and fold into the mixture, a third at a time, adding enough milk to give a soft dropping consistency.
 Divide the mixture between 10 to 12 dariole or castle pudding moulds, which have been well greased and dusted with flour. Place in a preheated moderate oven (180°C/350°F, Gas Mark 4) and bake for 15 to 20 minutes or until golden brown.
 Turn out of the moulds, upside down, and leave to cool. If necessary, trim the bases to give them a flat surface on which to stand. Spear each separately on a fork, then brush with the jam and roll in the coconut. Decorate the tops with half a glacé (candied) cherry and a few angelica 'leaves'.
Makes 10 to 12

Ginger nuts

METRIC/IMPERIAL
100g/4oz self-raising flour
1 × 2.5ml spoon/½ teaspoon bicarbonate of soda
2 × 5ml spoons/2 teaspoons ground ginger
1 × 5ml spoon/1 teaspoon ground cinnamon
2 × 5ml spoons/2 teaspoons sugar
50g/2oz butter
5 × 15ml spoons/
5 tablespoons golden syrup

AMERICAN
1 cup self-rising flour
½ teaspoon baking soda
2 teaspoons ground ginger
1 teaspoon ground cinnamon
2 teaspoons sugar
¼ cup butter
⅓ cup light corn syrup

Sift the flour, soda and spices into a mixing bowl. Stir in the sugar. Melt the butter with the syrup, then stir into the flour mixture. Roll into small balls and place well apart on greased baking sheets. Flatten the balls slightly.
 Bake in a preheated moderately hot oven (190°C/375°F, Gas Mark 5) for 15 to 20 minutes. Cool on the baking sheets before transferring to wire racks to cool completely.
Makes about 24

Date crunchies

METRIC/IMPERIAL
100g/4oz plain flour
175g/6oz rolled oats
225g/8oz butter or margarine
225g/8oz stoned dates, chopped
2 × 15ml spoons/
 2 tablespoons water
1 × 15ml spoon/
 1 tablespoon lemon juice
1 × 15ml spoon/
 1 tablespoon clear honey
pinch of ground cinnamon

AMERICAN
1 cup all-purpose flour
1¾ cups rolled oats
1 cup butter or margarine
1¼ cups chopped pitted dates
2 tablespoons water
1 tablespoon lemon juice
1 tablespoon clear honey
pinch of ground cinnamon

Sift the flour into a mixing bowl. Stir in the oats. Cut the butter or margarine into the flour mixture and rub in well. Divide the dough in half and press one half into a greased 18cm/7 inch square cake tin.
 Put the dates in a saucepan with the water and bring to the boil. Simmer until very soft, then remove from the heat and allow to cool. Stir in the lemon juice, honey and cinnamon. Spread the date mixture over the dough in the tin. Cover with the remaining dough.
 Bake in a preheated moderate oven (180°C/350°F, Gas Mark 4) for 25 minutes. Cut into fingers (bars), then allow to cool in the tin.
Makes 12 to 14

Bran teabread (page 338)

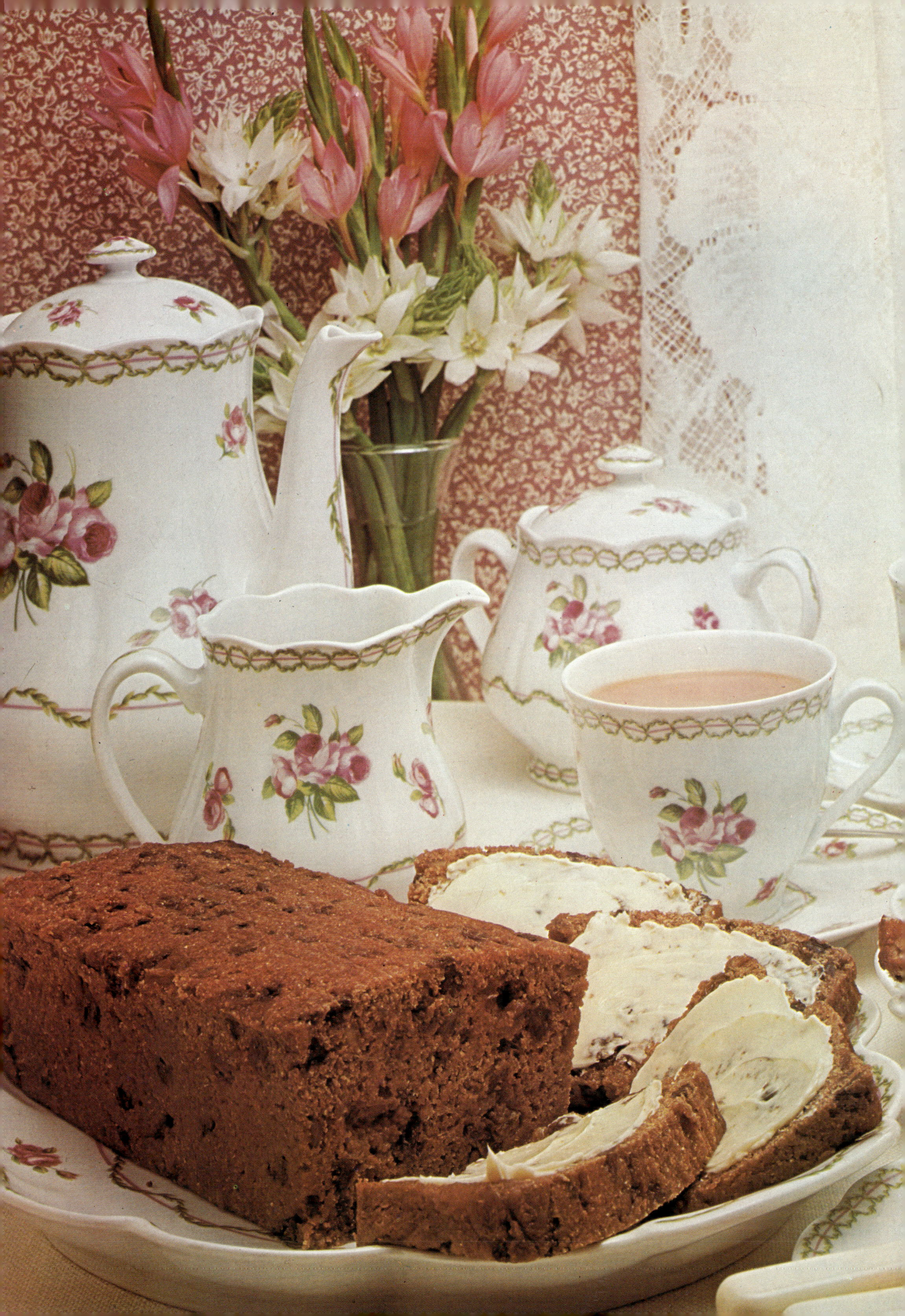

English madeleines (page 323); Yorkshire apple tart (page 281)

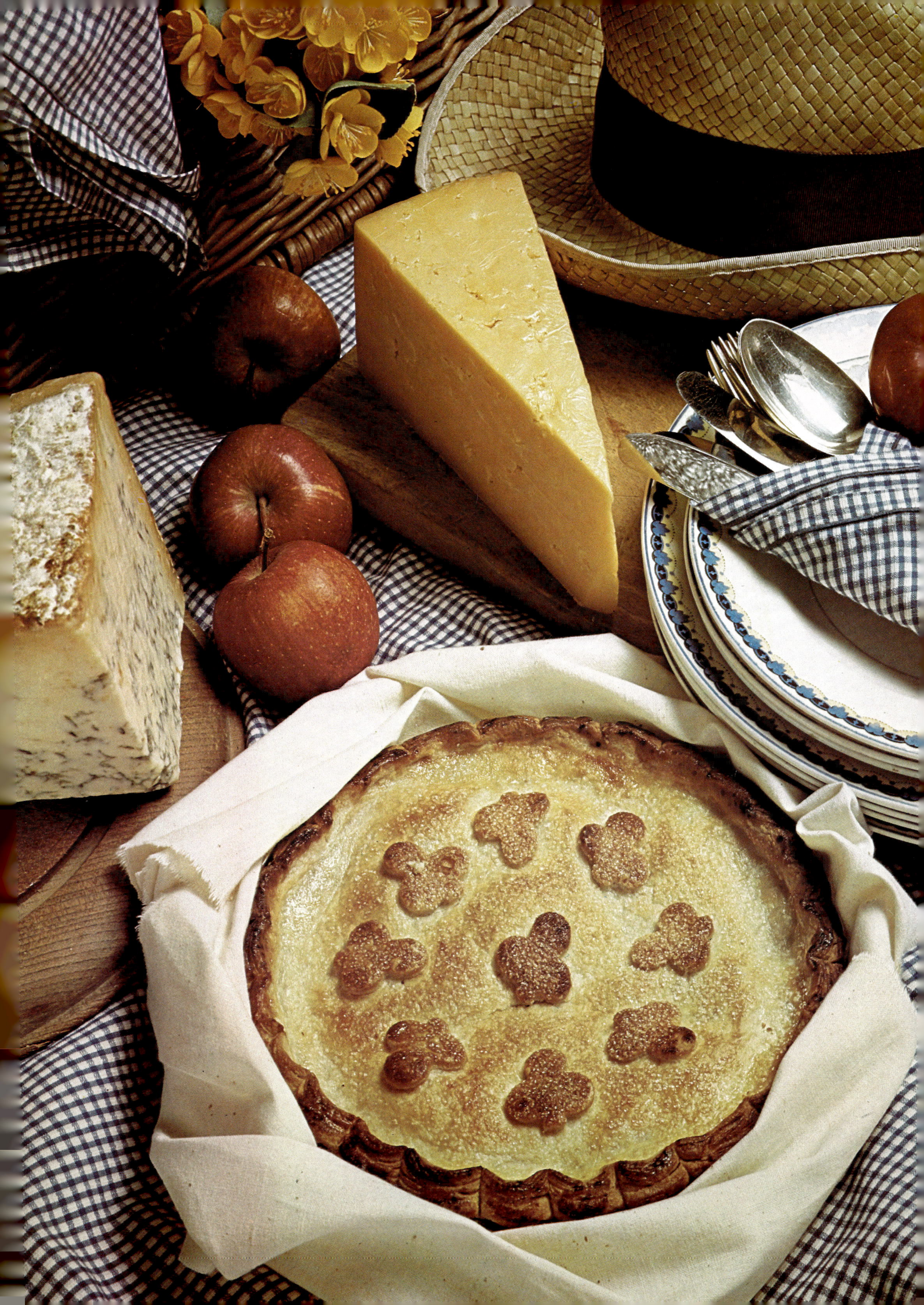

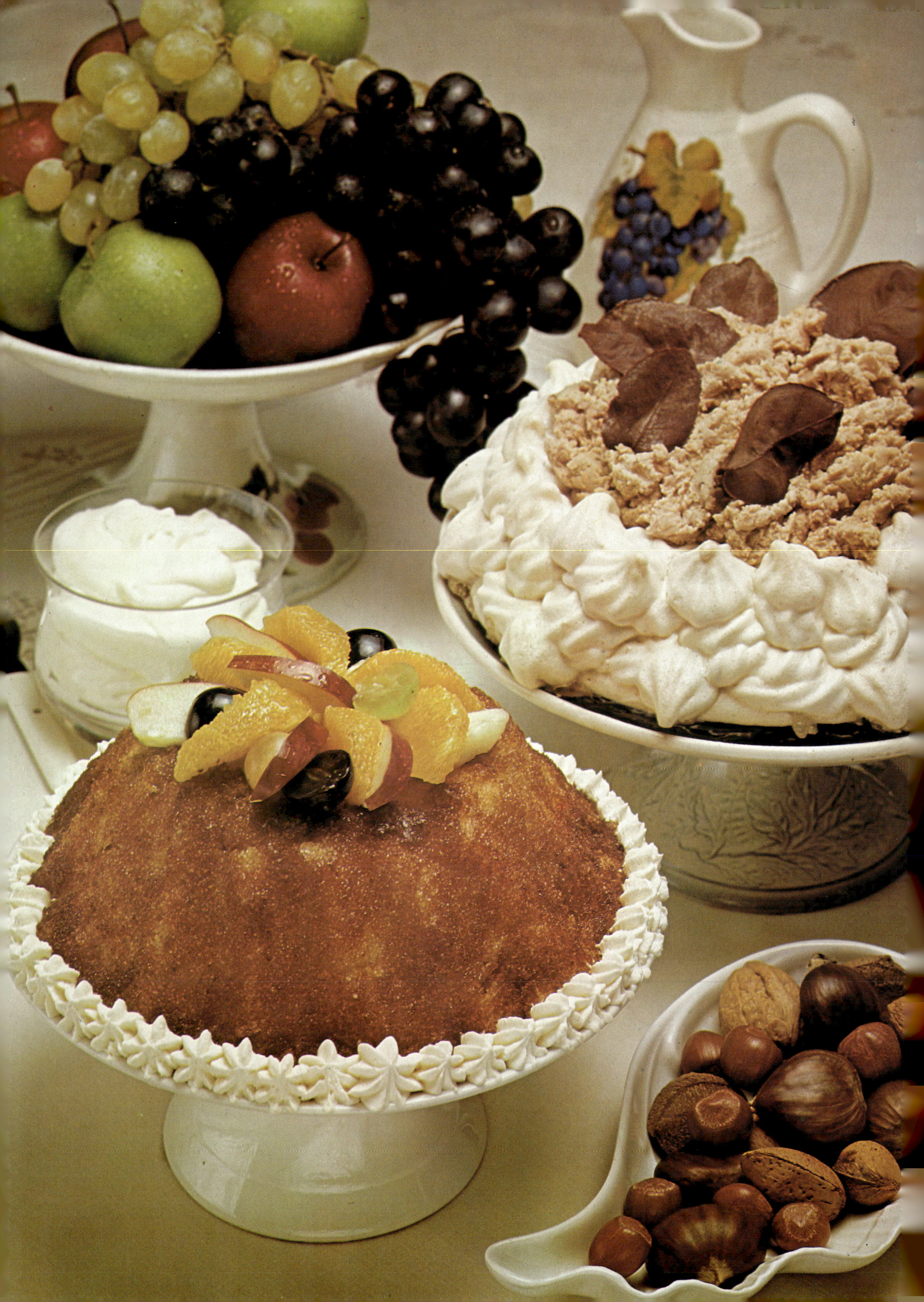

Chocolate flakes

METRIC/IMPERIAL
225g/8oz plain chocolate, broken into small pieces
2 × 15ml spoons/2 tablespoons golden syrup
50g/2oz butter
50g/2oz cornflakes

AMERICAN
8 squares semisweet chocolate, broken into small pieces
2 tablespoons light corn syrup
¼ cup butter
2 cups cornflakes

Melt the chocolate gently and stir in the syrup and butter. When the butter has melted and the mixture is well blended, remove from the heat. Fold in the cornflakes. Spoon the mixture into 12 paper cases and leave to set.
Makes 12

Shrewsbury biscuits (cookies)

METRIC/IMPERIAL
175g/6oz butter
175g/6oz sugar
few drops of vanilla essence
350g/12oz plain flour
1 egg, lightly beaten

AMERICAN
¾ cup butter
¾ cup sugar
few drops of vanilla extract
3 cups all-purpose flour
1 egg, lightly beaten

Cream the butter, sugar and vanilla together until the mixture is light and fluffy. Gradually sift in the flour and fold into the creamed butter mixture. Add enough of the egg to bind the mixture and knead well. If the dough is too dry to handle, add a little milk.

Roll out the dough to about 5mm/¼ inch thick. Cut into rounds, fingers (bars) or decorative shapes and place on baking sheets. Bake in a preheated moderate oven (180°C/350°F, Gas Mark 4) for 12 to 15 minutes or until light golden brown.

Allow to cool slightly on the baking sheets, then transfer to wire racks to cool completely.
Makes about 60

Fruit savarin (page 299) and Hazelnut and chestnut meringue (page 295)

Shortbread

METRIC/IMPERIAL
150g/5oz plain flour
pinch of salt
25g/1oz ground rice
50g/2oz caster sugar
100g/4oz butter, chilled
sugar for sprinkling

AMERICAN
1¼ cups all-purpose flour
pinch of salt
¼ cup rice flour
¼ cup sugar
½ cup butter, chilled
sugar for sprinkling

Sift the flour, salt and ground rice (rice flour) into a mixing bowl. Stir in the sugar. Rub in the butter until the mixture resembles breadcrumbs and knead until well mixed. Chill the dough for 30 minutes.

Press the dough out to an 18cm/7 inch diameter round and place on a greased baking sheet. Flute the edge. Prick all over with a fork, then mark into 8 triangular portions. Chill for 30 minutes.

Bake in a preheated moderate oven (160°C/325°F, Gas Mark 3) for 40 to 45 minutes or until pale golden. Allow to cool slightly on the baking sheet, then transfer to a wire rack to cool completely. Sprinkle with sugar. Break into the portions to serve.
Makes 8

Eclairs

METRIC/IMPERIAL
65g/2½oz quantity choux pastry★
150ml/¼ pint double cream
1 × 15ml spoon/
1 tablespoon caster sugar
Chocolate icing:
50g/2oz plain cooking chocolate
15g/½oz butter
2 × 15ml spoons/
2 tablespoons water
175g/6oz icing sugar

AMERICAN
10 tablespoon quantity choux pastry★
⅔ cup whipping cream
1 tablespoon sugar
Chocolate icing:
2 squares semisweet chocolate
1 tablespoon butter
2 tablespoons water
1⅓ cups confectioners' sugar

Pipe the pastry dough onto a dampened baking sheet in fingers about 7.5cm/3 inches long. Allow room between each finger for expansion. Bake in a preheated moderately hot oven (200°C/400°F, Gas Mark 6) for 25 to 30 minutes or until well risen and crisp.

Remove from the oven and slit the side of each éclair to allow the steam to escape. Cool on a wire rack.

To make the icing, break the chocolate into small pieces and put into a heavy-based saucepan with the butter and 1 × 15ml spoon/1 tablespoon of the water. Melt over a gentle heat, stirring frequently. Remove from the heat and gradually sift in the icing (confectioners') sugar, beating well. If the icing is too thick, add the rest of the water.

Whip the cream with the sugar until thick. Fill each éclair with the cream, then ice the tops with the chocolate icing. Allow to set for a few minutes, then serve.
Makes about 8

Chocolate chip cookies

METRIC/IMPERIAL
225g/8oz self-raising flour
pinch of salt
150g/5oz butter
100g/4oz caster sugar
1 egg, lightly beaten
50g/2oz plain chocolate, grated

AMERICAN
2 cups self-rising flour
pinch of salt
$\frac{2}{3}$ cup butter
$\frac{1}{2}$ cup sugar
1 egg, lightly beaten
$\frac{1}{3}$ cup chocolate chips

Sift the flour and salt into a mixing bowl. Cut the butter into the flour and rub in until the mixture resembles breadcrumbs. Stir in the sugar, then mix to a stiff dough with the egg. Fold in the chocolate, kneading it in to distribute evenly. Chill the dough for 30 minutes.

Roll out the dough, then cut into 5cm/2 inch rounds or decorative shapes. Place on greased baking sheets, well spaced apart. Prick with a fork. Bake in a preheated moderate oven (180°C/350°F, Gas Mark 4) for 10 to 12 minutes or until golden.

Cool on a wire rack.
Makes about 30

Icebox cookies

METRIC/IMPERIAL
225g/8oz plain flour
4 × 15ml spoons/
 4 tablespoons semolina
175g/6oz butter or margarine
150g/5oz sugar
1 egg, separated
2 × 15ml spoons/
 2 tablespoons water
beaten egg white to glaze
walnut halves to decorate

AMERICAN
2 cups all-purpose flour
4 tablespoons cream of wheat
$\frac{3}{4}$ cup butter or margarine
$\frac{2}{3}$ cup sugar
1 egg, separated
2 tablespoons water
beaten egg white to glaze
walnut halves to decorate

Sift the flour into a mixing bowl. Stir in the semolina (cream of wheat). Rub in the butter or margarine until the mixture resembles breadcrumbs. Stir in the sugar. Beat the egg yolk with the water and use to bind the dry ingredients to a stiff dough.

Divide the dough in half and shape each piece into a roll about 5cm/2 inches in diameter. Chill for 3 hours.

Cut off as many thin slices from a roll as you wish to make biscuits (cookies). Return any remaining dough to the refrigerator and store until required.

Arrange the dough slices on a greased baking sheet and brush with beaten egg white. Top each with a piece of walnut or walnut half. Bake in a preheated moderately hot oven (200°C/400°F, Gas Mark 6) for 8 to 10 minutes or until golden. Cool on a wire rack.
Makes about 5 dozen

Almond slices

METRIC/IMPERIAL
175g/6oz quantity shortcrust pastry★ (made with 175g/6oz flour, etc.)
2 × 15ml spoons/ 2 tablespoons jam
100g/4oz sugar
100g/4oz icing sugar
100g/4oz ground almonds
3 × 15ml spoons/ 3 tablespoons semolina
1 egg
1 egg white
1 × 5ml spoon/1 teaspoon almond essence
2 × 15ml spoons/ 2 tablespoons blanched halved almonds

AMERICAN
1½ cup quantity pie pastry★ (made with 1½ cups flour, etc.)
2 tablespoons jam
½ cup sugar
⅔ cup confectioners' sugar
1 cup ground almonds
3 tablespoons cream of wheat
1 egg
1 egg white
1 teaspoon almond extract
2 tablespoons blanched halved almonds

Divide the pastry dough in half and roll out each piece to a strip about 30 × 10cm/12 × 4 inches. Transfer to a greased baking sheet and spread each piece with jam. If you like, crimp the edges for a decorative effect.

Mix together the sugar, icing (confectioners') sugar, ground almonds and semolina (cream of wheat). Stir in the egg, egg white and almond essence (extract) and mix well. Spread over the pastry strips and decorate with the almond halves.

Bake in a preheated moderately hot oven (200°C/ 400°F, Gas Mark 6) for 20 to 25 minutes or until pale golden brown. Cool before cutting into fingers (bars).
Makes 24

Coconut crispies

METRIC/IMPERIAL
175g/6oz self-raising flour
225g/8oz sugar
1 egg, lightly beaten
100g/4oz butter, melted
150g/5oz desiccated coconut

AMERICAN
1½ cups self-rising flour
1 cup sugar
1 egg, lightly beaten
½ cup butter, melted
1⅔ cups shredded coconut

Sift the flour into a mixing bowl. Stir in the sugar, then beat in the egg and melted butter. Form into small balls and roll in the coconut to coat well. Arrange the balls on baking sheets, well spaced apart.

Bake in a preheated moderate oven (180°C/350°F, Gas Mark 4) for 10 to 15 minutes or until golden brown. Cool on a wire rack.
Makes about 32

Lemon butter biscuits (cookies)

METRIC/IMPERIAL
175g/6oz butter
100g/4oz plus 2 × 15ml spoons/2 tablespoons sugar
2 × 5ml spoons/2 teaspoons finely grated lemon rind
225g/8oz plain flour
pinch of salt

AMERICAN
¾ cup butter
½ cup plus 2 tablespoons sugar
2 teaspoons finely grated lemon rind
2 cups all-purpose flour
pinch of salt

Cream the butter and 100g/4oz/½ cup of the sugar together until the mixture is light and fluffy. Beat in the lemon rind. Sift in the flour and salt and mix together well to form a dough.

Divide the dough in half and shape each portion into a sausage shape. Roll in the remaining sugar.

Thinly slice the dough and arrange the slices on baking sheets. Bake in a preheated moderate oven (180°C/350°F, Gas Mark 4) for 15 to 20 minutes or until golden brown. Cool on a wire rack.
Makes about 32

Meringues

METRIC/IMPERIAL
2 large egg whites
150g/5oz caster sugar
300ml/½ pint double cream

AMERICAN
2 large egg whites
⅔ cup sugar
1¼ cups whipping cream

Beat the egg whites until stiff. Add 4 × 5ml spoons/4 teaspoons of the sugar and continue beating for 1 minute or until the mixture is very stiff and glossy. Carefully fold in the remaining sugar.

Spoon or pipe the meringue mixture in 8 mounds on a baking sheet lined with lightly oiled greaseproof paper or non-stick parchment. Dry out in a preheated very cool oven (120°C/250°F, Gas Mark ½) for 1¼ to 1½ hours, or until the meringues are set and light beige in colour.

Remove from the oven and allow to cool on the baking sheet.

Whip the cream until thick. Remove the meringues from the baking sheet and sandwich together pairs of meringues with the cream.
Makes 4

Cherry boats

METRIC/IMPERIAL
Pastry:
*175g/6oz plain flour
pinch of salt
75g/3oz margarine
25g/1oz caster sugar
1 egg yolk
water*
Filling:
*225g/8oz black cherries, stoned
4 × 15ml spoons/ 4 tablespoons redcurrant jelly
1 × 15ml spoon/ 1 tablespoon fruit juice*

AMERICAN
Pastry:
*1½ cups all-purpose flour
pinch of salt
⅓ cup margarine
2 tablespoons sugar
1 egg yolk
water*
Filling:
*½lb black cherries, pitted
4 tablespoons redcurrant jelly
1 tablespoon fruit juice*

Sift together the flour and salt. Cut the margarine into the flour and rub in until the mixture resembles fine breadcrumbs. Stir in the sugar. Add the egg yolk and enough water to bind to a stiff dough. Roll out the pastry on a floured surface and use to line twelve 10 × 5cm/4 × 2 inch boat tins. Prick well and bake blind in a preheated moderately hot oven (190°C/375°F, Gas Mark 5) for 10 minutes. Leave to cool then remove from the tins.

Fill the pastry shells with the cherries. Melt the jelly with the fruit juice over a very low heat and carefully brush over the cherries. Serve cold with whipped cream, if liked.
Makes 12

Butterscotch brownies

METRIC/IMPERIAL
*100g/4oz butter or margarine
100g/4oz soft brown sugar
2 eggs
1 × 5ml spoon/1 teaspoon vanilla essence
75g/3oz self-raising flour
50g/2oz walnuts, chopped*

AMERICAN
*½ cup butter or margarine
⅔ cup brown sugar
2 eggs
1 teaspoon vanilla extract
¾ cup self-rising flour
½ cup chopped walnuts*

Cream the butter or margarine and sugar together until the mixture is light and fluffy. Gradually beat in the eggs and vanilla. Sift in the flour and fold in with the walnuts.

Pour into a greased 18cm/7 inch square cake tin. Bake in a preheated moderate oven (160°C/325°F, Gas Mark 3) for 35 to 45 minutes or until well risen and firm to the touch.

Cool in the tin before cutting into squares.
Makes about 12

Maids of honour

METRIC/IMPERIAL
175g/6oz quantity rich shortcrust pastry★
4 × 15ml spoons/ 4 tablespoons raspberry jam
50g/2oz butter
50g/2oz sugar
1 × 2.5ml spoon/½ teaspoon vanilla essence
1 egg
50g/2oz self-raising flour

AMERICAN
1½ cup quantity rich pie pastry★
4 tablespoons raspberry jam
¼ cup butter
¼ cup sugar
½ teaspoon vanilla extract
1 egg
½ cup self-rising flour

Roll out the pastry dough to about 5mm/¼ inch thick. Cut out 12 rounds about 7.5cm/3 inches in diameter and use to line 12 greased patty (muffin) tins. Put a spoonful of jam into each pastry case.

Cream the butter and sugar together until the mixture is light and fluffy. Beat in the vanilla and egg, then sift in the flour. Fold together well. Spoon into the pastry cases over the jam.

Bake in a preheated moderate oven (180°C/350°F, Gas Mark 4) for 20 to 25 minutes or until set and golden brown.
Makes 12

Cream horns

METRIC/IMPERIAL
350g/12oz quantity puff pastry★ (made with 350g/12oz flour, etc.)
1 egg, lightly beaten
3 × 15ml spoons/ 3 tablespoons sugar
100g/4oz jam
Filling:
300ml/½ pint double cream
1 × 5ml spoon/1 teaspoon vanilla essence
1 × 15ml spoon/ 1 tablespoon icing sugar

AMERICAN
3 cup quantity puff pastry★ (made with 3 cups flour, etc.)
1 egg, lightly beaten
3 tablespoons sugar
⅓ cup jam
Filling:
1¼ cups heavy cream
1 teaspoon vanilla extract
1 tablespoon confectioners' sugar

Roll out the pastry dough to about 5mm/¼ inch thick and cut 12 strips 2.5cm/1 inch wide. Brush one side of each strip with water and wind around 12 greased cream horn moulds, overlapping the dough slightly. Arrange the moulds on a dampened baking sheet. Brush the dough with the egg and sprinkle with sugar.

Bake in a preheated hot oven (230°C/450°F, Gas Mark 8) for 20 to 25 minutes or until puffed up and golden brown. Remove from the oven and allow to cool.

When the pastry horns are cold, carefully remove the moulds. Put a little of the jam into the tip of each horn.

Beat together the ingredients for the filling until the mixture is thick. Fill the horns and serve.
Makes 12

BREADS & TEABREADS

Barm brack

METRIC/IMPERIAL
350g/12oz mixed dried fruit
200g/7oz brown sugar
450ml/¾ pint cold strong tea
275g/10oz self-raising flour
1 egg, lightly beaten

AMERICAN
2 cups mixed dried fruit
1 cup plus 2 tablespoons brown sugar
2 cups cold strong tea
2½ cups self-rising flour
1 egg, lightly beaten

Put the dried fruit in a mixing bowl. Sprinkle with the sugar and pour over the tea. Leave to soak overnight.

Sift the flour into a mixing bowl. Beat in the egg, then gradually fold in the dried fruit mixture. Spoon into a well-lined 1kg/2lb/9 × 5 × 3 inch loaf tin. Bake in a preheated moderate oven (180°C/350°F, Gas Mark 4) for 1½ hours or until a skewer inserted into the centre comes out clean. Cool on a wire rack.

Serve sliced with butter.
Makes one 1kg/2lb/9 × 5 × 3 inch loaf

Apricot and walnut bread

METRIC/IMPERIAL
15g/½oz fresh yeast
150ml/¼ pint lukewarm water
225g/8oz plain flour
1 × 5ml spoon/1 teaspoon salt
25g/1oz sugar
25g/1oz butter or lard
100g/4oz dried apricots, chopped
50g/2oz walnuts, chopped
Topping:
25g/1oz butter
25g/1oz sugar
40g/1½oz plain flour

AMERICAN
½ cake compressed yeast
⅔ cup lukewarm water
2 cups all-purpose flour
1 teaspoon salt
2 tablespoons sugar
2 tablespoons butter or shortening
⅔ cup chopped dried apricots
½ cup chopped walnuts
Topping:
2 tablespoons butter
2 tablespoons sugar
6 tablespoons all-purpose flour

Cream the yeast with a little of the water, then stir in the remaining water.

Sift the flour and salt into a mixing bowl and stir in the sugar. Rub in the butter or lard (shortening) until the mixture resembles breadcrumbs, then stir in the apricots and walnuts. Make a well in the centre and add the yeast mixture. Mix to a soft scone- (biscuit-) like dough.

Put the dough in a greased 1kg/2lb/9 × 5 × 3 inch loaf tin, filling it two-thirds full. Leave to rise in a warm place for 30 minutes or until the dough rises to the top of the tin.

Rub together the ingredients for the topping and sprinkle over the loaf. Bake in a preheated moderately hot oven (200°C/400°F, Gas Mark 6) for 40 to 45 minutes. Serve warm, sliced with butter.
Makes one 1kg/2lb/9 × 5 × 3 inch loaf.

Banana walnut bread

METRIC/IMPERIAL
50g/2oz butter
150g/5oz sugar
3 eggs
4 bananas, mashed
225g/8oz self-raising flour
pinch of salt
1 × 2.5ml spoon/½ teaspoon ground cinnamon
100g/4oz walnuts, chopped

AMERICAN
¼ cup butter
⅔ cup sugar
3 eggs
4 bananas, mashed
2 cups self-rising flour
pinch of salt
½ teaspoon ground cinnamon
1 cup chopped walnuts

Cream the butter and sugar together until the mixture is light and fluffy. Gradually beat in the eggs, then the bananas. Sift in the flour, salt and cinnamon and fold in with the walnuts.

Spoon into a greased 0.5kg/1lb/4½ × 2½ × 1½ inch loaf tin. Bake in a preheated moderate oven (180°C/350°F, Gas Mark 4) for 1 hour or until a skewer inserted into the centre comes out clean. Cool in the tin. Serve sliced with butter.

Makes one 0.5kg/1lb/4½ × 2½ × 1½ inch loaf

Orange teabread

METRIC/IMPERIAL
50g/2oz butter
175g/6oz sugar
1 egg
grated rind of ½ orange
2 × 15ml spoons/ 2 tablespoons orange juice
2 × 15ml spoons/ 2 tablespoons milk
225g/8oz plain flour
2.5 × 5ml spoons/ 2½ teaspoons baking powder
pinch of salt

AMERICAN
¼ cup butter
¾ cup sugar
1 egg
grated rind of ½ orange
2 tablespoons orange juice
2 tablespoons milk
2 cups all-purpose flour
2½ teaspoons baking powder
pinch of salt

Cream the butter and sugar together until the mixture is light and fluffy. Beat in the egg, then the orange rind and juice. Beat in the milk. Sift in the flour, baking powder and salt and fold into the orange mixture.

Spoon into a greased and lined 20 × 10cm/8 × 4 inch loaf tin. Bake in a preheated moderately hot oven (190°C/375°F, Gas Mark 5) for 40 to 50 minutes or until a skewer inserted into the centre comes out clean.

Cool on a wire rack, then store the cake in an airtight tin. Keep for 1 to 2 days before eating. Serve sliced with butter.

Makes one 20 × 10cm/8 × 4 inch loaf

Lardy cake

METRIC/IMPERIAL	AMERICAN
15g/½oz fresh yeast	½ cake compressed yeast
300ml/½ pint lukewarm water	1¼ cups lukewarm water
0.5kg/1lb plain flour	4 cups all-purpose flour
2 × 5ml spoons/2 teaspoons salt	2 teaspoons salt
100g/4oz lard, cut into pieces	½ cup shortening, cut into pieces
4 × 15ml spoons/ 4 tablespoons sugar	4 tablespoons sugar
1 × 5ml spoon/1 teaspoon mixed spice	1 teaspoon apple pie spice

Cream the yeast with a little of the water, then stir in the remaining water.

Sift the flour and salt into a mixing bowl. Make a well in the centre, stir in the yeast liquid and mix to a dough. Knead until the dough is smooth and elastic. Put in a lightly greased polythene (plastic) bag and leave to rise in a warm place for 1½ hours.

Roll out the dough to a large oblong. Using half the lard (shortening), cover the top two-thirds of the dough with pieces of fat. Sprinkle over half the sugar and spice. Fold up the bottom third, then fold down the top third and turn so that an open edge faces you. Roll out again into an oblong and repeat the process.

Roll out the dough into a 1cm/½ inch thick oval and transfer to a greased baking sheet. Leave to rise in a warm place for 30 minutes.

Bake in a preheated hot oven (220°C/425°F, Gas Mark 7) for 30 minutes. Serve warm.
Makes one oval cake

Bran teabread

METRIC/IMPERIAL	AMERICAN
100g/4oz bran	¼lb bran
100g/4oz soft brown sugar	⅔ cup brown sugar
225g/8oz mixed dried fruit	1⅓ cups mixed dried fruit
300ml/½ pint milk	1¼ cups milk
175g/6oz self-raising flour, sifted	1½ cups self-rising flour, sifted

Mix together the bran, sugar and dried fruit in a bowl. Stir in the milk and stand for 1 hour. Add the flour and transfer the mixture to a greased 1kg/2lb/9 × 5 × 3 inch loaf tin. Place in a preheated moderate oven (180°C/350°F, Gas Mark 4) and bake for 1 hour or until a skewer inserted into the centre comes out clean. Serve sliced with butter.
Make one 1kg/2lb/9 × 5 × 3 inch loaf.

Date and nut bread

METRIC/IMPERIAL
350g/12oz self-raising flour
2 × 5ml spoons/2 teaspoons ground cinnamon
175g/6oz butter
175g/6oz sugar
175g/6oz walnuts, chopped
175g/6oz stoned dates, chopped
300ml/½ pint apple purée
1.5 × 5ml spoons/ 1½ teaspoons bicarbonate of soda
150ml/¼ pint warm milk
1 egg, beaten
Topping:
2 × 15ml spoons/ 2 tablespoons chopped walnuts
2 × 15ml spoons/ 2 tablespoons chopped stoned dates
2 × 5ml spoons/2 teaspoons sugar
1 × 2.5ml spoon/½ teaspoon ground cinnamon

AMERICAN
3 cups self-rising flour
2 teaspoons ground cinnamon
¾ cup butter
¾ cup sugar
1½ cups chopped walnuts
1 cup chopped pitted dates
1¼ cups applesauce
1½ teaspoons baking soda
⅔ cup warm milk
1 egg, beaten
Topping:
2 tablespoons chopped walnuts
2 tablespoons chopped pitted dates
2 teaspoons sugar
½ teaspoon ground cinnamon

Sift the flour and cinnamon into a mixing bowl. Rub in the butter until the mixture resembles breadcrumbs. Stir in the sugar, walnuts, dates and apple purée (applesauce). Dissolve the soda in the milk and stir into the mixture with the beaten egg.

Pour into a greased and lined 20cm/8 inch round cake tin. Mix together the ingredients for the topping and sprinkle over the top. Bake in a preheated moderate oven (180°C/350°F, Gas Mark 4) for 1 hour. Cover the top of the cake with foil, reduce the heat to 160°C/325°F, Gas Mark 3 and bake for a further 15 minutes. Cool on a wire rack.
Makes one 20cm/8 inch round teabread

Spicy teabread

METRIC/IMPERIAL
0.5kg/1lb self-raising flour
1 × 5ml spoon/1 teaspoon salt
1 × 2.5ml spoon/½ teaspoon ground cinnamon
1 × 2.5ml spoon/½ teaspoon ground cloves
1 × 2.5ml spoon/½ teaspoon grated nutmeg
175g/6oz soft brown sugar
100g/4oz butter
2½ eggs, lightly beaten
2 × 15ml spoons/ 2 tablespoons treacle
300ml/½ pint milk

AMERICAN
4 cups self-rising flour
1 teaspoon salt
½ teaspoon ground cinnamon
½ teaspoon ground cloves
½ teaspoon grated nutmeg
1 cup brown sugar
½ cup butter
2½ eggs, lightly beaten
2 tablespoons molasses
1¼ cups milk

Sift the flour, salt and spices into a mixing bowl. Stir in the sugar. Rub in the butter until the mixture resembles breadcrumbs, then stir in 2 of the beaten eggs. Add the treacle (molasses) with half the milk and beat until smooth. Gradually stir in the remaining milk.

Pour into a greased 1kg/2lb/9 × 5 × 3 inch loaf tin. Bake in a preheated moderately hot oven (190°C/375°F, Gas Mark 5) for 30 minutes.

Brush with the remaining beaten egg and bake for a further 15 to 30 minutes or until a skewer inserted into the centre comes out clean. Cool on a wire rack.

Serve sliced with butter.
Makes one 1kg/2lb/9 × 5 × 3 inch loaf

English muffins

METRIC/IMPERIAL
25g/1oz fresh yeast
6 × 15ml spoons/
 6 tablespoons lukewarm
 water
0.5kg/1lb plain flour
1 × 5ml spoon/1 teaspoon
 salt
150ml/¼ pint lukewarm
 milk
1 egg, lightly beaten
25g/1oz butter, melted

AMERICAN
1 cake compressed yeast
6 tablespoons lukewarm
 water
4 cups all-purpose flour
1 teaspoon salt
⅔ cup lukewarm milk
1 egg, lightly beaten
2 tablespoons butter, melted

Cream the yeast and the lukewarm water together.
 Sift the flour and salt into a mixing bowl. Add the yeast liquid, milk, egg and melted butter and mix to a soft dough. Knead for about 10 minutes or until the dough is smooth and elastic. Put in a polythene (plastic) bag and leave to rise in a warm place for 1½ hours.
 Knead the dough lightly and roll out to about 1cm/½ inch thick. Cut out 12 rounds, 8.5cm/3½ inches in diameter. Arrange on greased and floured baking sheets and sprinkle with flour. Leave to rise in a warm place until doubled in size.
 Bake in a preheated hot oven (230°C/450°F, Gas Mark 8) for 5 minutes. Turn the muffins over and bake for a further 5 minutes.
 To serve, toast on both sides, pull apart and butter.
Makes 12

Bran muffins

METRIC/IMPERIAL
200g/7oz plain flour
1 × 5ml spoon/1 teaspoon
 salt
2 × 15ml spoons/
 2 tablespoons baking
 powder
100g/4oz ready-to-eat bran
450ml/¾ pint milk
50g/2oz butter
50g/2oz sugar
2 eggs, lightly beaten

AMERICAN
1¾ cups all-purpose flour
1 teaspoon salt
2 tablespoons baking powder
1 cup ready-to-eat bran
2 cups milk
¼ cup butter
¼ cup sugar
2 eggs, lightly beaten

Sift the flour, salt and baking powder into a mixing bowl. Soak the bran in the milk for 5 minutes. Meanwhile, cream the butter and sugar together until the mixture is light and fluffy. Gradually beat in the eggs. Add the egg mixture and bran mixture to the flour and stir until just mixed.
 Spoon into 20 greased deep muffin tins (about 6cm/2½ inch diameter), filling the tins only two-thirds full. Bake in a preheated moderately hot oven (200°C/400°F, Gas Mark 6) for 25 minutes or until well browned.
 Serve warm with butter.
Makes 20

Apple muffins

METRIC/IMPERIAL
225g/8oz self-raising flour
pinch of salt
50g/2oz brown sugar
1 × 2.5ml spoon/½ teaspoon
 ground cinnamon
2 eggs, lightly beaten
50g/2oz butter, melted
150ml/¼ pint milk
2 dessert apples, peeled,
 cored and grated

AMERICAN
2 cups self-rising flour
pinch of salt
⅓ cup brown sugar
½ teaspoon ground cinnamon
2 eggs, lightly beaten
¼ cup butter, melted
⅔ cup milk
2 dessert apples, peeled,
 cored and grated

Sift the flour, salt, sugar and cinnamon into a mixing bowl. Add the eggs, melted butter and milk and mix to a smooth batter. Fold in the grated apples. Pour into 12 greased patty (muffin) tins.
 Bake in a preheated moderately hot oven (190°C/375°F, Gas Mark 5) for 20 to 25 minutes or until cooked. Serve warm.
Makes 12

Buttermilk scones (biscuits)

METRIC/IMPERIAL
225g/8oz plain flour
1 × 5ml spoon/1 teaspoon
 bicarbonate of soda
1 × 5ml spoon/1 teaspoon
 cream of tartar
25g/1oz butter
150ml/¼ pint buttermilk

AMERICAN
2 cups all-purpose flour
1 teaspoon baking soda
1 teaspoon cream of tartar
2 tablespoons butter
⅔ cup buttermilk

Sift the flour, soda and cream of tartar into a mixing bowl. Rub in the butter, then gradually stir in the buttermilk to make a soft dough.
 Roll out the dough to about 2cm/¾ inch thick and cut into 5cm/2 inch rounds. Arrange on a floured baking sheet.
 Bake in a preheated hot oven (220°C/425°F, Gas Mark 7) for 10 minutes or until well risen and golden. Allow to cool slightly before serving warm, or serve cold.
Makes about 12

Griddle scones (biscuits)

METRIC/IMPERIAL
100g/4oz self-raising flour
pinch of salt
pinch of bicarbonate of soda
3 × 15ml spoons/
 3 tablespoons sugar
150ml/¼ pint buttermilk
1 egg, lightly beaten
2 × 5ml spoons/2 teaspoons
 melted butter

AMERICAN
1 cup self-rising flour
pinch of salt
pinch of baking soda
3 tablespoons sugar
⅔ cup buttermilk
1 egg, lightly beaten
2 teaspoons melted butter

Sift the flour, salt, soda and sugar into a mixing bowl. Add the buttermilk, egg and melted butter and mix to a batter.

Heat a lightly greased griddle or heavy frying pan (skillet). Drop spoonsful of the batter onto the griddle, well spaced apart, and cook until the tops are bubbly and the undersides golden brown. Turn over and brown the other sides.

Serve warm or cold.
Makes about 15

Treacle scones (molasses biscuits)

METRIC/IMPERIAL
225g/8oz plain flour
1 × 5ml spoon/1 teaspoon
 cream of tartar
1 × 5ml spoon/1 teaspoon
 bicarbonate of soda
pinch of salt
25g/1oz butter
2.5 × 15ml spoons/
 2½ tablespoons treacle
4 × 15ml spoons/
 4 tablespoons milk

AMERICAN
2 cups all-purpose flour
1 teaspoon cream of tartar
1 teaspoon baking soda
pinch of salt
2 tablespoons butter
2½ tablespoons molasses
4 tablespoons milk

Sift the flour, cream of tartar, soda and salt into a mixing bowl. Put the butter and treacle (molasses) in a saucepan and heat gently until the butter has melted. Add to the dry ingredients with the milk and knead gently to a soft dough.

Roll out the dough to about 2.5cm/1 inch thick and cut out about 8 rounds 5cm/2 inches in diameter. Arrange the rounds on a baking sheet.

Bake in a preheated moderately hot oven (200°C/400°F, Gas Mark 6) for 10 to 15 minutes or until risen and golden brown. Serve warm.
Makes about 8

Cheese scones (biscuits)

METRIC/IMPERIAL
225g/8oz self-raising flour
1 × 5ml spoon/1 teaspoon baking powder
pinch of salt
1 × 5ml spoon/1 teaspoon dry mustard
40g/1½oz butter
50g/2oz Cheddar cheese, grated
about 150ml/¼ pint milk

AMERICAN
2 cups self-rising flour
1 teaspoon baking powder
pinch of salt
1 teaspoon dry mustard
3 tablespoons butter
½ cup grated Cheddar cheese
about ⅔ cup milk

Sift the flour, baking powder, salt and mustard into a mixing bowl. Rub in the butter until the mixture resembles breadcrumbs. Stir in the cheese, then enough of the milk to give a soft light dough.
   Roll out the dough to about 2cm/¾ inch thick and cut out about 9 rounds with a 6cm/2½ inch cutter. Place the rounds on a baking sheet and bake in a preheated hot oven (220°C/425°F, Gas Mark 7) for 10 minutes. Cool on a wire rack.
Makes 9

Savoury teabread

METRIC/IMPERIAL
25g/1oz butter
1 small onion, peeled and finely chopped
3 celery sticks, finely chopped
0.5kg/1lb self-raising flour
pinch of salt
freshly ground black pepper
50g/2oz lard
175g/6oz cooked ham, finely chopped
150ml/¼ pint milk
1 egg, beaten

AMERICAN
2 tablespoons butter
1 small onion, peeled and finely chopped
3 celery stalks, finely chopped
4 cups self-rising flour
pinch of salt
freshly ground black pepper
¼ cup shortening
¾ cup finely chopped cooked ham
⅔ cup milk
1 egg, beaten

Melt the butter in a frying pan (skillet), add the onion and celery and cook gently for 5 minutes. Remove from the pan and allow to cool.
   Sift together the flour and salt and a little pepper. Rub in the lard (shortening), then stir in the ham and the onion and celery. Add the milk and egg and mix to a soft dough. Turn out onto a lightly floured surface and knead lightly. Shape into a rectangle and place in a well-greased 1kg/2lb/9 × 5 × 3 inch loaf tin. Bake in a preheated moderately hot oven (190°C/375°F, Gas Mark 5) for 1 hour. Cool on a wire rack for at least 15 minutes. Serve warm or cold.
Makes one 1kg/2lb/9 × 5 × 3 inch loaf.

Basic white bread

METRIC/IMPERIAL
15g/½oz fresh yeast
450ml/¾ pint lukewarm water
0.75kg/1½lb strong plain flour
1 × 15ml spoon/ 1 tablespoon salt
15g/½oz lard

AMERICAN
½ cake compressed yeast
2 cups lukewarm water
6 cups strong bread or all-purpose flour
1 tablespoon salt
1 tablespoon shortening

Cream the yeast with a little of the water, then stir in the remaining water.

Sift the flour and salt into a mixing bowl. Rub in the lard (shortening). Stir in the yeast mixture and mix to a firm dough. Turn the dough out of the bowl and knead for about 10 minutes or until smooth and elastic. Form into a ball.

Put the dough in a lightly greased polythene (plastic) bag and leave to rise in a warm place for 1½ to 2 hours or until doubled in bulk.

Knead the dough again and shape into a loaf. Place in a 1kg/2lb/9 × 5 × 3 inch loaf tin (or 2 smaller loaf tins) and leave to rise again in a warm place for about 30 minutes.

Bake in a preheated hot oven (230°C/450°F, Gas Mark 8) for 30 to 40 minutes or until well risen and golden brown. To test if the bread is cooked, knock the bottom with your knuckles: it should sound hollow. Cool on a wire rack.
Makes one 1kg/2lb/9 × 5 × 3 inch loaf

Wholemeal (wholewheat) bread: Make as for basic white bread using wholemeal (wholewheat) flour instead of plain (all-purpose) and adding 1 × 15ml spoon/1 tablespoon sugar with the salt.

Quick brown bread

METRIC/IMPERIAL
225g/8oz wholemeal flour
225g/8oz plain flour
1 × 5ml spoon/1 teaspoon salt
1 × 5ml spoon/1 teaspoon bicarbonate of soda
1 × 5ml spoon/1 teaspoon cream of tartar
150ml/¼ pint lukewarm milk
300ml/½ pint lukewarm water
1 × 15ml spoon/ 1 tablespoon golden syrup
1 × 5ml spoon/1 teaspoon vinegar

AMERICAN
2 cups wholewheat flour
2 cups all-purpose flour
1 teaspoon salt
1 teaspoon baking soda
1 teaspoon cream of tartar
⅔ cup lukewarm milk
1¼ cups lukewarm water
1 tablespoon light corn syrup
1 teaspoon vinegar

Sift the flours, salt, soda and cream of tartar into a mixing bowl. Mix together the remaining ingredients and gradually stir into the dry ingredients. Pour into a greased 1kg/2lb/9 × 5 × 3 inch loaf tin.

Bake in a preheated moderately hot oven (200°C/400°F, Gas Mark 6) for 20 minutes, then reduce the temperature to moderate (180°C/350°F, Gas Mark 4). Continue baking for 30 minutes or until the bread is cooked.
Makes one 1kg/2lb/9 × 5 × 3 inch loaf

Boiled fruit cake (page 317)

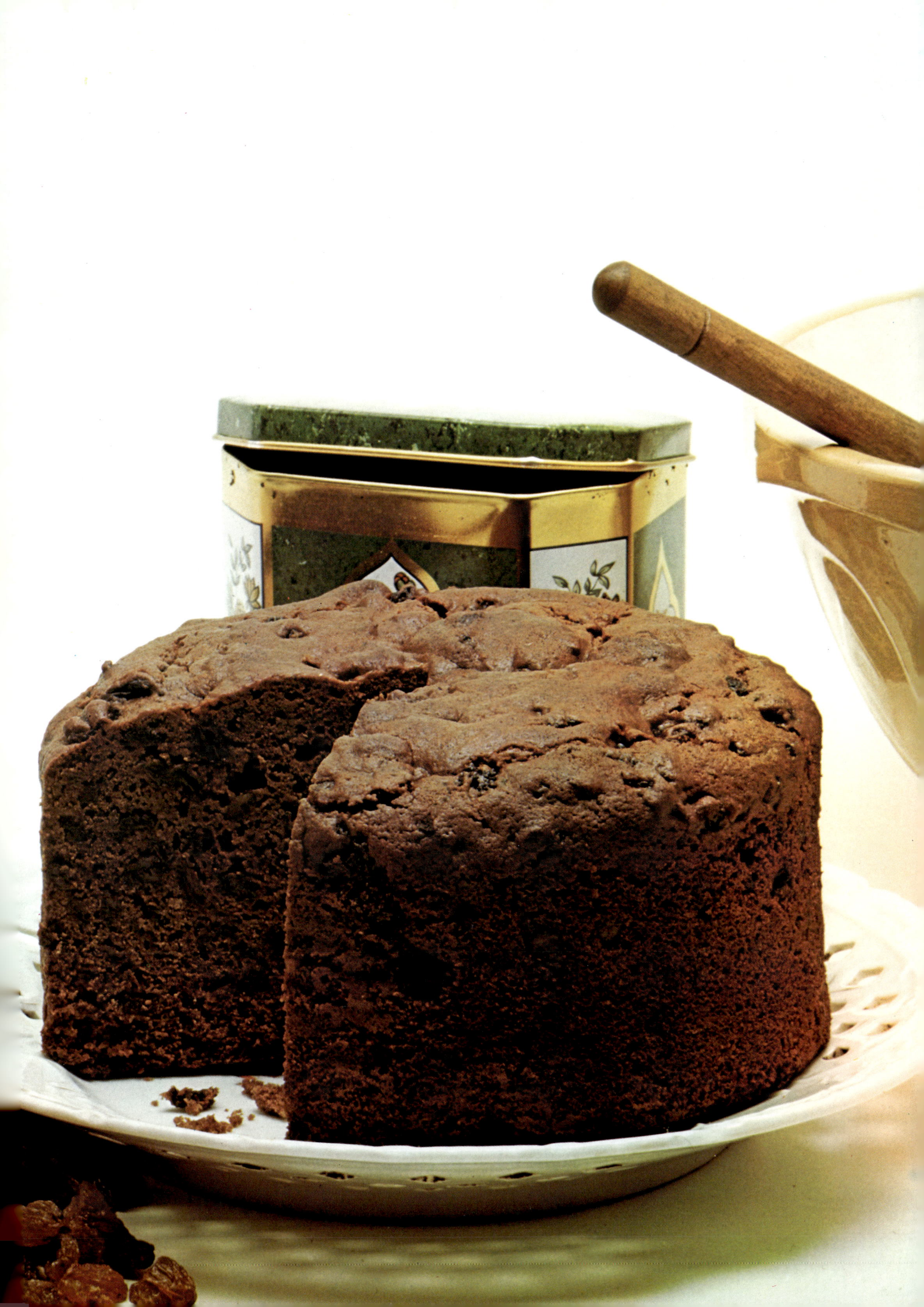

Flapjacks (page 322) and Date crunchies (page 324); Meringues (page 333)

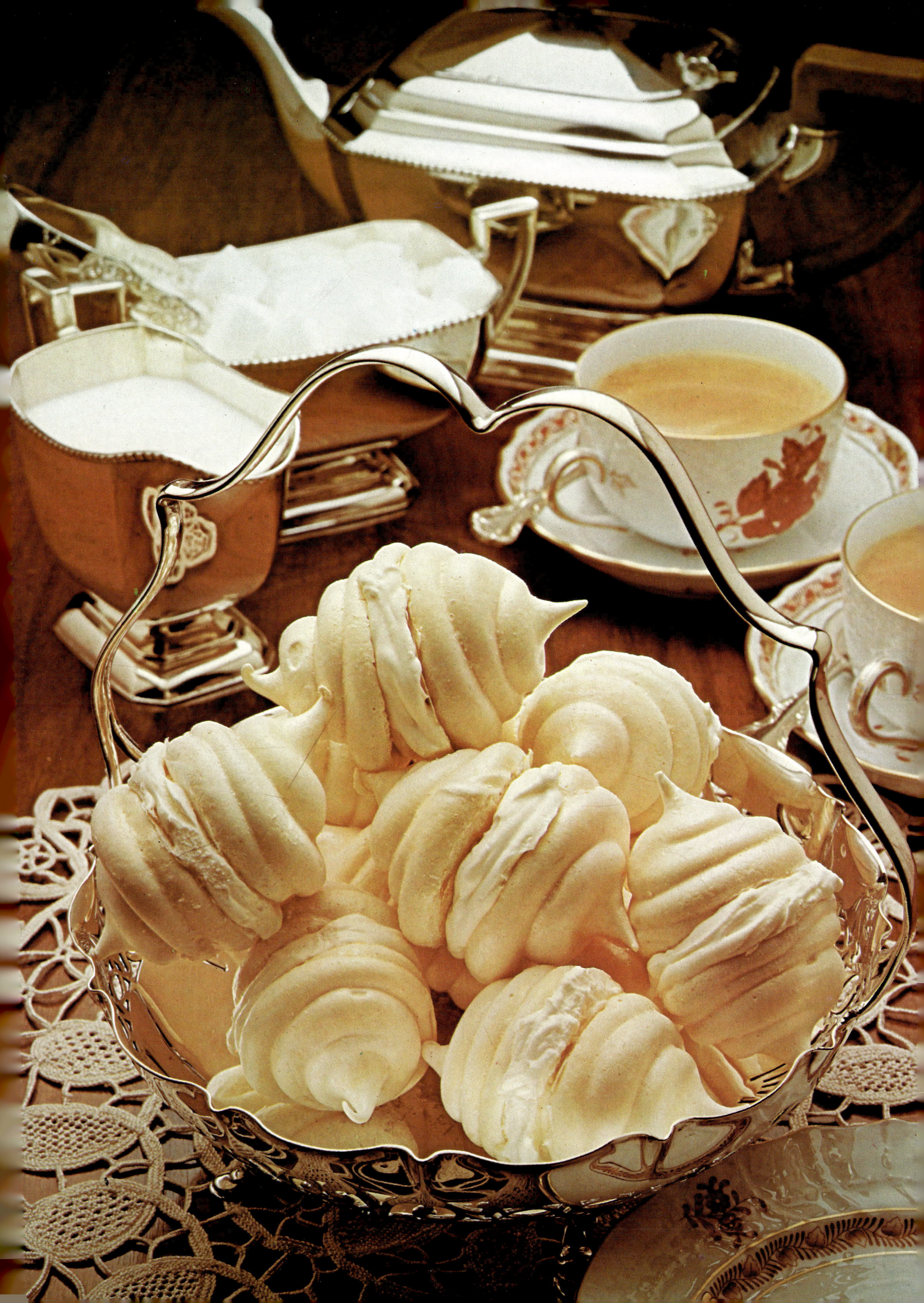

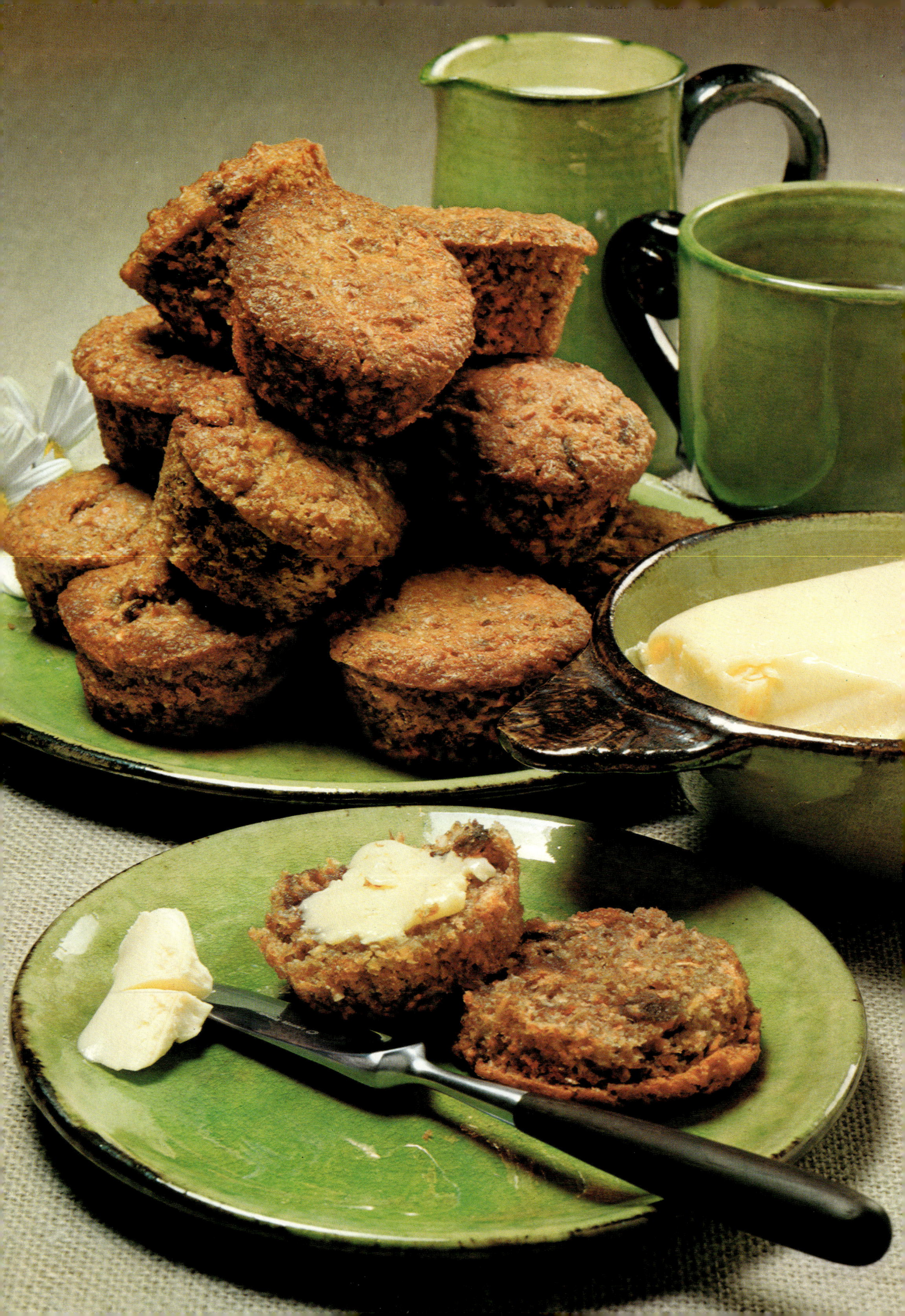

Soft milk bread

METRIC/IMPERIAL
15g/½oz fresh yeast
300ml/½ pint lukewarm milk
0.5kg/1lb plain flour
1 × 5ml spoon/1 teaspoon salt
2 × 5ml spoons/2 teaspoons sugar
50g/2oz butter, melted

AMERICAN
½ cake compressed yeast
1¼ cups lukewarm milk
4 cups all-purpose flour
1 teaspoon salt
2 teaspoons sugar
¼ cup butter, melted

Cream the yeast with a little of the milk, then stir in the remaining milk.
Sift the flour, salt and sugar into a mixing bowl. Make a well in the centre and add the melted butter and yeast mixture. Mix together to form a dough, then knead for 10 minutes or until smooth and elastic.
Put the dough in a polythene (plastic) bag and leave to rise in a warm place for 1½ hours or until doubled in bulk.
Knead the dough lightly and shape into a loaf. Put into a 1kg/2lb/9 × 5 × 3 inch loaf tin and leave to rise in a warm place for a further 45 minutes.
Bake in a preheated hot oven (230°C/450°F, Gas Mark 8) for 15 minutes, then reduce the temperature to 220°C/425°F, Gas Mark 7. Continue baking for 25 minutes or until the bread is cooked.
Makes one 1kg/2lb/9 × 5 × 3 inch loaf

Rye bread

METRIC/IMPERIAL
15g/½oz fresh yeast
450ml/¾ pint lukewarm water
0.5kg/1lb rye flour
225g/8oz plain flour
1 × 5ml spoon/1 teaspoon salt
2 × 5ml spoons/2 teaspoons brown sugar
2 × 5ml spoons/2 teaspoons oil

AMERICAN
½ cake compressed yeast
2 cups lukewarm water
4 cups rye flour
2 cups all-purpose flour
1 teaspoon salt
2 teaspoons brown sugar
2 teaspoons oil

Cream the yeast with a little of the water, then stir in the remaining water.
Sift the flours, salt and sugar into a mixing bowl. Make a well in the centre and add the yeast mixture and oil. Mix together to form a dough, then knead for 10 minutes or until the dough is smooth and elastic.
Put the dough in a polythene (plastic) bag and leave to rise in a warm place for 1½ hours.
Knead the dough again, then shape into a loaf. Put in a 1kg/2lb/9 × 5 × 3 inch loaf tin and leave to rise in a warm place for a further 45 minutes.
Bake in a preheated moderately hot oven (200°C/400°F, Gas Mark 6) for 40 minutes or until cooked. Cool on a wire rack.
Makes one 1kg/2lb/9 × 5 × 3 inch loaf

Bran muffins (page 340)

Challah (egg bread)

METRIC/IMPERIAL
15g/½oz fresh yeast
175ml/6fl oz lukewarm milk
0.5kg/1lb plain flour
1 × 5ml spoon/1 teaspoon salt
4 eggs, lightly beaten
1 × 15ml spoon/
 1 tablespoon sugar
2 × 15ml spoons/
 2 tablespoons poppy seeds

AMERICAN
½ cake compressed yeast
¾ cup lukewarm milk
4 cups all-purpose flour
1 teaspoon salt
4 eggs, lightly beaten
1 tablespoon sugar
2 tablespoons poppy seeds

Cream the yeast with a little of the milk, then stir in the remaining milk.

Sift the flour and salt into a mixing bowl. Make a well in the centre and add 3 of the eggs, the sugar and yeast mixture. Mix to a dough, then knead for 10 minutes or until smooth and elastic. Put the dough in a polythene (plastic) bag and leave to rise in a warm place for 1½ hours or until doubled in size.

Knead the dough lightly and divide into 3 portions. Roll out each portion into a sausage shape about 30cm/12inches long. Join the pieces together at one end, then plait (braid) the 3 strands. Join the other end to seal the plait (braid). Place the loaf on a baking sheet and leave to rise in a warm place for a further 45 minutes.

Brush the loaf with the remaining beaten egg and sprinkle with the poppy seeds. Bake in a preheated hot oven (220°C/425°F, Gas Mark 7) for 15 minutes, then reduce the temperature to moderately hot (190°C/375°F, Gas Mark 5). Continue baking for 20 to 30 minutes or until the loaf is cooked.
Makes 1 large loaf

Irish soda bread

METRIC/IMPERIAL
1kg/2lb plain flour
2 × 5ml spoons/2 teaspoons bicarbonate of soda
2 × 5ml spoons/2 teaspoons salt
350ml/12fl oz milk

AMERICAN
8 cups all-purpose flour
2 teaspoons baking soda
2 teaspoons salt
1½ cups milk

Sift the flour, soda and salt into a mixing bowl. Stir in the milk and mix to a soft dough. Shape the dough into a flat round and place on a baking sheet. Make a deep cut in the centre in the shape of a cross.

Bake in a preheated hot oven (220°C/425°F, Gas Mark 7) for 35 minutes or until golden brown. Cool on a wire rack.
Makes 1 large round loaf

Corn bread

METRIC/IMPERIAL
175g/6oz corn meal
100g/4oz plain flour
2 × 5ml spoons/2 teaspoons baking powder
1 × 5ml spoon/1 teaspoon salt
50g/2oz butter, melted
175ml/6fl oz milk
2 eggs, lightly beaten

AMERICAN
1 cup plus 3 tablespoons corn meal
1 cup all-purpose flour
2 teaspoons baking powder
1 teaspoon salt
¼ cup butter, melted
¾ cup milk
2 eggs, lightly beaten

Sift the corn meal, flour, baking powder and salt into a mixing bowl. Mix together the melted butter, milk and eggs. Add to the corn meal mixture and mix well. Spoon into a 20cm/8 inch square cake tin.

Bake in a preheated moderately hot oven (200°C/400°F, Gas Mark 6) for 20 to 25 minutes or until a skewer inserted into the centre of the bread comes out clean.

Serve warm, cut into squares.
Makes about 12 squares

Cheese bread

METRIC/IMPERIAL
7g/¼oz fresh yeast
150ml/¼ pint lukewarm water
225g/8oz strong plain flour
1 × 5ml spoon/1 teaspoon salt
pinch of dry mustard
pinch of freshly ground pepper
75g/3oz Cheddar cheese, grated

AMERICAN
¼ cake compressed yeast
⅔ cup lukewarm water
2 cups strong bread or all-purpose flour
1 teaspoon salt
pinch of dry mustard
pinch of freshly ground pepper
¾ cup grated Cheddar cheese

Cream the yeast with a little of the water, then stir in the remaining water.

Sift the flour, salt, mustard and pepper into a mixing bowl. Add all but 2 × 15ml spoons/2 tablespoons of the cheese and the yeast mixture and mix to a firm dough. Turn the dough out of the bowl and knead for about 10 minutes or until smooth and elastic. Form into a ball.

Put the dough into a lightly greased polythene (plastic) bag and leave to rise in a warm place for 1½ to 2 hours or until doubled in bulk.

Knead the dough lightly and form into a loaf. Place in a 0.5kg/1lb/4½ × 2½ × 1½ inch loaf tin. Leave to rise in a warm place for a further 30 minutes.

Sprinkle the reserved cheese over the loaf and bake in a preheated moderately hot oven (190°C/375°F, Gas Mark 5) for 45 minutes.
Makes one 0.5kg/1lb/4½ × 2½ × 1½ inch loaf

Baps

METRIC/IMPERIAL
15g/½oz fresh yeast
150ml/¼ pint lukewarm water
150ml/¼ pint lukewarm milk
0.5kg/1lb strong plain flour
1 × 5ml spoon/1 teaspoon salt
50g/2oz lard

AMERICAN
½ cake compressed yeast
⅔ cup lukewarm water
⅔ cup lukewarm milk
4 cups strong bread or all-purpose flour
1 teaspoon salt
¼ cup shortening

Cream the yeast with a little of the lukewarm water, then stir in the remaining water and milk.

Sift the flour and salt into a mixing bowl. Rub in the lard (shortening) until the mixture resembles breadcrumbs. Make a well in the centre and gradually stir in the yeast mixture to form a firm dough.

Turn the dough out of the bowl and knead for 5 minutes. Place in a lightly greased polythene (plastic) bag and leave to rise in a warm place for 1½ hours or until doubled in size.

Divide the dough into 16 portions and shape each into a ball. Roll out each ball until it is about 2.5cm/1 inch thick and arrange on a floured baking sheet. Sprinkle the tops of the baps with flour. Leave to rise in a warm place for a further 45 minutes.

Bake in a preheated moderately hot oven (200°C/400°F, Gas Mark 6) for 15 to 20 minutes or until golden brown. Cool on a wire rack.
Makes 16

Jam doughnuts

METRIC/IMPERIAL
15g/½oz fresh yeast
6 × 15ml spoons/6 tablespoons lukewarm milk
225g/8oz plain flour
1 × 2.5ml spoon/½ teaspoon salt
25g/1oz butter or margarine
1 egg, lightly beaten
jam
vegetable oil for deep frying
50g/2oz sugar
1 × 2.5ml spoon/½ teaspoon ground cinnamon

AMERICAN
½ cake compressed yeast
6 tablespoons lukewarm milk
2 cups all-purpose flour
½ teaspoon salt
2 tablespoons butter or margarine
1 egg, lightly beaten
jam
vegetable oil for deep frying
¼ cup sugar
½ teaspoon ground cinnamon

Cream the yeast and the lukewarm milk together.

Sift the flour and salt into a mixing bowl. Rub in the butter or margarine, then stir in the yeast liquid and egg to make a soft dough. Knead for about 10 minutes or until smooth and elastic. Put in a polythene (plastic) bag and leave to rise in a warm place for 1½ hours.

Knead the dough and divide into 12 portions. Roll each into a ball. Make a deep indentation in each ball and fill with a little jam. Pinch the dough around the jam to enclose completely. Leave in a warm place to rise until doubled in size.

Heat the oil in a deep frying pan (deep fat fryer) until it is 190°C/375°F. Fry the doughnuts for about 4 minutes or until they are puffed up and golden brown. Drain on absorbent paper.

Mix the sugar and cinnamon together and roll the warm doughnuts in this mixture to coat on all sides.
Makes 12

Croissants

METRIC/IMPERIAL
25g/1oz fresh yeast
200ml/⅓ pint lukewarm water
0.5kg/1lb plain flour
2 × 5ml spoons/2 teaspoons salt
200g/7oz butter
1 egg, lightly beaten
Glaze:
1 egg
1 × 15ml spoon/
 1 tablespoon water
1 × 2.5ml spoon/½ teaspoon sugar

AMERICAN
1 cake compressed yeast
⅞ cup lukewarm water
4 cups all-purpose flour
2 teaspoons salt
¾ cup plus 2 tablespoons butter
1 egg, lightly beaten
Glaze:
1 egg
1 tablespoon water
½ teaspoon sugar

Cream the yeast and the lukewarm water together.

Sift the flour and salt into a mixing bowl. Add 25g/1oz/2 tablespoons of the butter and rub into the flour until the mixture resembles breadcrumbs. Stir in the egg and the yeast mixture and knead to a smooth dough. Turn out of the bowl and knead for 10 minutes.

Roll out the dough to a rectangle 50 × 20cm/ 20 × 8 inches and 1cm/½ inch thick.

Divide the remaining butter into 3 portions and cut each into small pieces. Dot one portion over the top two-thirds of the dough rectangle. Fold up the bottom third, then fold down the top third. Give the dough a quarter turn and roll out again into a rectangle. Dot another portion of butter over the top two-thirds of the rectangle and fold as before. Chill for 20 minutes.

Roll out the dough into a rectangle and dot with the remaining butter, as before. Fold, turn and roll out, then fold and chill for 1 hour.

Roll out the dough to a rectangle about 58 × 35cm/23 × 14 inches. Trim to 53 × 30cm/ 21 × 12 inches. Divide in half lengthways, then cut each strip into 6 triangles.

Mix together the ingredients for the glaze and brush over the triangles. Roll up each triangle loosely, finishing at the point. Curve into a crescent and place, point underneath, on a baking sheet. Brush again with the glaze. Leave in a warm place to rise for 30 minutes or until puffed up.

Bake in a preheated hot oven (220°C/425°F, Gas Mark 7) for 20 minutes. Serve warm.
Makes 12

Brioches

METRIC/IMPERIAL
15g/½oz fresh yeast
2 × 5ml spoons/2 teaspoons lukewarm water
225g/8oz plain flour
1 × 2.5ml spoon/½ teaspoon salt
1 × 2.5ml spoon/½ teaspoon caster sugar
2 eggs, lightly beaten
50g/2oz butter, melted and cooled
Glaze:
1 egg
pinch of salt
1 × 15ml spoon/
 1 tablespoon water

AMERICAN
½ cake compressed yeast
2 teaspoons lukewarm water
2 cups all-purpose flour
½ teaspoon salt
½ teaspoon sugar
2 eggs, lightly beaten
¼ cup butter, melted and cooled
Glaze:
1 egg
pinch of salt
1 tablespoon water

Cream the yeast and lukewarm water together.

Sift the flour, salt and sugar into a mixing bowl. Add the yeast mixture, eggs and melted butter and mix together to form a soft dough. Turn out of the bowl and knead for 5 minutes. Place the dough in a lightly greased polythene (plastic) bag and leave to rise in a warm place for 1 to 1½ hours.

Divide the dough into 12 portions. Shape three-quarters of each portion into a ball and place in a greased 8cm/3 inch diameter fluted brioche tin. Press a hole in the centre with your finger. Shape the remaining quarter of each portion into a ball with a tapering end and press into the ball in the tin. Put the filled tins on a baking sheet and leave to rise in a warm place for a further 1 hour or until doubled in size.

Mix together the ingredients for the glaze and brush over the brioches. Bake in a preheated hot oven (230°C/450°F, Gas Mark 8) for 10 minutes. Serve warm.
Makes 12

Fruit plait

METRIC/IMPERIAL
1 × 5ml spoon/
  1 teaspoon sugar
200ml/⅓ pint mixed warm
  milk and water
2 × 5ml spoons/
  2 teaspoons dried yeast
350g/12oz strong plain
  flour
1 × 2.5ml spoon/
  ½ teaspoon salt
50g/2oz margarine
50g/2oz dried apricots,
  chopped
50g/2oz sultanas, chopped
1 egg, lightly beaten

AMERICAN
1 teaspoon sugar
⅞ cup mixed warm milk
  and water
1 package dried yeast
3 cups strong bread or
  all-purpose flour
½ teaspoon salt
¼ cup margarine
⅓ cup dried apricots,
  chopped
⅓ cup seedless white
  raisins, chopped
1 egg, lightly beaten

Stir the sugar into the milk and water. When the sugar has dissolved, sprinkle over the dried yeast and leave in a warm place for about 10 minutes or until frothy. Sift the flour and salt into a bowl and rub in the margarine. Add the apricots and sultanas (raisins) and mix well. Make a well in the centre and pour in the egg and the yeast liquid. Mix to a soft dough, then turn out onto a lightly floured surface and knead for 10 minutes or until smooth and elastic. Cover with a damp cloth and leave for 5 minutes.

Divide the dough into 5 and roll each piece out to make a rope 30cm/12 inches long. Plait (braid) 3 ropes together, then twist the remaining 2 together and place carefully on top. Place on a greased and floured baking sheet, cover with a damp cloth and leave to rise in a warm place until doubled in bulk. Place in a preheated hot oven (220°C/425°F, Gas Mark 7) for 10 minutes, then reduce the heat to moderately hot (190°C/375°F, Gas Mark 5) and bake for a further 20 minutes, or until the loaf is golden brown and sounds hollow when tapped. Place on a wire rack to cool.
Makes 1 large loaf.

Butterscotch buns

METRIC/IMPERIAL
1 × 5ml spoon/
  1 teaspoon sugar
150ml/¼ pint lukewarm
  milk
2 × 5ml spoons/
  2 teaspoons dried yeast
225g/8oz strong plain flour
pinch of salt
25g/1oz butter
1 egg, lightly beaten
50g/2oz butter
100g/4oz brown sugar
1 × 15ml spoon/
  1 tablespoon golden syrup

AMERICAN
1 teaspoon sugar
⅔ cup lukewarm milk
1 package dried yeast
½lb strong bread or
  all-purpose flour
pinch of salt
2 tablespoons butter
1 egg, lightly beaten
¼ cup butter
⅔ cup brown sugar
1 tablespoons light corn
  syrup

Stir the sugar into the milk. When the sugar has dissolved, sprinkle over the yeast and put in a warm place until frothy – about 10 minutes. Sift the flour with a good pinch of salt, then rub in the butter. Make a well in the centre and pour in the yeast liquid and egg. Mix to a soft dough, then turn out onto a lightly floured surface and knead until smooth and elastic. Put the dough in a lightly oiled polythene (plastic) bag and leave to rise until double in bulk.

Put the butter, sugar and syrup into a pan and heat until the sugar has dissolved. Grease an 18cm/7 inch square cake tin and pour in half the syrup mixture. Turn the risen dough onto a lightly floured surface and knead for 1 minute. Roll the dough out to a rectangle about 35 × 23cm/14 × 9 inches and spread with the remaining syrup mixture. Roll up like a Swiss (jelly) roll and cut into 9 rolls. Place the rolls in the tin, cut sides down, cover with a damp cloth and leave to rise in a warm place until doubled in bulk. Place in a moderately hot oven (200°C/400°F, Gas Mark 6) and bake for 30 minutes or until golden. Allow to cool in the tin for 10 minutes then turn out onto a wire rack.
Makes 9

Bara brith

METRIC/IMPERIAL
25g/1oz fresh yeast
175ml/6fl oz lukewarm water
0.5kg/1lb plain flour
1 × 5ml spoon/1 teaspoon salt
1 × 2.5ml spoon/½ teaspoon ground cinnamon
pinch of ground cloves
pinch of grated nutmeg
75g/3oz butter or margarine
75g/3oz soft brown sugar
0.75kg/1½lb mixed dried fruit
1 large egg, lightly beaten
1 × 15ml spoon/
 1 tablespoon clear honey to glaze

AMERICAN
1 cake compressed yeast
¾ cup lukewarm water
4 cups all-purpose flour
1 teaspoon salt
½ teaspoon ground cinnamon
pinch of ground cloves
pinch of grated nutmeg
⅓ cup butter or margarine
½ cup brown sugar
4 cups mixed dried fruit
1 egg, lightly beaten
1 tablespoon clear honey to glaze

Cream the yeast with a little of the water, then stir in the remaining water.

Sift the flour, salt and spices into a mixing bowl. Rub in the butter or margarine until the mixture resembles breadcrumbs. Stir in the sugar and dried fruit. Make a well in the centre and add the yeast mixture and egg and mix to a dough. Knead for 20 minutes or until the dough is smooth and elastic. Put in a polythene (plastic) bag and leave to rise in a warm place for 1½ hours.

Knead the dough again. Divide in half and shape each piece into a loaf. Place in well-greased 0.5kg/1lb/4½ × 2½ × 1½ inch loaf tins. Leave to rise in a warm place for 30 minutes.

Bake in a preheated moderate oven (180°C/350°F, Gas Mark 4) for 50 to 60 minutes. Cool slightly in the tins, then turn out onto a wire rack to cool completely. Brush with the honey to glaze.
Makes two 0.5kg/1lb/4½ × 2½ × 1½ inch loaves

Sally Lunn

METRIC/IMPERIAL
50g/2oz butter
200ml/⅓ pint milk
1 × 5ml spoon/1 teaspoon sugar
2 eggs, lightly beaten
15g/½oz fresh yeast
0.5kg/1lb plain flour
1 × 5ml spoon/1 teaspoon salt
Glaze:
1 × 15ml spoon/
 1 tablespoon sugar
1 × 15ml spoon/
 1 tablespoon water

AMERICAN
¼ cup butter
⅞ cup milk
1 teaspoon sugar
2 eggs, lightly beaten
½ cake compressed yeast
4 cups all-purpose flour
1 teaspoon salt
Glaze:
1 tablespoon sugar
1 tablespoon water

Melt the butter in a saucepan. Remove from the heat and stir in the milk, sugar and eggs. Stir in the yeast, creaming until smooth. Sift the flour and salt into a mixing bowl. Make a well in the centre and add the liquid mixture. Mix well and knead lightly to a smooth dough.

Divide the dough in half and put each portion into a greased 12.5cm/5 inch diameter cake tin. Leave to rise in a warm place for about 1 hour or until the dough has risen to fill the tins.

Bake in a preheated hot oven (230°C/450°F, Gas Mark 8) for 15 to 20 minutes. Transfer to a wire rack.

To make the glaze, boil the sugar and water together for 2 minutes. Remove from the heat and brush over the hot loaves.
Makes two 12.5cm/5 inch round loaves

SPECIAL OCCASIONS

Potted shrimps

METRIC/IMPERIAL
175g/6oz unsalted butter
1 × 2.5ml spoon/½ teaspoon ground mace
freshly ground black pepper
pinch of cayenne pepper
pinch of grated nutmeg
225g/8oz peeled shrimps
lemon wedges to serve

AMERICAN
¾ cup unsalted butter
½ teaspoon ground mace
freshly ground black pepper
pinch of cayenne pepper
pinch of grated nutmeg
1 cup shelled shrimp
lemon wedges to serve

Melt the butter in a saucepan and stir in the mace, pepper to taste, cayenne and nutmeg. Add the shrimps and cook gently for 5 minutes. Remove from the heat.

Divide the shrimp mixture between 4 individual ramekin or other small serving dishes. Allow to cool and set.

Serve garnished with lemon wedges.
Serves 4

Avocado stuffed with crab

METRIC/IMPERIAL
150ml/¼ pint white sauce★
3 tomatoes, peeled, deseeded and finely chopped
2 × 15ml spoons/ 2 tablespoons tomato purée
salt
freshly ground black pepper
pinch of grated nutmeg
75g/3oz crabmeat, flaked
2 avocado pears
juice of ½ lemon
To garnish:
lemon slices
parsley sprigs

AMERICAN
⅔ cup white sauce★
3 tomatoes, peeled, deseeded and finely chopped
2 tablespoons tomato paste
salt
freshly ground black pepper
pinch of grated nutmeg
½ cup crabmeat, flaked
2 avocado pears
juice of ½ lemon
To garnish:
lemon slices
parsley sprigs

Mix together the white sauce, tomatoes, tomato purée (paste), salt and pepper to taste and the nutmeg until well blended. Fold in the crabmeat.

Halve the avocado pears and remove the stones (seeds). Rub the cut surfaces with lemon juice to prevent discoloration. Fill the hollows in the avocados with the crab mixture. Place on a serving dish and garnish with lemon slices and parsley sprigs. Serve at room temperature.
Serves 4

Smoked trout pâté

METRIC/IMPERIAL
2 large smoked trout,
  skinned, boned and flaked
freshly ground black pepper
pinch of cayenne pepper
1 × 2.5ml spoon/½ teaspoon
  grated lemon rind
1.5 × 5ml spoons/
  1½ teaspoons lemon juice
150ml/¼ pint double cream

AMERICAN
2 large smoked trout,
  skinned, boned and flaked
freshly ground black pepper
pinch of cayenne pepper
½ teaspoon grated lemon
  rind
1½ teaspoons lemon juice
⅔ cup heavy cream

Put the fish, pepper to taste, cayenne, lemon rind, lemon juice and a little of the cream in the goblet of an electric blender. Blend until smooth.

Whip the remaining cream until it is thick and fold into the trout mixture. Put into a serving dish and chill until firm.

Serves 4

Pâté de foie

METRIC/IMPERIAL
0.5kg/1lb calf's or chicken
  liver, minced
100g/4oz pork fat, minced
1 garlic clove, crushed
pinch of dried thyme
salt
freshly ground black pepper
2 × 15ml spoons/
  2 tablespoons water
50g/2oz cooked tongue,
  finely chopped
1 × 5ml spoon/1 teaspoon
  finely chopped truffle
  (optional)
parsley sprigs to garnish

AMERICAN
2 cups ground calf or
  chicken liver
½ cup ground pork fat back
1 garlic clove, crushed
pinch of dried thyme
salt
freshly ground black pepper
2 tablespoons water
¼ cup finely chopped
  cooked tongue
1 teaspoon finely chopped
  truffle (optional)
parsley sprigs to garnish

Mix together the liver, pork fat, garlic, thyme and salt and pepper to taste. Heat a frying pan (skillet) and add the liver mixture. Fry until the mixture has changed colour, then stir in the water. Cook for a further 5 minutes.

Spoon the liver mixture into the goblet of an electric blender and blend to a smooth purée. Alternatively, push through a sieve (strainer) until smooth.

Stir the tongue into the liver mixture and spoon into a small serving dish or 6 individual ramekin dishes. Press the truffle into the top, if using. Chill until firm.

Serve garnished with parsley sprigs.

Serves 6

Jerusalem artichoke soup

METRIC/IMPERIAL
25g/1oz butter
1kg/2lb Jerusalem artichokes, peeled and chopped
1 large onion, peeled and chopped
2 celery sticks, chopped
900ml/1½ pints chicken stock
salt
freshly ground black pepper
1 × 2.5ml spoon/½ teaspoon dried thyme
150ml/¼ pint single cream or milk
150ml/¼ pint double cream
toasted croûtons to garnish

AMERICAN
2 tablespoons butter
2lb Jerusalem artichokes, peeled and chopped
1 large onion, peeled and chopped
2 celery stalks, chopped
3¾ cups chicken stock
salt
freshly ground black pepper
½ teaspoon dried thyme
⅔ cup light cream or milk
⅔ cup heavy cream
toasted croûtons to garnish

Melt the butter in a saucepan. Add the vegetables and cook gently until they are soft but not brown. Stir in the stock with salt and pepper to taste and the thyme. Bring to the boil, then cover and simmer for 30 minutes.

Pour the vegetable mixture into the goblet of an electric blender and blend until smooth. Return to the saucepan.

Stir in the single (light) cream or milk and double (heavy) cream and reheat gently, stirring. Serve hot, garnished with toasted croûtons.
Serves 6

Melon with Parma ham

METRIC/IMPERIAL
1 medium honeydew or cantaloup melon, chilled
8 thin slices Parma ham

AMERICAN
1 medium honeydew or cantaloup melon, chilled
8 thin slices Parma ham

Halve the melon and scoop out the seeds. Cut into slices about 5cm/2 inches wide and remove the flesh from the skin. Cut the flesh into 5cm/2 inch cubes.

Cut the ham into strips and wrap one around each melon cube. If necessary, secure with wooden cocktail sticks (toothpicks). Divide the melon and ham cubes between 4 serving dishes and serve.
Serves 4

Lobster bisque

METRIC/IMPERIAL
50g/2oz butter
1 large carrot, peeled and chopped
1 large onion, peeled and chopped
1 small lobster, shell split lengthways and claws cracked
3 × 15ml spoons/ 3 tablespoons brandy
300ml/½ pint dry white wine
100g/4oz long-grain rice
1.75 litres/3 pints court bouillon★
150ml/¼ pint single cream
salt
cayenne pepper

AMERICAN
¼ cup butter
1 large carrot, peeled and chopped
1 large onion, peeled and chopped
1 small lobster, shell split lengthwise and claws cracked
3 tablespoons brandy
1¼ cups dry white wine
⅔ cup long-grain rice
7½ cups court bouillon★
⅔ cup light cream
salt
cayenne pepper

Melt 25g/1oz/2 tablespoons of the butter in a saucepan. Add the carrot and onion and cook gently for 3 minutes. Remove the coral from the lobster and place the lobster, cut side down, on the vegetables. Cover and cook for 2 minutes.

Warm the brandy and ignite. Pour flaming over the lobster, then pour over the wine. Bring to the boil, cover and simmer gently for 15 minutes, shaking the pan occasionally.

Meanwhile, cook the rice in 600ml/1 pint/2½ cups of the court bouillon for 20 minutes or until it is tender and the liquid has been absorbed.

Shell the lobster, discard the intestine and stomach sac and finely chop the meat. Put into the goblet of an electric blender with the coral, vegetables, cooking liquid, and rice. Blend until a smooth purée. Stir in 300ml/½ pint/1¼ cups of the remaining court bouillon, then strain the lobster mixture and return to the saucepan. Stir in the remaining court bouillon.

Reheat the soup gently, then beat in the remaining butter in small pieces. Stir in the cream and season to taste with salt and cayenne. Serve hot.
Serves 6 to 8

Chilled avocado soup

METRIC/IMPERIAL
3 medium avocado pears
juice of 1 lemon
600ml/1 pint chicken stock
150ml/¼ pint natural yogurt
salt
freshly ground black pepper
chopped spring onions to garnish

AMERICAN
3 medium avocado pears
juice of 1 lemon
2½ cups chicken stock
⅔ cup unflavored yogurt
salt
freshly ground black pepper
chopped scallions to garnish

Halve the avocado pears and remove the stones (seeds). Scoop the flesh into the goblet of an electric blender. Add the lemon juice, stock, yogurt and salt and pepper to taste and blend until smooth.

Alternatively, rub the avocado flesh through a nylon sieve (strainer), then stir in the remaining ingredients, except the spring onions (scallions).

Pour the soup into individual soup bowls and chill for at least 30 minutes. Serve garnished with chopped spring onions (scallions).
Serves 4 to 6

Cold poached salmon with mayonnaise verte

METRIC/IMPERIAL
900ml/1½ pints court bouillon★
1 × 2.75kg/6lb salmon, cleaned and scaled
1 cucumber, thinly sliced
12 radishes, thinly sliced
watercress
Mayonnaise verte:
600ml/1 pint mayonnaise★
6 watercress sprigs, finely chopped
2 fresh tarragon sprigs, finely chopped
2 fresh chervil sprigs, finely chopped
1 × 15ml spoon/
 1 tablespoon chopped fresh parsley

AMERICAN
3¾ cups court bouillon★
1 × 6lb salmon, cleaned and scaled
1 cucumber, thinly sliced
12 radishes, thinly sliced
watercress
Mayonnaise verte:
2½ cups mayonnaise★
6 watercress sprigs, finely chopped
2 fresh tarragon sprigs, finely chopped
2 fresh chervil sprigs, finely chopped
1 tablespoon chopped fresh parsley

Put the court bouillon in a fish kettle and bring to the boil. Lower the salmon into the kettle, cover and simmer gently for 10 minutes. Remove from the heat, uncover and allow the salmon to cool in the liquid.

Remove the salmon from the fish kettle and carefully take off the skin. Place the salmon on a serving plate and garnish with the cucumber and radish slices and watercress.

Mix together the mayonnaise, watercress, tarragon, chervil and parsley. Spoon into a serving bowl and serve with the salmon.
Serves 8 to 10

Lobster thermidor

METRIC/IMPERIAL
2 × 1kg/2lb lobsters, shells split, claws cracked and intestine and stomach removed
100g/4oz butter
1 medium onion, peeled and finely chopped
50g/2oz plain flour
300ml/½ pint milk
50g/2oz Cheddar or Gruyère cheese, grated
2 × 15ml spoons/
 2 tablespoons dry white wine
pinch of paprika
salt
freshly ground black pepper
50g/2oz Parmesan cheese, grated
To garnish:
lemon wedges
watercress

AMERICAN
2 × 2lb lobsters, shells split, claws cracked and intestine and stomach removed
½ cup butter
1 medium onion, peeled and finely chopped
½ cup all-purpose flour
1¼ cups milk
½ cup grated Cheddar or Gruyère cheese
2 tablespoons dry white wine
pinch of paprika
salt
freshly ground black pepper
½ cup grated Parmesan cheese
To garnish:
lemon wedges
watercress

Remove the lobster meat from the shells and claws and cut into small pieces. Clean out the shell halves and rub them with oil to make them shine.

Melt 50g/2oz/¼ cup of the butter in a frying pan (skillet). Add the lobster meat and cook gently for 3 to 4 minutes.

Meanwhile, melt the remaining butter in a saucepan. Add the onion and fry until it is soft but not brown. Stir in the flour and cook, stirring, for 1 minute. Remove from the heat and gradually stir in the milk. Return to the heat and bring to the boil, stirring. Simmer until thickened. Stir in the Cheddar or Gruyère cheese, wine, paprika and salt and pepper to taste. Pour the sauce over the lobster in the frying pan (skillet) and stir well. Cook gently for 2 minutes.

Arrange the lobster shell halves in a grill (broiler) pan and spoon the lobster mixture into them. Sprinkle over the Parmesan cheese. Grill (broil) until the top is browned and bubbling. Transfer to a warmed serving dish and garnish with lemon wedges and watercress. Serve hot.
Serves 4

Scampi provençale

METRIC/IMPERIAL
25g/1oz butter
1 medium onion, peeled and chopped
1 garlic clove, crushed
100g/4oz mushrooms, sliced
0.5kg/1lb tomatoes, peeled, deseeded and chopped
1 × 15ml spoon/
 1 tablespoon tomato purée
1 × 5ml spoon/1 teaspoon dried oregano
salt
freshly ground black pepper
2 × 5ml spoons/2 teaspoons cornflour
150ml/¼ pint dry white wine
juice of ½ lemon
25g/1oz plain flour
0.5kg/1lb shelled scampi or Dublin Bay prawns
2 × 15ml spoons/
 2 tablespoons olive oil

AMERICAN
2 tablespoons butter
1 medium onion, peeled and chopped
1 garlic clove, crushed
1 cup sliced mushrooms
2 cups peeled, deseeded and chopped tomatoes
1 tablespoon tomato paste
1 teaspoon dried oregano
salt
freshly ground black pepper
2 teaspoons cornstarch
⅔ cup dry white wine
juice of ½ lemon
¼ cup all-purpose flour
1lb shelled jumbo shrimp
2 tablespoons olive oil

Melt the butter in a saucepan. Add the onion and garlic and fry until the onion is soft but not brown. Stir in the mushrooms and cook for 3 minutes. Add the tomatoes, tomato purée (paste), oregano and salt and pepper to taste.

Dissolve the cornflour (cornstarch) in the wine and add to the pan with the lemon juice. Bring to the boil, cover and simmer for 25 minutes.

Mix the flour with salt and pepper and use to coat the scampi (jumbo shrimp). Heat the oil in a frying pan (skillet). Add the scampi (jumbo shrimp) and fry until golden brown on all sides. Pour over the tomato sauce and simmer for a further 5 minutes. Serve hot, on a bed of boiled rice.
Serves 4

Tournedos béarnaise

METRIC/IMPERIAL
4 × 175g/6oz tournedos
salt
freshly ground black pepper
50g/2oz butter
120ml/4fl oz warm béarnaise sauce★
watercress to garnish

AMERICAN
4 × 6oz tournedos
salt
freshly ground black pepper
¼ cup butter
½ cup warm béarnaise sauce★
watercress to garnish

Rub the tournedos with salt and pepper. Melt the butter in a frying pan (skillet). Add the tournedos and fry for 3 to 4 minutes on each side. This will produce rare steaks; increase the time if you prefer the meat medium or well-done.

Transfer the tournedos to a warmed serving dish and spoon over the béarnaise sauce. Garnish with watercress and serve.
Serves 4

Beef Wellington

METRIC/IMPERIAL
100g/4oz butter, softened
1 × 1.25kg/2½lb fillet of beef
1 small onion, peeled and finely chopped
100g/4oz mushrooms, thinly sliced
50g/2oz pâté de foie gras
0.5kg/1lb quantity puff pastry* (made with 0.5kg/1lb flour, etc.)
salt
freshly ground black pepper
1 egg yolk, lightly beaten
2 × 15ml spoons/ 2 tablespoons plain flour
300ml/½ pint beef stock
2 × 15ml spoons/ 2 tablespoons port wine
watercress to garnish

AMERICAN
½ cup butter, softened
1 × 2½lb beef fillet (tenderloin)
1 small onion, peeled and finely chopped
1 cup thinly sliced mushrooms
¼ cup pâté de foie gras
4 cup quantity puff pastry* (made with 4 cups flour, etc.)
salt
freshly ground black pepper
1 egg yolk, lightly beaten
2 tablespoons all-purpose flour
1¼ cups beef stock
2 tablespoons port wine
watercress to garnish

Spread 25g/1oz/2 tablespoons of the softened butter over the beef and place in a roasting tin. Roast in a preheated hot oven (220°C/425°F, Gas Mark 7) for 15 minutes or until evenly browned. Remove from the oven and allow to cool. Reserve the meat juices.

Melt 25g/1oz/2 tablespoons of the remaining butter in a saucepan. Add the onion and fry until it is soft but not brown. Add the mushrooms and fry for a further 3 minutes. Remove from the heat.

Mix the remaining butter with the pâté. Roll out the pastry dough to an oblong large enough to enclose the beef. Place the beef in the centre and spread with the pâté mixture. Top with the onion and mushroom mixture and sprinkle with salt and pepper.

Bring up the dough around the beef and press the edges together to seal and make a neat parcel. Make a few slits in the dough and brush with the beaten egg yolk. Place on a baking sheet and bake in a preheated hot oven (230°C/450°F, Gas Mark 8) for 10 minutes, then reduce the temperature to 220°C/425°F, Gas Mark 7. Continue baking for 10 to 15 minutes.

Pour the reserved meat juices into a saucepan and stir in the flour. Cook, stirring, for 2 minutes, then gradually stir in the stock. Bring to the boil, stirring, and simmer until thickened. Stir in the port. Serve the beef with the sauce and garnish with watercress.
Serves 6

Lamb noisettes provençale

METRIC/IMPERIAL
25g/1oz butter
1 × 15ml spoon/ 1 tablespoon olive oil
1 onion, peeled and finely chopped
1 garlic clove, crushed
8 lamb noisettes
2 × 15ml spoons/ 2 tablespoons tomato purée
4 × 15ml spoons/ 4 tablespoons Pernod
4 tomatoes, peeled, deseeded and chopped
3 large courgettes, sliced
1 × 2.5ml spoon/½ teaspoon dried basil
salt
freshly ground black pepper

AMERICAN
2 tablespoons butter
1 tablespoon olive oil
1 onion, peeled and finely chopped
1 garlic clove, crushed
8 lamb noisettes (boned chops)
2 tablespoons tomato paste
4 tablespoons Pernod
4 tomatoes, peeled, deseeded and chopped
3 large zucchini, sliced
½ teaspoon dried basil
salt
freshly ground black pepper

Melt the butter with the oil in a frying pan (skillet). Add the onion and garlic and fry until the onion is soft but not brown. Add the noisettes to the pan, in batches, and brown on both sides. Remove the noisettes from the pan as they are browned.

Stir the tomato purée (paste) and Pernod into the onions. Add the tomatoes and courgettes (zucchini) with the basil and salt and pepper to taste. Return the noisettes to the pan and spoon the vegetable mixture over them. Stir in enough water to cover the lamb.

Bring to the boil, then cover and simmer for 45 minutes or until the lamb is tender and the vegetable mixture is cooked and thickened. Serve hot.
Serves 4

Crown roast of pork with rice stuffing

METRIC/IMPERIAL
1 crown roast of pork
  (14 chops)
50g/2oz dripping, melted
salt
freshly ground black pepper
300ml/½ pint pork or beef
  stock
1 × 15ml spoon/
  1 tablespoon sherry
watercress to garnish
Stuffing:
50g/2oz butter
1 small onion, peeled and
  finely chopped
3 celery sticks, finely
  chopped
pinch of hot curry powder
350g/12oz long-grain rice
750ml/1¼ pints pork or
  beef stock
finely grated rind and juice
  of 2 large oranges
175g/6oz raisins

AMERICAN
1 crown roast of pork
  (14 chops)
¼ cup drippings, melted
salt
freshly ground black pepper
1¼ cups pork or beef stock
1 tablespoon sherry
watercress to garnish
Stuffing:
¼ cup butter
1 small onion, peeled and
  finely chopped
3 celery stalks, finely
  chopped
pinch of hot curry powder
2 cups long-grain rice
3 cups pork or beef stock
finely grated rind and juice
  of 2 large oranges
1 cup raisins

Place the crown roast in a roasting tin and fill the cavity with crumpled foil. Brush the outside of the meat with the dripping and season with salt and pepper. Cover the tops of the bones with foil. Roast in a preheated hot oven (220°C/425°F, Gas Mark 7) for 2¼ hours.

Thirty minutes before the pork is ready, make the stuffing. Melt the butter in a saucepan. Add the onion and celery and fry until the onion is soft but not brown. Stir in the curry powder, then stir in the rice. Pour in the stock and orange juice and bring to the boil. Cover and simmer for 20 minutes or until the rice is tender and the liquid has been absorbed. Season well and stir in the orange rind and raisins. Heat through gently, then remove from the heat and keep hot.

Transfer the crown roast to a warmed serving plate. Keep hot.

Pour off the fat from the roasting tin. Add the stock to the sediment and season well. Bring to the boil, stirring, and boil for 3 minutes to reduce slightly. Stir in the sherry and strain into a gravy boat. Keep hot.

Remove the foil from the pork and from the tips of the bones. Fill the centre with the orange rice and put frills on the bone tips. Garnish with watercress and serve with the sauce.
Serves 6 to 8

Poussins Véronique

METRIC/IMPERIAL
4 sprigs of fresh thyme
4 poussins
50g/2oz butter
2 celery sticks, chopped
1 small onion, peeled and chopped
150ml/¼ pint dry white wine
salt
freshly ground black pepper
about 300ml/½ pint milk or single cream
25g/1oz plain flour
100g/4oz large green grapes, halved and deseeded

AMERICAN
4 sprigs of fresh thyme
4 broilers
¼ cup butter
2 celery stalks, chopped
1 small onion, peeled and chopped
⅔ cup dry white wine
salt
freshly ground black pepper
about 1¼ cups milk or light cream
¼ cup all-purpose flour
1 cup large green grapes, halved and deseeded

Put a sprig of thyme in each poussin (broiler). Melt half the butter in a flameproof casserole. Add the celery and onion and fry until the onion is soft but not brown. Push the vegetables to one side and add the poussins (broilers) to the casserole. Brown well on all sides, adding more butter if necessary.

Pour in the wine and bring to the boil. Add salt and pepper to taste, then cover and simmer for 20 to 25 minutes or until the poussins (broilers) are cooked through.

Transfer the poussins (broilers) to a warmed serving dish and keep hot. Strain the cooking liquid and make up to 450ml/¾ pint/2 cups with milk or cream.

Melt the remaining butter in a saucepan. Add the flour and cook, stirring, for 1 minute. Remove from the heat and gradually stir in the cooking liquid mixture. Return to the heat and bring to the boil, stirring. Simmer until thickened and smooth, then stir in the grapes. Heat through gently. Taste and adjust the seasoning. Pour the sauce over the poussins (broilers) and serve.
Serves 8

Tarragon chicken

METRIC/IMPERIAL
100g/4oz butter
3 × 15ml spoons/ 3 tablespoons chopped fresh tarragon
1 × 5ml spoon/1 teaspoon lemon juice
salt
freshly ground black pepper
1 × 1.75kg/4lb chicken
1.5 × 15ml spoons/ 1½ tablespoons plain flour
150ml/¼ pint double cream

AMERICAN
½ cup butter
3 tablespoons chopped fresh tarragon
1 teaspoon lemon juice
salt
freshly ground black pepper
1 × 4lb chicken
1½ tablespoons all-purpose flour
⅔ cup heavy cream

Cream the butter until softened, then beat in the tarragon, lemon juice and salt and pepper to taste. Loosen the skin on the breast of the chicken and stuff half the butter mixture under it. Form the remaining butter mixture into a ball and put inside the chicken.

Place the chicken in a roasting tin and cover with foil. Roast in a preheated moderately hot oven (190°C/375°F, Gas Mark 5) for 1½ to 2 hours or until the chicken is cooked.

Transfer the chicken to a warmed serving dish and keep hot.

Pour the cooking juices into a saucepan. Dissolve the flour in the cream and stir into the cooking juices. Cook gently, stirring, until the sauce thickens. Serve hot, with the chicken.
Serves 4 to 6

Poussins Véronique (page 364)

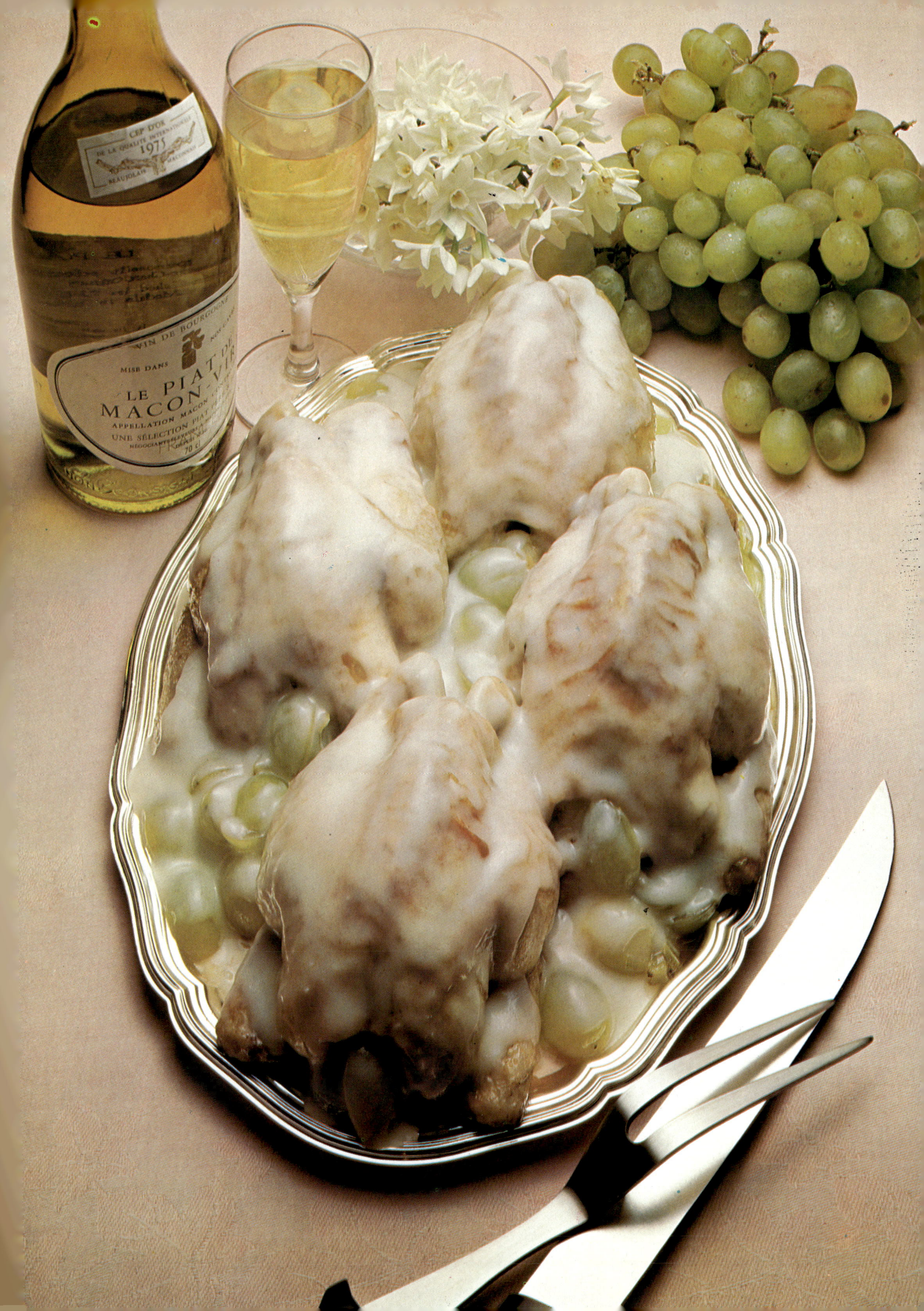
CEP D'OR
1975
VIN DE BOURGOGNE
MISE DANS

Christmas cake (page 378); Christmas pudding (page 377)

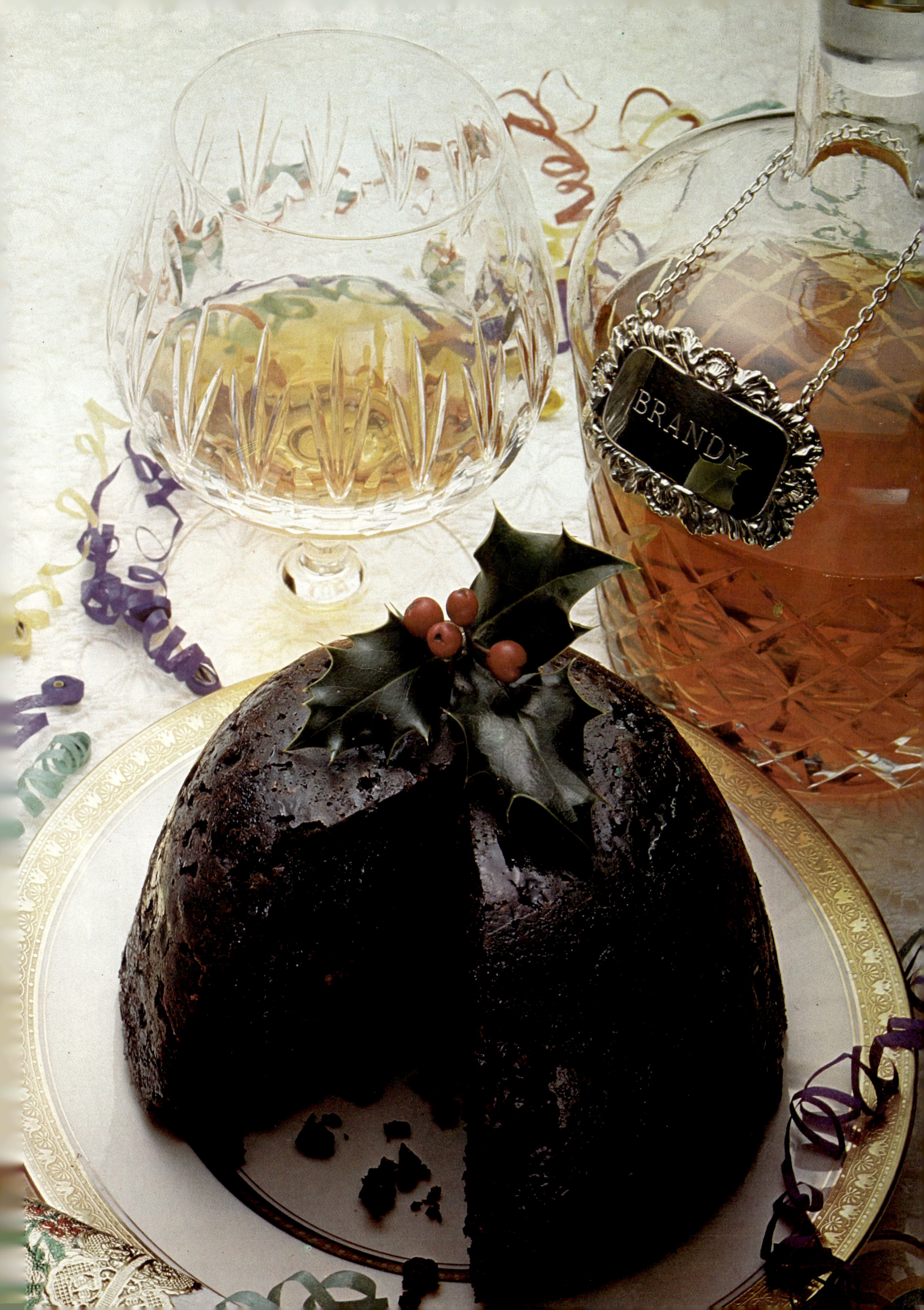
BRANDY

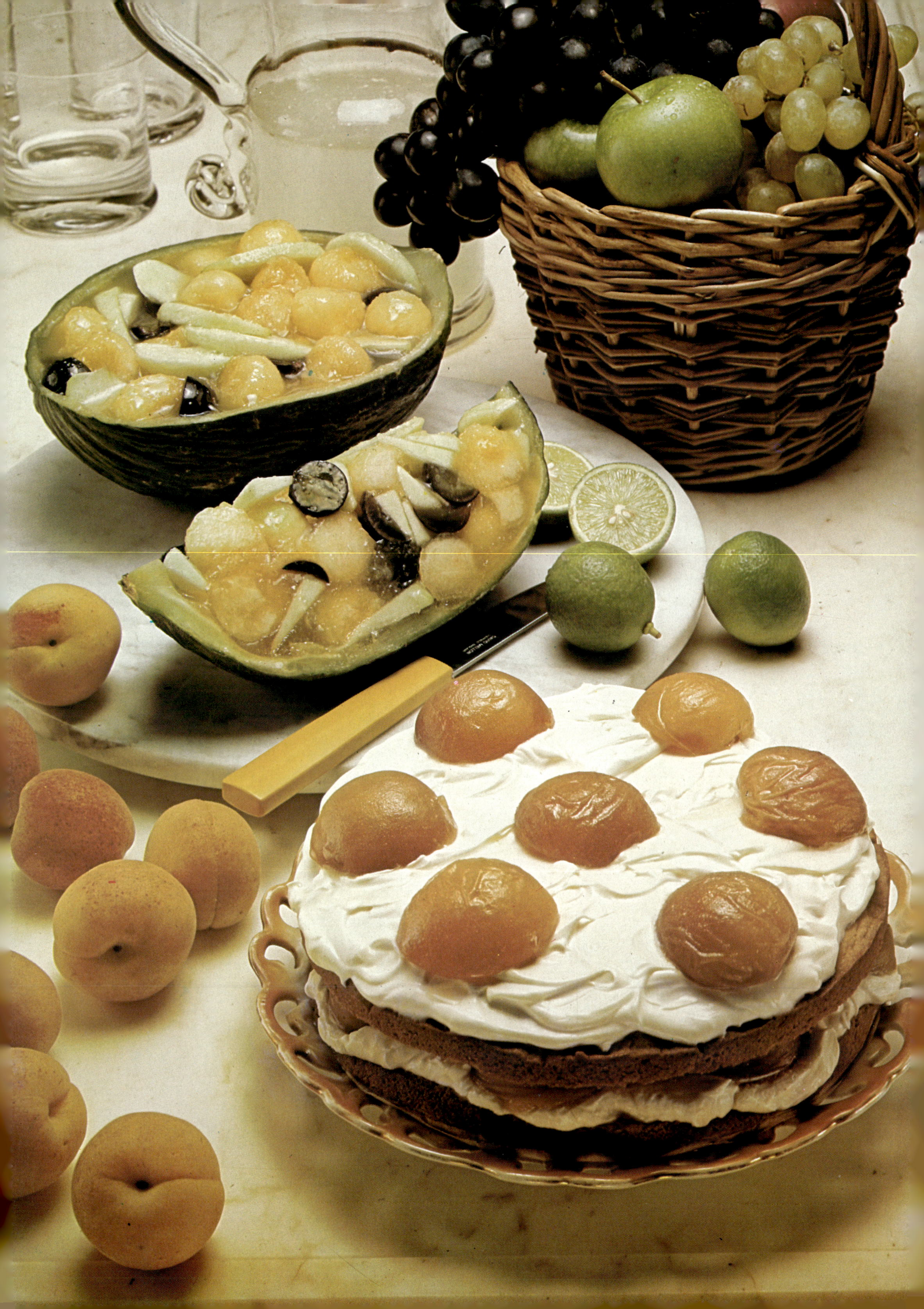

Pork fillets (tenderloin) in sherry sauce

METRIC/IMPERIAL
25g/1oz butter
2 pork fillets, halved crossways
1 garlic clove, crushed
1 × 15ml spoon/ 1 tablespoon paprika
150ml/¼ pint medium sherry
100g/4oz button mushrooms, sliced
1 × 15ml spoon/ 1 tablespoon plain flour
salt
freshly ground black pepper
150ml/¼ pint single cream
watercress to garnish

AMERICAN
2 tablespoons butter
2 pork tenderloin, halved crosswise
1 garlic clove, crushed
1 tablespoon paprika
⅔ cup medium sherry
1 cup sliced button mushrooms
1 tablespoon all-purpose flour
salt
freshly ground black pepper
⅔ cup light cream
watercress to garnish

Melt the butter in a flameproof casserole. Add the pork fillets (tenderloin) and garlic and fry until the pork is browned on all sides. Remove the pork from the pot.

Stir the paprika into the fat in the casserole, then stir in the sherry. Add the mushrooms. Return the pork to the casserole and bring to the boil. Cover and transfer to a preheated moderate oven (160°C/325°F, Gas Mark 3). Cook for 1 hour or until the pork is tender.

Transfer the pork to a warmed serving dish and keep hot. Mix the flour and salt and pepper to taste with half the cream and stir into the cooking liquid in the casserole. Simmer gently, stirring, until the liquid is slightly thickened. Pour this sauce over the pork, then pour over the remaining cream. Garnish with watercress and serve.

Serves 4

Roast duck with sage and Marsala

METRIC/IMPERIAL
2 fresh sage leaves
1 garlic clove, halved
1 × 1.75kg/4lb duck
salt
freshly ground black pepper
5 × 15ml spoons/ 5 tablespoons Marsala

AMERICAN
2 fresh sage leaves
1 garlic clove, halved
1 × 4lb duck
salt
freshly ground black pepper
⅓ cup Marsala

Put the sage and garlic in the cavity in the duck. Prick the duck all over and rub with salt and pepper. Place on a rack in a roasting tin. Roast in a preheated moderately hot oven (190°C/375°F, Gas Mark 5) for 30 minutes.

Pour off all the fat from the roasting tin. Pour the Marsala over the duck and continue roasting for 1 hour. Baste frequently with the Marsala during the roasting.

Serve hot.

Serves 4

Melon and grape jelly (page 374) and Apricot shortcake (page 372)

Courgettes (zucchini) with almonds and cream

METRIC/IMPERIAL
25g/1oz plain flour
salt
freshly ground black pepper
0.5kg/1lb courgettes, cut into 1cm/½ inch slices
75g/3oz butter
50g/2oz blanched almonds, flaked
150ml/¼ pint single cream

AMERICAN
¼ cup all-purpose flour
salt
freshly ground black pepper
1lb zucchini, cut into ½ inch slices
⅓ cup butter
½ cup blanched slivered almonds
⅔ cup light cream

Mix the flour with salt and pepper and use to coat the courgette (zucchini) slices. Melt the butter in a frying pan (skillet). Add the courgettes (zucchini) and fry until golden on all sides and tender. Remove from the pan and drain on absorbent paper. Pile onto a warmed serving dish and keep hot.

Add the almonds to the pan and fry until lightly browned. Drain off the fat from the pan and stir in the cream with salt and pepper to taste. Heat through gently, stirring. Pour over the courgettes (zucchini) and serve hot.

Serves 4

Mediterranean artichokes

METRIC/IMPERIAL
2 globe artichokes
1 garlic clove, halved
100g/4oz mushrooms, sliced
4 medium tomatoes, peeled, deseeded and thinly sliced
salt
freshly ground black pepper
pinch of dried oregano
pinch of dried basil
150ml/¼ pint dry white wine

AMERICAN
2 globe artichokes
1 garlic clove, halved
1 cup sliced mushrooms
4 medium tomatoes, peeled, deseeded and thinly sliced
salt
freshly ground black pepper
pinch of dried oregano
pinch of dried basil
⅔ cup dry white wine

Trim off the sharp points of the artichoke leaves. Cut off the stalks at the base. Quarter the artichokes and discard the hairy chokes. Blanch in boiling water for 10 minutes. Drain well.

Rub the inside of a casserole with the cut sides of the garlic. Discard the garlic. Mix together the mushrooms, tomatoes, salt and pepper to taste, the herbs and wine. Spoon into the casserole and spread out. Lay the artichoke quarters on top and cover tightly with a lid or foil. Bake in a preheated moderate oven (180°C/350°F, Gas Mark 4) for 1 to 1½ hours or until tender. Serve hot, from the casserole.

Serves 4

Potatoes dauphinois

METRIC/IMPERIAL
1kg/2lb potatoes, peeled and thinly sliced
25g/1oz butter, cut into small pieces
1 large onion, peeled and finely chopped
225g/8oz Gruyère cheese, grated
salt
freshly ground black pepper
150ml/¼ pint single cream

AMERICAN
2lb potatoes, peeled and thinly sliced
2 tablespoons butter, cut into small pieces
1 large onion, peeled and finely chopped
2 cups grated Gruyère cheese
salt
freshly ground black pepper
⅔ cup light cream

Make a layer of potato slices in a greased flameproof casserole. Sprinkle with a few pieces of butter, a little onion and cheese and salt and pepper. Pour over about one-quarter of the cream. Continue making layers, ending with a layer of cheese with the remaining cream poured over the top.

Cover and bake in a preheated moderately hot oven (190°C/375°F, Gas Mark 5) for 1 hour or until the potatoes are tender.

Uncover and grill (broil) for 5 minutes or until lightly browned and bubbling.

Serve hot, from the casserole.
Serves 4 to 6

Beans with bacon

METRIC/IMPERIAL
0.5kg/1lb French beans
salt
25g/1oz butter
½ small onion, peeled and chopped
100g/4oz streaky bacon rashers, rinds removed and diced
freshly ground black pepper
4 × 15ml spoons/ 4 tablespoons sour cream

AMERICAN
1lb green beans
salt
2 tablespoons butter
½ small onion, peeled and chopped
¼lb bacon slices, diced
freshly ground black pepper
4 tablespoons sour cream

Cook the beans in boiling salted water for 12 to 15 minutes or until they are just tender.

Meanwhile, melt the butter in a frying pan (skillet). Add the onion and bacon and fry until the onion is golden and the bacon is crisp.

Drain the beans and stir into the onion and bacon mixture. Add salt and pepper to taste. Stir in the sour cream and heat through gently. Serve hot.
Serves 4

Apricot shortcake

METRIC/IMPERIAL
75g/3oz butter
225g/8oz self-raising flour
pinch of salt
150g/5oz sugar
1 egg, beaten
1–2 × 15ml spoons/
  1–2 tablespoons milk
350g–0.5kg/12oz–1lb
  fresh apricots, halved and stoned
300ml/½ pint double cream, whipped

AMERICAN
⅓ cup butter
2 cups self-rising flour
pinch of salt
⅔ cup sugar
1 egg, beaten
1–2 tablespoons milk
¾–1lb fresh apricots, halved and pitted
1¼ cups heavy cream, whipped

Rub the butter into the flour and salt until the mixture resembles fine breadcrumbs. Stir in 75g/3oz/⅓ cup of the sugar. Gradually add the egg until the mixture binds together. If necessary, add a little milk.

Transfer the mixture to a floured board and knead carefully until smooth. Shape into a round and roll out until 20cm/8 inches in diameter. Press into a greased 20cm/8 inch loose-bottomed cake tin. Chill in the refrigerator for 20 minutes.

Meanwhile, stew the apricots in their own juice with the remaining sugar (or to taste). Stew for 10 to 12 minutes until they are just tender, but still hold their shape. Cool.

Put the shortcake in a moderately hot oven (190°C/375°F, Gas Mark 5) and bake for 20 minutes until golden brown and firm. Leave to cool for 10 minutes, then turn out of the tin and cool on a wire rack. When completely cold, carefully split the cake in half using a sharp knife. Spread one half with half the cream and arrange two-thirds of the apricots on top. Place the second shortcake round on top. Cover with the remaining cream and decorate with the remaining apricot halves.
Serves 6 to 8

Baked Alaska

METRIC/IMPERIAL
100g/4oz trifle sponge cakes, halved
2 × 15ml spoons/
  2 tablespoons brandy or sweet sherry
3 egg whites
175g/6oz caster sugar
600ml/1 pint block vanilla ice cream, frozen solid

AMERICAN
4 thick slices pound cake, halved
2 tablespoons brandy or sweet sherry
3 egg whites
¾ cup sugar
2½ cup block vanilla ice cream, frozen solid

Arrange the cake pieces on an ovenproof serving plate. Sprinkle the cake with the brandy or sherry.

Beat the egg whites until stiff, then add 75g/3oz/⅓ cup of the sugar. Continue beating for 1 minute or until the mixture is very stiff and glossy. Carefully fold in the remaining sugar.

Place the block of ice cream on the cake leaving a 1cm/½ inch margin around the edge. Cover with the meringue, bringing it down to the plate to seal in the ice cream completely. Bake in a preheated hot oven (220°C/425°F, Gas Mark 7) for 4 to 5 minutes or until the meringue is lightly browned and crisp on the outside. Serve immediately.
Serves 6

Strawberries Romanoff

METRIC/IMPERIAL
0.5kg/1lb strawberries, hulled and sliced
4 × 15ml spoons/ 4 tablespoons port wine
4 × 15ml spoons/ 4 tablespoons caster sugar
300ml/½ pint double cream
1 × 2.5ml spoon/½ teaspoon vanilla essence

AMERICAN
1lb strawberries, hulled and sliced
4 tablespoons port wine
4 tablespoons sugar
1¼ cups whipping cream
½ teaspoon vanilla extract

Put the strawberries in a glass serving bowl and pour over the port wine. Sprinkle with half the sugar and fold gently through the strawberries. Leave to soak for at least 1 hour.
  Whip the cream with the remaining sugar and the vanilla until it is thick. Pile on top of the strawberries and serve.
Serves 4

Cold peach and apple soufflé

METRIC/IMPERIAL
2 large cooking apples, peeled, cored and sliced
150ml/¼ pint water
4 peaches, peeled, stoned and sliced
6 eggs, separated
275g/10oz caster sugar
2 × 15ml spoons/ 2 tablespoons lemon juice
5 × 5ml spoons/5 teaspoons gelatine
2 × 15ml spoons/ 2 tablespoons orange-flavoured liqueur
150ml/¼ pint single cream
300ml/½ pint double cream

AMERICAN
2 large baking apples, peeled, cored and sliced
⅔ cup water
4 peaches, peeled, pitted and sliced
6 eggs, separated
1¼ cups sugar
2 tablespoons lemon juice
5 teaspoons unflavored gelatin
2 tablespoons orange-flavored liqueur
⅔ cup light cream
1¼ cups heavy cream

Put the apples and all but 3 × 15ml spoons/ 3 tablespoons of the water in a saucepan. Cook gently until the apples are soft. Pour the apples into the goblet of an electric blender and add the peach slices. Blend until smooth.
  Put the egg yolks, sugar and lemon juice in a heatproof bowl over a pan of hot water. Beat until the mixture is thick and will make a ribbon trail on itself when the beater is lifted. (If using an electric beater no heat is necessary.) Remove from the heat and continue beating until cool.
  Dissolve the gelatine in the reserved 3 × 15ml spoons/3 tablespoons water. Beat the fruit purée into the egg yolk mixture, then strain in the dissolved gelatine. Stir well and stir in the liqueur.
  Whip the creams together until thick. Fold into the fruit mixture. Beat the egg whites until stiff and fold into the fruit mixture. Spoon into a 1.5 litre/2½ pint/ 6¼ cup soufflé dish fitted with a paper collar. Chill until set. Remove the paper collar before serving.
Serves 6

Melon and grape jelly

METRIC/IMPERIAL
1 large melon, halved and deseeded
2 dessert apples, peeled, cored and sliced
175g/6oz black grapes, halved and deseeded
grated rind and juice of 2 limes
15g/½oz gelatine
2 × 15ml spoons/ 2 tablespoons water
4 × 15ml spoons/ 4 tablespoons honey

AMERICAN
1 large melon, halved and deseeded
2 dessert apples, peeled, cored and sliced
1½ cups black grapes, halved and deseeded
grated rind and juice of 2 limes
2 envelopes unflavored gelatin
2 tablespoons water
4 tablespoons honey

Scoop the melon into balls and mix with the apples and grapes. Scoop out any remaining melon flesh and chop roughly. Add the grated rind and juice of the limes to the melon balls and apples. Dissolve the gelatine in the water in a bowl set over a pan of hot water. Stir the gelatine into the fruit mixture and add the honey. Put the chopped melon in the bottom of the melon shells, spoon over the fruit and jelly (gelatin) mixture and put in a cool place to set. Serve cut into slices, with whipped cream if liked.
Serve 4 to 6

Chestnut vacherin

METRIC/IMPERIAL
6 large egg whites
350g/12oz caster sugar
300ml/½ pint double cream
1 × 250g/9oz can sweetened chestnut purée
1 × 15ml spoon/ 1 tablespoon dry sherry
3 marrons glacés
25g/1oz plain chocolate

AMERICAN
6 large egg whites
1½ cups sugar
1¼ cups whipping cream
1 × 9oz can sweetened chestnut purée
1 tablespoon dry sherry
3 marrons glacés
1 square semisweet chocolate

Line 3 baking sheets with non-stick parchment. Draw a 23cm/9 inch circle on each sheet.

Beat the egg whites until stiff. Add 3 × 15ml spoons/ 3 tablespoons of the sugar and continue beating for 1 minute or until the mixture is stiff and glossy. Carefully fold in the remaining sugar.

Pipe the meringue mixture onto the non-stick parchment to fill the circles. Reserve a little of the meringue mixture to pipe 6 small shells for the top decoration.

Bake in a preheated very cool oven (120°C/250°F, Gas Mark ½) for about 4 hours. Halfway through the baking, reverse the top and bottom meringue rounds. Remove from the oven and allow to cool slightly, then peel away the paper. Cool on a wire rack.

Whip the cream until thick. Set aside about 7 × 15ml spoons/7 tablespoons of the cream and fold the chestnut purée and sherry into the remainder.

Place a meringue round on a flat serving plate. Spread with half the chestnut cream. Cover with another meringue round and then with the remaining chestnut cream. Put the third meringue round on top. Secure the meringue shells to the top round with a little of the reserved cream. Pipe the remaining cream decoratively between the shells. Place the marrons glacés in the centre.

Melt the chocolate gently, then pipe a decorative pattern over the top in a thin line. Allow to set before serving.
Serves 8 to 10

Gâteau St. Honoré

METRIC/IMPERIAL
100g/4oz quantity French flan pastry★
65g/2½oz quantity choux pastry★
225g/8oz sugar
120ml/4fl oz water
Crème pâtissière:
600ml/1 pint milk
100g/4oz caster sugar
50g/2oz plain flour
15g/½oz cornflour
2 large eggs
50g/2oz butter

AMERICAN
1 cup quantity French flan pastry★
10 tablespoon quantity choux pastry★
1 cup sugar
½ cup water
Crème pâtissière:
2½ cups milk
½ cup sugar
½ cup all-purpose flour
2 tablespoons cornstarch
2 large eggs
¼ cup butter

Roll out the flan pastry dough to a round about 21cm/8½ inches in diameter. Place on a baking sheet and prick with a fork. Crimp the edge for a decorative finish. Bake in a preheated moderate oven (180°C/350°F, Gas Mark 4) for 20 minutes or until pale golden and set. Cool on the baking sheet.

Meanwhile, mark a 21cm/8½ inch circle on a dampened baking sheet. Pipe two-thirds of the choux pastry dough on the circle in a ring. Pipe the remaining choux dough into 16 small buns on another dampened baking sheet. Bake in a preheated hot oven (230°C/450°F, Gas Mark 8) for 15 minutes, then reduce the temperature to moderately hot (190°C/375°F, Gas Mark 5). Bake for a further 20 minutes. Slit each bun and the base of the ring to allow the steam to escape and cool on a wire rack.

Put the sugar and water in a saucepan and heat gently, stirring to dissolve the sugar. Bring to the boil and boil until the syrup reaches 130°C/260°F. Remove from the heat.

Dip the tops and sides of the choux buns in the syrup. Place the pastry round on a flat serving plate and put the choux ring on top. Arrange the glazed buns on the ring.

To make the crème pâtissière, scald the milk in a saucepan. Mix together the sugar, flour, cornflour (cornstarch) and eggs in a mixing bowl and stir in a little of the hot milk. Add the mixture to the milk in the saucepan and heat gently, stirring, until it thickens. Add the butter and beat well. Remove from the heat and allow to cool.

Spoon the crème pâtissière into the centre of the gâteau. Serve the same day.
Serves 8

Gâteau au chocolat

METRIC/IMPERIAL
4 eggs
100g/4oz caster sugar
75g/3oz unsalted butter, melted and cooled
50g/2oz plain flour
25g/1oz cocoa powder
Filling and icing:
75g/3oz sugar
75g/3oz butter
3 × 15ml spoons/ 3 tablespoons milk
225g/8oz icing sugar, sifted
1.5 × 15ml spoons/ 1½ tablespoons cocoa powder
100g/4oz plain chocolate

AMERICAN
4 eggs
½ cup sugar
⅓ cup unsalted butter, melted and cooled
½ cup all-purpose flour
¼ cup unsweetened cocoa powder
Filling and icing:
⅓ cup sugar
⅓ cup butter
3 tablespoons milk
1¾ cups confectioners' sugar, sifted
1½ tablespoons unsweetened cocoa powder
4 squares semisweet chocolate

Put the eggs and sugar in a large heatproof bowl over a pan of hot water. Beat until the mixture is pale and thick and will make a ribbon trail on itself when the beater is lifted. (If using an electric mixer, no heat is needed.) Remove from the heat and continue beating for 4 minutes. Add half the butter, then sift in the flour and cocoa powder. Fold into the egg mixture, then mix in the remaining butter.

Divide the batter between 2 greased and lined 18cm/7 inch diameter sandwich (layer) cake tins. Bake in a preheated moderate oven (180°C/350°F, Gas Mark 4) for 20 to 25 minutes or until just firm to the touch. Cool on a wire rack.

To make the filling, put the sugar, butter and milk in a saucepan and heat gently, stirring to dissolve the sugar. Bring to the boil and boil for 1 minute. Remove from the heat and cool quickly by standing the pan in cold water. Stir occasionally.

Sift together the icing (confectioners') sugar and cocoa powder. Stir in the cooled mixture, then beat well until thick and fluffy.

Cut each of the cake layers in half to make 4 layers. Use three-quarters of the chocolate filling to sandwich the layers together. Spread the remaining quarter around the sides of the cake.

Melt the chocolate gently. Spread half over the top of the cake. Spread the remainder onto a sheet of foil and allow to cool and set. Cut into squares and use to decorate the sides of the cake.
Makes one 18cm/7 inch round cake

FEAST DAYS

Roast turkey

METRIC/IMPERIAL
1 × 3.5kg/8lb turkey
chestnut and sausage meat stuffing★
50g/2oz butter, melted
Celery and apple stuffing:
50g/2oz butter
1 medium onion, peeled and finely chopped
3 celery sticks, finely chopped
1 medium cooking apple, peeled, cored and diced
175g/6oz fresh breadcrumbs
finely grated rind and juice of 1 small lemon
2 × 5ml spoons/2 teaspoons dried sage
3 × 15ml spoons/ 3 tablespoons turkey or chicken stock
salt
freshly ground black pepper

AMERICAN
1 × 8lb turkey
chestnut and sausage meat stuffing★
¼ cup butter, melted
Celery and apple stuffing:
¼ cup butter
1 medium onion, peeled and finely chopped
3 celery stalks, finely chopped
1 medium baking apple, peeled, cored and diced
3 cups fresh breadcrumbs
finely grated rind and juice of 1 small lemon
2 teaspoons dried sage
3 tablespoons turkey or chicken stock
salt
freshly ground black pepper

First make the celery and apple stuffing. Melt the butter in a frying pan (skillet). Add the onion and celery and fry until the onion is soft but not brown. Stir in the apple and fry for 3 minutes. Remove from the heat and stir in the remaining stuffing ingredients with salt and pepper to taste. Allow to cool.

Stuff the vent end of the turkey with the chestnut and sausage meat mixture. Use the celery and apple stuffing for the neck end. Truss the turkey with trussing needle and thread or with skewers. Place in a roasting tin and brush all over with melted butter. Sprinkle with salt and pepper.

Cover the turkey with foil and roast in a preheated hot oven (230°C/450°F, Gas Mark 8) for 2½ hours, or until the juices are clear when the thigh is pierced. Remove the foil for the last 30 minutes to brown the breast.

Transfer the turkey to a carving board or serving platter. Serve with sausages, Brussels sprouts and roast potatoes.

Serves 8 to 10

Christmas roast goose

METRIC/IMPERIAL
1 × 3.5-4kg/8-9lb goose
1 lemon, quartered
salt
freshly ground black pepper
spiced crabapples to garnish
Stuffing:
25g/1oz butter
1 onion, peeled and finely chopped
1kg/2lb pork sausage meat
2 × 0.5kg/1lb cans apricot halves, drained and chopped
50g/2oz fresh breadcrumbs
1 × 2.5ml spoon/½ teaspoon dried thyme
pinch of grated nutmeg
6 × 15ml spoons/ 6 tablespoons double cream

AMERICAN
1 × 8-9lb goose
1 lemon, quartered
salt
freshly ground black pepper
spiced crabapples to garnish
Stuffing:
2 tablespoons butter
1 onion, peeled and finely chopped
2lb pork sausage meat
2 × 1lb cans apricot halves, drained and chopped
1 cup fresh breadcrumbs
½ teaspoon dried thyme
pinch of grated nutmeg
6 tablespoons heavy cream

Prick the goose all over and rub with 3 of the lemon quarters. Sprinkle with salt and pepper. Squeeze the remaining lemon quarter inside the goose.

To make the stuffing, melt the butter in a frying pan (skillet). Add the onion and fry until it is soft but not brown. Add the sausage meat and brown lightly. Remove from the heat and stir in the remaining stuffing ingredients with salt and pepper to taste. Allow to cool.

Spoon the stuffing into the goose and secure the opening with a skewer or trussing needle and string. Place the goose, on its breast, on a rack in a roasting tin. Roast in a preheated hot oven (230°C/450°F, Gas Mark 8) for 15 minutes, then reduce the temperature to moderate (180°C/350°F, Gas Mark 4). Continue roasting for 2½ to 3 hours or until the goose is cooked. Remove the fat from the tin from time to time and turn the goose onto its back halfway through the cooking period.

Transfer the goose to a carving board and remove the skewer or trussing string. Serve hot, garnished with crabapples.

Serves 6 to 8

Christmas pudding

METRIC/IMPERIAL
100g/4oz self-raising flour
1 × 2.5ml spoon/½ teaspoon salt
1 × 2.5ml spoon/½ teaspoon grated nutmeg
1 × 2.5ml spoon/½ teaspoon ground cinnamon
1 × 2.5ml spoon/½ teaspoon ground cloves
175g/6oz fresh white breadcrumbs
175g/6oz shredded beef suet
225g/8oz brown sugar
225g/8oz currants
225g/8oz sultanas
0.5kg/1lb raisins
50g/2oz candied peel, chopped
25g/1oz blanched almonds, flaked
25g/1oz glacé cherries, chopped
1 medium cooking apple, peeled, cored and shredded
finely grated rind and juice of ½ lemon
finely grated rind and juice of ½ orange
3 eggs
5 × 15ml spoons/ 5 tablespoons stout
holly leaves to decorate

AMERICAN
1 cup self-rising flour
½ teaspoon salt
½ teaspoon grated nutmeg
½ teaspoon ground cinnamon
½ teaspoon ground cloves
3 cups fresh white breadcrumbs
1 cup plus 3 tablespoons shredded beef suet
1⅓ cups brown sugar
1⅓ cups currants
1⅓ cups seedless white raisins
2⅔ cups raisins
⅓ cup chopped candied peel
¼ cup blanched slivered almonds
2 tablespoons chopped candied cherries
1 medium baking apple, peeled, cored and shredded
finely grated rind and juice of ½ lemon
finely grated rind and juice of ½ orange
3 eggs
⅓ cup stout or dark beer
holly leaves to decorate

Sift the flour, salt and spices into a mixing bowl. Stir in the breadcrumbs, suet, sugar, dried fruit, nuts, cherries, apple and lemon and orange rind. Mix together the lemon and orange juice, eggs and stout (or beer) and stir into the mixing bowl. Mix well. Spoon into a greased 1.75 litre/3 pint/7½ cup pudding basin (steaming mold). Cover securely with greased greaseproof paper, or non-stick parchment, and foil and tie on with string.

Steam for 6 hours, replenishing the boiling water when necessary. Allow the pudding to cool, then cover with a fresh lid of greased greaseproof paper, or non-stick parchment, and foil. Store in a cool dry place.

To prepare for Christmas, allow a further 3 hours steaming. Turn out onto a serving plate and flame with warmed brandy. Decorate with holly leaves and serve with brandy butter.

Serves 8 to 10

Christmas cake

METRIC/IMPERIAL
275g/10oz plain flour
pinch of salt
1 × 2.5ml spoon/½ teaspoon baking powder
1 × 2.5ml spoon/½ teaspoon ground cinnamon
1 × 2.5ml spoon/½ teaspoon grated nutmeg
1 × 15ml spoon/
 1 tablespoon cocoa powder
0.5kg/1lb sultanas
350g/12oz currants
350g/12oz raisins
225g/8oz glacé cherries, chopped
100g/4oz blanched almonds, chopped
225g/8oz butter
225g/8oz soft brown sugar
4 eggs, lightly beaten
finely grated rind and juice of 1 lemon
1 × 15ml spoon/
 1 tablespoon treacle
3 × 15ml spoons/
 3 tablespoons brandy
1 quantity almond paste★
1 quantity royal icing★

AMERICAN
2½ cups all-purpose flour
pinch of salt
½ teaspoon baking powder
½ teaspoon ground cinnamon
½ teaspoon grated nutmeg
1 tablespoon unsweetened cocoa powder
2⅔ cups seedless white raisins
2 cups currants
2 cups raisins
1 cup candied cherries, chopped
1 cup chopped blanched almonds
1 cup butter
1⅓ cups brown sugar
4 eggs, lightly beaten
finely grated rind and juice of 1 lemon
1 tablespoon molasses
3 tablespoons brandy
1 quantity marzipan★
1 quantity royal icing★

Sift the flour, salt, baking powder, spices and cocoa powder into a mixing bowl. Stir in the dried fruits, cherries and nuts.

In another bowl, cream the butter and brown sugar together until the mixture is light and fluffy. Gradually beat in the eggs, then gradually fold in the flour mixture. Stir in the lemon rind and juice, treacle (molasses) and brandy. If the mixture is too dry, add a little milk.

Pour into a greased 23cm/9 inch diameter deep cake tin that has been double-lined with greaseproof paper, non-stick parchment or foil. Bake in a pre-heated cool oven (150°C/300°F, Gas Mark 2) for 1 hour, then reduce the temperature to 140°C/275°F, Gas Mark 1. Continue baking for 3 to 3½ hours or until a skewer inserted into the centre comes out clean.

Allow to cool in the tin.

Turn the cake out of the tin and peel off the paper or foil. Divide the almond paste (marzipan) in half and roll out one half to a 23cm/9 inch diameter round. Place on top of the cake and press on firmly.

Roll out the remaining almond paste (marzipan) to a strip long enough to go around the side of the cake. Press onto the cake and leave to dry for 2 to 3 days.

Cover the top and side of the cake with the icing and decorate with Christmas ornaments.
Makes one 23cm/9 inch round cake

Mince pies

METRIC/IMPERIAL
350g/12oz quantity rich shortcrust pastry* (made with 350g/12oz flour, etc.)
350g/12oz mincemeat*
sugar

AMERICAN
3 cup quantity rich pie pastry* (made with 3 cups flour, etc.)
2 cups mincemeat*
sugar

Roll out two-thirds of the pastry dough and cut out 20 rounds 7.5cm/3 inches in diameter. Use these to line twenty 6cm/2½ inch diameter patty (muffin) tins. Fill each pastry case (shell) two-thirds full with mincemeat.

Roll out the remaining dough. Cut out 20 rounds 6cm/2½ inches in diameter. Use these as lids and press the edges together to seal. Make a small slit in the top of each pie and sprinkle with sugar.

Bake in a preheated moderately hot oven (200°C/400°F, Gas Mark 6) for 20 minutes or until golden brown. Serve warm.
Makes 20

Mincemeat

METRIC/IMPERIAL
350g/12oz raisins, chopped
225g/8oz sultanas, chopped
350g/12oz currants, chopped
2 medium cooking apples, peeled, cored and grated
0.5kg/1lb brown sugar
0.5kg/1lb shredded suet
1 × 5ml spoon/1 teaspoon grated nutmeg
1 × 2.5ml spoon/½ teaspoon ground cinnamon
grated rind and juice of 1 lemon
grated rind and juice of 1 orange
250ml/8fl oz brandy

AMERICAN
2 cups raisins, chopped
1⅓ cups seedless white raisins, chopped
2 cups currants, chopped
2 medium baking apples, peeled, cored and grated
2⅔ cups brown sugar
3 cups plus 3 tablespoons shredded suet
1 teaspoon grated nutmeg
½ teaspoon ground cinnamon
grated rind and juice of 1 lemon
grated rind and juice of 1 orange
1 cup brandy

Mix together all the ingredients. Cover and leave overnight.

Stir well and spoon into jam jars. Cover as for jam and store in a cool dry place. Allow to mature for at least 2 weeks before using.
Makes about 2.75kg/6lb

Hot cross buns

METRIC/IMPERIAL
25g/1oz fresh yeast
150ml/¼ pint lukewarm milk
6 × 15ml spoons/ 6 tablespoons lukewarm water
0.5kg/1lb plain flour
1 × 5ml spoon/1 teaspoon salt
1 × 2.5ml spoon/½ teaspoon grated nutmeg
1 × 2.5ml spoon/½ teaspoon ground cinnamon
1 × 2.5ml spoon/½ teaspoon ground cloves
50g/2oz caster sugar
50g/2oz butter, melted and cooled
1 egg, lightly beaten
100g/4oz currants
25g/1oz chopped mixed candied peel

Glaze:
2 × 15ml spoons/ 2 tablespoons milk
2 × 15ml spoons/ 2 tablespoons water
40g/1½oz caster sugar

AMERICAN
1 cake compressed yeast
⅔ cup lukewarm milk
6 tablespoons lukewarm water
4 cups all-purpose flour
1 teaspoon salt
½ teaspoon grated nutmeg
½ teaspoon ground cinnamon
½ teaspoon ground cloves
¼ cup sugar
¼ cup butter, melted and cooled
1 egg, lightly beaten
⅔ cup currants
3 tablespoons chopped mixed candied peel

Glaze:
2 tablespoons milk
2 tablespoons water
3 tablespoons sugar

Cream the yeast with a little of the milk, then stir in the remaining milk and water.

Sift the flour, salt, spices and sugar into a mixing bowl. Make a well in the centre and add the butter, egg and yeast mixture. Gradually draw the flour mixture into the liquids and continue mixing until the dough comes away from the sides of the bowl. Knead in the currants and candied peel.

Turn out of the bowl and knead the dough until it is smooth and elastic. Return to the bowl, cover and leave to rise in a warm place for 1 to 1½ hours or until doubled in size.

Knead the dough again for about 5 minutes. Divide it into 12 portions and shape into buns. Arrange the buns, well spaced apart, on floured baking sheets. Cover and leave to rise in a warm place for a further 30 minutes.

Cut a cross in the top of each bun and bake in a preheated moderately hot oven (190°C/375°F, Gas Mark 5) for 15 to 20 minutes.

Mix together the ingredients for the glaze. Remove the buns from the oven and brush twice with the glaze. Allow to cool on a wire rack.

Makes 12

Easter biscuits (cookies)

METRIC/IMPERIAL
75g/3oz butter
75g/3oz caster sugar
1 egg, beaten
175g/6oz self-raising flour
pinch of salt
pinch of grated nutmeg
pinch of ground cinnamon
50g/2oz sultanas, roughly chopped
1–2 × 15ml spoons/ 1–2 tablespoons milk
1 egg white, lightly beaten
caster sugar for sprinkling

AMERICAN
⅓ cup butter
⅓ cup sugar
1 egg, beaten
1½ cups self-rising flour
pinch of salt
pinch of grated nutmeg
pinch of ground cinnamon
⅓ cup roughly chopped seedless white raisins
1–2 tablespoons milk
1 egg white, lightly beaten
sugar for sprinkling

Put the butter and sugar in a bowl and cream together until the mixture is light and fluffy. Add the egg and beat well. Sift together the flour, salt and spices and fold into the creamed mixture with the sultanas (raisins). Beat well and add enough milk to make a soft dough. Knead lightly until smooth, then roll out on a floured surface until 6mm/¼ inch thick. Using a biscuit (cookie) cutter, cut into rounds. Place on greased baking sheets, leaving enough room to allow for expansion. Put in the centre of a preheated moderate oven (180°C/350°F, Gas Mark 4) and bake for 10 minutes. Remove from the oven, brush with the egg white and sprinkle with sugar. Return to the oven and cook for a further 10 minutes or until golden. When cooked, leave to cool for a few minutes, then transfer to a wire rack to cool completely.
Makes 16 to 18

Simnel cake

METRIC/IMPERIAL
225g/8oz plain flour
pinch of salt
1 × 2.5ml spoon/½ teaspoon grated nutmeg
1 × 2.5ml spoon/½ teaspoon ground cinnamon
225g/8oz currants
100g/4oz sultanas
75g/3oz chopped mixed candied peel
100g/4oz glacé cherries, quartered
175g/6oz butter
175g/6oz caster sugar
3 eggs
1 quantity almond paste★
1 egg white

AMERICAN
2 cups all-purpose flour
pinch of salt
½ teaspoon grated nutmeg
½ teaspoon ground cinnamon
1⅓ cups currants
⅔ cup seedless white raisins
½ cup chopped mixed candied peel
½ cup candied cherries, quartered
¾ cup butter
¾ cup sugar
3 eggs
1 quantity marzipan★
1 egg white

Sift the flour, salt and spices into a mixing bowl. Stir in the currants, sultanas (raisins), candied peel and cherries. Cream the butter with the sugar until the mixture is light and fluffy. Gradually beat in the eggs, then fold in the flour and fruit mixture. Spoon half into a greased and lined 18cm/7 inch diameter deep cake tin.

Roll out one-third of the almond paste (marzipan) into a circle slightly smaller than the diameter of the tin. Place in the tin. Cover with the remaining cake mixture and smooth the top.

Bake in a preheated cool oven (150°C/300°F, Gas Mark 3) for 2½ to 3 hours or until the cake is firm to the touch. Remove from the oven and allow to cool on a wire rack.

Divide the remaining almond paste (marzipan) in half. Roll out one piece to a round just large enough to cover the top of the cake. Divide the other piece into 11 portions and shape each into a ball.

Brush the top of the cake with egg white and place the almond paste (marzipan) round on top. Arrange the balls around the top edge. Brush the top and balls with egg white. Grill (broil) gently until lightly browned.
Makes one 18cm/7 inch round cake

Kreplach

METRIC/IMPERIAL
Dough:
1 egg
salt
freshly ground black pepper
75g/3oz plain flour
Filling:
225g/8oz cooked meat, minced
1 small onion, peeled and grated
1 egg

AMERICAN
Dough:
1 egg
salt
freshly ground black pepper
¾ cup all-purpose flour
Filling:
1 cup ground cooked meat
1 small onion, peeled and grated
1 egg

Beat the egg with salt and pepper to taste. Gradually sift in the flour, beating to form a stiff dough. Knead well and roll out very thinly. Leave to dry for 1 hour.

Cut the dough into 7.5cm/3 inch squares.

Mix together the ingredients for the filling with salt and pepper to taste. Divide between the dough squares. Dampen the edges and fold over to form triangles. Press the edges together to seal. Leave to dry for 30 minutes.

Lower gently into boiling salted water, or soup, and simmer for 15 minutes. Serve hot, in the soup, or with a mushroom or tomato sauce.

Makes about 18

Lekach (honey cake)

METRIC/IMPERIAL
0.5kg/1lb honey
250ml/8 fl oz oil
2 × 5ml spoons/2 teaspoons instant coffee powder
150ml/¼ pint boiling water
225g/8oz dark brown sugar
4 eggs
0.5kg/1lb self-raising flour
1 × 5ml spoon/1 teaspoon bicarbonate of soda
1 × 5ml spoon/1 teaspoon ground cinnamon
1 × 2.5ml spoon/½ teaspoon ground cloves
1 × 2.5ml spoon/½ teaspoon grated nutmeg
1 × 5ml spoon/1 teaspoon ground ginger

AMERICAN
1lb (1⅓ cups) honey
1 cup oil
2 teaspoons instant coffee powder
⅔ cup boiling water
1⅓ cups brown sugar
4 eggs
4 cups self-rising flour
1 teaspoon baking soda
1 teaspoon ground cinnamon
½ teaspoon ground cloves
½ teaspoon grated nutmeg
1 teaspoon ground ginger

Mix together the honey and oil. Dissolve the coffee powder in the boiling water and add to the honey mixture with the sugar. Beat in the eggs. Sift together the flour, soda and spices and fold into the honey mixture. Pour into a greased shallow 30 × 25cm/12 × 10 inch cake tin.

Bake in a preheated moderate oven (160°C/325°F, Gas Mark 3) for 1 to 1¼ hours. Allow to cool in the tin, then cut into squares to serve.

Makes about 30 squares

Carrot pudding

METRIC/IMPERIAL
50g/2oz butter or margarine
50g/2oz sugar
2 eggs, separated
50g/2oz potato flour
1 × 5ml spoon/1 teaspoon ground cinnamon
225g/8oz carrots, peeled and grated
1 × 15ml spoon/
 1 tablespoon chopped walnuts
4 × 15ml spoons/
 4 tablespoons dry red wine
grated rind and juice of 1 lemon
pinch of salt

AMERICAN
¼ cup butter or margarine
¼ cup sugar
2 eggs, separated
½ cup potato flour
1 teaspoon ground cinnamon
½lb carrots, peeled and grated
1 tablespoon chopped walnuts
4 tablespoons dry red wine
grated rind and juice of 1 lemon
pinch of salt

Cream the butter or margarine with the sugar until the mixture is light and fluffy. Beat in the egg yolks. Sift in the potato flour and cinnamon and fold in with the carrots, walnuts, wine, lemon rind and juice and salt. Beat the egg whites until stiff and fold into the carrot mixture. Pour into a greased baking dish.

Bake in a preheated moderate oven (180°C/350°F, Gas Mark 4) for 45 minutes.

Serve hot, from the dish.

Serves 4 to 5

Spinach and matzo bake

METRIC/IMPERIAL
1kg/2lb spinach
2 × 15ml spoons/
 2 tablespoons oil
1 onion, peeled and grated
salt
freshly ground black pepper
50g/2oz butter, melted
3 eggs
3 matzo, dipped in cold water
100g/4oz Cheddar cheese, grated

AMERICAN
2lb spinach
2 tablespoons oil
1 onion, peeled and grated
salt
freshly ground black pepper
¼ cup butter, melted
3 eggs
3 matzo, dipped in cold water
1 cup grated Cheddar cheese

Cook the spinach for about 7 minutes or until it is tender. (Do not add any water: there should be enough left on the leaves after washing.)

Meanwhile, heat the oil in a frying pan (skillet). Add the onion and fry until it is soft but not brown. Remove from the heat.

Drain the spinach, pressing out all excess moisture. Chop finely and mix with the onion and salt and pepper to taste.

Put half the butter in a square baking dish and tilt to coat the bottom and sides. Beat together the eggs and salt and pepper. Dip one matzo in the egg and arrange in the dish. (The matzo should fill the dish so, if necessary, cut another matzo to fill any gaps.)

Spread over half the spinach mixture and one-third of the cheese. Dip the second matzo in the egg and place on the cheese. Cover with the remaining spinach mixture and another third of the cheese.

Add the final matzo, dipped in egg, and pour over any remaining beaten egg and the remaining butter. Sprinkle over the remaining cheese.

Bake in a preheated moderately hot oven (190°C/375°F, Gas Mark 5) for 30 minutes. Cut into squares and serve hot.

Serves 4

Cinnamon balls

METRIC/IMPERIAL
2 egg whites
100g/4oz caster sugar
225g/8oz ground almonds
1 × 15ml spoon/
 1 tablespoon ground
 cinnamon
icing sugar

AMERICAN
2 egg whites
½ cup sugar
2 cups ground almonds
1 tablespoon ground
 cinnamon
confectioners' sugar

Beat the egg whites until stiff. Beat in half the sugar and continue beating for 1 minute or until the mixture is stiff and glossy. Fold in the remaining sugar with the almonds and cinnamon.

Roll gently into small balls and arrange on a greased baking sheet. Bake in a preheated moderately hot oven (200°C/400°F, Gas Mark 6) for 10 to 15 minutes.

Roll in icing (confectioners') sugar while still warm.
Makes about 24

Cherry and apple strudel

METRIC/IMPERIAL
Dough:
175g/6oz plain flour
pinch of salt
1 × 15ml spoon/
 1 tablspoon oil
1 egg
4 × 15ml spoons/
 4 tablespoons lukewarm
 water
4 × 15ml spoons/
 4 tablespoons melted butter
Filling:
50g/2oz fresh breadcrumbs
50g/2oz sultanas
1 large cooking apple,
 peeled, cored and chopped
1 × 225g/8oz can cherries,
 drained, stoned and
 chopped
50g/2oz sugar
grated rind and juice of ½
 lemon
pinch of ground cinnamon

AMERICAN
Dough:
1½ cups all-purpose flour
pinch of salt
1 tablespoon oil
1 egg
4 tablespoons lukewarm
 water
4 tablespoons melted butter
Filling:
1 cup fresh breadcrumbs
⅓ cup seedless white raisins
1 large baking apple,
 peeled, cored and chopped
1 × ½lb can cherries,
 drained, pitted and
 chopped
¼ cup sugar
grated rind and juice of ½
 lemon
pinch of ground cinnamon

Sift the flour and salt into a mixing bowl. Add the oil, egg and water and mix to a soft dough. Knead until smooth, then cover and leave in a warm place for 30 minutes.

Divide the dough in half and roll out one half on a floured sheet of greaseproof (waxed) paper. Roll until paper thin. Brush with 1 × 15ml spoon/1 tablespoon of the melted butter.

Sprinkle over half the breadcrumbs. Mix together the remaining filling ingredients, adding more sugar according to taste. Put half the filling on the rolled out dough and spread to within 1cm/½ inch of the edge. Roll up, using the paper to lift the dough, and press the edges together to seal. Place on an oiled baking sheet and brush all over with another 1 × 15ml spoon/1 tablespoon of the butter. Repeat this process with the other piece of dough.

Bake in a preheated hot oven (220°C/425°F, Gas Mark 7) for 40 minutes basting occasionally with the butter. If the pastry is browning too quickly, reduce the temperature after 30 minutes.
Makes about 12 slices

Stollen (German Christmas bread)

METRIC/IMPERIAL
25g/1oz fresh yeast
200ml/⅓ pint lukewarm milk
0.5kg/1lb plain flour
1 × 5ml spoon/1 teaspoon ground cinnamon
1 × 5ml spoon/1 teaspoon ground allspice
175g/6oz sugar
2 eggs, lightly beaten
100g/4oz chopped mixed candied peel
100g/4oz raisins
75g/3oz walnuts, chopped
Icing:
225g/8oz icing sugar
25g/1oz butter, melted
1 × 15ml spoon/1 tablespoon lemon juice
1 × 2.5ml spoon/½ teaspoon vanilla essence
1 × 15ml spoon/1 tablespoon hot water

AMERICAN
1 cake compressed yeast
⅞ cup lukewarm milk
4 cups all-purpose flour
1 teaspoon ground cinnamon
1 teaspoon ground allspice
¾ cup sugar
2 eggs, lightly beaten
⅔ cup chopped mixed candied peel
⅔ cup raisins
¾ cup chopped walnuts
Icing:
1¾ cups confectioners' sugar
2 tablespoons butter, melted
1 tablespoon lemon juice
½ teaspoon vanilla extract
1 tablespoon hot water

Cream the yeast with a little of the milk, then stir in the remaining milk.

Sift the flour and spices into a mixing bowl, then stir in the sugar. Make a well in the centre and add the eggs and yeast mixture. Mix well to a soft dough, then knead for 10 minutes or until smooth and elastic. Knead in the candied peel, raisins and walnuts until evenly distributed. Put in a polythene (plastic) bag and leave to rise in a warm place for 1½ hours or until doubled in size.

Knead the dough lightly, then shape into a flat crescent. Place on a baking sheet and leave to rise in a warm place for a further 45 minutes.

Bake in a preheated moderately hot oven (200°C/400°F, Gas Mark 6) for 10 minutes, then reduce the temperature to moderate (180°C/350°F, Gas Mark 4). Continue baking for 35 minutes. Cool on a wire rack.

To make the icing, sift the icing (confectioners') sugar into a mixing bowl and stir in the remaining ingredients. Spread the icing over the cooled bread and allow to set. Serve cut into thin slices.

Makes one large loaf

Pumpkin pie

METRIC/IMPERIAL
225g/8oz quantity rich shortcrust pastry★ (made with 225g/8oz flour, etc.)
1 × 0.75kg/1½lb can puréed pumpkin
100g/4oz brown sugar
1 × 5ml spoon/1 teaspoon ground allspice
1 × 2.5ml spoon/½ teaspoon ground ginger
2 eggs, lightly beaten
250ml/8fl oz single cream

AMERICAN
2 cup quantity rich pie pastry★ (made with 2 cups flour, etc.)
1 × 1½lb can puréed pumpkin
⅔ cup brown sugar
1 teaspoon ground allspice
½ teaspoon ground ginger
2 eggs, lightly beaten
1 cup light cream

Roll out the pastry dough and use to line a 20cm/8 inch diameter flan ring (pie pan).

Mix together the pumpkin, sugar, spices, eggs and cream and pour into the pastry case (pie shell). Bake in a preheated moderately hot oven (190°C/375°F, Gas Mark 5) for 40 to 45 minutes or until the filling is set and the pastry is golden brown. Allow to cool before serving.

Makes one 20cm/8 inch pie

PARTY SNACKS

Camembert cream

METRIC/IMPERIAL
75g/3oz Camembert cheese, rind removed
15g/½oz butter, melted
15g/½oz Petit Suisse or cream cheese
3 × 15ml spoons/ 3 tablespoons double cream
1 × 5ml spoon/1 teaspoon made French mustard
1 × 5ml spoon/1 teaspoon chopped fresh parsley
watercress to garnish

AMERICAN
3oz Camembert cheese, rind removed
1 tablespoon butter, melted
1 tablespoon Petit Suisse or cream cheese
3 tablespoons heavy cream
1 teaspoon prepared French mustard
1 teaspoon chopped fresh parsley
watercress to garnish

Beat the Camembert with the butter until smooth. Beat in the Petit Suisse or cream cheese, then the cream, mustard and parsley. Spoon into a small serving dish and chill until firm.
    Serve chilled, garnished with watercress, with small savoury biscuits (crackers).

Cheese and walnut dip

METRIC/IMPERIAL
0.5kg/1lb mild soft cheese
450ml/¾ pint single cream
½ small onion, peeled and grated
2 × 5ml spoons/2 teaspoons tomato purée
salt
freshly ground black pepper
40g/1½oz walnuts, finely chopped

AMERICAN
1lb mild soft cheese
2 cups light cream
½ small onion, peeled and grated
2 teaspoons tomato paste
salt
freshly ground black pepper
⅓ cup finely chopped walnuts

Beat the cheese until it is soft and smooth. Gradually beat in the cream, then the onion, tomato purée (paste) and salt and pepper to taste. Fold in the walnuts.

Bagna cauda

METRIC/IMPERIAL
75g/3oz unsalted butter
5 × 15ml spoons/ 5 tablespoons olive oil
1 × 50g/2oz can anchovy fillets, drained and finely chopped
2–6 garlic cloves, finely chopped
To serve:
raw vegetables (e.g. carrot sticks, celery sticks, red or green pepper strips)

AMERICAN
⅓ cup unsalted butter
⅓ cup olive oil
1 × 2oz can anchovy fillets, drained and finely chopped
2–6 garlic cloves, finely chopped
To serve:
raw vegetables (e.g. carrot sticks, celery stalks, pimiento or green pepper strips)

Put the butter, oil, anchovies and garlic in a saucepan and cook gently for 15 minutes. Pour into a heatproof serving dish and place over a lighted spirit burner. Serve hot with the vegetables.

Sour cream and garlic dip

METRIC/IMPERIAL
300ml/½ pint sour cream
2 garlic cloves, crushed
salt
freshly ground black pepper

AMERICAN
1¼ cups sour cream
2 garlic cloves, crushed
salt
freshly ground black pepper

Mix together all the ingredients with salt and pepper to taste. Chill for at least 30 minutes before serving.

Hot mustard dip

METRIC/IMPERIAL
25g/1oz butter
3 × 15ml spoons/
  3 tablespoons plain flour
300ml/½ pint chicken stock
1 × 15ml spoon/
  1 tablespoon made mild mustard
2 × 5ml spoons/2 teaspoons made English mustard
2 × 15ml spoons/
  2 tablespoons vinegar

AMERICAN
2 tablespoons butter
3 tablespoons all-purpose flour
1¼ cups chicken stock
1 tablespoon prepared mild mustard
2 teaspoons prepared English mustard
2 tablespoons vinegar

Melt the butter in a saucepan. Stir in the flour and cook, stirring, for 1 minute. Remove from the heat and gradually stir in the stock. Return to the heat and bring to the boil, stirring. Simmer until thickened and smooth.
  Remove from the heat and stir in the mustards and vinegar. Serve hot with small sausages, meatballs and vegetables for dipping.

Blue cheese dip

METRIC/IMPERIAL
100g/4oz cream cheese
100g/4oz blue cheese
150ml/¼ pint sour cream

AMERICAN
½ cup cream cheese
¼lb blue cheese
⅔ cup sour cream

Cream all the ingredients together until well mixed. Serve lightly chilled, with savoury biscuits (crackers).

Guacamole

METRIC/IMPERIAL
2 large avocado pears, peeled and stoned
3 large tomatoes, peeled, deseeded and finely chopped
1 small onion, peeled and grated
150ml/¼ pint sour cream
1 × 15ml spoon/
  1 tablespoon lemon juice
3 × 15ml spoons/
  3 tablespoons mayonnaise★
salt
freshly ground black pepper
few drops of Tabasco sauce

AMERICAN
2 large avocado pears, peeled and deseeded
3 large tomatoes, peeled, deseeded and finely chopped
1 small onion, peeled and grated
⅔ cup sour cream
1 tablespoon lemon juice
3 tablespoons mayonnaise★
salt
freshly ground black pepper
few drops of Tabasco sauce

Mash the avocado flesh, then beat in the tomatoes, onion, sour cream, lemon juice, mayonnaise and salt and pepper to taste. Add enough Tabasco to make the dip slightly hot, or to your taste. Serve soon after making to prevent discoloration.

Liver pâté dip

METRIC/IMPERIAL
350g/12oz liver pâté
1 × 5ml spoon/1 teaspoon brandy
50g/2oz butter, softened
freshly ground black pepper
large pinch of mixed spice
double cream

AMERICAN
¾lb liver sausage
1 teaspoon brandy
¼ cup butter, softened
freshly ground black pepper
large pinch of apple pie spice
heavy cream

Beat together the liver pâté (sausage), brandy, butter, pepper to taste and the spice. Stir in enough cream to make a soft consistency. Spoon into a serving bowl and serve with crisps (potato chips), savoury biscuits (crackers) and raw vegetables.

Houmous

METRIC/IMPERIAL
100g/4oz dried chick peas, soaked overnight and drained
salt
pinch of garlic salt
freshly ground black pepper
juice of 1 lemon
pinch of paprika
2 × 15ml spoons/ 2 tablespoons olive oil
black olives to garnish

AMERICAN
½ cup dried chick peas (garbanzos), soaked overnight and drained
salt
pinch of garlic salt
freshly ground black pepper
juice of 1 lemon
pinch of paprika
2 tablespoons olive oil
black olives to garnish

Put the chick peas in a saucepan and cover with fresh water. Add salt and bring to the boil. Simmer for about 1 hour or until tender. Drain well.

Put the chick peas in the goblet of an electric blender with the remaining ingredients, except the olives, and blend until smooth. If necessary, add more oil to make a soft creamy consistency.

Serve garnished with olives.

Cheese straws

METRIC/IMPERIAL
225g/8oz plain flour
pinch of salt
pinch of freshly ground black pepper
pinch of cayenne pepper
pinch of dry mustard
100g/4oz butter or lard
75g/3oz Parmesan cheese, grated
2 egg yolks
water
egg white, lightly beaten

AMERICAN
2 cups all-purpose flour
pinch of salt
pinch of freshly ground black pepper
pinch of cayenne pepper
pinch of dry mustard
½ cup butter or shortening
¾ cup grated Parmesan cheese
2 egg yolks
water
egg white, lightly beaten

Sift the flour and seasonings into a mixing bowl. Rub in the butter or lard (shortening) until the mixture resembles breadcrumbs. Stir in the cheese. Add the egg yolks with enough water to bind the mixture to a soft dough.

Roll out the dough until it is about 1cm/½ inch thick. Cut into narrow fingers and arrange on greased baking sheets. Brush with egg white. Bake in a preheated hot oven (220°C/425°F, Gas Mark 7) for 8 to 10 minutes or until golden brown.

Allow to cool on the baking sheets. Serve fresh.
Makes about 60 straws

Cheese fritters

METRIC/IMPERIAL
100g/4oz butter
75g/3oz plain flour
600ml/1 pint milk
salt
freshly ground black pepper
1 × 5ml spoon/1 teaspoon dry mustard
350g/12oz Edam cheese, rind removed and diced
350g/12oz small button mushrooms
2 eggs, lightly beaten
100g/4oz dry breadcrumbs
vegetable oil for deep frying

AMERICAN
½ cup butter
¾ cup all-purpose flour
2½ cups milk
salt
freshly ground black pepper
1 teaspoon dry mustard
¾lb Edam cheese, rind removed and diced
3 cups small button mushrooms
2 eggs, lightly beaten
1 cup dry breadcrumbs
vegetable oil for deep frying

Melt the butter in a saucepan. Add the flour and cook, stirring, for 1 minute. Remove from the heat and gradually stir in the milk. Return to the heat and bring to the boil, stirring. Simmer until thickened and smooth. Season to taste with salt and pepper and add the mustard. Remove from the heat.

Stir the cheese and mushrooms into the sauce. Allow to cool, then shape into small fritters. Coat with the beaten egg, then in the breadcrumbs.

Heat the oil in a deep frying pan (deep fat fryer) until it is 180°C/350°F. Fry the fritters for 5 minutes or until they are golden brown. Drain on absorbent paper and serve hot.
Serves 8

Cream cheese puffs

METRIC/IMPERIAL
65g/2½oz quantity choux pastry★
100g/4oz cream cheese
50g/2oz butter
1 × 15ml spoon/ 1 tablespoon lemon juice
salt
freshly ground black pepper
2 × 15ml spoons/ 2 tablespoons chopped fresh chives

AMERICAN
10 tablespoon quantity choux pastry★
½ cup cream cheese
¼ cup butter
1 tablespoon lemon juice
salt
freshly ground black pepper
2 tablespoons chopped fresh chives

Pipe the choux pastry dough into about 24 walnut-sized balls on a dampened baking sheet. Bake in a preheated moderately hot oven (200°C/400°F, Gas Mark 6) for 15 to 20 minutes or until golden brown. Remove from the oven and make a slit in the side of each puff to allow the steam to escape. Leave to cool.

Cream together the cream cheese, butter, lemon juice and salt and pepper to taste. Stir in the chives.

Fill the choux puffs with the cream cheese mixture.
Makes 24

Hot cheese bites

METRIC/IMPERIAL
5 slices of white bread, crusts removed
50g/2oz butter
2 × 15ml spoons/ 2 tablespoons olive oil
100g/4oz Bel Paese cheese
10 anchovy fillets, halved

AMERICAN
5 slices of white bread, crusts removed
¼ cup butter
2 tablespoons olive oil
¼lb Bel Paese cheese
10 anchovy fillets, halved

Cut each slice of bread into quarters. Melt the butter with the oil in a frying pan (skillet). Add the bread squares, in batches, and fry until they are crisp and golden brown on both sides. Drain on absorbent paper.
  Cut the cheese into thin slices and then into squares the same size as the bread squares. Top each bread square with a square of cheese and arrange on a grill (broiler) rack. Grill (broil) until the cheese melts. Top each with an anchovy fillet half and serve hot.
Makes 20

Cheese olives

METRIC/IMPERIAL
225g/8oz cream cheese
15 pimento-stuffed olives
40g/1½oz walnuts, finely chopped

AMERICAN
1 cup cream cheese
15 pimiento-stuffed olives
⅓ cup finely chopped walnuts

Divide the cheese into 15 portions and use to cover the olives. Roll the cheese balls in walnuts to cover on all sides. Chill for 1 hour.
  To serve, cut each cheese ball in half.
Makes 30

Liptauer cheese dip

METRIC/IMPERIAL
top of the milk
225g/8oz curd cheese
1 gherkin, finely chopped
5 black olives, stoned and finely chopped
2 anchovy fillets, finely chopped
1 × 2.5ml spoon/½ teaspoon caraway seeds
paprika

AMERICAN
half-and-half
1 cup curd cheese
1 small dill pickle, finely chopped
5 black olives, pitted and finely chopped
2 anchovy fillets, finely chopped
½ teaspoon caraway seeds
paprika

Add enough top of the milk (half-and-half) to the cheese to moisten, and beat well. Stir in the remaining ingredients with paprika to colour to a pale pink.

Stuffed pepper slices

METRIC/IMPERIAL
2 red peppers
2 green peppers
175g/6oz cottage cheese
175g/6oz cream cheese
2 × 15ml spoons/ 2 tablespoons chopped fresh chives
2 × 15ml spoons/ 2 tablespoons chopped fresh parsley
salt
freshly ground black pepper

AMERICAN
2 pimientos
2 green peppers
¾ cup cottage cheese
¾ cup cream cheese
2 tablespoons chopped fresh chives
2 tablespoons chopped fresh parsley
salt
freshly ground black pepper

Cut the tops off the peppers and scoop out the seeds and white pith. Beat together the remaining ingredients with salt and pepper to taste. Fill the peppers with this mixture and chill for at least 30 minutes or until firm.
  To serve, slice the peppers and halve the slices. Arrange in rows on a serving plate.
Serves 20

Anchoïade

METRIC/IMPERIAL
2 × 50g/2oz cans anchovy fillets, drained
5 × 15ml spoons/ 5 tablespoons milk
8 slices of brown bread, crusts removed
50g/2oz unsalted butter
1 garlic clove, crushed
freshly ground black pepper

AMERICAN
2 × 2oz cans anchovy fillets, drained
⅓ cup milk
8 slices of brown bread, crusts removed
¼ cup unsalted butter
1 garlic clove, crushed
freshly ground black pepper

Soak the anchovies in the milk for 30 minutes. Drain well.
Toast the bread under a grill (broiler) on one side only. Remove from the heat. Butter the untoasted sides.
Pound the anchovies with the garlic to a paste and season to taste with pepper. Spread the buttered sides of the bread with the anchovy paste. Cut into small squares and arrange on a baking sheet.
Bake in a preheated moderately hot oven (200°C/400°F, Gas Mark 6) for 10 minutes or until crisp. Serve hot.
Serves 8 to 10

Sausage savouries

METRIC/IMPERIAL
24 small cocktail sausages
French mustard
175g/6oz Cheddar cheese, cut into 24 fingers
12 streaky bacon rashers, rinds removed and halved crossways

AMERICAN
24 small cocktail sausages
French mustard
6oz Cheddar cheese, cut into 24 fingers
12 bacon slices, halved crosswise

Grill (broil) the sausages until they are well browned and cooked. Spread one side of each sausage with mustard and press a cheese finger onto it. Wrap each sausage in a piece of bacon and secure with a wooden cocktail stick (toothpick).
Grill (broil) until the bacon is crisp and golden brown. Serve hot.
Makes 24

Fish goujons

METRIC/IMPERIAL
50g/2oz plain flour
salt
freshly ground black pepper
0.5kg/1lb white fish fillets (sole, whiting, etc.), skinned and cut into small strips
2 eggs, lightly beaten
100g/4oz dry breadcrumbs
vegetable oil for deep frying

AMERICAN
½ cup all-purpose flour
salt
freshly ground black pepper
1lb white fish fillets (sole, whiting, etc.), skinned and cut into small strips
2 eggs, lightly beaten
1 cup dry breadcrumbs
vegetable oil for deep frying

Put the flour and salt and pepper in a polythene (plastic) bag. Add the fish strips and shake to coat with the seasoned flour. Dip each fish strip in the beaten egg, then coat in the breadcrumbs.
Heat the oil in a deep frying pan (deep fat fryer) until it is 190°C/375°F. Fry the fish strips until they are golden brown.
Drain on absorbent paper and serve hot with tartare sauce★.
Serves 8 to 10

Onion biscuits (crackers)

METRIC/IMPERIAL
225g/8oz plain flour
pinch of salt
pinch of freshly ground black pepper
150g/5oz butter or margarine
1 onion, peeled and finely grated
2 eggs, lightly beaten

AMERICAN
2 cups all-purpose flour
pinch of salt
pinch of freshly ground black pepper
⅔ cup butter or margarine
1 onion, peeled and finely grated
2 eggs, lightly beaten

Sift the flour, salt and pepper into a mixing bowl. Rub in the butter or margarine until the mixture resembles breadcrumbs. Stir in the onion and enough beaten egg to bind to a stiff dough. Knead lightly.
Roll out the dough and cut into 5cm/2 inch squares. Arrange on a baking sheet. Brush with the remaining beaten egg. Bake in a preheated moderately hot oven (200°C/400°F, Gas Mark 6) for 15 to 20 minutes.
Makes about 24

DRINKS

Irish coffee

METRIC/IMPERIAL
4 sugar lumps
4 × 15ml spoons/
 4 tablespoons water
120ml/4 fl oz Irish whiskey
300ml/½ pint hot strong
 black coffee
120ml/4 fl oz double cream

AMERICAN
4 sugar lumps
4 tablespoons water
½ cup Irish whiskey
1¼ cups hot strong black
 liquid coffee
½ cup heavy cream

Put the sugar lumps and water in a saucepan and heat gently, stirring to dissolve the sugar. Divide between 4 stemmed heatproof glasses. Add 2 × 15ml spoons/ 2 tablespoons whiskey to each glass and top up with hot coffee. Stir well.
 Pour the cream carefully into each glass so that it floats on top of the coffee. Serve hot.
Serves 4

Hot rum toddy

METRIC/IMPERIAL
120ml/4 fl oz dark rum
2 × 5ml spoons/2 teaspoons
 clear honey
2 strips of thinly pared
 lemon rind
boiling water

AMERICAN
½ cup dark rum
2 teaspoons clear honey
2 strips of thinly pared
 lemon rind
boiling water

Divide the rum, honey and lemon rind between 2 small mugs and top up with boiling water. Stir well and serve hot.
Serves 2

Banana milk shake

METRIC/IMPERIAL
600ml/1 pint milk
2 bananas, sliced
1 × 5ml spoon/1 teaspoon
 clear honey

AMERICAN
2½ cups milk
2 bananas, sliced
1 teaspoon clear honey

Put all the ingredients in the goblet of an electric blender and blend until smooth and frothy. Serve immediately.
Serves 2

Mulled cider

METRIC/IMPERIAL
1.2 litres/2 pints cider
225g/8oz brown sugar
1 × 5cm/2 inch cinnamon
 stick
6 allspice berries
whole cloves
1 orange, sliced
1 lemon, sliced

AMERICAN
5 cups hard cider
1⅓ cups brown sugar
1 × 2 inch cinnamon stick
6 allspice berries
whole cloves
1 orange, sliced
1 lemon, sliced

Put the cider, sugar, cinnamon stick and allspice berries in a saucepan. Heat gently, stirring to dissolve the sugar. Bring almost to boiling point. Remove the cinnamon and allspice with a slotted spoon.
 Place a clove in each of the orange and lemon slices. Float on top of the cider and simmer for 5 minutes longer. Serve hot.
Serves 6

Huckle-my-buff

METRIC/IMPERIAL
1.2 litres/2 pints draught
 beer
6 eggs, lightly beaten
50g/2oz sugar
1 × 5ml spoon/1 teaspoon
 grated nutmeg
2 × 15ml spoons/
 2 tablespoons brandy

AMERICAN
5 cups draught beer
6 eggs, lightly beaten
¼ cup sugar
1 teaspoon grated nutmeg
2 tablespoons brandy

Put 600ml/1 pint/2½ cups of the beer, the eggs and sugar in a saucepan and heat gently, stirring. Do not allow to boil. When the mixture is very hot, remove from the heat and stir in the remaining beer, the nutmeg and brandy. Serve hot.
Serves 6

Glühwein

METRIC/IMPERIAL
8 whole cloves
1 orange
1½ bottles dry red wine
150ml/¼ pint orange juice
2 × 15ml spoons/
 2 tablespoons lemon juice
2 × 15ml spoons/
 2 tablespoons sugar
2 cinnamon sticks

AMERICAN
8 whole cloves
1 orange
1½ bottles dry red wine
⅔ cup orange juice
2 tablespoons lemon juice
2 tablespoons sugar
2 cinnamon sticks

Stick the cloves into the orange. Put the wine, orange juice, lemon juice and sugar in a saucepan and heat gently, stirring to dissolve the sugar. Add the orange and cinnamon sticks and heat through slowly. Serve hot.
Serves 6 to 8

Negus

METRIC/IMPERIAL
thinly pared rind and juice
 of 2 lemons
450ml/¾ pint water
75g/3oz sugar
grated nutmeg
1 bottle port wine

AMERICAN
thinly pared rind and juice
 of 2 lemons
2 cups water
⅓ cup sugar
grated nutmeg
1 bottle port wine

Put the lemon rind, water and sugar in a saucepan and heat gently, stirring to dissolve the sugar. Add the lemon juice, a generous pinch of grated nutmeg and the port and stir well. Heat through slowly. Serve hot, topped with a little more nutmeg.
Serves 10 to 12

Spiced orange juice

METRIC/IMPERIAL
600ml/1 pint orange juice
4 cinnamon sticks
grated nutmeg

AMERICAN
2½ cups orange juice
4 cinnamon sticks
grated nutmeg

Put the orange juice and cinnamon sticks in a saucepan and heat very gently for about 10 minutes. Remove the cinnamon sticks and pour into glasses. Top each serving with a pinch of nutmeg. Serve hot.
Serves 6

Iced tea

METRIC/IMPERIAL
1 litre/1¾ pints strong tea
sugar
6 lemon slices
6 mint sprigs

AMERICAN
4½ cups strong tea
sugar
6 lemon slices
6 mint sprigs

Sweeten the tea to taste with sugar and allow to cool.
Put 3 or 4 ice cubes in each of 6 tall glasses. Pour in the tea. Garnish each serving with a lemon slice and a mint sprig.
Serves 6

Sangria

METRIC/IMPERIAL
4 × 15ml spoons/
 4 tablespoons sugar
juice of 1 lemon
1.5 litres/2½ pints dry red
 wine
300ml/½ pint water
1 orange, sliced
1 lemon, sliced

AMERICAN
4 tablespoons sugar
juice of 1 lemon
6¼ cups dry red wine
1¼ cups water
1 orange, sliced
1 lemon, sliced

Put the sugar and lemon juice in a punch bowl and stir to dissolve the sugar. Add the wine and water and mix well.
Float the fruit slices on the surface and add a few ice cubes.
Serves 12

Summer wine cooler

METRIC/IMPERIAL
1 bottle medium sweet white wine, chilled
4 × 15ml spoons/ 4 tablespoons orange-flavoured liqueur
4 × 15ml spoons/ 4 tablespoons brandy
juice of 1 lemon
600ml/1 pint tonic or soda water
To garnish:
orange slices
lemon slices
mint sprigs

AMERICAN
1 bottle medium sweet white wine, chilled
4 tablespoons orange-flavored liqueur
4 tablespoons brandy
juice of 1 lemon
2½ cups tonic or soda water
To garnish:
orange slices
lemon slices
mint sprigs

Put the wine, liqueur, brandy and lemon juice in a punch bowl and stir well. Add some crushed ice and stir in the tonic or soda water. Add the fruit slices and mint sprigs and serve immediately.
Serves 6 to 8

Strawberry wine cooler

METRIC/IMPERIAL
1 bottle Beaujolais, chilled
2 × 15ml spoons/ 2 tablespoons brandy
100g/4oz strawberries, hulled and sliced
1.2 litres/2 pints lemonade, chilled

AMERICAN
1 bottle Beaujolais, chilled
2 tablespoons brandy
¼lb strawberries, hulled and sliced
5 cups lemonade, chilled

Put the wine, brandy and strawberries in a punch bowl and stir well. Leave in a cool place for 30 minutes.
Just before serving stir in the lemonade.
Serves 12

Gin fruit punch

METRIC/IMPERIAL
450ml/¾ pint water
100g/4oz sugar
juice of 6 oranges
juice of 6 lemons
600ml/1 pint tea
½ bottle gin
2.25 litres/4 pints soda water, chilled

AMERICAN
2 cups water
½ cup sugar
juice of 6 oranges
juice of 6 lemons
2½ cups tea
½ bottle gin
5 pints soda water, chilled

Put the water and sugar in a saucepan and heat gently, stirring to dissolve the sugar. Bring to the boil and boil for 10 minutes. Remove from the heat and allow to cool.
Pour the syrup into a punch bowl and stir in the orange and lemon juices, tea and gin. Leave to stand for 1 hour.
Just before serving, stir in the soda water.
Serves 25

Egg nog

METRIC/IMPERIAL
1 egg
1 × 15ml spoon/ 1 tablespoon sugar
2 × 15ml spoons/ 2 tablespoons brandy
200ml/⅓ pint milk
grated nutmeg

AMERICAN
1 egg
1 tablespoon sugar
2 tablespoons brandy
⅞ cup milk
grated nutmeg

Beat together the egg and sugar, then stir in the brandy. Heat the milk until it is very hot but not boiling. Pour into the egg mixture, stirring. Strain into a glass and serve hot, sprinkled with nutmeg.
Serves 1

Hot spiced tea

METRIC/IMPERIAL
1.2 litres/2 pints water
1 × 1cm/½ inch cinnamon stick
3 whole cloves
15g/½oz tea leaves
50g/2oz sugar
5 × 15ml spoons/
 5 tablespoons orange juice
juice of 1 lemon

AMERICAN
5 cups water
1 × ½ inch cinnamon stick
3 whole cloves
2½ tablespoons tea leaves
¼ cup sugar
⅓ cup orange juice
juice of 1 lemon

Put the water, cinnamon stick and cloves in a saucepan and bring to the boil. Put the tea in a mixing bowl and pour on the spiced water. Allow to infuse for 5 minutes.
 Stir the sugar into the tea mixture, then stir in the orange and lemon juices. Pour the tea mixture back into the saucepan and reheat without boiling. Strain and serve hot.
Serves 6

Tomato juice cocktail

METRIC/IMPERIAL
1kg/2lb tomatoes, peeled and chopped
1 small green pepper, pith and seeds removed and chopped
1 small onion, peeled and chopped
1 × 15ml spoon/
 1 tablespoon Worcestershire sauce
4 × 15ml spoons/
 4 tablespoons lemon juice
salt
freshly ground black pepper

AMERICAN
4 cups peeled and chopped tomatoes
1 small green pepper, pith and seeds removed and chopped
1 small onion, peeled and chopped
1 tablespoon Worcestershire sauce
4 tablespoons lemon juice
salt
freshly ground black pepper

Put the tomatoes, green pepper and onion in the goblet of an electric blender and blend until smooth. Strain into a jug and stir in the Worcestershire sauce, lemon juice and salt and pepper to taste. Serve chilled.
Serves 4 to 6

Lemonade

METRIC/IMPERIAL
600ml/1 pint water
100g/4oz sugar
finely grated rind and juice of 6 large lemons
water or soda water

AMERICAN
2½ cups water
½ cup sugar
finely grated rind and juice of 6 large lemons
water or soda water

Put the water and sugar in a saucepan and heat gently, stirring to dissolve the sugar. Add the lemon rind and bring to the boil. Boil for 3 to 4 minutes. Remove from the heat and allow to cool.
 Stir in the lemon juice. Strain the mixture into a glass container. Dilute to taste with water or soda water.
Serves 12 to 16

Ginger beer

METRIC/IMPERIAL
225g/8oz sugar
50g/2oz fresh root ginger, crushed
1 × 15ml spoon/
 1 tablespoon cream of tartar
grated rind and juice of 1 lemon
2.75 litres/5 pints boiling water
7g/¼oz fresh yeast

AMERICAN
1 cup sugar
2oz green ginger, crushed
1 tablespoon cream of tartar
grated rind and juice of 1 lemon
6 pints boiling water
¼ cake compressed yeast

Mix together the sugar, ginger, cream of tartar, lemon rind and boiling water, stirring to dissolve the sugar. Allow to cool.
 Crumble in the yeast and stir well. Leave in a warm place for 2 days or until the mixture stops frothing.
 Strain into a jug and stir in the lemon juice. Pour into stoppered bottles.
Makes about 2.75 litres/5 pints/6 pints

INDEX

Aïoli 15
Almond:
  Almond macaroons 321
  Almond paste 18
  Almond slices 332
  Almond spice bars 321
  Courgettes (zucchini) with almonds and cream 370
  Frozen almond meringue desserts 289
  Green beans with almonds 256
  Pear and almond crêpes 283
  Trout with almonds 53
Anchovy:
  Anchoïade 391
  Baked anchovy tomatoes 27
Angel food cake 302
Apple:
  Apple dumplings with walnut sauce 278
  Apple muffins 341
  Apple sauce 10
  Apple-stuffed steaks 83
  Applesauce spice cake 315
  Blackberry (bramble) and apple sponge 282
  Casseroled pigeons with apples and cider sauce 172
  Cherry and apple strudel 384
  Chilled apple and orange soup 46
  English apple pie 279
  French apple tart 297
  German apple cake 303
  Orange baked apples 277
  Red cabbage with apples 261
  Stuffed apple jelly 291
  Yorkshire apple tart 281
Apricot:
  Apricot and apple soufflé 294
  Apricot fool 288
  Apricot sherbet 293
  Apricot shortcake 372
  Apricot and walnut bread 336
  Chicken with apricots 161
  Loin of pork with apricot stuffing 134
  Roast leg of lamb with apricot stuffing 113
Artichoke:
  Artichoke omelette 200
  Jerusalem artichoke soup 358
  Mediterranean artichokes 370
  Stuffed globe artichokes 221

Asparagus:
  Asparagus hollandaise 260
  Ham and asparagus rolls 145
Aubergine (Eggplant):
  Aubergine and cheese casserole 189
  Aubergines with tomato sauce 248
  Lamb and aubergine casserole 112
  Stuffed aubergines 200
Avocado:
  Avocado with cheese dressing 32
  Avocado stuffed with crab 356
  Chicken and avocado casserole 152
  Chilled avocado soup 359
  Guacamole 387

Bacon:
  Bacon filling for baked potatoes 220
  Bacon and green bean quiche 221
  Beans with bacon 371
  Beef and bacon rolls 88
  Leek and bacon cheese 226
  Liver and bacon hotpot 178
  Liver, bacon and mushrooms 179
  Liver and bacon rolls with Marsala sauce 178
  Scallops and bacon 68
  Spaghetti with bacon and onion 228
Bagna cauda 386
Baked Alaska 372
Bakewell tart 309
Banana:
  Banana milk shake 392
  Banana walnut bread 337
  Bananas baked with rum 276
Baps 352
Bara brith 355
Barbecues and picnics 202–11
Barm brack 336
Batter for deep frying 12
Bean:
  Bean salad 274
  Beans with bacon 371
  Boston baked beans 258
  Broad (lima) bean and ham salad 264
  Cod and bean pie 225
  Green beans with almonds 256
Bean sprouts, lamb cutlets with 127
Béarnaise sauce 10
Béchamel sauce 8
Beef:
  African beef curry 91
  Apple-stuffed steaks 83
  Argentinian beef stew 74

Baked marinated steak 85
Beef and apricot stew 74
Beef and bacon rolls 88
Beef carbonnade 75
Beef and kidney pie 227
Beef, mushroom and olive casserole 75
Beef and spinach curry 73
Beef stock 6
Beef stroganoff 81
Beef-stuffed courgettes (zucchini) 223
Beef upside-down pie 72
Beef Wellington 362
Boeuf bourguignonne 81
Boeuf catalan 90
Boiled beef with dumplings 76
Braised beef topside 87
Chilli con carne 73
Cornish pasties 208
Cottage crêpes 217
Fondue bourguignonne 82
French beef stew 76
Goulash 91
Greek meatballs 90
Hamburgers 203
Indonesian beef satay 207
Neapolitan steak 83
Peppered steak 86
Quick-fried steak with celery and cabbage 82
Roast beef 87
Spaghetti bolognese 228
Steak and kidney pie 89
Steak and kidney pudding 72
Steaks with mustard sauce 84
Stuffed beef fillet 86
Stuffed beef rolls 88
Sukiyaki 85
Sweet and sour meatballs 89
Tournedos béarnaise 361
Tournedos provençale 84
Beetroot (Beet):
  Beetroot and apple moulded salad 273
  Sweet and sour beetroot and onions 254
Blackberry (bramble) and apple sponge 282
Blue cheese dip 387
Blue cheese mousse 29
Bobotee 112
Bortsch 34
Bouillabaisse 68
Brains in lemon sauce 187
Bran muffins 340
Bran teabread 338
Brandy butter 19
Brandy, orange and raisin cake 316
Bread sauce 7
Breads and teabreads 336–55
Brigade pudding 280
Brioches 353
Broccoli ring 253
Brown bread, quick 344
Buttermilk scones 341
Butters 8, 19

Butterscotch brownies 334
Butterscotch buns 354

Cabbage:
  Cabbage rolls 212
  Red cabbage with apples 261
  Sweet and sour Chinese cabbage 261
Cakes and cookies 211, 302–35, 378, 381
Camembert cream 386
Cannelloni with tomato stuffing 232
Caper sauce 126
Caramel cake 314
Carrot:
  Carrot pudding 383
  Carrots Vichy 248
  Thick carrot, leek and potato soup 34
Cassoulet 218
Cauliflower:
  Cauliflower cheese surprise 190
  Cauliflower fritters 257
  Egg and cauliflower salad 201
  Italian cauliflower salad 265
Celeriac rémoulade 32
Celery:
  Celery with cheese sauce 248
  Cream of celery and tomato soup 35
Challah (egg bread) 350
Charlotte russe 290
Cheese:
  Aubergine (eggplant) and cheese casserole 189
  Blue cheese dip 387
  Blue cheese mousse 29
  Cauliflower cheese surprise 190
  Celery with cheese sauce 248
  Cheddar soup 42
  Cheese bread 351
  Cheese charlotte 245
  Cheese and courgette (zucchini) quiche 247
  Cheese fondue 246
  Cheese fritters 389
  Cheese kebabs 204
  Cheese olives 390
  Cheese omelette 238
  Cheese and onion casserole 191
  Cheese scones (biscuits) 343
  Cheese slaw 265
  Cheese soufflé 244
  Cheese straws 388
  Cheese and walnut dip 386
  Cheesy Scotch eggs 207
  Cottage cheese and nut salad 245
  Cream cheese fritters 247
  Cream cheese puffs 389
  Herb cheese fondue 246
  Hot cheese bites 390
  Liptauer cheese dip 390

Macaroni cheese 230
Mornay sauce 9
Pork filiet (tenderloin) with cheese 139
Cheesecakes 298
Chef's salad 210
Cherry:
   Cherries jubilee 292
   Cherry and apple strudel 384
   Cherry boats 334
   Cherry cake 318
   Leg of lamb with cherry sauce 124
Chestnut:
   Chestnut and sausage meat stuffing 13
   Chestnut vacherin 374
   Hazelnut and chestnut meringue 295
   Mocha chestnut cake 314
   Pork with chestnuts and spinach 133
Chick pea and vegetable casserole 189
Chicken:
   Barbecued chicken drumsticks and sausages 202
   Chicken with apricots 161
   Chicken and avocado casserole 152
   Chicken breasts with herbs 160
   Chicken breasts Parmesan 163
   Chicken cacciatora 150
   Chicken chop suey 159
   Chicken and corn chowder 40
   Chicken dhansak 157
   Chicken and ham gougère 224
   Chicken with ham sauce 150
   Chicken Kiev 160
   Chicken liver and mushroom risotto 234
   Chicken livers on toast 180
   Chicken Maryland 161
   Chicken mille feuilles 164
   Chicken with orange and almond sauce 152
   Chicken pie 146
   Chicken pilau 236
   Chicken salad paradiso 159
   Chicken stock 6
   Chicken and walnuts 151
   Chilled cream of chicken soup 46
   Chopped chicken livers 25
   Cock-a-leekie 39
   Cold chicken with sherry sauce 164
   Coq au vin 149
   Crispy herb chicken 157
   Curried chicken 147
   Devilled chicken 148
   Hindle wakes 147
   Italian chicken casserole 158

   Lemon chicken 162
   Marsala chicken 148
   Normandy chicken 151
   Paella 162
   Paprika chicken 158
   Pâté-stuffed chicken 163
   Poulet bonne femme 149
   Poussins Véronique 364
   Roast chicken with sweetsour stuffing 146
   Tandoori chicken 202
   Tarragon chicken 364
Chicory:
   Braised chicory (endive) 256
   Chicory and orange salad 275
Chilli con carne 73
Chocolate:
   Chocolate chip cookies 331
   Chocolate flakes 329
   Chocolate frosting 19
   Chocolate and orange mousses 285
   Chocolate sauce 12
   Chocolate Swiss (jelly) roll 310
   Gâteau au chocolat 375
   Steamed chocolate pudding with rum sauce 281
Choux pastry 17
Christmas cake 378
Christmas pudding 377
Cider crumble cake 317
Cigarettes russe 323
Cinnamon balls 384
Clam chowder 41
Clams au gratin 67
Cock-a-leekie 39
Coconut crispies 332
Cod:
   Cod and bean pie 225
   Cod with curry topping 49
   Cod and green pepper sauté 51
   Cod with green sauce 50
   Italian-style cod steaks 50
Coeur à la crème 300
Coffee:
   Coffee brandy cake 304
   Coffee cream mousse 291
   Coffee ginger cake 313
   Irish coffee 392
Coleslaw 266
Cookies see Cakes etc.
Corn bread 351
Corn and cabbage salad 267
Corn-on-the-cob 260
Cornish pasties 208
Cottage crêpes 217
Courgette (Zucchini):
   Beef-stuffed courgettes 223
   Cheese and courgette quiche 247
   Courgette and carrot soup 37
   Courgettes with almonds and cream 370
   Courgettes à la grecque 255

   Quick courgette and tomato bake 197
   Stuffed courgettes 31
Court bouillon 7
Crab:
   Avocado stuffed with crab 356
   Crab soufflé 65
   Quick crab bisque 42
Cranberry lamb stew 115
Cranberry sauce 9
Cream horns 335
Crème brûlée 299
Crème caramel 287
Crêpes 14
Crêpes Suzette 283
Croissants 353
Cucumber:
   Chilled cucumber soup 45
   Portuguese-style cucumber 273
Cumberland sauce 11
Curried dishes:
   African beef curry 91
   Beef and spinach curry 73
   Curried chicken 147
   Curried eggs 243
   Curried scrambled eggs 242
   Curried turkey balls 166
   Lamb curry 116
   Shrimp curry 66
   Vegetable curry 192
Custard sauce 12
Custard tart 297
Cut and keep cake 315

Danish layer cake 320
Date crunchies 324
Date and nut bread 339
Desserts 276–301, 372–5, 377
Devil's food cake 312
Dips 286–7, 390
Dolmades 219
Doughnuts 352
Dressings 15–16
Drinks 392–5
Duck:
   Chinese duck casserole 167
   Duck with orange 167
   Duck with sweet and sour sauce 168
   Duck with turnips 168
   Roast duck with sage and Marsala 369
Dundee cake 320

Easter biscuits (cookies) 381
Eclairs 330
Egg:
   Artichoke omelette 200
   Baked eggs in tomato shells 188
   Baked eggs and tomatoes 242
   Baked potatoes and eggs 188
   Cheese omelette 238
   Cheesy Scotch eggs 207
   Convent eggs 240
   Curried eggs 243

   Curried scrambled eggs 242
   Egg bread 350
   Egg and cauliflower salad 201
   Egg croquettes 227
   Egg mayonnaise 25
   Egg mousse 243
   Egg nog 394
   Egg salad with yogurt dressing 241
   Eggs Lorraine 239
   Oeufs florentine 198
   Omelette aux fines herbes 238
   Pipérade 241
   Potato omelette 239
   Scrambled eggs with chicken livers 181
   Smoked salmon eggs 28
   Spanish omelette 197
   Stuffed baked eggs 240
   Watercress eggs 25
Eggplant see Aubergine
Ertwensoep 40

Finnan haddie 56
Fish. See also Cod etc.
   Bouillabaisse 69
   Creamy fish mould 63
   Crispy skin fish 70
   Fish cakes 56
   Fish goujons 391
   Fish in a jacket 70
   Fish meunière 63
   Fish and pepper kebabs 206
   Fish pie 71
   Fish stock 6
   Grilled (broiled) marinated fish 48
   Spiced fish soup 41
Flaky pastry 16
Flapjacks 322
Floating islands 293
Flounder see Plaice
Fondues 82, 246
French dressing 15
French flan pastry 17
French loaf, stuffed 210
Fritters:
   Cauliflower fritters 257
   Cheese fritters 389
   Cream cheese fritters 247
   Pineapple liqueur fritters 278
Fruit. See also Apple etc.
   Boiled fruit cake 317
   Fruit plait 354
   Marinated fruit salad with vanilla ice cream 284

Game casserole 177
Game pie 171
Gammon (Ham):
   Gammon braised in beer 142
   Gammon French-style 143
   Glazed baked gammon 141

Spiced orange gammon 142
Garbure 199
Garlic mayonnaise 15
Gâteau au chocolat 375
Gâteau St. Honoré 375
Gazpacho 45
Gin fruit punch 394
Ginger beer 395
Ginger nuts 324
Gingerbread 211
Gingered grapefruit 33
Glühwein 393
Gnocchi alla romana 233
Goose, Christmas roast 376
Goulash 91, 103
Grapefruit:
   Gingered grapefruit 33
   Grilled (broiled) grapefruit 33
   Prawn and grapefruit cocktails 27
Greek meatballs 90
Griddle scones (biscuits) 342
Guacamole 387

Haddock:
   Finnan haddie 56
   Haddock with fennel and celery sauce 51
   Haddock with green sauce 50
   Smoked haddock and cheese flan 244
   Smoked haddock kedgeree 225
Halibut with egg and lemon sauce 64
Ham. *See also* Gammon
   Chicken with ham sauce 150
   Ham and asparagus rolls 145
   Ham with corn sauce 143
   Ham Italiana 144
   Ham in Madeira sauce 145
   Ham mousse 30
   Ham and mushroom crêpes 222
   Ham rolls with curried rice 144
   Ham, tuna and fennel appetizer 30
Hamburgers 203
Hare:
   Hare in Madeira sauce 171
   Hare terrine 31
   Jugged hare 170
Hazelnut and chestnut meringue 295
Hearts, stuffed lambs' 186
Herring:
   Herrings in cider 62
   Pickled herring salad 26
Hindle wakes 147
Hollandaise sauce 8
Honey cake (Lekach) 382
Horseradish sauce 7
Hot cross buns 380
Hot mustard dip 387

Hot rum toddy 392
Houmous 388
Huckle-my-buff 392
Hungarian goulash 103

Icebox cookies 331
Icings 19
Irish coffee 392
Irish soda bread 350
Irish stew with parsley dumplings 121

Jam doughnuts 352
Jam roly poly 280
Jugged hare 170

Kebabs 204–6
Kedgeree 225
Kidney:
   Devilled kidneys 183
   Kidney crêpes 223
   Kidneys milanaise 182
   Kidneys in sour cream and whisky sauce 182
   Kidneys in white wine 184
   Lemon garlic kidneys 184
   Sherried kidneys 183
Kipper pâté 20
Kreplach 382

Lamb:
   Barbecued leg of lamb 203
   Bobotee 112
   Boiled breast of lamb with caper sauce 126
   Braised orange lamb 124
   Cranberry lamb stew 115
   Crumbed lamb chops 111
   Dolmades 219
   Grilled (broiled) marinated lamb chops 108
   Irish stew with parsley dumplings 121
   Lamb and aubergine (eggplant) casserole 112
   Lamb and bean stew 115
   Lamb curry 116
   Lamb cutlets with bean sprouts 127
   Lamb noisettes provençale 362
   Lamb noisettes with tomato sauce 127
   Lamb and orange stew 123
   Lamb rissoles 111
   Lamb stew 122
   Lamb stew with dumplings 122
   Lamb and yogurt casserole 123
   Lancashire hotpot 121
   Leg of lamb with cherry sauce 124
   Lemon and ginger chops 110
   Lyonnaise lamb chops 109
   Marinated lamb kebabs 205
   Milanaise lamb noisettes 110

   Mixed grill maître d'hôtel 108
   Moussaka 219
   Roast leg of lamb with apricot stuffing 113
   Roast leg of lamb with Marsala 113
   Shashlik 206
   Shepherd's pie 217
   Spanish lamb stew 116
   Spring lamb 114
   Stuffed breast of lamb 126
   Stuffed leg of lamb en croûte 125
   Stuffed shoulder of lamb 114
   Turkish lamb 109
Lardy cake 338
Lasagne al forno 232
Leek:
   Leek and bacon cheese 226
   Leek and tomato salad 209
   Leeks mornay 248
Lekach (honey cake) 382
Lemon:
   Brains in lemon sauce 187
   Lemon butter biscuits (cookies) 333
   Lemon chicken 162
   Lemon chiffon cake 302
   Lemon garlic kidneys 184
   Lemon and ginger chops 110
   Lemon meringue pie 295
   Lemonade 395
Lentil and vegetable stew 190
Liver:
   Chicken livers on toast 180
   Chopped chicken livers 25
   Italian-style liver 181
   Liver and bacon hotpot 178
   Liver, bacon and mushrooms 179
   Liver and bacon rolls with Marsala sauce 178
   Liver kebabs 205
   Liver with orange 179
   Liver pâté dip 387
   Liver soufflé 180
   Scrambled eggs with chicken livers 181
Lobster bisque 359
Lobster thermidor 360
Loganberry cheesecake 298

Macaroni:
   Frankfurter macaroni 231
   Macaroni cheese 230
   Macaroni and mushroom salad 231
Mackerel baked with tomatoes 62
Madeira cake 316
Madeleines, English 323
Maids of honour 335
Maître d'hôtel butter 19
Marble cake 313

Marrow (Squash):
   Marrow soufflé 191
   Stuffed baked marrow 218
Marsala chicken 148
Marzipan 18
Mayonnaise 14
Mayonnaise verte 360
Meat loaf 208
Melba sauce 12
Melon:
   Melon and grape jelly 374
   Melon with Parma ham 358
   Melon vinaigrette 33
   Minted melon cocktail 33
Meringues 333
Milk bread, soft 349
Mince pies 379
Mincemeat 379
Minestrone 38
Mint sauce 8
Mocha chestnut cake 314
Molasses biscuits 342
Mornay sauce 9
Moussaka 219
Mousse:
   Blue cheese mousse 29
   Chocolate and orange mousses 285
   Coffee cream mousse 291
   Egg mousse 243
   Ham mousse 30
Muffins 340–1
Mulled cider 392
Mushroom:
   Mushroom fritters 29
   Mushroom soufflé 199
   Mushrooms à la grecque 29
   Scallops in mushroom sauce 68
   Veal chops with creamy mushroom sauce 96
Mussels or clams au gratin 67
Mustard butter 8

Negus 393

Omelette aux fines herbes 238
Onion:
   Baked stuffed onions with tomato sauce 192
   French onion soup 38
   Onion biscuits (crackers) 391
   Stuffed onion casserole 212
Orange:
   Baked orange rhubarb 276
   Braised orange lamb 124
   Brandy, orange and raisin cake 316
   Chicken with orange and almond sauce 152
   Chilled apple and orange soup 46
   Duck with orange 167
   Lamb and orange stew 123
   Liver with orange 179
   Orange baked apples 277

Orange-braised pork chops 130
Orange and gooseberry crêpes 284
Orange ice cream 276
Orange refrigerator cheesecake 298
Orange stuffing 363
Orange teabread 337
Orange yogurt cake 311
Orange yogurt sorbet 294
Pork and orange stew 137
Spiced orange gammon (ham) 142
Spiced orange juice 393
Veal and orange casserole 104
Osso bucco 101
Oxtail and grape casserole 185
Oxtail soup 39
Oxtail stew 185

Paella 162
Paprika chicken 158
Parkin 319
Parma ham, melon with 358
Parsley dumplings 121
Parsley and thyme stuffing 13
Partridge with cabbage 177
Pastry 16–18
Pâté-stuffed chicken 163
Pâtés 20, 25, 357
Pea:
 Braised peas 262
 Pea soup 36
 Petits pois à la française 262
Peach:
 Cold peach and apple soufflé 373
 Sour cream peaches 296
 Stuffed baked peaches 288
 Stuffed peaches 32
Pear:
 Pear and almond crêpes 283
 Pears with blue cheese dressing 32
 Pears poached in red wine 277
 Poached minty pears 286
Peperonata 255
Pepper:
 Pork-stuffed peppers 222
 Stuffed pepper slices 390
Peppered steak 86
Pheasant casserole 172
Pies:
 Beef and kidney pie 227
 Beef upside-down pie 72
 Chicken pie 146
 Cod and bean pie 225
 English apple pie 279
 Fish pie 71
 Game pie 171
 Lemon meringue pie 295
 Mince pies 379
 Pumpkin pie 385

Shepherd's pie 217
Steak and kidney pie 89
Veal and ham pie 107
Pigeons, casseroled, with apple and cider sauce 172
Pineapple:
 Pineapple and cabbage salad 267
 Pineapple gâteau 309
 Pineapple liqueur fritters 278
 Pineapple salad 268
 Pineapple upside-down cake 311
 Pineapple and walnut cake 319
Pipérade 241
Pissaladière niçoise 71
Pizza, Neapolitan 233
Plaice (flounder) rolls with tomato sauce 48
Plum:
 Chinese plum sauce 9
 Plum slices 282
 Plums baked with port 276
Pork:
 Alsace-style pork 134
 Baked pork chops with fruit cocktail sauce 128
 Braised loin of pork Normandy 135
 Chinese quick-roast pork 139
 Chinese-style quick-fried pork 132
 Cold loin of pork oriental 135
 Crown roast of pork with rice stuffing 363
 Deep-fried Chinese pork 131
 Loin of pork with apricot stuffing 134
 Marinated pork chops 204
 Marinated roast loin of pork 133
 Orange braised pork chops 130
 Pork 'n' beans 129
 Pork with chestnuts and spinach 133
 Pork chop casserole 130
 Pork chops with spicy plum sauce 129
 Pork in creamy prune sauce 138
 Pork fillet (tenderloin) with cheese 139
 Pork fillet (tenderloin) with vermouth 138
 Pork fillets (tenderloin) in sherry sauce 369
 Pork and ham loaf 209
 Pork and mushroom stew 132
 Pork and orange stew 137
 Pork-stuffed peppers 222
 Pork and vegetable casserole 131
 Roast leg of pork 136
 Spareribs with maple syrup sauce 141

Spicy pork chops 128
Stuffed pork rolls 136
Sweet and sour pork 137
Sweet and sour spareribs 140
Potato:
 Baked potatoes and eggs 188
 Creamy potato soup 37
 Potato omelette 239
 Potatoes dauphinois 371
 Rosemary potatoes 258
 Savoyarde potatoes 259
 Scalloped herb potatoes 259
 Stuffed baked potatoes with bacon filling 220
Potted shrimps 356
Poussins Véronique 364
Prawn (Shrimp):
 Butterfly prawns 67
 Chilled prawn soup 43
 Prawn and grapefruit cocktails 27
 Prawns with tarragon dressing 65
Prune:
 Pork in creamy prune sauce 138
Puddings see Desserts
Puff pastry 17
Pumpkin pie 385
Pumpkin soup, chilled 47

Queen of puddings 277

Rabbit:
 Rabbit with mustard cream sauce 170
 Rabbit stew 169
 Rabbit in white wine 169
Raspberry and honey ice cream 290
Ratatouille 254
Red mullet (snapper) provençale 52
Redcurrant compote 285
Rhubarb:
 Baked orange rhubarb 276
 Rhubarb crumble 279
Rice:
 Chicken liver and mushroom risotto 234
 Chicken pilau 236
 Chinese rice and vegetable salad 263
 Hungarian veal risotto 235
 Rice and apricot stuffing 13
 Rice and bean casserole 237
 Rice pudding 277
 Risi e bisi 235
 Salmon rice salad 237
 Seafood risotto 234
 Vegetable pilaff 236
Rich shortcrust pastry 18
Rock cakes 322
Rosemary potatoes 258
Rough puff pastry 17
Royal icing 19
Rum bavarois 292
Rye bread 349

Sage and onion stuffing 13
Salads:
 Bean salad 274
 Beetroot (beet) and apple moulded salad 273
 Broad (lima) bean and ham salad 264
 Cheese slaw 265
 Chef's salad 210
 Chicken salad paradiso 159
 Chicory (endive) and orange salad 275
 Chinese rice and vegetable salad 263
 Coleslaw 266
 Corn and cabbage salad 267
 Cottage cheese and nut salad 245
 Egg and cauliflower salad 201
 Egg salad with yogurt dressing 241
 Italian cauliflower salad 265
 Leek and tomato salad 209
 Macaroni and mushroom salad 231
 Mixed salad 275
 Pickled herring salad 26
 Pineapple and cabbage salad 267
 Pineapple salad 268
 Salmon rice salad 237
 Sausage and bean salad 220
 Spinach slaw 274
 Tomato and endive salad 268
 Tomato and mushroom salad 264
 Tuna and bean salad 26
 Waldorf salad 266
Salami hors d'oeuvre 29
Sally Lunn 355
Salmon:
 Cold poached salmon with mayonnaise verte 360
 Salmon rice salad 237
 Salmon steaks with herbs 52
Saltimbocca 92
Sandwich cake 211
Sangria 393
Sauces 7–12, 126
Sausage:
 Barbecued chicken drumsticks and sausages 202
 Frankfurter macaroni 231
 Pork sausages in white wine sauce 140
 Sausage and bean salad 220
 Sausage savouries 391
 Toad in the hole 224
Savarin, fruit 299
Savoury teabread 343
Scallops and bacon 69
Scallops in mushroom sauce 69
Scampi, fried 66
Scampi provençale 361

Scones (biscuits) 341–3
Seafood quiche 68
Seafood risotto 234
Shashlik 206
Shellfish cocktail 28
Shepherd's pie 217
Sherried kidneys 183
Sherry trifle 289
Shortbread 330
Shortcrust (pie) pastry 18
Shrewsbury biscuits (cookies) 329
Shrimp:
   Potted shrimps 356
   Shrimp curry 66
Simnel cake 381
Smoked salmon eggs 28
Smoked trout with hot sauce 28
Smoked trout pâté 357
Sole:
   Sole Colbert 54
   Sole dugléré 55
   Sole with Marsala cream sauce 54
   Sole with sherry sauce 55
Soufflé:
   Apricot and apple soufflé 294
   Cheese soufflé 244
   Cold peach and apple soufflé 373
   Crab soufflé 65
   Liver soufflé 180
   Marrow (squash) soufflé 191
   Mushroom soufflé 199
Soups 34–47, 358–9
Sour cream and garlic dip 386
Sour cream peaches 296
Spaghetti with bacon and onion 228
Spaghetti bolognese 228
Spaghetti with ham and tomato sauce 229
Spanish omelette 197
Spareribs with maple syrup sauce 141
Spicy teabread 339
Spinach:
   Beef and spinach curry 73
   Chilled cream of spinach soup 44
   Italian spinach and cheese crêpes 198
   Oeufs florentine 198
   Spinach and matzo bake 383
   Spinach niçoise 257
   Spinach slaw 274
Squash see Marrow
Steak see Beef
Stocks 6
Stollen 385
Strawberry:
   Strawberries Romanoff 373
   Strawberry choux puffs 286
   Strawberry ice cream cake 301

Strawberry meringue gâteau 296
Strawberry shortcake 304
Strawberry wine cooler 394
Stuffings 13, 363
Suet crust pastry 18
Sukiyaki 85
Summer pudding 300
Summer wine cooler 394
Sweet and sour beetroot (beet) and onions 254
Sweet and sour Chinese cabbage 261
Sweet and sour meatballs 89
Sweet and sour pork 137
Sweet and sour spareribs 140
Sweetbreads, deep-fried 186
Syllabub 287

Tagliatelle with chicken liver sauce 230
Tagliatelle Riviera 229
Tandoori chicken 202
Taramasalata 28
Tarragon chicken 364
Tartare sauce 9
Tarts:
   Bakewell tart 309
   Custard tart 297
   French apple tart 297
   Yorkshire apple tart 281
Tea, hot spiced 395
Tea, iced 393
Teabreads see Breads etc.
Thick carrot, leek and potato soup 34
Thousand island dressing 16
Toad in the hole 224
Tomato:
   Aubergines (eggplant) with tomato sauce 248
   Baked anchovy tomatoes 27
   Baked eggs in tomato shells 188
   Baked eggs and tomatoes 242
   Baked stuffed onions with tomato sauce 192
   Cannelloni with tomato stuffing 232
   Chilled tomato and parsley soup 43
   Mackerel baked with tomatoes 62
   Plaice (flounder) rolls with tomato sauce 48
   Thick tomato soup 36
   Tomato and endive salad 268
   Tomato juice cocktail 395
   Tomato and mint soup 47
   Tomato and mushroom salad 264
   Tomato sauce 11
   Tomatoes baked with herbs 253
Tongue with raisin sauce 187
Tournedos béarnaise 361

Tournedos provençale 84
Treacle scones 342
Trout:
   Stuffed trout braised in white wine 53
   Trout with almonds 53
Tuna:
   Ham, tuna and fennel appetizer 30
   Tuna and bean salad 26
   Tuna crêpe cake 226
   Tuna mould 61
   Tuna provençale 61
   Vitello tonnato 107
Turbot steaks with mussel and shrimp sauce 64
Turkey:
   Curried turkey balls 166
   Roast turkey 376
   Turkey croquettes 166
   Turkey à la king 165
   Turkey suprême 165
Turnips, duck with 168

Vanilla mille feuilles 310
Veal:
   Blanquette de veau 102
   Emincé de veau 104
   Escalopes (scallops) bolognese 94
   Escalopes (scallops) Parmesan 95
   Fricadelles de veau smetana 105
   Hungarian goulash 103
   Hungarian veal chops 96
   Hungarian veal risotto 235
   Italian veal stew 102
   Osso bucco 101
   Roast stuffed shoulder of veal 105
   Saltimbocca 92
   Stuffed loin of veal 106
   Veal casserole with dumplings 103
   Veal chops with creamy mushroom sauce 96
   Veal Cordon Bleu 93
   Veal escalopes (scallops) with vermouth 93
   Veal and ham pie 107
   Veal and orange casserole 104
   Veal Orloff 106
   Veal parcels with yogurt sauce 92

Veal paupiettes 94
Veal stew niçoise 101
Vitello tonnato 107
Wiener schnitzel 95
Vegetables. See also Artichoke etc.
   Chick pea and vegetable casserole 189
   Chinese rice and vegetable salad 263
   Garbure 199
   Lentil and vegetable stew 190
   Pork and vegetable casserole 131
   Vegetable curry 192
   Vegetable hotpot 201
   Vegetable pilaff 236
   Vegetable stock 6
Vichyssoise 44
Victoria sandwich (layer) cake 302
Vinaigrette dressing 15

Waldorf salad 266
Walnut:
   Apple dumplings with walnut sauce 278
   Apricot and walnut bread 336
   Banana walnut bread 337
   Cheese and walnut dip 386
   Chicken and walnuts 151
   Pineapple and walnut cake 319
   Walnut ring 318
   Walnut spice cake 303
Watercress eggs 25
Watercress soup 35
White bread, basic 344
White sauce 7
Whiting braised with vermouth 49
Wiener schnitzel 95

Yogurt:
   Lamb and yogurt casserole 123
   Orange yogurt cake 311
   Orange yogurt sorbet 294
   Yogurt dressing 16

Zabaglione 301
Zucchini see Courgette

Acknowledgments

The publishers would like to thank the following organizations and individuals for their kind permission to reproduce the photographs in this book:

Bryce Attwell 271; Rex Bamber 22, 57, 79, 269, 307, 326, 327, 328, 347, 368; Theo Bergström 1–3; Barry Bullough 77; Melvin Grey 155, 173, 174, 175, 195, 213, 215, 272, 308; Paul Kemp 23, 58, 80, 100, 117, 119, 120, 154, 155, 176, 194, 196, 214, 216, 250, 251, 252, 270, 365, 367; Neil Lorrimer 99, 153; Octopus Library 21, 24, 97, 346; Roger Phillips 4, 59, 60, 98, 118, 193, 345, 366.

Line drawings by Su Turner